THIRD EDITION INFORMATION SYSTEMS: THEORY AND PRACTICE

JOHN G. BURCH, JR.
East Texas State University
Texarkana, Texas

FELIX R. STRATER
The Standard Oil Company (Ohio)
Cleveland, Ohio

GARY GRUDNITSKI
The University of Texas at Austin
Austin, Texas

JOHN WILEY & SONS
New York·Chichester·Brisbane·Toronto·Singapore

Production Supervised by Cathy Starnella
Text Design by Mark E. Safran

Copyright © 1979, 1983 by John Wiley & Sons, Inc.

All rights reserved. Published simultaneously in Canada.

Reproduction or translation of any part of this work beyond that permitted by Sections 107 and 108 of the 1976 United States Copyright Act without the permission of the copyright owner is unlawful. Requests for permission or further information should be addressed to the Permissions Department, John Wiley & Sons.

Library of Congress Cataloging in Publication Data:

Burch, John G.
   Information systems.

   Includes index.
   1. Management information systems. I. Strater, Felix R. II. Grudnitski, Gary. III. Title.
T58.6.B87   1983   658.4′0388   82-19962
ISBN 0-471-06211-1

Printed in the United States of America

10 9 8 7 6 5 4 3

To our wives, Glenda, Judy, and Mary

ABOUT THE AUTHORS

John G. Burch, Jr. is a professor and head of accounting and information systems at East Texas State University in Texarkana. He also has taught at the University of Massachusetts and Louisiana State University. Dr. Burch has instructed graduate and undergraduate courses in accounting, administrative controls, computer auditing and control, computer programming, and information systems in his ten-year career. Prior to his academic career, he worked in general accounting and managerial positions in the construction and oil industries.

A native of Texas and Louisiana, Professor Burch earned his Ph.D. in business from the University of Alabama and his undergraduate degree from Louisiana Tech. He is a member of several professional organizations and also holds membership in Beta Alpha Psi, Beta Gamma Sigma, Phi Beta Phi, and Delta Sigma Pi. He has written many articles that have appeared in professional journals. He has presented a number of papers at several conferences. Dr. Burch has been coauthor of two texts, *Information Systems: A Case Workbook* and *Computer Audit and Control: A Total Systems Approach*.

Many of the concepts of the present textbook are a direct result of consulting and training activities. In addition to continuing education seminars, Dr. Burch has conducted several computer control training sessions for the state of New York. He has also worked with a number of students on a variety of information systems projects in hospital, service, merchandising, and manufacturing organizations.

Felix R. Strater has held a variety of positions in the field of information systems during the past twenty years. He has performed as a programmer, analyst, and systems designer for the steel, plastic, and petroleum industries. He has held a variety of management positions in the areas of systems design, data center operations, software management, and data base development. More recently, Mr. Strater has held a variety of management positions in transportation and distribution functions. He is involved continuously as a guest lecturer in corporate training programs, in industry seminars, and in various university courses. He received his B.S. degree from John Carroll University, and he is a certified data processor (CDP).

Gary Grudnitski is associate professor of accounting at the University of Texas at Austin. He received his B. Comm. and M.B.A. degrees from the University of Saskatchewan, Canada, and his Ph.D. degree from the University of Massachusetts, Amherst. He has worked as a systems analyst for Bell Canada and the Government of Saskatchewan developing applications that ranged from customer billing to driver registration. At the University of Texas, Dr. Grudnitski has instructed information systems courses at the undergraduate, master, and doctoral level. He also taught a graduate consulting course. He belongs to several organizations including the American Accounting Association, American Institute of Decision Sciences, Society for Management Information Systems, and the EDP Auditors Association.

Preface

This third edition of our book follows the format of the previous edition closely. All chapters have been revised to include additional examples, to explain the chapter content better, and to aid students in working the assignments. Some of the assignments have been changed so that students will be better able to come to grips with and derive solutions for them but, because systems work is not cut and dried, room for imagination and analysis still exists. For those who want to stress definition and proficiency in the application of techniques, we continue to include a large number of review questions and exercises that call for specific answers and solutions. Finally, a wealth of discussion questions appear at the end of the chapters.

Whereas the previous edition was divided into four main parts with three appendixes, this edition has three main parts and two appendixes. Parts I and II, of the second edition (the theory material), are now combined in a streamlined Part I in this edition. The building-block concept, a key element of information systems theory, has been refined in this edition to show its role and application more clearly. The theoretical underpinnings of systems are used throughout the book to support the practical side of information systems development. Chapter 5, the final chapter of Part I, brings together the concepts presented in the first four chapters and applies them to a real-world situation.

In the second edition, Part III presented data base concepts and techniques. This fundamental design block is now treated in Part II, which we have restructured, clarifying the definitions and incorporating new ideas from the literature and practice. Much of the new material is devoted to logical data structures.

Part III, the last main part of the present edition presents the Systems Development Methodology. The primary objective of this part is to describe each of the phases of analysis a systems analyst goes through in the development and design of an information system. Practical facets of systems work are tightly linked to the theory presented in Part I.

Structured analysis, design, and programming receive more detailed treatment in this edition. The section on systems testing has also been rewritten to provide a more complete presentation.

In Part III the Pelican case replaces the TIS case study. The Pelican case stresses how systems analysts go about, on a step-by-step basis, developing information systems. Pedagogically, the main purpose of the case is to show students how the Systems Development Methodology is applied. It deals with an organizational situation all students can understand.

Material from Appendix C of the second edition is incorporated in Part III of this edition. Appendixes A and B have been updated and remain intact. Like the second edition, their purpose is to provide review and reference.

This book is designed so that the material in each chapter can be presented in sequence with the material in the appendixes being referenced throughout the text as necessary. Instructors may want to use various other approaches, however, depending on the background of their students and the objectives of the course. For example, the material in the appendixes can be presented first as a quick review. Or, Appendix A can be given more emphasis and presented with the material in Chapters 2 and 3, while the material in Appendix B can be emphasized during the discussion of Chapter 4. Although a progressive development of ideas and vocabulary from chapter to chapter is made, other alterations in chapter presentation might be appropriate as well.

This book is intended for a one-semester course for students in accounting, business, computer science, engineering, finance, management, and marketing, who have at least an introductory background in computers and business. Students in these and in other disciplines need to understand information systems, their role in organizations, and how they are developed.

We recommend three methods for teaching a course using this book: (1) a conventional classroom approach with heavy emphasis on assignments from each chapter and two or three exams; (2) a seminar/empirical approach with some assignments and an outside systems project, with special attention given to the Pelican case; or (3) a rigorous/theoretical research approach with extensive assignment of problems and topics for library research and a comprehensive qualifying exam. Some instructors use a combination of methods in two 3-hour courses, applying method (3) in the first course and method (2), in the follow-on course.

We gratefully acknowledge the reviews and suggestions offered by Ulric J. Gelinas, Jr., Myron H. Goldberg, Ronald J. Kizior, Sung W. Kim, Jan Pipkin, and Durwin Sharp. Their contributions enhanced several parts of this book. But, as is customary, we are responsible for all errors.

We are fortunate to have Wiley as our publisher and to have had several talented members of its staff working with us on this edition. Special recognition and thanks are due Lucille Sutton, our editor, for her support and encouragement.

We express appreciation to Jill Bedgood, Linda Parker, Sharon Caputo, Bonnie Miller, and Barbara Beeman for their typing and copying work, and for making those mad dashes to the post office for last-minute mailings.

Finally, we express thanks to our many students in regular courses and participants in special seminars. They kept us thinking and searching for ways to improve this book. We hope that we have not disappointed them.

John G. Burch, Jr.
Felix R. Strater
Gary Grudnitski

Contents

PART I   INTRODUCTION TO INFORMATION SYSTEMS   1

1 Information Systems Concepts   3

1.1 Introduction   3
1.2 Data and Information   3
1.3 The Systems Concept   8
1.4 Information Systems Development   17

2 Information Requirements for Modern Organizations   31

2.1 Introduction   31
2.2 Information Requirements—An overview   31
2.3 Management Requirements   38
2.4 Decision-Making Requirements   44
2.5 Operations Requirements   47

3 Designing Information Outputs—A User Orientation   63

3.1 Introduction   63
3.2 Filtering Method   64
3.3 Key Variable Reporting Method   67
3.4 Monitoring Method   68
3.5 Modeling Method   74
3.6 Interrogative Method   79
3.7 Strategic Decision Center Method   82

4 An Overview of Modern Data Processing Resources — 97

4.1 Introduction 97
4.2 Data Processing Resources 97
4.3 Organizing Data Processing Resources 108
4.4 Selecting Data Processing Resources 124

5 Lone Star Manufacturing Company: An Information Systems Case Study — 143

5.1 Introduction 143
5.2 The Demand Blocks 143
5.3 The Design Blocks 147

PART II DATA BASE DEVELOPMENT AND DESIGN — 161

6 Data Base Concepts — 163

6.1 Introduction 163
6.2 The Ultimate Data Base 163
6.3 Overview of the Data Base 164
6.4 Application Versus Data Base Processing 167
6.5 Data Base Management Systems 173

7 Coding, Sorting, and Searching Data — 185

7.1 Introduction 185
7.2 Coding Considerations 185
7.3 Types of Code Structures 190
7.4 Sorting Data 198
7.5 Searching Techniques with Sorted Codes 202

8 Logical Data Organization — 213

8.1 Introduction 213
8.2 Models of Logical Representations 214
8.3 Tree Structures 216
8.4 Network Structures 218
8.5 Relational Structures 218
8.6 Relational Operators 223

9 Physical Data Organization — 237

9.1 Introduction 237
9.2 Computer Storage Media 237
9.3 Addressing Methods 241
9.4 Pointers, Chains, and Rings 245
9.5 Physical Representation of Trees and Networks 246

9.6 Multiple Key Retrieval 251

10 File Storage and Processing Considerations 267

10.1 Introduction 267
10.2 An Introductory Example 267
10.3 Sequential Versus Direct Data Organization and Processing 269
10.4 Classification of Data Files 278
10.5 Selection Considerations for File Media and File Organization Methods 279
10.6 File Design Considerations 282

PART III INFORMATION SYSTEMS DEVELOPMENT METHODOLOGY 295

11 System Analysis 297

11.1 Introduction 297
11.2 Preparing to Conduct Systems Analysis 297
11.3 Sources of Study Facts for Systems Analysis 301
11.4 Frameworks for Fact Gathering 304
11.5 Techniques for Gathering and Analyzing Study Facts 309
11.6 Communicating the Findings 339

Pelican Case 357
Phase 1 Systems Analysis 357

12 General Systems Design 373

12.1 Introduction 373
12.2 The Design Process 373
12.3 Basic Design Alternatives and the General Systems Design Proposal Report 382
12.4 Systems Design—An Example 385

Pelican Case 397
Phase 2 General Systems Design 397

13 Systems Evaluation and Justification 407

13.1 Introduction 407
13.2 General Systems Design Requirements 407
13.3 Approaches to Obtaining Equipment Proposals 407
13.4 The Evaluation Process 409
13.5 Acquisition Considerations 414

13.6 Cost/Effectiveness Analysis   418

Pelican Case   *434*

Phase 3 Systems Evaluation and Justification   *434*

14 Detail Systems Design—Controls   449

14.1 Introduction   449
14.2 Control Points   449
14.3 Security Controls   464

15 Detail Systems Design—Forms, Programs, and Procedures   481

15.1 Introduction   481
15.2 Forms/Reports Design   481
15.3 Human Procedures   486
15.4 Program Specifications   488
15.5 Programming Techniques   493

Pelican Case   *498*

Phase 4 Detail Systems Design   *498*

16 Systems Implementation   509

16.1 Introduction   509
16.2 Training and Educating Personnel   509
16.3 Testing the System   513
16.4 Systems Conversion   522
16.5 Follow-up to Implementation   526

Pelican Case   *533*

Phase 5 Systems Implementation   *533*

17 Management Considerations of the Information System   541

17.1 Introduction   541
17.2 Managing Maintenance   541
17.3 Auditing Considerations   545
17.4 Project Management Systems   551
17.5 Managing Change   554

Appendixes   567

Appendix A   Logico-Mathematical Models   569
Appendix B   The Computer and Related Technology   597

Index   625

PART I

Introduction to Information Systems

CHAPTER 1

Information Systems Concepts

1.1 • INTRODUCTION

As a nation we are fond of using labels to characterize a significant aspect, event, or emotion for a given time period. Examples of these labels are, "The Dark Ages," "The Stone Age," "The Age of Chivalry," "The Roaring 20's," and "The Depression." A survey of current literature is likely to find references to "The Computer Age," "The Information Age," and "The Systems Age." Whether these labels are fads or of historical importance is not known nor necessarily important to know at this time. However, to more than half of the persons employed in this country today, developing and operating computer-based information systems are what they do for a livelihood.

The long talked about growth of computers and the "information explosion" are today's realities in our social and economic institutions. The purpose of this text is to provide the fundamental knowledge to enable one to participate in the development and use of information systems in modern organizations. Before we discuss the variety of information requirements and the sophisticated ways in which these requirements are satisfied in modern organizations, we first examine the basic concepts underlying information systems. The specific objectives of this chapter are:

1. To develop a descriptive and functional definition of data and information.
2. To analyze systems and their use in developing the information systems concept.
3. To present an overview of the information systems development methodology.

1.2 • DATA AND INFORMATION

Our analysis of information systems begins with functional definitions of data and information and a discussion of their relationship. This initial understanding is enhanced by distinguishing between formal and informal information, discussing the attributes which give value to specific information, and analyzing how information is produced from data.

Basic Definitions

The terms data and information are often used interchangeably, but they refer to two distinct concepts. **Data** are language, mathematical, and other symbolic surrogates which are generally agreed upon to represent people, objects, events, and concepts. Simply stated, data are raw facts. **Information** is data placed into a meaningful context for its recipient. The following examples illustrate these concepts and their relationship:

> ... let's consider the implications to various people of a train whistle penetrating the evening dusk. To the saboteur crouching in a culvert, it might signify the failure of his mission because the whistle indicates that the train has already passed over his detonating charge without causing an explosion. To the playboy, it might presage the imminent arrival of the transgressed husband ... To the lonely wife it means the return of her traveling husband. To the man with his foot caught in the switch down the track, it preshadows doom ... [1]

It is also likely that others who hear the train whistle associate nothing of value to its sound. Perhaps, some within range of the whistle do not even hear it!

The single most important transaction to any company is the receipt of a customer order. The information value of a specific customer order, however, will vary among the employees of the company. Those individuals most directly responsible for processing customer orders (e.g., credit clerks, inventory pickers, packagers, shipping clerks, etc.) will value the contents of a specific order as necessary information to perform their respective jobs. Individual salespersons will likely be interested in only those orders pertaining to their customers and, perhaps, only the aggregate of all orders received in a given time period (i.e., daily, weekly, monthly). The sales manager may be interested in all customer orders but only values these data when reported or presented in reference to quotas, forecasts, or budgets. Accountants view customer orders as data until such time as they represent or are processed into billable shipments, accounts receivables, monthly revenues, and so forth. Others in the company such as employee relations, research, and engineering personnel routinely are not interested in customer order data.

The sound of a train whistle and a customer order are two examples of data. Whether or not these data are to be valued as information, as the above examples illustrate, depends upon each recipient's specific situation, which includes their particular set of attitudes, emotions, and goals. The amount of data available at any time to each of us, whether it be in our classroom endeavors, recreational pursuits, or job responsibilities is virtually unlimited. Unless we have identified information requirements to satisfy, the sheer volume of available data represents a time and economic burden impossible to overcome. Therefore, if we want to provide information rather than data to individuals, it is necessary to have analyzed their specific situation and determined their specific information requirements.

Formal Versus Informal Information

Formal information systems are based on the supposition that we can identify individuals' information requirements and that we can also determine the methods of producing

---

[1] Edward D. Dwyer. "Some Observations on Management Information Systems," in *Advances in EDP and Information Systems* (New York: American Management Association, 1961), pp. 16 and 17. Used with permission of the American Management Association.

information from data to satisfy these requirements. The distinction between formal and informal information is a third important concept.

Examples of **formal information** include: legal requirements, government legislation, union contracts, accounting procedures, planning requirements, organizational budgets, job demands, communication requirements, control needs, stockholders and creditor demands, problem situations, and general decision-making processes. Paychecks, invoices, purchase orders, and receiving tickets are all examples of structured forms of formal information. Status reports, variances, probabilities, return on investment, reorder points, contribution margins, and traditional accounting statements are highly formalized forms of information. In contrast, **informal information** includes opinions, judgments, hunches, intuition, hearsay, personal experiences, "grapevines," "rules of thumb," gossip, assumptions, and so forth.

From the examples presented, the difference between formal and informal information should be clear. Formal information allows us to extract from the recipient the processing or conversion procedures for producing information from data. On the other hand, the value of informal information is arbitrarily assessed by its recipient. The form and content of informal information are both subjective and unstructured, and the process which converts data to information cannot be separated from the recipient.

Both types of information may be essential to the management and operation of an organization, but formal information is the only valid output of a formal information system, and the only valid information discussed in this text. It should be noted, however, that advances in accounting, operations research, finance, and statistics have resulted in formalizing some of what was previously regarded as informal information (e.g., human resource accounting, management forecasts, probability theory).

Information Attributes

Many attributes or qualities associated with the concept of information assist us in identifying and describing specific information requirements. Figure 1.1 illustrates several attributes of information.

As we move from the concept of providing generalized information to providing specific information to an individual, determining the values for the various information attributes illustrated in Figure 1.1 is necessary. This is not an easy task. Some of the attributes are difficult to state and almost impossible to measure objectively. For example, assume you are responsible for scheduling ships in a large shipping company. It is likely that one of your major responsibilities would be to know where each ship is at any given time. It is also likely that you would be routinely asked the location of a given ship by a variety of people. Your response could be any of the following: "At sea," "In the Atlantic," "On her way to Gibraltar," "Three days out of New York," "Latitude 38°N, longitude 51°W."

While each response is accurate and timely, it may or may not satisfy the information requirements of the individual because it fails to satisfy other attributes. The nature of each response presupposes that you have determined each individual's "meaningful context" and that you have determined the relevance of each attribute to that context. To the extent your judgment is correct, you have provided information. To

6 Information Systems Concepts

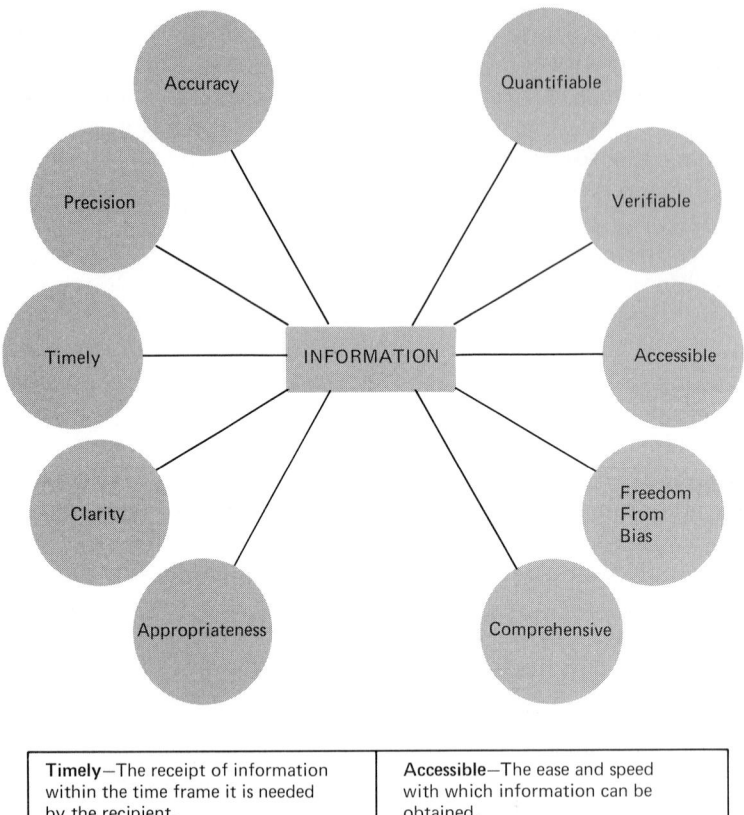

Timely—The receipt of information within the time frame it is needed by the recipient.	**Accessible**—The ease and speed with which information can be obtained.
Precision—The measurement detail used in providing information.	**Freedom From Bias**—The absence of intent to alter or modify information in order to influence recipients.
Accuracy—The degree of the absence of error in information.	**Comprehensive**—The completeness of the information.
Quantifiable—The ability to state information numerically.	**Appropriateness**—How well the information relates to a user's requirement.
Verifiable—The degree of consensus arrived at among various users examining the same information.	**Clarity**—The degree to which information is free from ambiguity.

FIG. 1.1 Information attributes.

the extent you have misunderstood the individuals' needs or failed to consider correctly the importance of the attributes, you have provided data and are likely to hear the following: "Can you be more precise?," "Will you clarify that?," "May I have the exact location," "When did she last report?," or "Is that in the Atlantic or Pacific?"

As we identify and define specific information requirements, it is essential that we describe these requirements in terms of information attributes as best we can. Properly analyzed, information attributes which are related to specific information requirements, begin to formulate a demand on the overall design of an information system. A demand, simply put, means to get the right information to the right person at the right time!

Producing Information from Data

To the extent that we can identify an individual's information requirements, it is possible to provide the information necessary to satisfy these requirements. The ways in which data become or are converted into information are almost as numerous as the specific situations we can identify. Our emphasis here, however, is on organizations and the information requirements of members of these organizations. Even with this qualification it would appear that the ways to convert data into information are almost endless. For example, examine the variety and number of course offerings in your business or management curriculum that are intended to provide information on how organizations operate. We can reduce this apparent variety by using a different conceptual approach to describe information and the ways it is produced. Producing information involves concepts and techniques as simple as communicating previously received data in a timely fashion or as complex as the development of a linear program. In Appendix A we provide brief descriptions of a variety of logico–mathematical models which produce information from data and have widespread applicability in various types of organizations. The models presented in Appendix A are merely representative of what is available to designers of modern information systems. We will refer to these models throughout the text and will also use them in some exercises and problems.

Basically, data must be processed to be considered information by recipients. Where the processing appears to be complex, the complexity can be reduced by breaking the process down into several simpler components. Ignoring, for the moment, the mechanisms of how data are processed, we can identify ten unique logical processing steps or operations taken to convert data into information. Any one operation or any combination of these operations can produce information from data. These **data operations** are:

1. *Capturing.* This operation refers to the recording of data from an event or occurrence, in some form such as sales slips, personnel forms, purchase orders, meters, gauges, and so forth.

2. *Verifying.* This operation refers to the checking or validating of data to ensure that it was captured and recorded correctly. Examples of verification might be one person reviewing another's work, the use of check digits in coding structures, or cross-footing.

3. *Classifying.* This operation places data elements into specific categories which provide meaning for the user. For example, sales data can be classified by inventory type, size, customer, salesperson, warehouse shipped from, or any other classification that will give the sales data more meaning.

4. *Arranging.* (Sorting.) This operation places data elements in a specified or predetermined sequence. An inventory

file, for example, can be arranged by product code, activity level, dollar value, or by whatever other attribute is coded in the file and deemed desirable by a user.

5. *Summarizing.* This operation combines or aggregates data elements in either of two ways. First, it accumulates data in a mathematical sense. For example, when a balance sheet is prepared, the aggregate figure of the category current assets represents a number of specific and more detailed accounts. Second, it reduces data in the logical sense, as in the example where the personnel manager wants a list of names of employees assigned to Department 23.

6. *Calculating.* This operation entails the arithmetic and/or logical manipulation of data. For example, computations must be performed to derive employees' pay, customers' bills, students' grade point averages, and so forth. In many instances, very sophisticated calculations must be performed to manipulate the data in management science models such as PERT, linear programming, forecasting, and so on.

7. *Storing.* This operation places data onto some storage media such as paper, microfilm, or magnetic tape, where the data can be retrieved when needed.

8. *Retrieving.* This operation entails searching out and gaining access to specific data elements from the medium where it is stored.

9. *Reproducing.* This operation duplicates data from one medium to another, or into another position in the same medium. For example, a file of data stored on a magnetic disk may be reproduced onto another magnetic disk or onto a magnetic tape for further processing or for security reasons.

10. *Disseminating/Communicating.* This operation transfers data from one place to another. It can take place at a number of junctures in the data processing cycle. For example, data can be transferred from a device to a user in the form of a report or a display on the screen of a computer-controlled terminal. The ultimate aim of all information systems is to disseminate information to the final user.

The role of these ten data operations in an information system is similar to the role of the six simple machines identified by the physical scientist. Just as all larger, more complex machines are composed of the lever, pulley, screw, incline plane, wheel and axle, and wedge in a variety of combinations, all complex information systems are composed of some combination of the ten simple data operations.

1.3 ▪ THE SYSTEMS CONCEPT

The term system has become quite popular in recent years. It has been used to describe many different things, particularly those activities required for data processing. Early attempts to apply technology to data processing centered around the development of machines which were capable of performing a single data operation more efficiently (e.g., typewriters, calculators, mechanical files, microfilm, and copy machines). The introduction of the punched card as a recording medium resulted in the development of various machines (e.g., keypunch, sorter, collator, printer) which perceived the conversion of data into information as a process (hence the term data processing). The development of the digital computer and its related technology popularized the use of the word systems and a methodology for the development of "systems" to satisfy the information requirements of modern organizations. We begin this section with a brief explanation of systems. We then use a systems context to analyze organizations. Finally, we conclude this section with a discussion of the information systems concept.

Systems

A *system* can be defined as any set of objects and ideas, and their interrelationships which are ordered to a common goal or purpose. Figure 1.2 illustrates a conceptual model of a system. In this illustration the various symbols *A* through *I* represent the components of the system. The lines connecting the symbols represent the relationships among components. Identical symbols represent a unique relationship among one or more components, which can be termed a **subsystem.** The use of the term subsystem facilitates analysis or communication. For example, we can describe the system by its components *A, B, C, . . ., I* or by its subsystems *ABC, DEFG, HI,* whichever serves our purposes better. With complex systems, we can divide the analysis and design of the system into subsystems for control and implementation purposes.

A system and any of its components and subsystems may be found as such in reality or they may be purely logical in nature. For example, a person can be viewed as a system. We might begin to describe or analyze a person by identifying and listing physical components (e.g., toe, eye, ear, heart). On the other hand, if this is too cumbersome or

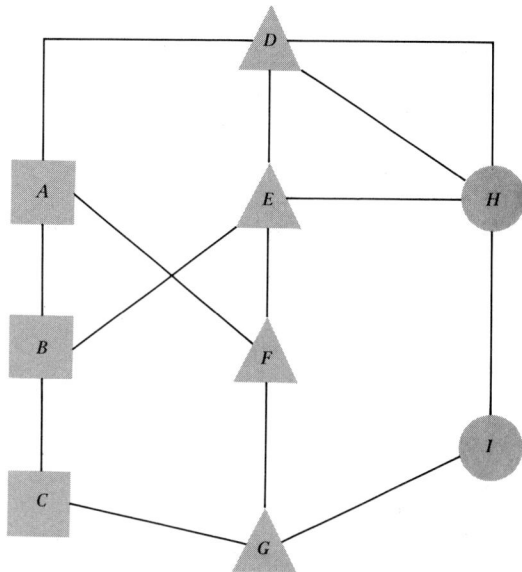

FIG. 1.2 Conceptual model of a system.

represents unwanted detail, we might identify major subsystems (e.g., respiratory, reproductive, endocrine). Another description of a person as a system might perceive the physical, intellectual, moral, and emotional aspects as either components or subsystems.

The first way of describing a person coincides fairly directly with what we find in reality: a set of physical organs. The second way implies the existence of physical organs and adds an awareness of specific relationships among these organs. The third perception represents logical entities. Each way would have value depending on our analytical or communication goals.

The value of approaching reality from a system's perspective can be as simple as just another technique to analyze or design complex machines, projects, or theories; or, on another level, we could argue that the true value of this perception of reality lies in the fact that the "Whole is greater than the sum of its parts." In other words, the effectiveness of components considered collectively as a system may be greater than the sum of the effectiveness of each component considered separately. The added measure of value or effectiveness is called the *synergistic effect*.

Organizations Perceived as Systems

Any organization can be viewed as a system composed of three subsystems, namely, the operations subsystem, the management subsystem, and the information subsystem. For the local corner drugstore all of the subsystems may reside within one person plus several filing cabinets and a typewriter. In a large drug manufacturing and distribution organization these three systems are separate and well-defined, but highly related. This relationship is depicted in Figure 1.3.

The **management subsystem** includes all the people and activities directly related to determining the planning, controlling, and decision-making aspects of the operations subsystem. For example, determining what services to market, deciding how many warehouses to have and the location of each, outlining the responsibilities and composition of a steering committee, and the like, are functions of the management subsystem.

The **operations subsystem** includes all of the activities, material flow, and people directly related to performing the primary functions of the organization. For example, selling the finished product or service, producing finished goods, warehousing inventory, delivering health care services, designing products, purchasing raw materials, engineering, and so forth, are functions of the operations subsystem.

The **information subsystem** is an assemblage or collection of people, machines, ideas, and activities that gather and process data in a manner that will meet the formal information requirements of an organiza-

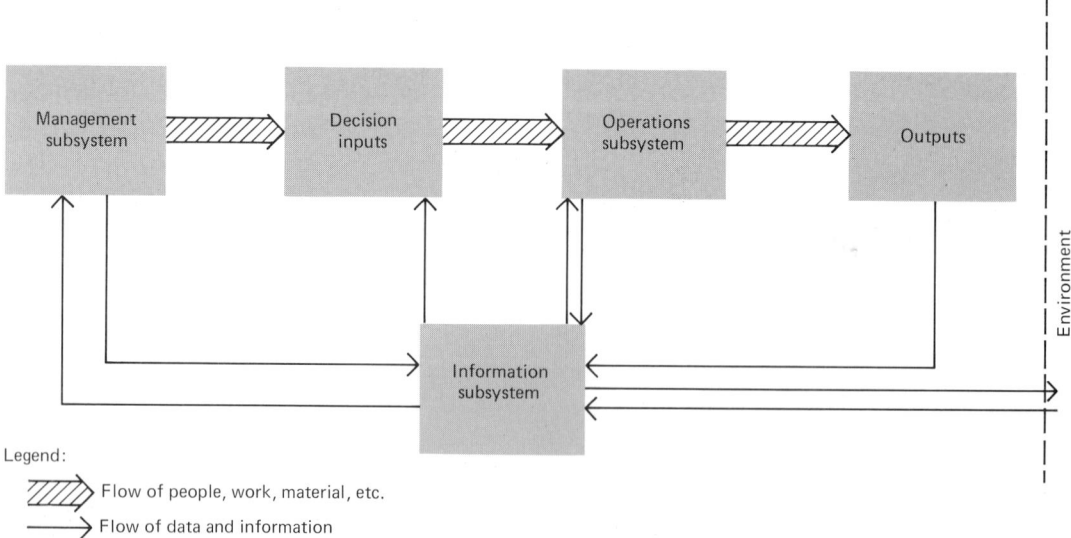

FIG. 1.3 Example of the relationship between the management, operations, and information subsystems of an organization.

tion. Its purpose is to satisfy information requirements including accounting and routine operational needs; planning, controlling, and decision-making needs of all levels of management; and the needs of concerned parties external to the organization.

Analyzing the interactions of these three subsystems allows us to make several key observations. First, the actual performance of the operations subsystem is represented by a variety of data input to the information subsystem. The information subsystem processes these data and produces information for the management subsystems (e.g., all forms of performance reporting), other segments of the operations subsystem (e.g., a customer order is input and processed or is converted to a production order or inventory withdrawal notice), or external users (e.g., a vendor purchase order, a customer invoice, a government report, or the financial statements). Second, the needs and requirements of external users in the environment within which the organization exists, interface with the information subsystem as a series of data inputs (e.g., customer order, governmental reporting requirements, industry statistics). These inputs are also processed and provide information either for the operations or the management subsystems. Finally, the management subsystem provides a variety of data inputs to the information subsystem which will affect the operations subsystem, external users, and other levels of management. These inputs might be objectives, budgets, forecasts, schedules, work orders, and so forth.

Viewed as a system, both the organization and its information subsystem are highly integrated. The information subsystem serves all departments or functions (i.e., horizontal integration) and all levels of management (i.e., vertical integration).

In most organizations, for example, inventories of finished goods, raw materials, in-process goods, supplies, etc., must be maintained. Depending on several management or organizational factors, the responsibility for maintaining physical inventories can reside in the marketing, purchasing, production, or materials department. Regardless of the department responsible for maintaining inventory, the need for information concerning inventory levels exists throughout the organization. Using product inventory and the information concerning inventory levels, we can demonstrate the integrated nature of the information system. Figure 1.4 illustrates the horizontal or interdepartmental integration.

Clearly, inventory planners need to know current inventory levels. Accountants need inventory level information for reporting purposes. A purchasing agent may need to know what is currently available to replenish the stock of raw material. A salesperson

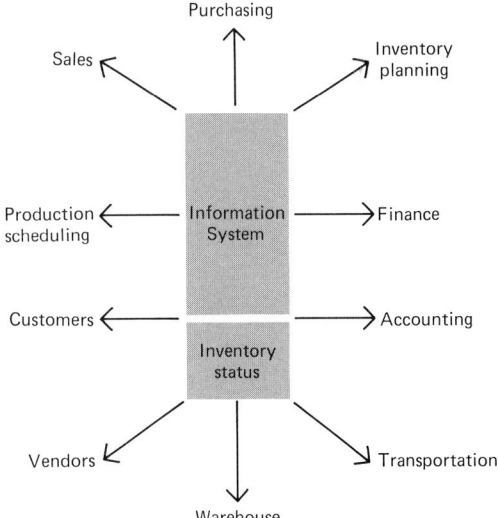

FIG. 1.4 Integrated nature of the information system as it relates to the functional units of the organization.

needs to know current inventory levels to commit to a delivery schedule for a customer. A production scheduler must know what inventory is available at various levels before assigning or scheduling other resources such as direct labor and machines. The finance department, when determining an organization's short-term cash requirements, includes the value of present inventories in their analysis. To arrange for proper warehouse space or freight schedules, other departments also must know current inventory levels. This integration does not mean that all departments or all levels of management use the resources of the information system in the same way. From department to department and from level to level, differences, as expressed by the information attributes, result in a multiplicity of information requirements.

The Information Systems Concept

All organizations have an information system. This information system is a formal entity composed of a variety of logical and physical resources. From organization to organization, these resources are arranged or structured in an infinite number of ways. Moreover, because organization and information systems are dynamic resources, a structure we construct one day may not necessarily reflect the actual arrangement of these resources the next day. Thus we need a concept that logically portrays the structure of an information system, reflects all of its physical resources, is appropriate for any size information system in any type of organization, and remains relatively constant. Figure 1.5 illustrates such a logical structure for information systems in terms of a series of building blocks.

Understanding the concepts represented by each of the building blocks shown in Figure 1.5 and their interrelationships, provides the basic knowledge for describing or developing the information system in all organizations. The material discussed in this text will expand your understanding of the logical content of each building block, its

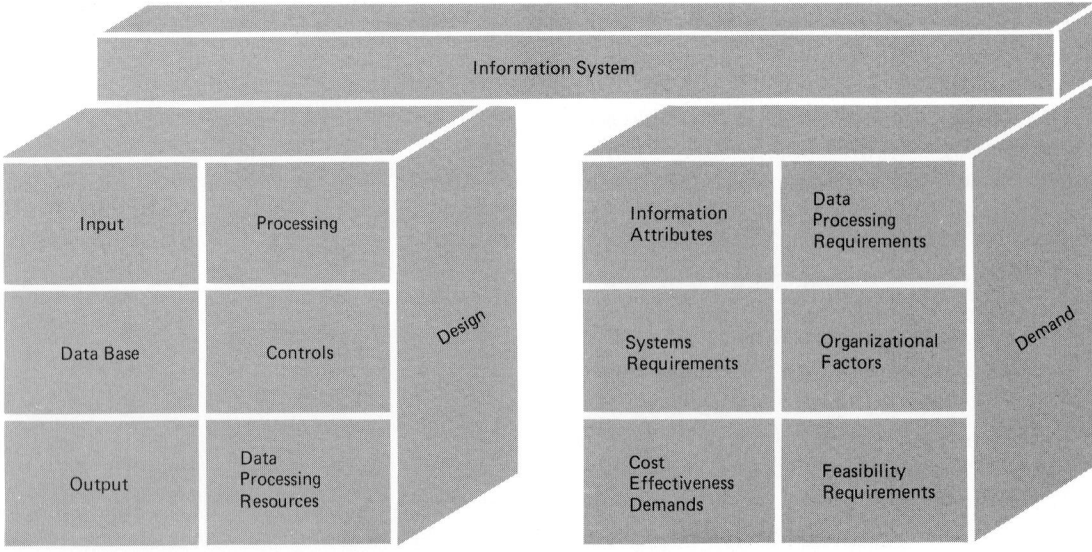

FIG. 1.5 The logical structure of an information system perceived as a series of building blocks.

relationship with the other building blocks, and provide you with a methodology for applying this knowledge on a practical level.

Illustrated in Figure 1.5 are 12 building blocks grouped into two columns labeled **design** and **demand.** The design blocks represent the logical and physical resources that must be ordered or arranged to produce information from data. The demand blocks represent the reasons for or causes to be considered when arranging the design blocks of an information system. Clearly, before we can design an information system (i.e., arrange the design blocks), we must ascertain the needs and requirements of the organization (i.e., the specific values of the demand blocks). The specific values that each building block contains in a given information system, is the result of a specific study performed within and for an organization. In Part III we provide a methodology for determining the specific values of both the design and demand building blocks.

Figure 1.6 expands the concepts of the design blocks with more detail or examples of the entities which they represent.

1. *Input block.* The input block illustrates the variety of data which are input into an information system. Generally, the required data to be input into a system are derived from specific information requirements. Throughout the text, and particularly in solving the exercises and problems at the end of each chapter, we will become more familiar with determining input data. In Chapter 4 we will discuss the impact of modern technology on the input design block.

2. *Processing block.* In the previous section we discussed the processing block in terms of data operations. We also referred to Appendix A, where a variety of logico–mathematical models are discussed. As with the input block, the specific values of the processing block are derived from specific information requirements and considerable opportunities will be given throughout the text for you to become adept at developing specific values for this block.

3. *Data base block.* A broad all-encompassing definition is that a data base is a

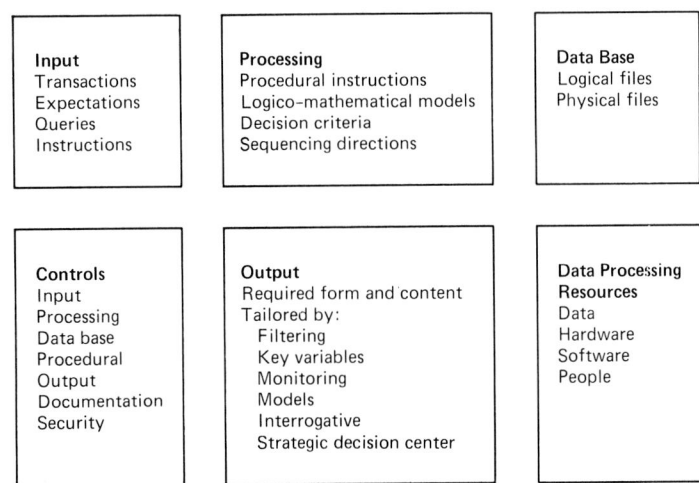

FIG. 1.6 Detail components of the design building blocks.

repository of all data of interest and value to the users of the information system. As noted in Figure 1.6, its two important dimensions are logical and physical files. Files are a concept of structuring data contained within the data base. Logical files refer to the inherent or implied relationships among the data, while physical files are associated with the way in which data are organized physically on specific storage devices or media. Part II in the text is dedicated to analyzing and illustrating the data base block.

4. *Controls block.* An information system is a complex and dynamic resource. As with any other resource, we need a way to ensure that it is operating as it was designed to operate. The controls block represents the concepts, techniques, and devices that ensure the integrity of the operations of the information systems. Some of these controls act as filters which prevent errors from entering or being processed through the system. Other controls alert the systems operators and users to potential or actual problems. Several sections in Part III provide an indepth discussion of practical controls for information systems.

5. *Output block.* The output block refers to the form and content of the actual information given to the users of the information system. The importance of this building block is stressed throughout the text and emphasized in the next two chapters. In Chapter 2 we analyze information requirements for modern organizations. In Chapter 3 we discuss a variety of techniques, listed in Figure 1.6, which can be used to tailor information outputs to specific information requirements.

6. *Data processing resources block.* The final design block is labeled data processing resources. The physical implementation of the other design blocks is expressed in terms of a particular set and arrangement of data, hardware, software, and people. In Chapter 4 we present an overview of the role of modern data processing resources in organizations. Appendix B provides brief descriptions of major components of the hardware resource. Aspects of data base hardware and software are discussed in Part II.

Figure 1.7 expands the concepts of the demand blocks with more detail (or examples of the entities which they represent). As noted previously, the demand blocks determine the form and substance of the design blocks.

1. *Information attributes.* The foremost demand on the information system is derived from the specific information requirements of the users. As we discussed previously, these requirements are stated in terms of information attributes listed in Figure 1.7.

2. *Data processing requirements.* This demand summarizes the impact of providing specific information requirements for one or more users of a system. Furthermore, an assessment of data processing requirements implies alternatives to satisfy more efficiently or effectively these requirements for both the individual user and the organization. These demands will be defined in Chapter 4 and discussed throughout Part III.

3. *Systems requirements.* This demand is somewhat similar to data processing requirements. Systems require-

ments recognize the dynamic nature of the organization and its information system, and the costs of the data processing resources with which the logical aspects of the system are implemented. Systems requirements are defined in Chapter 4 and referenced throughout the text.

4. *Organizational factors.* Every organization develops and operates an information system to satisfy its specific information requirements. The quantity and quality of user requirements are often dictated by broader organizational theories and practices. In Chapters 2 and 4 we analyze the organizational factors noted in Figure 1.7 and assess their impact on the design and development of information systems.

5. *Cost/effectiveness demands.* Information and the information system are resources. The acquisition or building of resources in organizations is normally done with an idea to make or to save money.

Thus it is necessary to identify the costs and benefits to be derived before expending significant funds for developing information systems. In Part III we analyze how this justification process is conducted.

6. *Feasibility requirements.* All of the specific values of the other demand blocks are expressed in terms of feasibility requirements. As previously noted, compromises among demands and among their implementation in the design blocks must be achieved from various points of view before a system can be designed and implemented. Feasibility requirements are defined and discussed in Part III.

In summary, when we make a judgment that an information system is good or bad, effective or ineffective, efficient or inefficient, we are comparing the specific values of the design blocks to specific values of the demand blocks for that system. This concep-

Information Attributes	Data Processing Requirements	Systems Requirements
Timely	Volume	Reliability
Precision	Complexity	Cost
Accuracy	Time	Installation schedule
Quantifiable	Computational	Flexibility
Verifiable		Life expectancy
Accessible		Growth potential
Freedom from bias		Maintainability
Comprehensive		
Appropriateness		
Clarity		

Organizational Factors	Cost/Effectiveness Demands	Feasibility Requirements
Nature	Direct costs	Technical
Size	Indirect costs	Economic
Structure	Direct benefits	Legal
Management style	Indirect benefits	Operational
		Schedule

FIG. 1.7 Detail components of the demand building blocks.

tual view of the information system and its development serves as our guide throughout the text.

An Analogy

At this point we have introduced the basic concepts of information systems, the foundation upon which any information system is developed regardless of size, orientation, or complexity. With these concepts, you have the framework and guidelines to keep you on track. In the final analysis, however, the specific system you design or implement depends on how well you determine and structure the specific values for each concept.

Architects design buildings to serve many purposes. Systems analysts design information systems to serve many organizations. The Roman Architect Vitruvius described the goals of architecture as use, strength, and beauty. These three goals continue to guide architects today.

The design of every building includes four components: (1) space, (2) materials, (3) light, and (4) style. The way these components or design blocks are arranged results in the kind of building that is constructed. The architect encloses space with walls and it flows through openings called doors and windows. The physical property of the building is made up of the materials used such as timber, steel, glass, concrete, and so forth. The architect must know the texture and structural properties of materials to use them properly. Light influences the appearance of a building's spaces and materials. Inside or outside, the architect uses materials to reflect or absorb light as it changes or to change the character of a room. There have been many architectural styles throughout history. Needs of people, their environment, and their tastes in fashion influence the development of styles. Some architects have broken with traditional styles stressing for example, organic architecture where a building, like a living organism, must "grow" out of its surroundings. No doubt there will be different styles in the future to accommodate structures such as ground homes designed to meet energy conservation demands. However, irrespective of the architectural styles, all buildings will still be designed and built using the basic concepts discussed here.

Many architects would say that there are form and function demands on the design components. They agree that form (the appearance of the building) and function (the purpose of the building) go hand in hand. Form is the way an architect puts together the design elements or design blocks. Function determines how well a building serves its purposes. Because of these two demands and their different levels of influence, the form design blocks of space, materials, light, and style can be arranged in different ways and take on different values.

The demands of form and function can be further subdivided. For example, a partial listing of demand blocks could be: aesthetics, shelter, efficient use of land, cost/effectiveness, safety, comfort, energy conservation, heat, ventilation, privacy, freedom of movement, single family dwelling, cooperative housing, building codes, zoning laws, permanent, mobile, temporary, environment planning, city planning, and so forth.

The building that is finally designed will be controlled by the specific values identified for the demand blocks listed above. For example, note that two demand blocks are aesthetics and efficient use of land. In cities, pleasing design and efficient use of land are strong demands. Architects have met this challenge by building impressive skyscrapers. Where land is more plentiful, architects design buildings with the land use demand less important compared to other demands. In this situation, architects normally design buildings with a pleasing horizontal look. In the development of buildings, architects have design and demand blocks which guide them in their work. So too, designers of information systems have design and demand concepts to guide them.

1.4 ▪ INFORMATION SYSTEMS DEVELOPMENT

The importance of information systems and their development can be seen in many different trends during the past 10 to 20 years. The emergence and growth of companies involved in the development of information technology is the most obvious. Within most other organizations, this growth is mirrored by the growth of data processing and information systems departments. The increased number of publications, both journals and textbooks, coupled with more course offerings in colleges and universities, represent added testimony to the increasing importance of information systems.

In Section 1.3 we presented a view of the information system as a series of building blocks representing design and demand components. By providing specific values for each block, we are able to analyze or design any information system. How one goes about providing these specific values within an organizational setting is what is called the systems development methodology. Part III of this text, as we have alluded to before, describes such a methodology. Here we discuss the need for an information systems development methodology in modern organizations, provide an overview for the methodology presented, and examine the role of the systems analyst in this methodology.

A Project Perspective

Organizations are comprised of many resources. There are tangible resources such as land, machines, materials, tools, people, and money. There are also intangible resources such as trademarks, patents, copyrights, manufacturing processes, skill level of a work force, and information. Indeed, information and the information system, are valuable organizational resources.

Both tangible and intangible resources have value and costs associated with them. In general, when we acquire or develop resources, we prefer not to incur costs greater than the value we receive. To ensure that resources are acquired or developed efficiently and effectively, many organizations use a project concept.

Projects are logical entities having specific beginnings and ends. The project concept is a useful management technique or device. In addition to being an efficient and an effective way to manage change, many other benefits accrue to the users of the project concept when acquiring, modifying, or developing resources. The project concept allows all of the costs and benefits associated with the acquisition, modification, or development of a resource to be identified and described in monetary terms. This allows management to determine not only if that specific project is cost/effective, but it allows them to compare the cost/effectiveness of all proposed projects to determine organizational priorities. Thus, the project concept directly supports the classical responsibility of management to allocate scarce resources.

The use of the project concept permits and encourages the sharing of organizational resources which normally or routinely are responsible to different administrative units within the organization. This is especially true in regards to personnel skills such as engineering, financial, technical, and management. Moreover, the project concept allows management to subdivide complex activities into smaller, simpler, and doable activities which can be planned and controlled effectively. The relatively short life of a project, as contrasted with the ongoing purpose of the organization, provides achievable goals and objectives. In fact, the development and evaluation of projects can be described as an important task of any organization's management.

While the original use of the project concept was popularized in the development of tangible resources (e.g., constructing new facilities) it has proven quite useful in the development of intangible resources (e.g., implementation of a new manufacturing process, revision of a marketing strategy, incorporation of a new employee fringe benefit) as well. The development and modification of information systems make good use of the project concept.

The Systems Development Life Cycle

Like any other resource, an information system must be developed and maintained to satisfy the requirements of the organization it serves. Just as factories must be modernized, buildings must be renovated, and ships must be refitted, so must information systems be modified to meet continuously changing conditions. Examples of just a few of the many changes that impact an organization and its information system are: New products being developed routinely; old production facilities replaced by new facilities; new management structures and philosophies introduced periodically; existing government requirements changed and new ones imposed; a renegotiated labor contract goes into effect; a new computer, reportedly faster and less expensive than the existing computer, is announced; sales volumes increase.

Required and desired modifications to an information system for whatever reasons are continuous. Where these modifications are minor they are regarded as maintenance to the system and routinely incorporated into the day-to-day activities of the organization. However, proposed modifications or new enhancements to the system requiring large expenditures of time, effort, and money are often viewed as a project.

A five-phase project life cycle adapted to an information system development is illustrated in Figure 1.8. The activities included in the first four phases of the depicted life cycle are directed to providing the specific values for the design and demand blocks. Grouping these activities into phases is important. Each phase is associated with one or more communication points critical to the development cycle. The communication points are characterized in Part III by the preparation of formal reports. These reports have two significant roles. First, they allow the organizations' managements to direct and monitor the systems development project. Second, these reports provide a continuing opportunity for potential systems users to evaluate the systems goals and the proposed ways in which these goals will be accomplished. Thus, the needs and concerns of each person affected by the information system can be acknowledged and, if possible, accommodated.

It is widely accepted that the persons who have the title ***systems analyst*** are responsible for performing many of the activities in this methodology. The label *user* describes those individuals in the management and operations of the organization for whom the information system is implemented. While the role of both the systems analyst and the user are important to the successful development of the information systems, we analyze the major activities of this life cycle from the perspective of the systems analyst.

The Role of the Systems Analyst

Let us again use the example of architects and their work to gain both a better understanding of the systems development life cycle and a perspective on the systems analyst's work. Systems analysts and architects go about their work using what is called a systems development methodology derived from Figure 1.8.

Let us assume that an architect has been commissioned to design a new university building. A meeting with university officials is scheduled. The architect interviews them to determine their needs and goals. Questions are asked such as: "How many classrooms are needed?," "What size classes will there be?," "What number of students are expected?," "How many faculty and staff?," "What special rooms and facilities are needed?," "For what purposes?"

Next, the architect does extensive research. Other buildings are observed and a

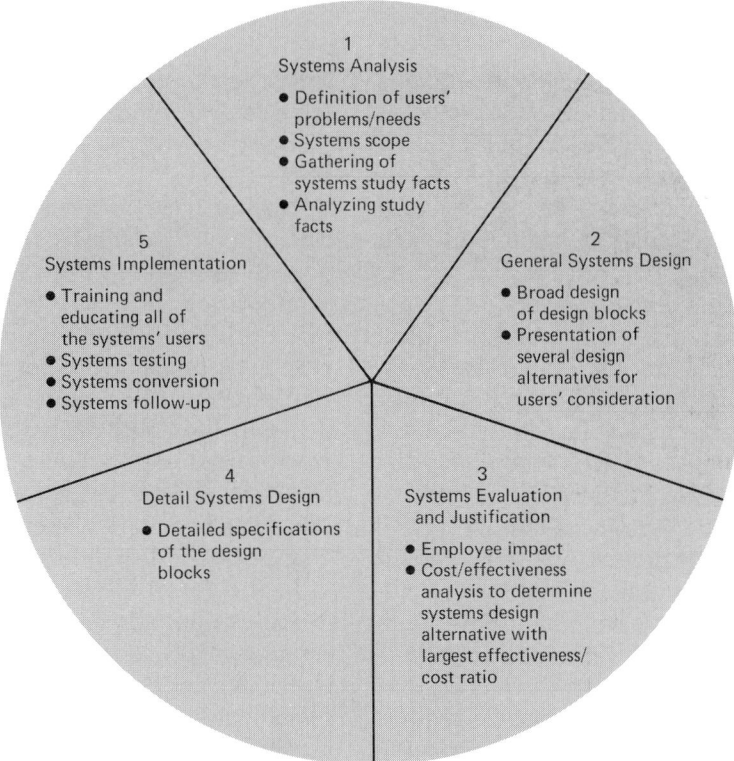

FIG. 1.8 The systems development life cycle showing five major phases and the major activities associated with each.

preliminary visit is made to the proposed site. What the architect is trying to determine is the scope of the project and any constraints that might be imposed on the work to be done. Some assumptions must be made at this point because a final answer on several issues may be pending. After interviewing, researching, and observing, many study facts will be gathered. These facts will have to be analyzed to define clear measurable objectives and performance requirements.

After completing the analysis phase, the architect's findings will be presented to officials of the university so that any misunderstandings or differences can be resolved. It is important to test the analysis and for the architect to receive feedback from all parties concerned so that a "Taj Mahal" is not designed when a functional structure is all that is wanted. The process of testing and feedback is done to see how demands (e.g., efficient use of land, safety, cost/effectiveness) impact upon design blocks (e.g., space, materials, light, style). Ideally, it should be done continuously; at the very least, it should be done at the end of each phase.

Assuming that the architect has completed the analysis phase successfully, work at the drawing board begins. **General design** alternatives are evolved that will meet objectives and various demands. The architect draws "plans" which show how the rooms on each floor of the building will be arranged. A sketch is made of how the inside of the building will look and how it will appear from the outside. Even a three-dimensional model of each alternative plan may be constructed. These plans and models are presented to university officials so that they may select the "best" design, or require the architect to "go back to the drawing board" to develop a better design. If a proper presentation is made in the analysis phase and the architect obtains sufficient and candid feedback, then the chance of having to go back to the analysis phase is reduced.

During the design phase and especially at its completion, strong consideration is given to the many *demand* blocks. After careful consideration, university officials will approve a design alternative or have the architect combine aspects of several alternatives into one. In any event, the architect comes out of the general design phase with a clear understanding of what is wanted in the detail design phase.

It should be emphasized at this point that the architect will often use specialists in the design work. These specialists may include interior designers, materials specialists, landscapers, and various engineers. The systems analyst does the same. The analyst's staff, for example, may include management scientists, computer programmers, forms specialists, and data communications experts.

Evaluation and justification should be performed continuously throughout the systems development life cycle. For the purpose of emphasis, however, we have presented this work as a separate phase. Also, from a practical viewpoint, after one general design alternative is selected, a more comprehensive, acid-test evaluation can then be done to ensure that this particular alternative will meet all demands. This phase should be completed before the long and arduous task of detail design is started.

In the detail design phase, the architect is ready to prepare detail plans for the builders who will construct the building. In these plans, the architect shows the size of each room; where the desks are located; the lighting, heating, plumbing, and air conditioning systems; and perhaps, even where each telephone jack is to be installed. Specifications are prepared which describe the sizes, kinds, and quantities of materials to be used. What kind of paint and how many coats will be applied to a particular surface may also be specified. The architect prepares documents that stipulate the rights and duties of the university, of the architect, and of the building contractor. The architect sees to it that the building is constructed in accordance with the detail design. It should be noted that the architect does not actually construct the building, but instead monitors this phase. Again, like the architect, the systems analyst also oversees the work of specialists.

In the implementation phase, the architect will make sure that skilled personnel are used. Certain tests are set up to see that proper materials are used and various systems, such as lighting, heating, and ventilation, work.

By following a well-defined methodology, the university building is finally constructed. After the building is completed, all components are tested together to see if the total system works. Assuming that all tests are passed, the new building may be moved into overnight. Or, the new building may be moved into in phases, such as one floor at a time. Or, it could be that both the old and new buildings are used in parallel.

After the new building has been in use for a short time, the architect performs a final inspection. If the development methodology described above has been followed, this final inspection should result in only minor adjustments being made.

Over time, because of increasing enrollment, additions must be made. An architect is hired, possibly the same one, to design an expansion. The systems development cycle is repeated. With very little effort we can substitute information systems terminology for the architect's work and have an accurate description of what the systems analyst does and how he or she goes about developing information systems, as shown in the following paragraphs:

During the **systems analysis phase** the systems analyst is involved with assisting the user in identifying what information is needed. This is often different from what users think they need, since frequently they have preconceived notions of what can be provided. The analyst is also concerned with identifying and quantifying the specific values of the other demand blocks.

In essence, the analyst is responsible for formalizing the specific purpose and scope of the new system or of the proposed modification or addition to the old information system. At the completion of the systems analysis phase a formal report is prepared by the systems analyst detailing the identified user requirements. It is the responsibility of the user to understand and approve these requirements before general design alternatives are prepared.

During the **general systems design phase,** specifications are developed that capture the conceptualizations formed during the systems analysis phase. The main aspect of this phase is to equate the user's requirements with all of the design blocks that satisfy the demand blocks. In effect, the analyst has assigned specific values to each of the design blocks based on his or her understanding of the demand blocks. The analyst must formalize these values in such a way that each is a viable work assignment. Again, a formal report detailing the specific design proposals must be prepared by the analyst and approved by the users.

The systems analyst presents to the users several design alternatives for comparison, selection, and further analysis, especially concerning cost/effectiveness and the impact the new or modified system will have on the organization as a whole. This work is performed in the **systems evaluation and justification phase.** One general systems design alternative is selected for detail design. In the **detail design phase** every design block is given precise specifications.

All of the analysis and design efforts come to a climax during the **systems implementation phase.** The analyst must identify cutoff dates, train and coordinate user personnel, instruct computer personnel, install new procedures and forms, test the new system, and be alert to significant oversights or omissions from earlier phases. Unfortunately, more than one well-designed information system has been scrapped due to poor conversion and implementation.

After conversion, the analyst should follow up to see that the system is operating as expected. The analyst should also monitor the system, seeking ways to improve its performance and to make modifications as users' needs change. Finally, at some point, the analyst will again review the system to recommend a new, greatly improved information system or subsystem for the organization; and the life cycle is repeated.

The role of the information systems analyst just presented is, of course, a composite picture. In a large organization the information system is a vast, complex entity, and many analysts are involved in designing and implementing even one subsystem of the organization's overall information system. At a given point in time, an analyst might well be executing activities related to more than one phase of the system's development methodology and these activities must be properly coordinated.

To make the system more effective, the systems analyst will be engaged in a wide spectrum of activities ranging from formal to informal, quantitative to qualitative, structured to unstructured, specific to general, and traditional to revolutionary. In performing these activities, the analyst may use: flowcharts, data flow diagrams, decision tables, matrices, graphs, narrative reports, interviews, logico–mathematical models, and so forth. The application of these techniques reinforce one another and, when viewed in combination, provide the basic tools for systems work.

SUMMARY

Data and information are different but related concepts. Data are the raw material from which information is produced. Formal information, as distinguished from informal information, is the legitimate product of an information system. Specific information requirements are defined by identifying information attributes. Information is produced in a variety of ways ranging from very simple to complex processing procedures. Data operations are a way of analyzing all information processing.

A system is a set of objects and their interrelationships which are ordered to a common goal. A synergestic effect results from a perception of a structure which emphasizes the totality of entities when viewed as components of a whole. An organization can be viewed as being comprised of three major subsystems. The information system is one major subsystem of an organization. The components of an information system can be thought of as a series of building blocks which represent the resources to be structured or designed and the reasons or demands for this structure.

The development or modification of information systems is often termed a project. Projects can be viewed as having life cycles, which in the case of information systems, can be divided into five phases. These five phases provide a methodology for managing and developing information systems. The functional role of the systems analyst is the catalyst for implementing this methodology.

REVIEW QUESTIONS

1.1 Define the terms "data" and "information." If we want to supply information rather than data to individuals, what must be done?

1.2 How is informal information different from formal information? Why might information that is considered to be informal today, be considered formal tomorrow?

1.3 Why might your response to a question be information to one person but not to another?

1.4 Identify and describe the data processing operations.

1.5 What is a "system?" Why do we divide complex systems into subsystems? Why adopt a systems perspective?

1.6 List and explain the three major subsystems of an organization. Provide an example that will help illustrate their overlapping nature.

1.7 What does "horizontal" and "vertical" integration imply in an information subsystem context?

1.8 Compare and contrast the two kinds of information systems building blocks.

1.9 List and define the design blocks. The demand blocks.

1.10 What are projects? Why is the project concept a useful management technique?

1.11 Why might "perfectly good" information systems be modified? When should modifications of the systems be viewed as a project? What phases are appropriate for describing the modification process?

Information Systems Concepts

1.12 What is a "systems analyst?" a "user?"

1.13 Describe the role of the systems analyst in each phase of the systems life cycle.

QUESTIONS FOR DISCUSSION

1.1 Discuss the statement: "Information is the cement that bonds an organization together."

1.2 Overheard at a three martini lunch: "I get all my important information from Washington, D.C. and on the golf course." Discuss the type of information to which this statement refers.

1.3 Given the same job in two different organizations which are similar in nature, one is highly computerized and one is not; one involves a great deal of formal reporting and the other does not; and one emphasizes the use of logico–mathematical models and the other does not. Discuss the probable reasons as to why this might be true.

1.4 Referencing the information attributes presented, evaluate the examples listed below. Identify the attribute(s) you would consider particularly significant, important, or most difficult to ascertain for each example.

(a) Testimony to Congress on proposed social legislation.
(b) Landing instructions to the pilot of a 747.
(c) Job instructions to each worker on a mass production line.
(d) Brochure for a proposed two-week trip to Europe next summer.
(e) Directions for driving from New York to Los Angeles.
(f) Advice on buying/selling stocks and bonds.

1.5 "In today's hectic environment, we cannot manage effectively if we depend solely on intuition and personal judgment." Would the author of this statement support or protest the usefulness of formal information systems? Would the author consider such systems as necessary or optional?

1.6 Assume that a particular data processing configuration is obtained to satisfy the data processing requirements of an organization. Does it follow that all the information needs for the organization have also been met?

1.7 "Data processing projects are not unique. These projects must compete with other large capital projects proposed within the organization." Discuss.

1.8 "Systems analysts are programmers who do not or cannot code." "Systems analysis requires a great deal of creativity and, as such, a person cannot be taught how to conduct systems analysis." "Systems Analysis is a new term for an old activity." Discuss these statements.

1.9 Using accounts payable information, discuss the dimensions of horizontal and vertical integration.

1.10 "Traditional organizational concepts (e.g., assigning responsibility and accountability, delegating authority, span of control) are time proven concepts. However, these concepts when implemented in an organization prohibit the effective use of the systems concept on a practical level." Discuss.

EXERCISES

1.1 Review the information attributes illustrated in Figure 1.1 and attempt to describe a system of measurement for each attribute. It may be helpful to use specific information to explain your answer.

1.2 From the library, obtain financial reports from *Standard and Poors* or *Moodys* on a particular company of your choice and decide whether or not you would invest in this company based on the information furnished by the financial reports. Using a scale of 1–10 (1 = poor, 10 = excellent), evaluate these reports in terms of the information attributes discussed in this chapter.

1.3 List and discuss the data processing operations required: (a) to prepare a payroll check, (b) to prepare a financial statement, and (c) to prepare an inventory status report.

1.4 Selecting several logico–mathematical models from Appendix A, describe how they produce information for organizational users.

1.5 Investigate an organization of your choice and describe its information system in terms of the design and demand building blocks.

1.6 Interview a variety of individuals (e.g., a businesswoman, a blue-collar worker, a professor of accounting, a military officer) and ask them to describe an information system. Prepare a presentation which compares and contrasts their descriptions with one another, and with that provided in this chapter.

1.7 Using the systems requirements illustrated in Figure 1.7, prepare a presentation for the head of a monastery as though you were selling typewriters and copy machines to replace pen and ink.

1.8 Many information systems are intended to provide an organization with a competitive edge in the market place. Select an organization and ascertain the way in which its information system helps to achieve a competitive edge.

PROBLEMS

1.1 Visit the local government office(s) responsible for issuing licenses for operating motor vehicles and registering motor vehicles. Evaluate the literature you obtain there and answer the following questions:

(a) Are these two functions administered separately or as a single department?

(b) How many information systems operate to perform both functions?

(c) To what degree are the systems integrated if there are more than one?

(d) If more than one system exists, what difficulties might prevent the designing of an integrated system?

(e) From your point of view, what commonalities exist between the data collected for each function?

1.2 The purpose of a city government is to provide public services desired or demanded by its citizens. These services include such things as law enforcement, fire protection, garbage pickup, gas and electric utilities, recreational facilities, and so forth. As cities grow, services often expand in terms of size and variety. This growth is often unplanned (e.g., neighborhood development) and responsibility is often achieved by adding new departments, or adding to existing departments for political reasons rather than based on efficient organizational principles. Using a hypothetical city with a population of 250,000 or more, list the kinds of services these cities are likely to offer. Then using the systems concept, reorder these services as you view their natural relationships for effective and efficient administration.

1.3 You have been asked by your boss to respond to a recent intracompany memo indicating your department would be billed $240 for keypunching of a 16,000-card job. A friend on your bowling team has supplied you with the following cost data on the last ten jobs performed by the keypunch section:

Job Size (In Thousands of Cards)	Cost
15	$180
30	320
12	140
18	240
20	230
9	110
17	190
22	270
12	160
25	300

Required: Prepare an appropriate response. (Hint: The least-squares model, illustrated in Appendix A, may be useful.)

1.4 Prepare a diagram illustrating the flow of data and information from and to the following components of the organization's information system*:

1. An order entry component that accepts sales orders.
2. A finished goods inventory component that processes the orders to determine if the ordered items are available for shipment.
3. A production scheduling component that schedules the resources of the manufacturing process to produce the items that the finished goods inventory system identifies as being unavailable.
4. A raw materials inventory component that is consulted by the production scheduling component to determine if adequate raw materials are on hand for input to the manufacturing processes.
5. A purchasing component that creates purchase orders for mailing to vendors requesting shipment of any raw materials found to be unavailable by the raw materials inventory system. The accounts payable component is notified of the financial obligations incurred by the firm.

* Adopted from Irvine Forkner and Raymond McLeod, Jr. (*Computerized Business Systems*, John Wiley & Sons, New York. 1973), Chapter 17.

6. A receiving component that receives the raw materials into raw material inventory when they arrive from the vendor and that notifies the accounts payable component so that the vendor might be reimbursed.
7. A production control component that monitors the manufacturing process to ensure that standards for time and cost are met. The manufacturing process is not begun until all of the needed raw materials are available and production scheduling has finalized the production schedule. When the production process is complete, the finished goods inventory component is notified of the availability of the finished goods. The production control component also enters information into the general accounting component so that production cost and inventory information from the manufacturing processes can be summarized.
8. A personnel component that advises payroll of any changes (additions, deletions, or other changes) to the personnel resources of the firm.
9. A billing component that prepares invoices for mailing to customers when items are identified by the finished goods inventory component as being available. Copies of the invoices are used by the warehouse stock clerks to select the items for shipment.
10. An accounts receivable component that has the responsibility of following up on the outstanding amounts owed the company, as established by the billing component. The output of the accounts receivable component becomes input to the consolidated financial records of the firm.
11. An accounts payable component that makes payments to vendors for the raw materials received, and that enters a summary of these transactions into the general accounting component.
12. A payroll component that pays employees for their services and enters information into the general accounting component.
13. A general accounting component that consolidates that data from the various input sources and prepares the financial reports for the firm.

BIBLIOGRAPHY

Davis, *Computer Data Processing,* Second Edition, New York: McGraw–Hill Book Company, 1973.

Davis, *Management Information Systems: Conceptual Foundations, Structure, and Development,* New York: McGraw–Hill Book Company, 1974.

Dwyer, "Some Observations on Management Information Systems," *Advances in EDP and Information Systems,* New York: American Management Association, 1961.

Forkner and McLeod, Jr., *Computerized Business Systems,* New York: John Wiley & Sons, Inc., 1973.

Hudson, "Determining Organizational Information Requirements," *Journal of Systems Management,* January 1981.

Kirk, *Total System Development for Information Systems,* New York: John Wiley & Sons, Inc., 1973.

Langefors & Samuelson, *Information and Data In Systems,* New York: Petrocelli Charter, 1976.

Lasden, "Overcoming Obstacles to Project Success," *Computer Decisions,* December 1981.

Lucas, *The Analysis, Design, and Implementation of Information Systems,* New York: McGraw–Hill Book Company, 1976.

Miller, "Problem Avoidance in the User/Analyst Relationship—Part 1," *Journal of Systems Management,* May 1981.

Murdick and Ross, *Information Systems for Modern Management,* Second Edition, Englewood Cliffs, NJ: Prentice–Hall, Inc., 1975.

Murdick and Ross, *Introduction to Management Information Systems,* Englewood Cliffs, NJ: Prentice–Hall, Inc., 1977.

Sadek and Tomeski, "Different Approaches to Information Systems," *Journal of Systems Management,* April 1981.

Sutherland, *Systems—Analysis, Administrations and Architecture,* New York: Van Nostrand Reinhold, 1975.

Weinberg, *An Introduction to General Systems Thinking,* New York: John Wiley & Sons, Inc., 1975.

CHAPTER 2

Information Requirements for Modern Organizations

2.1 ▪ INTRODUCTION

Information systems produce information to satisfy the needs of both the management and operations subsystems, as well as the needs of parties external to the organization. This information reflects the internal activities of the organization, competitive actions, environmental and sociological interests, and political and financial trends. It must represent what has happened, what is happening, and, perhaps most important of all, what will happen. This information requirement exists with equal importance in private industry, educational institutions, governmental agencies, the military, hospitals, and various other organizations.

An exhaustive list of specific information needs appropriate for any and all organizations does not exist. However, general information requirements are common to most organizations. An understanding of these requirements provides a conceptual basis to help us identify the specific information requirements for a particular organization. The objectives of this chapter are:

1. To provide an overview of the information requirements of organizations.
2. To analyze the role of management and its dependency on information.
3. To discuss the role of information in the decision-making process.
4. To identify the need for information in the day-to-day operations of an organization.

2.2 ▪ INFORMATION REQUIREMENTS—AN OVERVIEW

The growth of data and information processing is related directly to the growth of the organizations which comprise society in general. Since the formation of small, loosely organized tribes in prehistoric days, civilization has evolved slowly but continuously into societies of organizations. This trend toward organization affects all aspects of our lives. For example, most of us are employed by organizations, educated and trained by organizations, governed by a series of organizations, worship in organizations, and even spend a large amount of our leisure time in a manner specified by organizations. The evolution of organizations has two dimensions: there are more organizations, and they are becoming larger and more complex. To operate, control, and use these organizations efficiently and effectively, it is necessary to process data and produce information accordingly.

Pressures for More Information

Before the eighteenth century data were processed for two primary reasons. First, there was a natural desire by individuals to provide an account of their possessions and wealth. Babylonian merchants, for example, were keeping records as far back as 3500 B.C.

In the fifteenth century, Luca Pacioli developed the double entry bookkeeping system. This method permitted economic events to be recorded in monetary terms by using a series of expense and equity accounts. It remains the foundation of our financial accounting systems today.

The second reason for processing data before the eighteenth century was governmental requirements. As tribes grew into nations, the authorities of these nations—Egypt, Israel, Greece, etc.—compiled administrative surveys to be used for raising taxes and conscripting soldiers.

In the mid-eighteenth century there developed still more pressures for formally processing data. The Industrial Revolution had removed the basic means of production from the home and the small shop and put them into the factory. The development of large manufacturing organizations led to the development of service industries such as marketing and transportation. The increased size and complexity of these organizations prohibited any one individual from obtaining information to manage the organization effectively without data processing.

Furthermore, with the advent of the large factory systems and mass production techniques, the need for more sophisticated capital goods necessitated large investments and these large capital needs forced the separation of investor (owner) from management (manager). On one hand, management needed more information for internal decisions, while on the other hand, investors needed information about the organization and about management's performance.

As new business policies emerged, the need to process data also increased. For example, the granting of credit created a need to maintain accounts receivable, accounts payable, and credit statistics information. The procedures of financial accounting, which continued to be refined and expanded upon, also required more data processing. To produce greater efficiency in production, the pioneers of "scientific management" identified the need for still more data and information processing.

Regulation by government agencies forced not only corporations but society in general to adopt up-to-date processing practices and reporting systems. In the United States, such agencies include several state regulatory commissions; the Interstate Commerce Commission; the Internal Revenue Service; the Securities and Exchange Commission; environmental control boards; the Department of Energy, and so on. All of these agencies require a variety of reports from many organizations throughout the country. Therefore, not only does the reporting organization have to maintain a sound data processing system, but the regulatory bodies must maintain similar systems to handle the large volumes of data. It is not surprising, then, that the United States government is by far the largest data processor in the country.

Advances in technology, particularly as they affect the very nature of work itself, have rapidly transformed us from a people who survive on long hours of physical effort into a work force that is dependent on knowledge. Consequently, our ability to process data rapidly to provide necessary information is an essential element of the overall trend in society, rather than a recent fad or a result of the advent of computers. While we may lament the razing of the corner store or the family farm, and be discouraged by the red tape and bureaucracy of large organizations, the trend to greater complexity of organizations continues. The need to produce the necessary information becomes a requirement of survival rather than just a desirable goal to improve efficiency.

Organizational Factors

In Chapter 1 we introduced four organizational factors: nature, size, structure, and management style as comprising one of the six demand building blocks of the information systems. The demands of these organizational factors on the development of information systems is twofold. First, organizational factors provide a general framework which helps to determine the specific information requirements for an organization. Second, these factors influence the design of the physical structure of the information system in an organization. Although at this time we are concerned with how organizational factors determine the specific information requirements of organizations, in Chapter 4 we will analyze their influence on the physical structure of the information system.

The very *nature* or purpose of an organization is one major factor contributing to the information requirements of the organization. For example, while there will be obvious differences in the content or specific values of information required in a variety of manufacturing firms (e.g., steel, aluminum, plastic, chemicals, petroleum, rubber, etc.), the manufacturing process dictates a commonality of information requirements concerning planning, scheduling, controlling, and so forth. However, a real estate firm, an insurance company, or a transportation firm is unlikely to be comparable to a manufacturing firm in terms of many major information requirements. Certainly there are some similarities for all organizations in areas such as payroll, accounts receivable, accounts payable, purchasing, and so forth. However even in these "basic information systems," such characteristics as retail or wholesale oriented, unionized or not unionized, and service or product oriented, make for substantial differences in information requirements among organizations.

In most organizations information and data processing activities are viewed as support functions to the primary purpose of the organization. However, for some organizations (e.g., credit bureaus, libraries, and governmental agencies) the production of information for other organizations is their primary function. For still others, their primary product or service is related so closely to information processing (e.g., banks, insurance companies, securities brokers, etc.) that it is extremely difficult to separate the two. Consequently, to identify and understand the information requirements of a specific organization, it is first necessary to understand its nature and the inherent relationships to data and information processing.

The *size* of the organization is another factor affecting information requirements.

The larger an organization becomes the greater is its formal data processing and information requirement. Several characteristics associated with size alone are noteworthy. First, as organizations grow, they normally become segmented according to traditional business functions. For example, manufacturing, marketing, purchasing, accounting, and so forth, emerge as suborganizational units. Specific information tends to be identified with these individual units (e.g., purchasing information, engineering information, sales information).

Secondly, levels or tiers of management evolve, each having varying scopes of responsibility and authority. In a small manufacturing firm a production manager may be responsible for all aspects of production, including purchasing raw material, scheduling work, inventory control, machine maintenance, etc. There may be one or two persons performing each function, or one person performing two or more functions. In a large manufacturing firm scheduling work may be assigned to several different groups (e.g., daily scheduling, short-term scheduling, long-range scheduling). Each group may have a supervisor/manager who in turn reports to a general manager of scheduling, who reports to the production manager, who reports to the vice-president of production, and so forth. The information requirements for each level of management differ in terms of the specific values for the various information attributes.

A third characteristic associated with the size of an organization is that routine communications become more formal. At the local corner store, we simply walk in, ask for or select the product we want, pay for it, and the business transaction is complete. However, when one large organization conducts business with another large organization, this simple transaction becomes more complex. For example, a formal customer order, a packing slip, a bill of lading, and an invoice are usually prepared by the selling firm. The buying firm usually prepares a requisition, a purchase order, a receiving report, a receipt to inventory, and a check to the vendor, as a minimum, to effect a relatively simple and straightforward business transaction. Additionally, both firms keep other statistical and accounting records concerning this transaction. In practice the processing effort of even one of these simple communication documents is often a complicated information or data processing system in its own right.

The *structure* of the organization is the third inherent organizational factor affecting information requirements. While structure is in some ways related to size, it is a separate factor since two organizations of exactly the same size (i.e., sales, capital, personnel, etc.) can differ radically in their structure. Normally, we think of centralized or decentralized as the basic element of structure. However, the growth of conglomerates, franchises, licensees, and international organizations have initiated specific information requirements due entirely to their structure. Moreover, organizations are usually structured in varying degrees of centralization. For example, within a given organization, manufacturing may be decentralized by both product and region, marketing may be centralized by product and be decentralized by region, and accounting centralized in total.

The structure of specific business functions is also subject to variation from organization to organization. Responsibility for inventory management, as an example, can be part of manufacturing, purchasing, marketing, or materials management units within similar organizations. The use of matrix or project management structures also creates unique information requirements.

The *management style* or philosophy governing the organization is the fourth inherent organizational factor affecting information requirements. A management philosophy incorporating budgets or standard cost concepts generally requires more data and information processing than operating in an environment where only actual costs are measured. A controller approach requires different information than a simple bookkeeping approach. Any management philosophy emphasizing the development of extensive and intensive planning will have a concomitant requirement for formal information.

Early in the systems analysis phase of the systems development life cycle, the systems analyst should attempt to define and evaluate organizational factors. Not only will this awareness provide a framework for identifying specific information requirements, but it will ultimately become part of the criteria or demands against which proposed systems designs will be evaluated and selected.

Classifications of Information

Modern organizations have a multiplicity of information requirements. Moreover, one universally accepted classification scheme of information suitable for all situations does not exist. Descriptive phrases such as "management information," "production information," "real time information," "simulated information," and so forth, represent attempts to classify information according to various frames of reference. Many of these terms have widespread usage in the information systems field.

The distinction between formal and informal information, discussed previously, is the broadest and, perhaps, most critical classification. Categories such as management and operations information are very broad and will be treated more fully later in this chapter.

A functional classification of information (i.e., purchasing, accounting, scheduling, financial, marketing, etc.) is popular where information systems development projects have a functional orientation. A primary thrust of systems analysis at the practical level is to detail fully the information needed for each potential function. This frame of reference has several serious drawbacks for use in a textbook, however. First, the activities included in a particular function (e.g., purchasing) often differ radically from organization to organization. Second, the form of information requirements for many different functions is often similar. The apparent differences among functions are in the specific data values and the terminology employed by each function. For example, information reflecting inventory status is usually associated with the physical inventory function. However, the functions of finance, accounting, purchasing, employee relations, etc., also have a basic inventory and requirements for information regarding it. This commonality of form will be discussed in more detail when we analyze the information requirements of the operating subsystems. Third, the information produced by or for one function is often required by several other functions. This multiple use of the same information was described earlier as the horizontal and vertical integration characteristics of the information system. Thus, to treat the subject of information systems from an "accounting information systems," "marketing information systems," "production information systems," etc., viewpoint is too narrow in scope.

Time provides a frame of reference for classifying information that is appropriate in any organization. Viewing information as it relates to time is illustrated in Figure 2.1. Information which reflects past periods is normally defined as *historical information;* information reflecting the current period is considered *control information;* and, information representing the future is often termed *planning information*. No rigid lines separate time periods, since they may be different for each individual in an organization. Thus, even this frame of reference must be used judiciously. It is important to note that both the management and operation subsystems have information requirements representing all points on the time continuum.

It is necessary to include another dimension of time to satisfy all organization information requirements concerning the control function. This information is termed *expectations,* and it satisfies the question of "what should be?" The control function requires that actual information be compared to information reflecting expectations in order to be useful. While expectations often are expressed as plans, budgets, schedules, forecasts, etc., developed as part of the planning function, expectations may also be represented by engineered standards, policies, and practices governing the performance of organizational resources.

In a manufacturing environment, for example, the production of finished products is often described in a standard format at a point in time. This description includes what resources are used, how much are used, and in what sequence each resource is used. A document commonly called the "bill of material" describes the raw material quantities required to produce each item of finished goods. A routing sequence is the order in which material and labor enter into the manufacturing process. A rate table shows the amount of time and effort required at each work station in the process. Given these expectations for the process, future oriented information is developed using customer order or forecast information to produce plans, schedules, quotas, and work orders. Well-defined expectation information is a quantitative picture of how the organization interrelates. It is a model of the organization. Consequently, it can be used to help develop future alternatives and provide insights into a broad category of questions that begin with "What if. . . ." Control is implemented by comparing the expectations with information reflecting actual happenings during the process. Last, these expectations are used for both performance and financial accounting purposes to represent the process when it is completed.

Another useful frame of reference involves resources. Much information is generated, within and outside of organizations, that is related to tangible and intangible

Time / System	Past	Present	Future
Management System	Historical	Control	Planning
Operations System	What happened	What is happening	What will happen

FIG. 2.1 The classification of information as it relates to time.

resources. Tangible resources include employees, machines, facilities, materials, money, etc. Intangible resources include customers, processes, projects, vendors, stockholders, etc. This perspective also reflects the integrated nature of the information system, as can be seen by an analysis of customer-related information.

Information concerning a customer as a prospective market for a new product is future oriented and, more than likely, considered the proper domain of market research, long-term planning, and similar organizational units. It represents only an expectation type of information. Once that customer places a formal order for a product(s), however, the information becomes more than an expectation. The transaction results in information being produced for other organizational units such as order entry, credit, production scheduling, and shipping. When the ordered product(s) is shipped, customer information concerning billing and accounts receivable is required. Finally, this transaction is added to other similar transactions in a sales history or marketing statistical file to be analyzed, explained, and perhaps used as a basis for the next period's forecast.

A customer is an organizational resource. Information concerning a customer is an organizational requirement. Various units within the organization require customer information represented by various values for the information attributes, such as completeness, timing, detail, and so forth. The design of an effective information system recognizes the totality of a given resource, as well as the individual information requirements concerning that resource.

A closely related classification of information deals with the dynamics of the information value associated with the resource. For example, some information about resources such as customers, vendors, and employees is closely related to their very existence (e.g., names, addresses, identification codes) and therefore is subject to little, if any, change. This descriptive information usually involves the development of elaborate coding and classification schemes, discussed later in the text. Descriptive information, because of its unchanging nature, can be contrasted to information that reflects change (e.g., hours worked, orders on hand, sales last period). The latter is variable, transactional, or status information, and is given meaning by descriptive information. The distinction between *descriptive* and *variable* information is illustrated in Figure 2.2.

The advent of computer technology has added several other terms that classify in-

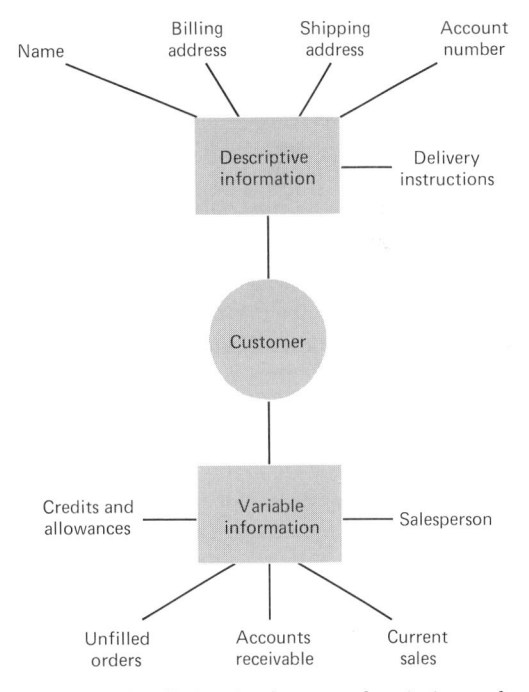

FIG. 2.2 The distinction between descriptive and variable information as each pertains to a resource.

formation. The manner in which data are collected and processed is referred to as **batch** or **random.** Batch is the processing of a collection of transactions at one time to improve the efficiency of the collection/processing operations. Random refers to the collecting and processing of data transactions as they occur. For example, if items are removed from inventory on a continuous basis but the inventory records are updated at a later time (e.g., at the end of the day), we call this updating batch processing. If the inventory records are updated with each inventory transaction, the process is random.

Real time and **online** are two additional terms that have received widespread attention in information systems literature and practice. One definition of real time is that information is made available within a time frame that permits the receiver to use or react to the information. By this definition, a monthly report is a form of real time information for an accountant. However, it is becoming popular to restrict the use of the term real time to information that is processed as it is received. Online information processing means collecting data or accessing information via a terminal device that is directly connected to a computer. As we shall discuss later, real time and online information are essential to some individuals in an organization, and are of little importance to others.

2.3 ▪ MANAGEMENT REQUIREMENTS

In the broadest sense, *management* refers to all of the individuals within an organization who are responsible for its actions and results. This includes presidents and vice presidents, as well as individuals such as supervisors and department managers.

Regardless of the title, those individuals charged with managing an organization are both vital consumers and producers of information. As producers of information, managers are part of the information system. As consumers of information, managers are key users of the information system.

The current trend to formalize and computerize the information system in large organizations has emphasized the role of the manager as a consumer. This movement is responsible for the description, **management information system** (MIS), so common in the literature. However, this same literature is replete with references of automated or computerized systems failing to meet management's information requirements adequately. A brief analysis of the function and role of a manager may provide some insights into why this is true. With this background, we can then briefly discuss the role of information in planning, controlling, and decision making.

The Management Function

Some authorities state that the essential function of management is to deal with changing conditions. Others say that the essential function is to recognize and assimilate technological changes in such a manner that practical items of value will be produced and disseminated to society in an orderly, timely, and economical manner. Still others state that management is simply "getting things done through the efforts of others."

The literature describes many tasks associated with the management function. Some of these tasks are planning, scheduling, directing, organizing, hiring, training, controlling, supervising, and so forth. More current studies emphasize the importance of decision making as an essential task of management. In all cases the importance of information attributes such as accuracy and timeliness are deemed necessary to perform these tasks effectively. However, as important as information is to performing these tasks, the gathering and processing of data to provide the information is usually considered only a minor concern of the manager.

A study by Mintzberg concerning the nature of managerial work, defines a manager in terms of ten distinct but interrelated roles.[1] The use of information in each of these different roles is viewed as the key ingredient of the power and authority associated with a manager. The author divides these ten roles into three groups: (1) interpersonal relationships, (2) transfer of information, and (3) decision making.

Within the interpersonal relationships group, he distinguishes three roles: (1) figurehead, (2) liaison, and (3) leader. As a figurehead, the manager formally represents the organization to all external parties. In the liaison role the manager interacts with external parties to exchange favors and information. The leader role includes all of the tasks directly involved with the traditional managing of subordinates within the organization. The importance of these interpersonal roles is that they allow the manager to access valuable information from sources both internal and external to the organization.

The second group, transfer of information, includes three informational roles: (1) monitor, (2) disseminator, and (3) spokesman. As a monitor the manager is a receiver of information regarding his or her own group's activities. In the role of disseminator, the manager is responsible for transmitting both internally and externally generated information to the organization. The spokesman role allows the manager to disseminate information concerning the activities of the manager's own group to external parties. Through these roles it is obvious that managers enjoy special access to information.

The final group, decision making, entails four roles: (1) entrepreneur, (2) disturbance handler, (3) resource allocator, and (4) negotiator. As an entrepreneur, the manager's function is to initiate change. In the role of disturbance handler, the manager is responsible for solving problems or unplanned changes within the organization. As a resource allocator, the manager decides where the organization will expend its efforts. Finally, in the negotiator role, the manager is required to participate in relationships or problems arising between the organization and external parties. The combination of status and unique access to information places the manager in the best position for making the necessary decisions to function well in these roles.

While all of the traditional managerial tasks can be identified and related to these ten roles, the significance of this view of the manager's function is the emphasis given to the value of information. Previously we stated that the information system concept defines the management of an organization as a primary user of the system. Certainly this present perspective reinforces that relationship. However, it is also obvious that as we design and implement an information system physically separate from the individual manager, we are removing an essential source of the manager's power and status. For in the development of formal but separate information systems (regardless of the

---

[1] H. Mintzberg, *The Nature of Managerial Work* (New York: Harper & Row Publishers, 1973).

level of automation involved), access to required information is available to *all* authorized persons within and outside of a specific organization.

The emphasis in early information systems development was on providing more efficient processing of what can be classified generally as routine operations or accounting information. More often than not, specific managers approved this developmental effort to improve efficiencies within their own unit. Recent attempts to develop more sophisticated information systems involve integrating data flows among individual units of an organization (horizontal integration) and between levels of management (vertical integration). It is in these latter endeavors where the more spectacular failures have occurred and have been well publicized. An awareness of the importance of information to management, both as consumer and as producer, will permit those who design and implement formal information systems to consider these nontechnical aspects in their overall analysis.

Planning

Planning is a task or activity that is required on a continuous basis of the management of all organizations. It is a task that is shared in varying degrees by all levels of management. The planning function is concerned with the future. When we plan we attempt to sketch out the things that will, might, or must happen to proceed from a given point to a desired point. While planning is future oriented, to do it well the planner must have an accurate assessment of the past and present situations of the relevant environment. Depending on the reasons for a plan, the timing requirements, or the magnitude of the action to be performed, the planner may require considerable formal information concerning the past and present situations. In addition, once the plan is developed it becomes necessary information for those individuals who will implement and control the proposed activity. The function of planning can be viewed as both a consumer and a producer of information that, in many instances, is provided by and required in the organization's formal information system.

The planning activity can be analyzed further as a series of five interactive steps. First the planner must establish goals or objectives. The process of selecting goals/objectives can be simple or complex. The final selection of a goal/objective may be the result of a large research effort involving an intricate decision-making process. Often a large requirement for information represents past and present situations concerning the proposed goal/objective, as well as requirement for information concerning the plans of other, related goals/objectives. The implications of existing plans, both long and short term, and the plans of related units within an organization, often must be considered and evaluated before a planner can state a final goal/objective. Thus, the availability of properly attributed information representing these existing plans is often a prerequisite to effective planning.

The second step in the planning process requires the planner to identify the events and activities that must be performed to achieve the stated goal/objective. This step is also an interactive process requiring evaluation and generation of a large quantity of information. In the third step, the planner describes the resources and/or talents necessary to perform each identified activity. The fourth step in the planning process is to define the duration of each activity identified. The final step involves determining in what sequence (if any) the identified activities must be performed. The last three steps in the planning process must be clearly stated so that once the plan is acted upon they can be used as the criteria for establishing a control scheme.

The design of a formal information system must take into consideration the requirements of the planning process if it is to support management. This includes supplying the information required by the planner at each step in the planning process, establishing procedures for processing the information at each step (including the means for viewing alternatives, which is often termed "what if"), providing for storing the approved plans as information for control purposes, and devising an efficient method for communicating the plans to other members of the organization. These requirements of the planning process are valid regardless of the level of automation involved in the implementation of the formal information system.

Controlling

Once a plan has been developed, approved, and implemented, it is necessary to evaluate the actual events as they occur. It is indeed rare when plans are implemented as they were originally developed. Deviations from plan result from many factors, including poor planning premises, erroneous estimates, miscommunication between planner and implementor(s), unforeseen events, and mistakes of implementors. Some deviations are minor and require little or no action by management. Other deviations require immediate management attention at various levels in the organization. However before any action can be taken, it is first necessary to identify the deviation. This is the primary function of the control process.

Controlling consists of three basic steps. First, it is necessary to become aware of what is actually taking place. Second, it is necessary to compare the actual with expected results. Third, it is necessary to take corrective action to alter either the actual results or the expectation. This control process is illustrated in Figure 2.3.

Expectations, or standards against which to measure, are developed in the planning process. These expectations may be time requirements, personnel, dollars, or any other resource measurement criteria. They may simply be referred to as "the plan," "the budget," or "the schedule," etc., or they may be quotas, estimates, engineered standards, specifications, and so forth. Regardless of what they are termed or how they are developed, expectations must exist if the control process is to be effective.

In many situations where detail planning is not formalized, these expectations exist only in the minds of the managers who plan or attempt to control activities. In simple endeavors or emergency actions this may be adequate. As a rule, however, the size and complexity of most organizations requires

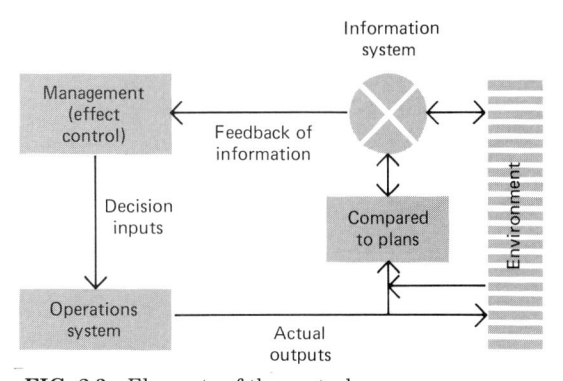

FIG. 2.3 Elements of the control process.

that these expectations be formalized and communicated to all individuals involved in executing the plan.

Given a set of quantified expectations, it is then possible for those responsible for controlling the implementation to identify and collect the appropriate data. Thus, an adequate feedback loop for the control process is actually initiated during the planning process.

In all organizations varying levels of control requirements on a given effort, in some way, relate to existing levels of management. The control requirements for a section supervisor on a right-of-way excavation project are different from those of the chief executive. An effective control system must contain the logic appropriate for reporting deviations to each level of management. In the absence of this control system mechanism, managers are often confronted with reviewing considerable amounts of meaningless data to determine whether it contains their appropriate control information, or they must rely on subordinates to communicate deviations on a "hit or miss" basis. Thus, meeting the requirements of an effective control system is as necessary as meeting the planning process requirements, regardless of the level of technology used in the design of the information system.

The successful development of highly automated control systems requires that expectations be well defined in terms of information attributes. It requires that the sensors used to collect actual data for the feedback loop be designed to match the attributes of the expectations. Last, it requires that the logic for reporting deviations to all levels of management be clearly developed prior to the actual occurrence of the deviations. These characteristics and capabilities must be designed into the formal information system to satisfy management's control requirements.

Decision Making

An activity common to all levels of management, and often considered to be management itself, is decision making. Within both the planning and the controlling processes, the manager is required to make decisions. The quality of managerial decisions is related directly to the information available to the decision maker. Decision making is the process of selecting the most desirable or optimum alternative to resolve a problem or to attain a goal. Managers must often make decisions to resolve problem confrontations or conflict situations. An orderly process of arriving at a decision contains four elements:

1. *Model.* The model represents a quantitative or qualitative description of the problem.
2. *Criteria.* The stated criteria represent goals or objectives of the decision problem (e.g., how to achieve maximum customer service). When several criteria are in conflict (e.g., increase customer service levels but also reduce inventory quantities), the decision maker must compromise.
3. *Constraints.* Constraints are limiting factors which must be considered in the solution of the decision problem. Lack of funds is an example of a constraint that most of us have.
4. *Optimization.* Once the decision problem is fully described (the model), the manager determines what is needed (the criteria), and what is permissible (the constraints). At this point the decision maker is ready to select the best, or optimum, solution.

Some decision problems and conflicts are simple and deterministic and have only minor ramifications. Others are complex and probabilistic and can have a significant impact. Decision making can be routine and structured, or it can be complex and ill-structured. In the broad terms introduced by Herbert Simon, decision making is either programmed or nonprogrammed.[2]

Programmed decision making refers to the process of dealing with well structured and repetitive decisions. To effect programmed decision making, the decision rules as well as the alternative courses of action pertaining to a decision must be completely defined. In many organizations, programmed decision-making opportunities are defined as standard operating practices, and an algorithm is developed describing how this decision is to be made. The execution of this decision process may be manual or computerized. A great challenge to those designing computer systems is to identify programmed decision opportunities and to develop computer programs to execute them. The process of this kind of decision making is illustrated in Figure 2.4.

Inventory activities provide an example of an opportunity for programmed decision making. An analysis of inventory activity to provide usage patterns, holding costs, replenishment costs, reorder points, reorder quantities, and safety stock levels must be accomplished. Once these components have been defined, we structure them into an algorithm so that each withdrawal from inventory triggers a comparison of the remaining inventory level against the predetermined reorder point. If the current inventory level is equal to or below the reorder point, the predetermined (economic) reorder quantity is generated as a replenishment order. If the remaining inventory level is above the predetermined reorder point, no replenishment order is produced. Safety stock provisions allow for random changes in the inventory withdrawal pattern.

All decisions that are routine and repetitive, with the potential for well-defined parameters, lend themselves to the development and implementation of programmed decision making. The payoff from implementing programmed decision making is that it frees management for more important tasks.

Nonprogrammed decision making or heuristic decision making, on the other hand, is the process of dealing with ill-defined problems. They are usually complex, only a portion of the set of total parameters is known, and many of the known parameters are highly probabilistic. It takes all the talent of a skilled decision maker plus the aid of a well-designed information system to make sound nonprogrammed decisions. Expansion of plant facilities, purchase versus lease, and merger transactions, are examples of nonprogrammed decision making.

Decision makers have individual information accumulation rates that determine their information processing efficiency. Past knowledge, coupled with present information processing efficiency, determines the in-

---

[2] Herbert A. Simon, *The New Science of Management Decision*, (New York: Harper & Row Publishers, 1960).

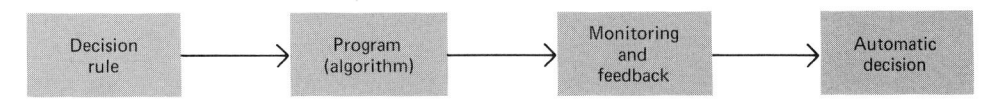

Decision rule → Program (algorithm) → Monitoring and feedback → Automatic decision

FIG. 2.4 A schematic diagram of the programmed decision-making process.

dividual's decision-making capacity. Faced with alternatives, decision makers identify an objective and then attempt to attain this objective by choosing the best alternative, based on their existing knowledge. If an individual is unable to come to grips with each alternative at the present level of knowledge, then additional information is sought. Insufficient information results from the inability of the sources of information to provide the information, or from the inability of decision makers to prescribe accurately their information requirements. An illustration of the decision-making process is shown in Figure 2.5.

This view of decision making is that it is a rational information-using process, not an emotional process. In this context, difficulties in decision making can be attributed to either inadequate information or to inadequately specified information objectives.

2.4 ▪ DECISION-MAKING REQUIREMENTS

The need for decision making at all levels of management on a continuing basis is emphasized throughout the literature. The importance of providing needed information to decision makers is also widely recognized. This section focuses on decision making in organizations and suggests ways of meeting information requirements. The analysis also points out why formal information systems have not been, and cannot be, successful in meeting *all* of the needs of decision makers.

Levels of Decision Making

We can classify decision making on three levels of a continuum: (1) strategic, (2) tactical, and (3) technical.[3]

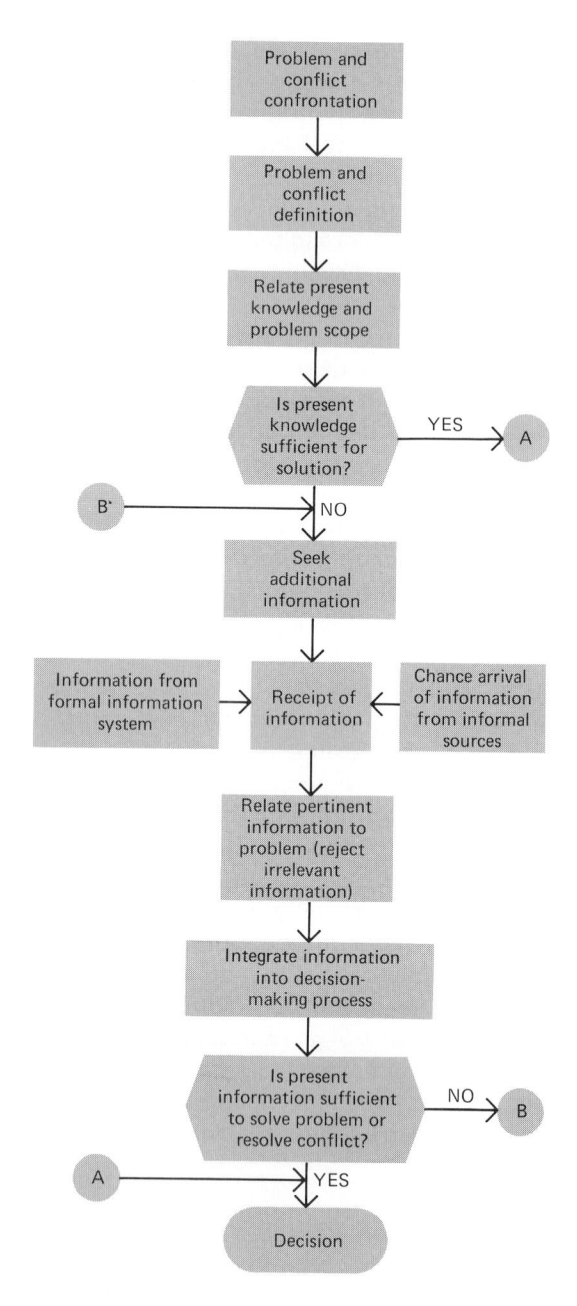

FIG. 2.5 Flowchart depicting the use of information in the decision-making process.

1. *Strategic level.* Strategic decisions are characterized by a great deal of uncertainty and are future oriented. They establish long-range plans which affect the entire organization. The goals of the organization are stated and a range of strategies is made. Goals and strategies might entail, for example, plant expansion, determination of product lines, mergers, diversification, capital expenditures, or the sale of the organization. The strategic level, therefore, includes establishing objectives, policy making, organizing, and attaining an overall effectiveness for the organization.

2. *Tactical level.* Tactical decision making pertains to short-term activities and the allocation of resources for the attainment of the objectives. This kind of decision making relates to such areas as formulation of budgets, funds flow analysis, deciding on plant layout, personnel problems, product improvement, and research and development.

    Where strategic decision making is largely a planning activity, tactical decision making requires a fairly equal mix of planning and controlling activities. This kind of decision making has little, if any, potential for programmed decision making. The decision rules in tactical decision making are, for the most part, ill-structured and not amenable to routine and self-regulation.

3. *Technical level.* At this level of decision making, standards are fixed and the results of decisions are deterministic. Technical decision making is a process of ensuring that specific tasks are implemented in an effective and efficient manner. This kind of decision making requires specific commands to be given that control specific operations. The primary management function is control, with planning performed on a rather limited scale. Examples of this kind of decision making are acceptance or rejection of credit, process control, scheduling, receiving, shipping, inventory control, and worker allocation.

Information Requirements

The different levels of decision making have different information requirements. Illustrated in Figure 2.6 are three aspects of decision making and their relationship to the levels of decision making. These schematics represent general concepts, and the lines in Figure 2.6 cannot be drawn precisely. The purpose of the illustration is to show not only the potential effectiveness of the formal information system but also its probable limitations. The literature is replete with grandiose promises of what information systems can do for management, but as shown in this illustration, many of these promises are far beyond the current state of the art. To the extent that decision making remains an art, nonprogrammed, and dependent on external information, formal information systems are limited in how effectively they can support decision making.

The matrix in Figure 2.7 relates some of the previously discussed classifications of information to the three levels of decision making. The nature of information requirements are related to the decision-making process. For each decision-making activity, a determination is made regarding the information required by the responsible man-

---

[3] The description of decision making within the two-dimensional framework of degree of structure and level of managerial activity was first presented by G. Anthony Gorry and Michael S. Scott Morton, "A Framework for Management Information Systems," *Sloan Management Review,* Fall 1971, pp. 55–70.

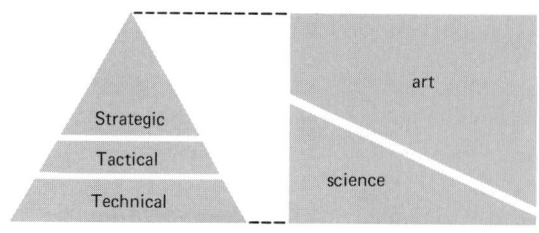

(a) Degree to which decision making is an art/science

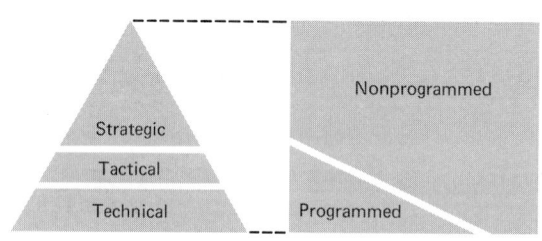

(b) Degree to which decision making can be programmed/nonprogrammed.

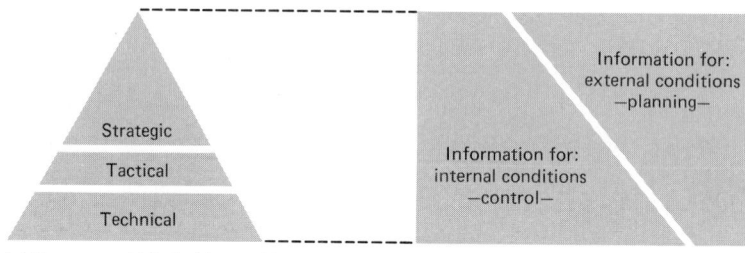

(c) Degree to which decision making requires internal or external information.

FIG. 2.6 Three aspects of decision making for the three levels of decision making. (a) The degree to which decision making is an art/science. (b) The degree to which decision making can be programmed/nonprogrammed. (c) The degree to which decision making requires internal or external information.

agers to enable them to effect planning, controlling, organizing, implementing of assignments, and so forth. For example, while it is technically possible to provide a cathode ray tube (CRT) to a strategic decision maker, the information needs at this decision level do not usually justify such an approach. While the person(s) who is responsible for the decision-making activity under analysis, and who will be the principal user of the information, should be given considerable latitude and help in determining their information requirements, both the analyst and the user must evaluate the range of information attributes for each identified information requirement.

Moreover, in many organizations the problem with providing users information is not due to the absence of information but rather to the abundance of available data or

Categories of Decision Making / Classification of Information	Technical	Tactical	Strategic
Dependence on External Information	Very low	Moderate	Very high
Dependence on Internal Information	Very high	High	Moderate
Information Online	Very high	High	Low
Information in Real Time	Very high	Very high	Very high
Information Reported Periodically	Moderate	High	Very high
Information That is Descriptive-Historical in Nature	Moderate	High	Low
Information That is Performance-Current in Nature	Very high	High	Moderate
Information That is Predictive-Future in Nature	Low	High	Very high
Information That is Simulated-What If in Nature	Low	High	Very high

FIG. 2.7 The classifications of information that meet the requirements of the three levels of decision making.

information. In Chapter 3 we discuss a variety of ways in which this problem can be solved. However using the direction given in Figure 2.7 can provide the analyst and user valuable assistance in formulating specific information requirements.

2.5 ▪ OPERATIONS REQUIREMENTS

The successful operation of many modern organizations is based on their ability to process simple, routine day-to-day information efficiently. In small organizations this information is highly informal and often is communicated verbally. However, as organizations grow, these simple and repetitive communications systems become quite structured and formal. Until recently, advances in modern data processing technology had little effect on this level of data processing and information requirement. Multiple copy forms often were used for the necessary flow of information among a number of organizational units. In emergencies or situations where timing was a major factor, personal meetings, the telephone, and the telegraph were the methods used.

In these latter cases informal communication was often documented later by the preparation of paperwork for accounting or other purposes, usually well after the action was initiated and completed. Early data processing endeavors were directed at reducing this "after the fact" paper processing. Thus, organizational units would forward copies of the transaction paperwork to a data processing unit, where it was encoded via a keying operation and entered into a computer system. This batch processing of routine information was effective for accounting purposes; however, it did nothing to improve the basic operations mode of the organization.

The state of the art in data processing and data communication technology has advanced to a point where online processing is not only feasible, but often the most efficient and effective method to use in providing operations level information. For example, the experimental airline reservation systems of the 60s are now commonplace in that industry, and in the automobile rental and the hotel/motel industries as well. Public utilities respond to work requests and customer account problems in an online mode using a variety of terminal devices, while their representatives communicate with customers via the telephone. Cashiers and service attendants receive real time credit clearances within minutes of querying on significant purchases. A telephone call about the problem with a major credit card account or billing item is often corrected or satisfied before the call is completed. In some organizations, production and shipping notices are directed to individual work stations via telecommunication terminals. It is now possible for a salesperson to verify an order status, an inventory level, or a credit approval, before leaving a customer's office.

These are just a few examples of how the operations of organizations have been improved and altered dramatically due to the implementation of advanced data processing and data communication technology. Moreover, this transactional level of data processing is often an essential input for preparing control level information for management. The information provided to management for short-term planning and control also is enhanced with improvements in operations oriented information. Industry forecasters are predicting still greater changes during the next decade in this dimension of information systems development.

The Communication Process

Effective communication is important not only in organizations but in all aspects of human pursuits. Communication takes place when information is transmitted from a source to a receiver via some channel. *Noise* is the term commonly used to describe anything that affects the quality of the information during this transmission. This classical view of the communication process is illustrated in Figure 2.8.

While there is a wide spectrum of communication systems ranging from simple person-to-person communication to highly complex electronic systems, we are concerned specifically with formal information

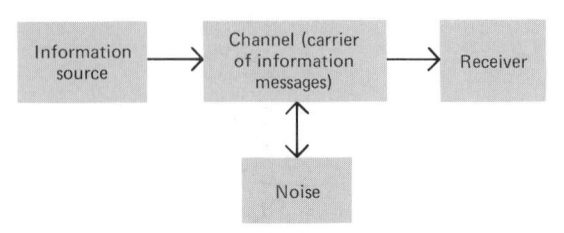

FIG. 2.8 The communication process.

and its communication in an organization by the formal information system. Noise is anything that interferes with accomplishing this.

The communication process illustrated in Figure 2.8 is only as effective as its least effective component—a chain is no stronger than its weakest link. If the source does not provide data with specific information attributes in mind, if the information is distorted or delayed in the channel, if the receiver cannot interpret or use the information, then the entire system is degraded to its lowest common denominator. The challenge to those designing information systems is to identify clearly what is required by the receiver to satisfy a specific information requirement, what can be done to ensure that the proper data are collected, and how the channel can be implemented to minimize the noise factor.

Transaction Processing

The information necessary for operating an organization is available in several different modes. The overall organizational structure, policy statements, position descriptions, and standard operating procedures provide much of the general information, answering such basic questions as "who does what?," "how is this done?," "when is this done?," "where is this done?," "how much is used?," "how long should it take?," "how much should it cost?," and so forth. A *transaction*, on the other hand, relates to the occurrence of an event that causes a specific action and specific work to be performed.

For example, a procedures manual describes how an organization purchases materials, supplies, and services. A purchase requisition is completed and is sent to the purchasing department, where a formal purchase order is prepared and sent to the vendor. Both the purchase requisition and the purchase order are part of the information flow necessary for the business transaction of acquiring a product or service by the organization. The purchase requisition tells the purchasing department what is needed, when, where, etc. Formalizing this information (i.e., preparing a purchase order) is the function of purchasing department personnel. Subsequently, the purchase order is forwarded to the vendor where it initiates the activity required to satisfy the customer request.

When goods are delivered to the receiving department of the customer organization, a copy of the purchase order provides the necessary approval to accept the goods and instructs the receiver where to send or inventory the goods. A receiving notice or a copy of the purchase order that reflects receipt of the ordered goods is matched with the vendor's invoice and initiates a check to be sent to the vendor. Notice of receipt and the vendor invoice are information necessary to complete the business transaction of acquiring products or services. This process is reflected in Figure 2.9.

The same business transaction viewed from the vendor's perspective may appear as follows. A customer's purchase order is received by the order processing unit. Upon receipt of this information, order processing clerks prepare a formal customer order that may be forwarded to either the shipping or the production scheduling unit, depending on the availability of the requested product. If the customer order is forwarded to the production scheduling unit, then it must be distributed to material handlers and production personnel in the form of a specific work assignment or scheduling request. After production, the goods must be invento-

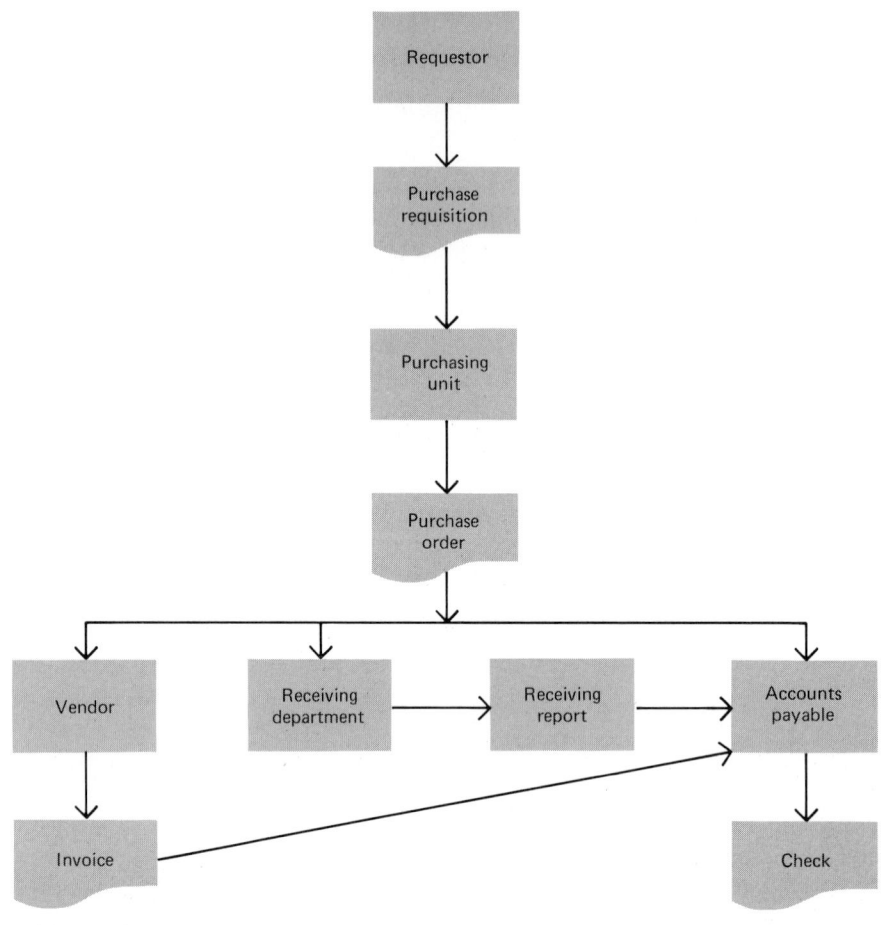

FIG. 2.9 The transaction processing for acquiring a product/service.

ried and shipping personnel notified, both of the customer order and of the product availability. They then ready the goods for shipment, prepare delivery instructions for the driver who is to deliver the goods, and notify the billing department of when, and to whom, the shipment was made. Once notified of a shipment, the billing department will formalize and issue an invoice to the customer and notify accounts receivable. The accounts receivable department will update their receivable files, and will complete the transaction when a customer payment is received. This transaction processing is illustrated in Figure 2.10.

These two examples illustrate the type of data processing and information requirements necessary for the successful operations of many organizations. The processing of transactional information is usually characterized by information attributes of rigid timing, simple but precise content, and a highly structured format. Transactional information usually passes from one organi-

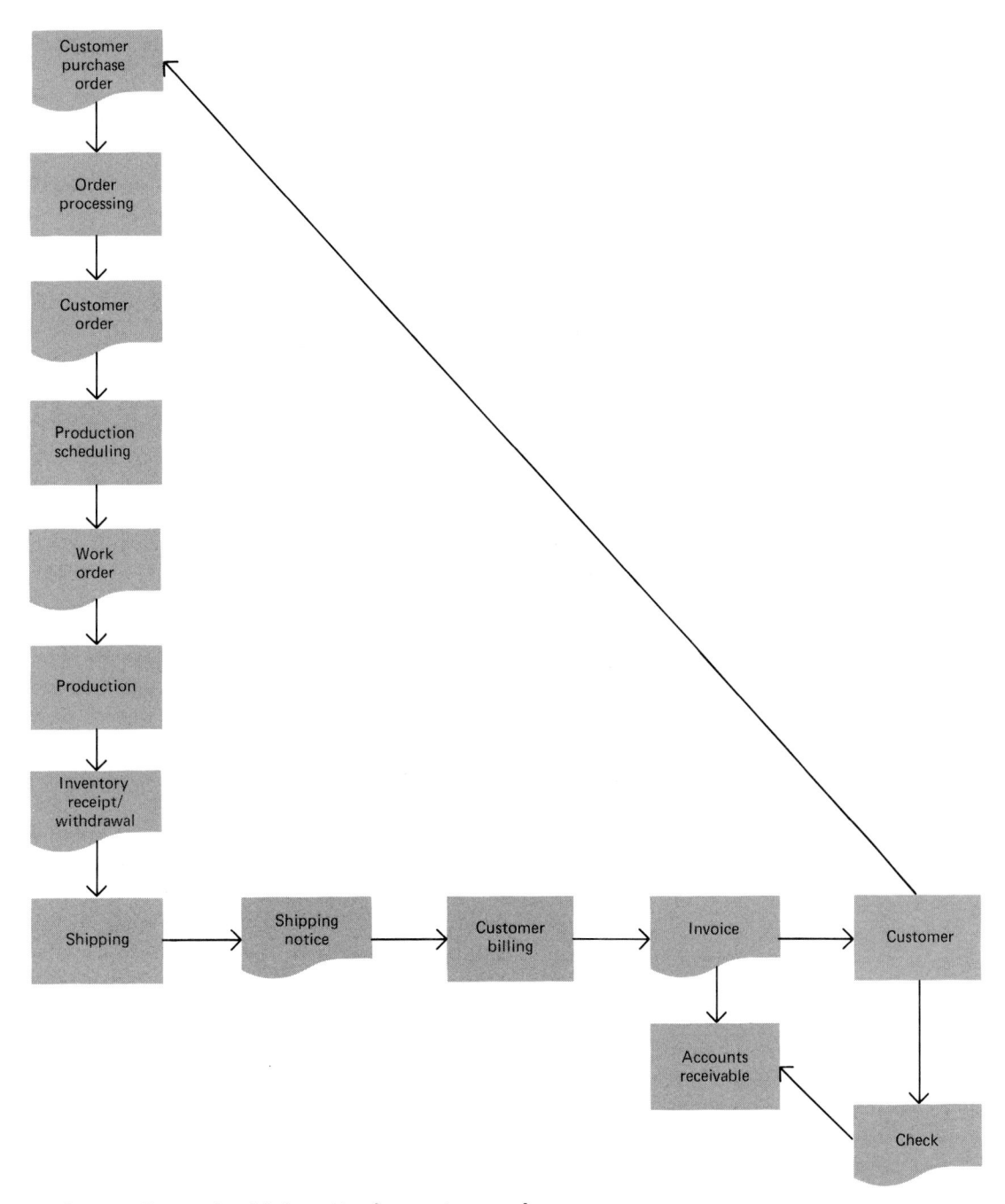

FIG. 2.10 Transactional information for a customer order.

zation unit to another, with each making important additions or modifications to its content. The information content is normally a combination of descriptive and variable data elements. Each version of the transaction serves as an initiator of some physical activity and provides the basic data elements for preparing the subsequent transaction. Systems development tasks that are process oriented are concerned with producing and processing each of these information transactions efficiently.

Status Information

The efficient processing of transactional information is the cement that bonds the organization together. However, the existence of transactions, and to some extent the efficiency with which they are processed, is closely related to the availability of what we term *status information*. Status information can either represent the status of the transaction, or reflect the status of the resources affected by the transaction.

Tracking the status of a transaction is a simple control problem that can become very complicated in large, complex operating systems. For example, a customer order is received and begins a transactional life which may be measured in minutes, days, weeks, or months. It may involve two or three physical activities, or it may involve several dozen physical activities. While the total transactions represent the organization's lifeblood, a specific transaction may be considered somewhat insignificant, mundane, and routine. But a query concerning that transaction (e.g., customer order) can result in a significant expenditure of resources to provide an answer. Our concept of how well an organization performs often is based on how well it is able to provide information concerning our transactions. In addition, a lost, misplaced, or erroneous transaction can be very expensive to an organization.

If the processing of a customer order, for example, is not performed efficiently, then several problem situations may occur. First, the order might never be filled and then the revenue associated with that order is lost. Potential future revenues from that customer may not be realized because of the way this transaction was handled. Second, the order may be filled as specified but be late. If it is refused by the customer, not only will its revenue be lost, but it is likely that charges for accepting returned goods will have to be paid by the organization. Third, the order might be processed twice; duplicate charges and expediting expenses will be incurred and the organization may lose customer goodwill.

In summary, the cost/value judgments related to developing information systems for satisfying status information requirements must consider all of these potential, as well as actual, costs. In Chapter 3 several techniques for satisfying these status information requirements are discussed.

The second form of status information is related to the resources that are affected by the processing of transactions. This type of information is similar to traditional inventory or balance sheet information. It satisfies the question, "how much?" While we commonly think of inventory as being materials, virtually all resources, tangible and intangible, have an inventory status. Thus, there is appropriate status information reflecting machine availability, personnel skills, accounts payable, accounts receivable, customer orders in process, purchase orders in process, budgetary dollars, storage space, and materials.

In the usual course of doing business, inventory balances experience constant change due to transactional processing. The use of modern data processing technology is particularly useful in satisfying this type of information need. The previous examples of real time reservation systems were nothing more than an attempt to provide inventory status information. Once we identify an information requirement as an inventory status requirement, it becomes a simple matter to identify the transactions that affect its status, and thereby provide the desired status information.

To many information theorists the prospect of providing information to meet the requirements of an organization's operations subsystem is not nearly as appealing as providing information for the management subsystem. Operations subsystem information normally does not require the use of complicated logico–mathematical models. Satisfying the information requirements of the operations subsystem, however, is perhaps most important in the short-term future of an organization.

SUMMARY

The growth in data and information processing is related directly to the growth of organizations. Pressures to produce more and more information come from both internal and external sources to an organization. While each organization has information requirements somewhat different from any other organization, commonalities can be found by analyzing four organizational factors. While one classification scheme for information does not exist, several classifications have a widespread use in designing information systems.

Management represents one large user group for formal information in all organizations. At the practical level managers can be perceived as both users and producers of information. Understanding this dual nature of management as it relates to the design of information systems provides a fundamental understanding of both the opportunities and problems associated with developing formal information systems. The key roles of management in planning and controlling an organization can be enhanced by developing efficient and effective information systems.

Decision making, if not synonymous with management, is essential to all managers. Moreover, good, sound decision making must be supported by information reflecting the proper attributes. Analyzing decision-making levels provides insights into how formal information systems can support decision making and how these systems are limited in supporting various types of decision making.

Those individuals involved in the actual operations of the organization represent the second large user group of formal information. The information requirements of these users tend to be characterized by simple and repetitive needs which are shaped by attributes of timeliness and precision. The development of the formal information system to satisfy these operations requirements can contribute greatly to the overall effectiveness of the organization, as well as provide the basis for information required by different levels of management.

REVIEW QUESTIONS

2.1 What were the reasons for processing data before the eighteenth century? After the eighteenth century?

2.2 List and describe the four factors that comprise the organizational demand block.

2.3 As organizations grow in size, what happens to their business functions? Levels or tiers of management? Routine communications?

2.4 Using time as a frame of reference, how might you classify information in an organization?

2.5 What is "batch" processing? "Random" processing? "Real time" and "online" systems?

2.6 What roles might a manager assume? How would each role affect a manager's access to information?

2.7 What steps are involved in the planning process? Controlling?

2.8 What requisite is necessary for automated control systems to be developed successfully?

2.9 Describe the four elements of decision making.

2.10 What is "programmed" decision making? "Nonprogrammed" decision making?

2.11 List and describe the three levels of decision making. How might the character of the information differ depending on the level it is intending to serve?

2.12 Within the context of the communication process, what is the challenge to the designer of information systems?

2.13 How would you characterize "transaction" processing?

2.14 What is meant by "status" information?

QUESTIONS FOR DISCUSSION

2.1 "The Federal Government is the single largest cause of the increasing requirements for data processing in most organizations. Organizations today spend $25 billion to $30 billion per year on government required paperwork. Processing this paperwork in various agencies of the Federal Government itself costs approximately $500 per year for every man, woman, and child in the United States." Provide some specific examples of government requirements.

2.2 "Certainly there are many reasons as to why our data processing costs are increasing, and requirements by various government agencies are no small part, but our own internal demands for more information and more timely information are probably the single largest reason for the increase." Compare the implications of this statement with that in Question 2.1.

2.3 While many people associate sophisticated data processing with large organizations, it should be clear in observing recent franchising trends that small organizations are, perhaps, even more dependent on efficient and effective information data processing. For example, 20 to 30 years ago "Mom and Pop stores" were replaced by large supermarkets. Today, a new breed of franchisor has brought back the "Mom and Pop" concept using very tight controls made possible through the use of well-designed data processing systems. From your own experiences, discuss how this is being accomplished.

2.4 "Controllers and budget directors are pushing such detailed financial reports at chief executives that long-range planning gets lost in the shuffle. The real problem is not that chief executives spend too much time on internal matters, but that, in fact, they spend too little time reviewing their internal operations." Compare and contrast these two observations.

2.5 "Tremendous progress was made in the use of computers in improving the efficiency of processing operating and accounting data. Probably because management has always thought of these activities as necessary evils, the failure of MIS's should have been predictable by those who understand the true nature of managerial work." Discuss.

2.6 "There is no need to plan since no one can predict the future." "The use of sophisticated information systems does not improve planning. It simply allows the use of more useless detail." "The use of the computer to support our planning function provides us with many more options for future activities." Compare and contrast these comments.

2.7 What level of decision making is required by investors who might want to develop more legalized gambling establishments in Atlantic City? Once the establishment is built and opens for business, what levels of decision making will be most prominent in its operation?

2.8 Evaluate this generalization. "A real time information system will always be able to serve its constituents better than a batch processing system."

2.9 A rather discouraging comment heard often today is, "I am sorry, I cannot help you, the computer is down." Why is this likely to be true or not true in the future?

2.10 "The ability of modern data processing technology to permit closer control for any organization cannot be truly utilized unless management has first determined the criteria against which to measure operations." Explain.

2.11 "The development of our new credit card application evaluation system has had several benefits. The cost to review each application has dropped 60 percent. Fraudulent and potentially high-risk applicants have been reduced significantly. And third, perhaps most important of all, each application is reviewed in exactly the same way. This standardization enables us to demonstrate to the government the objectivity of our acceptance practices." What concept is likely to have been implemented in this new system? Discuss.

2.12 "It is unfortunate that programmed decision making is so closely related to computer processing. Many organizations can benefit from defining their decision-making processes whether or not they use computers." Discuss how this might be done.

2.13 "In the first half of this century, we were able to improve productivity by simply automating our manufacturing processes. Real improvements to productivity in the last half of this century will be the result of using better information to plan and control our entire business." Comment.

2.14 Overheard in a check-in line at an airport, "The thought of airlines not having reservations systems computerized is like thinking of going across the country in a covered wagon." Ten minutes later, in the same line, from the same person, "What do you mean you don't have my reservation? My secretary made it three weeks ago! Your dumb computer made a mistake!" Discuss.

2.15 "In spite of the progress of the last 20 years, the automation of the transactions required for running our households will be such that, by the year 2000, methods and practices of today will appear to be so outmoded as to be hilarious." Comment with specific examples.

EXERCISES

2.1 Prepare a report describing the decision-making process you used when selecting your school.

2.2 From your own experiences, describe a present (or previous) job in terms of its information flow. Emphasize the information you require(d) from others to do your job, information you provide(d) to others to do their job, information your supervisor requires to understand how well you did your job.

2.3 Ten business applications or situations are listed below. Determine which represent significant opportunities for programmed decision making versus nonprogrammed decision making. Explain your choice.

    (a) Payroll processing
    (b) Advertising
    (c) Inventory control
    (d) Management development
    (e) Plant location
    (f) Shipping scheduling
    (g) Product development
    (h) Cash investing
    (i) Budgeting
    (j) Corporate planning

2.4 Five changes to organizations are described below. Evaluate these changes and their likely impact on the information system within that organization.

1. A national oil company drops the use of credit cards for customers at its gasoline stations.
2. A steel producing company acquires a department store chain.
3. An automobile manufacturer establishes a corporate budget division.

4. A furniture manufacturing firm is unionized.
5. A bank holding company expands its operations into four additional states.

2.5 From a survey of the literature, prepare a report comparing and contrasting what is meant by "Management Information Systems" (MIS) by various authors.

2.6 Examine a statement from a major credit card company (e.g., bank, oil company, department store) and determine what information concerning you, the customer, they would consider descriptive or variable.

2.7 Many organizational resources have an "inventory status." Certain transactions increase or decrease this inventory. Complete (1)–(10) in the following table:

Activity	Inventory status	Increase	Decrease
Physical inventory	Items on hand	Receipts	Withdrawals
Accounts receivable	(1)	Sales	Payments
(2)	Amount owed	Purchases	Payments
Customer orders	Unfilled orders	(3)	Shipments
Hotel rooms	Rooms available	Check-ins	(4)
Personal credit limit	(5)	Charges	Payments
Warehouse docks	Space available	(6)	Arrivals
Manufacturing process	Machine time	Completed jobs	(7)
Doctor's schedule	(8)	Cancellations	Appointments
(9)	Personnel availability	Applicants	Hires
Water system	Reservoir level	(10)	Usage

PROBLEMS

2.1 You have been made line manager responsible for the mixing department of the Cover-Up Paint Company. To improve control over your operation, you have decided to establish material usage standards and labor efficiency standards concerning your operation. Describe your approach to establishing these standards. Make any assumptions you feel are necessary.

2.2 Assume that you are the owner–manager of a high-volume discount department store. Reporting to you are the managers of three selling units, the credit department, security, purchasing, and customer services. Your cashiers use modern cash registers which are linked to a minicomputer in the store. The sale or return of an item is logged in the computer at the time of entry. What information would each departmental manager want: hourly? daily? weekly? monthly? What information would you require from these departments in the same time periods?

2.3 For each level of decision making, certain management activities are appropriate. Where indicated by a number, complete the following table:

Strategic	Tactical	Technical
Planning the organization	Planning staff levels	Controlling hiring
Setting personnel policies	(1)	Implementing policies
Setting financial policies	Working capital planning	(2)
(3)	Deciding on research projects	
Choosing new product lines	(4)	
	(5)	Controlling inventory
	Measuring, appraising, and improving management performance	(6)
(7)	Deciding on plant rearrangement	Scheduling production
Choosing company objectives	(8)	

2.4 An air traffic control system is composed of 21 Air Traffic Control (ATC) centers, each of which is further subdivided into sectors. The actual control of aircraft is performed by human controllers assigned to each sector. An aircraft enters the system by filing a flight plan at the departure airport. A flight plan includes: destination, route of flight, airspeed, requested altitudes, proposed takeoff time, estimated time enroute, and expected arrival. The flight plan is filed two hours prior to takeoff and stored in a computer at the ATC center of the departure airport. Five minutes prior to the takeoff time, an abbreviated version of the flight plan is transmitted to the controllers in the first sector who will control the aircraft. As the flight continues, the abbreviated flight plan is transmitted to the controller of each affected sector five minutes before the aircraft enters that sector. Five minutes before the aircraft leaves the departing ATC center, the flight plan is transmitted to the next ATC center computer.

A chronic problem in the air traffic control system is the bottleneck that occurs at high density airports. Aircraft stack up in holding patterns due to the inability of controllers to handle landing traffic as fast as it arrives. The information system notifies the ATC centers when landing delays are being experienced at specific airports, but only after the congestion occurs. Considering the basic description of this system, propose a systems improvement to make the feedback loop more responsive.

Two additional considerations are that it is considered more favorable to have aircraft delay their take-offs rather than aggravate the congested condition at a particular airport and that the ATC centers have varying traffic loads, with at least one center having excess computer capacity that could be further utilized.

2.5 A manufacturer of soap products in the midwest services over 20,000 retail establishments throughout the country. The company receives an average of about 800 customer orders per day. Finished goods are manufactured both to stock and to order, at a ratio of about 70:30. Shipping papers are prepared by a computer daily. The shipping department maintains a hardcopy file of orders to be shipped during the last five days and orders to be shipped, since it is not always possible (or necessary) to ship an order the same day it is received.

A computer-based inventory reporting system produces an inventory status report. This report is available each morning at 8 AM and includes production and shipping activity as of 5 PM yesterday. Production scheduling prepares a schedule each Friday indicating the products to be manufactured, the quantity, and production date for the following two-week period. The customer service department receives 25–50 calls per day concerning customer order status and finished goods availability.

Below are ten typical questions received by customer service. Indicate which questions can be answered by the available information described above and which questions require still other information.

1. Has my order of a week ago been shipped yet?
2. How much is my account balance?

3. Can you ship me 500 units of product X today?
4. I placed a customer order a month ago to be delivered next week. Can I cancel my order?
5. Why did I receive only a partial order last month?
6. Has my account been credited for the returns last week?
7. Do you have any of product Y available for shipment this month?
8. Is it possible to substitute product A for product B in my order next month?
9. What is my new salesperson's name?
10. Are you still selling product D?

BIBLIOGRAPHY

Anthony and Dearden, *Management Control Systems,* Fourth Edition, Homewood, IL: Richard D. Irwin, Inc., 1980.

Feigenbaum, "Effective Management Information Systems for Control," *Journal of Systems Management,* October 1979.

Forkner and McLeod, *Computerized Business Systems,* New York: John Wiley & Sons, Inc., 1973.

Fuchs, *Cybernetics for the Modern Mind,* New York: The Macmillan Publishing Co., 1971.

Gorry and Morton, "A Framework for Management Information Systems," *Sloan Management Review,* Fall 1971.

Hall, *The Management of Human Systems,* Cleveland, Ohio: Associates for Systems Management, 1971.

Kanter, *Management-Oriented Management Information Systems,* Englewood Cliffs, NJ: Prentice–Hall Inc., 1977.

Mintzberg, *The Nature of Managerial Work,* New York: Harper & Row Publishers, 1973.

Naylor, "Management is Drowning in Numbers," *Business Week,* April 6, 1981.

Simon, *The New Science of Management Decision,* New York: Harper & Row Publishers, 1960.

Wiest, "Heuristic Programs for Decision Making," *Harvard Business Review,* September–October 1966.

CHAPTER

3

Designing Information Outputs—A User Orientation

3.1 ▪ INTRODUCTION

The main purpose of an information system is to produce information to meet the needs of the management and operations of an organization. Substantial amounts of time and money are spent on devices that perform data processing operations more efficiently. Likewise, significant effort is often expended on designing the intricate logic necessary to produce information from data. These efforts are applauded because without advances in these areas, the ability to produce necessary information would be limited. However, systems analysts and users have traditionally given inadequate attention to the design of the specific outputs which represent the information. While the information system must be capable of carrying out basic data processing functions, obtaining meaningful information outputs is the primary reason why management spends money on information systems. Modern data processing technology has enhanced traditional techniques for producing information outputs and provided new methods for satisfying the information needs of users. In this chapter we present a variety of concepts and techniques which help to make information outputs more meaningful. Specifically, the objectives of this chapter are:

1. To explain how filtering data can provide information.
2. To show how information can be used to highlight key performance activities and identify potential opportunities.
3. To identify and describe the major ways the monitoring method can be implemented.
4. To introduce the use of logico-mathematical models as a method for providing information to decision makers.
5. To illustrate, based on the interrogative method, how information is provided.
6. To develop an awareness for the use of information reflecting events and activi-

ties external to the organization, and the application of the strategic decision center method.

3.2 ▪ FILTERING METHOD

In many large organizations, decision makers are subjected to an avalanche of data. Particularly where computers are used, great quantities of data are collected, processed, and reported. For a given decision maker, these reports might be meaningless, or some information may be found if the recipient is willing to spend the time searching the data for it. In the latter event, much of the recipient's available time is spent searching for needed information to make a decision, rather than in evaluating available information and the alternatives suggested. One approach to providing decision makers with less data but with more information, is to reduce or filter the amount of detail data provided to each level of decision making.

Levels of Detail

Filtering is a process of screening or extracting unwanted elements from some entity as it passes, or is communicated from one point to another. Data are filtered through summarizing and classifying operations that screen out unnecessary detail for a given level of decision making. The nature of this filtering process can be either logical or mathematical. The basic assumption supporting the filtering method is that different levels of decision making require different levels of detail. The relationship between levels of decision making and requirements for detail is illustrated in Figure 3.1.

As a rule, strategic decision making has a lower requirement for detail than either

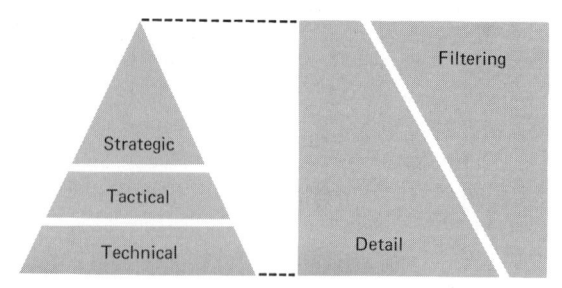

FIG. 3.1 The relationship between levels of decision making and requirements for detail.

tactical or technical decision making. For example, the president of a large manufacturing organization is certainly concerned with the sales of that organization; however, this concern does not necessarily require a daily listing of invoices; a monthly summary of total sales dollars might be satisfactory. It must be recognized, however, that requirements for detail vary significantly among individuals at the same level of decision making. Ideally, an information system is designed to permit the filtering of selected data elements from the data base so that each decision maker can obtain the level of detail appropriate to his or her individual needs. Traditionally, information is filtered at each subordinate–superior level in an organization. However, in modern organizations using modern data processing technology, there is an opportunity to include this filtering process as an essential element of the information system.

Examples of the Filtering Method

The filtering method has applicability in large organizations where current information reporting emphasizes the providing of large detail reports. All forms of transaction reporting lend themselves to filtering, and this can be illustrated with the reporting of cost and sales dollars.

In a construction company an awareness of actual costs incurred is an important aspect of each manager's job regardless of the manager's position in the organization. The president of the firm is likely to be concerned with the total costs incurred in a given time period. The vice president responsible for construction might require a further breakdown of total costs into prime costs and overhead costs. Each lower level of management would require a correspondingly higher level of detail concerning costs related to their activities only. In Figure 3.2 we illustrate how the filtering method is used to report construction costs to the various levels of decision makers.

Reporting sales activity in a large organization is another area where the filtering

President:				
Construction costs	7,200,000			
Manufacturing costs	xxxx			

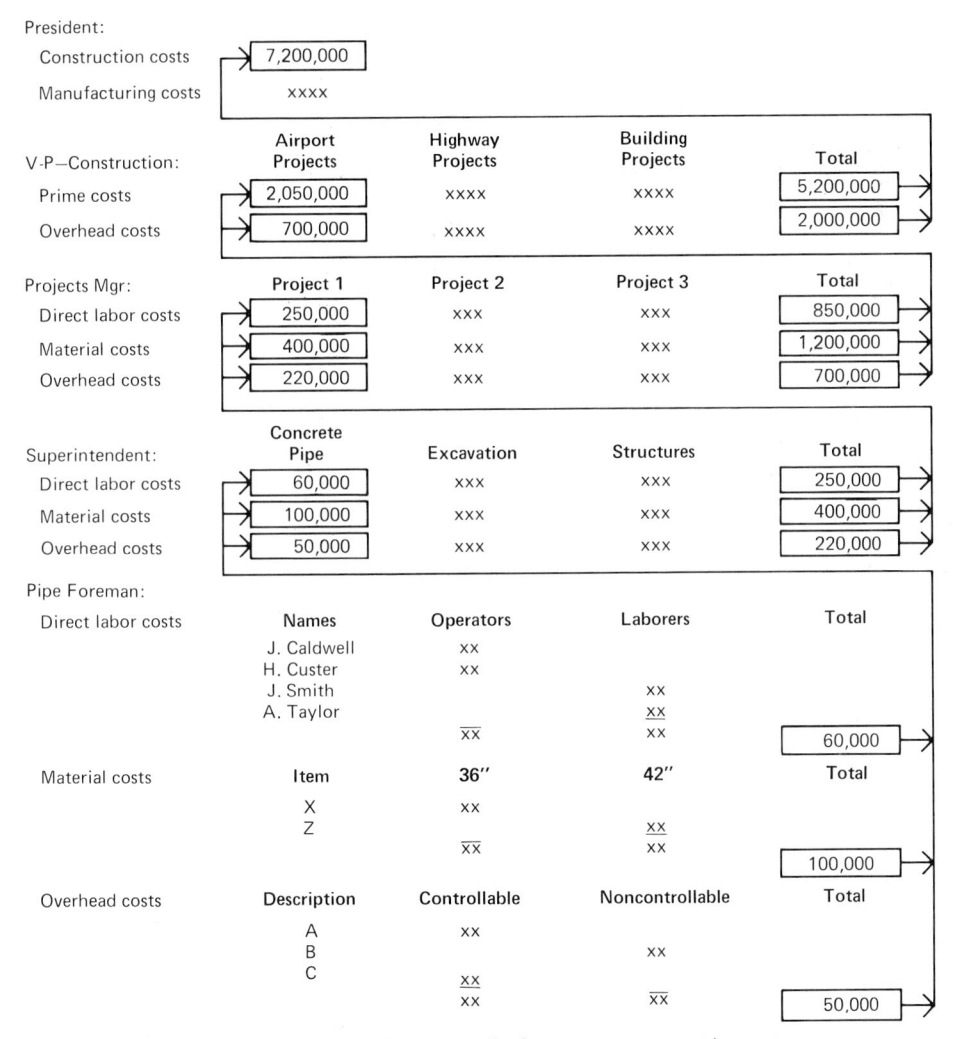

V-P—Construction:	Airport Projects	Highway Projects	Building Projects	Total
Prime costs	2,050,000	xxxx	xxxx	5,200,000
Overhead costs	700,000	xxxx	xxxx	2,000,000

Projects Mgr:	Project 1	Project 2	Project 3	Total
Direct labor costs	250,000	xxx	xxx	850,000
Material costs	400,000	xxx	xxx	1,200,000
Overhead costs	220,000	xxx	xxx	700,000

Superintendent:	Concrete Pipe	Excavation	Structures	Total
Direct labor costs	60,000	xxx	xxx	250,000
Material costs	100,000	xxx	xxx	400,000
Overhead costs	50,000	xxx	xxx	220,000

Pipe Foreman:

Direct labor costs	Names	Operators	Laborers	Total
	J. Caldwell	xx		
	H. Custer	xx		
	J. Smith		xx	
	A. Taylor		xx	
		xx	xx	60,000

Material costs	Item	36"	42"	Total
	X	xx		
	Z		xx	
		xx	xx	100,000

Overhead costs	Description	Controllable	Noncontrollable	Total
	A	xx		
	B		xx	
	C	xx		
		xx	xx	50,000

FIG. 3.2 Illustration of using the filtering method to report construction costs.

method is effective. In Figure 3.3 a series of reports are shown which describe the sales efforts of a company and the distribution of these reports.

The use of the filtering method requires the simplest understanding of an individual's information requirements. While it encompasses both logical and mathematical techniques, they are easily determined and quickly implemented.

Advantages and Disadvantages

Filtering, as a method for providing information to decision makers, represents a significant improvement over the production of

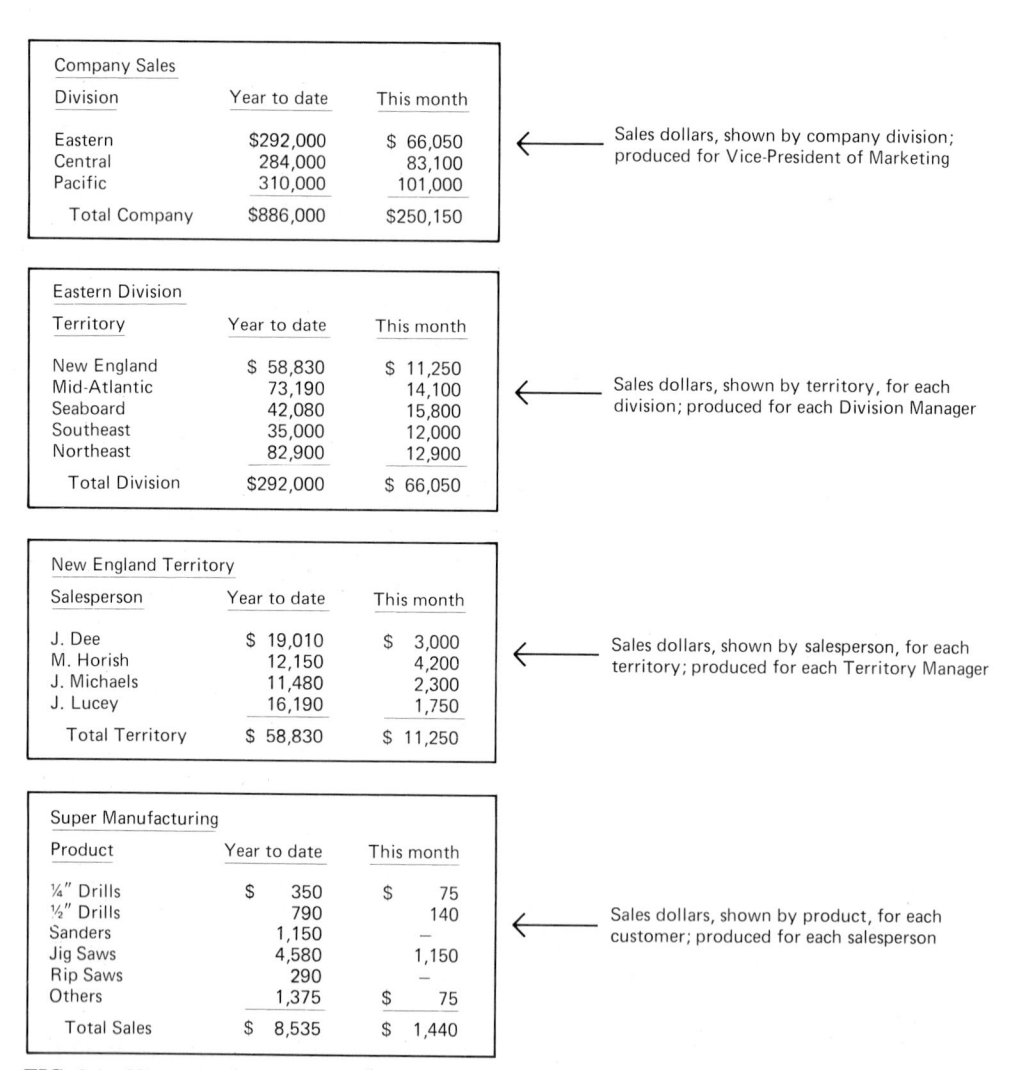

Company Sales

Division	Year to date	This month
Eastern	$292,000	$ 66,050
Central	284,000	83,100
Pacific	310,000	101,000
Total Company	$886,000	$250,150

← Sales dollars, shown by company division; produced for Vice-President of Marketing

Eastern Division

Territory	Year to date	This month
New England	$ 58,830	$ 11,250
Mid-Atlantic	73,190	14,100
Seaboard	42,080	15,800
Southeast	35,000	12,000
Northeast	82,900	12,900
Total Division	$292,000	$ 66,050

← Sales dollars, shown by territory, for each division; produced for each Division Manager

New England Territory

Salesperson	Year to date	This month
J. Dee	$ 19,010	$ 3,000
M. Horish	12,150	4,200
J. Michaels	11,480	2,300
J. Lucey	16,190	1,750
Total Territory	$ 58,830	$ 11,250

← Sales dollars, shown by salesperson, for each territory; produced for each Territory Manager

Super Manufacturing

Product	Year to date	This month
¼" Drills	$ 350	$ 75
½" Drills	790	140
Sanders	1,150	–
Jig Saws	4,580	1,150
Rip Saws	290	–
Others	1,375	$ 75
Total Sales	$ 8,535	$ 1,440

← Sales dollars, shown by product, for each customer; produced for each salesperson

FIG. 3.3 Using the filtering method to report sales dollars.

voluminous listings. Its disadvantages are few but important.

The major advantages to using the filtering method are that the amount of useless data provided to each decision maker is reduced considerably, since the level of detail received is based on individual requirements, and that organizational resources are conserved. Eliminating the need to produce massive reports conserves data processing resources; minimizing the need to search for information conserves decision makers' time. The disadvantages of using the filtering method are that implementation is difficult when the requirements for detail among decision makers at the same level varies considerably, that filtering alone does not provide adequate "action oriented" information to decision makers, and that it upsets the "political relationship" between each subordinate–superior level.

The real advantages to using the filtering method are often found when this method is combined with forms of the monitoring method discussed later in the chapter.

3.3 ▪ KEY VARIABLE REPORTING METHOD

With the filtering method, extraneous data are filtered from the report to tailor it to the specific needs of a particular user. The filtered report may consist of historical information that may not necessarily help the user to evaluate performance and provide information for action. In addition to reporting filtered statistical and traditional accounting information, the information system should be designed to report **key variables** that have a significant impact on the total performance and profitability of the organization.

Nature of Key Variables

The human body's condition can be determined to a great extent by the measurement of key variables—critical diagnostic factors such as pulse rate, blood pressure, and so forth. An automobile's condition can be measured by checking compression, oil pressure, ampere and voltage output, and so forth. There are usually at least five key variables (also called "key success factors," "key result areas," and "pulse points") for an organization as a whole.

Working with the users of the information system, the systems analyst can isolate most of these key variables. In addition, the analyst can examine how decisions are made, where the major decision points are, and the factors that management is concerned about in making decisions. After the key variables that determine the success of the organization are defined, the information system is designed to report their status, trends, and changes in trends.

Examples of Key Variables

Peter Drucker has stated that the key performance areas of an organization are typically market standing, profitability, innovation, productivity, physical and financial resources, motivation and organization development, and public responsibility.[1] These key performance areas act as a guide for the systems analyst to define precisely the key variables that support them. For example, key variables that help management to deal with market standing are: sales, market share, new orders, lost orders, and lost customers.

---

[1] Peter F. Drucker, *The Practice of Management* (New York: Harper & Row Publishers, 1954).

Some of these key variables can be used as predictors. If a leading manufacturer began to buy a large amount of machine tools, for instance, this could indicate future expansion in a particular market. Also, the reporting of key variables helps management zero in on a particular area for action. For example, from lost customer reports, management can formulate a strategy to recapture these customers. The lost customers become "target customers" that require immediate attention and the effort of everyone throughout the organization, including top management. To maintain attention on the lost customer problem and to assist in an effort to recapture them requires a reporting feedback system to be implemented in the information system. A simple report that illustrates this point is shown in Figure 3.4.

This report puts everyone on notice that the goal not only is to recapture lost customers, but to increase sales at the same time. On a weekly basis, the results of this effort are reported to all personnel involved (e.g., top management, sales manager, salespeople, and supporting personnel such as shipping clerks and desk salespeople).

Using Drucker's key performance areas as a guideline, examples of key variables that can be identified and reported on are shown in Figure 3.5.

With the reporting of key variables, management can see the direction of the current trends in all the key variables and determine whether they are moving the organization in the direction of its goals. Moreover, predictive key variables reveal developing opportunities that enable management to take early action to capitalize on them. This approach is better than waiting for results to be reported on the annual financial statements before taking action, even assuming that such information would be included in the financial statements, which might not be the case.

3.4 • MONITORING METHOD

The monitoring method is another alternative for reducing the amount of data decision makers receive while still increasing the amount of relevant information at their disposal. Instead of producing streams of data to be handled by a decision maker, the information system **monitors** the data and provides outputs to the decision maker on an automatic basis. Three basic ways to implement the monitoring method are: (1) variance reporting, (2) programmed decision making, and (3) automatic notification.

Target Accounts

Salesperson	Account	First quarter sales	*Second quarter sales	Third quarter sales goal
1	143	$ 9,000	$ -0-	$10,000
	156	12,000	-0-	15,000
2	176	6,000	100	8,000
	290	50,000	200	60,000
	294	24,000	-0-	30,000
3	179	18,000	-0-	25,000

*Period in which customers were "lost."

FIG. 3.4 Feedback report showing status of recapturing lost customers.

Key Performance Areas	Key Variables
Market standing	Sales
	Product margin
	New orders
	Lost orders
	Lost customers
Innovation	Number of new products
	New markets
Productivity	Capacity utilization
	Backlogs
	Backorders
	Manufacturing costs
	Yields
Physical and financial resources	Number of pieces of idle equipment
	Number of obsolete inventory items
	Accounts receivable turnover
	Inventory turnover
	Cash flow
	Working capital ratio
	Return on investment
Motivation and organization development	Absenteeism reports
	Number of personnel problems going to arbitration
	Number of personnel attending continuing education programs
	Labor turnover
Public responsibility	Number of employees involved in community programs
	Expenditures for pollution control
	Contributions to charitable organizations.

FIG. 3.5 Examples of key variables that can be reported by the information system.

Variance Reporting

This form of the monitoring method requires that data representing actual events be compared against data representing expectations in order to establish a *variance*. The variance is then compared to a control value to determine whether or not the event is to be reported. The result of this procedure is that only those events or activities that significantly deviate from expectations are presented to the decision maker for action.

For example, the XYZ Company develops and maintains standard costs for each product manufactured. The product line includes 23,000 different products. A cost variance report including each product requires more than 1000 pages. Many of the entries in this report show that the products were manufactured at, or very close to, the established standard. However, a much smaller report is produced if it were assumed that only products varying more than $\pm$ 5 percent from standard required management's attention. Moreover, each entry in the smaller report represents a need for either further analysis or action on the part of a decision maker.

In this example it is seen that the time spent by the human decision maker to identify every variance is eliminated. Such monitoring is still accomplished, but now it is performed by the information system, and the system in turn reports to the decision maker only those variances that are significant.

Another example of variance reporting is applied to sales reporting. In a sales organization where each salesperson is assigned a sales quota, the sales manager reviews only those who are well above or below their quota in any given time period. The sales manager assumes that the salespeople are operating satisfactorily when sales are within 10 percent of the quota. In Figure 3.6, the sales performance of one salesperson has been plotted for 12 months.

This chart shows that our salesperson exceeded the guidelines in the months of Feb-

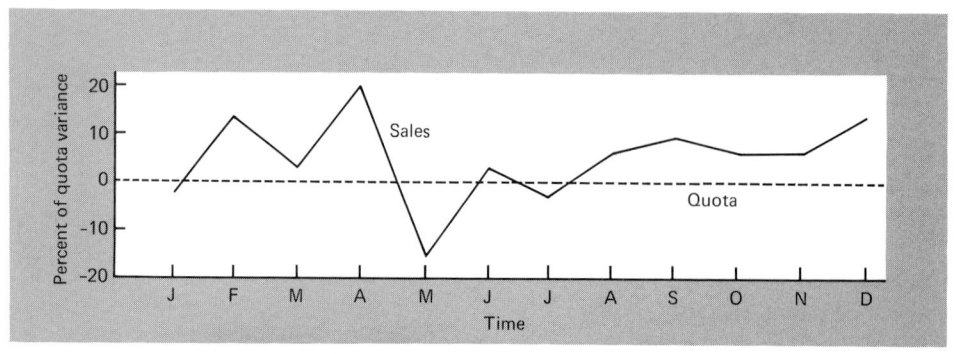

FIG. 3.6 A chart showing deviation from quota.

ruary, April, May, and December. Using the variance reporting method, the sales manager receives detailed sales reports on this individual's sales performance only at these times. In the remaining months the sales manager assumes that this particular salesperson is making sales according to expectations. In effect, the sales manager is freed from monitoring reports which contain little, if any, useful information; therefore, managers can better use their time and energy where they are most needed.

To implement this form of the monitoring method, the analyst executes the following procedures:

1. Establish the norm at which performance is anticipated (e.g., budget, plan, quota, schedule, standard, etc.).
2. Establish the amount of deviation from the norm which is considered acceptable. This deviation can be both above and below the norm, or only in one direction (the amount may be unequal, in that the deviation above the norm might be set at 30 percent and the deviation below might be set at 10 percent).
3. Establish a procedure for collecting actual performance data and comparing it to the norm.
4. Extrapolate past performance to see if trends can be highlighted (optional).
5. Disseminate the variance reports as they occur to the decision maker responsible for the performance.

Although variance reporting (also called exception reporting) represents a powerful tailoring technique, remember that management also needs periodic reports for decision making. Many managers are more comfortable if they know the overall status or general health of the organization. They feel that receiving information only when something has gone wrong or has fallen outside a predetermined limit does not indicate the gradual buildup of problems. Management must be in an informed position to anticipate situations. Variance reporting does not provide anticipatory information.

Programmed Decision Making

A second application of the monitoring method involves the development and implementation of *programmed decision making*. As described in Chapter 2, a significant part of technical decision making, and a small part of tactical decision making, involves routine repetitive decisions. By designing the information system to execute these routine decisions, the systems analyst has provided the human decision makers with more time to spend on less structured decisions. There are many opportunities to implement programmed decision making in most organizations.

For example, credit checking of customer orders is an important, but repetitive, decision-making process that can be programmed. Figure 3.7 illustrates one approach to programming this process. Once the credit manager is relieved of checking each customer order processed, he or she is able to concentrate on those orders that have a problem, such as collection, associated with them.

The purchasing function provides still another opportunity for the implementation of programmed decision making. Periodically, a purchasing agent must review all outstanding purchase orders to determine if some form of expediting is required to ensure that the purchase is delivered when needed. This process entails an examination of each purchase order and a comparison of the date the purchase is scheduled to arrive against the date when the purchase is required for use. Both dates are subject to continuous revision. In many organizations this process can be a tedious task since hundreds or thousands of purchase orders may be outstanding at any one time. Obviously, if the system is allowed to monitor outstanding purchase orders and the decision as to which orders are to be expedited is programmed, much time and effort is saved. Figure 3.8 illustrates one approach to programming this decision-making process.

In many manufacturing operations this method of providing information is used to automatically control the operation without manual intervention. *Process control,* as it

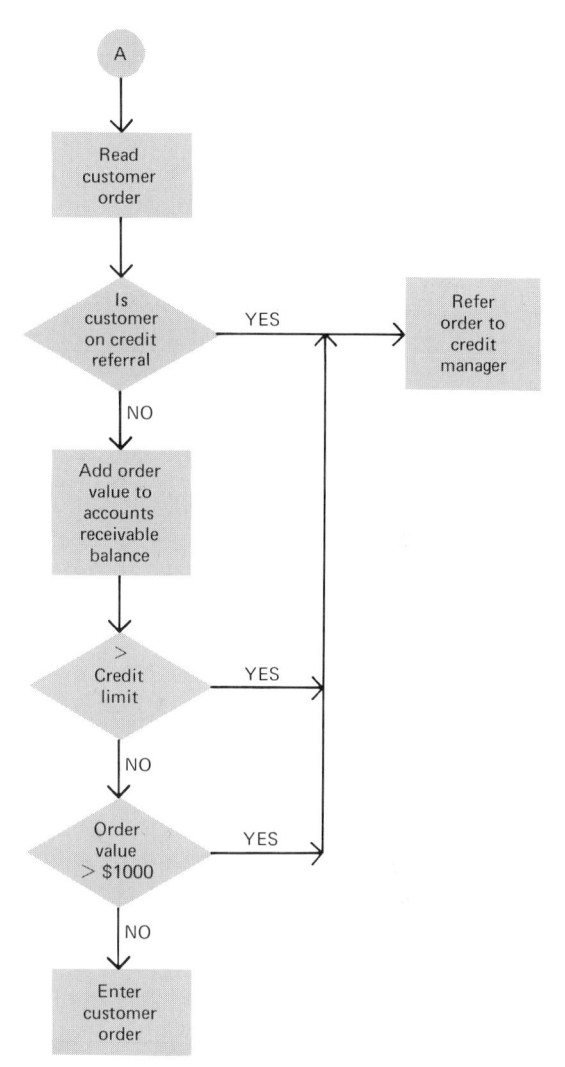

FIG. 3.7 An example of programmed decision making in the credit checking process.

is commonly termed, involves sensors which determine what is actually happening, and in turn, input this data into a programmed decision-making structure. Based on the logic programmed, the output may cause a valve to open or close, a bell to ring, or the operation to cease.

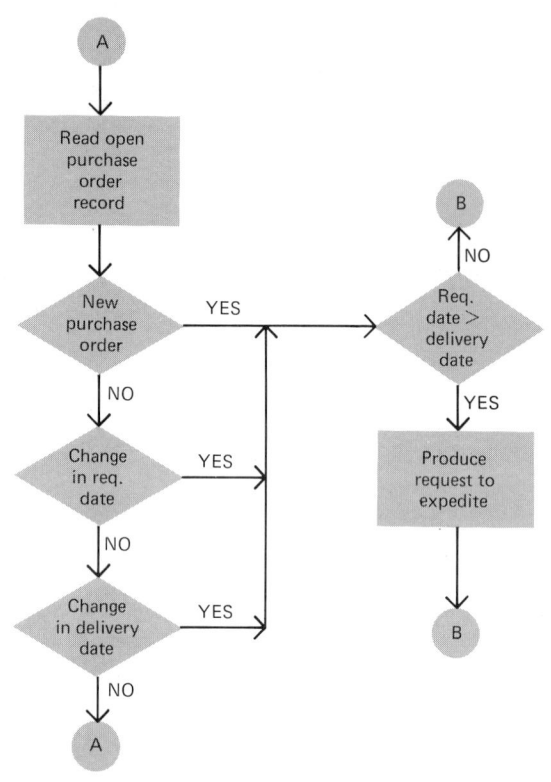

FIG. 3.8 An illustration of programmed decision making in the purchasing function.

In all of our examples the principle is identical. The system monitors the flow of data, and when an activity "triggers" or reflects a condition inside the programmed decision-making range, a decision is automatically made by the system based on predetermined conditions.

Automatic Notification

A third form of the monitoring method is termed *automatic notification*. In this approach the system does not make any decisions as such, but because it is monitoring the overall flow of data, it can release information at a predetermined time where needed. With this method the vast memory capabilities of computers are used to advantage to keep track of large amounts of detail information.

For example, in a large hospital the patients in a given area might be the responsibility of many different doctors. Each doctor has prescribed a definite schedule for administering medication, therapy, tests, and diets to each patient. Generally, a head nurse is responsible for monitoring these instructions and seeing that they are performed as scheduled in each area. In a twenty-four-hour period there are at least three head nurses involved; moreover, patients are coming and going, and doctors are continuously changing schedules.

If the doctor's instructions are input into a computer-based information system, specific information, in the form of instructions, can then be issued periodically to the head nurse via a CRT or teletype device. This automatic notification permits the nurse to spend time in other areas, providing patient service, rather than in keeping track of administrative details. The system can perform routines such as producing picking lists for loading medication carts, setting time schedules for the administration of drugs, preparing drug labels, checking for possible harmful effects because of the interaction of drugs, and the automatic charging of costs against each patient's account.

Patient monitoring systems rely on the computer for continuous surveillance of a patient's vital signs and automatic notification of physiological data for use by trained personnel. Figure 3.9 illustrates a typical medical monitoring system. The first step in the system is to capture data from monitoring devices connected to the patients and convert these analog signals to digital data for computer processing and CRT dis-

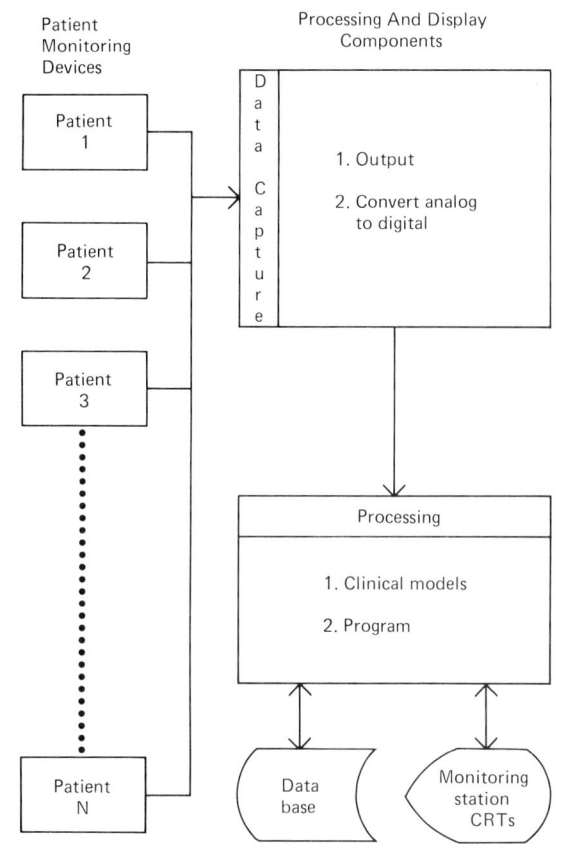

```
Patient              Processing And Display
Monitoring              Components
Devices
                    ┌─┬──────────────┐
┌─────────┐         │D│              │
│ Patient │────┐    │a│              │
│    1    │    │    │t│ 1. Output    │
└─────────┘    │    │a│              │
               │    │ │ 2. Convert analog│
               │    │C│    to digital │
┌─────────┐    │    │a│              │
│ Patient │────┤    │p│              │
│    2    │    │    │t│              │
└─────────┘    ├───▶│u│              │
               │    │r│              │
┌─────────┐    │    │e│              │
│ Patient │────┤    └─┴──────────────┘
│    3    │    │             │
└─────────┘    │             ▼
     ⋮         │    ┌──────────────────┐
               │    │    Processing    │
               │    │                  │
               │    │ 1. Clinical models│
               │    │                  │
               │    │ 2. Program       │
┌─────────┐    │    └──────────────────┘
│ Patient │────┘        ▲        ▲
│    N    │             ▼        ▼
└─────────┘         ┌──────┐  ┌─────────┐
                    │ Data │  │Monitoring│
                    │ base │  │ station │
                    │      │  │  CRTs   │
                    └──────┘  └─────────┘
```

FIG. 3.9 A patient monitoring system.

play. In addition to automatic notification, information is stored for periodic retrieval. Early warning information is given based on various clinical models and trend analysis. Various information is displayed periodically at monitoring station CRTs based on programmed decision rules.

In industry, this method of providing information is used to present work assignments to individual workers. For example, when workers complete their current assignment, they receive their next assignment notification automatically from the system. The allocation of other resources is also monitored. In a particular construction company an inventory schedule of heavy equipment is monitored. Periodically a notice is output which identifies machinery scheduled to be available for another project assignment.

In the above examples the system merely monitors a large file of data. The automatic notifications are issued based on some predetermined criteria, but the individual decision makers must decide whether any action is required.

Advantages and Disadvantages

To summarize the discussion of the monitoring method, its major advantages and disadvantages are presented here. The major advantages are that it:

1. Has widespread applicability.
2. Provides a high level of action-oriented information.
3. Relieves decision makers from routine and tedious decision-making activities.
4. Is adaptable to most approaches to management (e.g., management by objectives, management by costs, management by budget, etc.).
5. Improves usage of organizational resources.

The major disadvantages of the monitoring method are that it requires:

1. A high level of systems analysis and design.
2. A clear definition of how things are or should be.
3. A large amount of data collection, storage, and processing activity.
4. Sophisticated hardware and software development.

3.5 ▪ MODELING METHOD

The use of logico–mathematical models to transform data into information is becoming increasingly important as a means of providing information needed by tactical-level decision makers. In many instances modeling is the only method capable of providing this information. While some models require the model builder to possess a high degree of proficiency in mathematics, the vast majority of these models require a minimum of mathematical expertise. In this section a general overview of logico–mathematical models is provided to ensure the proper perspective on where these models apply in the development of information systems.

A Definition of Model

In the broadest sense a model is simply a representation of something else. To produce information, a **model** is usually a verbal or mathematical expression describing a set of relationships in a precise manner. A model can be useful simply in explaining or describing something, or it can be used to predict actions and events. Models can be classified in many different ways. In Figure 3.10, five different approaches to classifying models are illustrated.[2] Other attributes of a model could be chosen to provide still more classification schemes. It can be seen that in most organizations logico–mathematical models have a widespread applicability for providing information.

Appendix A provides a brief description of a selection of logico–mathematical models. The purpose of these descriptions is to convey an understanding of how these models are used to produce information, not to give the reader the necessary expertise to build or implement the models. However, the reader *is* encouraged to pursue a further understanding of various models and the model building process, by studying some of the many references indicated.

[2]Robert G. Murdick and Joel E. Ross, *Information Systems for Modern Management,* Second Edition, (Englewood Cliffs, NJ: Prentice-Hall, Inc., 1975), pp. 502–504. With permission from Prentice-Hall, Inc.

FIG. 3.10 Various ways in which models can be classified.

Class I—Function

Type	Characteristics	Examples
1. Descriptive	Descriptive models simply provide a picture of a situation and do not predict or recommend.	(a) Organization chart (b) Plant layout diagram (c) Block diagram representing the structure of each chapter of this book
2. Predictive	Predictive models indicate that "if this occurs, then *that* will follow." They relate dependent and independent variables and permit trying out "what if" questions.	(a) $BE = \dfrac{F}{1 - v}$, which says that if fixed costs *(F)* are given, and variable costs as a fraction of sales *(v)* are known, then break-even sales *(BE)* are predicted (deterministically)

Modeling Method

		(b) $S(t) = aS(t - 1) + (1 - a)S(t - 2)$, which says that predicted sales for period t depend on sales for the previous two periods.
3. Normative	Normative models are those that provide the "best" answer to a problem. They provide recommended courses of action.	(a) Advertising budget model (b) Economic lot size model (c) Marketing mix model

Class II—Structure

Type	Characteristics	Examples
1. Iconic	Iconic models retain some of the physical characteristics of the things they represent	(a) Scaled 3-dimensional mockup of a factory layout (b) Blueprints of a warehouse (c) Scale model of next year's automobile
2. Analog	Analog models are those for which there is a substitution of components or processes to provide a parallel with what is being modeled.	An analog computer in which components and circuits parallel marketing institutions and facilities and processes so that by varying electrical inputs, the electrical outputs provide an analog simulation of the marketing system outputs
3. Symbolic	Symbolic models use symbols to describe the real world.	(a) $R = a[ln(A)] + b$, which says in symbols that sales response (R) equals a constant times the natural log of advertising expenditure (A), plus another constant (b) $TC = PC + CC + IC$, which says in symbols that total inventory cost (TC) equals purchase cost (PC) plus carrying cost (CC) plus item cost (IC)

Class III—Time Reference

Type	Characteristics	Examples
1. Static	Static models do not account for changes over time.	(a) Organization chart (b) $E = P_1S_1 + P_2S_2$, which

FIGURE 3.10 *(continued).*

states that the expected profit *(E)* equals the probability *(P₁)* of the occurrence of payoff *(S₁)* multiplied by the value of the payoff *(S₁)*, plus the probability *(P₂)* of payoff *(S₂)* multiplied by the value of *(S₂)*,

    2. Dynamic   Dynamic models have time as an independent variable.

$dS/dT = rA(t)(m - S)/M - \lambda S$, which gives the change in sales rate as a function of a response constant *r*, advertising rate as a function of time *A(t)*, sales saturation *(M)*, sales rate *(S)*, and sales decay constant (λ)

Class IV—Uncertainty Reference

    Types   *Characteristics*   *Examples*

    1. Deterministic   For a specific set of input values, there is a uniquely determined output that represents the solution of a model under conditions of **certainty**   Profit = Revenue minus costs

    2. Probabilistic   Probabilistic models involve probability distributions for inputs or processes and provide a range of values of at least one output variable with a probability associated with each value. These models assist with decisions made under conditions of *risk*.

(a) Actuarial tables that give the probability of death as a function of age
(b) Return on investment is simulated by using a probability distribution for each of the various costs and revenues with values selected by the Monte Carlo (random) technique. ROI appears in graph form as return in dollars vs. probability of the various dollar returns

    3. Game   Game theory models attempt to develop optimum solutions in the face of complete ignorance or *uncertainty*. Games against nature and games of competition are subclassifications.

Two gasoline stations are adjacent to each other. One owner wonders: "Shall I raise or lower my price? If I raise mine, my competitor may raise or lower his. If I lower mine, he may raise or lower his. I know the gain or loss in any situation, but once each of us sets the price, we must keep it for the week. We can't collude."

Class V—Generality

Type	Characteristics	Examples
1. General	General models for business are models that have applications in several functional areas of business.	(a) Linear programming algorithm for all functional areas (b) Waiting line model. Applications appear in production, marketing, and personnel
2. Specialized	Specialized models are those that have application to a unique problem only.	(a) Sales response as a function of advertising may be based on a unique set of equations (b) The probabilistic bidding model has a single application to one functional area

The Model Building Process

The major steps involved in the model building process are illustrated in Figure 3.11.

The "real world" situation in step 1 represents the environment in which the analyst is working. At this point the problem to be solved must be defined and the essential variables related to the problem abstracted. In step 2, the analyst must sequence and quantify the identified variables. Testing the model requires that the analyst process some data through the model and compare the output with his or her expectations. If the model has produced acceptable output, the analyst may implement the model for use by organizational decision makers. On the other hand, if the outputs from the model are unacceptable, the analyst must continue to modify or add to the variables which comprise the model.

Advantages and Disadvantages

To summarize the discussion of the modeling method, the major advantages and disadvantages in using models are listed here.

The major advantages of using models are that they:

1. Provide action-oriented information.
2. Provide future-oriented information.
3. Permit alternative courses of action to be evaluated before implementation.
4. Provide a formal, structured description of a complex problem situation.
5. Represent a scientific approach to replace intuition and speculation.

The major disadvantages are that:

1. Users of the model tend to lose sight of the fact that the model represents an abstraction of reality and not reality itself.

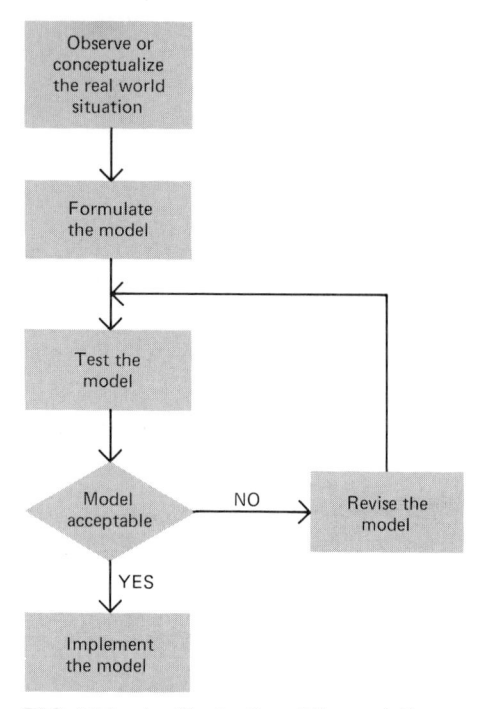

FIG. 3.11 An illustration of the modeling process.

2. Qualitative factors such as experience and judgment are minimized or eliminated.
3. The model building process is often very difficult and expensive.
4. Potential users of the model often have a fear or resistance to change which results in difficulties implementing the model.
5. Many models assume linearity, a condition that is not applicable to most "real world" situations.

To enjoy the successful implementation of the modeling method, the systems analyst must make sure that the user understands the model, what it does, what its limitations and constraints are, and how it is to be used. If users are not properly trained in these facets, they will not use models, and for all practical purposes, the modeling method becomes superfluous as a way to tailor the information system. The following examples illustrate this point.

In a food processing plant, a systems analyst developed an exponential smoothing model for forecasting sales, and a linear programming and EOQ model for raw material purchasing and control. The models worked and would have provided helpful information. However, company personnel did not understand the models and, therefore, did not use them. If the analyst had permitted the prospective users to participate in the development of the models, and had trained them in their usage, then the probability of successful implementation of the models would have been increased.

In a production and inventory control process, a sophisticated model was developed to account for speed of the production lines, work in process at various stages, setup scheduling, and labor smoothing. Ten control variables in the model helped it approximate reality. The model had both optimizing and simulation (what if) features. Not long after this model was implemented, the plant manager and other personnel ceased using it. Why? Because they did not understand it; and the large development effort went for naught.

The solution to the above real-world problems is threefold: (1) encourage the user to participate; (2) employ sufficient training about the model and its use; and (3) develop the model in stages, if possible. For example, an inventory control problem could be divided into three stages. The technique of forecasting could be presented first. When this was understood, then when to order (reorder point) would be presented, along with the idea of safety stock. Next, the how-much-to-order (economic order quantity) problem would be treated. After these stages were presented, the total inventory control model would be ready for implementation and use. If it were necessary to bring together and optimize several variables at the same time, then the model would be run in test or demonstration mode until the users understood it and were willing to accept results from it.

3.6 ▪ INTERROGATIVE METHOD

In all of the methods presented thus far in this chapter the information system disseminates information without any action on the recipient's part. In the interrogative method, the decision maker is required to request needed information from the system. This method of providing information is extremely valuable, since many decision makers are unable to identify what information is necessary to perform their duties until the situation confronts them.

Definition of the Interrogative Method

To interrogate means to question, and questioning is thus the basic premise of the interrogative method. The **interrogative method** is a micro, interactive concept applicable to any individual who requests a response based upon a specific interrogation of the data base. The essential elements of this method are: (1) the information users need only to format or structure their inquiry and submit it to some access mechanism or interface, and (2) the information is presented to the user in a viable format and in a relevant time period. To implement the interrogative method it is necessary that an extensive data base exist, organized in a manner where a variety of users can access needed data elements.

Examples of the Interrogative Method

The production or manufacturing environment in many organizations provides several opportunities to use the interrogative method. For example, employees can receive work assignments from a computer via a terminal device such as a teletype or CRT simply by identifying themselves and their work station, and requesting their next job assignment. A message is displayed giving the next job order number and operation, the location of the material, manufacturing information, and a list of necessary tools and their location.

In addition, employees use these terminals to record their attendance and overtime, job requests, job completions, material and tool receipts and issues, the results of all inspections, and their shift accomplishments as they leave for the day. In return the plant (and other) managers retrieve, via their own terminals, a broad spectrum of information, including:[3]

1. Long-term backlog behind critical facilities.
2. Short-term backlog behind each facility and work station.
3. Up-to-the-minute status of every order in process.
4. Promised dates on all orders.
5. Location of all tools in the plant.
6. Status of all purchase orders.

[3]T. A. LaRoe, "A Manufacturing Plant Information System," *Proceedings Third Annual Conference,* September 9 & 10, 1971 (Chicago, Illinois: The Society for Management Information Systems, 1971), p. 20. With permission.

80 Designing Information Outputs—A User Orientation

7. Complete inspection and quality control information.
8. Status of work in process as to percentage completion.

An order entry system provides a second example of the applicability of the interrogative method.[4] In the order entry system the salesperson or desk clerk in a field location communicates with the system via a CRT linked to the computer and common data base by a telephone line. Users complete a telephone connection with the computer and enter their identifying authentication. A list of functions available to the user is then displayed. For example, the user may enter a customer order into the file, cancel an order, alter an order, reschedule an order, or obtain an inquiry response relative to sales performance items. An example of a gross transaction display is illustrated in Figure 3.12.

The user makes a selection by depressing the appropriate key. If key "2" is depressed, an order entry transaction is displayed upon the screen. An example of this response is shown in Figure 3.13.

Next, an order entry form is displayed, providing a background form which consists of customer name, customer identification number, address, date, sales location, salesperson, purchase plan (such as sale or lease), plus the items ordered. When the operator depresses the "1" key, the form shown in Figure 3.14 is displayed on the CRT screen and the clerk makes the proper entries.

When an entry is completed, the order is checked against other constraints in the system such as credit status, inventory availability, and so on. If the final order is ac-

---

[4]This example based on Joseph F. Kelly, *Computerized Management Information Systems* (New York: The Macmillan Company, 1970), Chapter 4. With permission.

CRT Screen

Gross Transaction Display

1. Customer record control
2. Order entry control/old customer
3. Billing, taxes, and freight information
4. Sales administration
5. Inquiry
6. Order entry control/new customer
OPERATOR: MAKE A SELECTION

FIG. 3.12 CRT display of gross transaction.

CRT Screen

Order Entry Transaction Display

1. Order
2. Alteration
3. Cancellation
4. Reschedule
5. Special request message
6. Administration request message
OPERATOR: MAKE A SELECTION

FIG. 3.13 CRT display of order entry transaction.

CRT Screen

Order Entry Form Display

Customer Name	Customer Number
Address	Date
Sales Location	Salesperson
Purchase Plan	
Item Number	Quantity	Price

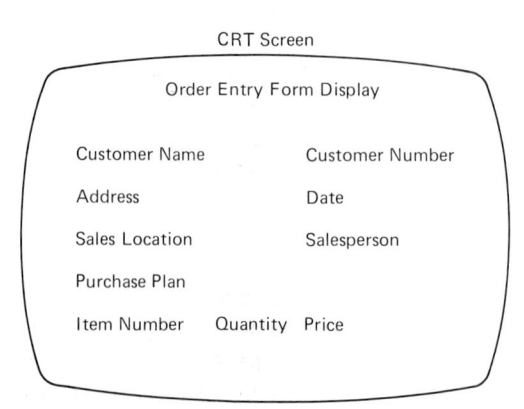

FIG. 3.14 CRT display of order entry form.

cepted by the system, then the order is processed in accordance with predetermined criteria. This process, incidentally, is an example of programmed decision making at the technical level. The order entry system is comprised of three files: the customer master file, inventory master file, and sales performance file. All three are updated, along with any others that are required. Also, all necessary documents are prepared for transactional data processing. This design concept reduces the amount of paper processing, especially in the branch office and warehouse locations. The inquiry capability into administrative areas replaces extensive file requirements and the need for operational and information clerical personnel in branch offices, various departments, and warehouses. For most organizations the order entry provides basic data because this event triggers an input into almost every functional area of the organization. It is possible to develop this method to fit the requirements of different decision makers by making it as complex (or simple) as can be economically justified.

These files must accommodate a series of transactions that can be accessed by users other than the sales department. For instance, the credit department needs the information illustrated in Figure 3.15.

An interrogative method such as that described above requires a method of ensuring data security and integrity. Certain changes are initiated by various operators throughout the organization. Control must be exercised, however, to ensure that a department or branch office changes only that part of the files over which it normally exercises control. For example, a branch office could change address data for a given customer but could not change the customer's credit status. The statistical data contained in the

CRT Screen

Display Customer Record

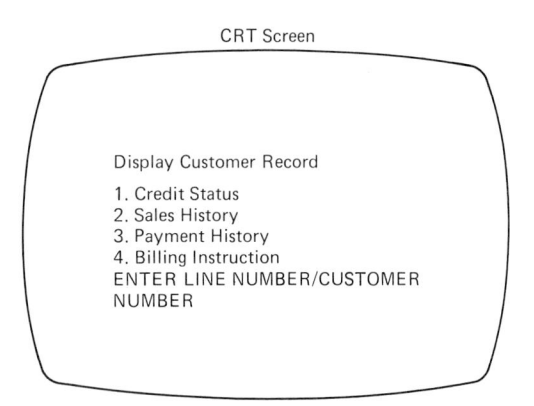

1. Credit Status
2. Sales History
3. Payment History
4. Billing Instruction
ENTER LINE NUMBER/CUSTOMER NUMBER

FIG. 3.15 CRT display of customer record.

sales performance file could not be changed from a local branch office, and so on.

The sales department has normally received its information based on a weekly report with a month-end summary. However, for information to be effective it must be not only relevant but also timely. Only the decision maker who knows what is happening in a department, as soon as it happens, can adjust effectively the means to the objectives. So, in addition to the periodic reports, action-oriented information is needed. Periodic reports provide a useful means of making historical analyses and highlighting present status and trends. These reports also can be easily provided via the remote terminal. Inquiry information is supplied to the user who requires responses from the system on a non-routine basis. This type of information gives to the user a specific response based on a specific inquiry, and usually results in some action being taken by the user.

The opportunities for implementing the interrogative method are restricted only by the imagination of the analyst. Financial data can be stored regarding closings and financial planning. Displays of orders entered for a specific time period, sales billed, and income/after/taxes to date, can all be made instantaneously. Sales managers can interrogate sales statistics files for information pertaining to product performance, market penetration, customer activity, and up-to-date forecasting information to mention only a few possibilities.

Advantages and Disadvantages

To summarize the discussion of the interrogative method, the major advantages and disadvantages related to its implementation and use are listed below.

The major advantages of the method are:

1. Widespread applicability.
2. Permits each decision maker to obtain relevant, specific information when it is required.
3. Allows previously unanticipated inquiries to be entered and processed.
4. Reduces paperwork (and paper pollution).
5. Reduces the time required to disseminate information.
6. Supports other methods of producing information such as filtering, monitoring, and modeling.
7. Alleviates organizational controversy by allowing each decision maker independent access to a common data base.

The major disadvantages of the interrogative method are:

1. Requires an expensive investment in data processing resources. This includes not only hardware, but also systems analysts and programmers who must design, develop, and implement this method.
2. Although sound in concept, it has proved to be almost impossible to provide the necessary data base required to respond to more than a small percentage of requests that one or more decision makers might make.

3.7 ▪ STRATEGIC DECISION CENTER METHOD

With rare exceptions, formal information systems have failed to provide information to assist strategic decision makers. This failure is due, mainly, to the very nature of strategic decision making. In general, strategic decision makers are concerned with decisions related to the overall development, growth, and plans of the organization. The forces which affect these decisions include political, social, economic, and competitive activities, in addition to various key variables of the organization itself. Most data bases do not include sufficient data to cover these areas.

The type of information useful to strategic decision makers is often referred to as "intelligence," and can be gathered from sources such as newspapers, trade journals, government reports, legislative chronicles, industry statistics, demographic studies, marketing surveys, and from the organization's data base. The systems analyst can be effective in providing this information by installing the following procedures:

1. Making publications available for quick dissemination through the use of collating, indexing, and document retrieval. In some instances top management may need to research a topic for a variety of reasons. The system could provide management with information about various topics, ranging from the Industrial Revolution to the 1950 World Series.

2. Gathering and summarizing documents from governmental agencies and other groups that affect the organization. Examples of strategic information resulting from this effort include truth in packaging, wage and price controls, foreign trade, economic indicators, consumer affairs, foreign exchange rates, tax rulings, stock exchange information, voting trends, cost of living indexes, labor trends, projected strikes, and developing technology.

3. Interfacing with the organization's data base to gather key variables. This information is presented to spotlight significant changes, exceptions, and variances (e.g., profits have fallen 30 percent in Division A during the first quarter). Much of this information is displayed to focus on trends and fluctuations, and to compare performance against plan. Also, management should have the ability to ask "what if" questions (and get timely answers), such as "What would be the result if we were to increase sales price by 4 percent and decrease our variable cost by 2 percent on product A?"

Logico–mathematical models can be stored in the system to give answers to "what if" questions that will, in turn, help management develop various scenarios. A simple example below uses a fundamental accounting model:

SALES REVENUE = VARIABLE EXPENSES + FIXED EXPENSES + PROFIT

The manager asks a series of "what if" questions and receives immediate results. For example:

"What is the new profit if we raise our sales price from $2.00 to $2.10 on a volume of 10,000 units, and decrease our variable expenses from $1.20 to $1.15 per unit with fixed costs remaining at $5000?"

$2.00 (10,000) = $1.20 (10,000) + $5000 + Profit
Old Profit = $3000

$2.10 (10,000) = $1.15 (10,000) + $5000 + Profit
New Profit = $4500

Another example of a "what if" question is: "Using the old figures, how many units do we have to sell to get a profit of $4600?"

$2.00 (UNITS) = $1.20 (UNITS) + $5000 + $4600
UNITS = 12,000

4. Gathering external data, storing it in the data base, and processing it via models or reformatting it in graphical form. Trade associations as well as private organizations[5] provide financial and market data in traditional report form or in a computer-readable format for input into the formal information system. This type of information shows such things as total sales, market trends, market share, developing markets, and industry averages. For example, census data, readily available from the Census Bureau, can be used to gauge potential markets; to make sales forecasts; to define sales territories; to allocate funds for advertising; to decide on locations for new plants, warehouses, or stores; and to provide general demographic analysis.

[5]For example, Sheshunoff & Company, Inc., of Austin, Texas, provides the following information concerning all banks within the state of Texas: (1) balance sheets and income statements, ranked by deposit size; (2) loan summary, ranked by deposit size; (3) employee expense analysis, ranked by deposit size; (4) correspondent banking and securities summary, ranked by deposit size; (5) high performance banking, ranked by return on average assets; (6) capital analysis, ranked by capital as a percentage of total assets; and (7) various other financial data and rankings. It is our understanding that bankers make heavy use of this external data in making strategic decisions and long-range plans.

Many commercial data bases, most of which are computerized, allow managers to retrieve a variety of data external to the organization. Some examples of these data bases are: location, size, and products of plants scattered across the country; statistics of the securities market; abstracts of legislative reports; abstracts of articles from magazines and newspapers; abstracts of medical literature; access to various economic data, appropriate logico–mathematical models, and computer programs to drive them; and business credit ratings.[6]

An example of strategic users of such data bases would be: corporate executives who want a list of potential merger or acquisition prospects, long range planners who want to estimate the effect of interest rates on their borrowing, productivity, energy costs, and labor costs; the marketing manager who wants to know the number, geographical location, and income levels of potential customers for a new product; and the financial executive who wants to evaluate various investment portfolios.

Some readers may wonder whether the **strategic decision center** (also referred to as the "Corporate War Room," "Decision Support Center," and the "Intelligence Center") method is a place, or a concept. It is a combination of both, subject to broad interpretation. It can be a physical location where top management personnel meet on a periodic basis to discuss issues, receive timely information that relates to these issues, and make strategic decisions. However, the same result can be accomplished by allowing top management to become involved from their individual offices via closed circuit television.

Equipment and media which can be used to support a strategic decision center include television, video and audio tape, computer output microfilm (COM), computers, movie projectors, telecommunications, and color graphs and tables displayed by cathode ray tube (CRT) devices. Management should be able to access information on their own through access codes provided to them in a directory. For example, to access the return on investment profile of Division A, a manager simply keys into a CRT the code ROI-A. Return on investment information for Division A, along with trends and comparisons, are displayed immediately in graphical form. Some other types of information (e.g., research material) might require assistance from support staff.

Computer vendors offer a variety of terminals and software designed to produce graphics. Users can obtain digital plotters for multicolor, camera-ready output and overhead transparencies, as well as hardcopy devices that reproduce paper copies of the screen at a touch of a button. Technology that uses color liquid-crystal displays or electroluminescent panels offers superb graphics resolution, better than that found on home television sets, and can generate all forms of graphs in eight or more colors.

Graphs, in the form of bar charts, trend charts, histograms, and pie charts are convenient and timely instruments for summarizing data in a format that gives management the "big picture." Management can spot trends quickly and get early warning signals. Since graphs filter out extraneous detail, they give strong support to the filtering method. Also, the information attributes of accessibility, comprehensiveness, appropriateness, timeliness, and clarity are

---

[6]For a detailed list, see Joel W. Darrow and James R. Belilove, "Keeping Informed," *Harvard Business Review,* November–December 1978, pp. 180–193.

strengthened. This is especially true when graphs are produced from internal data combined with appropriate external data.

Accounting is a traditional field that produces information for a variety of users. For years, financial statements have been presented in the form of pages with columns of numbers, often overwhelming management and hindering the interpretation of these numbers by financial analysts. These problems may be alleviated by the adoption of graphics for the presentation of financial information. Consider for example the sample balance sheet depicted in graphic form in Figure 3.16.

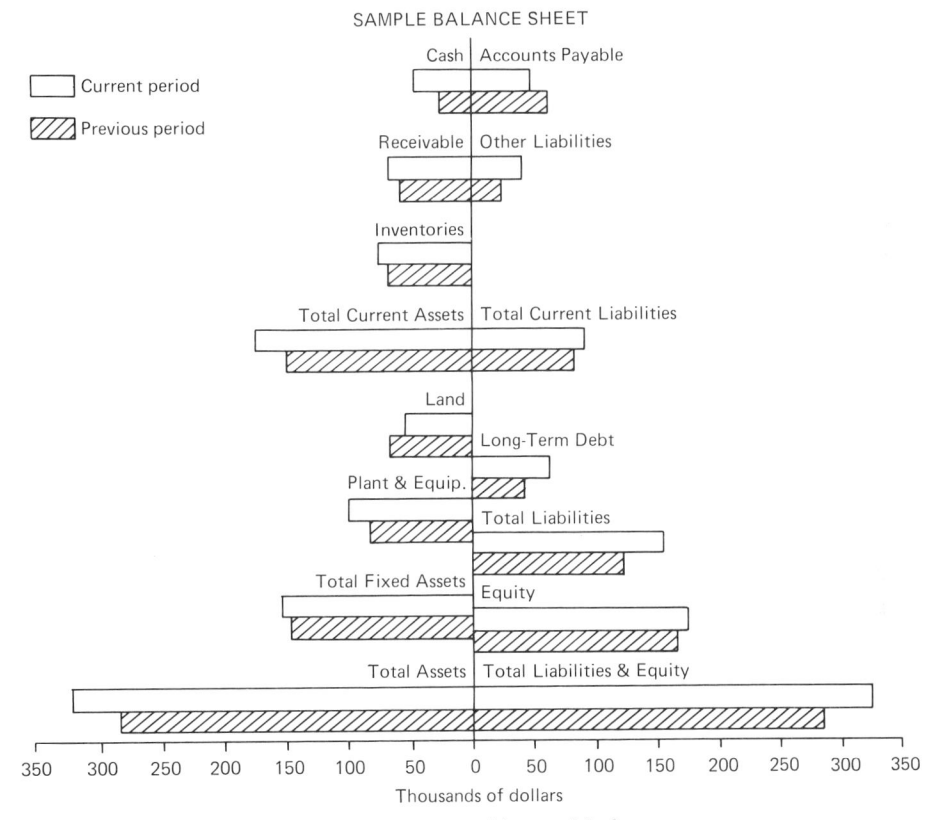

FIG. 3.16 Example of a balance sheet presented in graphic form.

SUMMARY

Information requirements at all levels are met more effectively if the analyst and the user work together to tailor the information output to fit the user's needs. Systems that produce and disseminate volumes of irrelevant data to users may be efficient data processors, but poor information providers. The systems analyst can improve the effectiveness of information output by employing one or more of the following six basic methods: (1) filtering method, (2) monitoring method, (3) modeling method, (4) interrogative method, (5) key variable reporting method, and (6) strategic decision center method.

The filtering method is based on the premise that various levels of decision makers require various levels of detail information to perform their duties. The higher the level of decision making, the less detail information required. The key variable reporting method assumes that the success of an organization is, in large measure, determined by how well it does on a few critical factors. The monitoring method allows the system to keep a close check on the flow of data, and automatically reports information only when certain criteria are met. The modeling method uses various logico–mathematical models to transform data into information. This method provides information which is predictive in nature. The interrogative method relies on the decision maker to format a specific query to the data base to meet a specific need to know. The strategic decision center method refers to gathering information from sources primarily outside of the organization to provide relevant information for strategic decision makers.

REVIEW QUESTIONS

3.1 What is the main purpose of an information system?

3.2 How are data "filtered?" What is the relationship between the level of decision making and requirement for detail?

3.3 List the major advantages of using the filtering method. The disadvantages.

3.4 What are "key variables?" What aspects of the key variables might an information system report?

3.5 List and describe the three ways of implementing the monitoring method.

3.6 Specify the procedures an analyst must execute to implement variance reporting.

3.7 What decision-making activities provide the best opportunities for the implementation of programmed decision making?

3.8 Define the term "automatic notification."

3.9 List the advantages and disadvantages of the monitoring method.

3.10 What is a model? How might models be classified?

3.11 List the major advantages and disadvantages of using models.

3.12 What are the essential elements of the interrogative method? What are its advantages and disadvantages?

3.13 To implement the strategic decision center method, what procedures might the systems analyst install?

QUESTIONS FOR DISCUSSION

3.1 "I am sure I have all the information I need in this situation; unfortunately, I have too much." Discuss this statement.

3.2 "It is prohibitively expensive to design reports for each manager. We provide periodic detailed listings representing major transactions affecting the organization and allow each manager to pick and choose what information they require." "We don't worry about designing information to fit a specific individual's needs. We store the data; when a manager wants a report, we generate it." Compare these philosophies.

3.3 Overheard at a bar, "I'm in deep trouble. My former boss never wanted any detail, in fact, all he ever wanted was a quick verbal update on the business. The new boss loves detail and he is killing me with questions about detail that I never worried about before." Explain what has happened and what the commentor must do differently now.

3.4 "The first year on this job, I took reports home each night and spent 2 to 3 hours reading them. Now I have eliminated all this reading because I figure there are only half a dozen factors I have to stay current on to realize that things are okay." "Just when I think I understand the business and can eliminate reviewing a lot of reports, my boss asks me a question about some detail of the business." Discuss these observations.

3.5 "The major difficulty with implementing programmed decision making is that few decision makers truly understand the decision making process." What is the systems analyst's role in this situation?

3.6 "Organizational decision makers must guard against an unconscious development of a narrow perspective when their primary source of information is provided on an exception basis." Discuss the implications of this statement.

3.7 "Since we put that new punch-up system in, the shipping department's on-time record has gone up 100 percent. The computer just won't let you forget when an order should be shipped." Explain the reporting method implied in this statement.

3.8 "When they installed the new credit collection system, management was excited about the ability to produce dunning letters automatically and regularly for all late paying customers. Now the switch board is lit up all day long with customers complaining about being dunned when they have paid their bills, returned merchandise, or received some other credit consideration." Explain what is likely to have happened in this organization.

3.9 "The use of models in assisting decision makers simply adds a scientific feeling to old-fashioned guessing." "The development of our production scheduling model 2 years ago has improved material and labor costs by 30 percent." "After 3 years and $200,000, management tossed out the model because it did not reflect enough of the critical factors that affect our business." Evaluate these statements.

3.10 "The interrogative method seems to be a sound concept, but it is not much use to we who manage small organizations and cannot afford sophisticated computer systems." Do you agree with this observation? Explain.

3.11 "Paperwork has been reduced by 90 percent since we installed the terminals throughout our warehouses and production facilities. The production and material transfer people simply enter their actions through the terminals rather than fill out paper forms and send copies to everyone." Which reporting method does this refer to?

3.12 "We use to have 300 clerks and a lot of expensive microfilm equipment to answer customer questions before our new system. Now we have 35 clerks with terminals connected directly to the computer. Response time that was measured in terms of hours is now measured in terms of seconds and our customers love it." "Last year when you called that company, they would give you an answer right away or get back to you within an hour. Now, every time I call, someone tells me they don't know because the computer is down." Compare and contrast these observations.

3.13 "We spend so much time analyzing and designing information systems, that by the time we implement a system, the users have changed and so have the information requirements." Evaluate.

3.14 "In this organization, my responsibility is long-range planning. I don't see how you (systems analyst) can help me directly." Provide some suggestions as to how this function can be assisted by a formal information system.

3.15 Discuss at least five sources of formal information that originate external to most organizations and which could be integrated into the formal information system of an organization.

EXERCISES

3.1 From the material in this chapter, plus the material in Appendix B, sketch a diagram of the computer hardware configuration required to support the interrogative method.

3.2 Assume you are responsible for the following businesses. Suggest several key variables which you might use to control each business.

1. a gasoline service station
2. a fast food restaurant
3. a travel bureau
4. a shopping mall
5. a resort hotel

3.3 Universities generally maintain a data base of class enrollments for each semester. Using the filtering method, develop a series of reports to be issued each semester for each of the following:

1. a professor's teaching assignment
2. a department head
3. a school dean
4. the registrar
5. the university president

3.4 For a hypothetical large organization, describe the changes that would be necessary or likely if suddenly no copy machines, carbon paper, or multiple copy forms (including computer printouts) were available for any reports *except* operations or transactional information. Note-user requirements for information should all be considered valid and unchanged by this disturbance.

3.5 Based on your own experiences or a survey of the literature, prepare a two–three page report describing the possible impact of modern word processing technology on information processing. Identify several traditional secretarial functions which can be implemented with this technology and use of the monitoring method.

3.6 Illustrate a rather descriptive model which could be used to guide taxpayers in completing a somewhat complex IRS 1040 form (i.e., use of itemized deductions, moving expenses, different forms of tax calculations, etc.).

PROBLEMS

3.1 Airline reservation systems are sophisticated, online, real time systems with elaborate computer and telecommunication capabilities. They are designed to be used interactively and to respond to simple inquiries. Using the interrogative method, structure the kinds of questions you would expect the systems to answer if you were: (a) a reservation agent answering the telephone, (b) a reservation agent at the boarding desk, (c) a tour planner in a travel agency, and (d) a vice president of operations for the airline.

3.2 You are a systems analyst for a municipal arena corporation and are asked to develop a ticket/reservation system. This arena is home for six different sporting teams and a hundred different entertainment events each year. For each event tickets are generally priced into four classifications (box seats, reserve seats, general admission, grand stand). Reservations and tickets are issued for any event within one year of the current date. Eighty percent of the reservations and ticket requests come in by telephone. The remainder arrive in the mail or in person at the arena. Describe how you might use each of the techniques and methods discussed in this chapter to provide information to: (1) the reservation clerk, (2) the events promoter, and (3) arena management.

3.3 Insurance agents are concerned not only with securing new policy holders, but also with maintaining and upgrading existing policy holders. Most companies maintain extensive computer data bases relating to existing policy holders. Focusing on the specific tailoring method of automatic notification, list several ways that the information system can assist an agent in identifying existing policy holders, who might be interested in new or additional insurance. For example, policy holders who change their address may require more or less home insurance.

3.4 The Blue Cab Company serves a large metropolitan area and employs approximately 200 cabs and 500 drivers. Recently, the accounting department reported that insurance coverage for Blue Cab is increasing at a rate 15 percent faster than comparable cab companies throughout the nation. Additionally, revenues, as a result of cab lower fares and reduced number of trips have been trailing company forecast by 17 percent. The president of Blue Cab feels that some of this lackluster performance is due to a less than aggressive policy of evaluating individual drivers' performance. Consequently, the president has requested that a reporting system be designed which would evaluate those aspects of a driver's performance most closely related to insurance premiums and requests for cab service.

The following statistics are made available to you, a systems analyst in the Blue Cab Company:

1. Traffic citations have averaged close to 1000 a year for the last 3 years.
2. Cabs are involved in an average of 37 accidents a week, 35 of which are considered minor "fender benders," and two per week involving some form of personal injuries claim.
3. Customer service people handle between 5 and 75 customer complaints for long waiting time, abusive language, poor service, etc. Complaints average about 25 per day. Each reported complaint, accident, and traffic citation is logged by day, by driver, by cab number, and by time of day.

From the above data, using the variances reporting method, develop a monthly report for the president reflecting driver performance.

3.5 Manufacturing processes generally require tight production controls to remain profitable. RUST-O Paint Mfg., Inc. produces 2 million gallons of various type paints annually. Management has decided to use production yields to help control over their manufacturing process. A yield in production is often expressed as the percentage actually obtained of the amount possible. (For a further discussion about yield, refer to Appendix A.) The standard product mix for a gallon of RUST-O's most popular paint includes two major components: resin and fish oil. One gallon of finished paint requires three pounds of resin and one quart of fish oil. Expected costs this year for these products are, resin at $1.30 per pound and fish oil at $1.00 per quart. Standard allowances for price variances are 10 percent; material usage variances are 50 percent. Standards are reviewed and established each year based on previous experience and purchasing forecasts.

Production runs are made in batches of 500 or 1,000 gallons at a time. Deliveries of raw material are generally scheduled for Mondays and Thursdays each week. For quantity control reasons, paint and the raw materials required in a batch are given a batch number. This batch number is also coded subsequently to the receiving report associated with the raw materials. Inventory tickets for both raw material withdrawals and paint receipts are completed for each batch.

Last month's production of paint amounted to 50,000 gallons and it was produced from the following input:

1. Resin—175,000 pounds at $1.41 per pound
2. Fish oil—64,000 quarts at $1.12 per quart

Prepare a report(s) for the production and purchasing managers which reflect those aspects of the operation which they control. Use one or more of the monitoring method techniques in the development of your report. Indicate the optimal timing for the report each manager receives to take corrective action (assume data processing can be accomplished over night if necessary). Illustrate your report using last month's actual data, assuming 80 percent of the batches produced were 500 gallons each.

3.6 Production can be divided into two phases: planning and execution. The data flow leads from an initial input of customer orders and statistical sales background data to the final shipment of an order.

Planning:

Planning begins with the preparation and projection of order forecasts. Stock availability and on-order status are screened across product inventory records. But component family characteristics of the product line must also be recognized. Product structure and bills of materials enter into these decisions.

After a determination of net requirements, an order quantity analysis takes place to ascertain lot sizes and lead times for two distinct groups: (1) those raw material items which must be purchased from outside sources, and (2) those raw material items which can be either assembled or fabricated internally.

Items required to be purchased are placed on a purchase requisition. At this point, prices are ascertained, delivery dates are negotiated, selection of a vendor is made, and a purchase order is released. Scheduled receipt documents may be prepared simultaneously with the release of the purchase order and forwarded to the inspection-receiving area of the warehouse. An open purchase order record is now established for follow-up procedures.

Internally made items are routed to production planning for assembly and fabrication. Some similarity exists between these two levels. An assembly order is generated for the assembly area, a shop order for the fabrication area. Material requisition and move tickets accompany both documents. Three basic types of records (standard routing, work center load, and open job order) permit assembly and fabrication to schedule, to load, and to level the line, or the shop, and to release the order paperwork.

Execution:

Execution begins at the purchasing level with the need for order follow-up and vendor expediting. The vendor ships material to the plant warehouse, accompanying the shipment with packing lists and an invoice.

Various execution functions are performed at the assembly and fabrication levels. Orders are dispatched, rescheduled, and expedited between work centers. In the meantime, current production reporting updates work center and open job order records.

Purchased items, along with components from the assembly and fabrication areas, move to the inspection area. These finished products move from final processing to the final inspection and receiving areas. The final cycle in this flow is a shipment authorization requesting the warehouse to pack and ship to a branch warehouse or to the customer.

Develop a production model (flow diagram) from the above information.

3.7 Old New England Leather is a large manufacturer and marketer of quality leather goods. Their product line ranges from wallets to saddles. Because of the prevailing management philosophy at Old New England Leather, the company will accept orders for almost any leather product to be custom made on demand. This is possible since the leather craftworkers employed by the company perform a job in its entirety (i.e., the company does not use production line techniques). Each leather craftworker is responsible for the complete manufacturing of a given product. Currently, the company employs about 150 leather craftworkers and has been growing at the rate of 20 percent per year over the last three years. Management does not anticipate this growth rate in the future, but instead sees a steady growth rate of 5 percent over the next decade.

Old New England Leather markets a proprietary line of leather goods worldwide. However, these stock products comprise only 50 percent of the output from the craftworkers. The remaining products are produced to special order. When a custom order is received, the specifications for the order are posted along with an expected shipping date. Each craftworker is then eligible to bid on all or part of an order. Once the bids are evaluated, the company determines which individuals have agreed upon the date, and accepts the lowest bid for production. It is this custom part of the business that has shown the greatest growth in recent years. During the last twelve months, there has been an average of 600 orders in process at any one time.

Along with growth, Old New England Leather management has experienced many problems related to providing consistent, on-time delivery. It appears that the skilled craftworkers often fail to report on a timely basis when a job is complete. Also, management has never had a satisfactory control for ensuring that orders are worked on in a priority sequence. Other problems, such as craftworkers overcommitting themselves in a given time period or simply losing an order, are also becoming serious.

The company leases a medium-sized computer configuration for processing payroll inventory, accounts receivable, accounts payable, and so forth. This configuration has capabilities for online processing with as many as twenty terminals. Currently, ten terminals are in operation throughout the plant.

Using the capabilities of the available computer configuration, propose a system for controlling custom orders that includes extensive use of the Monitoring and Interrogative Methods of providing information. Be sure that your proposed system benefits the craftworkers, management, and Old New England Leather's customers.

3.8 You are a systems analyst employed by a data processing service bureau. One of the specialties of your organization is to provide a data encoding service to other organizations in the area in addition to supporting your own operations. Much of this effort involves large jobs in short time periods. The goal of your organization is to provide a firm cost estimate for each job to the prospective customer. You employ approximately 100 data entry operators, both full- and part-time. The manager of the service bureau has requested you to design an information system which will assist him to plan and control the data entry operations. You have investigated the situation and determined the following:

1. A sampling of work indicates that there are three primary factors related to the time (and therefore cost) needed to complete a job: (a) the experience level of the operator; (b) the number of strokes per document; and (c) the format of the source document from which the data are entered.
2. You have classified operators as: trainees, juniors, and seniors. A trainee is considered to have a productivity factor of 75 percent, a junior 100 percent, and a senior 125 percent.
3. Source documents are classified as either formatted or mixed. A junior operator can key 10,000 strokes an hour from a formatted source document and 8,000 strokes an hour from a mixed document.
4. The keyboards are linked to a microcomputer, which can account for the number of strokes keyed in a job. When the operator indicates end of job, the micro will create a record that contains the number of strokes keyed for that job.
5. Approximately 40 percent of the data entry work done by the service bureau is repetitive.
6. The service bureau has a medium-sized computer with complete processing capabilities.

Requirements for Solution:
In your design proposal include the following:

1. An analysis of a simple planning model that could be used.
2. The informational outputs available for use in both planning and controlling activities.

BIBLIOGRAPHY

"America's Offices Enter a New Age," *Nations Business,* July 1981.

Alter, *Decision Support Systems: Current Practices and Continuing Challenges,* Reading, MA: Addison–Wesley Publishing Company, 1980.

Anthony and Dearden, *Management Control Systems,* Fourth Edition, Homewood, IL: Richard D. Irwin, Inc., 1980.

Carlson, "Decision Support Systems: Personal Computing Services for Managers," *Management Review,* January 1977.

Darrow, "Financial Data Banks: A Guide for the Perplexed," *Computer Decisions,* January 1975.

Drucker, *The Practice of Management,* New York: Harper & Row Publishers, 1954.

"Economic Census to Cover 1982 Activity," *Automation,* October 1972.

Getz, "MIS and the War Room," *Datamation,* December 1977.

Kilmann and Ghyman, "The MAPS Design Technology: Designing Strategic Intelligence Systems for MNCs," *Columbia Journal of World Business,* Summer 1976.

LaRoe, "A Manufacturing Plant Information System," *Proceeding of the Third Annual Conference,* Chicago, Illinois: The Society for Management Information Systems, 1971.

Laska, "All the News that's Fit to Retrieve," *Computer Decisions,* August 1972.

Lucas, *Information Systems Concepts for Management,* Second Edition, New York: McGraw–Hill Book Company, 1982.

Murdick and Ross, *Information Systems for Modern Management,* Second Edition, Englewood Cliffs, NJ: Prentice–Hall, Inc., 1977.

Pascarella, "Performance Feedback on Everything that Counts," *Industry Week,* September 20, 1976.

"Putting the Library on a Computer," *Business Week,* March 30, 1981.

"Today's Top Brass Eyeing War Room Graphics," *ComputerWorld,* August 3, 1981.

CHAPTER 4

An Overview of Modern Data Processing Resources

4.1 ▪ INTRODUCTION

A widespread misconception equates computer systems with information systems. The origin of this misconception can probably be traced to the tremendous impact computers have made on data and information processing during the last two decades. Thus far, our introduction to information systems has focused on information, systems, the information needs of organizations, and methods for tailoring information outputs for users. We have referenced specific data processing resources, only as it was necessary to demonstrate or explain another concept or technique.

In Chapter 1 we indicated that data processing resources are one of six design blocks comprising an information system. To participate in the development of information systems, it is not necessary to program or operate a computer. If we are to participate effectively, however, we must understand what data processing resources are available and what their capabilities are. Moreover, because the ultimate design of an information system is implemented in the form of these data processing resources, the manner in which these resources are selected and organized within an organization represents important decisions for both designers and users of information systems. The objectives of this chapter are:

1. To describe the basic data processing resources used in contemporary information systems.
2. To discuss the alternatives for organizing data processing resources in an organization.
3. To analyze the basis for selecting appropriate data processing resources to support the information system.

4.2 ▪ DATA PROCESSING RESOURCES

The design blocks of input, processing, data base, controls, and output are implemented in the form of four tangible data processing resources. These resources are data, hardware, software, and people. Although several of these terms are derived from and closely associated with computer technology, their use is appropriate for noncomputer systems as well.

The circle, traditionally thought of as a geometric symbol of strength, is used in Figure 4.1 to illustrate an information system in terms of its data processing resources. Each resource is viewed as an equal part of the system. The most advanced hardware is useless without equally good software development. Good software development occurs only through the efforts of good people. The success of the information system in satisfying users' requirements is attained only by collecting, storing, and processing the correct data. In this section we define and discuss each resource to understand its role and function in the design and development of information systems.

Data

The purpose of an information system is to produce information which satisfies the needs of its users. In Chapter 1 we stated that data, the symbolic representation of reality, derive value from their use as the raw material from which information is produced. The importance of understanding this relationship between data and infor-

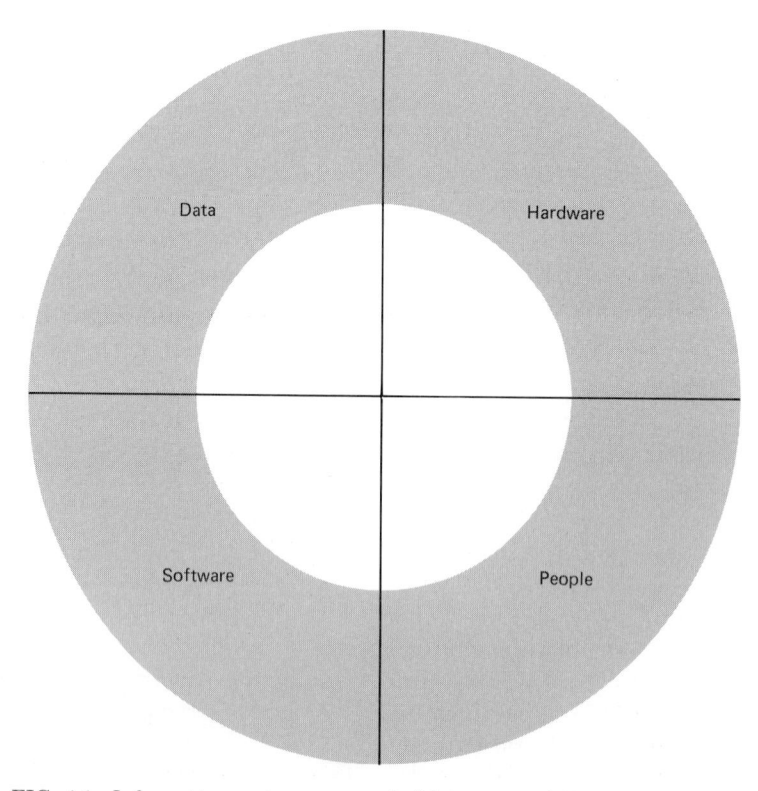

FIG. 4.1 Information system composed of data processing resources.

mation is increasing as more organizations perceive information as an organizational resource. To manage (i.e., plan and control) information as an organizational resource is, in reality, a requirement for managing data; this includes collection, processing, and storage.

In recent years, computing technology has been successfully applied to almost all forms of data processing. For example, the typewriter was introduced less than 100 years ago to replace manual transcription. The introduction of the electric typewriter earlier in this century represented a significant improvement over manual typewriters. In recent years, word processing machines (i.e., computer-based typewriters) have been implemented in many organizations to replace electric typewriters. Today, it is not uncommon for charts, graphs, and diagrams to be produced by computers as either hardcopy paper or in three-dimensional images on CRTs. The design and development of future information systems will include considerations for all forms of data representation and its related technology in order to achieve an organization's information objectives.

The variety of data required to be collected, processed, and stored in an organization correlates directly with the information requirements of the organization. For example, where management requires information concerning both internal and external activities, data must be collected from sources both internal and external to the organization; where accounting requires financial information concerning the use of organizational resources, the appropriate data must be collected; where planning requirements require information regarding the future, data representing future events or desires must be recorded. In Chapter 1, data input to an information system were classified as (1) transactions, (2) expectations, (3) queries, and (4) instructions.

Data representing transactions are numerous and include: personnel actions (e.g., hiring, promoting, firing, pay increases, job assignments, work locations); physical inventory movements (e.g., receipts, withdrawals, down time, maintenance activity); customer communications (e.g., orders, returns, payments, inquiries). Data reflecting expectations include plans, budgets, standards, and schedules. Queries represent data inputs that include requirements for periodic reports, special request reports, and specific information for specific questions. Instructions are data represented by both clerical procedures and computer programs.

Thus far, we have been discussing logical aspects of data. However, data exist physically in many forms or as many media. The most common media are the verbal and written word. The "paper explosion" we hear about or see in today's organizations refers to the abundance of written data. Experiences such as registering for classes, paying utility bills, and traveling on toll roads illustrate data in the form of punched holes in a paper card. (Ironically, this punched hole media has become familiar to the general public through the written words that often appear on the card, "Do not tear, fold, or mutilate.") Similarly, "ticker tape" parades have alerted us that data appear as punched holes in paper tape.

The growing use of tape recorders and video cassettes represents data recorded as magnetic spots on plastic tapes and disks—until recent years the "private" knowledge of computer specialists. Data are also represented by sensitized marks and bars as illustrated by bank checks and the labels on the goods we purchase at the supermarket.

Microfilm, a media often associated with government agents and espionage, has become an essential recording media in many organizations. Microfilm is not only an efficient form of recording for archival storage, but it can be useful for recording information needed in day-to-day operations. Blinking lights, pulsations, and meters are examples of other media on which data are recorded.

The variety of media used to record data represents the technology we have created to process data into information more efficiently than humans can do alone. Much of this new media and its related technology was developed specifically to improve the efficiency of data processing with computers. Early attempts at using data processing technology, however, had little effect on the initial recording of data. Initially, recorded data continued to be written or typed on paper or a form called a **source document**. The data from a source document were then reproduced or converted into other media until the data were in a media capable of being processed by a computer. Figure 4.2 illustrates this traditional media conversion sequencing for computer processing.

As illustrated, source documents are converted to punched cards, punched tape, or magnetic tape in a manual keying operation (e.g., keypunch, teletypewriter, key-to-tape). This media then enters the computer where the data are transferred to magnetic disk, drum, or tape. In subsequent processing, data from the magnetic media are converted to computer memory each time they are required for processing. Not illustrated in Figure 4.2 is the reversing of this conversion sequence. The data are returned to the magnetic media for storage, further processing, or conversion to another media for output (e.g., paper in the form of a report).

As illustrated in Figure 4.3, data no longer need to be recorded on paper and converted to computer readable media. In some

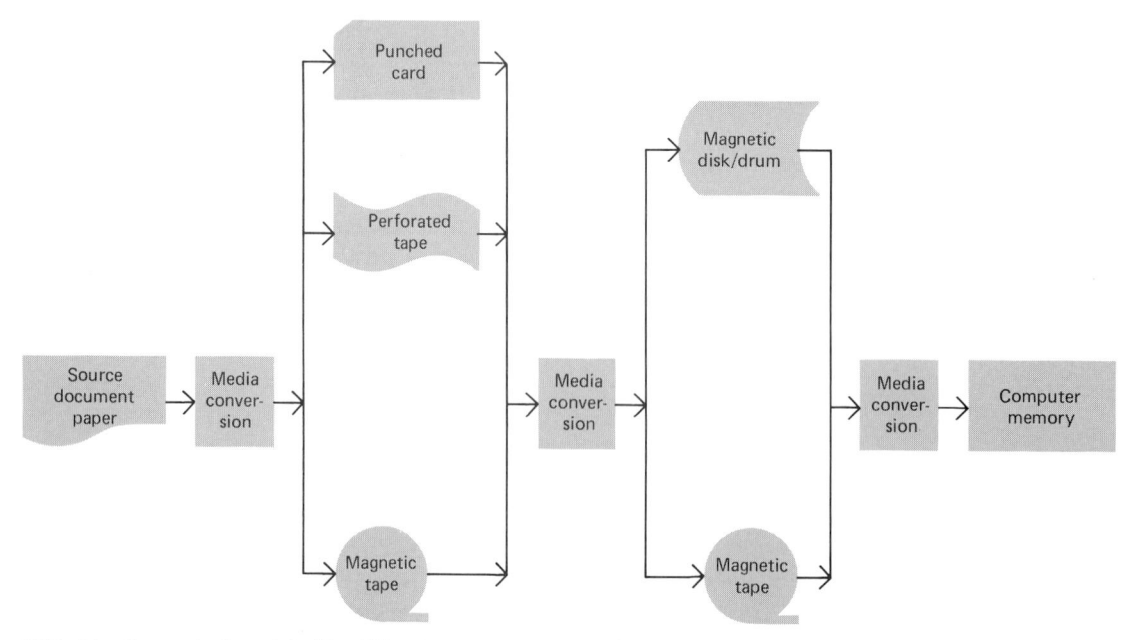

FIG. 4.2 Conceptual model of traditional process to convert data media.

situations, data are entered directly into computer memory using a variety of terminals; in other instances, the number of media conversion steps are reduced. With the use of still other devices or hardware, the initial recording of data input as a separate activity is eliminated. In these latter cases, data are recorded on media acceptable for computer processing as a by-product of the machine performing in the operations of the organization [e.g., cash registers and other point of sale (POS) devices, automatic bank tellers, and process control computers]. The use of devices and techniques to eliminate or minimize media conversions is termed **source data automation** (SDA).

In the development of information systems, considerations for both the logical and physical aspects of collecting data are essential design tasks. Given a set of user information requirements, it is necessary to determine first what data must be collected to produce the required information; second, where these data can be collected; and third, how these data can be collected. Modern information systems design includes the efficient collection of data to minimize both manual efforts and the amount of required media conversion activities. The use of concepts and techniques for SDA should be evaluated and implemented where feasible.

Traditional formal education emphasizes the use and structuring of data using verbal and written media. Although the use of these media will continue to be of paramount importance in the future, we must

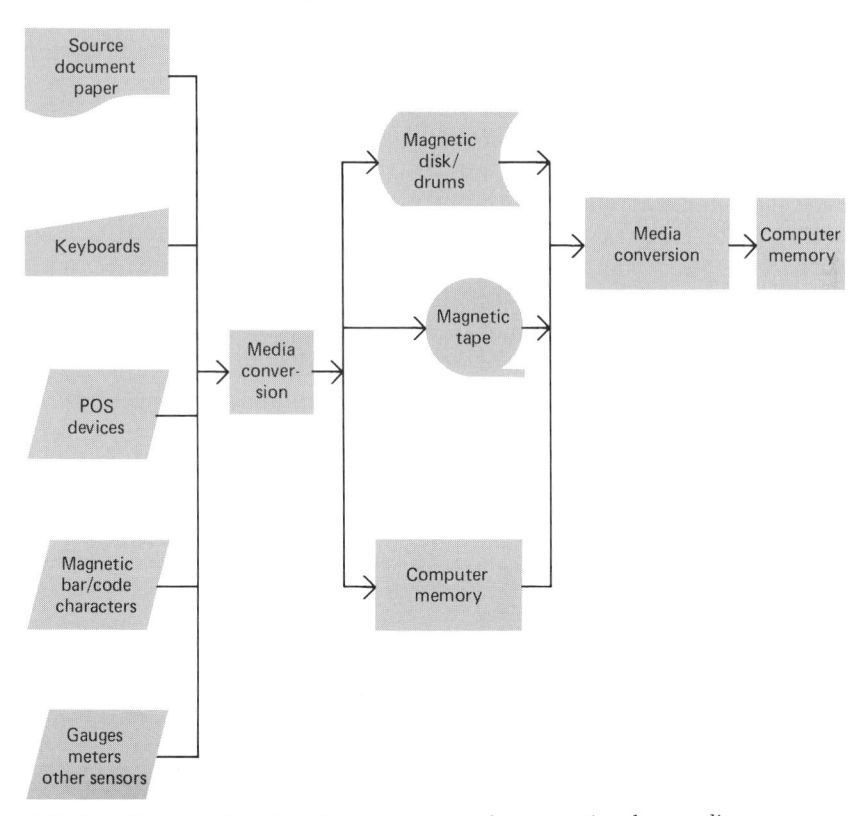

FIG. 4.3 Conceptual model of modern process for converting data media.

understand how to use and structure data with the modern media developed for efficient computer processing. Each of these media has capabilities providing comparative advantages and disadvantages to one another depending on our objectives. In Part II, we analyze these computer media, and the logical and physical structuring of data on this media.

Hardware

Hardware is a term used to describe any and all physical machines used in data processing. In a noncomputer system this might include pens, pencils, typewriters, calculators, file cabinets, and so forth. In a computer system, hardware refers to card readers, printers, tape units, disk drives, central processing units, consoles, terminals, modems, and so forth. In Appendix B, we provide brief but comprehensive discussions of computer hardware. The material in Appendix B can be easily incorporated at this time or simply reviewed quickly and referenced as necessary throughout the text. Some general comments concerning computer hardware, however, are appropriate at this point.

Figure 4.4 illustrates a conceptual model of a computer. A computer is composed of a **central processing unit** (CPU) having arithmetic and logical capabilities, a mechanism for placing data input into the processing unit, a mechanism for storage of data during processing, and a mechanism that allows the operator to obtain as output the information that has been processed. The computer's capabilities are limited to doing arithmetic calculations and executing decisions having only two alternatives. Combining the computer's basic capabilities of arithmetic calculations with a decision-making power, allows it to perform all of the data operations necessary to produce information.

Although we use the term computer as though it were a single machine, what we generally refer to as a computer is a series of machines or hardware units, more properly termed a computing system. The heart of a large computing system is the mainframe. The **mainframe** generally encompasses the CPU and a console, which is a hardware device (e.g., CRT, typewriter/printer) for limited input/output functions by the operator. The term **peripherals** is used to describe all of the additional hardware devices required for input, output, storage, and data communication functions.

This distinction between mainframe and peripherals in a computing system is significant for several reasons. First, whereas the internal speed of the CPU or mainframe is measured in fractions of a second, the speed of peripheral hardware is significantly slower and is directly related to the data media being used. Second, the performance capabilities of a modern computing system must be viewed as dynamic rather than static. Hardware can be upgraded or altered to provide increased performance capabilities in several ways: (1) the mainframe can be replaced by a larger, more powerful unit;

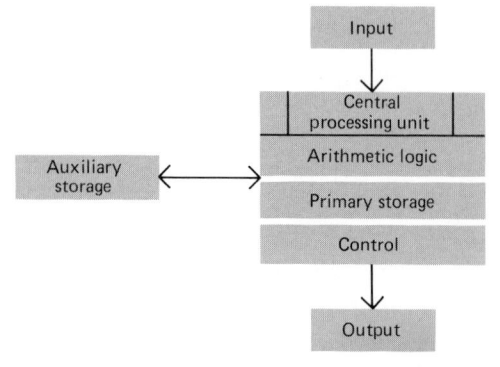

FIG. 4.4 Conceptual model of a digital computer.

(2) the existing mainframe can be enhanced by the addition of primary storage; and (3) the computing system can be enhanced by the addition of peripheral hardware. Third, computing systems can be designed using mainframes and peripherals from a variety of manufacturers. In the next section, we discuss computer software, but it is important to note at this time that in the evaluation of computers or computing systems, the performance capabilities of hardware are not necessarily viewed independently of the available software required to operate the hardware or process the data.

New computer hardware is introduced almost daily by a variety of vendors. Often this hardware is promoted as more capable and less expensive than the product it hopes to replace. This phenomenon is termed the "price/performance ratio." Although total sales for computer hardware are expected to exceed $100 billion in the mid-1980s, some industry experts estimate that the cost of computing has been declining at a rate of 20 percent per year for the last two decades. Others believe that hardware prices have dropped by a factor of 1000 since 1955.[1] These lower prices have resulted in more powerful large computers as well as the emergence of inexpensive, small computers known as "minicomputers," "microcomputers," "personal computers," and "desk top computers." The widespread availability of inexpensive small computers has reopened the controversy between proponents of one powerful mainframe computer for an organization and those who propose the use of many small computers distributed throughout the organization. We will examine this controversy later in this chapter.

[1]"Missing Computer Software," *Business Week*, September 1, 1980, pp. 46–56.

The emergence of small computers coupled with the impact of the "price/performance ratio" has put computing technology within the grasp of even the smallest organization. Consequently, understanding the capabilities of computer hardware is no longer restricted to computer specialists in large organizations. In the past, the literature and practice have seemed to emphasize the importance of hardware supporting the information system at the expense of, and often to the exclusion of, the other data processing resources. Perhaps this is why the industry is alleged to have implemented sophisticated computer hardware systems but ineffective information systems. Our approach in this book is not to downgrade the importance of the hardware, but, instead, to provide a balanced perspective in terms of all four data processing resources and their supportive role to the information system.

Software

Software is a computer-related term that originally referred to all of the data processing resources that were not hardware. More recently, its usage tends to be restricted to include the procedures or specific instructions that describe the operations of the information system. This includes both clerical and machine instructions (i.e., computer programs). Often, however, its usage refers only to computer programs. The term **documentation** is then used to describe clerical procedures and the English or people-version of the computer programs. We use software at this point in its most specific context (i.e., computer programs). Three general categories of software are: (1) programming languages, (2) operating systems, and (3) application and special service programs.

Programming Languages. Languages, or instructions that the computer can follow, are of three types: (a) machine language, (b) assembler language, and (c) compiler language. Machine language is binary code that the computer interprets directly. For humans, this language is tedious to write as it requires a programmer to keep track of storage locations of data and instructions in the form of strings of 0's and 1's. Machine language is efficient for the computer, but very inefficient for the programmer, and rarely used today to develop software.

Assembler languages were developed in the early 1950s to lessen the tedium and quicken the slow development process caused by having to write programs in machine language. Assembler languages are made up of mnemonic operation codes and symbolic addresses that human beings remember more easily than machine codes and addresses. However, these instructions must be translated into machine language that the computer understands. This translation is performed by an assembler program which converts the mnemonic operation codes and symbolic addresses (the source program) into machine processible form (the object program).

Compiler languages are also known as high level, or people oriented languages because the instructions resemble the English language or mathematical expressions used by people. However, the *source* program written by the human has to be compiled and translated into an *object* program that can be understood and executed by the computer. Compiler languages such as COBOL (an acronym for COmmon Business Oriented Language) have many advantages over machine and assembler languages for writing application programs. For example, they are relatively computer independent, easier to write, more human efficient, easier to read and maintain, and more readily understood than are assembler languages.

Operating Systems. When a computer is acquired, the user is not merely buying hardware but also a means of meeting his or her needs through application programs, without having to be too concerned about the internal operations of the computer. This internal operations interface, called the **operating system,** drives the computer in the most efficient manner. It is made up of an integrated system of complex, sophisticated programs (usually written in machine or assembler language) that supervise the operations of the CPU, control input/output (I/O) functions, translate assembler and compiler languages into machine language, and provide a host of other support services. An operating system attempts to maximize the use of the hardware by performing many of the functions that were formerly the responsibility of the computer operator. It performs activities such as freeing central processor storage locations after termination of a task, and scheduling jobs stacked in an input queue. It also performs *multiprogramming* and *paging functions*.

The key components of the operating system are control programs that include a supervisor, an I/O control system, data communications control, an initial program loader, and a job control program.

The *supervisor* is similar to a traffic cop in that it directs I/O activities and handles interrupt conditions, job scheduling, program retrieval, and primary storage allocation. The *I/O control system* handles I/O scheduling, I/O error corrections, and other data management functions.

Data communications control programs are included in systems that use a network of data communication channels and remote terminals. They perform such activities as data input, automatic polling, queuing and interrupt handling for competing terminals, message switching, and inquiry and transaction processing.

The *initial program loader* is a small control program that loads the supervisor control program from a systems residence device (e.g., a magnetic disk) into primary storage when the computer begins operations.

The *job control program's* function is to prepare the computer system for the start of the next job by executing job control language statements.

Application and Special Service Programs. Application programs can be classified into two broad categories. The first category of applications programs are those that are normally written by a programmer who works for the organization and are limited to a particular function within a particular environment. These types of programs are intended to take advantage of the unique way an organization conducts its activities (e.g., a sales analysis program for a specialty product). The second category of applications programs, known as generalized or "canned" programs, are developed by computer manufacturers, independent software vendors, or other computer users, and are directed toward serving the needs of many users. Applications of this type are linear programming, cash flow analysis, and demand deposit accounting.

Service programs include aids like the following: (a) subroutines that consist of a set of instructions that perform some common, subordinate function within another program and that can be called in by that program when needed; (b) librarian programs that catalog, control, and maintain a directory of programs and subroutines which are stored on the library (usually magnetic disk) of the computer system; (c) *utility* programs, a group of programs that perform various housekeeping functions such as sorts and merges, and file and memory dumps; and (d) various other services and aids such as simulators, emulators, statistical recording and reporting, and debug tools.

Some authorities predict that over 90 percent of the software currently programmed into systems will be in hardware form (some people use the terms *firmware, microprogram,* or *microcode*) by the early 1990s. This prediction assumes that a great deal of standardization and generalization of business data processing functions will occur among organizations in the future. For example, if every organization used the same kind of payroll system, then all payroll programs could be in firmware. This situation will probably never happen, but there will be movement toward the use of microprogramming, especially in the operating systems area. The use of microprograms or firmware will have two noticeable impacts: (1) it will improve significantly the cost/performance characteristics of computer systems, and (2) it will enhance the control of the system, since firmware is prepared by the computer vendor and normally can be changed only by the vendor.

People

The pace at which hardware and software resources are developed has often been a function of the availability of people who are trained to develop and operate the technology. Nevertheless, it is the exception rather than the rule to find an organization of any size that does not have a formal data processing or information systems department.

Figure 4.5 illustrates a variety of functional positions within the framework of a hypothetical department.

In any organization of people, those in positions of leadership are often referred to as managers. Depending on the size of the organization, it may be necessary to develop suborganizations and tiers of management. The responsibilities of information systems managers are identical to those of any manager in the organization (as described in Chapter 2). Information systems managers must plan, control, and effect decision making within and for their organizations. The high level of technology and technologically trained people involved causes problems and provides opportunities. In the final analysis, however, success is attained by the application of time-honored management practices.

The **steering committee** depicted in Figure 4.5 is similar to a management committee or board of directors for the larger or-

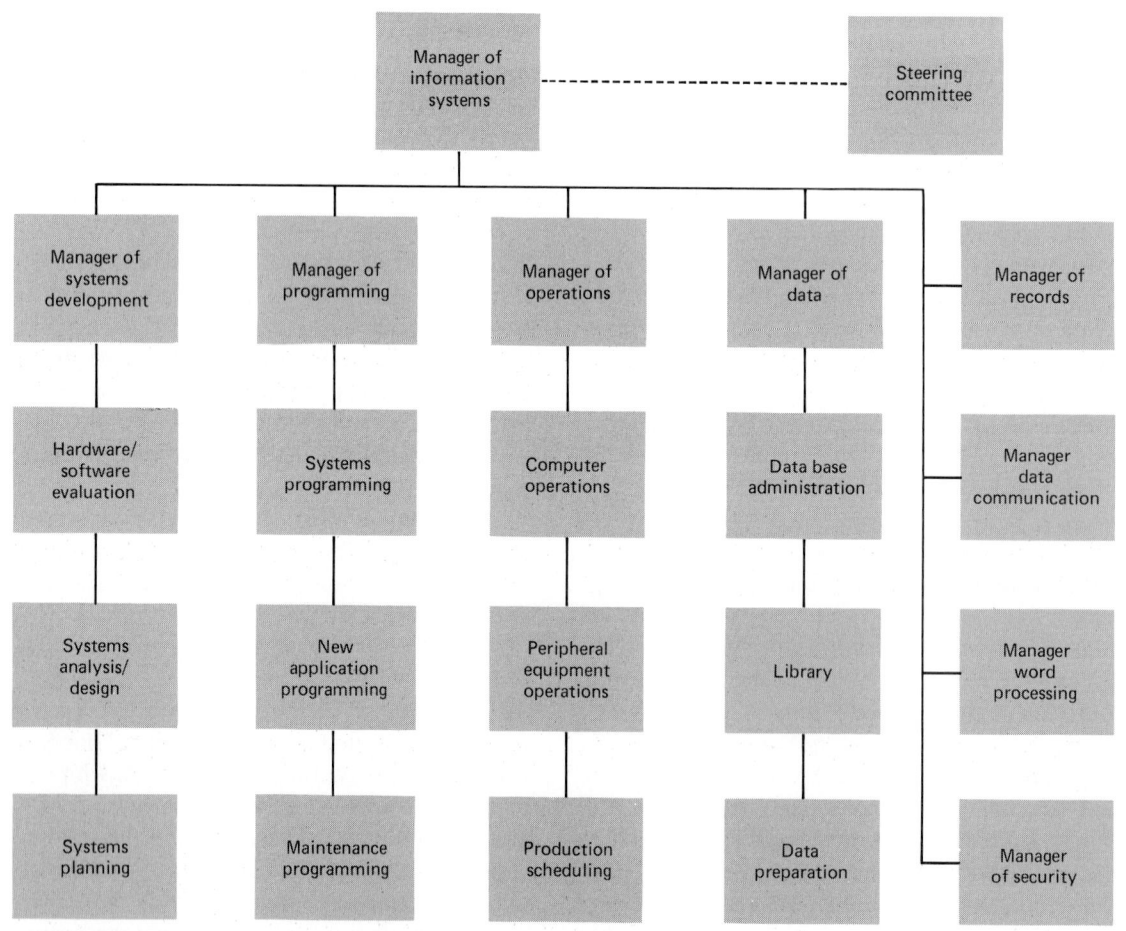

FIG. 4.5 Categories of jobs in a typical computer-based information system.

ganization. This committee, however, is comprised of representatives from the top management of the organization. Their primary function is to establish policy on aspects such as priorities for the development of systems, approval for capital expenditures related to the operation of the computer facility, charges for computer services, and so forth. With the use of a steering committee, developmental coordination is facilitated and communication is increased; different functional views are reconciled, and agreed on courses of action are established; widespread participation is encouraged and a forum is provided. Since information and the information system serves the entire organization, use of a steering committee is especially appropriate. Moreover, each individual participant's viewpoint is broadened as he or she gains an appreciation of other departments' problems, as well as those of the information system.

Systems development functions include hardware and software evaluation, analysis and design, and information systems planning. This may include operations research specialists who apply logico–mathematical models to the solution of different problems. Additionally, it may include clerical methods, procedures, and forms as part of the development of new or improved systems. The central figure in the system development category is the systems analyst discussed in Chapter 1. Through his or her information systems knowledge, the users' information requirements and other demands are translated into a comprehensive systems design.

Programming management supervises the personnel who are responsible for the development and maintenance of the software. *Systems programmers* develop and maintain the operating system and other technical systems software that controls the basic functions of the computer. They are highly trained individuals who have strong technical proficiency in hardware architecture and software. **Application programmers** code, test, and implement new or existing computer programs for specific user applications (e.g., accounts receivable, payroll). This activity is sometimes further subdivided into new application program development or maintenance. Where organizations have used computers for several years, a significant amount of programming effort is expended to maintain existing programs rather than to design new programs.

Operations management supervises hardware operators and schedules the tasks to be performed by the hardware and software resources. This job is analogous to that of a production superintendent in a manufacturing process. The *computer operators* monitor and control the computer through the central computer console. *Peripheral equipment operators*, in turn, assist the computer operators by setting up, operating, and unloading peripheral devices such as tape and disk drives, printers, card readers and punches, and so forth. The *production scheduler* coordinates and controls the mix of data processing jobs to achieve optimum equipment utilization and service to users. Large computing systems represent a very complicated and sophisticated operating environment.

The data manager supervises the handling of data that are processed by the system. A **data base administrator** (DBA) designs and controls the data base of the system. The DBA establishes and enforces standards for the use, control, and security of all files comprising the data base. The data library is a well constructed, secure structure used to house offline files, programs, documentation, and other sensitive material. It is under the control of a person, sometimes referred to as an *operations librarian*. Data preparation includes the people and machines that convert written source data into readable computer media.

As formal information systems evolve in their use of technology and in the numbers of people they employ, further specialization occurs. As represented in Figure 4.5, new categories of information specialists emerge and traditional categories undergo dramatic changes in emphasis related to the development of information systems. Some of these functional categories are as follows: (1) **Records** or records management refers generally to managing traditional media such as paper or micrographics (e.g., microfilm). (2) **Data communications** refers to the rapidly growing area of both voice and data transmittal. (3) **Word processing** is a term used to describe the technology replacing traditional office equipment such as typewriters. Finally, traditional concepts and practices of **security** within organizations have evolved to compensate for current developments in the use of modern information technology.

The organization chart represented in Figure 4.5 is not intended to propose the ideal organization for data processing people resources. Its intent is simply to illustrate the wide variety of talents that can comprise the development and operations of information systems. Information systems theorists and practitioners (including users) have ongoing debates about the organization or structuring of not just people resources but data processing resources as a whole. In the next section we analyze alternative structures for data processing resources.

4.3 ▪ ORGANIZING DATA PROCESSING RESOURCES

Organizing resources is a management task derived from the traditional responsibility to control. Organizing data processing resources is also an information systems design decision. The nature of this decision process is noneconomic, but it has both technological and political overtones. Technically, this decision process has been blurred by the mystique associated with data processing technology. In addition, the rapid pace of technological innovation and the equally rapid improvement in "price/performance ratio" of newer technology contribute variety to this decision process. Politically, organizational "battles" as to whether data processing resources should be a central organizational function (i.e., centralized) or dispersed to each department or location within the organization (i.e., distributed) also add confusion and complexity to the decision process. Continuing advancements in data processing technology, and changing organizations and information requirements fuel this controversy rather than solve it.

In this section we examine various approaches to organizing processing resources, and outline the advantages and disadvantages of alternative structures. We also provide a perspective on the current situation, discuss the factors that influence organizational selection, and present examples of selected organizational structures.

Alternative Organizational Structures

In Chapter 1 we analyzed the integrated nature of the information system when viewed as a major subsystem of an organization. This integrated nature of the information system is illustrated again in Figure 4.6.

Conceptually, the information system serves all levels of management and operations equally. At the practical level, data processing resources are implemented and used with varying degrees of efficiency and effectiveness.

For example, data originating in one functional area of an organization, may be required by individuals in other functional areas to perform their duties. If each user of information must collect and process the necessary data individually, the total cost of data processing for the organization is considerably greater than it need be. This situation represents an inefficient systems design. More important, inefficient data processing or a poor flow of information can result in users receiving information that is out of synchronization with the reality it purports to reflect. This information has a diminished value to the recipient, and it may represent a lost opportunity for the recipient to act on the flow of activity the information reflects.

Centralized, distributed, and hybrid are three alternative structures for data pro-

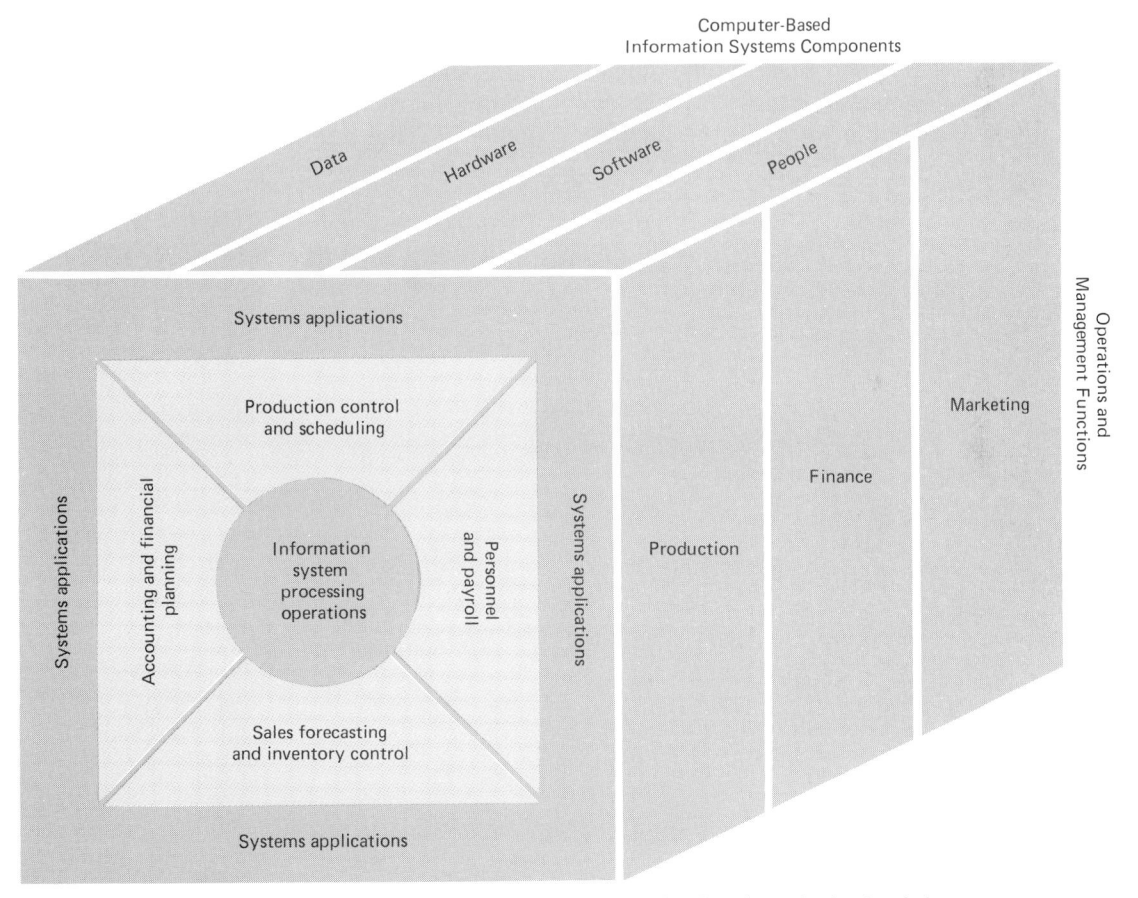

FIG. 4.6 Schematic diagram showing an information system, developed on the basis of the approach of keeping the operations and management systems in synchronization.

cessing resources. Figure 4.7 depicts each data processing resource as a two-directional flow line terminating at end points labeled as centralized or distributed structures. A **centralized structure** places data processing resources in a common physical location and administrative unit within an organization. A **distributed structure** disperses data processing resources to individual locations or administrative units within the organization. (*Note:* Organizations are often classified as centralized or decentralized. However, we prefer the use of the term "distributed" to decentralized when referencing data processing resources. Decentralized denotes independence and fragmentation. Data processing resources, a component of the information system, are centralized or distributed for the overall effectiveness of the system.) As illustrated, the physical structure of each resource in an organization can be designed independently of the other resources. In other words, some of the resources can be physically centralized and others can be distributed. Also, the flow lines represent an infinite number of possible structures for each resource (i.e., partially centralized and partially distributed). For our purposes, the structures represented by either a point on a flow line between the end points or a combination of end points, are termed **hybrid structures.**

Figure 4.8 illustrates a centralized data processing structure as a single functional or administrative unit within the organization. The characteristics of individual re-

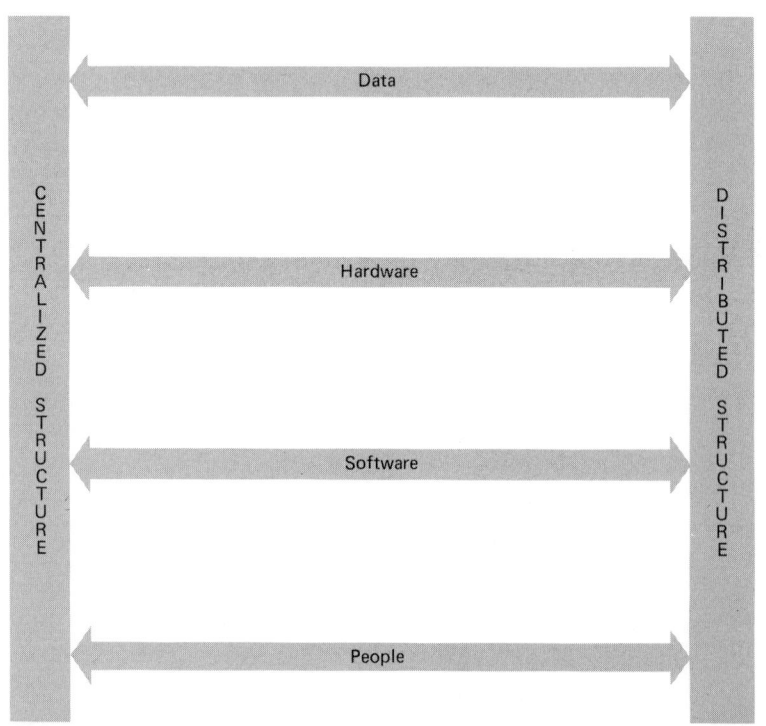

FIG. 4.7 Various approaches to organizing data processing resources in an information system.

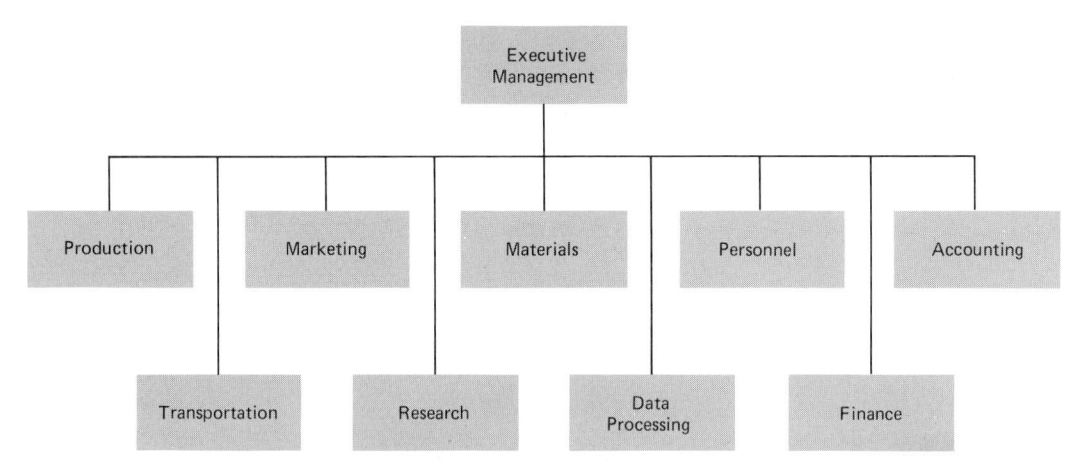

FIG. 4.8 A hypothetical organization with a centralized structure of data processing resources.

sources within this overall structure are as follows: (1) People. This organizational unit contains, for administrative purposes, all of the data processing and systems development personnel. The internal structure is generally some form of line (i.e., operations) and staff (i.e., developmental). Project leaders are designated to coordinate development activities for each of the organization's user functions and staffs. Skilled personnel are transferred or consult internally from project to project as developmental needs or operating problems require. (2) Hardware. A large, general purpose mainframe(s) and a large variety of related peripherals are housed in one physical area usually labeled the "Data center." (3) Software. Computer programs include vendor supplied (i.e., generally a sophisticated operating system), purchased (i.e., a variety of control programs and application systems), and inhouse developed application programs. (4) Data. The design of data flows attempts to minimize the amount of redundant input. Physically, data flows closely follow their logical relationships (e.g., data reflecting a raw material receipt is used in developing information for purchasing, inventory, accounts payable, and so forth). The physical structure of the organizations "common data base" is designed to support the logical relationships of the data and to minimize storing redundant data. Generally the data base is controlled through the use of a specially purchased computer program(s) called a **Data Base Management System** (DBMS). Information outputs are transmitted directly to individual users on a predetermined schedule.

An organization that incorporates a distributed structure for its data processing resources is illustrated in Figure 4.9. The characteristics of individual resources within this overall structure are as follows: (1) People. The necessary data processing and systems development personnel skills are located physically and administratively within the user functions. Depending on the size of the staff, individuals may share functional responsibilities (e.g., analyst/programmer). In fact, users may perform many of their own data processing tasks (e.g., system analysis, programming, data entry). (2) Hardware. The hardware configuration for

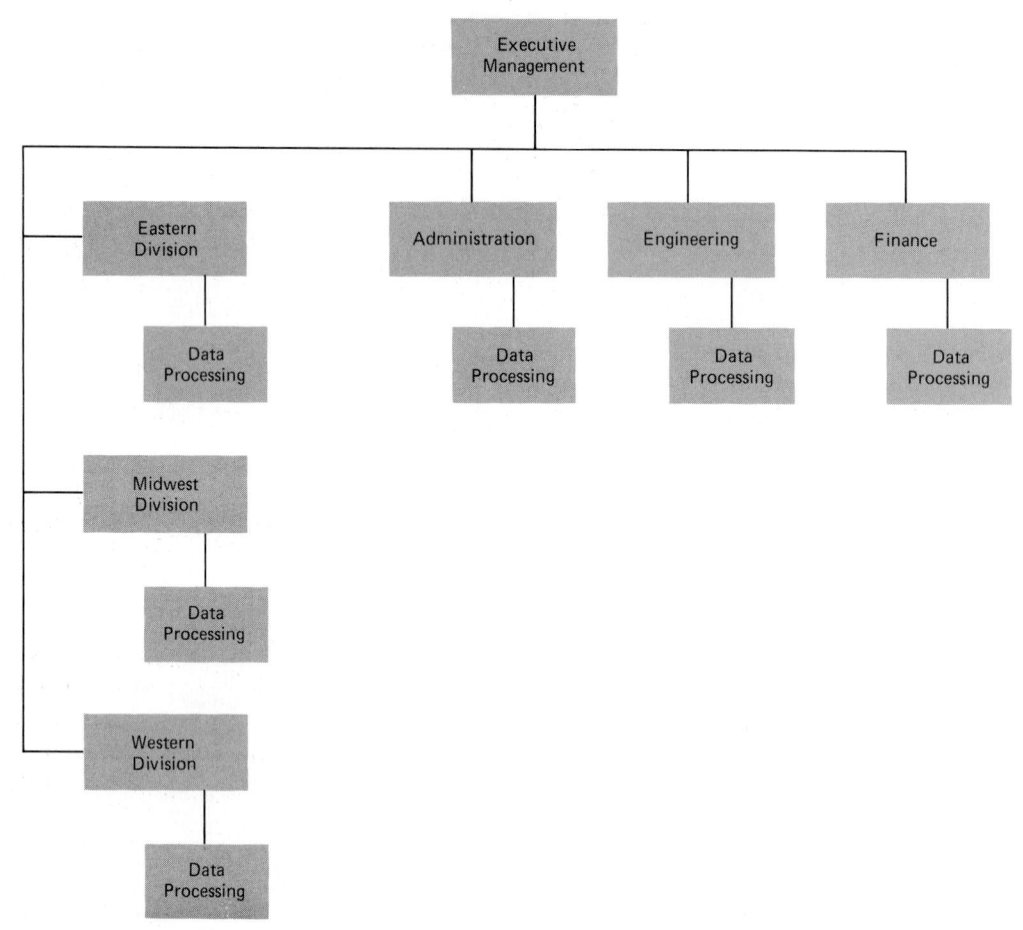

FIG. 4.9 A hypothetical organization with a distributed structure of data processing resources.

each user is tailored to his or her requirements. The mainframe or selected peripherals in each hardware configuration may be special purpose appropriate for processing the users' specific information requirements. (3) Software. It is required or developed in the same fashion as in a centralized structure, but limited to the scope of each user. (4) Data. Data are collected, stored, and processed to satisfy both the specific user area information requirements and identified requirements in other user areas. Conversely, data required from other users are obtained from them. With the distributed structure, data flows within the organization appear as illustrated in Figure 4.10. Advancements in small computers and data communication technology allow for efficient and effective flow of data from computer to computer.

A hybrid structure can be formed an endless number of ways. A common structure combines a centralized administrative unit with several distributed units. This form of

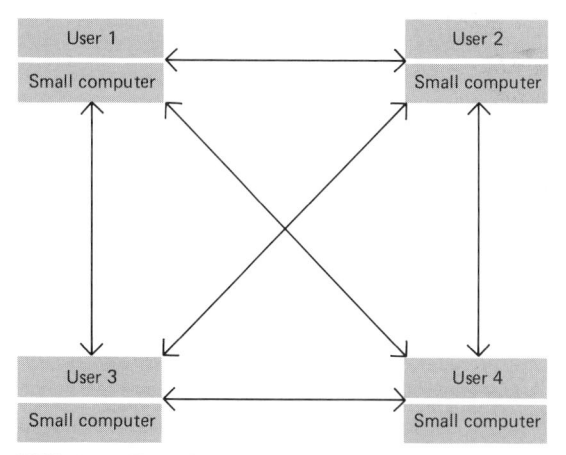

FIG. 4.10 Data flows within a distributed structure of data processing technology.

a hybrid structure is illustrated in Figure 4.11. As previously illustrated in Figure 4.7, each resource can be centralized or distributed, in part or wholly, as appropriate. For example, in large organizations, where the hardware, software, and staff support are centralized and some applications within the organization are sufficiently large and complex within themselves, there is minimum integration of data flows and data base design among applications. In other organizations, hardware components are being distributed to selected user departments, but the support staffs and software development are maintained in a centralized administrative unit. In these situations, data flows and structures are partially centralized and partially distributed. And in other organizations, the hardware, software, and data are centralized, but the people, particularly developmental support, are distributed to each user area.

Each structure is capable of satisfying an organization's information requirements. Each structure can be implemented to support the concept of integration. Each structure can provide a high degree of efficiency and effectiveness. In other words, the rationale for organizing data processing resources includes considerations beyond satisfying user information requirements, supporting systems integration, and implementing efficiency and effectiveness.

Historical Perspective

To gain insight into the current thinking pertaining to the organization of data processing resources, it is useful to develop a brief historical perspective concerning these resources. As organizations grew, and as pressures for more information developed, managers separated operation or production tasks from data processing tasks. In some instances, this separation was necessary to maintain or to improve operational productivity. In other instances, it was necessitated by the desire to have special skills or knowledge to perform the data processing tasks. Routine data processing tasks became the primary function of clerical groups. The more complex data processing tasks required to produce information for management became the domain for a variety of staff specialists (e.g., statisticians, industrial psychologists, accountants, and planners). These actions created line and staff as an organizational concept. The distinction between line and staff was reinforced by the concept of division of labor and went hand in hand with the introduction of automation of operations activities.

Organizations made great strides during the late nineteenth and early twentieth century toward automating their operations. Efforts to automate their data processing activities were also initiated. Typewriters, calculators, and reproduction machines are examples of this early automation. The in-

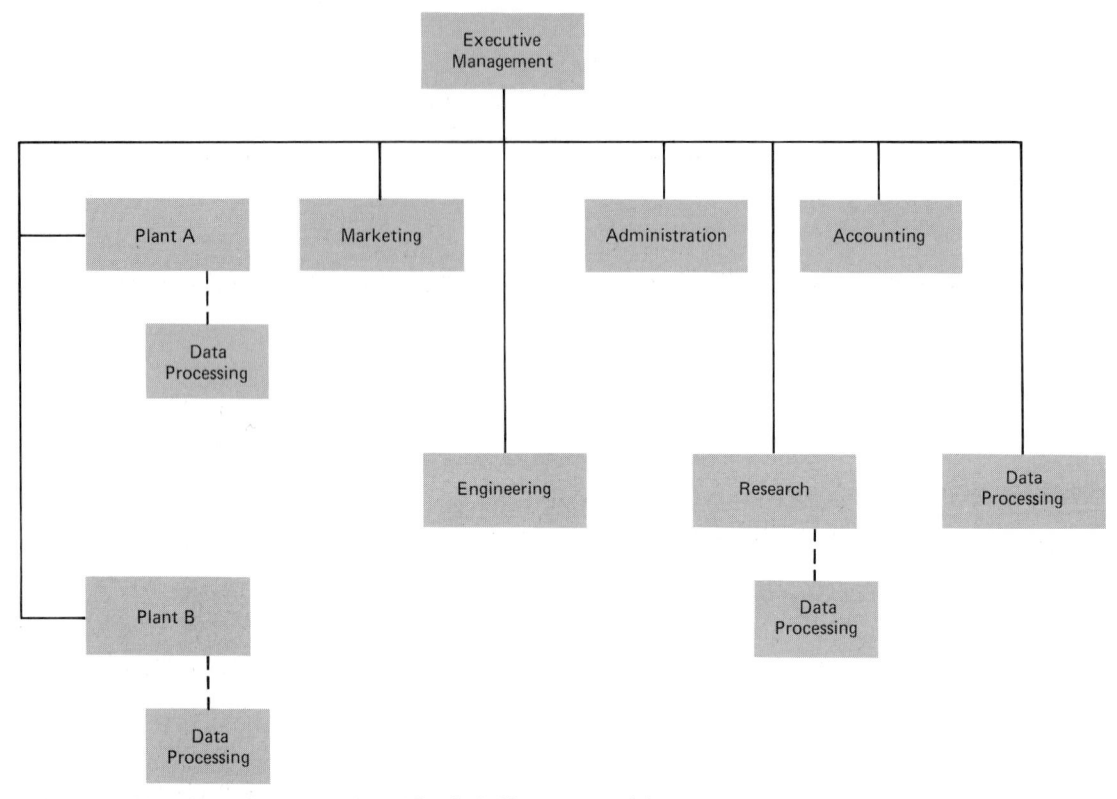

FIG. 4.11 Hypothetical organization with a hybrid structure of data processing resources.

troduction of punched card technology was another attempt to improve the efficiency of data processing activities. The relatively high cost of punched card technology, its requirements for a special environment, and its demand for skilled personnel, resulted in the creation of still another staff organization, called data processing, to serve line and other staff functions.

The introduction of computers followed the patterns established by punched card technology. First generation computers were large, expensive, highly sensitive to environmental conditions, and required a highly skilled work force. The use of this technology was restricted to a few governmental and commercial organizations. The availa-bility of second generation computers in the late 1950s and early 1960s produced several changes. The hardware was physically smaller and, per unit of work performed, was less expensive. It too, however, required a special environment and a highly skilled work force.

In the early 1960s, the introduction of third generation computers simply followed what was now a traditional organizational concept. Although the improved price/performance ratio allowed more organizations to adopt computer technology, the meaningful organizational structure remained a centralized staff function. In some very large organizations, for primarily geographical reasons, several functional units developed to provide data processing services. In essence, each unit served as a centralized staff in its geographical area, and the organization was said to have decentralized data processing.

Until recently, the cost of the hardware and the availability of people shaped the organizational structure of data processing. The availability of less expensive and smaller hardware, coupled with similar developments in data communications technology, have shifted that emphasis. Data structuring and software development considerations have now come to the foreground, and they may well be the primary forces in shaping the overall organizational approach.

The initial use of computing technology centered around organizations having either large volumes of data with simple data processing requirements or small volumes of data with complex processing requirements. In other words, computers were initially used for processing accounting or engineering data. Recent emphasis has shifted from using computers for merely processing data more efficiently to using computers to provide more effective information. This changing emphasis represents more than a simple change in terminology. As discussed in Chapter 2, the use and dissemination of information are essential tasks of management. Using computers to perform routine data processing more efficiently, by reducing clerical staffs, is one thing; but designing computer systems that disseminate information directly to those who require it, strikes at the very nature of management. It is often claimed that use of the computer frees management from routine data processing tasks so that they can concentrate on decision making and nonroutine activities. However, in many organizations the primary function of some managers is to provide information to others. The development of information systems in organizations where there is a centralized data processing structure, is often perceived as a "shifting of power."

This shifting of power is somewhat obvious in the development of so-called "management information systems." It is less obvious and can be more frustrating when centralized data processing organization is used in the development of "operation information systems." In these latter situations, a line or staff manager is responsible for a specific function (e.g., customer service, production scheduling). However, the availability of necessary status information and the capability for transaction processing to perform that function is highly dependent on the proper performance of the data processing resources. Hardware failures, out-of-date software, late projects, and a stream of untrained analysts and programmers are just a few examples of the "poor service" provided by centralized data processing. The attitude of many of these functional managers can be summarized as follows: "If I am to be held accountable for getting the job done, then I want responsibility for all of the resources I need to do the job." Right or wrong, a general feeling exists that "things will be better when I control them."

The evolutionary changes in software also contribute to the thinking that shapes the organizing of data processing resources. For example, as computer languages evolved from machine languages to user-oriented languages (e.g., COBOL, FORTRAN, BASIC), many individuals acquired programming skills. Although many of these individuals are employed by data processing organizations, many others hold positions in user departments. Users, having both knowledge of the computer's capability and skills to use this capability, are demanding access to the computing system. Equally important, operating systems have evolved to the point where access can be granted simultaneously for many types of users. For example, traditional batch processing of large volumes of data can be processed along with interactive processing from CRT and POS devices. Timesharing capabilities for new program development can be given to professional programmers as well as to qualified user personnel.

In summary, the success in using modern data processing resources, combined with the growing awareness by users of the capabilities of these resources, results in a rising level of expectation for the performance of data processing organizations. To control the use of these resources and at the same time satisfy user expectations, management must continuously evaluate the organizational structure of its data processing resources.

Advantages and Disadvantages

How an organization will structure its data processing resources is a decision comparable to developing marketing strategies, selecting plant sites, and establishing employee compensation programs. Ideally, these decisions are addressed and described in a long-range plan. This plan serves as an overall framework for decisions by lower levels of management. In the absence of a long-range plan, each systems development project proposal or new hardware or software announcement may prompt an organizational structure decision. In these situations, higher level management often forgoes their responsibilities, and information systems development begins to fragment and become disjointed. Although each organizational structure will support efficient and effective information development, there are certain advantages and disadvantages to each structure.

The following are advantages of a centralized structure:

1. It is readily applicable in organizations where most functional responsibilities are divided into line and staff for administrative purposes.
2. It supports the concept of economies of scale in the acquisition of hardware and software resources.
3. It permits the application of the division of labor principle by allowing individuals to specialize in either functional disciplines (e.g., finance, manufacturing, purchasing) or technological disciplines (e.g., programming, systems analysis, data base).
4. It facilitates standardization in the selection of hardware, development of software, training of personnel, and structure of data.
5. It supports the use of project management techniques and concepts in the development of information systems.
6. It provides job enrichment by permitting specialization and by providing career paths.

The following are disadvantages of a centralized structure:

1. Because of its size, its service levels are subject to the law of diminishing returns.
2. Its need for standardization often requires the use of rigid approaches to individual user needs and requests.
3. Its monolithic structure does not easily

accommodate the rapid changes often required by its users.
4. It requires total management involvement and commitment to be effective.
5. Its adoption and use of technology is often uneven (e.g., the latest mainframe but minimum SDA, POS, and COM equipment).
6. Its size and complexity are difficult to manage efficiently.

The following are advantages of a distributed structure:

1. It is easily adaptable where organizations are characterized by management style, service/product, or geographical diversity.
2. It supports the concept of matching responsibility and authority.
3. It permits a more flexible approach to solving individual user needs.
4. Its relative size and lack of complexity allow it to be more easily managed.
5. It provides job enrichment by allowing individuals to share or split responsibilities (e.g., programmer/analyst, programmer/operator).

The following are disadvantages of a distributed structure:

1. It requires extensive planning and coordination to prevent and minimize suboptimization and fragmentation in the development of the overall information system.
2. It generally requires maintaining redundant resources.
3. It is often difficult to attract and maintain talented people into a "small shop" environment.
4. Its technical performance is often poor, in spite of the appearance of acceptable service levels based on stated user satisfaction.
5. It is not always capable of taking advantage of the latest technology.

The main advantage of the hybrid structure is that it allows us to attain advantages from both the centralized and distributed structures as they appear applicable in the organization. Hopefully, with this structure, we also minimize the disadvantages associated with either of the other structures. The disadvantage to the hybrid structure is that it requires extensive organizational analysis and planning. In the absence of this planning, a proposed change to either the organization or the information system becomes an emotional rather than a rational decision.

Economic justification, as such, is not inherent in any of the structural alternatives. Certainly, a specific proposal to move from one structure to another can be justified with a cost/effectiveness analysis. For example, a poorly managed distributed system can be replaced effectively by the implementation of a better managed centralized or hybrid structure (or vice versa). But that same effectiveness or more could have been accomplished by improving management of the distributed structure. With an understanding of the advantages and disadvantages associated with each, we analyze some of the major factors that influence the choice of a given structure.

Factors That Influence Selection

The decision as to how to design or structure data processing resources promises to be as interesting and controversial in the near future as it has been in the recent past. The continuing advancements in technology and the future changes in organizations will require numerous evaluations of the organizational placement of data processing resources. Although there is not a "right" structure for all organizations, there is probably a "better" structure for an organization. Given our discussion to date, we can identify several factors that influence the choice of structure.

In Chapter 2 we discussed four organizational factors that affect specific information requirements and that also influence the decision process regarding the organization of data processing resources. These organizational factors are the nature of the organization, the size of the organization, the structure of the organization, and the management style or philosophy. Earlier, these organizational factors were identified as composing a demand block for the design of an information system. These factors are illustrated in Figure 4.12. In some cases various aspects of these organizational factors are identified to illustrate their influence on this structural decision. The top solid bar represents the organizational options. All the dashed lines running through the vertical arrow represent the organizational factors, and indicate their directional impact on the decision of structural design.

After analyzing the detail values of this demand block, if we determine that a preponderance of these values point to the left, as we view this chart, then our design proposals should emphasize a centralized structure. If these demand values point toward the right, then our design proposal should encompass a distributed structure. If there is no clear direction, as some of the values indicate centralized and others indicate distributed, our design proposal will recommend the implementation or use of the hybrid structure.

An Example of a Centralized and a Distributed Structure

To summarize our analysis of organizational structures, we present a description of two organizations and their approach to structuring data processing resources to support the information system. Background facts concerning each organization are provided so that you can understand how the factors influence structure selection. Emphasis is given to describing the makeup of the physical components and some indication of their logical relationships. In each example, the flow and structure of data representing a major application area are highlighted. Obviously, numerous other activities within these organizations are not explicitly discussed. However, it is our intent at this time to provide a "real world" flavor for the many ideas and concepts fundamental to the decision process of selecting an organizational structure.

1. *A Centralized structure.* General Hospital in Metropolis has developed a centralized data processing organization to service all functions performed by hospital administrators, technicians, doctors and nurses, and other service personnel. The configuration of the hardware includes a large mainframe and the following peripherals equipment: a card reader/punch unit, 12 high-speed tape drives, six large capacity disks, a high-speed printer, a communications controller, and a computer output microfilm device (COM). Data entry devices include: four keypunch/verifiers, six keyboard-to-tape machines, and a number of CRTs, which are located at various work stations throughout the hospital. With the exception of the CRTs, all of the hardware is housed in a specially provided area called the data center.

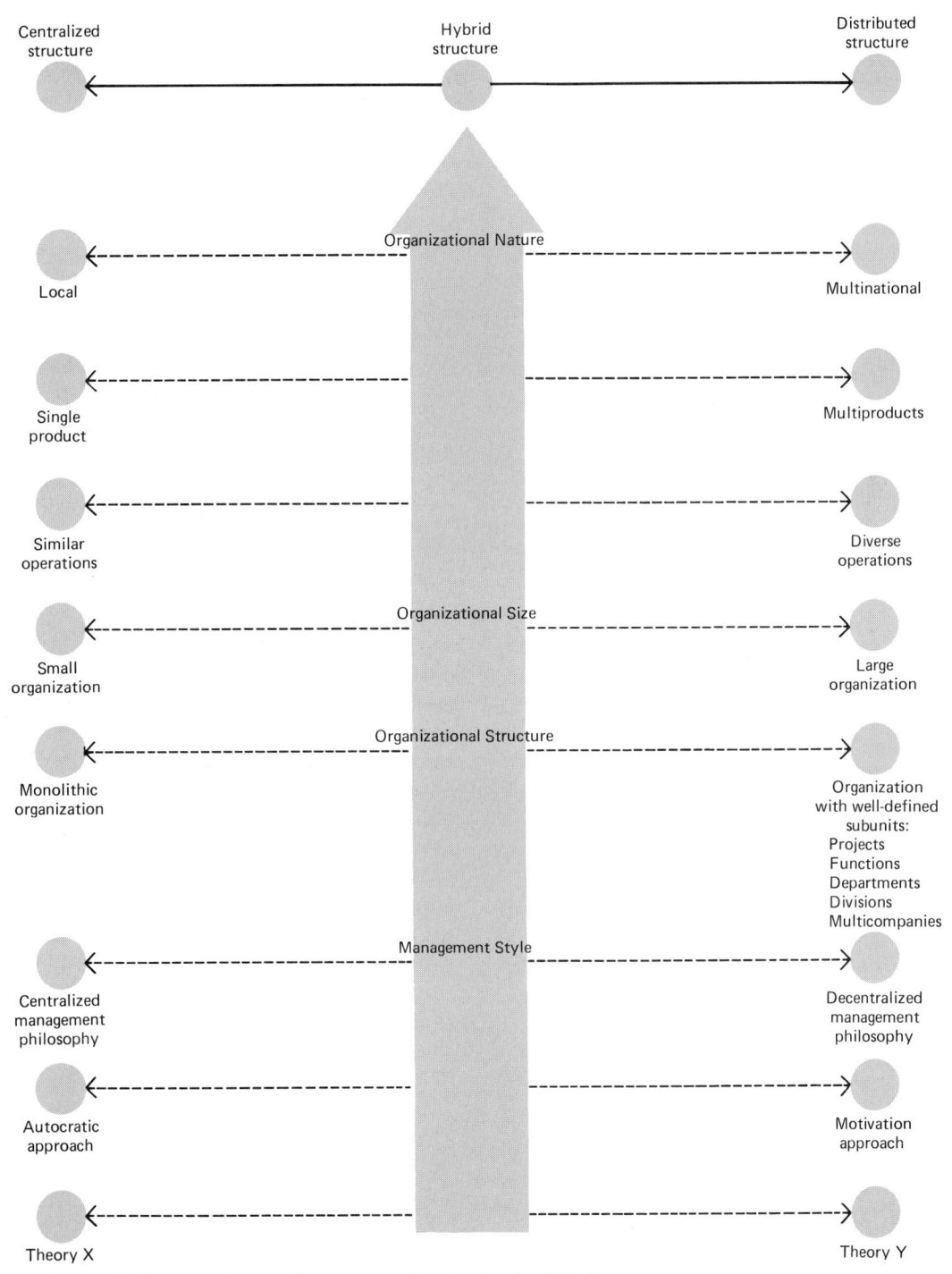

FIG. 4.12 Influencing factors that act as guides to structural design.

The software is composed of vendor-supplied, purchased, and hospital-developed programs. The operating system provided by the hardware vendor permits operating in a batch mode simultaneously with online processing. Purchased software includes a data base management system, a generalized report writer, a communications program, and a general accounting application package. Approximately 150 of the programs were developed internally.

The organization is managed by the Director of Data Services. She reports to the hospital administrator. Her organization is staffed to provide a 24-hour service. Reporting to the Director are the Data Center Manager, Systems Development Manager, and Data Entry Manager. Four shift supervisors report to the Data Center Manager. Each supervisor has responsibility for four to six operators. The Systems Development Manager has a staff of six systems analysts, 14 programmers, a data base administrator (DBA), and a data communications specialist. All of these individuals are capable of serving as a project leader as the workload demands. Data Entry has two shift leaders reporting to the Manager. Each shift leader supervises four to eight data entry clerks.

Traditionally the flow of data, including the input collection and data base design, was very application oriented. Early attempts and improving efficiency included passing data from one application to another via specially designed files. This improved processing by reducing redundant data input activities. Other data integration attempts involved one application using the master files from another application to verify certain data and to extract selected data elements for further processing. This limited integration of data flows improved overall data processing operations. However, the lack of standards governing file design proved to be a severe obstacle to further integration efforts.

With the recent upgrade of the mainframe and the operating system, the acquisition of the DBMS and CRTs, and approval to develop interactive online systems, the DBA was hired to develop and enforce standard data and file design. The recently developed Patient Control System (PCS) application is a good example of how this centralized structure provides efficient and effective use of the data processing resources.

As each patient is admitted to the hospital, the admissions agent inputs, via a CRT, various required data concerning the patient into the computer data base. The data base contains records for each patient, room, bed, medical service, and staff member. Once all the patient data are input, the logic in the PCS assigns a room (e.g., ward, semiprivate, private), a bed, and checks to see what services the admitting doctor has scheduled. To satisfy certain legal requirements, a small typewriterlike printer, attached to the admissions agent's CRT, immediately prints a hardcopy of all the data provided by the patient to be reviewed, acknowledged, and signed by the patient.

As various services are performed for the patient, data reflecting these services are input to the PCS using various methods. For example, data describing medicine and supplies provided by the hospital pharmacy are immediately input to the system via a CRT. Other services such as laboratory, X-ray, and therapy treatments are reported routinely on a standard charge ticket. A data entry clerk collects these tickets every four hours and delivers them to data entry for conversion to a computer media. They are input to the PCS in a batch processing mode at the end of each shift.

When a patient is discharged, a CRT printer located in the reception area of the patient accounting unit prints a detailed listing of the services rendered and the charges incurred.

PCS also provides a variety of other services and information to hospital administrators. A master file of all approved service charges in the hospital is referenced to calculate the charges for a specific patient. The status of rooms and beds is available on request. All charges billable to various health insurance companies are compiled and mailed daily. The status and activity reflecting the inventory of medicines and supplies in the hospital pharmacy are available for review on request. Future developmental efforts include additional SDA application at various service areas, including nurses' stations; preparing automatic purchase orders for pharmaceutical supplies; and, projecting hospital cash flows based on the payment record of various hospitalization programs.

2. *A Distributed structure.* Burstraski, Inc., is organized with three operating divisions and executive offices: the Texarkana Division fabricates structures for oilfield drilling rigs; the Cleveland Division is an industrial painting company that applies protective coatings to railroad boxcars; the Austin Division is a freight transfer company with a large public warehouse; executive offices are located in New York.

The management style at Burstraski encourages a high degree of independence, but emphasizes a spirit of cooperation among its operating divisions. There appears to be a real attempt to match authorities with responsibilities, but there is also a recognition of corporate responsibility. Consequently, although each division is allowed significant freedom in "running their own show," they are also responsible for satisfying minimum corporate goals. A management committee, comprised of the division presidents and three other corporate officers, meets quarterly to discuss operations. Annually they participate in updating the corporation's long-term plan and establish a budget for the next year.

Each operating division is responsible for providing their own data processing capabilities as they see fit with a few exceptions. Each division must provide to New York monthly financial data to allow for the preparation of consolidated financial statements, and weekly time cards and personnel action data for payroll processing.

The Texarkana Division has acquired hardware to perform both administrative data processing, and to provide computer control for a variety of operations equipment. Their hardware configuration includes a medium sized mainframe and the following peripheral equipment: a card reader/punch unit, a high-speed printer, 12 disk drives, two low-speed tape drives, a plotter, data communications controller, and an assortment of hardwire links to operate machines such as a tubular steel cutting machine, an electric welding machine, and a flat steel sheet grinding machine. In addition to the hardwire links, data entry is effected through six CRTs located in the engineering department and the factory control center, and four keypunch/verifiers located in the accounting department.

The software is composed of vendor-supplied and division-developed programs. The operating system will support six hardwire links and eight other terminals in an online mode while processing one job in a batch mode. Of the 200 homegrown programs, more than 60 percent provide specific engineering functions, and the balance provide general administrative and accounting data processing.

The data processing organization reports to the Administrative Manager of Engineering. There are two scientific programmers and a junior programmer who doubles as the computer operator. A process control specialist and an operations research analyst round out the staff. Most of the actual program development is done by the individual engineers. In addition, two analyst/programmers and three keypunchers report to the plant controller. They perform application development and program maintenance on all nontechnical systems.

A variety of data is processed and information is produced by these data processing resources. The first priority is the hardware/software support of the computer controlled operations cited above. In addition to controlling these operations, data concerning performance and utilization are recorded automatically. The second priority is to provide an efficient method of processing complex and voluminous engineering calculations. Lastly, this organization provides support for administrative data processing of all kinds.

The Austin Division has acquired data processing resources to manage its transportation and storage business better.

The hardware configuration includes two small CPUs. The smaller CPU has few peripherals. They include two CRTs, a slow speed printer, and two disk drives. The single purpose of this system is to keep track of the freight transfer business. The larger CPU has some additional peripherals; these include a communications unit, four disk drives, four tape drives, and a medium-speed printer. Four key-to-disk units are used for data entry.

The software includes programs that are vendor supplied, purchased, and division developed. The hardware and software of the smaller system was acquired from a firm that develops "turn key" systems for transportation firms. When the Austin Division requires a software change or incurs a hardware-software problem, they call on the systems vendor to make the necessary change. The larger system has an operating system and a DBMS provided by the vendor. All of the application programs (53) were developed by Austin personnel. A communications control program in the operating systems permits the two systems and the key-to-disk unit to "talk to each other" (i.e., transfer data) in a dial-up mode.

The smaller system is the direct responsibility of the operations manager in the freight transferring department. The other computing system is supported by two analyst/programmers and three key-to-disk operators. The key-to-disk operators run the computers as needed.

The data flows in this system are rather individual. The smaller system is dedicated to the freight transferring function. Requests for service, availability of transportation resources, and other pertinent data are keyed directly into the data base via CRTs operated by the dispatchers. Freight bills are printed on a small printer on request. Daily activity is transferred each night to the larger system where a variety of control, utilization, and accounting reports are produced. The larger system processes input data pertaining to the public warehouse operation, as it is entered by the key-to-disk units. Management, operations, and accounting information are all processed in a batch environment and output as hardcopy reports.

The Cleveland Division has taken a completely different approach to data processing. Several years ago, a jurisdictional battle between two unions representing employees in the Cleveland Division resulted in a two-month work stoppage in the then existing data processing department. Temporary relief was provided by a local service bureau providing computer data processing services. When the unions finally agreed between themselves as to who would represent data processing employees, most of the professional staff had resigned to seek other employment. Perhaps more importantly, management found that the service bureau provided better service at less cost than their internal staff. Consequently, they pulled out the computer hardware and its related technology and continued to use the service bureau.

Thus the Cleveland Division has no hardware, software, or data processing personnel. Each night, the appropriate source documents representing sales, production, personnel movements (including time cards), inventory receipts, transfers, and withdrawals are batched and sent by courier to the service bureau. The appropriate control and accounting reports are waiting on the receptionists' desks when management arrives in the morning. For a fee, the local bank processes accounts receivable, accounts payable, prepares checks, and supplies an activity register daily. Aged trial balances, dunning notices, and cash flow analysis and forecasts are provided monthly.

The executive offices in New York maintain a medium sized computing system capable of both batch and online processing. The hardware includes a CPU, a card reader/punch unit, communications unit, six disk drives, two tape drives, and eight CRT's. In addition to the vendor-supplied operating system and communication control program, there are a variety of purchased modeling packages and a DBMS, and numerous in-house developed programs. The data processing staff consists of four analyst/programmers, an operations research specialist, and a data communications specialist. The company subscribes to several outside data services that provide online stock market quotations, financial reviews, and real estate brokers industrial listings. In addition to providing payroll and personnel services for the operating divisions, this unit provides a variety of financial analysis, government reporting, and general accounting information for executive management.

Each of the computing systems can communicate directly with one another in a dial-up mode. (The service bureau in Cleveland also has this capability.) Currently, the Austin Division is developing an inventory control and accounting system that will be used by the other operating divisions. Many of the models in New York and the engineering programs in Texarkana are shared on request by the individual locations staff personnel.

4.4 ■ SELECTING DATA PROCESSING RESOURCES

Long before the age of computers, the selection of data processing resources was a decision process essentially concerned with the hiring and training of personnel. During the last 20 years, the emphasis of this decision process centered on whether or not to use computers. During this period of time, viable options to computers included continuing in a manual environment, adapting a variety of electromechanical devices, or using punch card equipment. The recent widespread availability of small, powerful, and inexpensive mini- and microcomputers minimizes the value of these other alternatives. Using some form of computer technology in the design of information systems appears feasible for all but a few organizations or a few applications within an organization. However, sorting through the wide assortment of hardware and software vendors, and their offerings of mainframes, peripherals, and software to select the right mix of resources, is a complex decision. Indeed, in small organizations, the technical nature and perceived complexity of this decision for noncomputer specialists often appears to be insurmountable or pure guesswork. In large organizations, on the other hand, staffs of hardware and software specialists are generally available to help develop the decision criteria. Conceptually, this decision process is the same for large organizations looking to add or to upgrade existing computing systems, as it is for small organizations choosing their first computing system.

Current trends in information systems development, (i.e., more user participation in systems design activities and the use of small computers for the first time in an organization) make a basic understanding of this decision process important to users and systems analysts, as well as hardware/software specialists. In this section we discuss the general framework of the decision process, emphasizing the role of various systems demand blocks. In Part III, we present a basic methodology for conducting a specific hardware/software evaluation and justification study.

Decision-Making Criteria

Although the organization of data processing resources is fundamentally noneconomic, the selection of data processing resources is basically an economic decision. In other words, to obtain information, a resource for which we perceive a value, we must acquire and use costly data processing resources. Logically, we do not want to pay more to acquire and use these resources than the value of the information they will produce.

To structure this economic or cost/effective decision, you first must determine what it is that the organization wants to accomplish. In Chapter 1, we introduced the concept of the demand building blocks. Essentially, identifying the details to the various demand blocks provides an understanding of what the organization wants to accomplish. This includes not only the specific information requirements but also a variety of organizational related requirements.

The demand blocks that have the largest role in this decision process are the data processing and systems requirements. Once we have a general understanding of these two demands, we can begin to evaluate the available data processing resources. An evaluation of these resources should produce an understanding of their performance capabilities. Comparing performance capabilities of data processing resources to the data processing and systems requirements of the organization is the first step in this decision-making process.

The nature of this decision has not really changed with the introduction of computing technology. What has changed is the nature of data processing resources. In previous years, an assessment of work to be performed required an understanding of the skill level of personnel necessary to perform the work. For example, a variety of data processing activities are performed in an accounting department. Some of these activities require the formal training of an accountant; other activities require the skill level of a bookkeeper; a final group of activities can be performed by a variety of clerical personnel. Before selecting personnel and assigning activities, it is necessary to understand the performance capability of each resource (i.e., accountant, bookkeeper, clerical).

Similar to individuals, hardware and software components in computing systems have specific performance capabilities. Before selecting and using these resources, their performance capabilities must be understood at some level. Obviously, the technical nature of computing resources requires a comparable background to facilitate understanding. However, the skills of an operator or a programmer are not necessary to obtain some level of understanding of the capabilities of most computing systems.

Once we have identified the data processing and systems requirements, and have identified several alternative configurations of data processing resources to satisfy these requirements, we can provide a cost/effectiveness statement. In manual systems, for example, accountants are capable of performing bookkeeper tasks. However, to do so, is a poor utilization of the accountant's time and skills. Any number of computer hardware and software configurations can usually satisfy an organization's requirements. What is necessary, is to identify the most economical configurations for satisfying these requirements. Ultimately, the functional description of an organization's requirements and the performance capabilities of the selected resources must be set in economic terms.

Data Processing Requirements

The most fundamental demand on an information system is that of the users' specific information requirements as expressed by the information attributes. The analysis of specific information requirements to determine what data must be collected and how these data must be processed to produce the desired information can also identify data processing requirements. Four broad categories of data processing requirements represent: (1) the volume of data involved, (2) the complexity of required data processing operations, (3) processing time constraints, (4) computational demands.

Volume refers to the amount of data that must be processed in a given period to achieve an information goal. One attempt at quantifying volume might be referencing organizational transactions (e.g., time cards, invoices, inventory transactions, budget items). Other measures might reference processing functions (e.g., 14 file updates per record, 3000 master records, 26 line-items per page).

Complexity refers to the number of intricate and interrelated data operations that must be performed to achieve an information goal. For example, to process a payroll properly it is necessary to calculate the correct gross pay for employees, and to account for federal, state, county, and city taxes, a variety of fringe benefits, union dues, investment programs, company purchases, and so forth, when calculating net pay.

Time contraints are defined as the amount of time permitted or acceptable between when data are available and when the information is required. Again, citing the payroll function, a union contract may state that all employees are to be paid in full by 9:00 AM Tuesday morning for work performed as of the preceding Friday midnight. Another example might be providing the inventory status of a product to a salesperson attempting to satisfy an urgent customer need. He or she needs to know the inventory status as of the last withdrawal or receipt, not as of last Friday or at month end.

Computational demands are a unique combination of volume, complexity, and time constraints, for a specific information requirement. For example, the computational demands to process a large linear programming model or to maintain a large on-line data base are considerable.

Given the general capabilities of computing systems and the wide variety of organizational data, the identification and quantifying of data processing requirements is a necessary first step to structuring a useful decision model. Many times, one of the data processing requirements in an organization is so dominant in a given situation that the others are not even included in the decision-making process. For example, a bank may process so many checks that volume alone is the deciding factor; an engineering firm may make its selection purely on the basis of massive computational requirements; an airline selects resources for handling airline reservations based entirely on time constraints; and a public warehouse chooses data processing resources because those resources are best suited for the complexity with which it must deal. In most organizations, however, the data processing requirements from a variety of users are accumulated as a demand to be satisfied in the selection of data processing resources.

Selecting the correct data processing resources to support an information systems design for an organization is a difficult decision under the best of circumstances. However, without a realistic statement of data processing requirements, it is impossible. Redefinition of these requirements may take place several times as we attempt to match them against the performance capabilities of various data processing resource alternatives. As difficult as it sometimes appears to be to identify and quantify these requirements, this process is fairly straightforward when it is compared with the process of determining other organizational requirements.

Systems Requirements

Systems requirements are derived from the dynamic nature of the organization and its information system. Organizations grow, develop new products, enter new territories, and acquire and divest entire operations. The increasing pressures for information, which are generated from sources both internal and external to an organization, were discussed in Chapter 2. An assessment of organizational change, its direction, its volume and its timing results in the formalizing of specific systems requirements. Several examples of these requirements were listed in the demand block in Figure 1.7.

Reliability refers to how dependable a resource performs its function when called upon. Some people are more reliable than others; some machines are more reliable than others. Producing some information requirements requires a higher degree of reliability in the operation of an information system than do other requirements. For example, online applications of all types require a higher degree of reliability from hardware and software than do batch-oriented applications. When selecting data processing resources, an attempt at describing or defining the expected reliability of each resource provides an important decision parameter.

The *cost* of developing and operating data processing resources is a systems requirement. Identifying and quantifying the various cost elements is often the most critical demand and is discussed further in Part III.

The *installation schedule* refers to the time frame that originates when an organization recognizes a need and that ends when the solution to that need is implemented. The development of an information system (the duration of the developmental life cycle) is often, but not always, a critical systems requirement. Considerations for acquiring and installing necessary data processing resources is an essential component of any installation schedule. Systems analysis and design might conclude with a recommendation that requires six months to develop and implement the optimum solution. The organization's need, however, may well require that a solution be implemented in one month. As we discussed in Chapter 1, the conflicting nature of the demand blocks forces some compromises in the ultimate form and value of the design blocks.

Flexibility refers to the capability of a resource to change or adjust to satisfy changes in users' requirements. The ability to adjust for wide fluctuations in data volumes to be processed in specific time periods, is an example of the demand for flexibility. The tentative and changing nature of users' information requirements, the role of judgment factors in determining data processing and systems requirements, and the relative permanence of data processing resources, are additional reasons for considering flexibility.

Life expectancy and *growth potential* are two examples of systems requirements that are closely related. Life expectancy refers to how long the organization's needs are expected to exist. Growth potential refers to how these needs will be met in the future. Although it is not always possible to match these systems demands perfectly with a specific set of data processing resources, a good attempt to assess formally these requirements will eliminate attractive looking, but impractical, alternatives.

Given that the establishment of the specific values for all of the demand blocks represents a perceived need at one point in time, or a rough approximation of future events, it is important to provide for changes or modifications to the tangible resources that support an information system.

Maintainability is the systems requirement that provides this consideration. Although we may initially think of maintenance as related to hardware, it is an equally important consideration for all data processing resources. For example, recent studies show that maintenance costs of software often exceed the initial cost of that software development by as much as 25 times.[2] (Structured programming, discussed in Part III, is one software development technique that is intended to make development more efficient and maintenance less costly.)

There are three possible outcomes when comparing data processing and systems requirements against the performance capa-

---

[2] Wendy Rauch-Hindin, "Some Answers to the Software Problems of the 1980's," *Data Communications*, May 1981, pp. 57–70.

bilities of data processing resources. First, several or all of the alternatives will satisfy the stated demands; second, none of the resource proposals satisfy the demands; and finally, one of the resource proposals satisfy the demands. The first two outcomes indicate that we must continue to evaluate both the demands and the data processing resource proposals. Often, prioritizing and redefining specific demands is a method for either reducing or increasing the variety of acceptable proposals. This is not always necessary. Generally, the evaluation of the demand values of cost/effectiveness demands eliminates otherwise acceptable proposals.

Systems requirements other than costs are often categorized as intangible or non-quantifiable demands. To the extent that we are aware of these requirements and provide some verbal or quantifiable description, we ensure a better decision-making process. In other situations, systems requirements are treated as indirect benefits based on the selection of a specific configuration of data processing resources. This treatment of systems requirements tends to bias the ultimate decision for the wrong reasons. This latter approach is analogous to the "tail wagging the dog." If we fail to give formal recognition to systems requirements as a legitimate criterion in the decision-making process, we fail to structure the proper decision model. This leads to an incorrect decision and to many organizational disappointments.

SUMMARY

Information systems are composed of logical and physical components. The physical components are called data processing resources and include data, hardware, software, and people. Data, the symbolic representation of reality, can appear in many different media. Some of those media were created to allow efficient processing with computers. The machines that compose a computing system are collectively termed hardware. Hardware is further classified as the central processing unit (CPU) or mainframe and the various input, output, and storage devices collectively referred to as peripherals. Although the term software can be used to describe all of the non-hardware items in a computing system, specifically, it refers to computer instructions. Three general categories of software include: programming languages, operating systems, and application and special service programs.

Data processing people possess a variety of skills. Many have the primary responsibility of designing and developing an information system. Others are responsible for operating the physical resources composing the information system. Management is responsible for organizing resources. This responsibility is derived from their function to establish necessary control.

Three broad categories of structure can be given to data processing resources. The centralized structure places all of the resources in one physical location and within one administrative unit. A distributed structure disperses the resources to user locations. A mix of the centralized and distributed structures results in a hybrid structure. Each resource can be structured to be somewhat independent of the other resources.

Selecting data processing resources is fundamentally an economic decision process. The parameters for this decision include the detail values of several of the demand blocks and the performance capabilities of the resources. The two demand blocks that have a primary role are the data processing and systems requirements. The data processing requirements are derived from the user information requirements and include volume, complexity, time constraints, and computational demands. Systems requirements are derived from a variety of other organizational needs and an assessment of future change. To satisfy these demands requires an evaluation of the capabilities of available data processsing resources. Ultimately, this decision is reduced to economics in a cost/effectiveness analysis.

REVIEW QUESTIONS

4.1 List and define the four tangible data processing resources.

4.2 List six media that can be used to represent data.

4.3 How do we classify data input to an information system? Give two examples of each.

4.4 Provide two examples of media conversions for data input to a computing system. Define "source data automation" (SDA). Cite an example of SDA.

4.5 Describe the primary functions of the central processing unit (CPU). Cite four examples of peripheral hardware in a computing system.

4.6 Why is it important to distinguish between mainframe and peripherals?

4.7 Explain the phrase "price/performance ratio."

4.8 What are the three general categories of software?

4.9 Describe the three types of programming languages.

4.10 Compare the function of the operating system to an application program.

4.11 Define the purpose of: (a) the steering committee, (b) production scheduling, (c) data base administration, (d) records management.

4.12 What is the ultimate purpose in organizing data processing resources?

4.13 Define each of the basic alternatives for organizing data processing resources.

4.14 What were the major considerations initially for choosing a data processing structure?

4.15 Discuss the reasons for users' "rising expectations."

4.16 Compare and contrast four of the advantages/disadvantages of the centralized and distributed structures.

4.17 Describe the role of the detail demand block values in the decision-making processes for structuring and selecting data processing resources.

4.18 List and define the four data processing requirements. How are they determined?

4.19 Identify and define six systems requirements. How are they determined?

4.20 How do we determine what performance capabilities are required from specific data processing resources?

QUESTIONS FOR DISCUSSION

4.1 Overheard at a CPA convention: "Computers are nothing more than fast calculators and sophisticated clerks." Reported at a convention of sociologists: "Computers have no morals or feelings." Comment from a computer salesperson: "Acquisition and installation of a computer will help to improve an organization's profit picture." Discuss these statements.

4.2 "Much discussion today centers around the notion that information is an organizational resource. However, the users in our company act as though the data generated in their departments and the data stored in their computer files belong to them and not the company." Discuss the conflicting nature of these two ideas.

4.3 "The punched card is as good as dead. Between our conversion to key-to-disk in data entry, the installation of SDA equipment in our users' departments, and the CRTs in the programmers' offices, I don't think there is one keypunch machine remaining in the entire company." Is it likely that the punched card will go the way of the passenger pigeon?

4.4 "There have been many changes to our corporate data center over the years. For example, we process 10 times as much work in about one-half the space. The mainframes are housed in a completely different room from the input/output peripherals. All the windows are gone and you need a badge to get in, but nobody has to go in anymore." Discuss the changes in hardware and software implied in this observation.

4.5 "In 1965, I spent three months developing a program to satisfy the needs of our claims department. It was a tricky piece of code, but it was very efficient using the computer memory and cycle times of the CPU. A year later, another programmer took six months to modify that program for the user. Today, I write very simple programs which any junior programmer can modify in a day or two." Explain the rationale implied in this comment.

4.6 "The art of programming is changing. Now the emphasis is placed on putting a running program into production as soon as possible. The things we worried about 10 years ago are not even important anymore. For example, why worry about using memory efficiently when the operating system has virtual memory capabilities? Why worry about processing storage files on alternate channels when the operating system assigns different tape drives each time the program runs?" Discuss.

4.7 "Promotions within the management of our data processing department are designed to alternate an individual between line and staff functions. In fact, if new employees are interested in managing within data processing, we encourage them to take an assignment with a user area at some time early in their career." "There is little correlation between an individual's technical competence or background and their success as a manager." "It is necessary that the programming manager be technically competent to ensure their group produces an efficient product." Compare and contrast these varying comments on management development.

4.8 "In the old days, we would call and ask for a programmer when we wanted something new or changed in our computer system. Now you talk to a systems analyst, who talks to a programmer, who talks to a data base something or another, who talks, I guess, to the computer. It is a nightmare trying to get anything accomplished anymore." Discuss the possible pros and cons to this criticism.

4.9 "In our organization data processing is a centralized function. However, to avoid political battles and to expedite implementing new applications, data flows and data bases are designed separately for each user. Now if we can just figure out how to get more programmers or to reduce maintenance it will be a good operation." How would you respond to this comment?

4.10 "The cost of acquiring hardware is only a minor consideration in the development of information systems. The cost of developing the software is an increasingly important aspect." Explain this comment.

4.11 "Before we acquired these new businesses and expanded our marketing efforts, it made sense to have a centralized support function. However, our budget for data communications and personnel travel is skyrocketing and has management up in arms." Discuss.

4.12 "Down time on the mainframe in a centralized information system can be catastrophic; and the one thing you can depend on is it will go down and at the worst possible time." "Our data center has four large mainframes linked together by a sophisticated operating system. If any one of the mainframes fails and goes down, we can be back up and running again in a matter of 15 minutes." Does the second comment represent a solution to the concern in the first comment? Why or why not?

4.13 "In 1967, I was a member of a task force that recommended establishing regional data processing centers. In 1975, I was a member of a task force that recommended a centralized data processing organization at headquarters. In early 1982, I headed up a task force which recommended distributed processing for each division. Each task force found that it's recommendations were economically justified." Discuss.

4.14 "We have the best track record for systems up time in the industry. No one is perfect, but no matter how well we perform, our users take every opportunity to complain to management about our service level." Discuss this problem and suggest at least two ways in which it can be addressed.

4.15 "We have made some recent changes to improve user satisfaction levels. For example, we have given each user area their own systems analyst(s) and at least one programmer to accomplish routine maintenance. As their developmental projects require, we will provide a variety of programming and other technical support personnel. We are maintaining a centralized data base function to develop and coordinate record and file design." Discuss potential advantages/disadvantages to this approach.

4.16 "Every staff group with a new 'hot shot' starts to clamor for their own computer. In the beginning, it seemed like a good idea. Then some of these folks move on to other departments or out of the company. Every time users need a change to their programs, guess who they called? We seldom find any documentation and the programming logic uses no conventions." Discuss several actions that can be taken to prevent this situation.

4.17 "Management no longer trusts our computer usage forecast. Seven years in a row we have exceeded our capacity by more than 20 percent. It seems that no matter what the users tell us they need for next year's budget, their actual usage is always greater." What is the likely problem in the company? How might it be minimized or eliminated?

4.18 "Some of the programming models that engineering develops make you wonder what they did before computers. Personally, I think they are having a contest to see who can create the biggest monster to use more of the computer at any one time." Discuss.

4.19 "Several vendors offer similar products at lower prices than the equipment we use. However, when you consider our remote location and our need for 24-hour service, lower prices are not enough." Explain.

4.20 "Most people think that raw CPU power is the biggest factor in choosing a computer; but it is not. The design of the operating system is far more important. We modified our operating system six months ago and immediately we picked up 35 percent more running capacity. Our CPU might as well be half the size that it is. Most of the time it's I/O bound anyway." Discuss.

EXERCISES

4.1 Examine the 10 functions described below and indicate in which software category each function would most likely take place: (a) computer language, (b) operating system, and (c) application or special service program.

1. Scheduling jobs in the Engineering Department.
2. Logic for searching a three-dimensional table.
3. Recording the utilization of computer storage units.
4. Limiting the absolute size of a data field.
5. Scheduling jobs for the computing system.
6. Logic for calculating an Internal Rate of Return (IRR).

7. Defining the way to move data fields from location to location.
8. Recording the utilization of manufacturing facilities.
9. Indicating acceptable methods of data file organization.
10. Mapping computer instructions into real addresses.

4.2 From the facts given in the two examples in this chapter (Metropolis General Hospital and Burstraski, Inc.) for structuring data processing resources, prepare:

1. An organization chart for each example that highlights data processing resources.
2. An organization chart that reflects the personnel assignments within data processing units.
3. An illustration of the hardware configuration in each example.

4.3 Royal Processing in Cincinnati is a data processing service bureau that specializes in providing computer services to small banks within the area. One of Royal's major services is the processing of credit card tickets submitted to banks by their merchant customers. Daily credit card activity is collected by each bank and delivered by courier to Royal each night between 8:00 PM and midnight. Royal is required to process the tickets to a clearinghouse for the credit card syndicate by 8:00 AM the next morning. The volume of tickets to be processed nightly averages 50,000 and it ranges between 25,000 and 90,000. Royal is currently evaluating equipment from three vendors which reads the credit card tickets and converts them to magnetic tape for computer processing. They have determined essential performance capabilities of each vendor's equipment to be as follows:

	Vendor A	Vendor B	Vendor C
Equipment cost per unit	$15,000	$ 8000	$ 4000
Life expectancy	5 yrs	4 yrs	3 yrs
Processing rate	12,000/hr	7000/hr	4000/hr
Mean time between failures	60 hrs	40 hrs	30 hrs
Average fail time	4 hrs	4 hrs	6 hrs

Additional Notes

1. Royal's operating system can support as many as six readers simultaneously.

2. Royal is forecasting an increase in the processing rate of 10 percent annually.
3. Vendor A offers a 20 percent discount on additional units.
4. Vendor products cannot be mixed in a system.
5. Royal has a 5-year contract with the banks.
6. The management at Royal Processing has indicated that they place a high premium on system reliability, but are equally concerned with attaining low-cost processing.

Required: Prepare an evaluation of each vendor and your recommendations. Your analysis should include a specific configuration and considerations for reliability, growth, flexibility, and costs.

4.4 Listed below are 10 typical applications in a manufacturing organization with a brief description of their functions. Additionally, 10 business transactions are listed. For each transaction, indicate the potential logical relationship to each application.

Applications

1. *Purchasing.* Prepares a purchase order to be sent to a vendor. Keeps track of purchase orders placed.
2. *Inventory Control.* Keeps track of current inventory status for raw materials, work in process, and finished goods.
3. *Production Scheduling.* Assigns people, machines, and material according to customer orders received or an inventory replenishment plan.
4. *Machine Utilization.* Keeps track of machine usage in terms of hours available, hours running, and hours down.
5. *Accounts Payable.* Keeps track of monies owed by the organization for products/services received from vendors. Prepares a check for payment.
6. *Accounts Receivable.* Keeps track of monies owed to the organization for products/services provided to customers. Prepares invoices and statements.
7. *Bill of Material.* Maintains the composition (recipe) of each finished good item, in terms of the type and quantity of raw material or subassembly material.

8. *Sales Reporting.* Maintains a record of sales to customers by various selling units.
9. *Payroll.* Processes time cards to prepare paychecks for employees. Maintains records concerning various deductions from gross pay to calculate net pay.
10. *Personnel.* Maintains employment records for each employee including a variety of descriptive information, job performance, and salary history.

Transactions

1. Receipt of a customer order.
2. Receipt of a raw material.
3. Receipt of an invoice by a customer.
4. Notification of an employee change of address.
5. Notification of a customer change of address.
6. Realignment of sales territories.
7. Physical shipment of goods to a customer.
8. Notification of a substitute raw material.
9. Machine repair report.
10. Receipt of return goods.

4.5 Many financial institutions issue what is termed a "bank card." This card allows their customers to accomplish a variety of traditional bank services 24 hours a day at machines (i.e., automatic bank tellers) located throughout their business area. Other institutions are introducing "charge cards," which have a predetermined and paid for credit limit encoded on them. This credit limit is reduced each time the card is used. Still other banks and retail establishments are experimenting with a credit instrument called a "debit card." This card permits the immediate transfer of funds between the customer's account and the retail establishment's account at the time of purchase. Using whatever additional research you need, prepare a report that emphasizes the impact that these new approaches will have on data processing resources and applications such as credit card systems, checking account processing, and so forth.

PROBLEMS

4.1 Select at least two different approaches to Source Data Automation (SDA) discussed in this chapter or in Appendix B and research them in the literature. Prepare a three-to-four page report comparing the advantages/disadvantages in their use for collecting data.

4.2 Fedco Credit Union has 40 offices located throughout the Northeastern United States. Since all Fedco Credit Union customers are employees of Fedco Food Marts, Inc., there is a heavy emphasis on payroll deductions for loan payments and saving deposits. In fact, 90 percent of all transactions in the offices involves preparing either checks or receipts. At present, every check and receipt is typed by hand. At the end of a day, tellers bundle the day's paperwork for the branch and ship it to Philadelphia for processing on Fedco Food's central computers. Within 48 hours of receipt, Philadelphia mails an updated statement of account to the employee and the local credit union branch.

1. What is the current structure of data processing resources in Fedco?
2. Given the brief description of the Credit Union's operations, the restructuring of which resources should be reevaluated?
3. Provide a diagram indicating the flow of data and the hardware configuration you might recommend for Fedco.

4.3 Gamma Electronics, Inc., is a $500 million, multilocation manufacturer of specialized electronic equipment. It is organized into four divisions, with three divisions responsible for manufacturing and one division responsible for assembly. Presently, each division is designated as a profit center, with a manager in charge of its data processing operations. Because of high data processing costs in each division, a proposal for the reorganization of data processing activity has been offered. In essence, the proposal advocates a centralized structure (under the leadership of a vice president of data processing) supported by divisional processing centers (under the direction of a divisional data processing manager). Prepare a brief memorandum to the president of Gamma Electronics analyzing this proposal. Discuss the potential advantages/disadvantages of the proposed new structure in terms of each of the data processing resources. Make any assumptions you feel are appropriate.

4.4 The Louisiana Yam Company has three plants for processing and canning yams. These plants are located in Louisiana, Mississippi, and Alabama. The relative activity at each plant is as follows:

	Louisiana	Mississippi	Alabama
Raw material lots purchased per day	15	8	35
Finished cans produced per day	5000	2000	20000
Average number of shipments per day	50	10	75
Employees	20	12	40

The home office of Louisiana Yam is located in Monroe, Louisiana. In addition to performing general accounting (e.g., preparing bills, payroll), the home office also receives, processes, and distributes customer orders, and keeps inventory records for all three plants' warehouses.

The owner/operator has an office located in Monroe. Under her direction are three plant managers, one for each plant. By tradition each manager has a staff who maintain inventory records, perform various clerical duties, and periodically prepare sales and production performance reports. Plant managers are expected to purchase raw produce for the necessary production of their respective plants. Raw produce is supplied by a variety of growers throughout the Mis–Lou–Ala area. The owner/operator of Louisiana Yam requests that you submit two alternatives for an information systems design using computers.

Discuss the structure you propose in terms of each data processing resource. Indicate your recommendation and why.

4.5 In the consumer goods manufacturing environment, customer order servicing is an important set of activities that is highly dependent on efficient flows of data and timely communications. Viewed as a system, order servicing is composed of three subsystems: order entry, order processing, and customer inquiry.

The purpose of the order entry subsystem is to prepare a standardized customer order based on the customer's request. This request may be received by telephone, mail, in person, or via a salesperson. The specific products required and their quantities are fundamental data. Additionally, correct shipping and billing instruction must be included. All of these data must be entered usually with an approved data coding system.

The order processing subsystem uses this customer order data to prepare additional communication documents that may include an acknowledgment of the received order which is sent to the customer, picking instructions for warehouse personnel, shipping instructions for shipping personnel (which includes two documents that go with the shipment, a bill of lading, and a packing list), and a notification to the billing department to prepare a customer invoice. To ensure that only customer orders that can be shipped are forwarded to be shipped, this subsystem requires timely access to data representing product availability, customer credit worthiness, and shipping schedules.

Providing status of the order to salespersons, customers, and the like, is the function of the third subsystem called customer inquiry. This function needs to access data about a specific order from the time it is placed until the goods are delivered to the customer.

Below we describe three such organizations with varying resource structure. Analyze each structure in terms of the customer order processing system. Prepare a flowchart representing the data flows and a configuration diagram describing the computer hardware required to efficiently support each data flow.

1. *Firm A.* One manufacturing facility with an attached warehouse and order entry office.
2. *Firm B.* One manufacturing facility with two geographically separated warehouses and four order entry offices.
3. *Firm C.* Two manufacturing facilities, six geographically separated warehouses, and one order entry office.

4.6 Litigants in criminal cases are experiencing delays of two or more years before their cases can be adjudicated. These delays do not support a defendant's constitutional right to a speedy trial and due process of the law. In some situations, the accused are released without a trial because of the delays. In other situations, either dangerous criminals are free on bond or innocent persons who cannot post bond are held in jail for lengthy time periods before a trial is provided. In still other situations, because of delays, justice is altered because witnesses are unable to recall significant details, or they move or die before the trial. The delays result in an inefficient and ineffective use of various legal resources (e.g., judges, lawyers, police, and facilities).

Some of the reasons for delays are justified whereas others are not. Legitimate requests for delays due to appeals, illnesses, conflicting schedules, and so forth are further complicated by poor communications, clerical errors, and generally the complexity of scheduling required resources. For example, the schedules of judges, prosecution attorneys, defense attorneys, courtrooms, and witnesses (including policemen) must all be coordinated into a trial docket in several types of courts (e.g., county, district). In felony cases, it is often necessary to schedule grand jury hearings or trials as well.

The overall responsibility for this scheduling usually resides in the office of the clerk of courts. Assume funds are available to develop an improved information system using computer technology for the clerk of courts in a given city. Prepare the following:

1. Several examples of information likely to be requested by users of this system.
2. A list of probable systems requirements other than specific information.
3. A schematic diagram of hardware configurations to support a centralized, distributed, and hybrid structure.

BIBLIOGRAPHY

"A Case Against Large-Scale Computers," *Infosystems,* August 1975.

Acree and Lynch, "Ring Network Architecture Supports Distributed Processing," *Data Communications,* March/April 1976.

Anthony and Dearden, *Management Control Systems,* Fourth Edition, Homewood, IL.: Richard D. Irwin, Inc., 1980.

Arnold, "Online at the Factory," *Computer Decisions,* March 1975.

Ashenhurst and Vonderohe, "A Hierarchical Network," *Datamation,* February 1975.

Benedon, "The Records Center—A Continuing Role," *Information and Records Management,* June 1976.

Bowers, "Data Communications, A Systems Mentality Is Needed," *Modern Data,* April 1975.

Bowers, "Small-Scale Computing, It's Like Doing Your Laundry," *Modern Data,* May 1975.

Burch, "An Independent Information System," *Journal of Systems Management,* March 1972.

Canning, "Improvements in Man/Machine Interfacing," *EDP Analyzer,* April 1975.

Connell, "Information Resource Management," *Business Week*, March 29, 1982.

de Cillia, "The Office of the Future will Integrate Systems and Information Management," *Information and Records Management*, February 1982.

"Distributed Computing: A Growing Concept," *Infosystems*, August 1975.

Farber, "A Ring Network," *Datamation*, February 1975.

Fraser, "A Virtual Channel Network," *Datamation*, February 1975.

International Business Machines Corporation, *Customer Information Control System/Virtual Storage (CICS/VS)* General Information Manual, Publication No. GH20-1287-3, White Plains, N.Y.: 1975.

Lasden, "Avoid the Empire-Building Image," *Computer Decisions*, October 1981.

Lasden, "Should MIS Report to the President," *Computer Decisions*, August 1980.

Lasden, "Update on Data Entry," *Computer Decisions*, April 1981.

LaVoie, "Distributed Computing, Systematically," *Computer Decisions*, March 1977.

Llewellyn, *Information Systems*, Englewood Cliffs, NJ.: Prentice-Hall, Inc., 1976.

"Missing Computer Software," *Business Week*, September 1, 1980.

"Moving Away From Mainframes," *Business Week*, February 15, 1982.

Mueller, "Integrating Information Processing Technologies," *Information and Records Management*, February 1982.

"Planning for the Fourth Generation," *Computer Decisions*, January 1975.

Rauch-Hindin, "Some Answers to the Software Problems of the 1980's," *Data Communications*, May 1981.

Rhodabauger, "Are They Calling You a Bureaucrat," *Computer Decisions*, March 1981.

Rothman and Mosmann, *Computers and Society*, Chicago: Science Research Associates, Inc., 1972.

Seaman, "Easy Efficient Ways to Link Offices," *Computer Decisions*, April 1981.

Severino, "Databases and Distributed Processing," *Computer Decisions*, March 1977.

Snyders, "Managing Systems and Data," *Computer Decisions*, November 1981.

Special Report, "Discussing Computer Software," *Business Week*, September 1, 1980.

Special Report, "The Small Computer Stands Tall," *Nations Business,* November 1981.

Special Report Section of *Computerworld,* August 30, 1976.

Whieldon, "Organizing MIS/DP to Meet the New Challenges," *Computer Decisions,* October 1981.

CHAPTER 5

Lone Star Manufacturing Company: An Information Systems Case Study

5.1 ▪ INTRODUCTION

Throughout Part I, we have described concepts and techniques to improve the efficiency of data processing and to provide more effective information for decision making. Specific examples have been given to illustrate the use of each concept and technique. However, it may be difficult to understand how all of the techniques and concepts fit together. The purpose of this chapter is to illustrate, by a case study, the integration of these concepts and techniques.

The case is about the Lone Star Manufacturing Company, a fabricator of steel fittings. One of Lone Star's systems involves the activities necessary to service a customer order. The design of this system is intended to satisfy management, operations, and accounting information requirements.

In a typical retail or merchandising operation, such as a clothing store, drugstore, or grocery store, handling customer orders is a fairly simple process. Items are bought from wholesalers and stocked in inventory for resale. When an item is sold, it is removed from inventory. In a manufacturing organization, as you will see, this process is significantly more complex. To illustrate this process, we will describe the Lone Star Manufacturing Company and its information system in terms of the detail values for the demand and design building blocks.

5.2 ▪ THE DEMAND BLOCKS

Before we examine and describe the information subsystem of Lone Star, we must understand something about the operations of the company. One way to gain this understanding is to become familiar with the company's detail values for its *demand building blocks*.

143

Organizational Factors

The Lone Star Manufacturing Company's business is to fabricate steel fittings. This involves purchasing a variety of steel products (e.g., coils, bars, sheets) from steelmaking companies and converting the bulk steel into a variety of finished goods (e.g., fasteners, angle irons, hinges). Lone Star's product line consists of low-cost, high-quality steel fittings. The company prides itself on its ability to respond to customer needs rapidly.

Figure 5.1 illustrates the physical *structure* of Lone Star. Each of three fabricating plants provide finished goods inventory for two or three warehouses. Customer orders can be received at a warehouse or a fabricating plant.

The approach of Lone Star's management is to view each plant and warehouse location as a separate profit center, while encouraging a degree of mutual cooperation. This approach is affected by encouraging each location manager to be innovative, but enforcing standard operating practices at all locations, (e.g., the product coding structure, finished goods inventory records, and customer order processing are standardized for all locations).

Order Processing System

The transaction processing illustrated in Figure 5.2 begins with the receipt of a customer's order. This order enters the system via the business function known as order entry. The primary purpose of order entry is to translate data from the customer's order into a standard coding format and terminology familiar to Lone Star personnel. Triggered by customer order data in conjunction with status data representing inventory quantities, physical location of inventory, packaging requirements, and so forth, several other transactions or documents must be generated. For example, a shipping schedule is developed to inform shipping personnel what goods will be delivered, who will deliver them, and when they will be

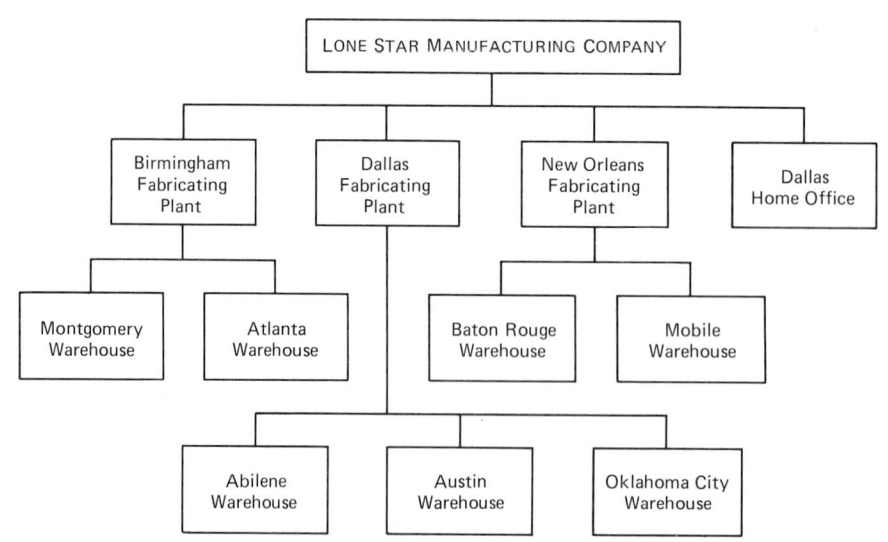

FIG. 5.1 The organization of Lone Star Manufacturing Company.

delivered. Additional documents, such as bills of lading for the carrier and packing lists for the customer, accompany each physical shipment.

Prior to shipping a customer's order the requested goods must be assembled (picked) and packed. The original customer order triggers the generation of a picking list. The picking list identifies the products to be shipped and the required quantities. The list is ordered in sequence comparable to the physical storage locations of the inventory items. Once the goods are shipped to the customer, the shipping department notifies the billing department. This notification results in the preparation of a customer invoice and an entry made to debit accounts receivable.

Information Attributes

To process a customer order efficiently, order entry, warehouse, shipping, and accounting personnel must have ready access to status

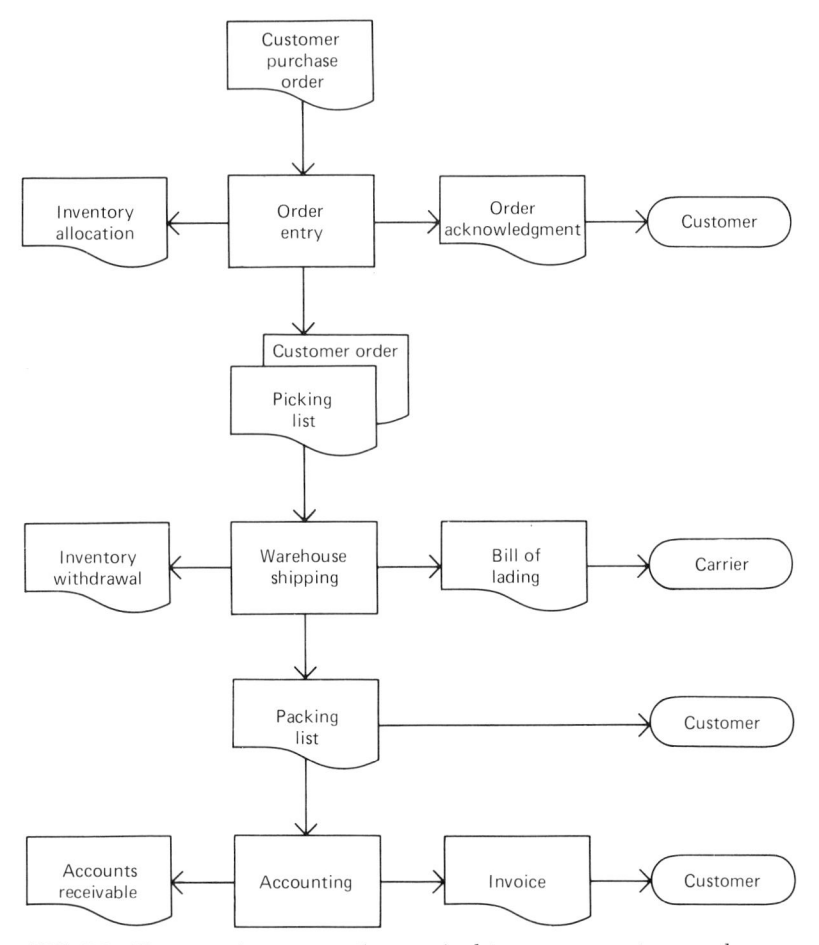

FIG. 5.2 The operations transaction required to process a customer order.

information concerning available inventory, manufacturing schedules, inventory locations, product pricing, trucking schedules, and the customer order itself. The information requirements for Lone Star were originally defined as a set of user specific informational outputs. These outputs reflected necessary *information attributes* such as timeliness, accuracy, and appropriateness. For our purposes, we can categorize these requirements into planning, control, and accounting information.

The various transactions described above are instrumental in the development of short-term plans or schedules. Examples of these plans or schedules include: (1) the shipping schedule, (2) the production plan, (3) personnel planning, (4) facilities planning, and (5) maintenance scheduling. Generation of each planning document includes the capability for measuring actual performance against plan. By using expectations from the plan along with status information, and by applying programmed decision-making and monitoring methods, Lone Star management should be provided with effective control reporting.

Each sales order and inventory transaction ultimately represents an accounting transaction. Accounting transactions affect the status of the general ledger accounts or "financial inventories." Ultimately, the general ledger is used to prepare the balance sheet and the income statement.

Management can also receive, as necessary, additional accounting reports, such as aging reports, that show amounts owed Lone Star in 0–30, 31–60, 61–90, and over 90-day categories; monthly customer statements; and late payment notices (e.g., dunning letters). Changes to finished goods inventory are reflected not only physically for operations personnel but financially for accounting purposes. Therefore, transactions representing inventory receipts (e.g., produced-to-inventory) and inventory withdrawals (e.g., shipped-to-customers) must be dollarized accordingly. Periodically, Lone Star management may also obtain information on key variables such as inventory turnover, lost customers and new customers, and an assortment of financial ratios (e.g., current assets to current liabilities, return on investment).

Data Processing Requirements

Various data processing requirements were identified by assessing users' specific information requirements. Each location receives between 50 and 200 orders per day. Orders may contain a request for a single, custom-made item or more than a dozen shelf products. Data *volumes* may not appear to be a major consideration initially. With the occurrence of multiple items per order, however, volume considerations become significant.

Although each step in the processing of a customer order is somewhat simple, because of the number and interrelatedness of the steps, there is considerable *complexity* in the overall system. *Time constraints*, particularly the rapidity of response desired by management, is an overwhelming data processing requirement. *Computational demands* in this system are relatively minor in nature.

Systems Requirements

The roots of the current system evolved from a systems study performed three years ago. At that time, Lone Star operated somewhat individually at each location. Warehouses were strictly manual and various computer configurations existed at each fabricating plant. Each plant developed its own data processing capabilities, emphasizing an application orientation in a batch environment. One of management's systems requirements was that the proposed system be standardized at all locations to ensure *reliability* in processing of customer orders.

Lone Star predicts a 10 to 15 percent annual *growth* in the number of customer orders over the next decade. Management believes that whatever system is implemented must also be capable of handling this growth. It was recognized that the new system should contain sufficient *flexibility* to allow for frequent changes of business practices. For example, expanding sales territories, adding new product lines, and frequent modifications to product specifications should be handled routinely by the system.

Three years ago, a significant factor appeared to be the added *cost* of a new system compared with the cost of the old system. Management's first thought was that any proposed system should be no more expensive than the existing system. However, they realized that to achieve both specific information, data processing, and other systems requirements, it would be necessary to spend more money on a new system.

Feasibility Requirements

Initially, the study addressed the following feasibility requirements:

1. *Technically,* the use of computer and data communications technology could accomplish Lone Star's goals.
2. Although at first online computing technology did not appear *economically justifiable,* management's redefinition of acceptable cost levels permitted its use.
3. Management expressed concerns over the *operational* feasibility of using computers. They requested that the system's designers recognize the talents and skill levels of each person who would interact with the system. Moreover, simplification of use of the system for the operating personnel was emphasized.
4. Once management approved the general systems design, the need for immediate improvements was reflected in a decision to *schedule the implementation* in phases. While this decision recognized that the cost of systems development was likely to be greater, it also recognized that some of the potential benefits could be realized earlier.

Cost/Effectiveness Demands

As noted above, management was willing to accept a higher operating cost for the new system because they perceived that many of their requirements were unattainable with the existing system. Thus, much of the justification for the new system was based on management's assessment of cost savings from fewer canceled orders and returned goods, and less expensive transportation. They also believed that intangible benefits from an improved service image would accrue to Lone Star because of the new system. It was formally agreed on that a postaudit would be conducted at the end of each implementation phase to determine if future phases should be discontinued, implemented as proposed, or implemented in a modified form.

5.3 ▪ THE DESIGN BLOCKS

Thus far we have discussed Lone Star Manufacturing Company and its customer order processing in terms of the demand blocks. Only a few key items or factors for each block were highlighted; numerous others were omitted. We should have a sufficient understanding at this point, however, to evaluate how the detail values of the design blocks were developed to satisfy these demands. Again, only selected points in each design block will be discussed.

Data Processing Resources

The data processing resources in Lone Star are best described as a *hybrid structure*. The Home Office and each plant has its own computing system. The computing systems are compatible with one another and can be interconnected by dial-up telephone lines. The size of the processors and the extent of the peripheral equipment at each location varies according to need, but all computing systems have direct access storage devices (DASDs), and permit online and batch processing simultaneously. Each location contains 4 to 10 input/output devices, such as cathode ray tubes (CRTs) and printer/keyboard devices.

Each computing system contains software to perform data processing locally in a standalone mode or remotely in a communications mode. The software at each location includes a vendor-supplied operating system, purchased software, such as a data base management system (DBMS), and numerous programs and subroutines developed by Lone Star. One of the purchased software applications allows noncomputer personnel to input data or to access data using prompting formats (i.e., the computer asks a specific question) or selection formats (i.e., the computer offers a "menu" of alternatives).

The majority of information systems personnel at Lone Star are located at the Home Office. Each plant has one or two systems analysts/programmers, however, to provide immediate maintenance and troubleshooting support to field personnel.

The data flows at Lone Star are currently mixed. In some instances, the data flow is highly integrated and, in others, it is customized for individual location needs. For the customer order subsystem, the data flows are highly integrated, and the data base is distributed among the locations.

Input

The design of the *input block* in this system recognizes that modern data processing resources can support and enhance the performance of each operating unit and each employee. The strategic use and placement of CRT and keyboard/printer terminals throughout Lone Star's physical environment provides several advantages. Obviously, operating data can be recorded, collected, and made available to all users more quickly. Paperwork, with all of its related handling and filing, can be minimized. Finally, the reduction of media conversion steps results in more efficient data processing.

Although we emphasize transactions inputs, a full range of queries and expectation inputs is also supported. For example, managers can access status and transaction information via terminals in their offices; various staff personnel, such as industrial engineers and production and inventory planners, can develop their expectations (e.g., routing sequence, bills of material, staffing levels) online by using terminals at their desks.

A number of transaction inputs can be made to the system. They include payments received and made, purchases of raw mate-

```
┌─────────────────────────────────────────┐
│           ORDER TRANSACTIONS            │
│ The following options are available:    │
│                                         │
│  1. Input new order                     │
│  2. Revise existing order               │
│  3. List orders input today             │
│  4. List unfilled orders for this customer │
│  5. New customer                        │
│  6. Return to main program              │
│                                         │
│ ENTER YOUR SELECTION:  1                │
└─────────────────────────────────────────┘
```

FIG. 5.3 Example of an order transaction menu displayed on a video screen.

rials, initializing customer records, posting items to appropriate accounts, inventory transfers, and recording shipments to customers.

To input an order transaction, the order entry clerk enters a secret code called a password, and requests the order transaction menu shown in Figure 5.3. Once this format is displayed, the order entry clerk selects from the available options and continues to interact with the system until the complete order is input.

The system processes the order in several interactive steps, eliminating paper handling and manual calculations for pricing and extensions. Inventory commitment, shipping document preparation, and account posting are done automatically by program logic. The menu approach increases the accuracy of inputs because errors and omissions are detected immediately by controls and edits at the point the order data are input. Moreover, many data fields, such as customer names, addresses, account titles, item descriptions, and prices, already exist in the data base; they do not have to be reentered for each order. Thus, the order entry clerk need only input certain identifying numbers (e.g., customer identification number, product code) plus variable data, such as purchase order numbers, requested ship date, and quantities. A typical new order transaction form is revealed in Figure 5.4. This form is displayed as a result of the selection made from the order transaction menu in Figure 5.3.

For a new customer, a new customer form is requested and the blanks are "filled in" by keying the appropriate data. The person entering the data is guided by the system in completing the form. It automatically advances the cursor to the next character, or if a field is complete, automatically advances the cursor to the next appropriate field.

Processing

This design block includes a variety of concepts and techniques that convert data into

```
┌─────────────────────────────────────────────────────┐
│                  NEW ORDER FORM                     │
│  DATE ORDER RECEIVED: _____       │
│  REQUESTED SHIP DATE: _____       │
│  CUSTOMER ID NUMBER: _____       │
│  CUSTOMER PURCHASE ORDER NUMBER: _____      │
│  ITEM NUMBER: _____       │
│  QUANTITY ORDERED: _____       │
│  MORE THAN ONE ITEM NUMBER? (Y = YES; N = NO): ___  │
│  END OF ORDER? (Y = YES; N = NO): _____      │
└─────────────────────────────────────────────────────┘
```

FIG. 5.4 Example of a new order transaction form displayed on a video screen.

information. Numerous computer and human procedures provide detailed instructions as to who, what, when, where, and how things are to be done. The design of this system calls for a high degree of interaction between the computer and user personnel via terminals. Although the use of prompting and menus makes the process somewhat self-documenting and simple, specific manual activities must be explained, and what the system does with each input must be described. This material is contained in a set of procedure manuals.

The design of the customer order system is modeled after the physical activity required to service a customer order. Within this model many procedures are coded in the software and performed automatically for each transaction. Six examples of processing customer orders will give you a flavor for these procedures.

1. *Credit checks.* Lone Star's policy is that each customer order received must be reviewed for credit approval. In the past, each order prepared by order entry was forwarded to the credit department for review. This meant that all customer orders were held for at least one working day and often longer before they were released for shipment. During the *systems analysis phase,* it was determined that 90 percent of all orders were acceptable for shipment after routine processing.

The current system provides shared access to customer information by order entry, credit, and accounting personnel. Although order entry maintains customer name and address, pricing information, and so forth, the credit department periodically updates the various credit terms, credit limit, and overall credit status. Both can access the accounts receivable amount due and payment status, although these data are the responsibility of the accounting department. Consequently, when an order entry clerk inputs order data, the following actions take place automatically: (a) the price of each product is obtained from a standard pricing file and each line item is extended by multiplying the quantity by the price; (b) the line items are summed and the appropriate credit terms/discounts for the customer (as indicated in the customer file) are applied to the order giving an order amount; (c) this order amount is added to the current accounts receivable amount and compared against a predetermined credit limit for that customer; (d) the accounts receivable file is also checked for its current payment and credit status.

Customer orders failing either of the two credit tests (c) and (d), and all first-time orders, are automatically printed at a terminal in the credit department for further review and action. Processing continues on all other orders.

2. *Availability determination.* A second procedure involves determining the availability of inventory to be shipped within the time frame requested by a customer. Again, order entry has access to inventory data and the production scheduling file. If a requested product is not in current inventory, or indicated by the production scheduling file as being available within the customer's requested time frame, the system will maintain the order in a special "backorder" status. The customer is then notified of the status of the order. Three responses to a backorder are: (a) the customer indicates "no backorder," and the order is canceled; (b) only part of the order can be shipped, shipping documents are processed for available

items, and the rest of the order is backordered in the form of a new order; (c) the customer indicates "ship complete," and the order is held until all items are available.

Availability determination eliminates preparing orders and forwarding them to the shipping department when the product is not available. On the other hand, availability determination affords Lone Star the opportunity to prepare an order acknowledgment, which indicates to the customer that the order has been received and will or will not be shipped as requested. Of course, it also allows order entry to call a customer and suggest a different time frame or substitute an item. Since the system maintains unfilled orders and backorders, these data can also become valuable input to the preparation of future production schedules and plans.

3. *Orders for future deliveries.* Customer orders specifying future delivery dates allow a lead time before the actual shipment must be made. This kind of order may be supplied from on-hand inventory, planned production, or future production not yet planned. Commitment of current inventories to an order that is to be shipped far in the future can cause another order for the same item to be backordered or canceled. If a customer sends in an order two months in advance, however, and on the date of the requested shipment the system backorders it because of an out-of-stock situation, customer dissatisfaction and frustration is likely. To prevent this occurrence, the system continuously monitors current inventory and production schedules. At the beginning of a work day, the system allocates both inventory and near-term production to existing unfilled orders. As new orders arrive and are entered, the system provides an opportunity for changing individual order priorities by listing conflicting order requirements. Thus, although the system allocates inventory in routine situations by preparing an automatic notification of conflicts, it permits management to exercise their authority on an exception basis.

4. *Unfilled order file monitoring.* Once order entry inputs a customer order, credit approval is given, and inventory allocation is made, the order is monitored by the system until it is due to be picked, packed, and shipped. Each day, or on request, the system prepares outputs indicating what customer orders are to be shipped that day, or the next day, or the next week. For example, by requesting a list of orders to be shipped in a two- or three-day period, shipping is able to schedule an entire trailer rather than a series of part loads to make deliveries to customers in a similar geographical location. Or, each time a special request is made by a customer or when a production schedule changes, the effect on the status of all other unfilled orders can be evaluated.

5. *Billing release.* When it is time to ship an order that has been picked, packed, and staged at the shipping dock, shipping personnel simply enter that order number into the system and request a bill of lading and packing list to be printed. On the unfilled order file, that order is noted accordingly as "shipped." Each day at 5:00 PM, a program scans the unfilled order file and produces invoices and customer statements for all orders shipped that day. At the same time that the unfilled order file is purged, the accounts

receivable file is updated, and a hardcopy of the billing transaction is prepared for accounting control purposes. As payments are received, accounts receivable personnel simply input the payment amount by order number to update the proper account.

6. *Changes to orders.* Customers request all kinds of changes to previously submitted orders. For example, customers may want a change in requested delivery date, an increase or decrease of quantity, an addition of an item, or an order cancellation. These changes can be handled easily, often while the customer is still on the telephone, by simply requesting the "revise order" menu indicated in Figure 5.3. At that time, the program logic will reverify inventory availability and provide automatic notification to production scheduling where a custom item is involved.

Data Base

The old system at Lone Star used a fragmented approach in the design of the data base, as depicted in Figure 5.5. For example, accounting programs accessed accounting files, order entry programs accessed order entry files, inventory control programs accessed inventory files, manufacturing pro-

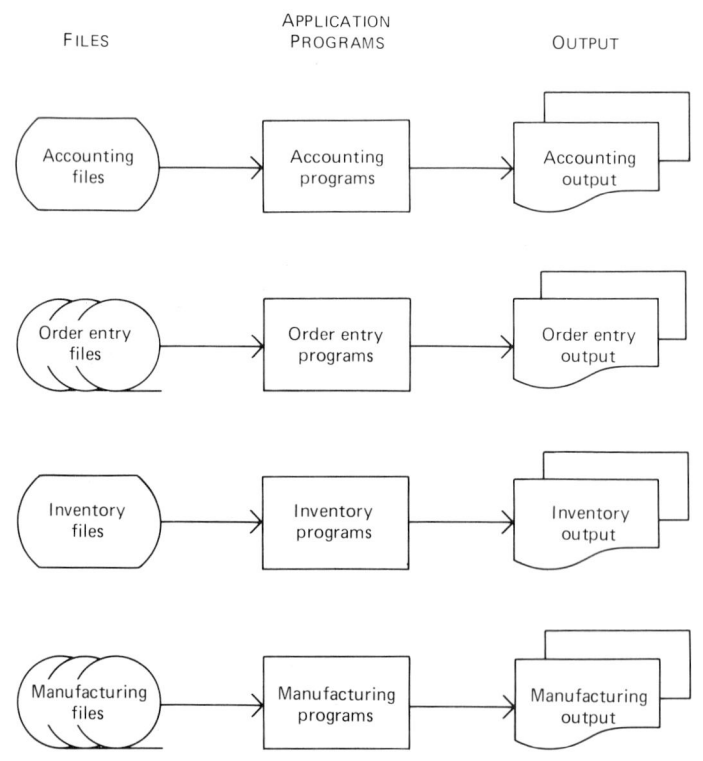

FIG. 5.5 Example of a data base designed using the application approach.

grams accessed manufacturing files, and so forth. Much of the data in each set of functional files were identical, but each file required individual updating procedures. Often, identical data fields were defined differently from file to file and from program to program. Attempts to obtain reports that combined data from different files required that new programs be written. This programming effort was obviously both time-consuming and expensive. Moreover, the value of similar data fields in different files was not always identical because of the different timings of updating procedures.

Lone Star's new data base is designed with data integration and the minimization of redundancy. The data base management system (DBMS), which was purchased, encourages and facilitates the integration and standardization of data definition. Conceptually, the result is shown in Figure 5.6. Data are monitored and processed by the DBMS, not by individual application programs. Compatibility exists in both programs and data fields; the sharing of common data thus eliminates a great deal of needless data redundancy.

Several methods of logically and physically associating data are discussed in the next part of this text. Because of the technical nature of associating data, a more detailed description of Lone Star's data base

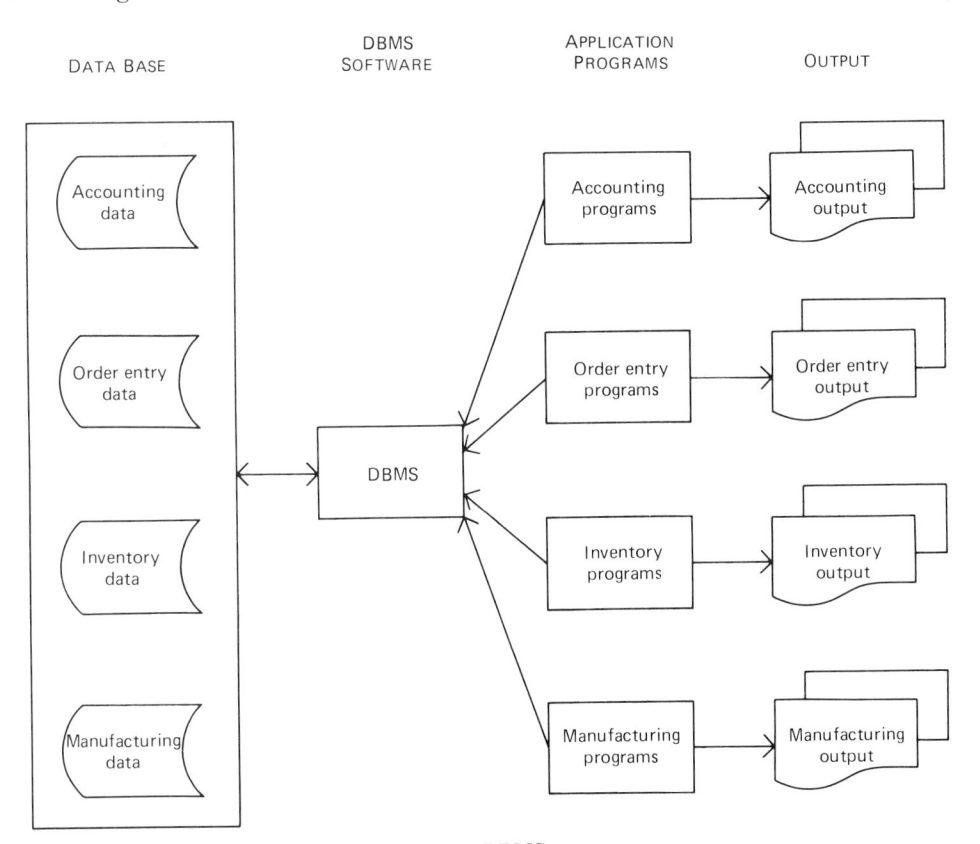

FIG. 5.6 Example of a systems design using DBMS.

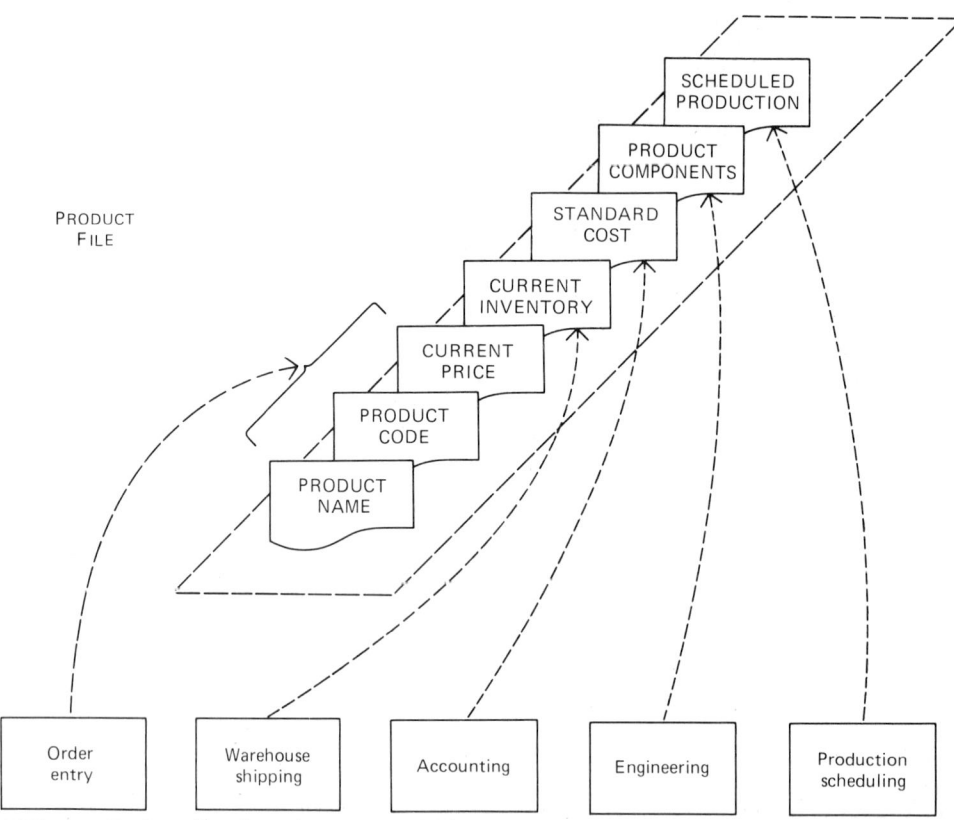

FIG. 5.7 Product file whose data are available to all users and where each functional unit has a maintenance responsibility for different data fields.

will be omitted. In Figure 5.7, however, we illustrate how each functional area is responsible for providing and maintaining data that then can be accessed by any other functional area.

Controls

The purpose of this design block is to focus on the techniques and concepts that ensure that the customer order system operates as designed. This involves both preventing data errors from entering the system and identifying problems that occur within it. The concept of controls is analyzed later in Part III of this book. Some of the basic controls in Lone Star's information system, however, are discussed below.

Before the customer order is input to the system, the following controls are established to ensure that all data are entered completely:

1. The date of receipt by Lone Star is stamped on the customer order by a mail clerk.

2. Serial numbers for the orders received are logged on a daily register. This register is compared with the unfilled order file at the end of the day to ensure that all orders were entered.

3. Control totals within the order are established, such as the total number of lines on an order or the total quantity of items ordered. The terminal operator uses these totals to help ensure that all ordered items are entered into the system.
4. Special requests by customers are highlighted, such as extra copies of the invoice, unusual packing or shipping instructions, and so forth. Highlighting may take the form of underlining or circling the request on the customer purchase order, or indicating the presence of special requests in any way that will ensure the order entry clerk's attention.

Once the order reaches the order entry clerk, the first test performed is to associate it with an approved customer master record. This function allows fast retrieval of information concerning all open orders for a customer. It also means that the information in the customer record can be retrieved quickly when preparing order documentation or handling a customer inquiry.

As previously discussed, the customer master record contains several data fields maintained by the credit department. These include:

1. *Credit limit.* The credit limit is the maximum credit granted to one customer at a given time after adding up all the open order amounts and the current accounts receivable amount due balance.
2. *D–U N–S.* This is a number assigned to the customer by credit companies so one can find out the credit position of the customer.
3. *Credit terms.* These are any special discounts or payment arrangements either negotiated or applied to this customer for marketing or financial reasons.

Using the credit limit and the current accounts receivable amount due to determine whether a customer order should be filled is another form of control. Similarly, using a common item master file to obtain standard prices and allocating available inventory before producing a shipping request also serves as a vital control.

The use of the *menu-driven software* with the terminals permits many potential input errors to be detected and corrected as a condition for acceptance by the system. Data field sizes and content can be rigorously controlled. For example, if insufficient, or too many characters are entered, the system is programmed to request immediate verification from the operator. Also, data fields that should be all numeric or all alphabetic are verified at the time of input. Finally, interactive systems limit data inputs to necessary identification and variable data, thereby minimizing data errors.

Audit trails for order entry are provided by transaction logs, which are maintained on magnetic disk. All transactions are written to a log in order of their occurrence. The log contains a wealth of information useful to auditors. For example, to satisfy auditors' information needs, transactions can be grouped by terminal, by type of transaction, by terminal user, by dollar amount, or by customer. Also, variance conditions can be displayed on request.

Besides a variety of locks and security devices, *access control* at Lone Star is handled by three levels of *passwords*. Level 1 passwords can enter transactions and change these transactions, if needed, during the normal business day. These passwords are assigned to order entry clerks, customer service personnel, and accounting clerks. Level 2 passwords can revise transactions that are currently input or have been input since the last accounting period. Also, this level can use a number of menu options to obtain various reports. Personnel assigned these passwords are middle- and upper-level managers. Level 3 passwords permit complete access to all operations in the system. Only a few selected top managers have this highest level access, and even then, access by them requires a dual user mode (i.e., two authorized users must use the system at the same time, similar to double-key entry in a safe-deposit box). This level allows extraordinary cash withdrawals, the printing of certain financial information, and other sensitive options. Also, data values, such as product prices and pay raises, can be changed by this level of passwords.

Reliable *backup procedures* are an essential control in any system. Sometimes weeks of work can be saved in the event of a disaster or malfunction. Daily, Lone Star copies all of their sensitive files so that the most that can be lost is one day's processing. Also, all software and documentation files are duplicated. Backup copies are routinely stored in bank vaults several miles from Lone Star's computer systems.

Output

This design block represents the product of the information system. Output for Lone Star ranges from many routine operations documents (e.g., picking list, bill of material, customer statements, and dunning letters) to a variety of complex management reports. This output can be presented almost instantly via CRT terminals or hardcopy terminals. The generation of outputs is customized to suit the user's needs. For example, some outputs are produced at predetermined time frequencies (e.g., daily, weekly, or monthly). Other outputs are produced because selected conditions or transactions occur (i.e., a customer order is not shipped by its requested ship date or a recorded shipment results in producing an invoice). Still other outputs are produced on request. In the following paragraphs, several of Lone Star's outputs are described.

1. *Order status.* The ability to answer customer questions quickly and accurately concerning price and delivery dates can significantly affect a company's success in securing and retaining customers. Nothing is more frustrating to customers than being told that no one knows the status of their order. Likewise, customers become upset if order data are incomplete or inaccurate. Previously, Lone Star took customer questions, searched a paper file, and called back customers with the answer to their inquiries; these efforts took time. The new customer order system provides the means to answer customer questions quickly and accurately. Responses may be related to information the customer needs to place an order, such as price, quantities, and delivery dates; status of an order currently pending shipment; and changes to existing orders. For example, whenever an inquiry is made about an existing order, the first step is to retrieve that order from the order file. The key to this file is the customer purchase order number. Once the appropriate customer order is found, the clerk can answer questions regarding the order. When the order status shows that the order is in the shipping room or has already been shipped, the probable delivery date can immediately be given. If the status shows that items are still in production, an estimated delivery date can be given to the customer. Most importantly, the customer's questions can be

answered within seconds or minutes by customer service clerks who access the data base by CRTs. This capability to query the data base for a specific output is valuable not only to answer customer questions, but to satisfy the information needs of Lone Star personnel at all levels.

2. *Standard reports.* Traditional accounting reports are generated by the system automatically at predetermined time intervals. However, because of the online input, processing, and output capabilities of the system, management may request specific reports at any time. The system allows users to format a report appropriate to their needs, thus *filtering* out extraneous data. In Figure 5.8, we illustrate a menu that provides a selection of financial reports.

3. *Ad hoc reports.* Besides getting standard financial reports, management can generate ad hoc reports, such as the movement of specific inventory items, the performance of a profit center, sales by customers, and variances from standards and budget. A few examples are shown in Figure 5.9. Bear in mind that even these reports can be easily changed (e.g., number of months, customers to inventory items, dollars to units, different levels of subtotals) by choosing different selection parameters, like a menu within a menu.

For inventory control purposes, Lone Star classifies inventory items into groups. This method, known as *ABC analysis,* is particularly helpful in situations where there are many different inventory items. (See Appendix A for an additional discussion of this method.) The ABC Inventory report received by management of Lone Star is shown in Figure 5.10.

Problems inherent in inventory control are reduced by establishing performance standards for certain functions and reporting variances from these standards to management on a timely basis. For example, at Lone Star, the standard for the number of orders shipped late is two per day. Any number over this standard reported to management automatically.

4. *Variance reports.* These Reports are generated automatically by the system for management and include the following:

1. orders pending because of:

FINANCIAL REPORTS MENU

The following options are available:

1. Print period-to-date income statement.
2. Print year-to-date income statement.
3. Print comparative income statement.
4. Print balance sheet.
5. Print comparative balance sheet.
6. Print statement of changes in financial position.
7. Print financial ratios.
8. Return to main program menu.

Enter Your Selection: ___

FIG. 5.8 Example of a report menu.

a. pricing,
b. credit approval,
c. backorders,
d. verification of order details,
e. equipment breakdown.

2. the number of orders shipped late;
3. the number of orders delayed in shipping room;
4. the average time to respond to customer interrogations;
5. the number of unsolved interrogations;
6. the percentage of rush orders;
7. the average response time to rush orders;
8. the percentage of orders shipped incomplete.

The above list is not exhaustive. The point we are trying to make is that with an efficient information system, management can either request or have the system monitor information that will allow them to react quickly to out-of-control conditions, or identify high- or low-performance areas. Thus management, by getting early warning signals, is able to take corrective action before significant problems occur.

CUSTOMER SALES PERFORMANCE (Dollars)

	CUSTOMER 1	CUSTOMER 2	CUSTOMER 3
January Sales	$10000.00	$20000.00	$ 5000.00
February Sales	12000.00	15000.00	10000.00
Increase	$ 2000.00		$ 5000.00
<Decrease>		$ 5000.00	
Change	20% +	25% −	100% +

PROFIT CENTER PERFORMANCE (Dollars)

	PROFIT CENTER 1	PROFIT CENTER 2	PROFIT CENTER 3
Item 1	$ 60000.00	$70000.00	$ 50000.00
Item 2	40000.00	20000.00	80000.00
SUBTOTAL	$100000.00	$90000.00	$130000.00
Item 3	$ 20000.00	$30000.00	$ 20000.00
Item 4	10000.00	40000.00	30000.00
SUBTOTAL	$ 30000.00	$70000.00	$ 50000.00

INVENTORY SALES FORECASTS (Units)

	19×1	19×2	19×3	19×4 Forecast*
Item 1	70000	75000	80000	87000
Item 2	60000	70000	90000	114000
Item 3	40000	50000	70000	95000

*Exponential smoothing model used. Weighting Alpha furnished by management.

FIG. 5.9 Examples of management reports.

The Design Blocks 159

PROFIT CENTER VARIANCE REPORT

	PLANNED		ACTUAL		VARIANCES	
	Amount	Percent	Amount	Percent	Amount	Percent
Profit Center 1	$ 60000.00	40.0	$ 58000.00	33.6	$ 2000.00 −	3.3 −
Profit Center 2	50000.00	33.3	64000.00	37.2	$14000.00 +	28.0 +
Profit Center 3	40000.00	26.7	50000.00	29.2	$10000.00 +	25.0 +
	$150000.00	100.0	$172000.00	100.0		

DAILY TRANSPORTATION REPORT

DATE DD/MM/YY

PURCHASE ORDER NUMBER	DATE SHIPPED	SHIPPED VIA	LOCATION CODE	TRANSPORTA- TION CHARGE	TRANSPORTA- TION ALLOWANCE	QUANTITY SHIPPED
XXXXXX	DD/MM/YY	XXXXXXX	XXX	$XXXX.XX	$XXXX.XX	XXXXX.XX
XXXXXX	DD/MM/YY	XXXXXXX	XXX	XXXX.XX	XXXX.XX	XXXXX.XX
XXXXXX	DD/MM/YY	XXXXXXX	XXX	XXXX.XX	XXXX.XX	XXXXX.XX
			TOTALS	$XXXX.XX	$XXXX.XX	XXXXX.XX

ORDER ACTIVITY REPORT

DATE DD/MM/YY

PURCHASE ORDER NUMBER	CUSTOMER ID NUMBER	ITEM NUMBER	DATE ORDERED	QUANTITY ORDERED	DATE SHIPPED	QUANTITY SHIPPED	QUANTITY BACKORDER	QUANTITY CANCELLED
XXXXXX	XXXXX	XXXXX	DD/MM/YY	XXXXX.XX	DD/MM/YY	XXX.XX	XXXXX.XX	XXXXX.XX
XXXXXX	XXXXX	XXXXX	DD/MM/YY	XXXXX.XX	DD/MM/YY	XXX.XX	XXXXX.XX	XXXXX.XX

CONTROL TOTALS:
SHIPPED QUANTITY TOTAL   XXXXXXX.XX
BACKORDER QUANTITY TOTAL   XXXXXXX.XX
CANCELLED QUANTITY TOTAL   XXXXXXX.XX

REGISTER FOR DAILY SHIPMENTS

SALESPERSON NUMBER	GROSS SALES	CREDIT ALLOWANCE	ADJUSTED GROSS SALES	SHIPPING CHARGES	GROSS INVENTORY AMOUNT
XXX	$XXXXX.XX	$XXXXX.XX	$XXXXX.XX	$XXXX.XX	$XXXXX.XXCR
XXX	XXXXX.XX	XXXXX.XX	XXXXX.XX	XXXX.XX	XXXXX.XXCR
XXX	XXXXX.XX	XXXXX.XX	XXXXX.XX	XXXX.XX	XXXXX.XXCR
TOTAL	$XXXXX.XX	$XXXXX.XX	$XXXXX.XX	$XXXX.XX	$XXXXX.XXCR

FIG. 5.9 (continued).

ABC INVENTORY REPORT FOR PROFIT CENTER 1			
Group	Number of Inventory Items	Percentage of Total Inventory Items	Total Sales ($)	Percentage of Total Sales
A	30,000	18.7	960,000	80.0
B	50,000	31.3	140,000	11.7
C	80,000	50.0	100,000	8.3
	160,000	100.0	1,200,000	100.0

FIG. 5.10 Example of ABC report.

Plans are underway at Lone Star to develop a *strategic decision center,* especially for long-range planning in the area of inventory and logistics. Several optimum transportation models based on different warehouse placement are being considered. Devices that convert digital output into multicolored graphs on large video screens are being tested to determine operational feasibility. These graphs will be used as the output medium to communicate to top management the results of a number of "what if" questions. Also, external data are being gathered concerning new packaging and loading techniques. Another task group is compiling technical and cost information about automated warehousing using robotics and microprocessors.

SUMMARY

Here we have shown how the concepts and methods discussed in the first four chapters are applied. The detail values of the demand and design blocks of Lone Star Manufacturing served as basic vehicles to facilitate this discussion. Lone Star's initial use of computers was application oriented; it was intended to improve the efficiency of specific data processing activities. When the flow of data was integrated in the new system, it was not only possible to continue to increase data processing efficiencies but also to provide more effective planning and control information for management.

PART II

Data Base Development and Design

CHAPTER 6

Data Base Concepts

6.1 ▪ INTRODUCTION

It has been emphasized that modern organizations have a continuing need to collect, process, and store large quantities of data to obtain that information necessary for effective decision making, planning, and control. Moreover, in most organizations, for reasons of volume, complexity, timing, and computational demands, this collected data must be organized in a manner to serve a variety of users' information requests.

In this chapter, general aspects of the *data base,* a key design block of the information system, are discussed. Chapter 7 is devoted to essential functions of coding, sorting, and searching data. The techniques used to associate data logically are analyzed in Chapter 8. In Chapter 9 the characteristics of physical storage devices are described, the most common methods of addressing are discussed, and mechanisms for representing logical structures physically are examined. In the last chapter of this part, a detailed presentation is made of file storage and processing considerations.

The specific objectives of this chapter are:

1. To present the basic concepts and functions of the data base.
2. To identify the descriptors and hierarchical grouping of data.
3. To contrast the application approach to the data base approach in data base design.
4. To present a general discussion of a data base management system (DBMS).

6.2 ▪ THE ULTIMATE DATA BASE

The term ***data base*** has no standard, precise definition. An all-encompassing definition is that a data base is a repository of interrelated data of interest and value to the users of the system. The physical storage media of the data base can be, among other things, groups of paper file folders in filing cabinets, journals, ledgers, punched cards, punched paper tape, magnetic tape, magnetic disk, and electrons in the human mind.

In a large, complex organization there are many users who simultaneously require access to information. Users include executives, division or department managers, accounting and auditing personnel, salespersons, production personnel, engineering staff, programmers, and so forth.

These users require many different levels of service, from simple inquiries taking a few seconds, to the generation of comprehensive reports requiring hours of file searching and manipulation.

Where volume, complexity, timing, and computational demands are low, the human mind represents the ultimate data base. Take, for example, a shoe cobbler prior to the Industrial Revolution. His entire business was located in a small shop. Several pairs of shoes representing his craft were displayed in a window for viewing by passersby. Finished goods inventory consisted of a few pairs of popular styles. Raw materials consisted of a few boxes of tacks, some twine, and several sheets of leather. His production facilities were simple—shoe lasts, cutting tools, hammers, stitching devices. Most of his sales were shoes made to order. The operating system, management system, and information system all resided in him.

Contrast the shoe cobbler's small business with the multinational footwear industry of today. Modern organizations are so complex that no one individual can know everything about his or her operation, as the shoe cobbler did.

In a way, we have come full circle. Today managers are trying to emulate the situation that existed with the shoe cobbler, that is, to capture the feeling that they are "on top of everything" and that they know what is going on at all times. To approach this goal, the data base that supports the information system should act as an extension of users' minds. It must attempt to match the *associative* abilities of the human mind to be effective. Although this goal may never be fully achieved, using this broad concept as a general guideline to designing the ultimate data base may be of benefit to you while reading the remaining material.

6.3 ▪ OVERVIEW OF THE DATA BASE

A data base consists of data elements organized into records and files in a way intended to meet users' information requirements. The totality of these data elements is the data base, the foundation of the information system.

Data Descriptions

Data are ideas and facts about things or entities; for example, people, places, or machines. Data act as surrogates of entities. A sales clerk may often need to know how many $3'' \times 4'' \times 20'$ pieces of angle iron are in stock. It would be impractical to have to go to the warehouse and count the number of items every time to know the quantity on hand. Instead, the clerk accesses data which represent the angle iron inventory.

Data are supposed to correspond to how we think about each thing and thus how it is described. To represent entities through data, we require three descriptors: (1) **data attribute,** (2) **data attribute value,** and (3) **data representation.** An example of how these descriptors are applied is shown in Figure 6.1.

If a user wishes to receive data about an entity, attributes that describe these data must be defined. For example, if the credit manager wants to know all customers by name with account balances greater than $1000.00, the data attributes names that are defined are CUSTOMER NAME and AMOUNT OWED. The AMOUNT OWED attribute value of each customer is compared against the $1000.00 parameter, and every AMOUNT OWED attribute value greater than this parameter is displayed to the credit manager along with the appropriate CUSTOMER NAME attribute value.

Overview of the Data Base

Descriptor / Entity	Data Attribute	Data Attribute Value	Data Representation (Maximum Length)
Customer	Customer number Customer name Amount owed Credit limit	12345 Nept. Inc. 01400.00 10000.00	5 Digits 30 Alphanumerics 7 Digits with 2 decimal places 7 Digits with 2 decimal places
Employee	Employee number Employee name Department number Hourly pay rate Job classification	135 J. Smith 764-B 07.00 Systems analyst	3 Digits 20 Alphabetics 5 Alphanumerics 4 Digits with 2 decimal places 20 Alphabetics
Inventory Item	Item number Size Description Price Unit of measure	117JP 2 × 2 × 20 Angle 00.80 Each	5 Alphanumerics 6 Alphanumerics 10 Alphabetics 4 Digits with 2 decimal places 4 Alphanumerics

FIG. 6.1 Data descriptors.

In some instances, data must be calculated from existing attribute values. For example, the credit manager may want to know the names of all customers who have an AMOUNT OWED within twenty percent of their CREDIT LIMIT. The system must subtract the value of AMOUNT OWED from the value of CREDIT LIMIT and divide the result by the value of CREDIT LIMIT. This calculated value is then presented to the credit manager. In a sophisticated information system, users are not aware of the calculations required to derive the information they request.

Note that data attribute names and representations are not recorded in the same place as the data attribute values. They are recorded elsewhere, perhaps in a **data dictionary,** which lists the attribute names and representations of all data items in the data base.

Hierarchy of Data

To gain an understanding of how data elements are structured to form a data base, refer to Figure 6.2.

Physical Storage of Data

Different words or terms are used to describe the physical storage of data. A brief definition of these terms follows.

1. *Physical record.* A physical record is the basic unit of data that can be written or

Data Base Concepts

Data base is a totality of all the items below, organized in a manner appropriate for providing information to users of the information system.

↑

File is a collection of records containing data about a related group of entities (e.g., CUSTOMER MASTER FILE).

↑

Record is a collection of fields relating to some entity. In the context of the users' needs, this record should identify and describe completely each entity (e.g., CUSTOMER RECORD).

↑

Nonelementary fields represent attributes, attribute values, and data representations that can be further subdivided (e.g., CUSTOMER ADDRESS). Nonelementary fields are also called *data aggregates*.

↑

Elementary fields represent attributes, attribute values, and data representations that cannot be further subdivided (e.g., CUSTOMER NUMBER). Elementary fields are also called *data items*.

↑

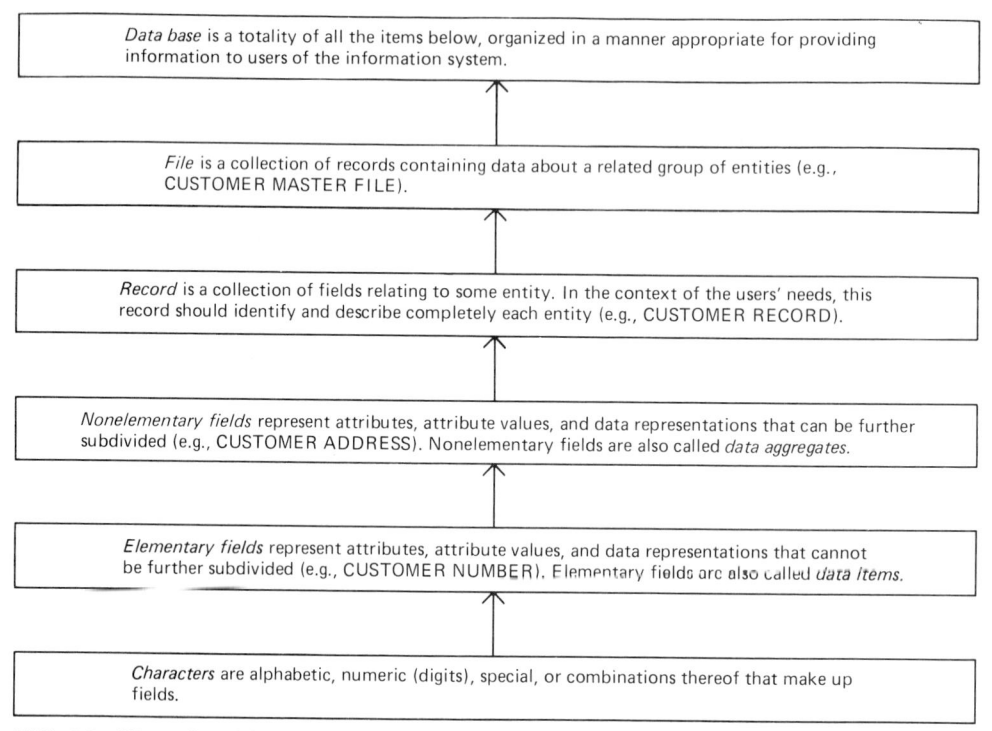

Characters are alphabetic, numeric (digits), special, or combinations thereof that make up fields.

FIG. 6.2 Hierarchy of data.

read by a single output or input command to the computer. If the data records are **blocked** (see Appendix B) multiple logical records would be contained in a single physical record.

2. *Extent.* Physical records that are contiguous in external storage are called an extent. Customer records stored on disk cylinders 005 to 010 inclusive are said, for example, to occupy an extent of six cylinders.

3. *Data set.* A data set is a named group of physical records. Included in a data set are any indices necessary for locating the data records of the data set. A data set may be made up of one or more extents.

Physical Versus Logical Files

The media used to store data come in a variety of **physical** forms. For example, paper file folders, index cards, and microfilm can all be used to store data, but any calculations performed on this data must be done by hand. Some other physical storage media are computer accessible, such as magnetic tape, disk, drum, paper tape, and punched cards.

The **logical** aspect of files relates to how data are associated to provide information to the user. A logical file may extend across more than one physical file; a physical file may contain only one logical file or multiple logical files. These situations are illustrated in Figure 6.3.

One Logical File over Multiple Physical Files

Logical file 1 of 1 — Physical file 1 of 3

Logical file 1 of 1 — Physical file 2 of 3

Logical file 1 of 1 — Physical file 3 of 3

One Physical File Containing Multiple Logical Files

Logical file 1
Logical file 2
Logical file 3
Physical file 1

One Logical File Contained in One Physical File

Logical file 1
Physical file 1

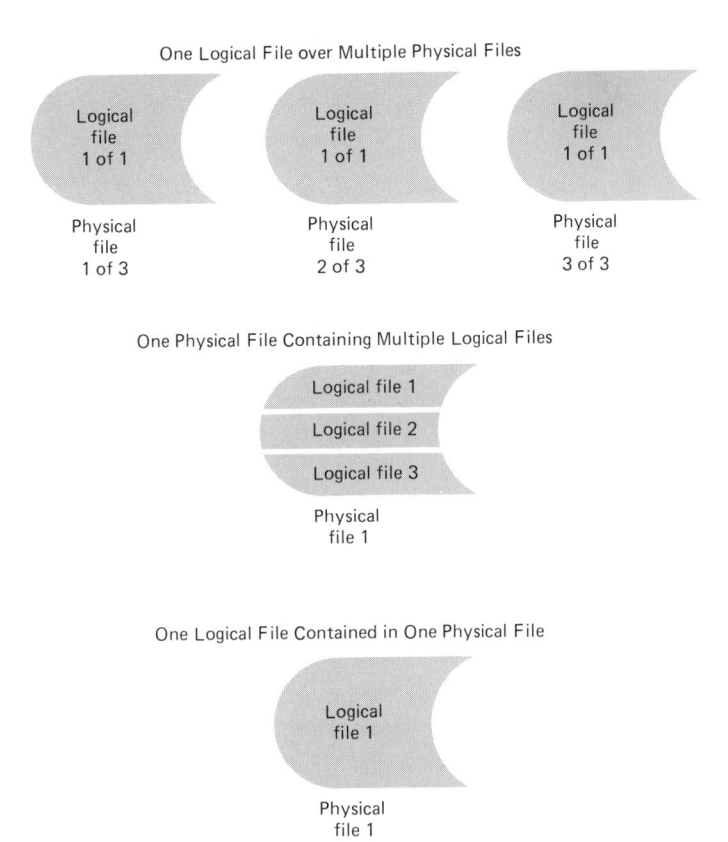

FIG. 6.3 Illustration of logical/physical file relationships.

It should be mentioned that prior to extensive application of direct access storage devices (DASDs) in computer-based applications, it was customary to have not more than one logical file per physical file.

In a data base the logical files, records, and/or fields should be logically associated in a manner that will accommodate the information needs of users. This interrelatedness of data elements is accomplished by pointers, indexes, and other techniques which will be discussed later. The users' information requirements are affected by logical methods that can permit any combination of data elements to be retrieved from any number of different (or single) physical storage media, in any manner or order desired. The task of conversion between a user's logical perception of the data and the manner in which the data are actually stored physically in the data base is accomplished by the data base software. An example of this logical–to–physical mapping is shown in Figure 6.4.

6.4 ▪ APPLICATION VERSUS DATA BASE PROCESSING

The **application approach** to data base design is traditional. Each application within the organization has its own file bearing lit-

168 Data Base Concepts

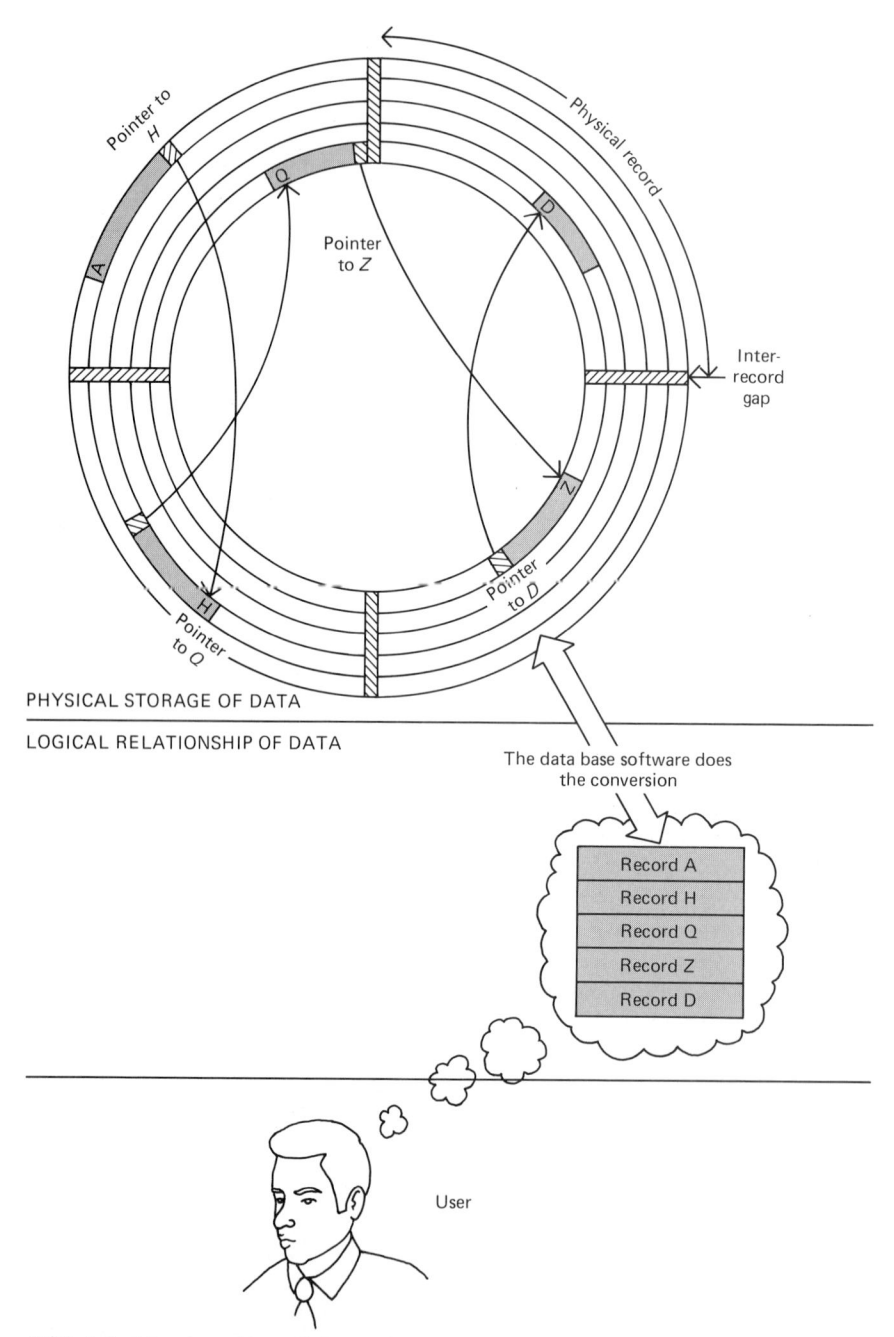

FIG. 6.4 Mapping of logical data relationship to physical storage of data.

tle, if any, relationship to other applications. The **data base approach** to data base design interrelates various files, records, and data elements to increase the associative ability of the data base. As indicated earlier in this chapter, the human mind represents an ideal data base and information system in that it has an amazing talent for associating facts. The data base approach strives to equal this ability.

General Overview

The basic problem in providing all users with a variety of information is the inflexibility of the application approach to designing the data base. The inputs and outputs are developed to perform a specialized function for a limited number of users. Every application area such as demand deposit accounting, savings, loans, accounts payable, accounts receivable, and inventory is developed strictly for that particular application with little or no relationship to other areas of the organization.

The form of input, layout, data attribute, data attribute value, data representation, and the way data are stored and coded may differ from one application to another. For example, a customer's data attribute, data attribute value, and data representation may be formulated differently in accounts receivable than in sales analysis applications. In accounts receivable, customer name may be given the data attribute of CUST-NAME with a value of first name first, middle initial, and last name. Data representation is alphabetic, with a maximum length of 30 characters. In sales analysis, the customer name may be given the data attribute of CUSTOMER-NAME with a value defined as last name first with first initial only. Data representation is alphabetic with a maximum length of 20 characters.

Such an approach limits the *logical association* of common data between different organizational areas. If the customer name differs, for example, the data cannot be shared, especially in a computer system, without significant changes being made. Consequently, data are fragmented over several incompatible application files. It is not impossible to eventually relate the application files and get the information needed. By simple brute force of repetitive searching, sorting, and merging several application files, information queries can be satisfied. In terms of setup costs, searching efficiency, and timeliness of the information a high price, however, must be paid.

Two Approaches Illustrated

The two extremes to data base design are illustrated in Figure 6.5. In the application approach, the order file, customer master file, inventory control file, and sales statistics file reside in physically separate files. Each file is specifically designed to meet its own application needs. Some of the fields in each file may represent the same thing (e.g., AB may represent an inventory item), but they may not be standard. The data base approach to data base design attempts to include and relate all elements into one logical file. This logical file may consist of a large number of physical files.

The application approach completely ignores the data base approach philosophy because little attempt is made to: (1) standardize record attributes, attribute values, and data representations; (2) associate common data elements logically; (3) synchronize file

170   Data Base Concepts

updates; and (4) minimize redundant data elements among files.

A very simple example of how to start designing data bases using the data base approach is depicted in Figure 6.6. In a typical banking operation, using the application approach to data base design, each functional area [demand deposit accounting (DDA), savings, and loans] is separated in its own file as shown in the BEFORE part of the figure. A person named J. Jones is a customer at this bank and she has a checking account, a savings account for a new home, and a commercial loan. Identifying data about Jones is duplicated in each application file. The DDA file is updated twice daily, the loan file each night, and the savings file twice a week. For all practical purposes, the bank's processing is handled as three distinct operations and Jones is

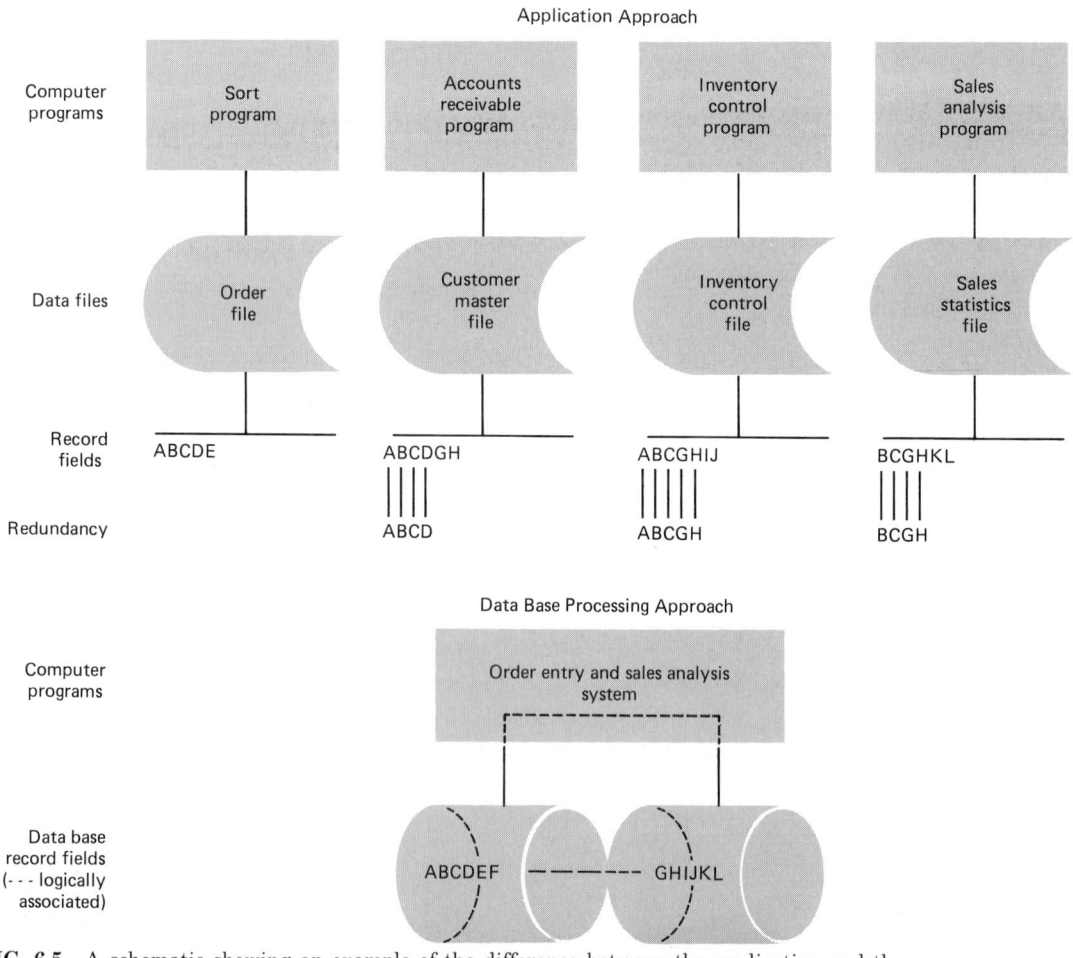

FIG. 6.5 A schematic showing an example of the difference between the application and the data base processing approach to data base design.

treated as three different customers. Any association between the files is difficult because the file updates are not synchronized. Although not shown in the example, different record formats between files also add to the problem of data association.

To eliminate some of the problems of the application approach, all common data concerning each customer are withdrawn from each file and included in one file. The customer number and name become the key data elements to coordinate and associate data pertaining to the bank's total operations. All transactions and inquiries about a customer are handled through the customer file. This file contains all customers of the bank. Each customer record contains a special field that points to or associates the customer record with all DDA, savings, and loan data, where appropriate. All transactions are updated as they occur. This results in a data base that is current and synchronized. Also, any transfer between accounts (e.g., a transfer from savings to DDA) is handled easily. And if any area of the bank requires specific information about a particular area, its request can also be provided.

The Changing User/System Interface

As stated earlier, we are moving into an era of user-oriented systems. A significant char-

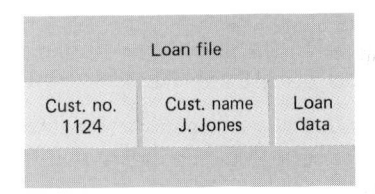

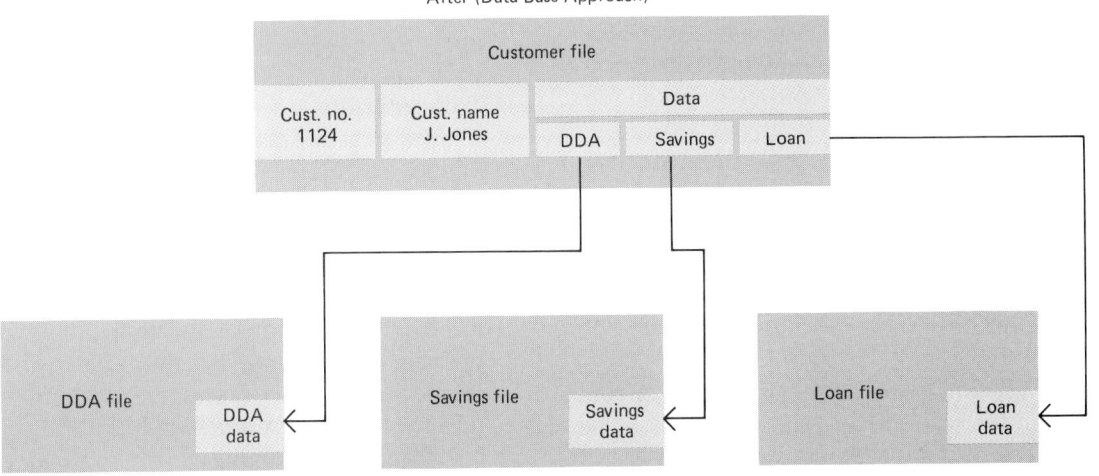

FIG. 6.6 A simple illustration of how to apply the data base processing approach to data base design.

acteristic that distinguishes information systems developed via the data base approach, as opposed to the application approach, is the difference in the user interaction capabilities. The introduction of online terminals, data communication, and DASD represent the technology that allows users to interact with the system. Well designed data bases with logical association supply the information needed by the user.

With application systems, the relationship between the users and the system is, at best, secondhand, with intermediaries providing a report at the conclusion of a predetermined processing cycle. Special requests for information can take days or possibly weeks.

Advantages of the Data Base Approach to Data Base Design

The advantages of the data base approach to data base design are summarized below.

1. *Associative data elements.* This approach provides a data base with the ability to associate data in a manner that is applicable to the interrelated functions of the organization. Broader, more coordinated, and more relevant information service can be provided users throughout the organization. Timeliness of information is increased because the updating of files occurs simultaneously (i.e., when a transaction occurs, all logical files affected by that transaction are updated). Thus, management is afforded a better opportunity to effect synchronized operations.

2. *Data independence.* Data independence allows changes in location and data representations of fields, without users (including application programmers) being aware of these changes. There are different levels of independence, such as: (a) user must know only the attribute name(s) of the data element(s) needed; (b) user must know attribute name, data representation, and file name; (c) user must know attribute name, data representation, file name, and data organization or association technique; and (d) user must know all of above plus physical storage device characteristics.

3. *Reduced data duplication.* More logical association of data elements minimizes data duplication. For example, with a data base approach a customer's name may be stored once, whereas it may be stored several times in a data base in which an application approach has been used. In addition to reducing the need for storage, reduction in data duplication helps to decrease errors and inconsistencies.

4. *Standardization.* Record formats and data names are standard throughout the organization for consistency in application.

5. *User/System interface.* The data base approach has the ability to provide users with a direct interface with the data base. This interface gives faster response and allows users to interrogate the data base and make inquiries that are basically unanticipated. For example, the personnel manager might interrogate the data base to determine how many electrical engineers the company has in its employ who are located in the midwest division, have ten years' experience, are unmarried, and speak French. The sales manager may wish to know the names and locations of customers who purchased over 100 cases of Product XYZ in the last 30 days. In a

matter of minutes, or even concurrently, other inquiries can be made that require a completely different response. Direct interface with the data base will help reduce voluminous reports because the user zooms in on only the information needed.

6. *Growth potential.* There is an ability to grow without a major overhaul of the system. Even with thorough systems analysis of users' needs, users cannot anticipate all requirements that they might have nor can they guarantee that present requirements will remain unchanged. If the data base is organized on the basis of functional relationships and common associations, thus modeling the operations of the organization and the flow of material and activities, then a major change in users of the system should not create a need for significant changes to be made in the data base design. For example, Manager B might replace Manager A, make many more requests than A, want more (or less) detail than A, and still be accommodated by the same data base design.

6.5 ▪ DATA BASE MANAGEMENT SYSTEMS

Data base management systems are large, complex software packages that are written in languages such as BAL (Basic Assembler Language), FORTRAN (FORmula TRANslator), COBOL (COmmon Business Oriented Language), or PL/1 (Programming Language 1). They have filled a large portion of the gap between the ordinary user (e.g., order entry clerk, marketing vice president), the application programmer, and the computer. Nonprogrammer users can now at least "shake hands" on their own with the computer. A data base management system (DBMS) can give these users (or nonprogrammer users) relatively powerful commands without having to be introduced by a programmer or some other technically proficient computer intermediary. Likewise, data base management systems have greatly extended the application programmer's ability to handle complex data association structures and to supply timely reports for a variety of users, with less difficulty and a smaller investment in programming time than ever before.

Specifically, the DBMS provides users with a set of language commands for the explicit purpose of accessing information from the data base. To the user of the DBMS, most of the internal operations and data structure are transparent (i.e., the users do not need to be concerned with the physical appearance of data, its physical storage location, and other technicalities). Although the degree of transparency varies among different packages, it has the net effect of isolating users from technical considerations.

Operational and Control Features

Users who possess a wide variety of technical skills have a common need. Each wants to obtain specific data from the data base in a certain form. To accommodate such needs, a DBMS has a number of operational and control features. The dimensions of each feature are described below:

1. *Access.* Method, mode, and type of access are the most important dimensions by which access to the data base can be achieved. Users direct the DBMS by employing either a *query* language, which is composed of special English-like statements, or a *host* computer language such as COBOL, FORTRAN, or BASIC. A

query language is best for users who do not possess a high degree of programming skill; a host language is more suitable for application programmers who practice their skills on a daily basis.

Mode of access to the data base through the DBMS can be either *batch* or *interactive*. Payroll is an example of an application that normally accesses the data base in batch mode. In contrast, travel agency personnel making airline reservations almost always require access to the data base in an interactive mode.

User requests can be classified as *static* or *dynamic*. Airline reservation agents are good examples of individuals who, through the touch of a key, make fixed requests concerning the availability of seats on a certain flight, the cost of a one-way, economy fare between two cities, the scheduled departure time for a certain flight, and so on. Agents are unlikely to have the capability of inquiring as to the number of hours flown in a week of each of the crew members on a flight. This last request is dynamic. It is composed to satisfy the *ad hoc* needs of users.

2. *Identification.* Users can identify data to a DBMS by one of three methods. The most basic method of data identification is *sequential*. Processing starts at the beginning of the data base and records are read until the desired data are found. Sequential identification implies that the data are ordered. It is appropriate only if all data records contain the same data fields.

Direct processing is a second way of identifying data. Discrimination among records is accomplished by users supplying unique keys. The system applies an algorithm to the key to convert it to a physical storage location. In this way only the data records desired are processed.

Identification by attribute is the final way a user can identify data. By this we mean that a user can obtain all records containing a specific data value. For example, a user might want records of all employees who have at least 10 years of service with the organization. Perhaps by means of a secondary index, only records containing the user-specified data value will be processed.

3. *Security.* A data base system may contain vast amounts of data. These data may summarize the condition of the organization and allow it to operate. Frequently, the data base is an organization's most prized asset.

As with anything of value to the organization, management wants to ensure that the data base will be as secure as possible.

To protect a data base from unauthorized intrusion and accidental or intentional alteration, password, log, edit check, and encryption techniques are used. *Passwords* are the most common techniques for making the data base secure. Before a user can obtain access to protected data, the correct password must be supplied; or, a password may allow data to be accessed, but not altered or deleted.

Logs are another security technique. Every time access/modification is made to the data base an entry is generated in a log. The entry includes date, time, user identification, program name, location, and access type. Periodically the log is examined for suspicious activity.

Edit checks are a third security technique. Edit checks prevent the unintentional modification of data by validating the accuracy of data entering the system. For example, edit checks prevent hourly pay rates from being established that are above a certain ceiling, say $15.00.

A final security technique is data encryption. A data value can be *encrypted* by squaring it, adding a constant to it, or by replacing one character with another. In this way, data are protected from line tapping and against access by programs outside the system.

4. *Concurrency.* A data base is a resource shared by many users. Sharing of data eventually leads to two or more users accessing, and attempting to modify the same data. When this happens the following sequence of activities is likely to occur:
   - User X retrieves data from the data base.
   - User Y retrieves the same data from the data base.
   - User X changes the data and returns the data to the data base.
   - User Y changes the data and returns the data to the data base.

What has happened is that user X's change has been lost because user Y did not modify the data modified by user X.

Compromise of integrity of the data due to concurrency can be prevented by lockout and notification. *Lockout* means that users are prohibited from accessing data that are currently being examined by another user. *Notification* means that the data base system notifies a user that previously retrieved data have been modified by another user. The notified user must then reissue the retrieve command to obtain the modified data.

5. *Backup and recovery.* A data problem may cause an erroneous piece of data to be obtained, a power failure may cause the system to "crash," or a program may incorrectly update an important data file. These are examples of problems that necessitate some type of *backup* and *recovery* system. Backup and recovery systems consist of two tasks. First, the data base is dumped periodically. That is, data are copied from their normal storage medium to a secondary storage medium (e.g., magnetic tape). Second, data base modifications are recorded in log files. When changes are made to the data base, the DBMS records the data before the change, after the change, or both.

Suppose data errors have been created by a program bug. By reapplying the before images contained in the log (*roll backward*) to the data base, a clean version of the data can be created. If a catastrophic system failure should befall the data base, recovery can be made by restoring the data base from the dump and applying all after images contained in the log (*roll forward*). The system is restarted using the restored data base.

DBMS Availability

What follows is a summary of five of the most popular, commercially available DBMSs. Figure 6.7 describes these DBMSs in terms of their operational and control feature.

1. *ADABAS* is supplied by Software AG of North America. It is supported for large IBM and IBM-compatible processors; it is used by more than 550 users. Monthly lease price is from $1875 to $2500.

2. *IDMS* is marketed by Cullinane Corporation. Like ADABAS, it is supported for

176 Data Base Concepts

DBMS	ACCESS: Access Method Query Language	ACCESS: Host Languages	ACCESS: Access Mode Batch/Interactive	IDENTIFICATION: Direct	IDENTIFICATION: Attribute	SECURITY	CONCURRENCY	BACKUP AND RECOVERY
ADABASE	ADASCRIPT	COBOL, PL/1, FORTRAN, Assembler	Yes/Yes	Yes	Secondary index for each field	Password for update at file and field level; encryption on a file basis	Yes	Before and after images are taken; automatic repair of the data base after a systems failure
IDMS	None	COBOL, PL/1, ASM FORTRAN, RPG II	Yes/Yes	Yes	No	Password protection, data base access mode restrictions (retrieval or update) and restricted processing options (exclusive, protected, unspecified)	Yes	Before and after images are taken, utilities to roll a file backward or forward
IMS	GIS	COBOL, PL/1, Assembler	Yes/Yes	Yes	Secondary indices	Password and terminal access control	Yes	Systems log to record data base modifications; roll forward or backward
SYSTEM 2000	SYSTEM 2000	COBOL, FORTRAN, PL/1, Assembler	Yes/Yes	Yes	Hierarchical, secondary keys	Password to field level	Yes	Transaction and activity log, roll forward
TOTAL	T-ASK	COBOL, FORTRAN, PL/1, Assembler, RPG II	Yes/Yes	Yes	No	Password to field level	Yes	Before and after images are taken, roll backward and forward

FIG. 6.7 Operational and control features of five DBMSs.

large IBM processors. The current number of users of IDMS is 460. The base rental price of IDMS is $50,000.
3. *IMS* is a product of IBM, designed to run on their large computers. About 1500 users pay a monthly license fee of from $1045 to $1265 for IMS.
4. *SYSTEM 2000* is supplied by Intel Systems Corporation. Besides large IBM processors, SYSTEM 2000 is supported for CDC Cyber series and Univac 1100 series processors. SYSTEM 2000 has a starting base price of $45,000 and has been sold to over 700 users.
5. *TOTAL* is supported for more types of processors than any other DBMS. In fact, TOTAL is supported for most major minicomputers. At present, users number 3000. The base price for TOTAL starts at $18,500.

SUMMARY

The data base is one design block of the information system. Some authorities have referred to it as the foundation of the information system. Physically, it may consist of a number of storage media, including various paper forms and filing cabinets, microfilm and microfiches, and magnetizable files. Logically, the data elements stored on the file media are associated to provide a variety of information to a number of users.

The traditional approach to data base design has been to develop a separate file for each application. This approach limits the ability to associate data of one application with data of other applications effectively. For example, sales reporting may be treated as one application with its own file and computer program. Inventory control may be treated as a separate application. Accounts receivable may be handled in yet another way; and so forth. Using the data base approach philosophy, however, these applications are interrelated to provide an associated data base that serves many users with a multiplicity of timely information. The data base approach to data base design also helps to standardize operations and data names, synchronize file updates, decrease data redundancy, reduce duplication of processing, and increase the ability of nonprogrammer users to interface in an online mode with the information system without help from professional intermediaries (e.g., programmers).

In a computer environment the logical association of data is realized through the use of special programs referred to as data base management systems. This data association transcends the physical limits of individual magnetic tape reels or disk packs.

REVIEW QUESTIONS

6.1 Define the term "data base."

6.2 Identify the ways in which the terms "data attribute," "data attribute value," and "data representation" differ. Give your own example of each.

6.3 Distinguish between logical and physical files.

6.4 Discuss the major differences between the application approach and the data base approach to data base development.

6.5 What are the major advantages and disadvantages associated with applying the data base approach to data base development?

6.6 List the significant operational features of a DBMS. The significant control features.

QUESTIONS FOR DISCUSSION

6.1 "Every organization maintains a large data base. The problem confronting both management and the systems analyst today is how to organize this data base so that it can be more effectively utilized." Discuss fully.

6.2 "Today we design a data base; a few years ago we designed files. The activities are still the same, whatever you choose to call them." Discuss.

6.3 "The data base is the underlying and basic component of an information system." Discuss fully.

6.4 "We spent nearly three years and $100,000 and have still not identified everything that should be in our data base." Discuss.

6.5 "Online processing and direct access to records requires sophisticated, elaborate, and expensive hardware and software." Discuss this statement.

6.6 "Most organizations operate under a great deal of pressure that emanates from competition. This pressure tends to limit the amount of time available for planning and the execution of plans. The pressure of competition forces quick decisions and quicker action. How does an organization meet its competition? By offering a good product at reasonable cost and by maintaining a high level of customer service. This last aspect can be achieved by providing answers to questions concerning a multiplicity of matters, such as order status, scheduled shipment date, method of transportation, inventory availability, pricing schedules, change orders, and so forth." Comment on this statement, especially as it relates to the design of the data base.

6.7 "A data base design which will satisfy the needs of every organization is a mirage. We don't read about engineers trying to build one manufacturing process to fit every organization." Discuss this rationale.

6.8 "The concepts related to retrieving data from a file are the same whether the file contains payroll data, purchasing data, or production data. It doesn't seem to make much sense, reinventing the wheel for each system designed in each organization." Discuss this rationale.

6.9 "Before the average organization attempts to implement an integrated, online data base, they will have to acquire personnel with a greater understanding of communication hardware and software." Explain.

EXERCISES

6.1 Interview a manager from a local organization (preferably someone knowledgable about data processing) which is large enough to utilize a computer for processing data and information, or review the literature for a report or article that describes the data processing activities in a particular organization. The objectives of your efforts are to determine: (a) what data are contained in the computer-accessible data base; (b) to what extent is this data base integrated; (c) what is the philosophy of the organization as it relates to the development of information systems; (d) what are the goals of management concerning future expansion of the data base; and (e) what is the present hardware configuration? Prepare a report describing your findings.

6.2 Using your own experiences and some library and field research, identify the types of data files and records likely to be found supporting the following organization's operations (ignore considerations such as payroll, inventory control, miscellaneous accounting, and so forth):

1. A personnel recruiting agency.
2. An independent credit bureau.
3. A dating and escort service.
4. A dog breeders association.
5. A custom/antique jeweler.

6.3 From journals and magazines related to information and data processing, research one or more data base management systems being offered for purchase. Evaluate these packages in terms of the capabilities and functions they propose to perform.

6.4 Listed below is a series of documents and reports prepared by various types of organizations. Evaluate these informational outputs and determine the following: (a) what type of data files must be maintained to produce the output; (b) what data could be entered once for many uses; (c) what data must be entered each time the document is produced; and (d) what relationships exist, if any, among the data files you have identified?

1. An employee paycheck.
2. A year-to-date sales report by customer.
3. A purchase order for raw materials and miscellaneous supplies.
4. An invoice to customers for purchases.
5. An analysis of records of work performed, against a planned work schedule.
6. A check to vendors.

PROBLEMS

6.1 Zoot Suit Tailors, Inc. makes four models of men's suits. A customer initiates an order by mailing to Zoot Suit a document specifying the model chosen, with a specification of measurement, and the material necessary to make the suit. Upon receipt of the document, the receiving clerk assigns a particular tailor a copy of the specifications along with the material. The tailors are paid on a job basis.

Besides preparing payrolls for all employees of Zoot Suit, the information system must handle the following types of requests for information: (1) date order received; (2) status of work-in-process, (3) projected completion dates, and (4) measurement specifications. Moreover, when the order is filled and shipped to the customer, billing and payment information is often requested.

In general terms describe the data base you would recommend for Zoot Suit.

6.2 Ark–La–Tex Airlines has recently incorporated and has been given permission to set up operations, transporting passengers and freight, in eight southern cities: Dallas, Houston,

Lake Charles, Lafayette, Baton Rouge, New Orleans, Shreveport, and Little Rock.

Among other assets, they have 24 large planes ready for commercial service. They have leased storage and maintenance hangars at Dallas, Shreveport, and New Orleans. In addition, they have also leased ticket counter and baggage handling facilities at each of the eight airports.

You have been brought in as a consultant to present, in broad outline form, the kind of information system you recommend plus the kind of data base and hardware support such a system will require. Assume you will be in another part of the country on a different job for the next week, which means that you will have to depend on a narrative and descriptive report for fully communicating to management your broad system design alternatives. In addition to this report, you feel that it is necessary to prepare a list of questions, that must be answered by management, before embarking on a more detailed study. For convenience, and for your reference, assume that the problems (e.g., scheduling, reservation, passenger service) of Ark–La–Tex will be similar to the problems of any other airline.

6.3 The capture of data and the dissemination of information is quite often a manufacturing organization's (as well as many other organizations') most difficult problem. Data are voluminous, scattered, and often difficult to obtain. Five general kinds of information dissemination exist: (1) replies to inquiries, (2) standard routine reports, (3) exception reports, (4) cost reports, and (5) special reports.

Implementation of an integrated data base, using the data base approach, normally can handle all the mainstream data needed for the operation of the organization. The data are stored on magnetic disk files and are, for the most part, online. Because of this structure, summary and detail information can be retrieved.

Each of the data base records is linked in a particular way wherein the user can make detail requests for reports and/or make specific interrogations. For example, a part number accessed from an item master record may lead to a bill of materials (or product structure), work-in-process and degree of completion, standard routing, an open purchase order status, cost data, and so forth. The illustration below is an example of an Item Master Record within the Item Master File.

182 Data Base Concepts

ITEM MASTER RECORD

Product Item Number	Description	Unit of Measure	Inventory Value Code	Engineering Cross Reference	
				To standard routing	To product structure

Order Policy	Forecasting	Lead Times	Unit Costs	Unit Prices	Parts Usage History	Current Period Inventory	Inventory on Hand (Qty. and locations)

Gross Requirements	Planned and Released Orders	Purchasing Cross Reference				Open Job Order Control Cross Reference		
		Total qty.	Purchase master	Vendor master	Detail requisitions	Total qty.	Order summary	Operation detail

The Item Master Record layout represents a typical record design with its cross references that allow the integration of the mainstream data flow. This cross referencing, or linkage, is the key reason why information is accessible via multiple points throughout the organization. With this cross referencing, no longer is it necessary to spend hours or days trying to capture and bring together data scattered in files, file drawers, or ledger cards. Moreover, the files are updated simultaneously.

The Item Master Record is stored in the Item Master File. Also, in this file module are the Work Center Master and the Tool Master. Three other file modules linked to the Item Master module include:

1. *Purchase Order Control.* This file module is composed of: (1) purchase master, (2) vendor master, (3) purchase on order, and (4) open purchase requisition.
2. *Open Job Order Control.* This file module represents production planned, and on order, and is made up of: (1) order summary and detail and (2) operation detail.
3. *Engineering Indices.* This file module is comprised of: (1) standard routing and (2) product structure (bill of materials).

Considering the above information, develop a schematic showing how these file modules should be linked for overall information access. Also, list the functional areas to which information from the data base will flow and examples of what kind of information it will be. Examples of functional areas and information flowing to these functional areas are:

1. *Work Center Control:* (1) labor reporting, (2) material movement and logistics, (3) work-in-process, (4) costing, and (5) reporting of variances.
2. *Capacity Planning:* (1) projected work center load report, (2) planned order load, (3) order start date, and (4) production leveling.

6.4 In a typical manufacturing organization the data flow, to one degree or another, affects eleven major areas:

1. Sales analysis for decision making for management objectives, determination of product line, market, advertising, sales promotion, and production scheduling.
2. Management control based on reporting of costs and variances from standards.
3. Engineering which includes research and development, product design, specifications, catalogs, and bills of materials.
4. Inventory control.
5. Manufacturing facilities which include plant and equipment personnel, maintenance, and machine loading schedule.
6. Purchasing, receiving, and shipping.
7. Payment to vendors.
8. Determination of income and preparation of reports to stockholders and governmental agencies.
9. Credit checking.
10. Handling customer orders.
11. Providing reports to management such as variance reports, sales statistics, market analysis, and income statements.

With these areas in mind, develop a flow diagram of how you visualize the mainstream flow of data and information would occur in this typical manufacturing organization. Make any assumptions that you deem necessary.

BIBLIOGRAPHY

"A Buyers Guide to Data Base Management Systems," *Datapro 70,* Delran, NJ.: Datapro Research Corporation, September 1980.

Beehler, "Integrated MIS: A Data Base Reality," *Journal of Systems Management,* February 1976.

Canning, "The Debate on Data Base Management," *EDP Analyzer,* March 1972.

CODASYL Data Base Task Group April 71 Report, New York: Association for Computing Machinery, 1971.

CODASYL System Committee Technical Report, *Feature Analysis of Generalized Data Base Management Systems,* New York: Association for Computing Machinery, 1971.

Cohen, *Data Base Management Systems,* Wellesley, MA.: Q.E.D. Information Sciences, Inc., 1976.

Donovan, "Database System Approach to Management Decision Support," *Database Systems,* December 1976.

Fry and Sibley, "Evolution of Data-Base Management Systems," *ACM Computing Surveys,* March 1976.

Gillenson, "Back to Data Bas(e)ics," *Computerworld,* December 8, 1980.

Hunter, "Decoding the CODASYL Database," *Computer Decisions,* January 1977.

Inmon, *Effective Data Base Design,* Englewood Cliffs, NJ.: Prentice-Hall, Inc., 1981.

Kroenke, *Database Processing,* Chicago: Science Research Associates, 1977.

Mader, *Information Systems,* Second Edition, Chicago: Science Research Associates, 1979.

Martin, *Computer Data-Base Organization,* Second Edition, Englewood Cliffs, NJ.: Prentice-Hall, Inc., 1977.

Prendergast, "Selecting a Data Management System," *Computer Decisions,* August 1972.

CHAPTER

7

Coding, Sorting, and Searching Data

7.1 ▪ INTRODUCTION

Data emanates from various transactions and events which occur in all organizations: a sale is made which must be recorded; a student enrolls in college and takes a variety of courses for which she receives credit; and a patient enters a hospital to receive certain treatment and medication that must be meticulously recorded. All of these transactions and events create voluminous amounts of scattered data which must be collected, processed, and retrieved from time to time.

Within an information system data can be stored in a myriad of devices such as library cards, file folders, documents, index cards, and computer accessible devices. Regardless of the devices used for storage, data are usually input into the system according to some predetermined structure which is based on future processing and retrieval requirements. It is fairly simple to collect data; however, if data items are not systematically coded and ordered it may be difficult, if not impossible, to gain access to the data once it has been collected and stored.

To design the complex information systems needed by organizations today, the systems analyst must understand thoroughly different coding structures, the processes by which data are ordered, and finally, the common methods employed to search data.

The objectives of this chapter are:

1. To identify the major considerations related to coding structures and their design.
2. To identify and explain the primary types of coding structures.
3. To provide a general understanding of internal and external sorting procedures.
4. To introduce several methods applicable to searching ordered codes.

7.2 ▪ CODING CONSIDERATIONS

Codes provide an abbreviated structure for classifying items to record, communicate, process, and retrieve data. Codes are designed to provide unique identification of the data to be coded. A person may be classified as female or male. The code that represents this classification is F or M. Codes can use letters, numbers, words, and special symbols, or any combination thereof; however, systems analysts are primarily concerned with code structures having numbers and letters. The use of computers has provided a strong impetus to incorporate codes, especially numercal codes, in the processing of information. In this section the functions of codes, the available coding symbols, and some considerations of code design are discussed.

Function of Codes

The function of a code is twofold: it provides a brief, unambiguous identification for a data item, record, or file, and it confers a special meaning to these data structures which will assist in retrieval and manipulation.

Considering the volume of data that already has to be processed in most organizations, lengthy definitions, descriptions, names, adversely affect both processing efficiency and accuracy. Efficiency is affected since as more characters are used in a name or description, more time must be spent in reporting, recording, acknowledging, and understanding. Moreover, the amount of space required to record or store the necessary characters or figures is important. This effect on efficiency occurs with manual operations and in machine execution. Accuracy, on the other hand, is almost impossible to achieve when a given name, description, or characteristic must be used by many different individuals in the processing of data. Standardization of data item identification is a must in computer processing.

The use of a properly designed coding structure helps to alleviate all of these problems. For example, a three-digit code uniquely and concisely identifies 1000 different items and, obviously, requires much less space than a language description for each of these items.

In addition to using codes for enhancing processing efficiency and accuracy, coding structures can be established to provide special meaning for the data item. For example, an employee might be coded on an employee master file for sex, age, education level, skill, residence, benefit program participation, and so forth. Once the coding has been accomplished, data concerning this employee can be sorted, summarized, or statistically analyzed according to certain prescribed algorithms.

Codes are required for both routine batch processing and online inquiry systems. The use of coding systems in modern organizations varies widely from very crude, simplistic structures to quite sophisticated systems. A well planned coding structure is an essential component of any viable information processing system today.

Coding Symbols

In selecting a given code format, the character set available must be considered. Analysts have a large number of symbols at their disposal. They have numbers, letters, and special characters (e.g., dollar sign, colon, period). However, numbers are by far the most widely used symbols in coding systems, especially where electromechanical and electronic equipment are utilized. This is true today because most computers on the market can store two digits in the same storage location as one alphabetic character. Consequently storage requirements are reduced and processing efficiency is increased.

A *numerical* code provides up to 10 classifications for each digit in the code. These codes are quite amenable to machine processing; however, if manually processed by clerks, large numerical codes are difficult to remember accurately. *Alphabetic* codes provide up to 26 classifications for each position in the code. Codes which use both numbers and letters are called *alphanumeric*. Numbers and letters can be mnemonically structured to help the user remember what the code stands for. For example, 3 BR CV, may represent a three-inch brass check valve.

While numeric, alphabetic, and alphanumeric codes comprise the majority of coding structures used in information processing today, future systems will most likely provide for data coded in special symbols which are understandable only by special scanning or sensing devices. Symbolic coding structures seem appropriate in many point-of-sale (POS) applications where vast amounts of data are available but quite costly to collect with present input methods and procedures.

Code Design

Many possible arrangements of digits, letters, and characters can be designed into codes. A great deal of thought, however, must go into the coding scheme if it is to satisfy a variety of users. The following considerations should be kept in mind when designing codes.

1. The coding scheme must logically fit the needs of the users and the processing method used. An arbitrary code, such as PDQ, assigned to represent an accounting class, is confusing to users.

2. Each code must be a unique representation for the item it identifies. For example, an inventory item number or employee identification code must identify one and only one inventory item or employee.

3. The code design must be flexible to accommodate changing requirements. It is too costly and confusing to have to change the coding structure every few months or years. The coding structure should not be so extensive, however, that part of it will not be used for a number of years. For example, if a 16-digit code will handle all processing needs for three or four years, then it would be costly to set up a code larger than sixteen digits. There is a basic trade-off in the length of the code. Normally, the shorter the code, the less is the cost of classification, preparation, storage, and transmission. On the other hand, the longer the code, the better the translation, and the wider the variety of data retrieval, statistical analysis, and information processing.

4. The code structure must be easily understood by various users in the organization. It should be simple, practical, and as meaningful as possible.

5. As discussed before in this text, a particular transaction can affect a number of files in the information system. For example, an order from a customer triggers changes in inventory, sales, accounts receivable, purchasing, shipping, etc., and requires credit checks. Therefore, a code structure must be designed to be meaningful in all related situations. Codes must pertain to the overall functions of the organization. It might not be feasible to design one code structure that would take care of all requirements for each individual function or subdivision in the organization. The structure, however, must be broad

enough to encompass all functions and provide a basic cross-reference for any additional special-purpose codes for a variety of processing requirements.

6. Standardization procedures should be established to decrease confusion and misinterpretation for persons working with the code structure. Some of the procedures that can be easily standardized in most systems are: (1) Elimination of characters which are similar in appearance: The range of permissible characters to be used should be selected on the basis of their dissimilarity to other characters. For example, the letters O, Z, I, S, and V may be confused with the digits 0, 2, 1, 5, and the letter U, respectively. (2) Gaps in code numbers should be avoided where possible. (3) Days and weeks should be numbered. For example, days are numbered one to seven and weeks are numbered consecutively beginning with the start of the fiscal period. (4) The use of a twenty-four hour clock alleviates the AM/PM confusion. (5) Dates should be designed by digits using the Year Month Day format YYMMDD, (where September 18, 1982, becomes 820918); or through the use of the Julian Calendar dating system.

7. Where possible, letters that sound the same should be avoided (e.g., B, C, D, G, P, and T, or the letters M and N). In alphabetic codes or portions of codes having three or more consecutive alphabetic characters, avoid the use of vowels (A, E, I, O, and U) to prevent inadvertent formation of recognizable English words. In cases where the code is structured with both alphabetic and numeric characters, similar character types should be grouped and not dispersed throughout the code. For example, fewer errors occur in a three-character code where the structure is alpha-alpha-numeric (e.g., WW2) than in a sequence of alpha-numeric-alpha (e.g., W2W).

8. The layout of the code itself should be equal in length. For example, a chart of accounts code should read 001–199 (for assets), not 1–199.

9. Codes longer than four alphabetic or five numeric characters should be divided into smaller segments (sometimes called **chunking**) for purposes of reliable human recording and display (it makes no difference to the computer because the computer likes to process contiguous data). For the human, 726–49–6135 is more easily remembered and is more accurately recorded than 726496135.

10. In instances where a long code is an essential element in processing information, particularly where financial control is involved or where humans are required to transcribe this code repeatedly, its accuracy is verified by using a check digit. The **check digit** is generated when the code is initially assigned to a data element, and, in fact, becomes part of the code itself. The check digit is determined by performing a prescribed arithmetic operation on the number. In subsequent processings, this same arithmetic operation can be performed to ensure that the number has not been recorded incorrectly.

A check digit guards against typical errors such as[1]:

[1] From *Systems Analysis,* edited by Alan Daniels and Donald Yeates. Copyright National Computing Centre, 1969. Adapted by permission of Sir Isaac Pitman and Sons, Limited. Reprinted by permission of Science Research Associates, Inc.

1. Transcription errors, in which the wrong number is written, such as 1 instead of 7.
2. Transposition errors, in which the correct numbers are written but their positions are reversed, such as 2134 for 1234.
3. Double transposition errors, in which numbers are interchanged between columns, such as 21963 for 26913.
4. Random errors, which are a combination of two or more of the above, or any other error not listed.

The Modulus 11 check digit method is the most frequently used method to generate check digits. Three different approaches to using Modulus 11 are illustrated below.

1. Arithmetic progression.
   Account number: 1 2 3 4 5
                        × × × × ×
   Multiply by: 6 5 4 3 2
   Add result of multiplication:
       6 + 10 + 12 + 12 + 10 = 50
   Subtract 50 from next highest multiple of 11: 55 − 50 = 5
   Check digit = 5
   New account number: 12345-5

2. Geometric progression.
   Account number: 1   2 3 4 5
                        ×   × × × ×
   Multiply by: 32 16 8 4 2
   Add result of multiplication:
       32 + 32 + 24 + 16 + 10 = 114
   Subtract 114 from next highest multiple of 11: 121 − 114 = 7
   Check digit = 7
   New account number: 12345-7

3. Prime number weighting.
   Account number: 1   2 3 4 5
                        ×   × × × ×
   Multiply by: 17 13 7 5 3
   Add result of multiplication:
       17 + 26 + 21 + 20 + 15 = 99
   Subtract 99 from next higher multiple of 11: 99 − 99 = 0
   New account number: 12345-0

It has been determined statistically that Modulus 11 with prime number weighting, a method developed by Friden, Inc., will detect all possible transposition and transcription errors..

It should be pointed out that under any Modulus 11 system a percentage of all numbers will have the number "10" as a check digit. Since the check digit must consist of one digit only, all numbers that lead to a check digit of 10 must be discarded and cannot be assigned.

Although it is most common that the check digit becomes the last digit of an account number, such placement is not necessarily imperative. As long as the check digit is placed in a constant position, most pieces of equipment can verify the correctness of the account number whatever the position of the check digit. In a manual or semiautomatic operation there are many advantages to be gained by separating the check digit from the main number by means of a hyphen, since it is much easier to sort and read the account number. In the case of fully automatic equipment and computers, the placing of the check digit should be dependent upon the type of equipment used and the system to be employed.

11. When calculating the capacity of a given code for covering all situations while still maintaining code uniqueness, the following formula applies: $C = S^p$, where C is the total available code combinations possible, S is the number of unique characters in the set, and p is the number of code positions. For example, a three-digit code with the char-

acters 0 through 9, would have 1000 = 10^3 unique code combinations. If the alphabetic characters O, Z, I, S, and V were eliminated from the permissible character set of an alphanumeric code of length two, then 961 (31^2) unique code combinations would be available.

Designing coding schemes is one of the most important tasks of the systems analyst. Any coding scheme should be designed for the organization as a whole. For example, a code for the chart of accounts should encompass all functions of the organization or should at least provide a cross-reference for more detailed, special-purpose coding systems.

The coding system must be designed to accumulate and classify all data of the organization, in the most efficient and economical way, and to respond to the informational requirements of a variety of users.

7.3 ▪ TYPES OF CODE STRUCTURES

Codes can be formatted in a variety of ways and selecting a specific *code structure* is critical. The choice of code structures is fairly extensive. In this section, several code types used in a number of organizations are discussed and an attempt is made to indicate the advantages and disadvantages of each. In practice, the systems analyst might select a code structure that is some combination of the following codes.

Sequential Code

A **sequential** (or **serial**) **code** represents a one-for-one consecutive assignment of numbers to such items as payroll checks, account numbers, inventory items, purchase orders, employees, and so on. Any list of items is simply numbered consecutively, usually starting with one. For example, a sequential coding scheme for inventory items might be structured as follows:

001	WRENCHES
002	HAMMERS
003	SAWS
.	.
.	.
.	.
678	VALVES

The advantages of a sequential coding scheme are that:

1. It is the scheme most commonly used, because of its simplicity.
2. It is short and unique.
3. It provides a simple way of locating records or documents on which the code appears, assuming that the requestor knows the code.
4. It is simple to administer.

The disadvantages of a sequential code are that:

1. It has no logical basis. It contains no useful information about the item except its order in the list.
2. It is inflexible because it cannot accommodate changes. Additions can be made only at the end of the numerical sequence. Vacant number codes must either remain open or wait for reassignment at a later date.

Frequently, the term random number code is mistakenly applied to the sequential code just described. The difference between a sequential and a random code is the number list from which the code values are assigned. The *random code* is drawn from a number list that is not in any detectable order or sequence. There are computer programs available to produce these random number lists. Each additional item to be coded is given the next number in the random list. This method forces the coder to look up the next number on the list because there is no logical way to predict what the next number will be when the last-used number is known. In a sequential list, if 200 were the last number assigned, the next one would be 201. The next number on a random list might be 163. This forced look-up is supposed to reduce errors in coding, but in actual practice it tends to introduce problems of control. Properly controlled sequential lists have proved less error-prone than random lists.

Block Code

The **block code** classifies items into certain groups where blocks of numbers (or letters) are assigned to particular classifications. The block representing a particular classification must be set up on the basis of an expected maximum utilization of that block.

A typical example of a block scheme is the ZIP Code (Zoning Improvement Plan) used by the United States Postal Service. This coding scheme uses a five-digit code divided into blocks as follows:

```
ZIP Code:  X  XX  XX
           |  |   |
           |  |   Sectional Center
           |  |   within State (Local
           |  |   Postal Station)
           |  |
           |  Sectional Sorting Center
           |  (State or Parts of State)
           |
           Major Regions or Geographical
           Areas of Country
```

For another example of a block code, suppose that customers are classified into five groups; wholesale, retail, educational, military, and government. In addition there is a classification according to amount of purchases for credit analysis. This classification could be handled as illustrated in Figure 7.1.

Type of Customer (first digit)		Amount of Purchases (second digit)	
Code	Classification	Code	Classification ($)
1	Wholesale	1	Up to 9999
2	Retail	2	10,000–29,999
3	Educational	3	30,000–49,999
4	Military	4	50,000–99,999
5	Government	5	Over 99,999

FIG. 7.1 Example of a block coding structure.

A simple two-digit code could be used to classify type of customer and amount of purchase. For instance, the code 34 might represent an educational customer with purchases of $50,000–$99,999.

The basic format of a simple block code is further illustrated in Figure 7.2.

The equipment is classified into meaningful categories so that a code number identifies certain attributes of a particular piece of equipment. For instance, in the equipment file, those bulldozers on a rental contract and held by the airport division can be determined by accessing all records with a "2" in position 1, a "3" in position 2, and a "1" in position 4. Or we can retrieve any information or make any statistical analysis desired just so long as the code contains the requisite classifications.

The advantages of a block code are:

1. The value and position of the numbers have meaning.

Code Number \ Code Position	1	2	3	4
1	Truck	Lease	Service contract	Airport division
2	Bulldozer	Purchase	No service contract	Highway division
3	Grader	Rent	—	—
4	Pile driver	—	—	—
5	Crane	—	—	—

FIG. 7.2 Block coding structure.

2. The coding structure is amenable to information processing, in that data items can be easily retrieved, manipulated, analyzed, sorted, and so on.
3. A category of the code can easily be expanded unless that category has reached its maximum limit (e.g., our equipment example can handle only ten pieces of equipment, 0–9).
4. Whole categories can be added or deleted.

The disadvantages of a block code are:

1. The code length will depend upon the number of attributes classified. As a result codes can become quite lengthy.
2. In many instances the code will contain spare numbers (e.g., in our equipment example attributes 2, 3, and 4 have spare slots); however, this condition may not always represent a disadvantage.
3. Block codes used as identifiers or record keys pose significant systems maintenance problems when they require modification.

Variations of Block Codes

Like a cut gem, many items handled by organizations possess different facets. A code that describes each facet of the item in question, is referred to by some authorities as a *faceted code.* With this method, items are classified so that each facet of every item has a place. Each facet is further subdivided into its different parts. For example, consider the structure illustrated in Figure 7.3, which is designed to show the various facets available relative to an inventory of steel products.

With such a coding system, domestic hot-rolled flat iron of size 1" × 8" × 20' is coded 21208. This system creates some redundancy because certain combinations of numbers are illogical. For example, angle iron is not cold drawn or cast and its size is meaningful only in terms of thickness, width of each flange, and length. (Angle iron sizes are not shown in the illustration.)

Hierarchial block codes are developed on the basis of ascending significance. Conventionally, this structure starts with the most general, or most significant, aspect of the item as the left-most group of characters, and moves toward the right as subclasses or less significant aspects are classified.

For example, the clearing of checks through the Federal Reserve check clearing system uses a coding system developed by the American Bankers Association. This

Facet A (Source)	Facet B (Method of Production)	Facet C (Type)	Facet D (Size)*
1 = Foreign 2 = Domestic	1 = Hot-rolled 2 = Cold drawn 3 = Cast	1 = Angle 2 = Flat 3 = Sheet 4 = Bar 5 = Tubing	00 = 1/16" × 20' 01 = 1/8" × 20' 02 = 1/4" × 20' 03 = 1/2" × 20' 04 = 3/4" × 20' 05 = 1/4" × 40' 06 = 1/2" × 40' 07 = 3/4" × 40' 08 = 1" × 8" × 20'

*Partial list of sizes.

FIG. 7.3 A facet coding structure.

code uses a combination of standardized magnetic ink characters which include ten digits (0–9) and four special symbols. These characters are printed at the bottom of the document in three specific areas, as illustrated in Figure 7.4.

The transit number code is printed near the left edge of the document (or check). This classification uses 11 characters; four digits for the transit number, five digits for the American Bankers Association number, and a beginning and ending transit number symbol. The next classification represents, in order, the transaction code and the customer account number. The right-most characters, which are not part of the coding scheme per se, represent the dollar amount of the document (not shown in the illustration).

The hierarchical scheme is also quite applicable to the area of accounting where the left-most digits represent the account classification. Subsequent digits represent the item identification, its location in the warehouse, user department, and so on.

Decimal codes, such as the Dewey Dec-

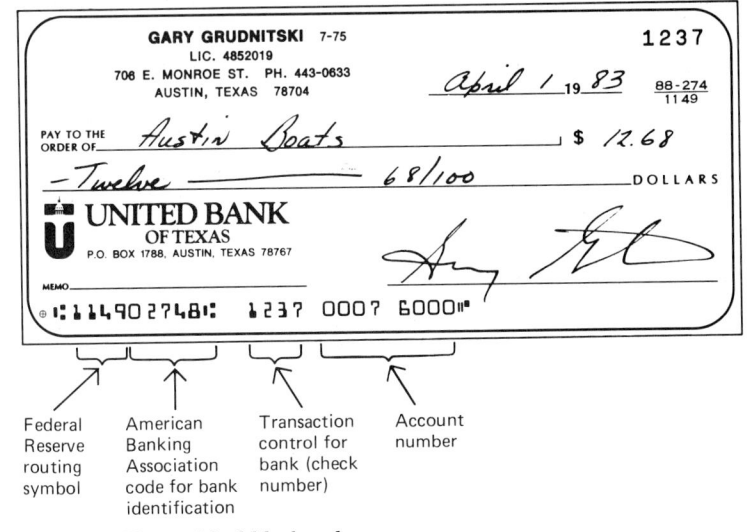

FIG. 7.4 Hierarchical block codes.

- Federal Reserve routing symbol
- American Banking Association code for bank identification
- Transaction control for bank (check number)
- Account number

Code	Field of Knowledge
600	Applied science
610.7	Health care
610.73	Nurses and nursing
610.732	Private duty nursing
610.733	Institutional nursing
610.734	Public health nursing
610.735	Industrial nursing
610.736	Special nursing
610.736.1	Psychological

FIG. 7.5 The use of decimal codes.

imal coding system, are basically hierarchical block codes, where the group of digits left of the decimal point represents the major classification and the digits to the right of the decimal point denote the subclassifications. As mentioned earlier, the Dewey Decimal system classifies books by dividing them into ten main knowledge groups. Each of these ten main groups is broken up into more specialized areas. For example, class 600–699, Applied Science is subdivided into ten special classes. And, in turn, each of these divisions is further subdivided. The numbers 630–639, for example, represent Agriculture, and are subdivided into such classes as Field Crops, Garden Crops, Dairy Products, and so on.

Using the area of applied science as an example this system can be subdivided into meaningful relationships in the field of nursing, as shown in Figure 7.5.

In addition, two similar areas may be related by linking two separate code numbers. For instance, human anatomy in the area of teratogenesis, coded 611.012, can be linked to biochemistry under human physiology, coded: 612.015, by use of a hyphen, resulting in 611.012–612.015, wherein these two linked codes signify that the designated book or article treats the first subject area from the viewpoint of the second.

Bar Codes

The example in Figure 7.6 represents an example of a bar code used in the grocery industry. This **bar code** is a computer-readable representation of the grocery industry's Universal Product Code (UPC), a voluntary ten-digit coding system used to identify grocery manufacturers and their products. The symbols can be easily read by the computer and converted into numbers that represent a particular code. The bars themselves merely represent the number code.

Each participating manufacturer is permanently assigned the first five digits of a ten-digit number. The number is similar to the sequential code discussed earlier. The last five digits (on the right) uniquely identify a particular manufacturer's product. For example, the manufacturer's number for Kellogg is 38000. Kellogg, in turn, assigns 01620 to Special K cereal in the 15-ounce box. Similarly, Hunt's tomato paste in the six-ounce can is 2700038815, where 27000 is Hunt's unique manufacturer's number and 38815 is the product's unique number. By changing the bar widths and spaces be-

FIG. 7.6 An example of a bar code used in the grocery industry.

tween the bars, all variations of products and sizes manufactured can be accommodated.

In a supermarket application, the computer matches the code to the correct price, product type, size, and other data already stored in the computer's data base. Results of each transaction are displayed and printed on a receipt at the same time. A typical receipt is shown in Figure 7.7.

This kind of point-of-sale (POS) system enables users to decrease checkout time; increase inventory control; eliminate the need for price marking individual items; improve resource and shelf allocation; reduce the probability of human error, pilferage, and fraud through cash register manipulations; and generally produce a broader range of more timely information to a variety of users. Some people, however, have discounted the usefulness of bar codes in supermarkets because: (1) items that are not easily coded (e.g., a sack of grapes) require special handling; (2) in some locations, consumer legislation requires each individual item to be marked; (3) optical or laser code readers are expensive; and (4) processing of customer purchases has not proven to be any faster than under conveneional methods.

A large number of effective applications of bar codes exist in other areas. For example, materials control personnel are using bar-coded labels and scanners in an integrated, online scheduling production control system. Each representative bar code is attached to specific components and subassemblies, which are monitored as they pass through production. These bar code labels contain mnemonic codes and color codes (e.g., red means chassis, blue means motor block) for human reading and identification. Such a system provides an accurate count and control of materials. It also provides

```
        HEB STORE #8
      2400 SOUTH CONGRESS
    07/06 16:34  5     219  62


          2 @ 1/.76
    PERRIER WTER       1.52*
    ALUMNUM FOIL        .49 TX
    GATORADE           3.39*
        MARKET         4.69*
    YACHTING           1.90 TX
        TOTAL         12.11
        CASH TEND     20.01

        SUBTOTAL      11.99
        TAX PAID        .12

    7.90 CHANGE

    BUY GOLD RUSH JEWELRY
```

FIG. 7.7 A typical grocery receipt.

timely performance, scheduling, and tracking information.

In other applications, bar codes are attached to windows on the sides of cars to identify authorized staff members for hospital parking lot control systems, where remote scanners read the bar code to activate entry and exit gates. Bar codes are attached to luggage in some airport terminals (e.g., Miami) for proper routing of luggage.

An endless number of possibilities exist for using the bar codes. For example, libraries can use them for circulation control. The dispensing of valuable resources, such as tools, equipment, drugs, and so forth, might be more effectively accounted for and controlled using bar codes.

Mnemonic Codes

A **mnemonic code** structure is characterized by the use of either letters or numbers or letter-and-number combinations that describe the item coded. The combinations are designed to aid memorization of the codes and association with the items they represent. For example, in our previous facet code for steel products, domestic hot-rolled flat iron size 1″ × 8″ × 20′ was coded 21208. But a code such as this may be meaningless to the human requestor. It may, therefore, be necessary to derive a mnemonic code (e.g., DFI-1 × 8 × 20) for efficiency of reference.

Mnemonic codes used in manual systems are not necessarily fixed length. To facilitate computer processing, high- or low-order blanks or zeros must frequently be added to make the code values a specified, constant length.

Some problems are connected with the use of mnemonic codes to identify long, unstable lists of items. Wherever item names beginning with the same letters are encountered, there may be a conflict of mnemonic use. To overcome this, the number of code characters is necessarily increased, thus increasing the likelihood that the combinations will be less memory-aiding for code users. Also, since descriptions may vary widely, it is difficult to maintain a code organization which conforms with a plan of classification.

Mnemonic codes are used to best advantage for identifying relatively short lists of items (generally 50 or fewer, unless the list is quite stable), coded for manual processing where it is necessary that the items be recognized by their code. A common problem, however, is that the code is likely to be misapplied when specific code values are subject to change and users rely too heavily on memory. Thus, to be effectively coded with mnemonics, entity sets must be relatively small and stable.

Phonetic Code

Under this method, a given name is analyzed according to certain rules (based on phonetic principles) and a code is derived that represents this name in abbreviated form. These codes are frequently used in applications that require the retrieval of persons by name rather than by a number (such as an account number). The code structure contains one letter followed by three digits, and has the form A123. Following is the "Soundex" code developed by Remington Rand.[2] The steps in deriving the code are:

1. Given any name, retain the first letter.
2. Delete the following: A E I O U Y W & H.
3. Assign numbers, as shown by the following list, to the remaining letters. Perform this procedure from left to right until three numbers are obtained. If the name is short and has insufficient consonants to generate three numbers, then insert zeroes to fill. The code now contains one letter plus three digits, or a four-position code.

Code Number	Letters To Be Included
1	B F P V
2	C G J K Q S X Z
3	D T
4	L
5	M N
6	R
0	Insufficient consonants

(Note: the digits 7, 8, and 9 are illegal in this scheme)

4. Example: By the rules above, the name BURCH is coded as B620, but that

---

[2] Remington Rand Brochure LVB809, "Soundex: Foolproof Filing System for Finding Any Name in The File."

code also represents BIRCH. The code for STRATER is S363, as it is for STRAITER. The code for GRUDNITSKI is G635, the same as the code for the name GRATON.

```
B U R C H
|   |  | |
B   6  2 0    (ZERO FILL)

S T R A T E R
|   | |   |
S   3 6   3

G R U D N I T S K I
|   | |   |
G   6 3   5
```

By this technique, names that sound the same will be given the same code number, or very closely related code numbers, regardless of minor variations in spelling. When sorted in order, the names will be adjacent, or nearly so, in the file. If a name code identification has several names included in its category, each of those names is then examined in detail to obtain the exact match required. The purpose of the code is to provide an approximate, if not an exact, location of the name even though slight differences in spelling may exist.

Advantages of this coding system are:

1. It provides a sound system for handling inquiries by phone or mail where only the name is known.
2. A reduction in the number of letters reduces the chance of spelling errors.
3. Similar-sounding names are placed together.
4. It works well in jobs that require extensive name and address processing.
5. The codes can be derived by computer.
6. The codes are short in length.

The disadvantages of a phonetic code are:

1. A particular code might not be unique, in that it can represent more than one name, resulting in a sequential search.
2. The codes are rather limited for general information processing application.

Color Codes

In manual-based information systems **color codes** are used to help identify records fast and efficiently. Color-coded devices for identification and control have always been available, but they were not used extensively in the past. Today, they are being used more frequently. There are many benefits, such as (1) increased filing accuracy, (2) speed in storage and retrieval, (3) increased security and control, and (4) automatic indication of misfiles.

Applications include using color to file by years, by department, by project, by accounting use, and so forth. Color by year (e.g., ten color stripes, one for the last digit in each year) speeds the transfer of data to inactive files and helps avoid misfiling one year's data with another (inadvertently filing a red year record into a blue year file is easily detected). Color by department helps avoid misdirection of information. Color by accounting use helps to separate information by function. For example, all incoming accounts receivable might go into green folders, accounts payable into red folders, credit memos into blue folders, and so forth.

Colors also are used for filing sequences. In such a system a different color is assigned to each digit, 0 through 9. Color coding for alphabetic filing is just as easy. Groups of letters are assigned specific colors. For example, in a doctor's office, small clinic, or neighborhood health center, it may be practical to file alphabetically, eliminating the need for a cross-reference index. A variety of simple color-code systems are now available for alphabetic filing, including self-labeling systems with A–Z self-adhesive labels; pre-color-coded alphabetic systems; and alphanumeric systems for larger volumes of records.

Folders are not the only record repositories that benefit from color. The use of computer printouts can be simplified considerably by using a color-coding system. Nylon post binders are available in a wide range of materials and colors, and users can create many different codes based on the nature of the information. Color also can enhance security in the use of computer reports. Reports can be cycled by color so that when a green report is delivered to a department, an old green report must be turned in. Similarly, color can be used to see that only authorized personnel have access to certain computer reports. If all payroll reports were in red binders, for example, then someone from sales who had authorization to get only blue sales binders, could not easily walk off with confidential payroll information.

The integrity of any storage and retrieval system depends on the ability to find any given record when it is needed. When any record card or folder is removed from the file, a signal or outmarker should be put in its place so that anyone else needing the same information will know where it is and when it was removed. Color outcards are vivid and obvious. Color can also be used to denote which day, week, or month applies to out-of-file material. It can help spot material that should have been returned earlier and initiate corrective action.[3]

[3] Condensed from "The Wonderful World of Color Makes Records Management Easier," *Information and Records Management,* October 1976, pp. 23–27.

7.4 • SORTING DATA

Throughout the first section of this chapter, the important concepts related to coding data have been presented. Closely related to these ideas are concepts related to manipulating data and accessing specific data records in a predetermined sequence for reporting. In this section, therefore the manipulation and association of data by the data operation of *sorting* is discussed.

Purpose of Sorting

One of the major activities performed in processing a list (file) of data records is the arranging of these data records into some predetermined order, using a field (or fields) in the record as a sorting key. If, for example, the list is an inventory file, it might be desirable to arrange it according to a sequence of largest-to-smallest selling items, by quantity-on-hand, or by dollar value of product classes. In an employee file, on the other hand, the records might be arranged in alphabetical order using employees' last names as the sorting key; or sequencing by age, skill type, and years of employment. The need to sort data records is universal in all organizations. Many ways are available to sort records, depending upon the file media and equipment used.

Although most computer manufacturers provide software packages for sorting data, many organizations choose to build their own sorting routines for specific processing tasks. The systems analyst must, therefore, be aware of different methods and, in particular, of which ones will help reduce sorting time.

Internal Sorting

Internal sorting by computers has made it almost routine to sort voluminous files of data records efficiently and quickly relative to other data processing methods. The major constraints, however, to the sorting of large files are: (1) the instruction repertoire of the computer, (2) the capacity of main storage, (3) the type of auxiliary storage devices used, and (4) the size of the data records to be sorted. In this section, specific constraints are ignored and two ways to perform an internal sort on a data file are discussed.

1. *The Selection technique.* In Figure 7.8 a list L with N numbers is to be sorted in ascending order. Another list, S, will eventually contain the sorted numbers, but which is presently either empty (as in our example) or contains extraneous data which will be destroyed as the selected numbers are moved to their proper locations.

   The method of selection sorting is the simplest and most straightforward. List L is examined, wherein the smallest element, $N = 2$, is selected and stored in list S at S_1. It is replaced in L by an arbitrarily large number R, as illustrated in Figure 7.9.

   List L is again examined for the smallest number and this number is then moved to S_2 and again replaced by R as illustrated in Figure 7.10. This process is repeated until all the numbers have been selected and moved to S in *ascending* order, as desired. Figure 7.11 shows the final results of the selected sort.

   The number of comparisons that would be needed to order a list (called the search effort) using the selection method is $[N(N-1)]/2$. For this case, 21 comparisons would be necessary to order the list. Moreover, selection sorting requires an additional list to which the selected numbers are moved.

2. *Selection with interchange technique.* The main objective in using selection with interchange sorting is to perform the sorting task by using only one area, as opposed to the two areas necessary with selection sorting. When one considers the amount of data that must be sorted in real-world applications during a sorting project, in addition to the storage required for the sorting algorithm, the concern for storage in many large applications can be critical.

   Perhaps the **bubble sort** algorithm is the simplest selection with interchange

L			S	
Physical Location	N		Physical Location	N
1	7		1	
2	4		2	
3	6		3	
4	2		4	
5	3		5	
6	8		6	
7	5		7	

FIG. 7.8 List to be sorted, L, and list S, which will eventually contain the sorted numbers.

L			S	
Physical Location	N		Physical Location	N
1	7		1	2
2	4		2	
3	6		3	
4	R		4	
5	3		5	
6	8		6	
7	5		7	

FIG. 7.9 Selection of first number from L; and moved to S_1.

Coding, Sorting, and Searching Data

L

Physical Location	N
1	7
2	4
3	6
4	R
5	R
6	8
7	5

S

Physical Location	N
1	2
2	3
3	
4	
5	
6	
7	

FIG. 7.10 Selection of second number from L; and moved to S_2.

L

Physical Location	N
1	R
2	R
3	R
4	R
5	R
6	R
7	R

S

Physical Location	N
1	2
2	3
3	4
4	5
5	6
6	7
7	8

FIG. 7.11 Lists L and S after the selection sort.

Original List L	After First Compare	After Second Compare	After Third Compare
7	7	7	7
4	4	4	4
6	6	6	6
2	2	2	2
3	3	3	3
8	5	5	5
5	8	8	8

FIG. 7.12 Partial result of a bubble sort.

made. The first pass of the list, which entails $N - 1$ comparisons, bubbles the smallest number to the top of the list. This is illustrated in Figure 7.13. After the list is passed a second time, the two smallest numbers are in their correct positions. The second pass requires only $N - 2$ comparisons.

The sort effort requires $[N(N - 1)]/2$ comparisons when the elements are in reverse order, $N - 1$ comparisons when the list is already in the proper order, and $[N(N - 1)]/4$ comparisons on average.

Sorting and Merging Using Auxiliary Devices

In practice a data file is normally too large

technique to apply. Successive pairs of elements in the list are compared and an interchange is made if the top element is the larger of the two. In this way, the small numbers are "bubbled" to the top of the list.

In our list L (see Figure 7.12), the numbers 5 and 8 are compared first. Since 8 is larger than 5, the elements are interchanged. Five is then compared to 3. No interchange is made. Three is compared to 2. Again, no interchange is

Original List L	After First Pass	After Second Pass
7	2	2
4	7	3
6	4	7
2	6	4
3	3	6
8	5	5
5	8	8

FIG. 7.13 Results of the first two passes of a bubble sort.

for all of it to be resident in main storage at one time and sorted internally. Therefore, a **sort/merge** technique is required to perform the sorting operation. This technique normally includes two phases: (1) from the original file to be sorted, small strings of data are input in main storage, sorted, and output on other devices; and (2) these strings are repeatedly merged with other strings until, finally, the entire original list is sorted.

What is called a two-way sort/merge will be used here to illustrate the concept of sorting with auxiliary devices. This method usually uses four devices and builds up a sorted file by merging strings of sorted records. With a two-way sort/merge, the original list of records is read from one file in strings, or sublists, of a predetermined size (in our example, two records to the string); sorted into ascending order, using an internal sorting routine (some of which we have already discussed); and output on alternate files.

In our example, it is assumed that four tape drives are available, designated Tape 1, Tape 2, Tape 3, and Tape 4. It is further assumed that the original, unordered tape file to be sorted is stored on Tape 1.

In Figure 7.14 a string of two records from Tape 1 is read into the input buffer area. These records are sorted and then written as a sorted string, S_1, onto Tape 2. Next, a second string of two records is read in the same way, sorted and output on Tape 3 as string S_1. This process is continued in the same way, writing alternate sorted strings on Tapes 2 and 3, until all the records on Tape 1 have been read, sorted, and written onto Tapes 2 and 3.

Now, we rewind Tapes 1, 2, and 3 and reverse their positions as shown in Figure 7.15. One string from Tape 2, string S_1 is read, and one string from Tape 3, string S_2 is read. The strings are merged and written as string SS_1 on Tape 1. This process is repeated for strings S_3 and S_4. The merged

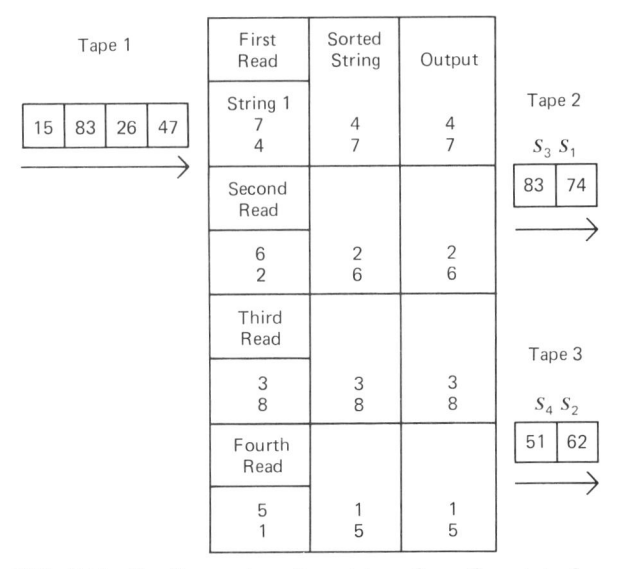

Tape 1	First Read	Sorted String	Output	Tape 2
15 83 26 47	String 1 7 4	4 7	4 7	$S_3\ S_1$ 83 74
	Second Read 6 2	2 6	2 6	
	Third Read 3 8	3 8	3 8	Tape 3 $S_4\ S_2$ 51 62
	Fourth Read 5 1	1 5	1 5	

FIG. 7.14 Reading and sorting strings from the original file and writing the output on alternative tapes.

202 Coding, Sorting, and Searching Data

Tape 2

S_3 S_1

| 83 | 74 |

→

First Read	Merge Pairs	Output
4		2
7	2	4
Second Read	4	
	6	6
2	7	7
6		

Tape 1

SS_1

| 76 | 42 |

→

Tape 3

S_4 S_2

| 51 | 62 |

→

Third Read		
3		1
8	1	3
Fourth Read	3	
	5	5
1	8	8
5		

Tape 4

SS_2

| 85 | 31 |

→

FIG. 7.15 Merge of tapes 2 and 3.

string SS_2 is written on Tape 4 because its right-most value (1) is less than the left-most value (7) of string SS_1.

Again the tapes are rewound, and their positions are reversed. Tapes 1 and 4 become input that is merged either on Tapes 2 or 3 (depending on where our final sorted list is to be sorted), because with this operation our file will be sorted fully. For illustrative purposes, it is assumed that Tape 2 will hold the sorted file. The final merge is shown in Figure 7.16.

Sorting data files is a time-consuming, expensive operation, but in the absence of more sophisticated chaining structures, sorting is an effective way to bring about necessary data associations. In many data processing operations, sorting data files consumes the largest percentage of processing time on the computer. This fact must be acknowledged by the systems analyst when he or she considers the various structures and associations required to achieve their informational outputs.

7.5 ▪ SEARCHING TECHNIQUES WITH SORTED CODES

Searching techniques are used to give the

Tape 1

SS_1

| 76 | 42 |

→

Tape 4

SS_2

| 85 | 31 |

→

First Read	Merge Pairs	Output
2		1
4	1	2
Second Read	2	
	3	3
1	4	4
3		
Third Read		5
6	5	6
7	6	
Fourth Read		7
5	7	8
8	8	

Tape 2 (sorted file)

| 87 | 65 | 43 | 21 |

→

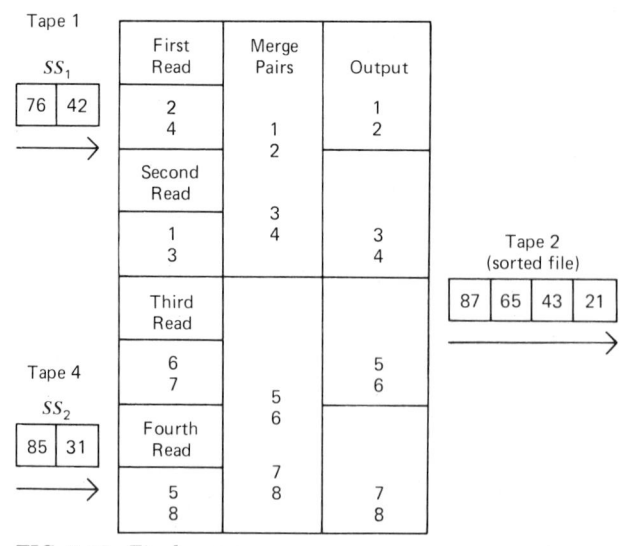

FIG. 7.16 Final merge.

user access to specified data elements, to delete or modify this data, or to answer a query. This section investigates how such access can be made when data are organized as a sorted sequential list.

Sequential Search

The simplest way we can search ordered data is **sequentially.** Starting from the beginning of the data, each value is compared to the one we are seeking until a match is found. For example, suppose that we are seeking data associated with the value 62. If the data were ordered as in Figure 7.17, then the data values 07, 09, 26, 51, and 57 would have to be compared before the desired data value, 62, was found.

Binary Search

The **binary search** technique provides a way to process a sequential list in somewhat of a random fashion. The middle of the list is located first to determine if the requested item is above or below the accessed element. In other words, a high/low comparison is made to determine if the requested record is in the top half or bottom half. The proper half of the list is then divided by half again. Another check is made to determine if the requested data value is above or below this entry. By continuing this searching pattern of halving the number of data values, the requested data value is located eventually. An example of the binary search is shown in Figure 7.18. The requested data value is identified with Code 21.

Block Search

With this search method the original data are partitioned into blocks. Then, only one value from each block has to be tested. If the value tested indicates that the desired data value may be in the block, then a sequential search of that block begins. An example of

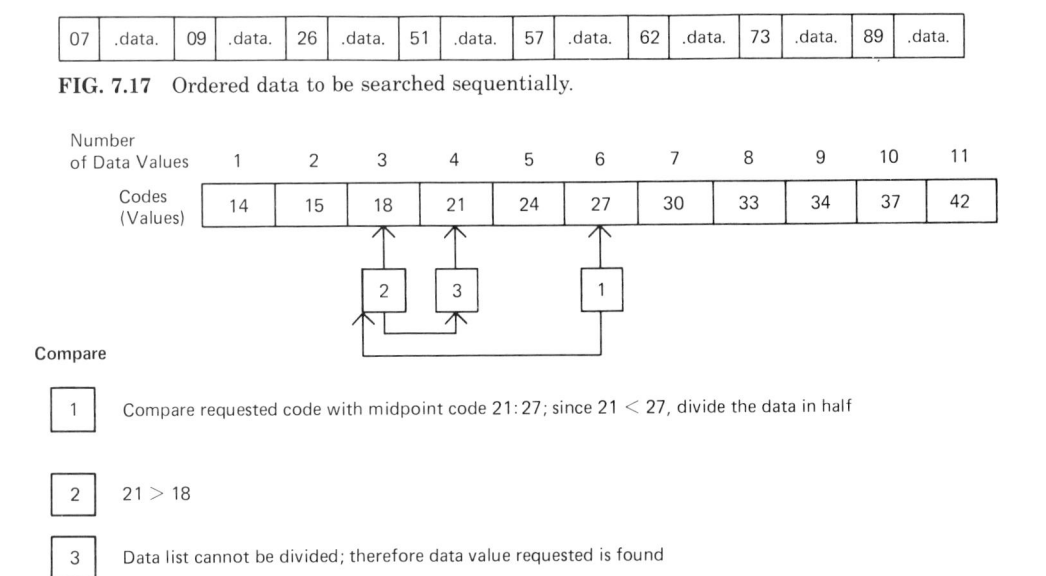

| 07 | .data. | 09 | .data. | 26 | .data. | 51 | .data. | 57 | .data. | 62 | .data. | 73 | .data. | 89 | .data. |

FIG. 7.17 Ordered data to be searched sequentially.

| Number of Data Values | 1 | 2 | 3 | 4 | 5 | 6 | 7 | 8 | 9 | 10 | 11 |
| Codes (Values) | 14 | 15 | 18 | 21 | 24 | 27 | 30 | 33 | 34 | 37 | 42 |

Compare

| 1 | Compare requested code with midpoint code 21:27; since 21 < 27, divide the data in half |

| 2 | 21 > 18 |

| 3 | Data list cannot be divided; therefore data value requested is found |

FIG. 7.18 An example of a binary search.

a block search is illustrated in Figure 7.19.

Search Methods Compared

One way to compare the various methods of searching is to examine estimates of how many searches must be performed before the data value we are seeking is found. For a good size list—say 10,000 items—we have on the average approximately 5000 searches ($N + 1$)/2, using a sequential search technique. Using the binary search method, the number of searches on that same list can be reduced to about 13 [$\log_2 (N + 1) - 1$]. (Remember though that *all data values to be searched must be in internal memory at the same time.*)

To calculate the average number of comparisons necessary using a block search, we must first determine the number of blocks and the number of data values in each block. Given N data values, the average number of compares for a block search is minimized when there are $\sqrt{N}$ blocks of block size $\sqrt{N}$ ($\sqrt{N}$ data values per block). The average number of compares then would be ($N + 1$)/2 for a search over the blocks plus ($N + 1$)/2 compares for a search within a block. This means, for example, that a list of 10,000 data values would on average require 2 [(100 + 1)/2] or 101 compares to find a specific data value.

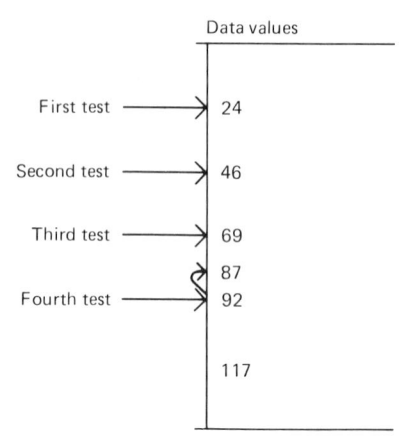

FIG. 7.19 A block search. The data values are in ascending order. We are seeking the data value 87.

SUMMARY

Codes are used to identify and to give meaning to data. Three basic sets of coding symbols are important to information processing: (1) numeric, (2) alphabetic, and (3) alphanumeric.

The two primary approaches to the development of code structures are sequential codes and block codes. Variations of block code structures include: (1) facet, (2) hierarchical, and (3) decimal. Special purpose codes include: (1) mnemonic, (2) color, and (3) phonetic. Mnemonic codes are used extensively in manual systems for aiding the memory of the human user. In manual information systems, color codes can be used effectively to assist in identifying records faster and more efficiently. Phonetic codes are used on systems where a need for accessing names exists. Bar codes, representing numbers that uniquely identify products, form the basis for point-of-sale retailing systems.

The use of a check digit in code structures provides a standardized procedure for validating codes.

Sorting is a major data operation used to structure data values in a predetermined sequence. Sorting can be accomplished either internally in storage, or externally via the use of auxiliary devices such as tapes or disks.

Searching a list of sorted codes can be done easily in a sequential fashion. Although simple in operation, this approach is not always the most efficient method. The binary search, or some form of block search is normally recommended for large data lists.

REVIEW QUESTIONS

7.1 Define coding.

7.2 What are the functions of codes?

7.3 Briefly explain the considerations involved in code design.

7.4 What are the advantages and disadvantages of sequential codes? Of block codes?

7.5 What is the key aspect that differentiates block codes from sequential codes?

7.6 What is a facet code?

7.7 Describe a hierarchical block code. Give an example of one besides that given in the chapter.

7.8 What is the purpose of a mnemonic code?

7.9 What is the purpose of a phonetic code?

7.10 Why should check digits be appended to code numbers? At the very minimum, how many times is the check digit calculated?

7.11 List the advantages of the grocery industry's POS system based on the bar code.

7.12 Why must data records be sorted?

7.13 List the major constraints of performing an internal sort on a large number of data values.

7.14 In the phrase, "two-way sort/merge," what does "two-way" mean?

7.15 List the advantages of the block search method of accessing data.

7.16 Define the term "block."

QUESTIONS FOR DISCUSSION

7.1 Why are not all data items simply given a sequential code number?

7.2 "What good are phonetic codes? You can't use them for basic data processing." Comment on this statement.

7.3 "The importance of using check digits for important codes is increasing. Recent developments in data entry devices (e.g., buffered keypunches) permit the automatic verification of codes with certain check digits at the time they are recorded. This valuable control concept should be used in the design of all new systems." Discuss.

7.4 "With recent advancements in computer technology, there is less need for using codes to identify certain data than ever before. Although use of codes is still more efficient than descriptive data, codes tend to depersonalize individuals. The inefficiencies related to processing noncoded data should be balanced against the benefits of minimizing feelings of depersonalization associated with computer processing." Discuss both the technical and nontechnical implications of this statement.

7.5 "It seems that no matter how many different ways we code a given element of data, someone in the organization needs it coded still another way." Discuss.

7.6 "If an individual would only examine the type of coding required to input data into the data base, he would understand the basic information available to him." Explain.

7.7 "Each new standardized coding system implemented in our society removes one more layer of an individual's privacy." Evaluate.

7.8 Why should a systems analyst be familiar with the different methods of sorting?

7.9 "Binary search is efficient because each successive search cuts in half the number of records to be considered. However, it is most useful for large files." Comment on this statement.

7.10 "The amount of sorting needed to be done is an important factor in the design of the basic system of data processing." Comment on this statement.

7.11 All other things being equal, a six-way sort/merge will be as fast as, and likely faster than, a three-way sort/merge. Explain why this statement is true.

EXERCISES

7.1 Using prime number weighting starting at 3 and Modulus 11, prepare a check digit for three account numbers of your choice. Then prepare a program, in the programming language of your choice, that verifies the accuracy of these numbers as they are read into the computer.

7.2 Using the Soundex System, prepare a code for your name.

7.3 Examine the subscription label from any magazine or journal in terms of the coding printed on that label. Identify, as well as you can, what each part of this code represents. What characteristics might you expect that the publishers would desire to be codified to assist their operations?

7.4 Examine the statement from a credit card system of your choice. Prepare a report which analyzes the coding found on the statement. Include in your report recommendations for additional coding schemes that might be implemented to provide additional information.

7.5 The emphasis on automotive safety has resulted in Detroit automobile manufacturers having to recall millions of automobiles for real and potential safety defects. Often the potential safety problem is related to a certain part made in a specific plant or during a specific time period. Obviously, if the automobile manufacturer could determine which automobiles had which parts, needless expense could be eliminated in many recalls. Moreover, structural defects in older cars could also be addressed, as they were determined. One suggestion offered by safety experts is the development of an identification number which could be imprinted on a metal plate and attached to each automobile. This number would be recorded by a dealer on all new sales and by the owner on all subsequent resales.

Using the above ideas and any additional assumptions or ideas of your own, prepare a proposal for a coding structure to be used by the automobile manufacturers.

7.6 If there are 5000 data values in a list and 10,000 accesses per week (assume uniform distribution) and each search costs $0.02; how much will it cost on the average to make these lookups if (1) a sequential search is used, (2) a binary search is used, and (3) a block search is used?

7.7 We have 1600 data values to store and search via a block method. What is the optimum division for blocks?

7.8 Prepare a flowchart for bubble sorting a list (L) of N elements into high-to-low sequence.

PROBLEMS

7.1 You are a systems analyst for the Bayou State Insurance Company of Ruston, Louisiana. Your job, among other things, is to design a coding structure for the Automobile Claims File. Following are items of the file that must be coded:

1. Identification of cities and towns in Louisiana.
2. Personal Injury Protection Deductible Coverage:
   Full Coverage
   $250 Deductible Name Insured
   $500 Deductible Name Insured
   $1000 Deductible Name Insured
   $2000 Deductible Name Insured
   $250 Name Insured and Members of Household
   $500 Name Insured and Members of Household
   $1000 Name Insured and Members of Household
   $2000 Name Insured and Members of Household
3. Bodily Injury Limits:
   5/10   50/100
   10/20   20/50
   15/30   100/300
   20/40   Excess of 100/300
   25/50   All other
4. Medical Payments Limits:
   $500 $3000
   750   5000 and Over
   1000   All Other
   2000   No Medical Payments
5. Property Damage:
   $5000 $ 50,000
   10,000   100,000
   15,000   300,000
   25,000   All Other
   35,000   No Propery Damage
6. Property Damage Coverage:
   Full Coverage + Option 1
   Full Coverage + Option 2
   Full Coverage + Option 3
   Deductible   + Option 1
   Deductible   + Option 2
   Deductible   + Option 3
   Full coverage
   Straight Deductible

Design a coding scheme to classify properly and make the above items more manageable, meaningful, and amenable to processing.

7.2 A transaction code has been developed for the Bow Shirt Company. It is illustrated below.

Position / Digit	1 Sleeve Length	2 Neck Size	3 Shirt Color	4 Style	5 Material	6 Market	7–8 Market[1] Region	9–10 Outlet[2]	11 Salesperson	12 Quantity[3]
1	28	14	White	Monogram	Cotton	South	Dallas	Neiman-Marcus	P. Newman	XXXX
2	30	14½	Ivory	Tapered	Polyester	West	Little Rock	Godchaux	J. Danelli	
3	32	15	Lime	Sport	Silk	Midwest	Memphis	Goldrings	T. Gretz	
4	34	15½	Gray	Dress	Other	Northeast	New Orleans	Homes	C. Griffin	
5	36	16	Blue	—	—	—	Birmingham	Palais-Royale	M. Kotecki	
6	38	16½	Orange	—	—	—	Jackson	etc.	B. Cushing	
7	40	17	Shale	—	—	—	Atlanta		J. Mandel	
8	42	17½	Pink	—	—	—	Richmond		E. Summers	
9	44	18	Yellow	—	—	—	Charlotte		J. Mathern	
0	Short	—	—	—	—	—	etc.		K. Larson	

[1]Market regions are sequence codes (00–99) within the market.
[2]Outlets are sequence codes (00–99) within the Market Region. Example: Market: South; Market Region: Dallas; Outlet; Holmes is 10104.
[3]Represents actual quantity—cannot exceed 9999.
In addition, cost and sales price is coded   1 2 3 4 5 6 7 8 9 0
Last two letters in code = cents   B O W S H I R T L N

What follows is a partial list of transactions for September:

Code	Quantity	Cost Code	Sales Price
23241301038	400	BWN	OLH
43222102044	300	OIR	SLH
55422307740	250	WNN	HLT
45422124937	500	WOI	ISN
45422236783	275	WOI	ISN
44423173047	800	OLN	HIL
43534407451	750	OTL	HRL
75741380415	450	SNH	RLH
53633407082	600	WNH	IOL
33422410121	950	OTH	HRH

Please answer the following questions based on the partial list of transactions for September:
1. What is the most popular color of shirt nationwide? In the Northeast?
2. What is the revenue obtained from the item having the partial code of 23241?
3. What salesperson produced the largest dollar sales? What salesperson sold the most shirts? What salesperson produced the largest profit?
4. What market is the most profitable?
5. What market purchases the most shirts having 16-inch necks?
6. How many shirts having 36-inch sleeves and 18-inch necks did J. Mandel sell this period?
7. How many shirts having 36-inch sleeves and 16-inch necks were sold during September?

7.3 A bank data base contains several files, one of which contains a complete customer profile. This file is stored on a DASD and is accessible by bank tellers via online inquiry devices. One way to access this file is by an abbreviated alphanumeric code. The last name of the customer is abbreviated by a computer-generated key based on eliminating certain letters and replacing others with phonetic symbols. Using this method, as outlined in the text, code the following names: RODRIGUEZ, BROWN, JOHNSON, COHEN. Would you code the names, RODRIGEZ, JONSON, and COHAN the same? If not, then how would you access, say, FRED COHEN, if you also have a FRED COHAN in the files?

7.4 Old Briar Patch, Inc. is a major corporation that acts as a holding company for numerous smaller corporations engaged in the distillation, blending, bottling, and distribution of spirits. Old Briar Patch controls 45 corporations, sells six basic spirit types (Gin, Bourbon, Scotch, Canadian, etc.), sells under sixty different brand names, bottles 26 sizes (from small one-drink bottles to gallons in various increments), engages in both domestic and export business, offers many special packages (Christmas, Father's Day, etc., as well as wooden crate, cardboard carton, and similar variations), and distributes in up to 1000 subclassifications of geographical area. Develop a product/customer-combination code.

The product code should uniquely identify each product sold, and, in addition, provide for statistical analysis by financial account, spirit type, brand, size, market, area sold, and so forth. Also, the combined customer code indicates at least three items, such as the major area within domestic and export class, subclass within major area, the customer serial within area subclass. (Adapted from: Van Court Hare, Jr., *Systems Analysis: A Diagnostic Approach* (New York: Harcourt Brace Jovanovich, 1967), pp. 501–503.)

7.5 Using the sort/merge technique described, sort the following list of numbers into high to low sequence. Assume the records are blocked 2, and 6 tapes are available:

17, 105, 34, 28, 1, 7, 45, 16, 88, 34, 29, 87, 112, 119.

7.6 Using both the sequential search technique and the binary search technique find the following numbers in list A: [3–35–87–49–98–17]. Compare the actual average searches needed for each technique to the average searches indicated by formulas given in the chapter.

List A: 1, 3, 4, 8, 10, 12, 17, 20, 24, 29, 31, 35, 38, 43, 49, 54, 57, 63, 69, 71, 74, 78, 83, 86, 87, 92, 98, 100.

7.7 Using the bubble sort technique described in this chapter, sort the following list of numbers into high-to-low sequence:

19, 4, 7, 5, 11, 12, 0.

BIBLIOGRAPHY

"A Standard Labeling Code for Food." *Business Week,* April 7, 1973.

Alan and Yeates, *Systems Analysis,* Palo Alto: California Science Research Associates, Inc., College Division, 1971.

"Bar-Encoded Labels Simplify Librarians' Duties," *Computerworld,* August 29, 1977.

Clifton, *Systems Analysis for Business Data Processing,* Philadelphia: Auerbach Publishers, 1970.

Data Processor, a newsletter published by the National Wholesale Druggists' Association, October 6, 1972.

Flores, *Computer Sorting,* Englewood Cliffs, NJ.: Prentice-Hall Inc., 1970.

Hare, *Systems Analysis: A Diagnostic Approach,* New York: Harcourt Brace Jovanovich, 1967.

Hussian and Hussian, *Information Processing Systems for Management,* Homewood, IL.: Richard D. Irwin, Inc., 1981.

Lewis and Smith, *Applying Data Structures,* Boston: Houghton Mifflin Co., 1976.

"Soundex: Foolproof Filing System for Finding Any Name in the File," Remington Rand Brochure LVB809.

"The Wonderful World of Color Makes Records Management Easier," *Information and Records Management,* October 1976.

CHAPTER

8

Logical Data Organization

8.1 ▪ INTRODUCTION

Logical data organization concerns how data are associated to meet user information requirements. *Physical data organization* is how these same data are stored on physical files, such as magnetic disks. It is coincidental when both are the same. A simple physical example may help explain the difference between logical and physical organization. Let us suppose that we have designed a toolroom using peg boards and hangers to store tools such as saws and hammers. Further, suppose that Joe Carpenter has a job to do, and that he has determined that he needs a hammer, saw, level, and square to do it. He will search through the stored tools to gather what he needs. In a little while, Jim Repairman goes to the tool storage area to get two pipe wrenches and a hacksaw. His route through the physical storage area is different from Carpenter's, but both have related together, from a single physical storage location, the tools necessary to do their jobs.

If the toolroom becomes large and complex, we will need to build a logical route, map, association, connection, structure or whatever you wish to call it, to speed up the gathering together of different sets of tools. As systems analysts, we face a similar challenge in getting all of the relevant data stored on physical media and developing logical structures to associate these data to meet a variety of needs. It can be effectively argued that anytime we gather and deal with data, a logical function has been performed. Certainly, when we classify and code data, as discussed in Chapter 7, we have logically related that data. The same occurs when we sort data. Even in Chapter 9, when we deal specifically with physical files, we will cover chains, pointers, rings, and lists, which are nothing more than logical ways to associate data. We believe that it is appropriate, however, to separate the logical from the physical as much as possible. That is why we devote this chapter to three logical data structures: trees, networks, and relations.

The objectives of this chapter are as follows:

1. To describe the rules that must be followed when describing the logical organization of data.
2. To present and analyze the basic structures of logical data organization.

3. To specify the processes applied to turn hierarchical structures into flat files.
4. To introduce relational operators that manipulate and transform flat files.

8.2 ▪ MODELS OF LOGICAL REPRESENTATIONS

A *schema* describes the overall logical organization of data. It gives the names of the data entities and attributes, and it specifies the associations that exist between them. Different users of the data need different information. They view data associations in different ways. These views, which tend to focus on only a subset of the data, can be expressed by *subschemas.* Figure 8.1 shows how subschemas of an instructor and of a custodian can be derived from an overall schema.

Schedule is fully described by associated data items: class, instructor, enrollment, room, and meeting times. These data items and their appropriate descriptors (remember data attributes, attribute values described in Chapter 7?), may be stored in this same sequence in one physical file or they may be stored across several physical files. The relevant thing is the way in which these data attributes are gathered together logically to provide various information. Instructors want to associate classes with their enrollment to determine how many assignment sheets to prepare. Custodians want to associate rooms with meeting times to schedule their custodial tasks.

Many different sets of rules for drawing a schema can be followed, depending on the type of DBMS examined. For simplicity, we will use the following ones:

1. Data items gathered into groups (records) should be placed in adjacent rectangles. Notice the example in Figure 8.1, in which the data items CLASS, INSTRUCTOR, ENROLLMENT, ROOM, and MEETING-TIMES are gathered together to form the record SCHEDULE.
2. The name of the data structure or record should appear above the first data item (e.g., the name of the data structure CUSTODIAN appears above the date item ROOM).
3. No two data items or records should have the same name.
4. A data item that is used to identify a specific record from a data file is called a *primary key.* Data values must not be repeated within a data item for that data item to qualify as a primary key. For example, for CLASS to qualify as a primary key in the subschema SCHEDULE, multiple sections could not exist. If there were multiple sections of a class, referring to *only* CLASS would not cause a record to be identified uniquely.
5. Data items are underlined to designate that they are primary keys.
6. The property of uniqueness of data values may be obtainable only by joining data items together. This operation, known as **concatenation** (associate or link together), is shown by underlining all of the data items comprising the primary key (e.g., ROOM and MEETING-TIMES in Figure 8.1).

If you keep these simple rules in mind, you can draw and interpret complex schema without ambiguity. Now let us discuss ways in which relationships between subschemas are portrayed here.

These relationships can be either one-to-one (1 : 1), one-to-many (1 : M), or many-to-many (M : M). For example, in Figure 8.2, we see that every class is taught by one, and

Models of Logical Representations 215

Schema—Overall Logical Data Base Description

SCHEDULE: CLASS | INSTRUCTOR | ENROLLMENT | ROOM | MEETING-TIMES

→ Instructor's Subschema

→ Custodian's Subschema

INSTRUCTOR: CLASS | ENROLLMENT

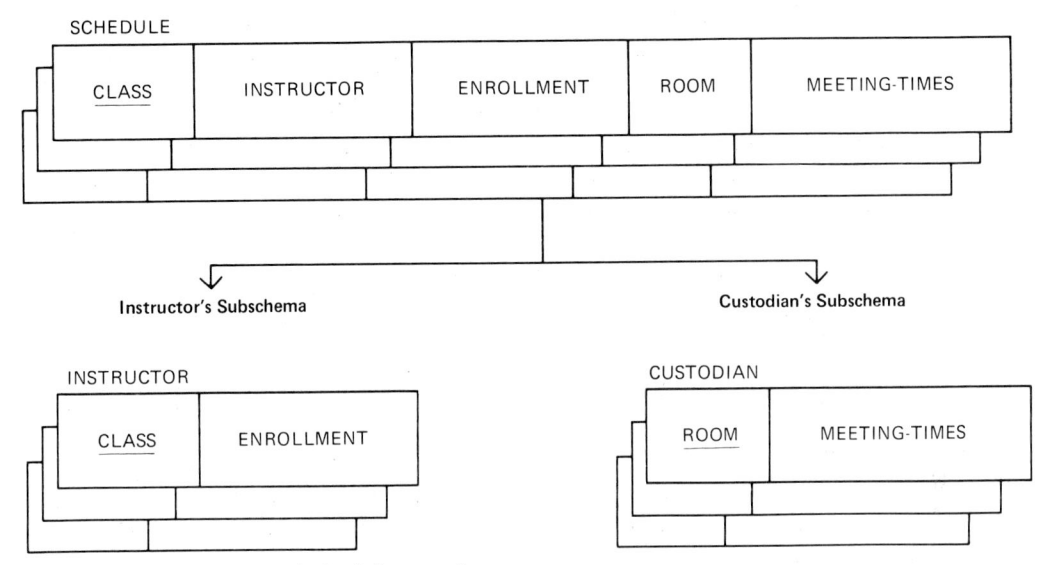

CUSTODIAN: ROOM | MEETING-TIMES

FIG 8.1 Two subschemas derived from a schema.

SUBSCHEMAS

INSTRUCTOR: NAME | OFFICE-#

↕ 1 : M

CLASS: UNIQUE-# | LOCATION

↕ M : M

TIME: TIME-OF-DAY | DAY-OF-WEEK

RELATIONSHIPS

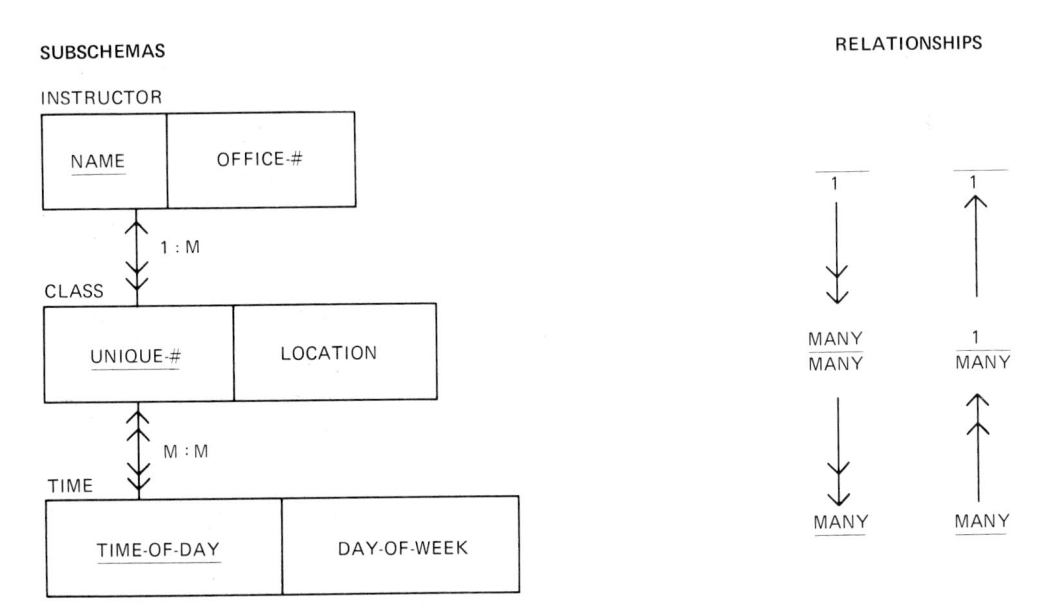

1 / MANY → MANY / MANY

1 / MANY ← MANY / MANY

FIG 8.2 Relationships between subschemas.

only one (1 : 1), instructor. Instructors, however, teach multiple classes (1 : M). Finally, all classes meet at multiple times during the week, and more than one class meets at any time during the day (M : M).

To elaborate further, instructor Boggs teaches three classes: two sections of introductory financial accounting and one section of advanced accounting. Hence, a one- (INSTRUCTOR) to-many (CLASS) relationship exists. Using the same connector, but going in the other direction, the advanced accounting class is taught by only one instructor, Boggs. To illustrate the many-to-many relationship, the advanced accounting class is taught at 9:00 AM, three times a week. Likewise, many different classes besides advanced accounting meet at 9:00 AM, three times a week.

8.3 ▪ TREE STRUCTURES

A **tree** is made up of a multilevel group of elements called *nodes*. A node is nothing more than a point at which subsidiary data originate. The reason this particular logical data structure is called a tree is simply because it looks like a tree, usually one turned upside down. Geneologists use a schema called a tree to show ancestoral descent of a person, family, or group. Data associated by a tree schema are *hierarchical*. They branch from a point or node without forming loops or polygons. Data presented in a tree structure must meet two conditions. First, the tree must have a single *root* node. Second, all nodes other than the root node must be related to one and only one higher level node.

In Figure 8.3, node ① is the root node. Notice that nodes ②, ③, and ④ are related to only one higher level node, ①. Nodes ②, ③, and ④ are called *children* of *parent* node ①. Similarly, nodes ⑤ and ⑥ are children of parent node ②.

Moving from trees grown from nodes to schemas built from records, consider the hierarchical structure illustrated in Figure 8.4. It represents the relationship of a university employing three general types of personnel: instructors, administrators, and support people. These relationships are all one-to-many. Both the relationships between INSTRUCTOR and CLASS, between ADMINISTRATOR and BUDGET, and between ADMINISTRATOR and JOB-HISTORY are one-to-many. The data structure SUPPORT has no children.

In Figure 8.5, sample data values are mapped into the schema of Figure 8.4. For example, the INSTRUCTOR, Jean Alexander, teaches two sections of introduction to financial management and one section of a class entitled, "Organization Structures." The sample data in the ADMINISTRATOR structure also indicate that the salary of Marg Ramirez, who is Director of the Computer Center, comes from four budget line items. These four line items sum to $42,285, her annual salary. She has also held five positions, the last of which is her present title.

One other point concerning Figure 8.4 is important. The second level of the tree, which describes university personnel, really contains three different types of records (children). The record types INSTRUCTOR, ADMINISTRATOR, and SUPPORT are fundamentally different. This cannot be said of the next lower, or third level. For example, the records of the entity CLASS are occurrences or repetitions of the same record type (a single child), with only the data values changing. The ability of trees to accommodate both **heterogeneous branches** and

Tree Structures 217

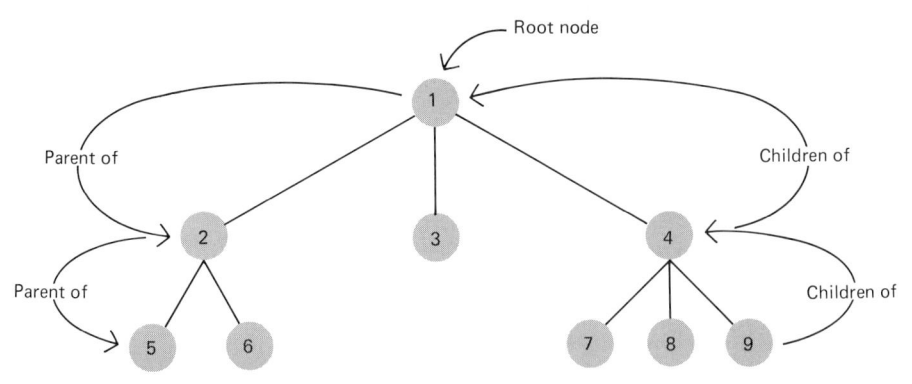

FIG 8.3 A tree structure.

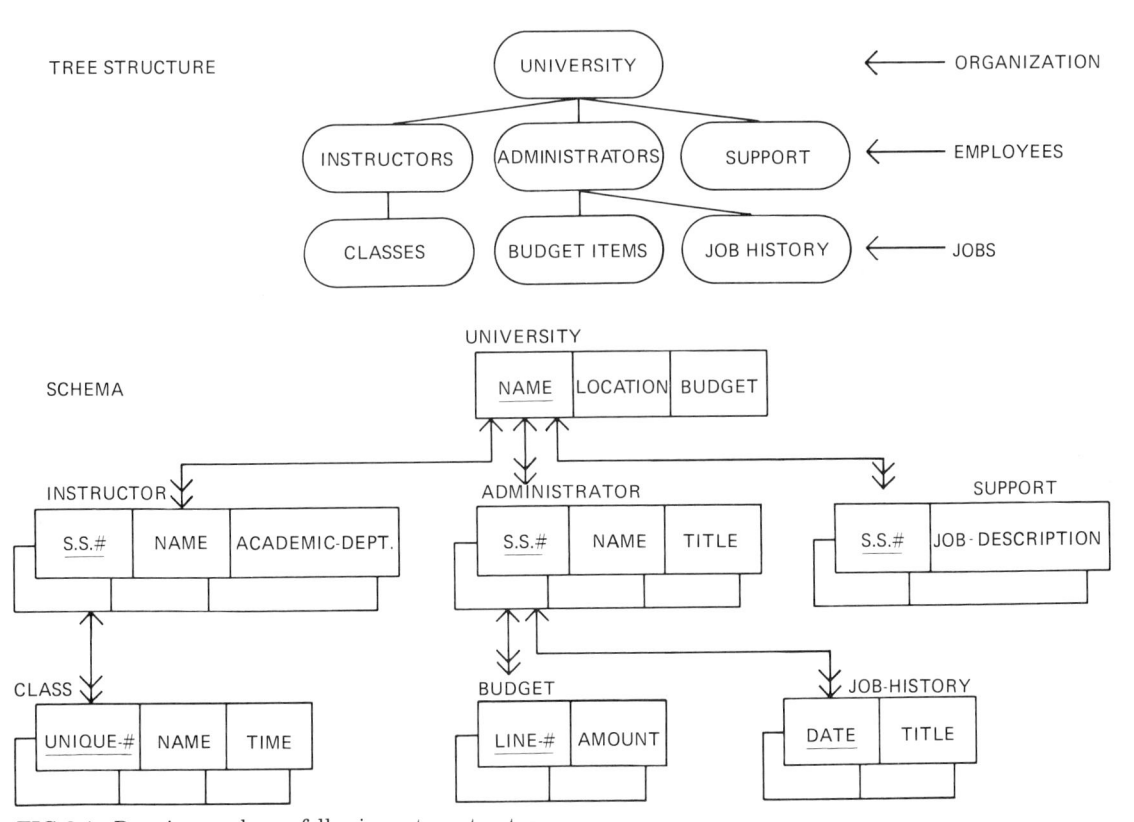

FIG 8.4 Drawing a schema following a tree structure.

218 Logical Data Organization

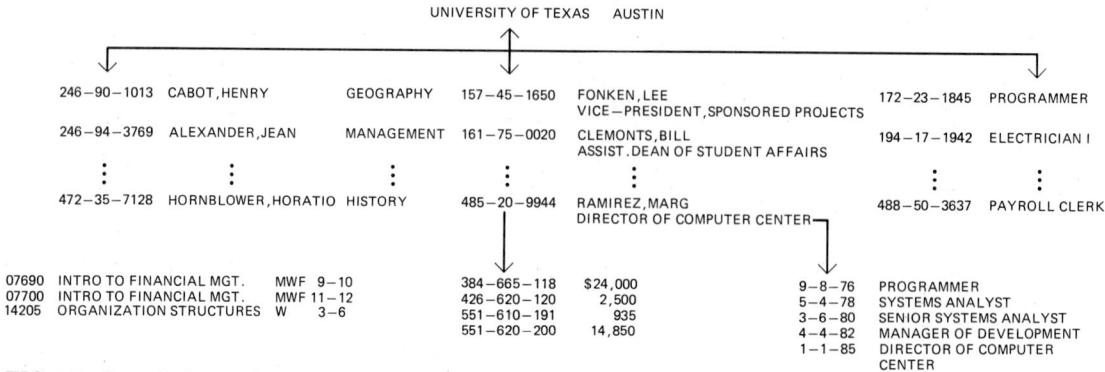

```
                          UNIVERSITY OF TEXAS     AUSTIN
        ┌──────────────────────┬──────────────────────┐
        ↓                      ↓                      ↓
246-90-1013  CABOT,HENRY    GEOGRAPHY  157-45-1650  FONKEN,LEE           172-23-1845  PROGRAMMER
                                                    VICE-PRESIDENT, SPONSORED PROJECTS
246-94-3769  ALEXANDER,JEAN MANAGEMENT 161-75-0020  CLEMONTS,BILL        194-17-1942  ELECTRICIAN I
                                                    ASSIST.DEAN OF STUDENT AFFAIRS
   :            :              :           :            :                   :            :
472-35-7128  HORNBLOWER,HORATIO HISTORY  485-20-9944  RAMIREZ,MARG         488-50-3637  PAYROLL CLERK
                                                     DIRECTOR OF COMPUTER CENTER
                                             ↓
07690  INTRO TO FINANCIAL MGT.    MWF  9-10     384-665-118   $24,000    9-8-76   PROGRAMMER
07700  INTRO TO FINANCIAL MGT.    MWF 11-12     426-620-120    2,500     5-4-78   SYSTEMS ANALYST
14205  ORGANIZATION STRUCTURES    W    3-6      551-610-191      935     3-6-80   SENIOR SYSTEMS ANALYST
                                                551-620-200   14,850     4-4-82   MANAGER OF DEVELOPMENT
                                                                         1-1-85   DIRECTOR OF COMPUTER
                                                                                  CENTER
```

FIG 8.5 Sample data values for data entities.

homogeneous occurrences, makes them appropriate vehicles for portraying a variety of user perspectives of the data base.

8.4 ▪ NETWORK STRUCTURES

Any data in a **network** may be related to any other data (see Fig. 8.6). A network is without a strict hierarchy as one finds with a tree. In a network, data entities can be related in an endless number of ways. A network may be *simple* or *complex.* By simple is meant that the mapping from one level to the next is 1 : M. If the relationship is described as M : M, then the network is said to be complex. In Figure 8.7, a complex network is illustrated. CLASS data are owned by both an INSTRUCTOR parent and a STUDENT parent. This makes the structure a network. The fact that the CLASS is team taught by multiple instructors, makes the structure a complex network.

8.5 ▪ RELATIONAL STRUCTURES

A systems analyst can easily become entangled in a network maze or confused by a bushy tree. One way to simplify the logical description of the data is through the process of normalization. **Normalization** is the step-by-step process for replacing tree and network structures with two-dimensional tables called *relations.* It is a process of associating data in such a manner that the result is independent of the order in which

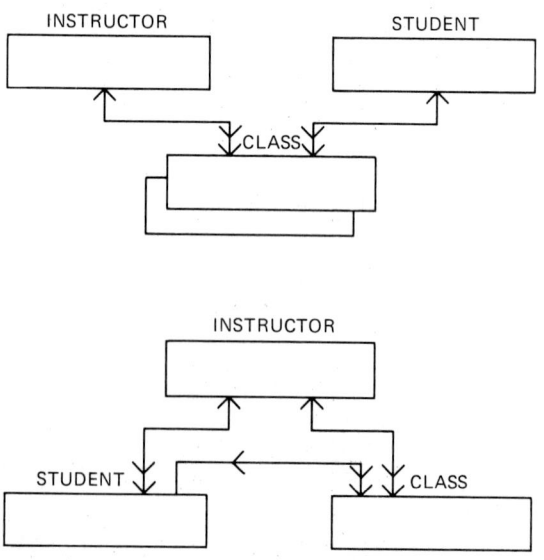

```
   ┌────────────┐              ┌────────────┐
   │ INSTRUCTOR │              │  STUDENT   │
   └────────────┘              └────────────┘
           ↑         ┌───────┐         ↑
           └─────────│ CLASS │─────────┘
                     └───────┘

              ┌────────────┐
              │ INSTRUCTOR │
              └────────────┘
                ↑    ↑    ↑
   ┌─────────┐           ┌─────────┐
   │ STUDENT │◄──────────│  CLASS  │
   └─────────┘           └─────────┘
```

FIG 8.6 Examples of network structures.

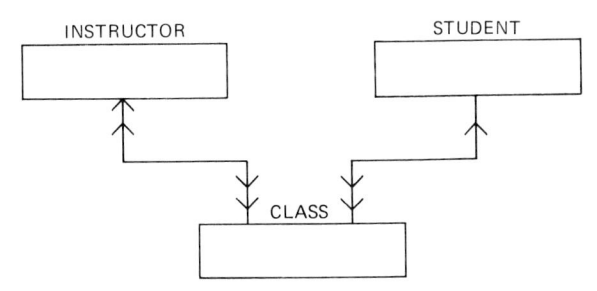

FIG 8.7 An M : M relationship between INSTRUCTOR and CLASS makes this network complex.

the data are taken. Before describing the steps in normalizing a structure, it is useful to describe the conditions that apply to a relation.

A relation, sometimes referred to as a *flat file,* is made up of columns and rows. Each column, which we can consider to be analogous to a data field, must be unique. That is, no two data fields in a relation can have the same name. Similarly, this rule is applicable to the rows. Each row, analogous to a record, must be distinct. This condition is achieved through the use of primary keys. Figure 8.8 illustrates a structure that fails to meet and satisfy one of these conditions. The data structure STUDENT–GPA has a group of data items, SEMESTER, G.P.A., that occurs more than once (also called a *repeating group*). The flat file equivalent of the data structure STUDENT–GPA is shown in the bottom half of Figure 8.8.

To avoid drawing pictures of flat files all the time, the following shorthand notation will be used:

STUDENT (STUDENT-#, SEMESTER, GPA)

The element preceding the parentheses is the name of the data structure or relation. Elements within parentheses are the names of the data items. In relational terms, the data items are known as *domains.* Finally, the data item or domain underlined is the primary key. The primary key is necessary to identify the records uniquely, (or again adopting relational terminology, *tuples*—rhymes with couples).

Normalizing Hierarchical Structures

The hierarchical structure to be normalized is one having a repeating group. Normalization is accomplished by removing the repeating group from the structure and making it a separate flat file. Referring to Figure 8.9, the structure ORDERS is normalized by creating a relation ORDER and a relation ORDER–ITEM. Using our shorthand notation, the following flat files result from the normalization process:

ORDER (ORDER-#, ORDER-DATE)
ORDER–ITEM (ORDER-#, PART-#, PRICE, QTY)

The new relation is called ORDER–ITEM. The tuples (records or rows) in ORDER–ITEM are uniquely identified by combining the domains ORDER-# and PART-#. Simplicity, which is the hallmark of normalization, has been achieved by repeating one or more domains in the new relation. The structure illustrated in Figure 8.9 is a homogeneous tree, in that PART-# could be

220 Logical Data Organization

STUDENT-GPA ← Not a Flat File

STUDENT-#	SEMESTER	G.P.A.	SEMESTER	G.P.A.	SEMESTER	G.P.A.	...	G.P.A.
164892	Fall 84	3.60	Spring 85	3.55	Fall 85	3.00		
165000	Spring 85	2.35						
389365	Fall 85	4.00	Spring 86	4.00	Fall 86	3.75		

STUDENT-GPA ← A Flat File

FIG 8.8 Data structure STUDENT-GPA illustrated as not a flat file and as a flat file.

STUDENT-#	SEMESTER	G.P.A.
164892	Fall 84	3.60
164892	Spring 85	3.55
164892	Fall 85	3.00
164892	Fall 86	2.92
165000	Spring 85	2.35
.	.	.
.	.	.
.	.	.
389365	Fall 85	4.00
389365	Spring 86	4.00
389365	Fall 86	3.75

Primary Key

considered to be an occurrence or a repetition of the relation ORDER. A heterogeneous tree structure can be normalized by applying the same basic process.

Figure 8.10 represents a heterogeneous tree structure. Two comments about it are appropriate. First, every DEPARTMENT numbers its jobs from 1 to N. Second, we would like to be able to reference the department in which an employee works. Considering these two comments, the tree structure in Figure 8.10 is normalized as follows:

DEPARTMENT (DEPT–#, DEPT–NAME, MANAGER, BUDGET)
JOBS (DEPT–#, JOB–#, JOB–DESCRIPTION)
EMPLOYEE (EMPLOYEE–#, EMPLOYEE–NAME, SALARY, DEPT–#)
HISTORY (EMPLOYEE–#, JOB–DATE, TITLE)
CHILDREN (EMPLOYEE–#, CHILD–NAME, CHILD–AGE, CHILD–SEX)

Notice that the domains DEPT–#, EMPLOYEE–#, and EMPLOYEE–# have been added to the relations JOBS, HISTORY, and CHILDREN, respectively, to make the tuples of the relations unique. Also, the domain DEPT–# has been added to the relation EMPLOYEE so that EMPLOYEE tuples can be tied back to DEPARTMENT tuples.

Another example of a tree structure is illustrated in Figure 8.11. Test yourself on the process of normalization. If you have learned the rules of normalization, you should have produced the following normalized relations:

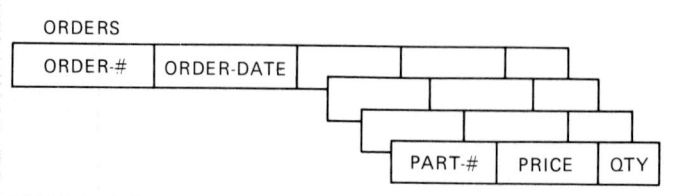

ORDERS
ORDER-#	ORDER-DATE				
				PART-#	PRICE	QTY

FIG 8.9 A data structure containing a repeating group.

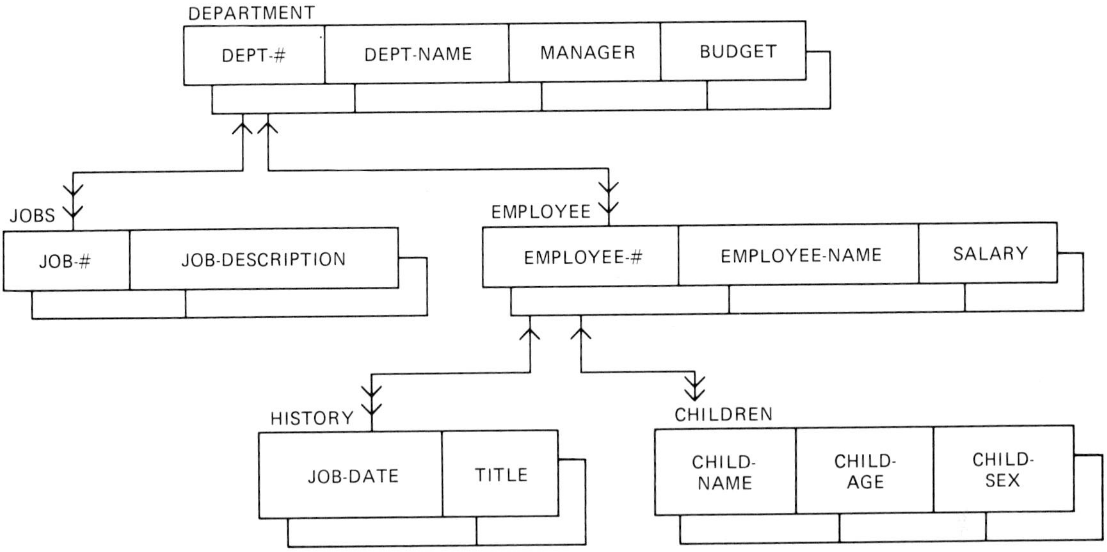
DEPARTMENT
DEPT-#
DEPT-NAME
MANAGER
BUDGET
JOBS
JOB-#
JOB-DESCRIPTION
EMPLOYEE
EMPLOYEE-#
EMPLOYEE-NAME
SALARY
HISTORY
JOB-DATE
TITLE
CHILDREN
CHILD-NAME
CHILD-AGE
CHILD-SEX

FIG 8.10 A tree structure.

DIVISION (DIVISION–#, DIVISION–NAME, DIVISION–HEAD)
OFFICE (DIVISION–#, OFFICE–NAME, LOCATION, ADDRESS, EMPLOYEE)
DEPARTMENT (DIVISION–#, DEPARTMENT–NAME, MANAGER)
PROJECT (DIVISION–#, DEPARTMENT–NAME, PROJECT–NAME, FINISH–DATE, BUDGET–AMT)

Congratulations! With the foundation of being able to normalize trees correctly, we next consider the normalization of networks.

Networks are normalized by first transforming them into trees, and then following the normalization process described above. In essence a network is changed into a tree by adding redundant nodes and by creating

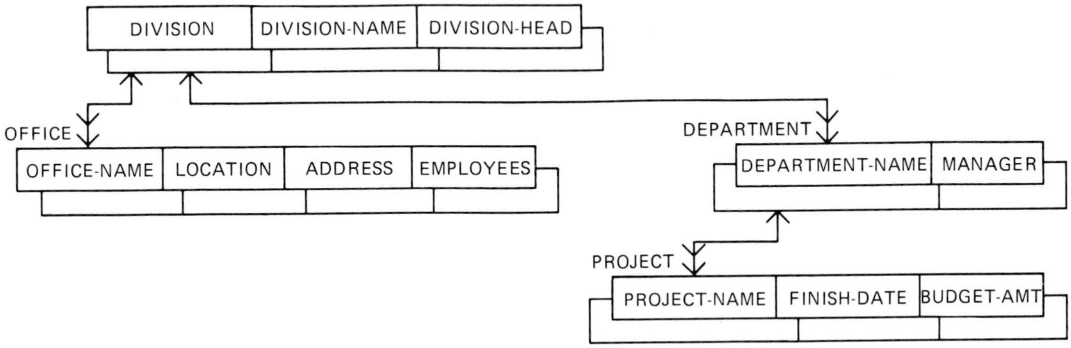
DIVISION
DIVISION-NAME
DIVISION-HEAD
OFFICE
OFFICE-NAME
LOCATION
ADDRESS
EMPLOYEES
DEPARTMENT
DEPARTMENT-NAME
MANAGER
PROJECT
PROJECT-NAME
FINISH-DATE
BUDGET-AMT

FIG 8.11 A schema for a tree structure.

222 Logical Data Organization

additional trees. Consider the networks portrayed in terms of nodes on the left side of Figure 8.12. The networks, by adding additional trees and redundant nodes, are represented on the right side of Figure 8.12 as tree structures.

The schema shown in the upper portion of Figure 8.13 represents a simple network. The parents of the structure CLASS are INSTRUCTOR and STUDENT. In the bottom portion of Figure 8.13 the network schema has been transformed into a tree structure by the addition of a redundant relation CLASS–TAKEN. The tree structure can then be normalized, again portraying the dependencies, as follows:

INSTRUCTOR (<u>INSTRUCTOR–ID</u>, INSTRUCTOR–NAME, OFFICE–#)
CLASS (<u>CLASS–ID</u>, CLASS–NAME, INSTRUCTOR–ID, LOCATION)
STUDENT (<u>STUDENT–ID</u>, NAME)
CLASS–TAKEN (<u>STUDENT–ID, CLASS–ID</u>)

Redundancy introduced into the relation CLASS–TAKEN is minimized by repeating only the primary key of the new relation. A complicating factor occurs between the relations INSTRUCTOR and CLASS when a course is team taught. That is, the relationship between INSTRUCTOR and CLASS changes for 1 : M to M : M. To normalize the new M : M relationship, the following relation is added:

FIG 8.12 Networks transformed into trees.

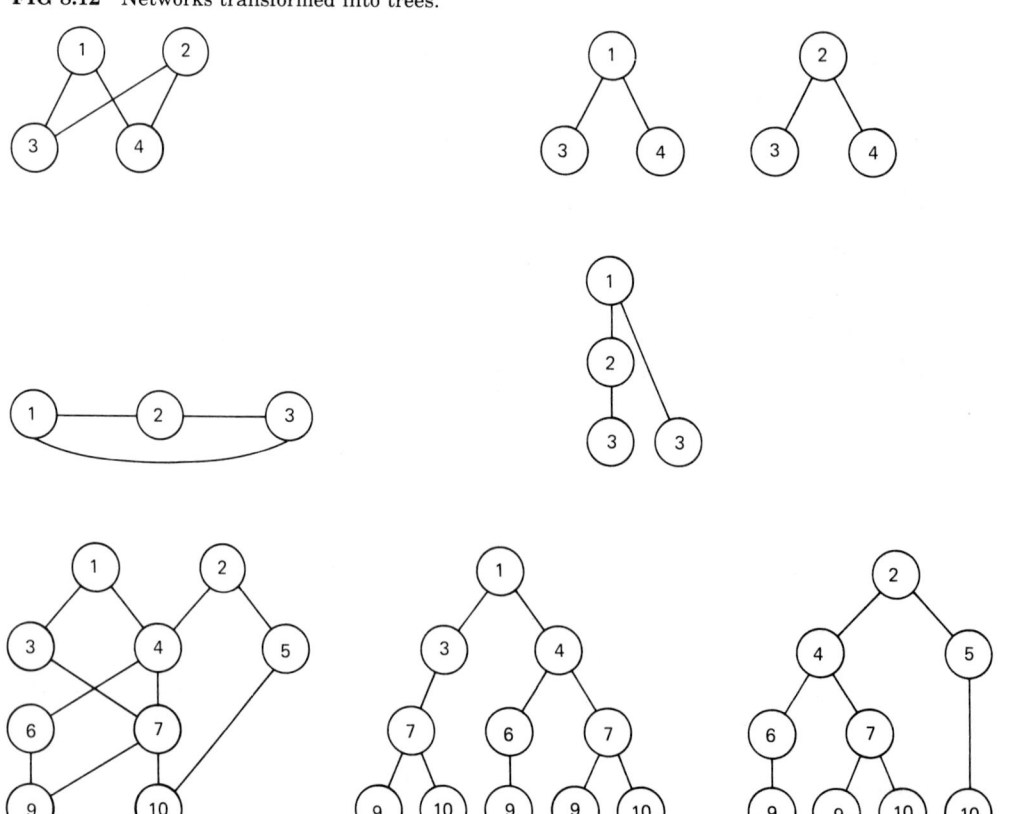

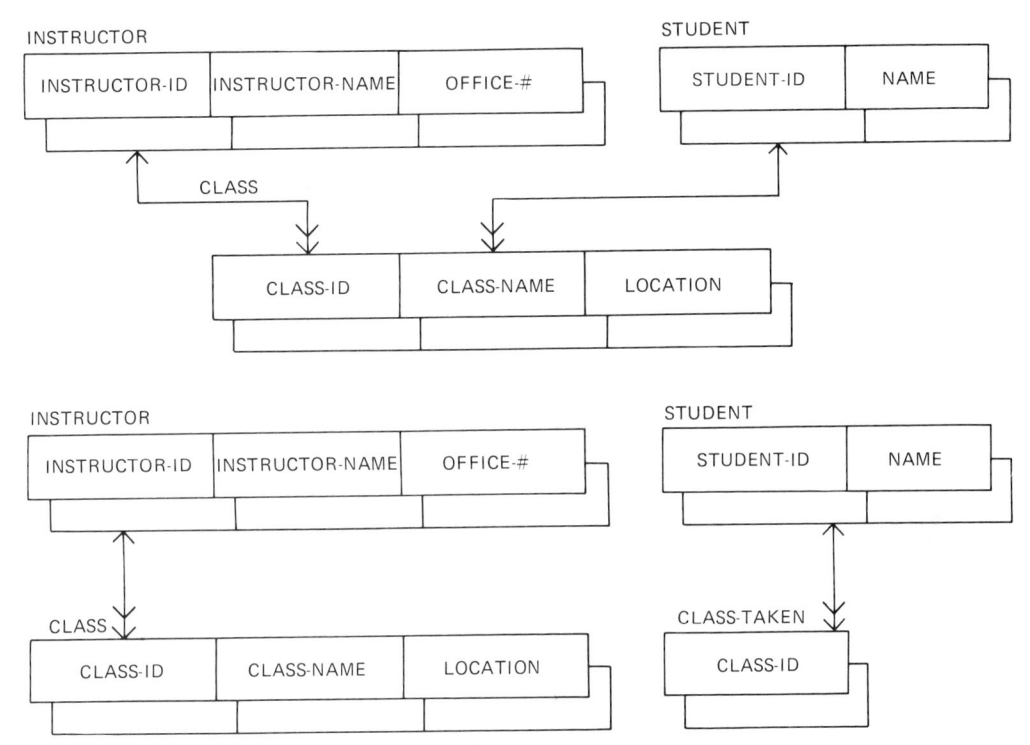

FIG 8.13 A network structure is transformed into a tree structure.

TEAM–TAUGHT (CLASS–ID, INSTRUCTOR–ID)

With the ability to normalize nonflat structures, we can now serve nontechnical users better. We can present them with a single and consistent data structure, one they will find easier to deal with and comprehend. This is especially important as the number of records increases and their relationships become more complex. Also, with hierarchical structures, we have a tendency to give preferential treatment to user requests that start at the root of the tree and move down its nodes. With a relational model, a user sitting at a CRT will not feel constrained to formulate questions that can be easily responded to by the data structure. Finally, once the contents of the data structures are normalized, application of powerful operators on easy to understand tables permits the derivation of a wide variety of tables. Such flexibility allows user queries such as "What are the multiple ship to points on this order?" or "What accounts or notes are related to a specific bank customer?" to be answered.

8.6 ▪ RELATIONAL OPERATORS

The key to flexibility in a relational data base lies in the ease with which relations can be manipulated by the user. A flat file can be "cut and pasted" by the user through the application of the *relational operators* of project and join.

Project

Suppose a user wishes to work with only a few domains from a relation. For example, from all the information stored about a company's customers, the sales manager might be interested only in their location. The process of shrinking the number of domains of a relation can be accomplished by using the relational operator *project*. In essence, the project operator enables us to select domains from a relation, and if we wish, to establish their order.

We examine two cases of the project operator in Figure 8.14. The first case shows the projection (signified by a π symbol),

EMPL–DEPT = π EMPLOYEES (DEPT–#)

EMPLOYEES

EMPLOYEE-#	EMPLOYEE-NAME	DEPT-#	LOCATION	TITLE
53702	MAY B	72	AUSTIN	PROFESSOR
53704	SUMMERS E L	72	AUSTIN	PROFESSOR
53791	WELSCH G W	07	TYLER	ASSOCIATE
53800	ROBERTSON J	40	TULSA	ASSISTANT
53805	SOMMERFELD R	72	AUSTIN	ASSISTANT
53806	DEAKIN E	40	TULSA	ASSOCIATE

EMPL-DEPT = π EMPLOYEES (DEPT-#)

EMPL-TITLE-LOC = π EMPLOYEES (TITLE, LOCATION)

EMPL-DEPT

DEPT-#
72
07
40

EMPL-TITLE-LOC

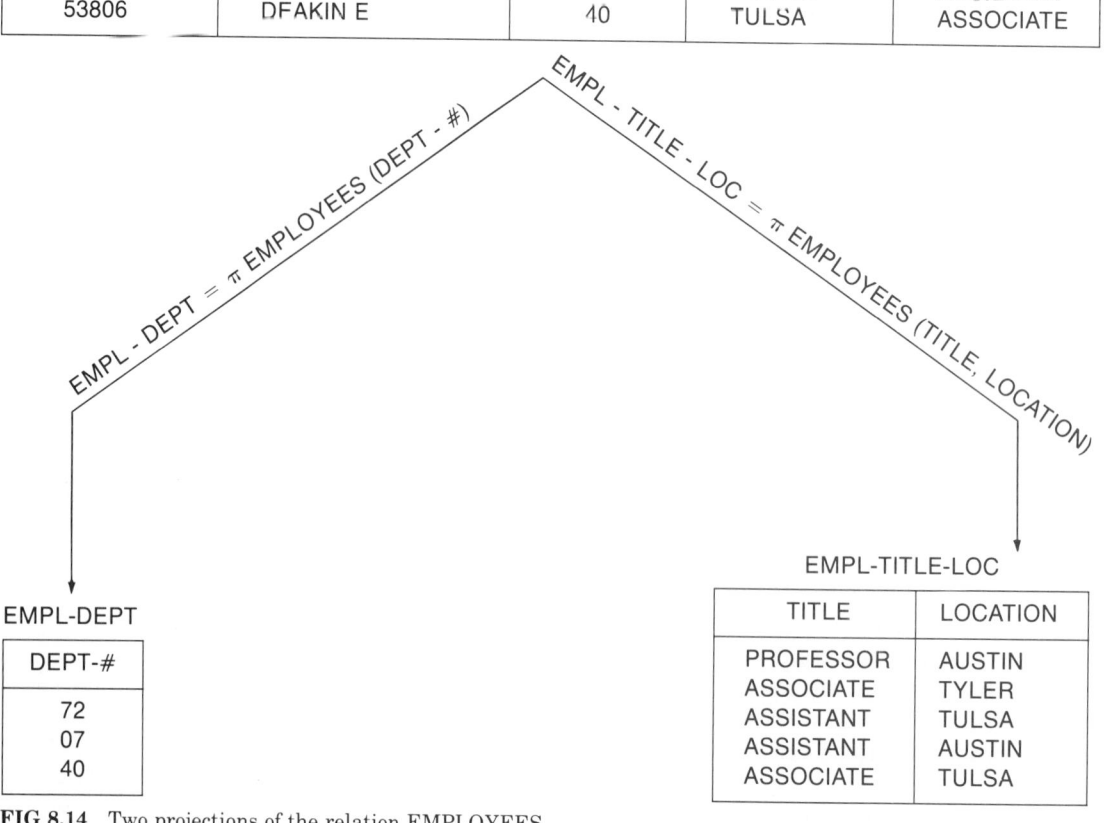

TITLE	LOCATION
PROFESSOR	AUSTIN
ASSOCIATE	TYLER
ASSISTANT	TULSA
ASSISTANT	AUSTIN
ASSOCIATE	TULSA

FIG 8.14 Two projections of the relation EMPLOYEES.

Relational Operators

The project operator is being applied to the relation EMPLOYEES to answer the question, "In what departments do our employees work?" Notice that because all we want is a list of departments, only the domain DEPT-# is selected (this is specified by enclosing it in parentheses) to appear in the newly created relation, EMPL-DEPT. Further, fewer tuples appear in the new relation EMPL-DEPT than in the original relation EMPLOYEES. This occurs because *a projection results in deletion of any tuples that are complete duplicates* (i.e., 72, 72, and 40).

Figure 8.14 contains a second projection operation,

EMPL-TITLE-LOC = π EMPLOYEES (TITLE, LOCATION)

It is intended to answer the question, "What job titles are held by our employees at different locations?" Note the order of the domains (i.e., TITLE then LOCATION) in the new relation EMPL-TITLE-LOC. Also note that because the tuple AUSTIN, PROFESSOR is a duplicate, the new relation contains one less tuple than the old relation EMPLOYEES.

Join

Because of the simplicity and streamlined nature of relational structures, it is uncommon for a single relation to contain all the data necessary to satisfy a user inquiry. Data scattered in two or more relations can be brought together by applying the second of relational operators called a join. We now discuss the mechanics governing a join operation.

Two relations can be joined when they share a *common* domain. In other words, the *join* operator brings domains from different relations together. (You might think of a join as the reverse of a project.)

The symbol commonly used to denote a join operator is an *. When relations are joined on a domain, only those tuples that share the same data values of the common domain appear in the resulting relation. For example, a user, working from a terminal, might devise the join of the relations INSTRUCTOR and STUDENT illustrated in Figure 8.15. The common domain here is CLASS-#. Tuples that share the same data values of the common domain make up the new relation CLASS-ROSTER. Notice that the tuple DEITRICK, JAMES | LAW 426 is missing from the relation CLASS-ROSTER because it does not have a common data value in the domain CLASS-# of the relation STUDENT. Likewise, the tuples CAUSEY, RICHARD | ACC 382 , JONES, MARK | BL 291 , and WARREN, GORMAN | MAN 336 are not in the relation CLASS-ROSTER because they do not have common data values in the domain CLASS-# of the relation INSTRUCTOR.

A user may want to project on a relation produced from a join operation. This can be done by appending, within parentheses, the domains on which a projection operation is to be performed. Referring to Figure 8.16,[1] the relations R1, R2, and R3 are joined and then projected on the domains, NAME, ZIP, PROFESSION, CONVICTION-TYPE, and CONVICTION-DATE by the following statement:

R4 = R1 * R2 * R3 (NAME, ZIP, PROFESSION, CONVICTION-TYPE, CONVICTION-DATE)

---

[1]Taken from James Martin, *Computer Data-Base Organization*, Englewood Cliffs, N. J.: Prentice-Hall, Inc., p. 220.

CLASS-ROSTER

INSTRUCTOR-NAME	CLASS-#	STUDENT-NAME
ANDERSON, JOHN	ACC 391	DOUGLAS, GOR
ANDERSON, JOHN	ACC 391	HANNEMAN, PAUL
ANDERSON, JOHN	ACC 391	WIELANSKY, CRAIG
CHENG, PETER	MAN 652	CARTER, MARGARET
CHENG, PETER	MAN 652	BUCHOLZ, ROBERT
CHENG, PETER	MAN 652	OETKING, PAULA
BLACK, ROBERT	ACC 384	CHUNG, PAUL
BLACK, ROBERT	ACC 384	BOWDEN, HIGHT
BLACK, ROBERT	ACC 384	NEUMANN, KATHY
BLACK, ROBERT	ACC 384	PILLIS, JAMES
FOWLER, ANNA	MKT 518	KOSTAS, CYNTHIA
FOWLER, ANNA	MKT 518	MAURICE, JEFFERY
FOWLER, ANNA	MKT 518	ROSS, YOLANDA

=

INSTRUCTOR

INSTRUCTOR-NAME	CLASS-#
ANDERSON, JOHN	ACC 391
CHENG, PETER	MAN 652
BLACK, ROBERT	ACC 384
DEITRICK, JAMES	LAW 426
FOWLER, ANNA	MKT 518

*

STUDENT

NAME	CLASS-#
CHUNG, PAUL	ACC 384
CAUSEY, RICHARD	ACC 382
CARTER, MARGARET	MAN 652
BUCHHOLZ, ROBERT	MAN 652
DOUGLAS, GOR	ACC 391
HANNEMAN, PAUL	ACC 391
KOSTAS, CYNTHIA	MKT 518
BOWDEN, HIGHT	ACC 384
JONES, MARK	BL 291
MAURICE, JEFFEREY	MKT 518
NEUMANN, KATHY	ACC 384
OETKING, PAULA	MAN 652
ROSS, YOLANDA	MKT 518
WARREN, GORMAN	MAN 336
WIELANSKY, CRAIG	ACC 391
PILLIS, JAMES	ACC 384

FIG 8.15 A join of the relations INSTRUCTOR and STUDENT to form the new relation CLASS-ROSTER.

R2

IDENTIFIC-ATION-#	NAME	ADDRESS	ZIP
817.53711	JENKINS L	10.E.51	70017
817.42815	SMITH A	24.E.51	70017
817.60712	ROPLEY ES	201.E.51	70017
817.31179	ELIOT K	402.E.51	70017
817.44051	DOE J	497.E.51	70017

R1

IDENTIFIC-ATION-#	CONVICTION-DATE	CONVICTION-TYPE	CONVICTION-LENGTH
817.42315	1.12.82	RAPE	12
817.42815	2.2.83	THEFT	24
817.43001	10.12.84	THEFT	36
817.44051	11.1.83	DRUGS	LIFE
817.46172	3.5.82	RAPE	363

R3

IDENTIFIC-ATION-#	NAME	PROFESSION	INCOME-RANGE
817.42815	SMITH A	ACCOUNTANT	20000
817.77112	WILLIAMS S	REALTOR	30000
817.73119	NELSON H	SAILOR	10000
817.44051	DOE J	DIPLOMAT	50000
817.91254	MARTIN P	PROGRAMMER	20000

R4 = R1 · R2 · R3 (NAME, ZIP, PROFESSION, CONVICTION-TYPE, CONVICTION-DATE)

NAME	ZIP	PROFESSION	CONVICTION-TYPE	CONVICTION-DATE
SMITH A	70017	ACCOUNTANT	THEFT	2.2.83
DOE J	70017	DIPLOMAT	DRUGS	11.1.83

FIG 8.16 A *join* operation, followed by a project *operation*.

Project and join operators are the backbone of relational data base management languages. For instance, *Query-by-Example* (QBE) developed by IBM, enables users who have never learned a formal programming language to formulate programs to create and drop tables interactively. Because QBE embraces the technology of flat files, this new class of user is given the preception of manual manipulation of the data base.

SUMMARY

The material in this chapter is new to most of you. It may even be slightly intimidating. It should not be. The purpose of it is to give you a rigorous way to associate logically data items in a data base. It is simply another design technique to help you prepare the "blueprint" of your information systems design. Actually, most of this material is formalized common sense.

As a systems analyst, you need precise ways to define logical data structures to meet a variety of information needs. A user wants to know how many instructors teach introductory accounting. Another wants to know how many rooms with a 20 or more seating capacity are available Tuesday night between 7 and 10 PM. The sales manager wants to know how many orders have been made by a particular salesperson. And so on. If all captured data were merely "dumped" in physical files, the systems analyst would not have to be concerned with data structures. Everything could be filed under "miscellaneous." At best, the above inquiries or any other inquiries could be answered by brute force search techniques. And if answers to inquiries were found, the timeliness of these responses would be so bad as to make them useless.

Obviously, it is better systems work to define data associations beforehand and implement these into the system either by preparing or purchasing appropriate computer programs (possibly in the forms of a DBMS package) to handle these structures. If one is designing a manual system, the same techniques apply by showing how filing cabinets and record-folders are associated to accomplish the same information objectives.

REVIEW QUESTIONS

8.1 What does a schema describe? In what terms?

8.2 How are different views of the schema expressed?

8.3 List the rules for drawing a schema.

8.4 Define what is meant when a data item is called a "primary key."

8.5 Why are data items "concatenated?"

8.6 Give an example of your own of one-to-one, one-to-many, and many-to-many relationships between subschemas.

8.7 A tree must meet two conditions. What are they?

8.8 What is the difference between heterogeneous branches and homogeneous occurrences of a tree?

8.9 When does a tree become a network? What is the difference between a simple and complex network?

8.10 What is meant by the term "normalization?"

8.11 What is another name for a two-dimensional table? A column of that table? A row of that table?

8.12 How is a network structure changed to a tree structure?

8.13 What is the affect of a "project" operator being applied to a relation?

8.14 Why might a projection of a relation result in a relation with fewer "tuples" than the original?

8.15 When two relations are "joined," what tuples appear in the resulting relation?

8.16 What form is used to specify a join operation that follows a project?

QUESTIONS FOR DISCUSSION

8.1 "It takes too much time to determine everyone's subschema. Instead, we believe that a single schema should be able to satisfy the needs of all users equally and completely." Explain why this viewpoint might cause user dissatisfaction.

8.2 If standards do not exist for drawing a schema, what problems might result?

8.3 "All logical structures can be expressed as trees." Comment on the validity of this statement.

8.4 "In a network it is difficult to distinguish parent and children nodes." Do you agree or disagree with this statement? Why?

8.5 "The benefits of normalization are not worth the effort." Under what conditions may this statement be true? Under what conditions may it be false?

8.6 Answer the user question, "Why are there so few records remaining after I selected a couple of fields from a file?"

8.7 What do you think happens when an attempt is made to join two relations that do not have a common domain?

8.8 "A relational system is not a viable alternative because commercially available DBMSs do not exist." Comment on the accuracy of this statement.

230 Logical Data Organization

EXERCISES

8.1 Construct a tree to depict the following network structure:

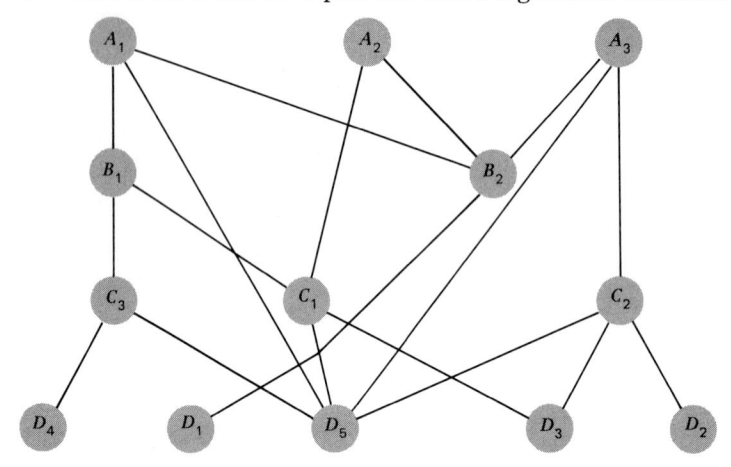

8.2 Given the relations below, completely describe the relations R_4 and R_5.

R_1 (A,B,C)

A	B	C
1	1	Y
4	J	Y
4	J	Y
6	L	Y
6	N	Y
7	N	Z

R_2 (A,E)

A	E
4	Y
6	K

R_3 (C,F)

C	F
Y	A
Z	B
P	C
Y	D

$$R_4 = R_1 * R_2 * R_3 \ (E,F)$$
$$R_5 = R_3 * R_1 * R_2 \ (A,\dot{B})$$

8.3 Draw this network as a tree structure.

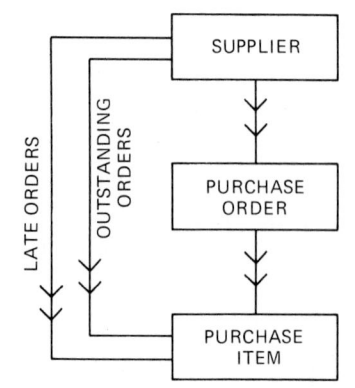

8.4 Draw a subschema to represent the following descriptions:

a. Each employee of the company has certain attributes, such as employee identification, employee name, and employee address. Employees may have worked at one or several jobs. Each job has a title and a starting date. Finally, in each job an employee may have one or more hourly rates and starting dates.

b. A bank has many customers, each of whom is identified by his or her name, business address, and home address. A customer may have one or more checking accounts and one or more saving accounts. Each account has an account number and a balance. Finally, debit and credit transactions make up an account. A transaction contains a date and a dollar amount.

8.5 Normalize the following tree structure:

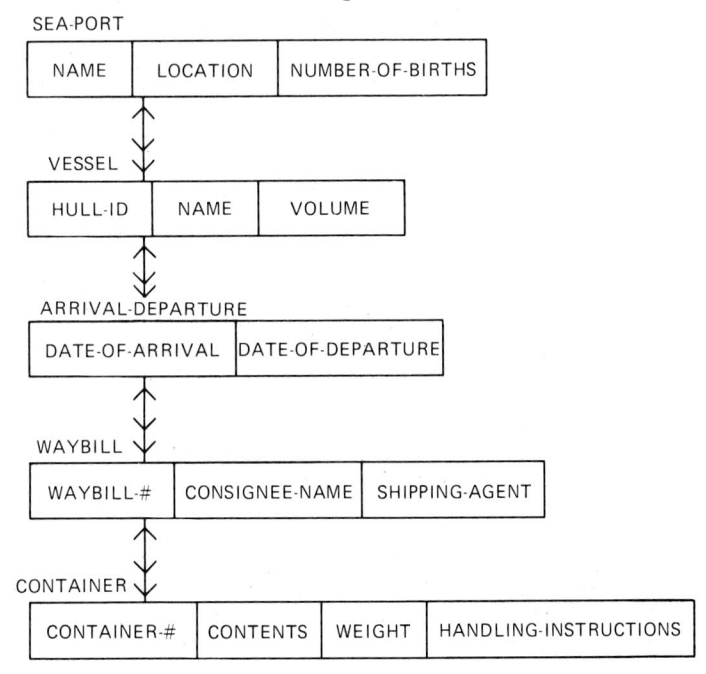

SEA-PORT

| NAME | LOCATION | NUMBER-OF-BIRTHS |

VESSEL

| HULL-ID | NAME | VOLUME |

ARRIVAL-DEPARTURE

| DATE-OF-ARRIVAL | DATE-OF-DEPARTURE |

WAYBILL

| WAYBILL-# | CONSIGNEE-NAME | SHIPPING-AGENT |

CONTAINER

| CONTAINER-# | CONTENTS | WEIGHT | HANDLING-INSTRUCTIONS |

8.6 Completely define the relation STUDENT–DESCRIPT = π STUDENT (MAJOR, GPA)

STUDENT

STUDENT-#	STUDENT-NAME	G.P.A.	MAJOR
234-90-1014	GNUFF, PETER	4.00	ACCOUNTING
421-50-9622	MARUM, LISA	2.50	FINANCE
425-40-8000	HUNG, SUSAN	3.80	MARKETING
427-32-4567	FRANK, JEROME	2.50	FINANACE
451-99-6625	YONEG, PATRICK	1.60	MANAGEMENT
451-99-7536	CLAY, MIFFY	4.00	ACCOUNTING

PROBLEMS

8.1 Prepare a schema for the following representation:

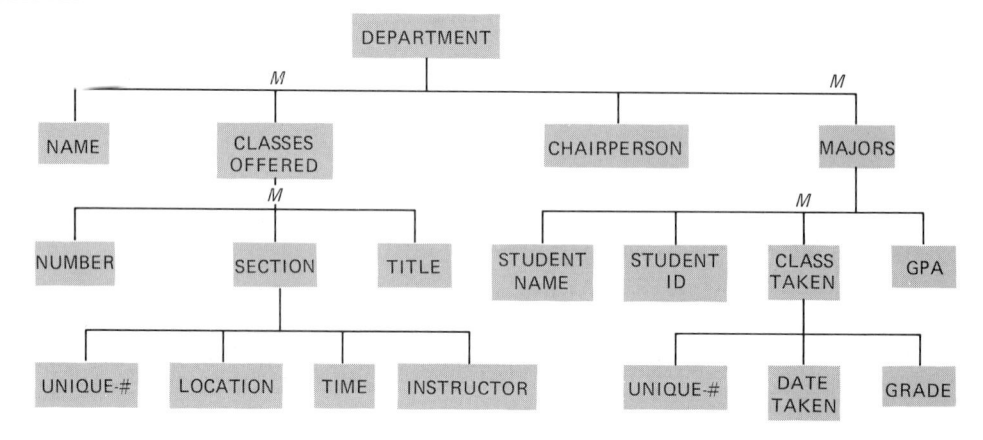

Note: M means a one-to-many relationship.

8.2 Normalize the following structure:

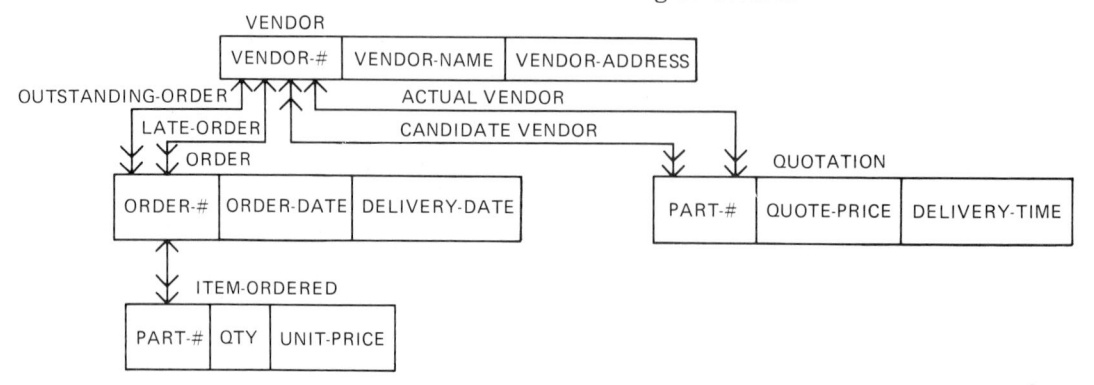

8.3 The following data base is set up to answer several queries. Study it and for each query, formulate the appropriate relational operations and specify the results of these operations.

PROFESSOR–STUDENT

PROFESSOR–ID	STUDENT–ID	COURSE
56	462	ACC 380
56	690	BL 382
56	700	BL 382
58	462	ACC 380
58	690	ACC 380
58	694	ACC 382
63	690	BA 384T
63	700	BA 384T
74	700	ACC 380
74	723	ACC 380
87	723	ACC 382

C–1

STUDENT–ID
462

C–2

COURSE
ACC 380
ACC 382

C–3

GOAL
Ph.D

PROFESSOR

PROFESSOR–ID	PROFESSOR–NAME	DEGREE-FROM
56	Black	Minnesota
58	Deakin	Illinois
63	Huber	Stanford
74	Robertson	North Carolina
87	Tabor	Florida

STUDENTS

STUDENT–ID	STUDENT–NAME	GOAL
462	Falk	Ph.D
690	Haegele	MPA
694	Kowalczyk	MPA
700	Slade	Ph.D
723	Wilkerson	Ph.D

(a) Obtain the professor identification number for all professors who taught student 462 and call the result relation X.
(b) Obtain a list of names of all professors who taught student 462.
(c) Obtain a list of the names of professors who taught the course ACC 380 or ACC 382.
(d) Obtain a list of the professor identification numbers for all professors who taught students whose goal is a Ph.D. degree. Also include in the list the courses involved.
(e) Obtain a list of names of professors who taught students whose goal is a Ph.D. degree.

8.4 Draw a schema for the following representation:

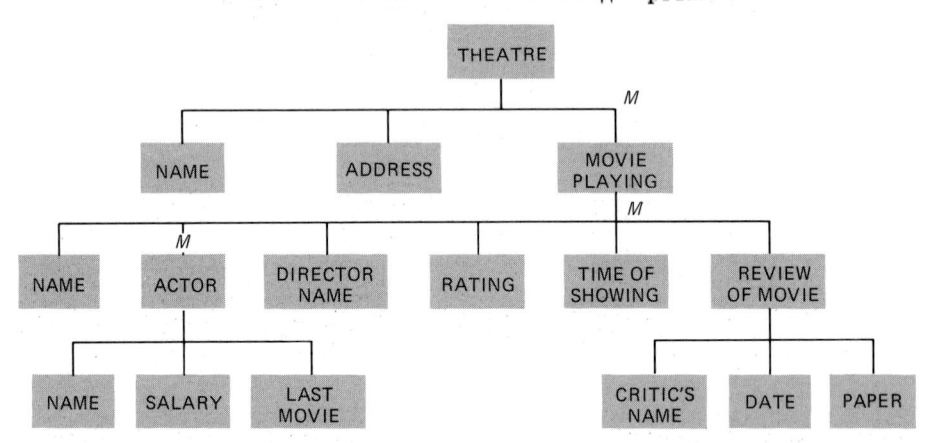

```
                    THEATRE
                       |
        ┌──────────────┼──────────────┐
                                      M
      NAME         ADDRESS       MOVIE
                                 PLAYING
                                    |
                                    M
   ┌────┬──────┬──────────┬────────┬──────────┐
        M
  NAME  ACTOR  DIRECTOR  RATING  TIME OF    REVIEW
               NAME              SHOWING    OF MOVIE
          |                                    |
     ┌────┼──────┐                    ┌────────┼────────┐
   NAME SALARY  LAST                CRITIC'S  DATE   PAPER
               MOVIE                 NAME
```

Note: M means a one—to—many relationship.

8.5 Consider the following relations:

ITEM

ITEM	NAME	WEIGHT
26	WINCH	8
38	TURNING BLOCK	4
52	ROD RIGGING	35

SUPPLIES

ITEM-#	SUPPLIER-#	QUANTITY
24	2	125
26	4	46
38	1	51
52	3	104
52	2	33
91	1	19

SUPPLIER

SUPPLIER-#	CITY	NAME
1	NEWPORT	SCHAFFER
2	BRISTOL	COMET
3	MIAMI	BARLOW
4	SAN DIEGO	TRAX
5	VANCOUVER	FAULTLESS

By an appropriate combination of join and project operations, show how to create a list of what items (names) can be supplied from what city.

BIBLIOGRAPHY

Date, *An Introduction to Data Base Systems,* Third Edition, Reading, MA.: Addison–Wesley Publishing Company, 1981.

Dieckmann, "Three Relational DBMS," *Datamation,* September 1981.

Cardenas, *Data Base Management Systems,* Boston: Allyn and Bacon, Inc., 1979.

Gillenson, "Back to Data Bas(e)ics," *Computerworld,* December 8, 1980.

Inmon, *Effective Data Base Design,* Englewood Cliffs, NJ.: Prentice-Hall, Inc., 1981.

Kroenke, *Database Processing,* Chicago: Science Research Associates, 1977.

Martin, *Computer Data-Base Organization,* Second Edition, Englewood Cliffs, NJ.: Prentice-Hall, Inc., 1977.

Zloof, "A Language for Office and Business Automation," IBM Research Report, RC 8091 (#35086), January 24, 1980.

CHAPTER 9

Physical Data Organization

9.1 ▪ INTRODUCTION

In the first part of this chapter we will look at how data are stored on and retrieved from physical storage media, and the characteristics of these media. If the data base could be supported by a storage device that had unlimited storage available at the instant it was needed by a program, then this chapter would not be needed. Thus far, technology has not provided an infinitely fast, unlimited size storage media, directly accessible by the user. The discussion that follows relates to the most popular physical media available to the systems analyst today.

In the second part of this chapter we examine the most common methods of addressing. Sequential, direct, hashing, and indexed sequential addressing methods are normally supplied by computer vendors via their operating systems.

The third part of this chapter discusses the techniques of using pointers, chains, and rings. These mechanisms allow us to represent physically the logical structures (trees and networks) described in detail in Chapter 8.

The last part of the chapter describes approaches that facilitate retrieval of data based on attributes. Having the capability of being able to retrieve physical records that have common data values is essential if an information system is to respond to the needs of many of its users.

The specific objectives of the chapter are as follows:

1. To review the primary computer storage media for data files.
2. To present the most commonly used methods of addressing data.
3. To describe the techniques that allow us to represent logical data structures physically.
4. To provide examples of network and tree structures represented physically.
5. To introduce approaches that allow retrieval of data based on common attribute value.

9.2 ▪ COMPUTER STORAGE MEDIA

Data files can be stored on a variety of hardware storage media accessible during computer processing. For a given system the storage media selected depends upon the detail values of the demand blocks. The characteristics of the various types of file storage media must first be understood before the systems analyst can make a logical determination as to how data files are to be organized and processed. One popular classification of storage media is based on the methods by which data can be accessed, and provides two broad categories: sequential and direct. **Sequential access** is merely serially searching through a file of records until the appropriate record has been found. On the other hand, records stored on a direct access storage device (DASD) have a unique address. Thus, records can be stored on a DASD in such a way that the location of any one record can be determined without extensive searching, so that records can be **accessed directly** rather than sequentially.

Figure 9.1 lists the basic storage media and indicates which access method is applicable. Note that while all storage media can be accessed sequentially, certain media cannot be accessed via the direct method.

Punched Cards and Punched Paper Tape

Two of the earliest developed and most widely used storage media are punched cards and punched paper tape. Although many small organizations still process their data via these storage media, they are seldom considered as desirable alternatives in more sophisticated data base applications. These media, however, are still extremely valuable as alternatives for inputting data transactions, particularly in batch processing environments.

Although many versions of **punched cards** are used for data processing, by far the most widely used card is known as the *Hollerith card,* named after its inventor. The Hollerith card provides storage for as many as 80 characters of data. These data are entered into 80 vertical columns with twelve

Media	Sequential access	Direct access
Punched cards	X	
Punched tape	X	
Magnetic tape	X	
Magnetic drum	X	X
Magnetic disk	X	X
Mass storage	X	X
Core (memory)	X	X
Computer output microfilm	X	X

FIG 9.1 Basic file media with method of access.

punching positions in each column. One or more punches in a single column represents a character. Figure 9.2 illustrates one coding structure for character designation. Data on a card might represent part of a record, one record, or more than one record. If a particular record contains more data than one card can hold, then two or more cards can be used. Continuity in the cards of one record is obtained by punching an identifying code in a specified column of each card.

Paper tape is a continuous storage medium. Consequently, paper tape can be used to store records of any length, limited only by the capacity of the buffer area of the equipment being used to process the tape. Paper tape can contain five or eight *channels* (punching positions) with which data can be represented. Certain combinations of punches in the channels provides a binary representation of characters which can subsequently be interpreted and processed.

Magnetic Tape

Magnetic tape[1] is also a continuous storage medium similar to the tape used in sound

---

[1] Magnetic storage media are discussed in more depth in Appendix B.

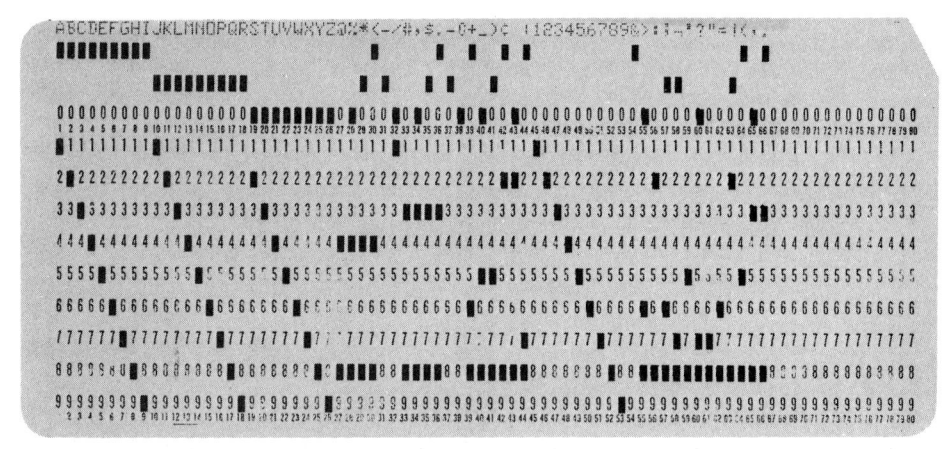

FIG 9.2 A Hollerith card showing how different characters are represented.

recorders. Data are stored in magnetized bits, are permanent, and can be retained for an indefinite period. As data are stored, the previous data are destroyed, thus permitting repetitive use of the tape.

A typical tape segment is shown in Figure 9.3. Each record is separated from the adjoining record by a blank section of tape known as the **interblock gap** (IBG). This interval between records allows for the start and stop operations of the tape drive. The size of tape records may vary from a few characters to several thousand and is restricted only by the capacity of the equipment that processes the tape.

Since the interblock gaps waste space, the logical records are usually "blocked" in groups of N physical records, where N represents the **blocking factor.** For example, the tape of Figure 9.3 could be blocked using a blocking factor of 4 as illustrated in Figure 9.4.

Although blocking conserves storage space and decreases the processing time required for reading and writing the tape, it adds to the core requirement of the program processing the file.

Magnetic Disk

A **disk** device is composed of magnetically coated platters, which are stacked on a rotating spindle. A movable access arm, containing read/write heads, passes between the physical disks. The surface of each disk is divided into concentric **tracks.** The tracks on each disk surface are located physically one above the other forming a series of concentric cylinders. A schematic diagram of a disk device is shown in Figure 9.5.

A *cylinder* of data is the amount that is accessible with one positioning of the access mechanism. The concept of a cylinder is an important one because the movement of the

FIG 9.3 Segment of magnetic tape.

FIG 9.4 Magnetic tape segment with blocked records.

access mechanism represents a significant portion of the time required to access and transfer data. A large amount of data can be stored in a single cylinder, thus minimizing the movements of the access mechanism. For example, the magnetic disk system in Figure 9.5 consists of ten separate horizontal recording surfaces. If there are 200 tracks on the recording surfaces, then from an access point of view, it consists of 200 separate vertical cylinders of ten tracks each. If each track can contain 3625 characters (bytes) of data, then a cylinder has a maximum capacity of 36,250 characters (3625 × 10).

Some disk devices use a single-arm access mechanism, which moves both horizontally and vertically to access any track within the disk file. However, most disk devices are equipped with a comb-type access mechanism in which the arms are arranged like the teeth on a comb and move horizontally between the disks. The read/write heads are aligned vertically and all move together. Thus, for each position of the access mechanism one entire cylinder surface is accessible to the heads. There are also disk devices which contain read/write heads permanently located at all cylinders, thereby eliminating any arm movement.

Data records stored on a DASD are recorded in locations that are identified by unique addresses. A **disk address** is a number that represents a particular cylinder on which a desired data record has been written or is to be written. For example, if a particular record is located in cylinder 84 of disk surface 3, then the actual **hardware address** (sometimes called the **relative address**) of the record is 843. The read/write heads are "told" to go to this particular address, whereupon the fourth read/write head either reads from or writes on this location.

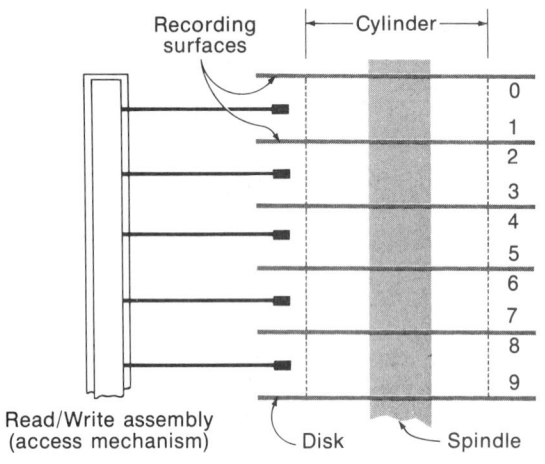

FIG 9.5 Magnetic disk system.

Computer Output Microfilm

Computer output microfilm (COM) represents a blend of microfilm and computer technology. Computer output that would normally be printed on paper is produced on microfilm. The production and use of COM provides significant user benefits in a wide range of systems applications. Some of these benefits are: (1) computer time reduced by bypassing the printer (impact printers represent a major bottleneck); (2) savings in file space (over 200 legal-sized pages can be copied on one 4" × 6" piece of microfilm); (3) cost of duplication and distribution is reduced; and (4) compared to paper documents, ease of use and speed of retrieval are increased. Components of a COM system are: recorder, duplicator, reader, and software for titling, indexing, editing, and data manipulation.

9.3 • ADDRESSING METHODS

The purpose of **addressing** is to transform unique identifier of records, called *keys,* into relative or absolute physical storage locations. In this section three of the most commonly used methods of addressing are examined.

Sequential Addressing

Sequential addressing is the simplest way of finding a record. Records in a file are stored in a predetermined order based on a key value, such as account number, social security number, or customer order number. A specific record is located by inspecting the key of one record after another until a match is found.

Indexed Sequential Addressing

In many instances, finding a specific record using sequential addressing may be too time-consuming. If a file is ordered by a key value, *indexed sequential* addressing can be used.

Indexed sequential search procedures can be compared to those we might use to find a book in a library. If you want to find a book in your library, you can go to the shelves and examine each book in sequence. This sequential examination would be extremely time-consuming. Instead, you can go to the card catalog, determine the approximate physical location of the book from the entry on the catalog card, and proceed to the shelf that holds the book.

We locate data using an indexed sequential method by following a similar procedure. A separate physical file, which is made up of an **index entry** for every *n*th data record rather than every data record in our library example, is created. It is first searched sequentially until the approximate location of the data record we are seeking is determined. Then, beginning at the location in the data file indicated by the index entry, the localized portion of the data file is searched sequentially until a match to the key value desired is found.

Let us work through an example showing how the above procedure is applied to locating data. The six entries in the index of Figure 9.6 indicate the ordered names of persons in the data segment or **sublist.** For example, suppose we wished to retrieve the data record having the key value "LARSON." We would begin by sequentially searching the index starting with the record having the key value "BARNES." The record "LARSON" may be in the first sublist. We know that it is not in the first sublist only when the second key value in the index "DEITRICK" is read. As we sequentially search through the index, we determine that if the record with the key "LARSON" exists, then it must be contained in the sublist headed by the data record with the key value "KELLOGG" (i.e., "KELLOGG" < "LARSON" < "NEWMAN"). Control is then transferred to relative address 19, the location of the data record "KELLOGG." The sublist of the actual data file is searched sequentially until, finally, a match is found at relative location 21.

Direct Conversion

Off all the addressing methods, **direct addressing** allows records to be found most quickly because the access mechanism must be moved only once. With direct addressing every possible key value must correspond to a unique storage address. Hence the *range* of the key value dictates the number of physical storage locations that must be reserved

242 Physical Data Organization

for the data file. A simple example illustrates a procedure that converts a key value to a physical address.

Suppose we wish to establish a file of data records for the telephone exchange 471. If the last four digits of the telephone number were the primary key, then we would need 10,000 physical storage locations to hold the data records (i.e., 471-0000 to 471-9999). Suppose further that each track of a disk could hold exactly 50 records and that a cylinder had 10 tracks, each holding 500 records. Doing a few calculations tell us we need 200 tracks or 20 cylinders to hold our data.

The cylinder address of any record relative to where our file begins is the *quotient* produced by dividing the last four digits of the key by 500. The *remainder* is divided by the records per track, 50, to determine the

Data List

INDEX

BARNES	01
DEITRICK	07
GRANOF	13
KELLOGG	19
NEWMAN	25
SUMMERS	31

Relative address

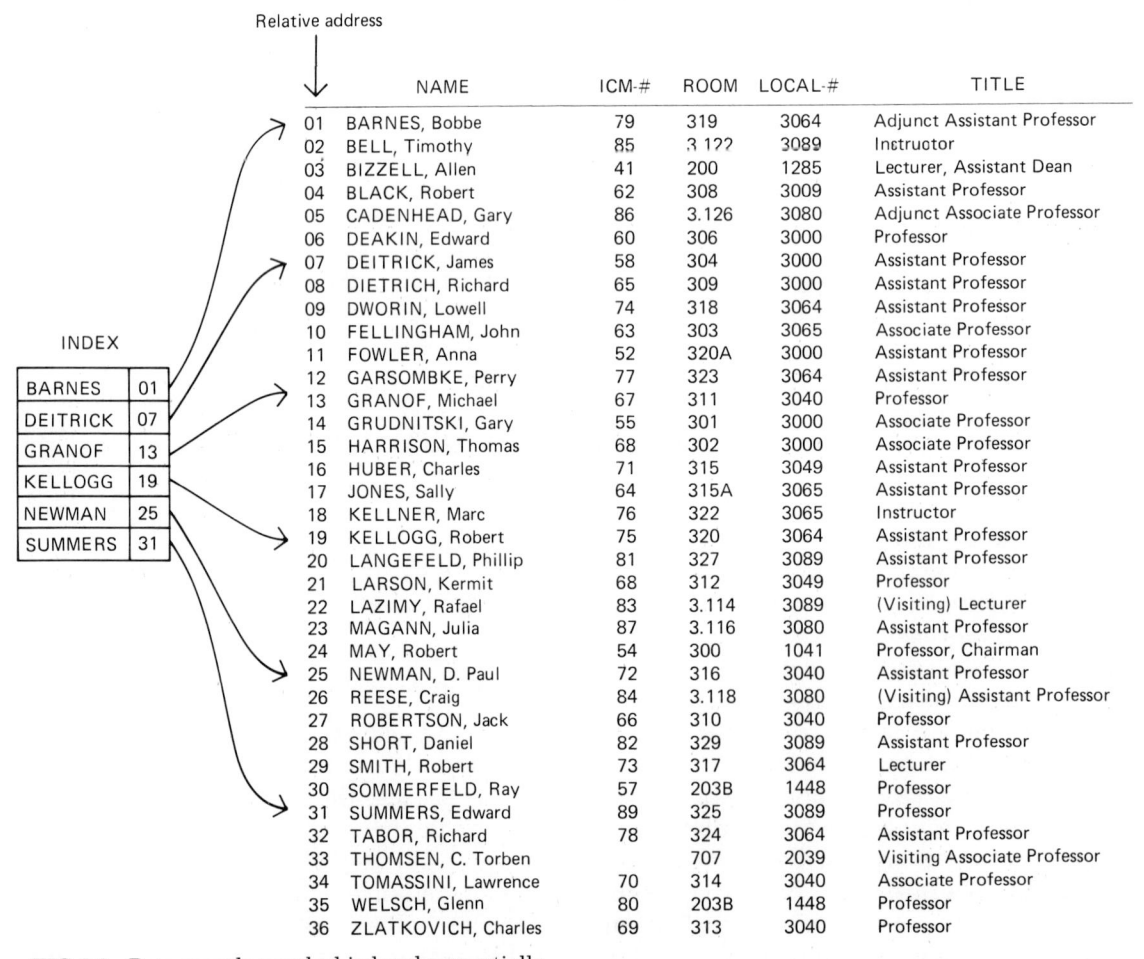

	NAME	ICM-#	ROOM	LOCAL-#	TITLE
01	BARNES, Bobbe	79	319	3064	Adjunct Assistant Professor
02	BELL, Timothy	85	3.122	3089	Instructor
03	BIZZELL, Allen	41	200	1285	Lecturer, Assistant Dean
04	BLACK, Robert	62	308	3009	Assistant Professor
05	CADENHEAD, Gary	86	3.126	3080	Adjunct Associate Professor
06	DEAKIN, Edward	60	306	3000	Professor
07	DEITRICK, James	58	304	3000	Assistant Professor
08	DIETRICH, Richard	65	309	3000	Assistant Professor
09	DWORIN, Lowell	74	318	3064	Assistant Professor
10	FELLINGHAM, John	63	303	3065	Associate Professor
11	FOWLER, Anna	52	320A	3000	Assistant Professor
12	GARSOMBKE, Perry	77	323	3064	Assistant Professor
13	GRANOF, Michael	67	311	3040	Professor
14	GRUDNITSKI, Gary	55	301	3000	Associate Professor
15	HARRISON, Thomas	68	302	3000	Associate Professor
16	HUBER, Charles	71	315	3049	Assistant Professor
17	JONES, Sally	64	315A	3065	Assistant Professor
18	KELLNER, Marc	76	322	3065	Instructor
19	KELLOGG, Robert	75	320	3064	Assistant Professor
20	LANGEFELD, Phillip	81	327	3089	Assistant Professor
21	LARSON, Kermit	68	312	3049	Professor
22	LAZIMY, Rafael	83	3.114	3089	(Visiting) Lecturer
23	MAGANN, Julia	87	3.116	3080	Assistant Professor
24	MAY, Robert	54	300	1041	Professor, Chairman
25	NEWMAN, D. Paul	72	316	3040	Assistant Professor
26	REESE, Craig	84	3.118	3080	(Visiting) Assistant Professor
27	ROBERTSON, Jack	66	310	3040	Professor
28	SHORT, Daniel	82	329	3089	Assistant Professor
29	SMITH, Robert	73	317	3064	Lecturer
30	SOMMERFELD, Ray	57	203B	1448	Professor
31	SUMMERS, Edward	89	325	3089	Professor
32	TABOR, Richard	78	324	3064	Assistant Professor
33	THOMSEN, C. Torben		707	2039	Visiting Associate Professor
34	TOMASSINI, Lawrence	70	314	3040	Associate Professor
35	WELSCH, Glenn	80	203B	1448	Professor
36	ZLATKOVICH, Charles	69	313	3040	Professor

FIG 9.6 Data records searched indexed sequentially.

Addressing Methods

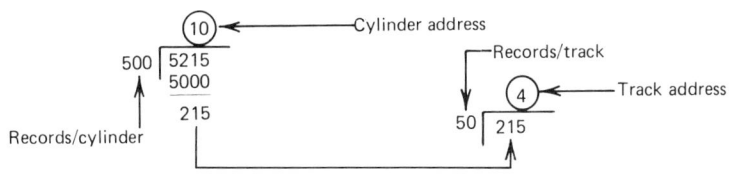

track address. Again, the *quotient* of our second division is the track where our data record is located. For the telephone number 471-5215, you should obtain the relative cylinder address 10, and relative track address 4.

Direct addressing usually means that the file is not completely filled with data records. Consider the situation where social security number is the key to a personnel file. One billion storage locations must be set aside because the keys have a possible range of from 000-00-0000 to 999-99-9999. If 10,000 records are in the file, utilization of the assigned memory is .001 percent. This poor utilization of storage space can be overcome by adopting an addressing method called hashing.

Hashing

The *hashing* method (also called algorithm, randomizing, or transformation method) of addressing records converts a key into a relative physical file address. Here the range of keys in a file is compressed into a smaller range of physical addresses. The main difficulty encountered with hashing is the problem of *synonyms* (records whose keys randomize to the same physical address). To minimize synonyms that cannot be written where they belong (**overflow** records), two techniques are used. With the first technique, hashing is to a track address rather than a record address. In this way not every synonym will produce an overflow. A second technique is to select a hashing algorithm that distributes records evenly over the file.

Of the many algorithms available, the most popular appears to be prime number division.

Using the **prime number division** technique and randomization to a track address, suppose that 6000, 200-byte records are to be addressed to a magnetic disk having a 5000-byte-per-track capacity. Therefore, 240 tracks would be required if all the records were evenly distributed. Since this ideal is seldom attained, more storage space—say 20 percent or a *loading factor* of 83 percent (240/288)—is added to handle synonyms. Now the total space allocated is 288 tracks. This means that if an even distribution of records to tracks was actually attained, approximately 21 out of the 25 possible storage locations of each of the 288 tracks would be occupied.

A prime number close to, but less than, 288 is now chosen—say 283. The prime number of 283 is then divided into a record's key value, say 1457. The quotient is discarded and the *remainder* of 042 is the relative address of the track for this record. An overflow condition will occur if more than 25 records happen to randomize to relative track address 042 (i.e., have a remainder of 42). Overflow may be handled by placing overflow records on another track of the same cylinder or by providing separate storage cylinders that are *independent* of the overflow record's track address.

Another example of hashing[2] which uses 25 percent more storage space to handle syn-

[2] Adapted from James Martin, *Computer Data-Base Organization*, Second Edition, Englewood Cliffs, New Jersey: Prentice-Hall, Inc., 1977.

244 Physical Data Organization

onyms, is illustrated in Figure 9.7. A maximum of two records are stored on each track. Tracks 29 to 32 hold *overflow synonyms*. Overflows are loaded on these tracks in the order in which they occur.

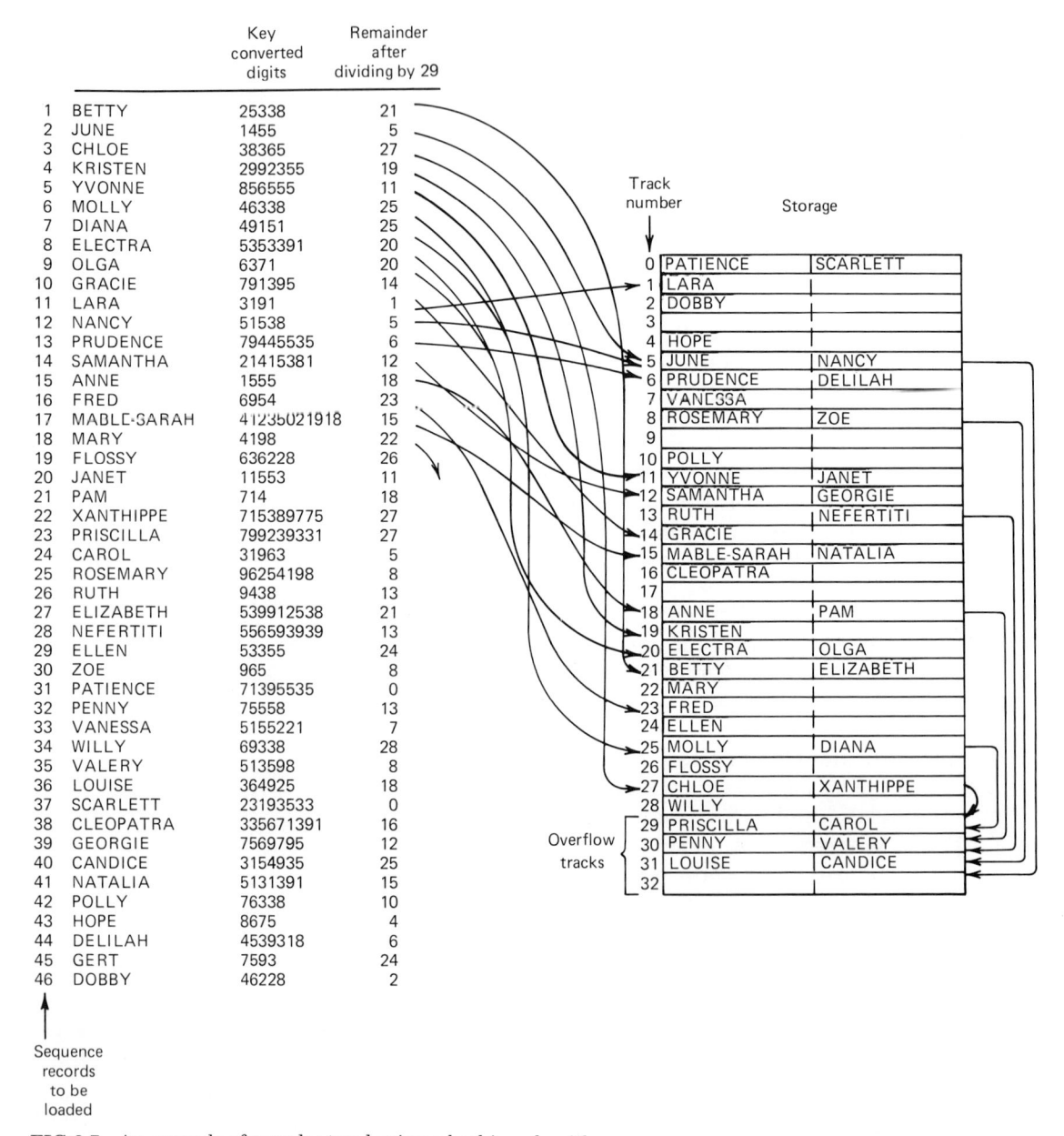

		Key converted digits	Remainder after dividing by 29
1	BETTY	25338	21
2	JUNE	1455	5
3	CHLOE	38365	27
4	KRISTEN	2992355	19
5	YVONNE	856555	11
6	MOLLY	46338	25
7	DIANA	49151	25
8	ELECTRA	5353391	20
9	OLGA	6371	20
10	GRACIE	791395	14
11	LARA	3191	1
12	NANCY	51538	5
13	PRUDENCE	79445535	6
14	SAMANTHA	21415381	12
15	ANNE	1555	18
16	FRED	6954	23
17	MABLE-SARAH	41235021918	15
18	MARY	4198	22
19	FLOSSY	636228	26
20	JANET	11553	11
21	PAM	714	18
22	XANTHIPPE	715389775	27
23	PRISCILLA	799239331	27
24	CAROL	31963	5
25	ROSEMARY	96254198	8
26	RUTH	9438	13
27	ELIZABETH	539912538	21
28	NEFERTITI	556593939	13
29	ELLEN	53355	24
30	ZOE	965	8
31	PATIENCE	71395535	0
32	PENNY	75558	13
33	VANESSA	5155221	7
34	WILLY	69338	28
35	VALERY	513598	8
36	LOUISE	364925	18
37	SCARLETT	23193533	0
38	CLEOPATRA	335671391	16
39	GEORGIE	7569795	12
40	CANDICE	3154925	25
41	NATALIA	5131391	15
42	POLLY	76338	10
43	HOPE	8675	4
44	DELILAH	4539318	6
45	GERT	7593	24
46	DOBBY	46228	2

Sequence records to be loaded

Track number / Storage:

Track		
0	PATIENCE	SCARLETT
1	LARA	
2	DOBBY	
3		
4	HOPE	
5	JUNE	NANCY
6	PRUDENCE	DELILAH
7	VANESSA	
8	ROSEMARY	ZOE
9		
10	POLLY	
11	YVONNE	JANET
12	SAMANTHA	GEORGIE
13	RUTH	NEFERTITI
14	GRACIE	
15	MABLE-SARAH	NATALIA
16	CLEOPATRA	
17		
18	ANNE	PAM
19	KRISTEN	
20	ELECTRA	OLGA
21	BETTY	ELIZABETH
22	MARY	
23	FRED	
24	ELLEN	
25	MOLLY	DIANA
26	FLOSSY	
27	CHLOE	XANTHIPPE
28	WILLY	
29	PRISCILLA	CAROL
30	PENNY	VALERY
31	LOUISE	CANDICE
32		

Overflow tracks: 29–32

FIG 9.7 An example of records stored using a hashing algorithm.

9.4 ▪ POINTERS, CHAINS, AND RINGS

We have alluded to the term pointer on several occasions without actually defining it. As you have probably already surmised, a **pointer** is anything that will allow the accessing mechanism to locate a specific record. Logical chaining associates records that have something in common according to the record content, whether those records are in the same physical file or in different files. A **chain** represents a logical path through the data base, thereby associating groups of records and fields within records to provide responses to information requests.

Figure 9.8 is a simple illustration of how a logical chain and pointer system works. In this example the file is sequenced alphabetically by employee name. The information request is to list all employees located in Boston. The pointer system provides for this information request by having associated Brown with Smith. No other record in the file represents a person living in Boston so termination of the chain is represented by an **asterisk** in the pointer for Smith.

For another example, assume that we have employee records stored on a DASD and that we wish to access all records with the data attribute "programmer." As illustrated in Figure 9.9, a total of seven employee records are in the data base. N gives the physical address of each employee's record, and the pointer provides the ability of software that supports the data base management system to retrieve only those employees who are programmers. We will assume that the starting location is the record located at physical address 2. Note that the pointer containing an asterisk indicates end of the logical chain that associates all programmers in the employee file.

Suppose that we wish to add another criterion that would give us only those programmers with five or more years' experience. We would have to add the number-of-years'-experience field to each record, and also add pointers to provide the chain that provides this kind of information. This physical data organization is shown in Figure 9.10. This example shows that by using more than one pointer in each stored record, *multiple associations* can be established with one physical organization of a file.

The use of chains and pointers alleviates the need to examine all records sequentially to gain specific information. A great deal of planning and work must go into the design of a data base to be able to tell how many programmers have five or more years' experience.

In a manual system, the number of logical associations would be limited because of the burdensome record keeping and pointer maintenance. In a computer-based system, logical data organization requires substan-

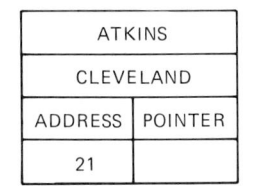

ATKINS		BROWN		JONES		SMITH	
CLEVELAND		BOSTON		DALLAS		BOSTON	
ADDRESS	POINTER	ADDRESS	POINTER	ADDRESS	POINTER	ADDRESS	POINTER
21		30	40	32		40	*

FIG 9.8 Simple illustration of a chain and pointer system.

246 Physical Data Organization

N	Social Security Number	Name	Title	Pointer
1	436339084	Custer H. L.	Systems analyst	
2	435779921	Tinsley W. A.	Programmer	7
3	237124444	Hamlin B. A.	Operator	
4	761234581	Pesnell B. R.	Programmer	5
5	477810020	Pesnell Glenda	Programmer	*
6	423871422	Powers Vesta	Scheduler	
7	400471748	Cranford H. L.	Programmer	4

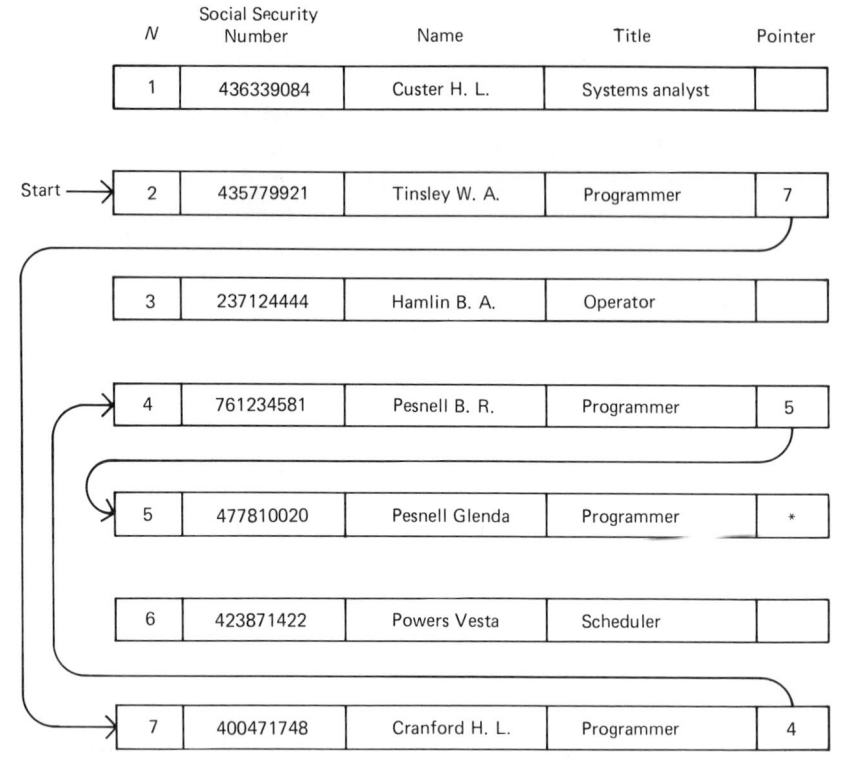

Start → 2

FIG 9.9 Simple chain structure that associates programmer records in an employee file.

tial logic and software support, a sophisticated I/O system, direct access storage, additional storage space for pointers, and a high level of maintenance (changing and keeping track) of pointers. Moreover, the entire file must be reorganized periodically, because *deleted* "dead" records waste space.

Rings are chains that do not have an end-of-chain indication (i.e., an asterisk) in the last record. Instead, the last record of the chain contains a pointer back to the entry record. An example of the "endless chain" principle can be seen in Figure 9.11.

A record within a chain may be at some distance from the *entry record;* when it is retrieved it may be useful to either go backward to the entry record or go directly to the entry record. This need to go backward can be satisfied by adding a pointer to each record to make a second chain. To go directly to the entry record without traversing the chain can be accomplished by adding a third pointer to each record. This third pointer would contain the address of the entry record. The addition of second and third pointers to each data record is shown in Figure 9.12.

9.5 ▪ PHYSICAL REPRESENTATION OF TREES AND NETWORKS

In Chapter 8, the logical structure of trees and networks was presented and discussed. Nothing was said, however, about the way

Physical Representation of Trees and Networks

N	Social Security Number	Name	Title	Years Experience	Pointer$_1$	Pointer$_2$
1	436449084	Custer H. L.	Systems analyst	4		
2	435779921	Tinsley W. A.	Programmer	6	7	6
3	237124444	Hamlin B. A.	Operator	2		
4	761234581	Pesnell B. R.	Programmer	5	5	*
5	477810020	Pesnell Glenda	Programmer	8	*	4
6	423871422	Powers Vesta	Scheduler	7		5
7	400471748	Cranford H. L.	Programmer	3	4	

FIG 9.10 A second chain that associates programmers with years of experience in an employee file.

these logical structures could be represented physically. In this section two methods of physically representing tree and network structures will be illustrated.

Figure 9.13 illustrates a tree structure. The link between *parent* and *child* could be made by attaching children pointers to the parent record. The use of multiple child pointers to represent relationships of the tree in Figure 9.13 is shown in Figure 9.14. Although the method of multiple child pointers allows us to go from parent to children quickly, it is rarely used because of the variable number of pointers attached to each parent. Pointer lists that are widely variable in length are difficult to handle when additions to and deletions from the file must be made.

To take advantage of the condition that each child in a tree structure has but a single parent, parent pointers might be considered. Figure 9.15 shows the outcome of using parent pointers in the tree structure illustrated in Figure 9.13. Although this method is certainly simpler than the method using multiple children pointers, it is limited to situations where only children-to-parent mapping is required. *Child-and-twin pointers* overcome both the complexity of multiple child pointers and the restriction of children-to-parent mapping. Here, two pointers are attached to each record; the first pointer of each record is the address of one child of the family, the second pointer indicates the location of a twin. The child-and-twin pointer method is illustrated in Figure 9.15

248 Physical Data Organization

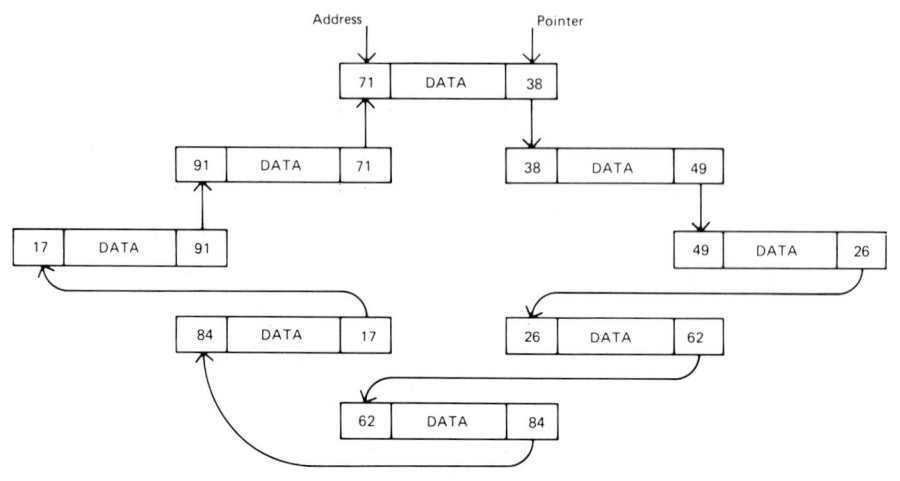

FIG 9.11 A one-way ring.

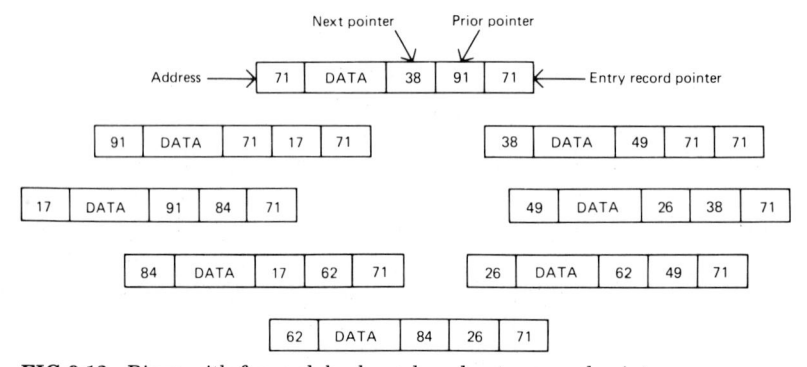

FIG 9.12 Rings with forward, backward, and entry record pointers.

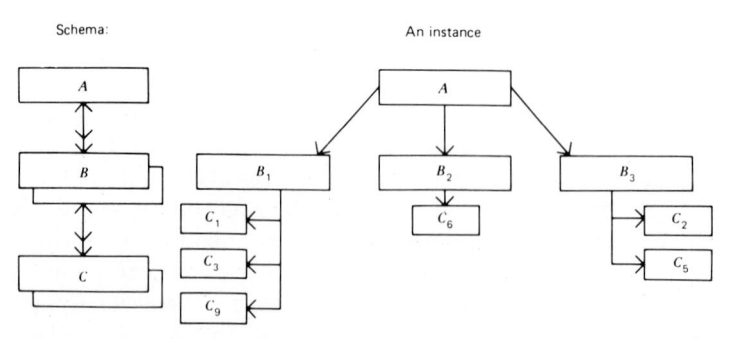

FIG 9.13 A representative tree structure.

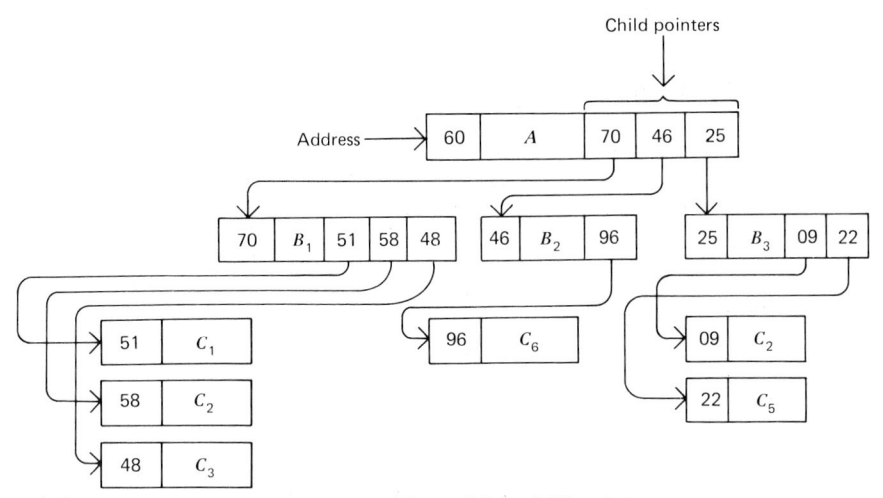

FIG 9.14 A tree structure represented by multiple child pointers.

for the tree structure portrayed in Figure 9.13.

The child-and-twin pointer method is not without its shortcomings. If the record has many children and we seek only one child, search of the chain may be extremely time-consuming.

A ring is an alternative method of representing free and network structures. Rings may be a straightforward mapping of children-to-parent relationships; they may be more complex, perhaps defining child-and-parent relationships. A ring structure depicting child-and-twin relationships is il-

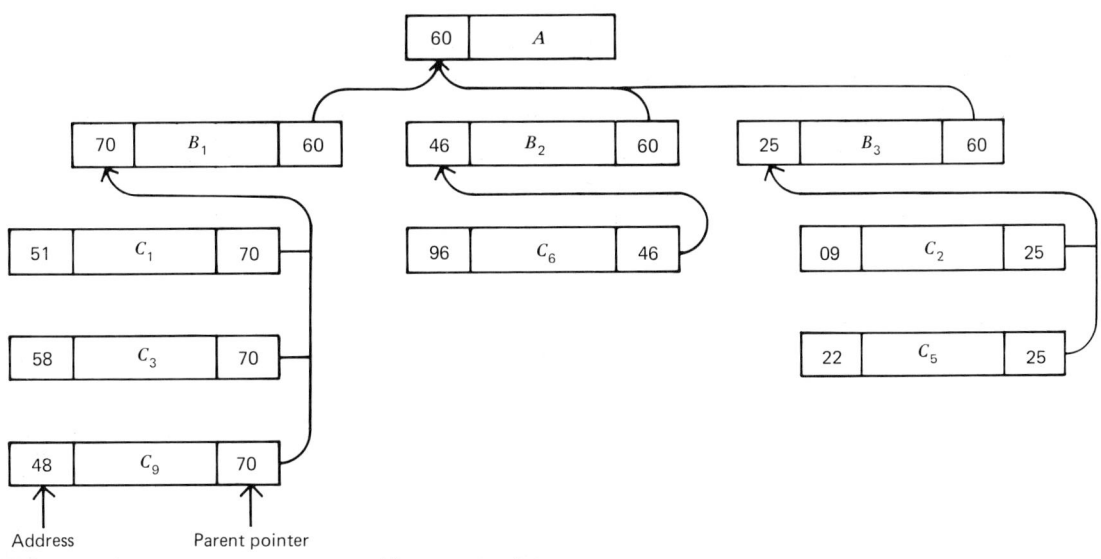

FIG 9.15 A tree structure represented by parent pointers.

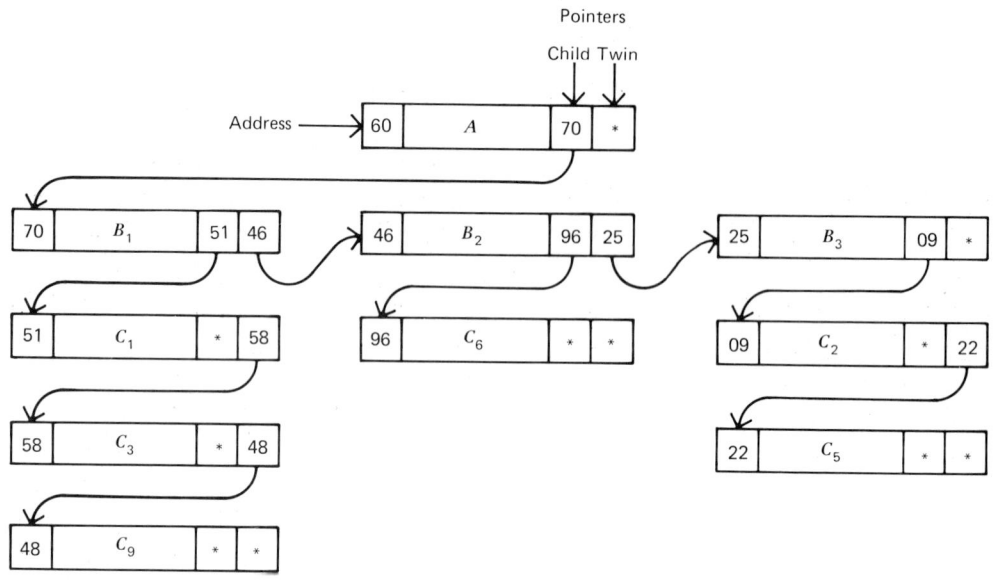

FIG 9.16 A tree structure represented by child-and-twin pointers.

lustrated in Figure 9.17. For a *childless* record the child pointer points back to its parent. For example, the first pointer of (childless) records C_1, C_3, and C_9 in Figure 9.17 contains the address of their parent B_1.

Up until now in our discussion, the pointers that link records together have been attached to the records. An alternative approach is the use of an index or directory. Here the pointers, which represent the relationship between records, are removed from the data records and placed in a separate **directory**. Being relatively compact, a slice of the directory can be brought into main memory and searched at high speed. This is not true for following chains embedded in the physical records. Representation of the tree structure of Figure 9.13 by a directory is shown in Figure 9.18. Frequently, an index is added to indicate the beginning location of each major segment of the directory (i.e., the A's, B's, and C's).

Networks

In Chapter 8 networks were differentiated from trees. In a *network,* children had more than one parent. Moreover, the relationship between parent and child was either multiple 1:M (simple network) or M:M (complex network).

Let us take the physical representation of a simple network first. *Pointers* might be used to represent the network illustrated in Figure 9.19. Figure 9.20 uses parent pointers to represent the network. Figures 9.21 and 9.22 use multiple child and child-and-twin pointers, respectively. In Figure 9.23, child, twin, and parent *rings* represent the network portrayed in Figure 9.19. Lastly, if

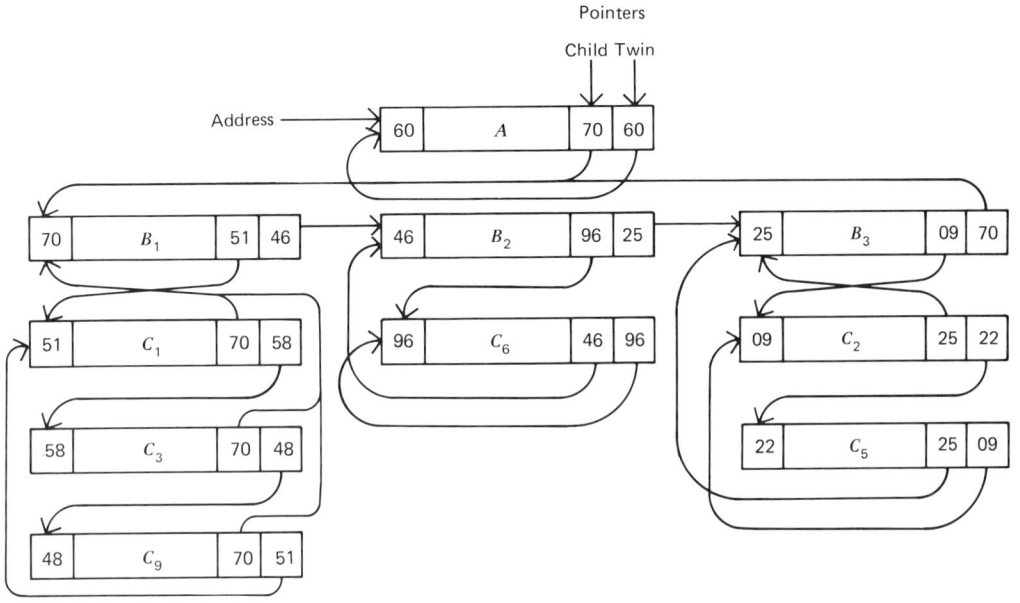

FIG 9.17 A tree structure represented by child-and-twin rings.

the pointers are removed from the network and placed in a *directory,* Figure 9.24 represents the network structure of Figure 9.19.

All methods that embed pointers within data records are nightmares to work with when a complex network must be represented physically. To update the embedded pointer file representing a complex network structure, the pointer lists must be expanded and contracted. Efficiency of processing demands that the added and deleted records be reorganized periodically which, in turn, becomes extremely difficult because record movement causes so many pointers to be changed.

Complex networks can be accommodated rather easily by applying the directory method. Note that the complex network relating products to subassemblies to components illustrated in Figure 9.25, can be represented simply by using directories (see Fig. 9.26). In general, the more complex the mapping, the stronger the argument for separating the data from the means by which their relationships are expressed.

9.6 ▪ MULTIPLE KEY RETRIEVAL

The methods of file organization we have examined to this point have contained records with a single key. Order entry, accounts payable, and airline reservation systems may function adequately by responding to such single key requests, as "What products were requested on customer order number

252 Physical Data Organization

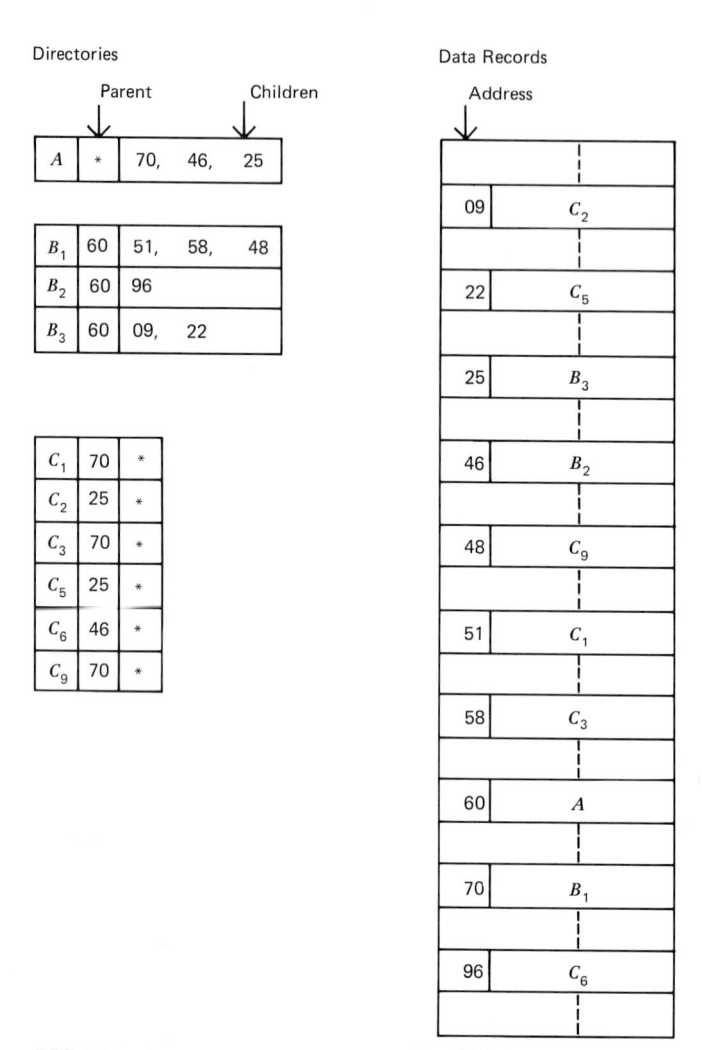

FIG 9.18 A tree structure represented by directories.

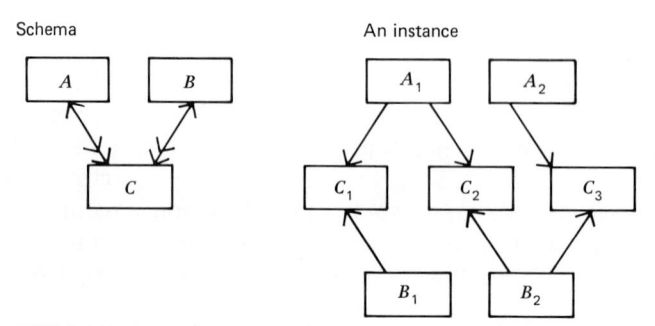

FIG 9.19 A simple network structure.

Multiple Key Retrieval

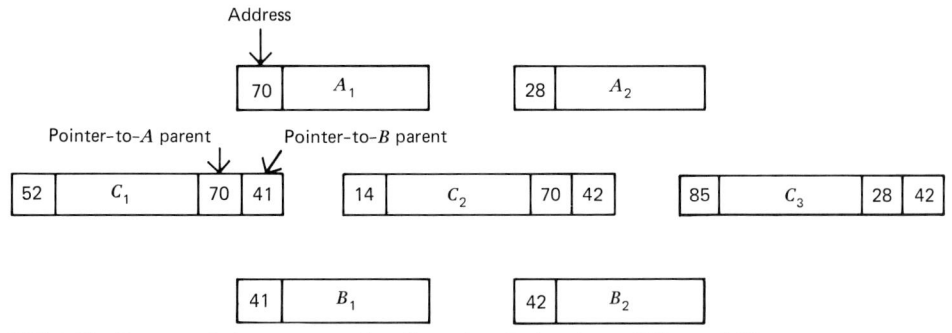

FIG 9.20 Parent pointers representing the network structure of Figure 9.19.

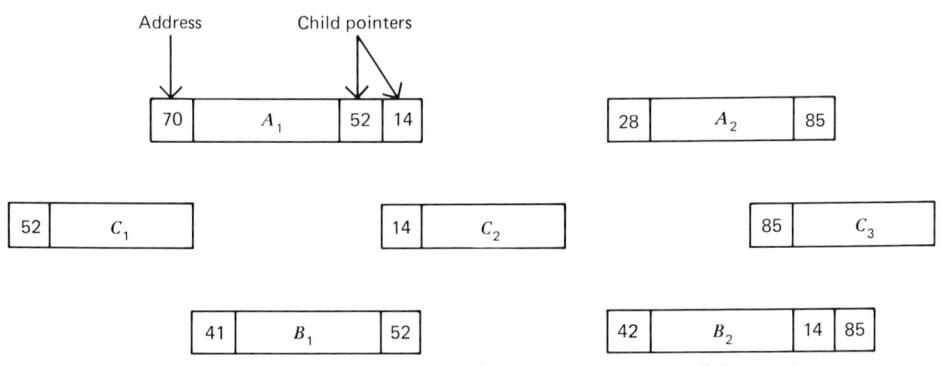

FIG 9.21 Multiple child pointers representing the network structure of Figure 9.19.

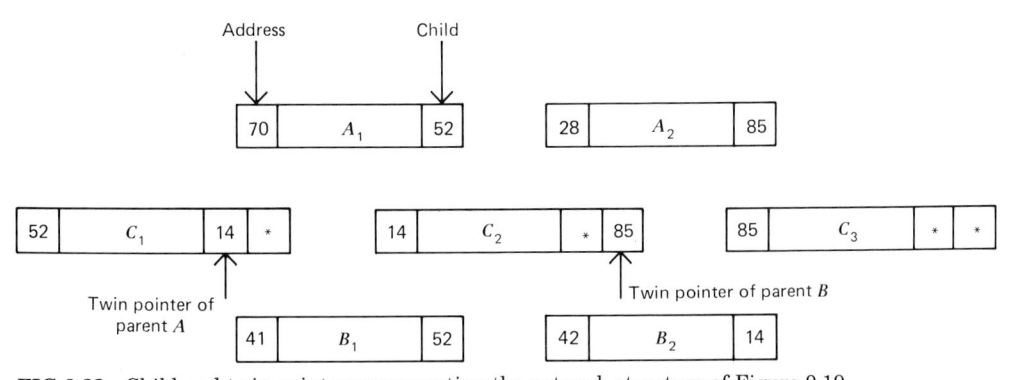

FIG 9.22 Child-and-twin pointers representing the network structure of Figure 9.19.

Physical Data Organization

07613?" "How much do we owe vendor 6422-3?" or "How many seats are left on Eastern, flight 71?" Often, however, systems must respond to a variety of inquiries about several different attributes of the data. These we will refer to as **multiple key retrieval systems.**

Multiple key retrieval systems use one or more secondary keys to answer requests. For example, the administrator's request, "How many upper division undergraduate courses have grade point averages in excess of 3.00?" can be answered by finding the intersection of data records that have a secondary key

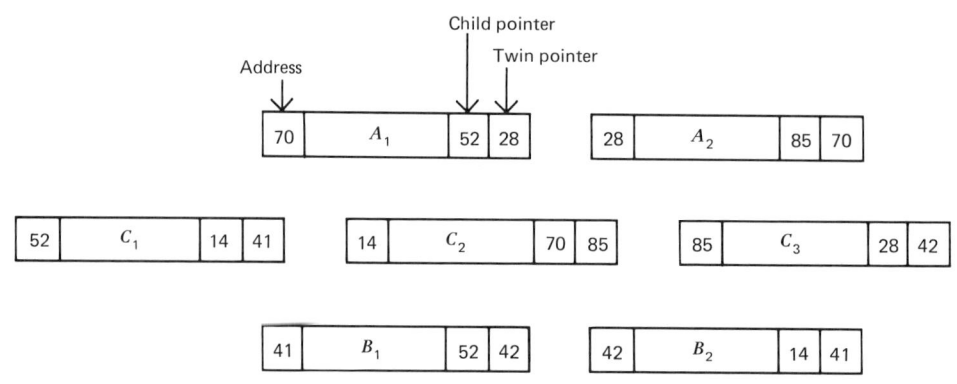

FIG 9.23 The network of Figure 9.19 represented by child, twin, and parent rings.

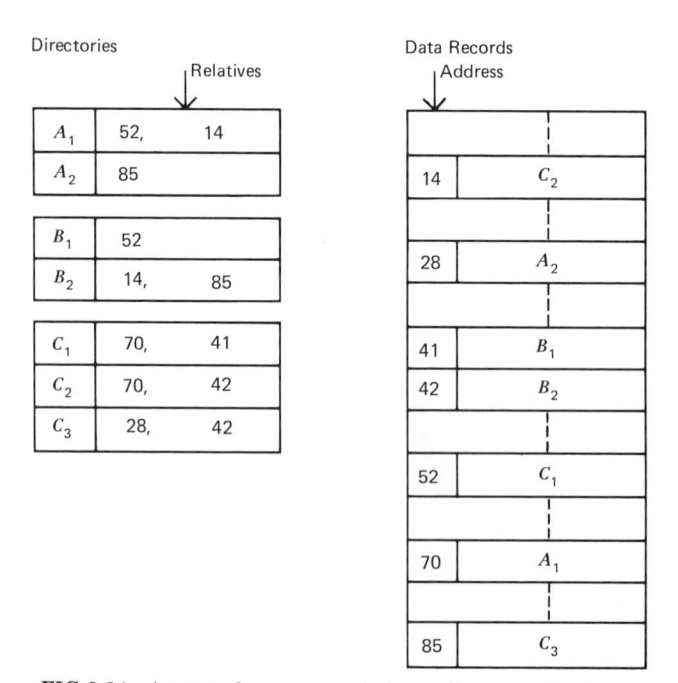

FIG 9.24 A network represented physically using directories.

value of upper division with data records that have another secondary key value of G.P.A. > 3.00.

Multiple key retrieval can be achieved by using multiple pointers, indices, or a combination of the two. We do not intend to

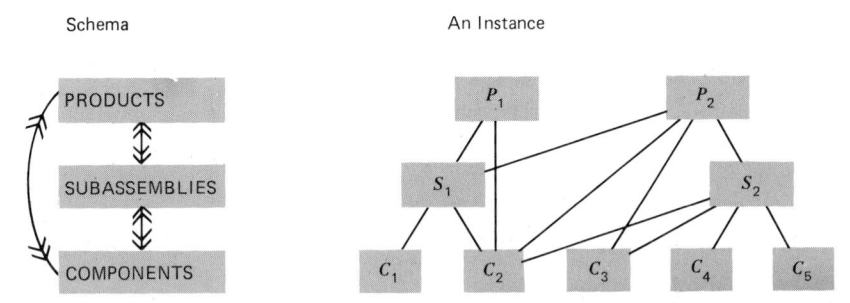

FIG 9.25 A complex network portraying a relationship between products, subassemblies, and components.

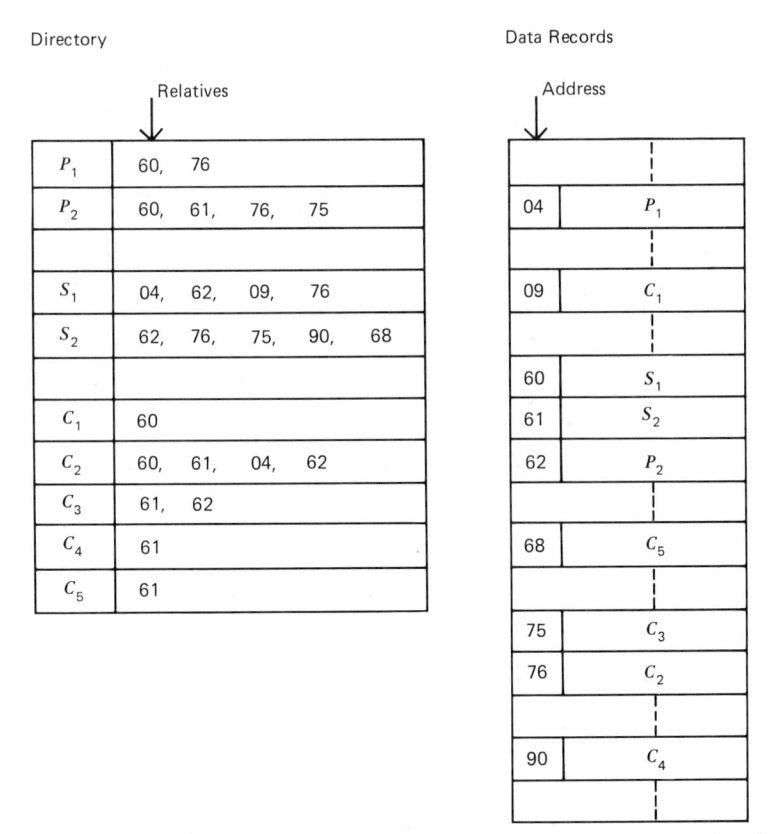

FIG 9.26 The directory method of depicting the physical representation of the complex network illustrated in Figure 9.25.

explore variations of the two physical representations here. Instead, the following example illustrates an "all purpose" way of representing data to be retrieved on the basis of multiple keys.

Figure 9.27[3] shows a data file of 28 records. Each record has five important attributes: employee number (the primary key), A_1 (the employee's name), A_2 (department number), A_3 (skill code of the employee, and A_4 (the employee's monthly salary).

Sample inquiries the data base system might be expected to respond to are as follows:

- What employees in department 220 are making less than $2000 per month?
- What employees, listed in alphabetical order, do not have a skill code of either PL or FI?
- Who are the three highest paid employees?

[3] Adapted from James Martin, *Computer Data-Base Organizations*, Second Edition, Englewood Cliffs, New Jersey: Prentice-Hall, Inc., 1977.

Employee number	A_1 Name	A_2 Department number	A_3 Skill code	A_4 Salary	Nonindexed details
07642	MARTJT	220	PL	1900	
07643	GREEJW	119	SE	2700	
07650	HALSPD	210	SE	2000	
07668	FEINPE	220	PL	1950	
07670	SCHAWE	119	AD	3100	
07671	MARSJJ	119	FI	1200	
07672	ALBEHA	210	SE	2100	
07700	LONDAJ	220	AD	3000	
07702	ANDEWF	119	FI	1000	
07710	MARTCH	220	PL	1750	
07715	FLINGA	119	AD	3000	
07716	MERLCH	220	FO	2200	
07740	JONEKB	119	PL	2200	
07761	REDFBD	119	SE	2650	
07780	BLANJE	220	FO	2100	
07805	ROPEES	220	PL	1900	
07806	KALNTD	119	MA	2300	
07815	EDWARB	220	PL	2040	
07850	DALLJE	119	FI	1050	
07883	JONETW	210	SE	2010	
07888	WEINSH	119	MA	2450	
07889	KLEINM	220	PL	1830	
07961	FREIHN	220	PL	1780	
07970	MANKCA	119	MA	2410	
07972	FIKETE	210	SE	2500	
08000	SCHEDR	210	FI	2100	
08001	FLANJE	119	PL	1920	
08100	JOOSWE	210	SE	3150	

FIG 9.27 A sample data file.

One way of responding to the above inquiries is to search the data file sequentially. Records could be retrieved sequentially and then tested to determine whether they have the attribute values specified in the inquiry. For a small data file, this uncomplicated method of answering inquiries may be satisfactory. If the data file is large, however, the sequential search method is very time-consuming and, hence, unlikely to be practical. A more feasible method for extracting data from large files involves using indices and embedded pointers. Each important attribute has an index entry, which consists of an attribute value, the address of the first occurrence of the attribute value in the data file, and a count of the number of data records with the same attribute value. Each important attribute also has an embedded chain representing it. Pointers in the chain indicate the address of the next occurrence of the same attribute value.

Figure 9.28 represents the data file illustrated in Figure 9.27 with indices and embedded chains added to facilitate multiple key retrieval.

Inverted Lists

When retrieval can be based on a large number of attributes, searching with embedded pointers becomes complicated and inefficient. Inverted lists provide an alternative way to obtain specific information more efficiently. With **inverted lists,** attribute data values are placed in an index. The index entries relate the search parameter to the *addresses of all* records that correspond to the search parameters.

A **completely inverted list** has a separate index for every field. This form of data organization works well where many unanticipated requests for information are made. However, an inverted list used where lengthy indices exist is impractical and

A_1 Index

First Letter of Name	Address of start of chain	Count
A	110	2
B	210	1
D	250	1
E	240	1
F	040	5
G	020	1
H	030	1
J	170	3
K	230	2
L	120	1
M	010	5
R	180	2
S	050	2
W	320	1

A_2 Index

Department number	Address of start of chain	Count
119	020	12
210	030	6
220	010	10

A_3 Index

Skill code	Address of start of chain	Count
AD	050	3
FI	060	4
FO	160	2
MA	230	3
PL	010	6
SE	020	7

A_4 Index

Salary	Address of start of chain	Count
1000≧ <1750	060	3
1750≧ <2000	010	7
2000≧ <2250	030	8
2250≧ <2500	230	3
2500≧ <3000	020	3
3000≧	050	4

Address	A_0 Employee number	A_1 Name	Chain address	A_2 Department number	Chain address	A_3 Skill code	Chain address	A_4 Salary	Chain address	Nonindexed details
010	07642	MARTJT	060	220	040	PL	040	1900	040	
020	07643	GREEJW	*	119	050	SE	030	2700	180	
030	07650	HALS PD	*	210	110	SE	110	2000	110	
040	07668	FEINPE	150	220	120	PL	140	1950	140	
050	07670	SCHAWE	370	119	060	AD	120	3100	120	
060	07671	MARSJJ	140	119	130	FI	130	1200	130	
110	07672	ALBEHA	130	210	310	SE	180	2100	160	
120	07700	LONDAJ	*	220	140	AD	150	3000	150	
130	07702	ANDEWF	*	119	150	FI	250	1000	250	
140	07710	MARTCH	160	220	160	PL	170	1750	220	
150	07715	FLINGA	340	119	170	AD	*	3000	390	
160	07716	MERLCH	350	220	210	FO	210	2200	170	
170	07740	JONE KB	310	119	180	PL	220	2200	210	
180	07761	REDFBD	220	119	230	SE	310	2650	360	
210	07780	BLANJE	*	220	220	FO	*	2100	240	
220	07805	ROPEES	*	220	240	PL	240	1900	330	
230	07806	KALNTD	330	119	250	MA	320	2300	320	
240	07815	EDWARB	*	220	330	PL	330	2040	310	
250	07850	DALLJE	*	119	320	FI	370	1050	*	
310	07883	JONETW	390	210	360	SE	360	2010	370	
320	07888	WEINSH	*	119	350	MA	350	2450	350	
330	07889	KLEINM	*	220	340	PL	340	1830	340	
340	07961	FREIHN	360	220	*	PL	380	1780	380	
350	07970	MANKCA	*	119	380	MA	*	2410	*	
360	07972	FIKETE	380	210	370	SE	390	2500	*	
370	08000	SCHEDR	*	210	390	FI	*	2100	*	
380	08001	FLANJE	*	119	*	PL	*	1920	*	
390	08100	JOOSWE	*	210	*	SE	*	3150	*	

FIG 9.28 The data file of Figure 9.27 physically represented to handle multiple key retrievals.

costly because the indices require a great deal of storage, and updating and maintenance activities become burdensome. A common compromise approach is to organize most of the data in a sequential or direct way, and to use inverted lists for selected search parameters only. **Partially inverted lists** require the systems analyst to be more effective in defining search parameters of users before hand, thus decreasing some of the unanticipated aspects of information need.

SUMMARY

Data can be stored in a variety of hardware storage units. With magnetic storage units it is important to make the distinction between logical and physical files and records. Two basic methods are available to the systems analyst to organize and process data entities physically: the sequential method and the direct method.

Records in a file are identified by a unique number or group of characters called a primary key. Given a primary key, the computer can locate the record for that key by applying a sequential, direct, hashing, or indexed sequential addressing technique. Each of these techniques has advantages and disadvantages associated with it. Selection of the best technique to apply in a particular situation requires the systems analyst to be well-versed in the physical structure of the data.

Whether the system is manual-based or computer-driven, it is essential for the analyst to be able to apply data association structures, in the form of trees and networks, to physical storage media. Chaining is a technique that links logical records together physically.

The vital element in chaining is the pointer. A pointer represents the address of a particular record. Pointers can be either embedded in the data records or removed from them and contained in a separate file called a directory.

For applications that require data selection on the basis of common attributes, a means must be provided for going directly from the inquiry to those records that permit the inquiry to be answered. Variants of multiple key retrieval enables the systems analyst to satisfy both anticipated and many unanticipated user inquiries.

REVIEW QUESTIONS

9.1 What is the basic classification of storage media as it relates to accessing data?

9.2 Which physical storage devices support direct access?

9.3 Can punched cards be used where the requirements for the data record exceed 80 characters? How?

9.4 What is the function of the interblock gap? Is this a real or a logical space on a magnetic tape?

9.5 What does the term "record" refer to? Give at least two examples of a record.

9.6 What is blocking? Why are logical records blocked? Why are printed materials not blocked? If blocked records are more efficient for processing than unblocked records, then why not combine all logical records into one superblock? What determines the maximum block length?

9.7 Distinguish between a track and a cylinder on a magnetic disk.

9.8 List the benefits provided by COM.

9.9 What determines the number of physical storage locations that must be reserved for the data file if direct addressing is used?

9.10 In a hashing context, what is a synonym? How can you avoid writing synonyms to overflow locations?

9.11 What is a pointer? A chain? A ring?

9.12 Using pointers, what are the three methods of representing tree structures?

9.13 What is the advantage associated with removing pointers from the data records and placing them in a separate directory?

9.14 As the mapping of networks becomes more complex, what is a good rule to follow regarding the physical location of pointers?

9.15 What reason might a systems analyst offer for a list to be completely inverted? Against the complete inversion of a list?

QUESTIONS FOR DISCUSSION

9.1 "Punched cards and tape no longer seem meaningful as storage media in the information system of large organizations." Discuss the validity of this statement.

9.2 Comment on the statement: "COM provides our organization with direct processing capability at a fraction of the cost of direct access storage devices."

9.3 "The progression from sequential, through list, to random, indicates a progression from simple data structures to complex data structures. Today's data management systems offer varying degrees of capability along this scale." Comment on this statement.

9.4 There are many applications for chaining techniques besides bill of materials applications. Discuss several.

9.5 "A major part in the design of any information system must be the study of how the data should be organized and structured." Discuss this statement.

9.6 "It is inconceivable to me how systems analysts can design highly integrated systems without understanding the restrictions of technology on data association." Discuss fully.

9.7 "The establishment of efficient directories is the key to implementing the interrogative approach for producing information." Explain this comment.

9.8 "A generalized data base management system must be able to process data in a variety of structures to be meaningful." Discuss.

9.9 "All files that are used for information purposes require some sort of inversion." Do you agree with this statement? Why?

EXERCISES

9.1 In designing a file it has been determined that there will be 75,000 records and that each record is 200 bytes. Calculate: (1) records per track, (2) number of tracks required, and (3) number of cylinders required. Assume the model of disk pack available has 200 cylinders, each cylinder has 10 tracks, and each track has a maximum capacity of 16,000 bytes.

9.2 Access motion time is negligible if a file is being processed in sequence. The significant time, in this case, is rotational delay and data transfer. If the full rotational delay is 8.5 milliseconds per track and the data transfer 1882 KB (thousands of bytes per second), then, using Exercise 9.1, calculate the time required to read all the records.

9.3 A disk pack has 200 cylinders. There are 10 recording surfaces or tracks, and each track can store a maximum of

16,000 bytes (characters). What is the maximum capacity of each cylinder? What is the maximum capacity of the disk pack?

9.4 There are 200 cylinders in a disk pack. Each cylinder has a maximum capacity of 320,000 data bytes. If there are 20 recording surfaces, what is the maximum capacity of each track?

9.5 Assume that a tape drive has a transfer rate of 60,000 bytes per second and a start/stop time at each IBG of 10 milliseconds. If this tape drive is to read 15,000 blocks and each block is 50 characters in length, how long will it take? This exercise, so far, represents 15,000 unblocked records. Suppose, however, that the 15,000 records to be read were blocked, 10 to a block. How would this blocking affect the total time to read the records from the tape?

9.6 A nine-track tape has 6250 CPI or BPI density and a tape unit speed of 60 inches per second. The number of blocks on the tape is 6000, the blocking factor is 4, and each logical record contains 25 bytes. The size of the IBG is 0.75 inch and the time to pass an IBG is 0.012 seconds. Calculate: (1) stated transfer rate, (2) size of each block, (3) total number of bytes, (4) total start/stop time, and (5) total time for reading data.

9.7 Assume the availability of 2400-foot magnetic tape reels with 6250 bytes-per-inch density. Further assume 200-byte logical records, blocked 5, 0.00016 inches per character, and a 0.60-inch IBG. On a 2400 foot reel, 28,440 inches are available for storing working records (2400-foot reel minus 30 feet of combined header and trailer records). Calculate the physical and logical records per reel.

9.8 A DASD has a capacity of 7200 bytes per track. There are 3600 200-byte records to be mapped with a 75 percent loading factor. How many record locations are required? How many tracks are required? Select a prime number for division.

9.9 What track address will be assigned to a record with a key of 29,864? Assume that: (1) the file contains 40,000 records; (2) 500 records can be placed on a track of a DASD; (3) an 80 percent loading factor is desired; and (4) a hashing technique is to be used.

9.10 An N room motel system is planning to install an online information system for handling room reservations. You have been hired to design the data file for this system. Some parameters which you should consider are:

1. Number of beds and type (single, double) in each room.
2. Cost of room.
3. Location of room (e.g., next to swimming pool, next to highway, etc.).
4. Special requests.
5. Checkout times (assume that a room can be rented when it is empty and has been cleaned, even though this condition may occur before the time of checkout designed by the patron during sign-in.)
6. Advance room reservations are permitted.

9.11 Design an information retrieval system for physicians in a hospital. By entering a physician's code number, a display will be made listing his or her patients, their room number and their present health condition.

9.12 Using a simple chain structure, design a file for a banking institution which will allow the user to access all depositers with average balances of $10,000,00 or more.

PROBLEMS

9.1 Represent the following tree by means of child-and-twin rings.

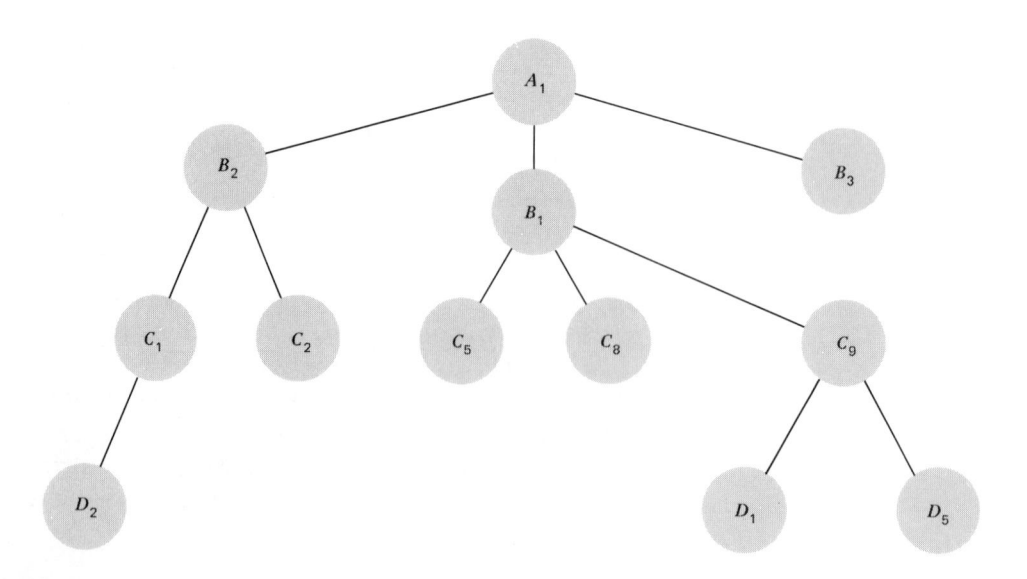

9.2 Design a file structure of an employment agency. It must be able to provide the following kinds of responses:
1. How many civil engineers do we have who are unmarried, speak French, and have over five years' experience?
2. Give me the name of a systems analyst who has an MS degree and belongs to a minority group.

9.3 Design a data file for a large nationwide construction company using a chain to maintain all employee records alphabetically. This file, on the average, contains 5000 employees, but because of the nature of the work, on the average, 200 employees quit and 200 new employees are hired each week. Use only 10–20 entries to illustrate your data structure. Would it be more efficient to maintain a sequential structure without pointers? Explain.

9.4 Design a vehicle registry file for the state registry which will contain the following attributes: (1) name of owner, (2) make of vehicle, (3) year, (4) model or type, (5) color, and (6) license number.

Types of inquiries:
1. Given a license number, display owner's name.
2. Given the owner's name, display make, year, model, color, and license number of vehicle.

Would you recommend sequential lists without pointers to meet the above requirements? Why? Why not?

9.5 Design a directory for part structure and where-used information for the following parts:

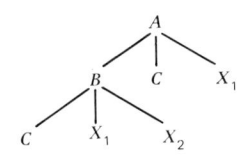

```
           A
         / | \
        B  C  X₁
       /|\
      C X₁ X₂
```

9.6 Design a personnel file by employee number, to answer the following inquiries:
1. Those employees who are married.
2. Those who have more than four dependents.
3. Those who make over $12,000 per year.

Use a structure other than inverted. For example, one solution to this problem is the application of a directory.

Physical Data Organization

9.7 Note the following schematic:

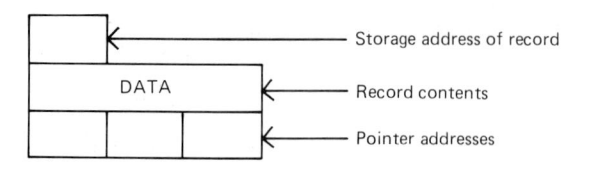

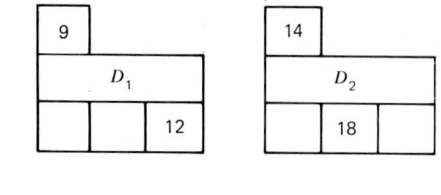

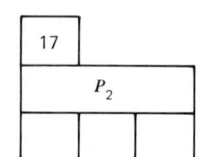

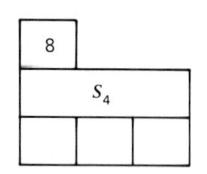

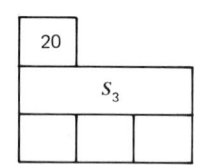

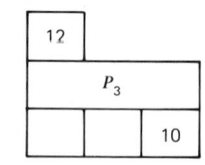

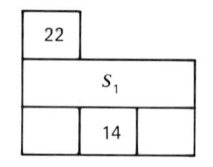

```
┌────┐
│    │ ←──────── Storage address of record
├────┴──────────┐
│     DATA      │ ←──────── Record contents
├──────┬────────┤
│      │        │ ←──────── Pointer addresses
└──────┴────────┘
```

9			14			17			10	
D_1			D_2			P_2			P_1	
	12			18						9

18			8			20			12			22	
S_2			S_4			S_3			P_3			S_1	
	22									10			14

Using the schematic as a guide and the following records: Please work the following exercises:

1. Assuming that D1 is the master record for construction division one, what projects are assigned to this division? P1, P2, P3, represent projects 1, 2, and 3, respectively.
2. What superintendents (S1, S2, S3, and S4) are working out of division two (D2)?
3. Inserting the proper pointers, illustrate how you would accommondate an inquiry concerning the projects handled by division two.
4. Suppose a listing is required indicating location of all projects (P1 and P2 are in the north, and P3 is in the south); add required chains to give this information.

9.8 Assume that the Iron Bolton Plate Company's files have been structured according to the following example:

For each of the following queries indicate the best access paths to follow.

(a) Obtain the names of the vendor companies that are located in Boston and supply 1" × 20' × 20' plate.

Problems

PURCHASE-ORDER-FILE

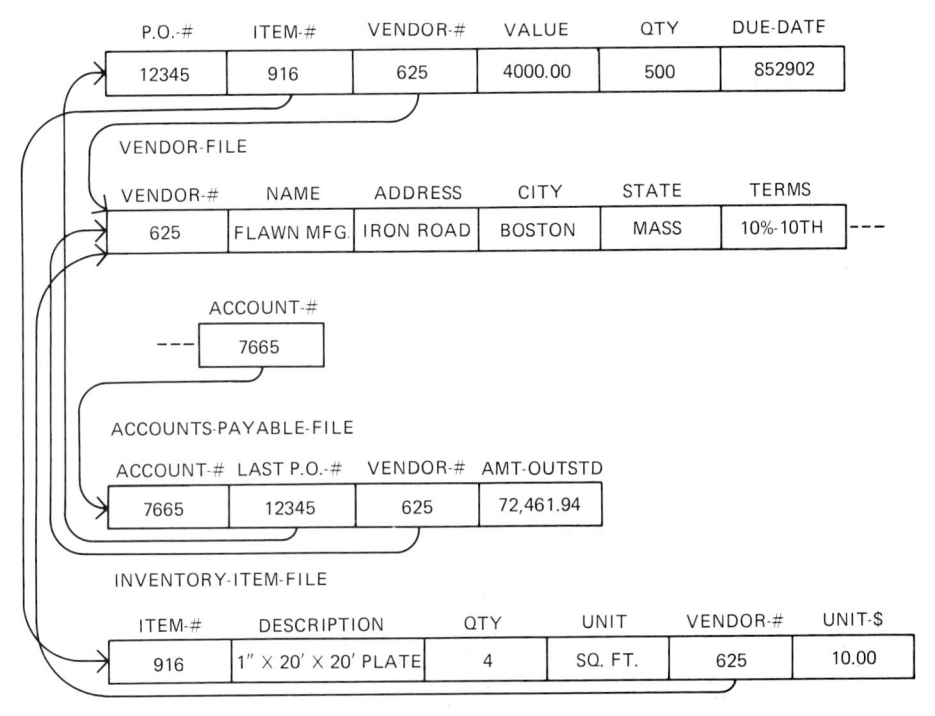

P.O.-#	ITEM-#	VENDOR-#	VALUE	QTY	DUE-DATE
12345	916	625	4000.00	500	852902

VENDOR-FILE

VENDOR-#	NAME	ADDRESS	CITY	STATE	TERMS
625	FLAWN MFG.	IRON ROAD	BOSTON	MASS	10%-10TH

ACCOUNT-#
7665

ACCOUNTS-PAYABLE-FILE

ACCOUNT-#	LAST P.O.-#	VENDOR-#	AMT-OUTSTD
7665	12345	625	72,461.94

INVENTORY-ITEM-FILE

ITEM-#	DESCRIPTION	QTY	UNIT	VENDOR-#	UNIT-$
916	1" × 20' × 20' PLATE	4	SQ. FT.	625	10.00

(b) Produce a copy of the purchase order records involving 1" × 20' × 20' plate.

(c) Generate a list of vendor names from whom 1" × 20' × 20' plate has been ordered in quantities greater than three.

9.9 Organize the following data using child, twin, and parent rings such that an inquiry can be made by office or by Department:

NAME	OFFICE	DEPARTMENT
Bretel	Dallas	Consulting
Casey	Dallas	Tax
Clement	Houston	Tax
Cohen	San Antonio	Tax
Fejer	Houston	Audit
Garza	Dallas	Audit
Han	Dallas	Consulting
Maloy	Houston	Audit
Todd	Houston	Audit

BIBLIOGRAPHY

Date, *An Introduction to Data Base Systems,* Third Edition, Reading, MA.: Addison–Wesley Publishing Company, 1981.

Cardenas, *Data Base Management Systems,* Boston: Allyn and Bacon, Inc., 1979.

Inmon, *Effective Data Base Design,* Englewood Cliffs, NJ.: Prentice-Hall, Inc., 1981.

Kroenke, *Database Processing,* Chicago: Science Research Associates, 1977.

Martin, *Computer Data Base Organization,* Second Edition, Englewood Cliffs, NJ.: Prentice-Hall, Inc., 1977.

CHAPTER 10

File Storage and Processing Considerations

10.1 • INTRODUCTION

In this chapter a discussion of the concepts related to file organization and processing is presented. It should be recognized that in file design, various tradeoffs must be made. When making these tradeoffs, however, one should not lose sight of the fact that the data base must be responsive to a variety of user demands. An efficient method of data storage and organization is not beneficial unless it is effective in meeting the important information needs of an entity.

The specific objectives of this chapter are as follows:

1. To present a comprehensive discussion of sequential and direct data organization and processing.
2. To describe the most common classifications used to describe data files.
3. To identify the basic criteria used to select file media, organization, and processing methods.
4. To summarize the primary considerations related to file design.

10.2 • AN INTRODUCTORY EXAMPLE

To help relate physical storage media concepts to logical data association structures, we have prepared a simple, practical example of such a relationship. Bear in mind that the physical storage media can be made of almost anything from clay tablets to magnetic tape and disks. In the following example, the physical storage media are pieces of paper in notebooks. The same system could be set up on magnetic disk files and manipulated by a computer via the necessary software. In either case, the following data base should provide the manager with necessary information to make decisions.

Assume that you have just purchased the Rocking B Ranch in Rhode Island. The ten-acre ranch is divided into two pastures, and you have acquired six brood cows (also called mother cows or dams). So far, your herd has produced five calves. Further, assume that you intend to breed these cows to famous bulls by artificial insemination, normally referred to as AIing. Assume that some cows have been bred, have calved, and have been

268 File Storage and Processing Considerations

bred again, while others have been bred but have not yet calved.

Your data base design includes three basic files: (1) calf master file, (2) dam master file, and (3) breeding master file. An example of these files is shown in Figure 10.1.

This figure shows only the records of dam 04; the record of her first calf, 04A; and her breeding record. That is, the complete files of all cows and calves are not shown. Also, only selected entries are made in these records for illustrative purposes. Obviously, in

CALF MASTER FILE INDEX

Attribute Value	Page Number
Sex: Male	01, 02, 05
Female	03, 04
205-Day Weight:	
400–500	02, 05
501–600	04
above 600	01, 03

CALF MASTER FILE

Calf Master Record — Page 03

Code*	Name	Birth Date	Birth Weight	Birth Condition	Sex
04A Green	Petunia	October 19X1			Female

205-day Weight	Sire	Dam Name	Dam Pointer
650	Sal	Bertha	08

*Code Structure:
04: Calf number matches dam number
A: First calf from dam 04,   B: Second calf, and so forth.
Green: Color green is for Herd 1 and yellow is for Herd 2.

DAM MASTER FILE INDEX

Attribute Value	Page Number
Expected calving:	
October	02, 06
November	08, 04
December	10, 12
Calving performance:	
01	06, 10
02	08, 02, 12
03	04

DAM MASTER FILE

Dam Master Record — Page 08

Code*	Calf Pointer	Name	Date of Purchase	Purchased From	Age at Purchase	Breeding Record Pointer
04 Green	03	Bertha	August 19X9			02

Medication History	Calving Performance**	Calf Name	Calf History Code	Pointer	Expected Calving Date
	02	Petunia	A	03	November

*Code Structure:
04: Unique dam number
Green: Color green is for Herd 1 and yellow is for Herd 2.

**Code Structure:
01: No difficulty
02: Some difficulty
03: Extreme difficulty

BREEDING MASTER FILE INDEX

Attribute Value	Page Number
Sires:	
Sal	01, 02
Aurato	05, 06
Neat	02, 04

BREEDING MASTER FILE

Breeding Master Record — Page 02

Code	Dam Pointer	Date Bred	AI Technician	Technician's Comments
04	08	February, 19X1	A. Jones	
		March, 19X2	B. Smith	

Sire	Vendor
Sal	Allied Breeders
Neat	Genetics, Inc.

FIG 10.1 Simple example on how to associate physical records logically to provide information.

a real situation, all attributes would normally have values. Also shown in the figure is an index for each master file. This index is in reality a page inserted in the cover of each independently paginated master file notebook. Its purpose is to aid information retrieval.

Assume further that some time has elapsed and one day you decide to take a look at your empire. You load your data base in your pickup truck and head for the north pasture. Approaching, you see that a calf has become separated from the herds. You wish to know which herd and cow this calf belongs to. One way to get this information is to look at a color-coded plastic tag inserted in the calf's ear. A similar tag is also inserted in the cow's ear. Upon closer observation, you notice that the lost calf's ear tag is green and has 04A written on it. You have two herds, herd one's tag is color-coded green and herd two's tag is color-coded yellow; so immediately you know that the calf belongs to herd one.

The cow herd that is color-coded green is located in the south pasture. So you load the calf into the pickup and head for the south pasture. Upon releasing the calf into the south pasture, instinct takes over and mother and calf are immediately and happily united. You wish to verify that your records are accurate. You locate the dam record that contains data about green 04 cow. This direct access is performed by multiplying the code 04 by 2, giving page number 08 of the dam master file. This transformation technique accesses the first page of the record for green 04 cow. Upon retrieving the green 04's record, a calf pointer is located that points you to page 03, the record address of the appropriate record in the calf master file. At this point, you have verified the accuracy of these records as far as the cow-calf relationship of green 04 and 04A is concerned (i.e., your records accurately show that Petunia is Bertha's calf).

Typical examples of the kinds of information that you would probably want about your herds are listed in Figure 10.2.

The data base for your beef ranch could be organized in a lot of ways, depending upon the kinds of information you need. Several things about this data base could be improved. A page address for each record of the calf master record could be included in the indexes. Other interrelationships could be made by adding additional pointers. Overall, however, the above example should give you a fairly good idea how records, fields within records, and addresses can be logically related to provide information, and also serve as an introduction to the following material. Incidentally, this example data base would be sufficient for most ranches using AI.

10.3 ▪ SEQUENTIAL VERSUS DIRECT DATA ORGANIZATION AND PROCESSING

Two basic methods are available to the systems analyst to organize and process data elements physically : sequential and direct. Other terms are used to describe these two methods. For example, sequential data organization and processing is also known as periodic, batch, serial, and offline, while direct is often called (with varying degrees of appropriateness) event processing, online, inline, random access, time-sharing, or online real time systems. Following are the characteristics, advantages, and disadvantages of both methods.

Sequential Data Organization

With the use of **sequential organization** of data records, these records are placed on the

270 File Storage and Processing Considerations

file using a key or code for sequencing (e.g., inventory item sequence). Usually before changing or updating the sequential file, all new items are first *batched* (grouped) and

Information Requested	Method of Retrieval
Calf 04's (Petunia) birth date.	Search sequentially through the dam master file. Calf pointer of the appropriate dam master record will give the page number of the calf master file.
	Answer: October 19X1.
Date of purchase of cow with code green 04.	Direct access. The transformation algorithm of multiplying 2 times the numeric code gives page number of sought record.
	After the record is accessed, the attributes are sequentially searched.
	Answer: August 19X9.
Date bred since last calf, sire bred to, and AI technician for cow green 04.	Breeding record pointer in dam master record addresses to appropriate breeding master record.
	Breeding record is sequentially read and relevant information is noted.
	Answer: March, 19X2, Neat, and B. Smith.
All calves with 205-day weight of 501-600 pounds.	Search calf master file index for appropriate attribute value.
	Each attribute has an appropriate pointer(s) that gives page number(s) that meet the attribute value.
	Answer: Calf at page number 04. This calf's name is Frosty but her record is not shown in the figure.
All male calves.	Calf master file index search.
	Answer: Three calves. Records at page numbers 01, 02, 05.
All cows expected to give birth in December.	Dam master file index search.
	Answer: Two cows. Records at page numbers 10, 12.
All cows with calving performance of 03.	Dam master file index search.
	Answer: One cow. Record at page 04.
All cows bred to Aurato.	Breeding master file index search.
	Answer: Two cows. Records at pages 05 and 06.

FIG 10.2 Typical requests for information and methods of providing such information.

sorted into the same sequence. To access any data record in the sequential file, all records preceding the one in question must first be passed. That is, to access record number 1000, the system must read past 999 records. An *insertion* of a data record means *creating* a new sequential file.

The sequence of the file is usually chosen according to some common attribute called a *key*. The sequence of a file may be changed by selecting a different key and *sorting* the stored records according to the values of the new key. In Figure 10.3(A), a file containing data about the customers of an organization is sorted according to the numerical values associated with the field CUSTOMER NUMBER. If the field CUSTOMER NAME were used as a key, then the stored records would be physically rearranged in the file illustrated in Figure 10.3(B). In some cases, using one data attribute as a sorting key is not sufficient to identify a given stored record. In this case, one or more additional data attributes would be concatenated to form the key. Figure 10.3(C) shows the same file sorted in ascending order according to the values of the data attribute SALESPERSON NUMBER. Notice that two stored records exist with the value of SALESPERSON NUMBER equal to 14. To ensure a unique sequence, the data attribute CUSTOMER NAME is concatenated to SALESPERSON NUMBER and the values of CUSTOMER NAME are placed in ascending order.

Sequential organization is an efficient method of data organization if a large volume of records and a reasonably high percentage of records are being processed each run. Sequential organization is applicable to preparing reports that must meet such information requirements as retrieving all stored records in ascending order by CUSTOMER NUMBER. It is not suited for information requests such as "retrieve only the record where CUSTOMER NUMBER is equal to 176." In both situations, all of the stored records must be accessed, but for the second request, the first six records accessed are of no value. So sequential organization offers rapid access to the next record in a file if the basis for retrieval is the same as the basis for the physical ordering of the file. In an information system meeting a variety of information needs, this is seldom the case.

If a group of stored records must be processed using more than one key to satisfy information requests, the stored records are sorted into different work files. For example, the files in Figure 10.3 represent three separate files. The contents of each file are the same, but the ordering is different for different purposes. This duplication of files wastes storage space and processing time.

Sequential Processing

With sequential processing (see Fig. 10.4), source document forms are prepared that represent a transaction or event (e.g., sales transaction, patient checking into a hospital, collection of cash). These forms are then keypunched and verified. The resulting punched cards are then validated to determine inaccuracies and omissions. Any inputs that fail the validation process are rerouted for correction. Validated batches of these transactions are sorted and merged into a transaction file in the same order as the old master file stored in the file library. Both files are mounted and processed by matching a transaction key in the transaction file with a key of a record in the old master file. In this way, the record is updated and written on a new master file in sequence. Also, any reports needed can be printed at the same time. The new master

(A)

Customer Number	Customer Name	Salesperson Number
123	BARCO	21
138	AJAX	14
142	ACME	16
144	TURF	14
151	BEACON	26
170	SALZ	15
176	CEZON	28

Sort Key (Customer Number)

(B)

Customer Number	Customer Name	Salesperson Number
142	ACME	16
138	AJAX	14
123	BARCO	21
151	BEACON	26
176	CEZON	28
170	SALZ	15
144	TURF	14

Sort Key (Customer Name)

(C)

Customer Number	Customer Name	Salesperson Number
138	AJAX	14
144	TURF	14
170	SALZ	15
142	ACME	16
123	BARCO	21
151	BEACON	26
176	CEZON	28

Concatenated Sort Key

FIG 10.3 Example of sorting a file in different sequences by using different sort keys.

file is returned to the library until the next process, where it becomes the old master file. In summary, characteristics of sequential processing systems are as follows:

1. *Job shop oriented.* Applications are viewed as individual jobs or batches, each of which receives varying degrees of attention. For example, all other jobs may be discontinued on Friday morning of every week to process payroll.
2. *File availability.* Files, as soon as they are updated, are returned to the library and are not available for processing until the next update cycle.
3. *Timing.* The rationale for sequential processing is that transactions should be grouped into batches and processed periodically according to a planned schedule. The new master file is created during the current update cycle (e.g., weekly payroll) by posting transactions that have accumulated during the period (e.g., daily time cards).
4. *Updating.* The master file is updated by creating a new file. This new file reflects unaltered old master file records that were unaffected by transactions, first-time master records that were created by transactions (additions), and altered old master file records (updates). It does not contain old master file records that were dropped as a result of transaction records (deletions).

The old master file is kept intact. For example, with magnetic tape processing, the old master file is mounted on a different tape unit than the new master file. When updating is completed, both the old and new master files exist, with the difference between the two being the changes from the transaction file.

5. *Organization of records.* Records are stored and processed in a predetermined sequential order, usually in ascending order based on a key such as account number. Before processing, both the transaction file and the master file must be in the same sequence. Processing begins at the first record in both files and the two files are next related to each other by their respective keys. When a match occurs, the transaction record is posted to the master record and the results written to the new master file. Processing ends when both files have been completely read from the first record to an end-of-file condition. Any file media can be used for sequential data organization (e.g., punched cards, magnetic tape, or magnetic disk).
6. *Interrelationship of processing functions.* Similar activities of the organization may be handled differently and at different times. For instance, a customer of a bank may have a savings account, a demand deposit account, and a loan. If three records are created, one for each file, then the processing function handles this customer as three different customers.

Direct Data Organization

Direct data organization (sometimes called random access) ignores the physical sequence of stored records in a file and accesses stored records on the basis of their physical hardware address in the storage device. Direct organization is applicable only to a DASD such as magnetic disks or drums. Records are stored on the physical file without regard to sequence. Any record can be retrieved with a single access without having to read many other records in the file. To store records on the file and subsequently retrieve them, addresses are generated for each record. Three methods,

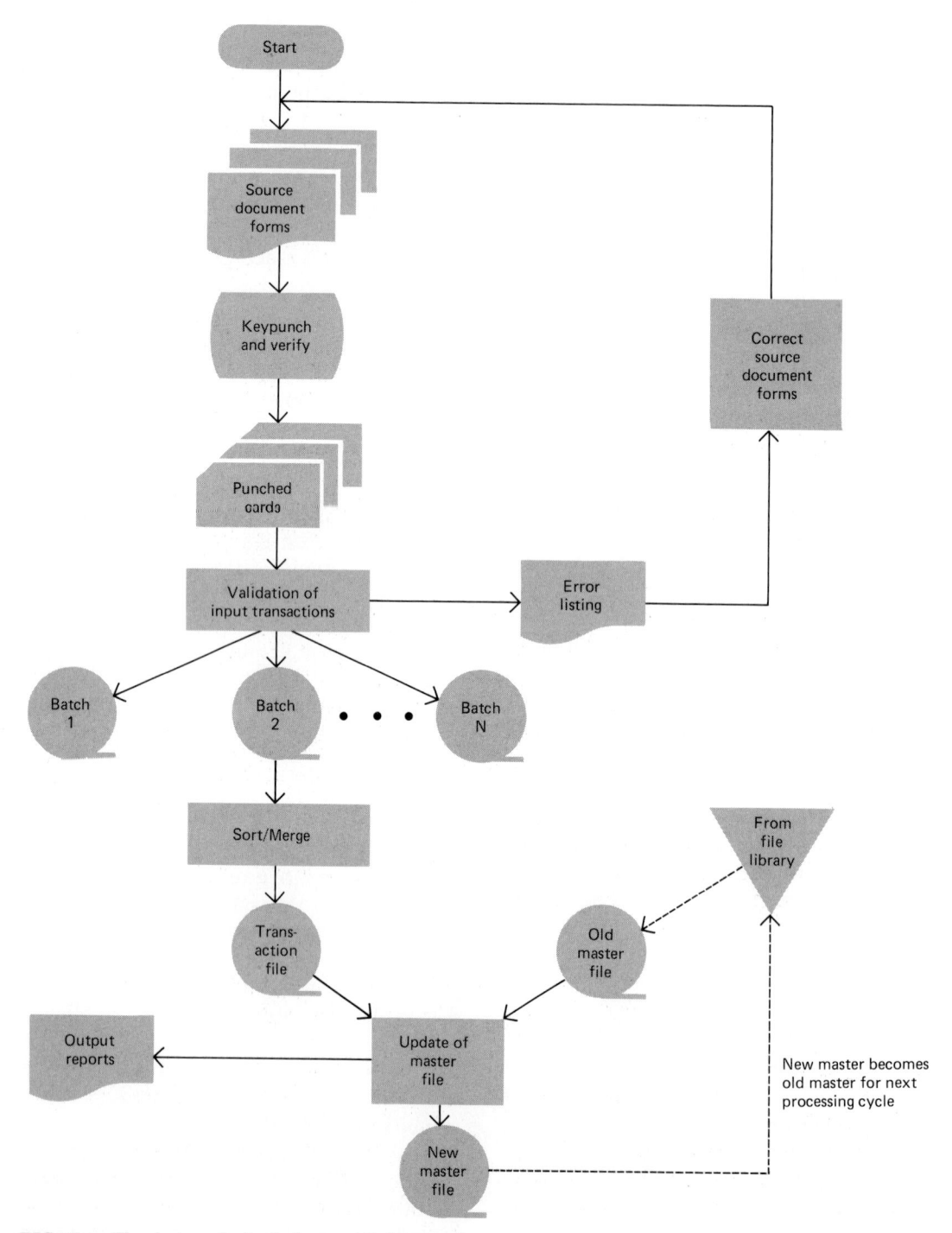

FIG 10.4 The design of a typical sequential processing system.

which are described in Chapter 9, are used to do this: (1) the programmer or data base administrator may assign an address to each record and make it part of each transaction record, (2) each record's key and its address are stored in a data base directory or index that can be searched prior to storage and retrieval of the record, and (3) an algorithm (set of mathematical or logical operations) can be applied to the key to transform it, either directly or indirectly through hashing, into a file address.

Direct Processing

With a direct processing system (see Fig. 10.5), transactions are input to master files as they occur without having to be presorted into batches. Each event location captures the transaction as it happens and inputs it by means of a terminal device connected to the central computer and data base. DASD data base files are available at all times to add, delete, or change a record. Many of the terminals are input/output devices (e.g., CRT) that can also be used for interrogative purposes, (i.e., a user can make a specific inquiry and receive a specific response). Typical applications include airline reservation systems, motel/hotel reservation and accounting systems, law enforcement systems, and savings, loan, and demand deposit accounting systems.

Summary characteristics of direct processing systems are as follows:

1. *Process oriented.* Data are processed on a continuous or "as-occurring" basis, contrasted to the processing of jobs on a periodic basis. The computer system acts as an integral part of the total operations of the organization.

2. *File availability.* Files are online and available to the system at all times for updating and inquiry purposes.

3. *Timing.* The direct processing system eliminates the time interval between the occurrence of an event, and the reflection of that event by the system.

4. *Updating.* When an event occurs that requires a change in the master files, a record is transferred from a file into the processing unit, updated, and transferred back to its original physical location. The original contents of the record are lost or destroyed, unless its before-image has been recorded on a transaction log in another file. This method of updating is called destructive or **overlay** updating and is utilized only with direct access storage devices (DASDs).

5. *Organization of records.* Records are stored on DASDs without regard to sequence. They are retrieved by the use of indexed sequential, direct, or indirect access techniques.

6. *Interrelationship of processing functions.* All similar activities of the organization are interrelated. For example, a sales transaction updates all pertinent files simultaneously (e.g., inventory, accounts receivable, sales, shipping).

Advantages of Sequential Processing Systems

1. Ideally suited to applications where the nature of the application relates to a definite cycle (e.g., payroll).

2. Ideally suited to applications where a large portion of records are processed each time the file is accessed or during each processing cycle. For example, if

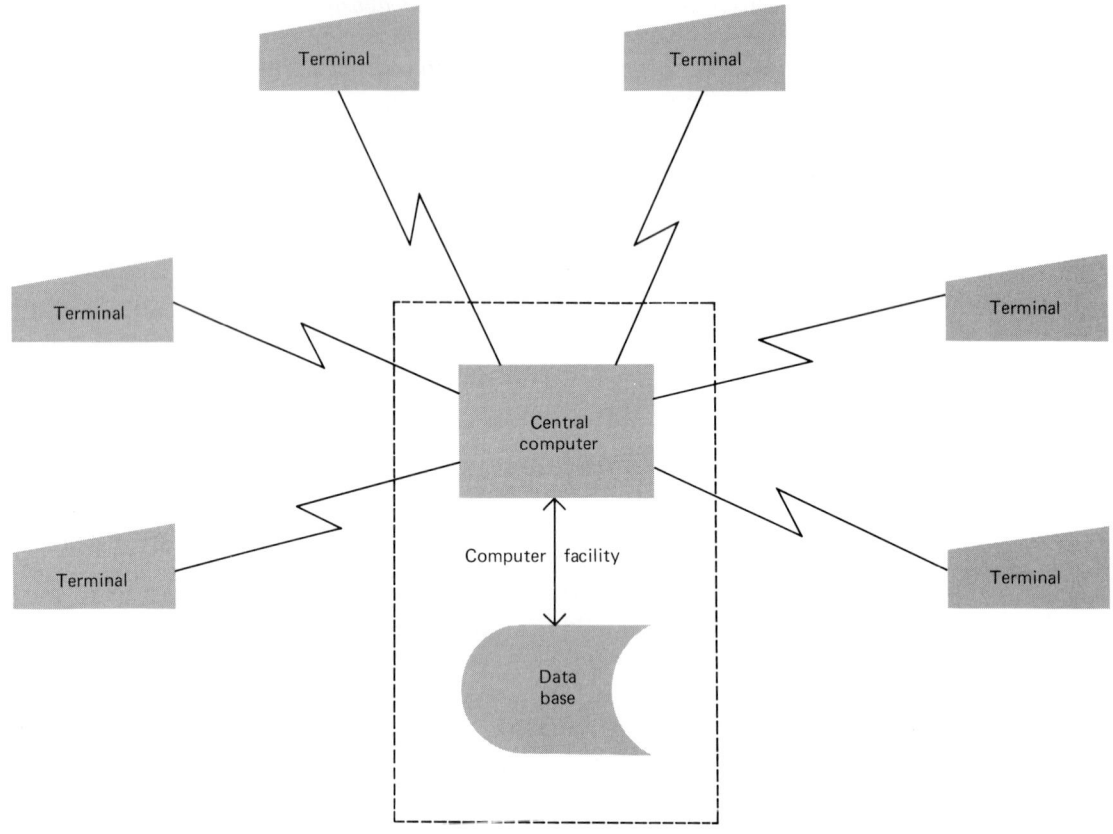

FIG 10.5 A typical direct processing system.

there are 5000 records in a payroll file and 4500 of them had activity for the week, then this represents an activity ratio of 45:50, or 90 percent. This means that 4500 records are changed in some way and the other 500 were merely read from the old master file and written on the new master file. As this *activity ratio* drops, it becomes less and less efficient to process using the sequential approach.

3. Requires less expensive equipment than direct processing and personnel who are less technically sophisticated.

4. Easier for many people to understand and work with because it is less integrated and complex.
5. Relates well to traditional accounting because all jobs and applications represent beginning and ending periods.

Disadvantages of Sequential Processing Systems

1. They are a poor application where instantaneous output must be produced.

For example, reports are available only on a periodic basis, making them irrelevant for some types of decisions. Any inquiry about the status of something may have to go unanswered until the processing cycle is completed.

2. Portions of the data base do not represent the current status of the organization (i.e., the system is constantly out of synchronization with the conditions in the organization). For example, an inventory file may show that 300 wrenches are in stock, but because 100 have been sold since the last update cycle, the system has overstated by 100 the number of wrenches on hand. Such out-of-date information can obviously cause a number of operational problems.

3. They are a poor application where the activity ratio is low. For example, if, during a day, sales transactions occur that represent only a 10 percent processing of a file, then the entire file would still have to be processed (10 percent would be updated and 90 percent would be written unchanged to the new file).

4. As indicated earlier, sequential processing requires that both transaction and master files be sorted in the same sequential order. Although normally only the transaction files need to be sorted during each processing cycle, sorting consumes large amounts of computing resources.

Advantages of Direct Processing Systems

1. Ideally suited where timeliness of response is imperative.
2. Ideally suited to master files that have a low activity ratio. Direct access storage devices provide for access to any record location without having to go through a sequential search.
3. By updating the files as pertinent events occur, the data base reflects the current status of the organization.
4. By logically relating and integrating files, the organization is viewed as a total system rather than as an aggregation of disjointed departments each working on its own. A single transaction can call into execution a number of programs, and can simultaneously affect a number of master files, which represent the interdependency of functioning within the organization. Overall, then, direct processing supports the data base approach to information systems design.
5. Less offline data conversion and human intervention is required. For example, in sequential processing the transaction may have to go through several stages before it can be read by the computer. With direct processing, the transaction is captured and input directly into the system.
6. If sequential ordering of files is appropriate in some situations, then direct access storage devices, particularly portable disk packs, can be efficiently used as sequential storage media. This capability obviously provides additional flexibility because sequential files, such as magnetic tape, cannot be used to support indexed sequential or direct organization.

Disadvantages of Direct Processing Systems

1. They can be expensive and complex, requiring highly skilled personnel.
2. They represent an expensive alternative

278 File Storage and Processing Considerations

where the activity ratio is high on all applications and where timeliness of information is not too important.
3. This approach, because of its high level of integration, requires stringent control procedures, especially in the areas of backup procedures and access security controls.

Hybrid Processing Systems

Although there is a strong movement toward direct processing systems, many organizations will not go all the way, but instead use a hybrid system encompassing both sequential and direct processing approaches exploiting the advantages of each.

Certainly, no organization has to use one approach or the other exclusively. In many organizations, if not most, a hybrid system can be set up in one of two ways: (1) processing activities can be performed at different times, such as online activities (e.g., inquiries) during the business day and all of the accumulated transactions at night; or (2) both types of processing activities can be executed concurrently. In the latter case, multiprogramming is required to dynamically give direct transactions priority over batched transactions. In this way, the computer system is used more efficiently; it does not sit idle, waiting for the next online inquiry or periodic update to be processed.

The possible need for a hybrid system is illustrated below by considering the requirements of a typical banking operation:
1. *Response time.* Response to a loan or demand deposit account status request by a teller must occur within a few seconds. The response time for other information requests (e.g., trust accounts) may not be as critical.
2. *Mixed transactions.* An online savings system may incorporate the processing of savings transactions, Christmas club payments, savings certificates, and mortgage payments in the transaction stream. It is likely, however, that only the savings transactions are posted immediately, all others being accumulated for subsequent periodic processing performed at night.
3. *Transaction queuing.* Bank transactions tend to peak during relatively short periods of the day (e.g., 9:30–11:00 AM and 1:30–3:30 PM). The direct processing system receives more dedicated support during these peak times.
4. *Data communications network.* A large bank with its many branches requires a network of data communications and many terminals.
5. *Complex operating system.* The operating system that controls and supervises all the operations must have the ability to set program partition sizes and priorities, interrupt and recovery procedures, paging, and the like.
6. *Systems dependability and integrity.* Since the lifeblood of a banking operation is the flow of data, it is imperative that the information system have a high degree of integrity and dependability. Any breakdown of the system, say for more than a day, would be catastrophic.

10.4 ▪ CLASSIFICATION OF DATA FILES

The way data files are used in an information system, together with the available hardware device characteristics, will help guide us in considering and selecting storage media and file organization. Following are some of the ways files are used according to contents, mode of processing, and organization.

Classification According to Contents

In this classification files fall into seven basic categories: (1) master files, (2) transaction files, (3) index files, (4) table files, (5) summary files, (6) archival (historical) files, and (7) backup files.

1. *Master files.* This category of file contains data records for basic identification as well as an accumulation of certain statistical data. Examples of master files are: customer file, employee file, vendor file, stockholder file, product file, and so forth. Descriptive data contained in these files might include: Customer file—name, address, credit rating, account number, billing and shipping instructions, etc.; Product file—product code, styles, components, packaging, weight, etc. Statistical data contained in these files are generally of the current status type, such as outstanding balance owed, quantity on hand, purchases to date, shares owned, and so forth. Master files can be utilized effectively in both offline and online processing to satisfy the organization's requirements.

2. *Transaction files.* If the method of updating is batch, then a transaction file is necessary to accumulate activity records that will be used to update the master file. The records in this file are usually created from source documents such as receiving reports, invoices, purchase orders, time cards, etc.

3. *Index files.* These files are used to indicate, via an index key or address, where specific records are located in other files.

4. *Table files.* These files provide fairly static reference data. For example, one may use a pay-rate table for preparations of payrolls, a freight-rate table for preparation of bills of lading, a premium table for insurance billing, and so forth.

5. *Summary files (report files or work files).* This file represents data extracted from other files and compiled into a more concise or meaningful form. For example, once data have been extracted and summarized from several accounting ledger files, then accounting reports can be prepared.

6. *Archival files (history files).* Often these files are also called master files (see item 1 above). They contain statistical data for *noncurrent* periods and are used as a basis for creating comparative reports, plotting trends, computing commissions, and so forth. Archival files are normally updated periodically and involve large volumes of data. In an online mode, they can be used for reference purposes.

7. *Backup files.* These are simply noncurrent files of any type which are stored in a file library and are used as a link in a file-creation process if a current file is destroyed.

Classification According to Mode of Processing

Files can be processed in three modes: (1) input, (2) output, and (3) overlay.

1. *Input.* The data from the file are input into the CPU and then operated upon. An output that can be placed in another

file results. For example, an old master tape file may be read into storage, along with the transaction file.

2. *Output.* Data are processed and are then transferred to another tape, resulting in a new master tape file.

3. *Overlay.* A record can be accessed from a file into main storage, updated, and placed back in its original location. The original value of the record is lost unless such updates are recorded (or logged) in another file. Only direct access storage devices can be used in overlay mode. An obvious advantage using this mode of processing is that it is possible to deal with only a specific record of the file without having to process the entire file. Countering this advantage is the risk of destroying data which cannot be recreated easily.

10.5 ▪ SELECTION CONSIDERATIONS FOR FILE MEDIA AND FILE ORGANIZATION METHODS

Selecting the most appropriate storage media, and the best file organization methods, for a particular computer configuration depends on a number of considerations based on application requirements and available resourses. A discussion of these considerations follows.

File Update

File update follows either the sequential or direct approach as discussed earlier.

File Size

Magnetic tape, removable magnetic disk packs, floppy disks, and punched cards, can provide unlimited offline storage. Small files can be combined on magnetic disk or they may be stored on punched cards and paper tape.

Magnetic tape is normally used with larger files, if the type of processing is sequential or if online processing is not needed. Volume of data is not restricted if processing is sequential. Magnetic disk can also store large volumes of data but at a higher cost per character stored than magnetic tape. In direct processing, the size of a file is limited to the amount of data that can be stored online.

The systems requirement of growth potential of the files is also an important consideration. Normally, the systems analyst should design files on the basis of their anticipated growth over a certain period of years.

File Interrogation

Interrogation is simply a referral to a specific record for a specific response without changing the record in any way. File interrogation can normally be handled more quickly and easily if direct access storage devices are used. Normally, a teletype or CRT device is used to input an inquiry specifying the information required to the CPU. The data base management system determines the location of the applicable record in the file, accesses it, and transfers it to the CPU to be communicated to the requestor. Usually this whole sequence is accomplished within seconds after the inquiry is made.

Examples which emphasize the significance of this interrogative method are: (1)

In banking, "What is the balance of account number 1385?"; (2) In airline transportation, "Is there a coach seat available on flight 27?"; (3) In inventory control, "What is the quantity on hand of inventory item number 91736?"; (4) In manufacturing, "What is the material price variance of product number 67641?", or "What is the level of completion of work-in-process of job lot 41?", or "What is the quantity on hand of subassemblies for assembly 734?"; (5) In financial control, "What is year-to-date profit of division 3?", or "What customers are ninety days overdue?"; and so forth. Any of these inquiries could eventually be answered using sequential storage media and batch processing. The question is, how long would it take and how many disruptions would it cause? Usually, a special interrogation would have to be handled at the end of a processing run. At that time the response for the inquiry might be outdated and, consequently, of no value.

File Activity

Activity is the proportion of records actually affected by an updating run. The **activity ratio** for a file is equal to the number of records affected compared to the number of total records in that file. For example, if in one processing run 100 records were added, 800 changed, and 100 deleted, then the activity ratio for a file of 5000 records would be 1:5, or 20 percent.

If the activity ratio is high, more than three records in ten, the processing run would probably be handled more economically and faster by using sequential rather than direct processing. An example of a file with a high activity ratio is a payroll file.

File Volatility

File volatility refers to the additions and deletions of records in a file during a specific time period. With sequential processing, the volatility of a file is a matter of concern only insofar as its effect on the amount of physical space occupied and processing time consumed. With direct processing, another dimension is added. Deleted records are not physically removed from the direct access storage device until the file is reorganized. Thus the file is usually not in a compact state. Furthermore, particularly with a file that has many additions, a change in the distribution of keys may alter the results of the addressing technique and adversely affect the speed of referencing records.

Response Time

If one of the design considerations is for a fast response, measured in seconds, then the logical storage media are direct access storage devices. The reasons for fast response may emanate from the need (1) for a quick response to a particular inquiry, as in an airline reservation system; (2) to bring the organization a competitive advantage (e.g., by providing customers with a fast response to inquiries about the status of accounts); and (3) to handle the high volatility of a file, as in the changing conditions of stock accounts in a stock exchange.

In the past, many applications were rejected for online processing because of the excessive volume of data required to be accessible for a response, and the cost of direct access storage devices. Not only is the cost of direct access storage devices diminishing

Methods of Organization and Media / File Usage Considerations	File Update Sequential	File Update Direct	Large File Size*	File Interrogation	Large File Activity Ratio	High File Volatility	Response Time	Cost	Software Support	Implementation
Sequential (Tape and Cards)	Excellent	N.A.	Unlimited	Poor	Excellent	Excellent	Poor	Modest	Low	Simple
Indexed Sequential	Good	Good	Moderately unlimited	Good	Good	Good	Good	High	Medium	Difficult
Direct	N.A.	Excellent	Limited	Excellent	Fair	Poor	Excellent	Very high	High	Very difficult

*Theoretically, all methods would have unlimited capacity, but from a practicable viewpoint unlimited file size for direct access would be cost prohibitive.

FIG 10.6 Comparison of file usage considerations with methods of file organization and file storage media.

but technological advancements in magnetic tape devices continue to improve the speed with which magnetic tape files can be processed. Both of these situations require the systems analyst to consider new requests for fast response systems carefully.

The table in Figure 10.6 helps spotlight some of the considerations one should be aware of when selecting the file organization methods and file storage media. In most cases, it is not a matter of selecting one method over another, but of selecting a combination of methods to meet the variety of demands imposed upon the information system.

Note that selections of hardware storage media and of the organization of data records, should place records with high volatility or frequent use where they can be located quickly and easily. While doing systems work it might be discovered, for example, that 10 percent of the inventory items give rise to 80 or 90 percent of the references made. (This is a classic example of the application of contribution analysis, also called ABC analysis, as described in Appendix A.) The analyst could apply this same idea by ascertaining those records that have the highest rate of access and organizing them for direct access. The remaining records would be organized sequentially or indexed sequentially.

10.6 ▪ FILE DESIGN CONSIDERATIONS

The file design considerations discussed in this section should not be viewed separately from the other items discussed throughout the text. Rather, these considerations should be viewed as the culmination and reinforcement of what has thus far transpired.

File Aspects

The basic approach to file design is to study the various aspects that relate to a particular file. On the basis of this study, findings should be recorded on a worksheet similar to the one illustrated in Figure 10.7.

File Design Considerations

File Design Worksheet

Date started _____
Date completed _____
File name _____ Analyst _____

File update	File organization	Process cycle	Activity ratio	Direct access	Volatility	Record characteristics		
Batch Direct	Sequential Indexed sequential Direct	On demand Hourly Daily Weekly Monthly Yearly	Low Medium High	Yes No Seldom	Low Moderate High	Type: fixed variable	Blocking factor	No. of characters

File dynamics		File size	File media
Yearly additions	Yearly deletions	Total characters = Number of records × number of characters per record	General description of storage media file specifications (hardware)
Source of data for processing	Type of information required and reported		General remarks

FIG 10.7 Analyst's file design worksheet.

Along with this worksheet, the analyst should include a specimen of each record layout. In this way, the file design worksheet describes the file, and the record layout describes, in detail, the records contained in the file.

General File Considerations

The following general considerations should be observed when designing files:

1. A classic tradeoff exists between the current status of a file, the storage capacity of a file, and its cost. All master files should be maintained at some level of up-to-dateness depending upon the timing requirements. Periodically, out-of-date items must be deleted from the file, and restructuring may be necessary to meet changing applications and requirements. The cost of frequent processing for batch operations must be measured against keeping current the status of the data items within files. In a batch processing system, a file is always out-of-date by some factor equal to the age of the items in the transaction batch. In many instances this condition is tolerable (e.g., in a payroll file).

2. All application and processing jobs that utilize a file must be doublechecked to ensure that no necessary data items have been omitted.
3. The analyst must anticipate future requirements of the present procedures. For example, it may be reasonable and less costly in the long run to include additional fields in a payroll file to handle changes in government requirements (e.g., deductions for Medicare and Medicaid). It is more efficient and less costly in many instances to include additional space rather than to restructure a file. Moreover, it avoids reprogramming or a patched-up record layout at a later date.
4. The analyst should study the feasibility of combining existing data files, applicable to a broad functional area, into a single, integrated file to eliminate redundancy of common data items.
5. The analyst should receive a verification from all designated users of a file that it meets their information requirements in terms of content.
6. The analyst should establish a plan of security and audit control to ensure the integrity of the data items stored in a file, in accordance with the degree of sensitivity and confidentiality of the data. No foolproof method exists for restricting access to unauthorized users. Those safeguards which are established via programming, for example, can be changed the same way, and those persons in charge of controlling security procedures can themselves allow access at their discretion.

SUMMARY

Two basic methods are available to the system analyst to organize and process data elements physically: the sequential method and the direct method.

Sequential organization is an efficient method if a large volume of records and a high percentage of records are being processed each cycle. On the other hand, direct organization is most suitable where timeliness of response to events is important and where file activity ratios are low. The advantages of sequential processing systems are that they: (1) are suitable to situations where the nature of the applications relates to a definite cycle, (2) are efficient in applications where a large portion of the records are processed each cycle, (3) require less expensive equipment and a lower degree of technical sophistication, (4) are easier for many people to understand, and (5) relate well to traditional applications that have specified period lengths. The advantages of direct processing systems are that they: (1) are suitable to situations where timely response to events is important, (2) are efficient with regard to low activity ratio files, (3) can reflect the current status of the organization, (4) support the systems approach to information systems design, (5) require less offline data conversion and human intervention, and (6) offer flexibility insofar as supporting sequential processing.

Files can be classified in three different ways, according to: (1) content, (2) mode of processing, and (3) organization. When selecting the media and organization to be used for a file, the systems analyst must measure the systems requirements against certain criteria, such as: (1) method of update, (2) size of file, (3) degree of interrogation, (4) activity and volatility rate, (5) file operations, and (6) response time.

REVIEW QUESTIONS

10.1 When is sequential organization an efficient method of data organization? When is it not?

10.2 Explain the steps involved in sequential processing.

10.3 Summarize the characteristics of direct processing systems.

10.4 List the advantages and disadvantages of sequential processing systems. Of direct processing systems.

10.5 What is a hybrid processing system?

10.6 What are the various classifications of data files based on their contents? Based on their mode of processing?

10.7 What is overlay? Is it feasible to use the overlay concept on sequential file media such as magnetic tape?

10.8 Differentiate between activity ratio and volatility. Give examples of both.

10.9 What is the basic difference between updating a payroll file and updating an inventory file? What kind of file storage media would you use for each process?

10.10 Explain how the following factors affect the selection of file storage media and file organization methods: (1) file update, (2) file size, (3) interrogation, (4) activity ratio, (5) volatility, (6) response time, (7) cost, (8) software support, and (9) implementation.

QUESTIONS FOR DISCUSSION

10.1 "Direct processing systems have advantages not found in sequential processing systems. Direct processing systems also require programming and systems considerations that are not required by sequential processing systems." Comment on this statement.

10.2 "Under program control, the computer system can, in milliseconds, access particular data from a DASD and display the results on an output device. In contrast, in a sequential processing system, much preprocessing and sorting must be done before the desired information is produced. Thus interrogations become somewhat impracticable using a sequential processing system. By use of interrogative capability, the direct processing system makes possible a completely different kind of information system." Comment on this statement.

10.3 "To sift out the information wanted from a sequentially organized file, a great deal of sorting (arranging) of data normally is required, and if only a small percentage of the records are affected in a processing run, then many records are read unnecessarily." Comment on this statement.

10.4 "I can furnish any information you want from my batch processing system. It may take me a little longer, but I can still perform any information processing tasks that they can perform in those fancy direct access systems." Comment on this statement.

10.5 "Although data files with direct organization are applicable in many situations, most organizations do not use this technique to organize their data files." Discuss fully.

10.6 "The benefits of direct processing should not be restricted to online processing only." Explain this comment.

10.7 "Many data files are organized sequentially because the analyst who designs the file does not understand what factors must be evaluated when choosing a file organization approach." Discuss why this statement may be true.

EXERCISES

10.1 Prepare a list of questions that a systems analyst might ask to determine the type of file organization that should be used in a particular application. Provide answers for this checklist of questions and, based upon these answers, indicate the appropriate file organization method. Give supporting reasons for choosing the particular method (examples of typical questions: "What is the expected activity ratio?" or "What is the time limit from initiation of a particular operation to its completion?").

10.2 The file dynamics are stated as follows: (1) number of records is 180,000, (2) yearly percent add is 26, and (3) yearly percent drop is 10. Calculate, on the average, two-year percent growth and total number of records.

10.3 An inventory contains 25,000 different items. Information about quantity on hand of each item is stored in a sequential list. A user may determine the quantity on hand of a particular item by keying in the item number via a terminal which is connected to the computer. The requested number is accessed via a sequential search. Can you suggest a better way?

PROBLEMS

10.1 Red River Data Service handles the billing operations for a number of businesses in the local community. There are 150,000 customer master records maintained and about 70,000–80,000 of these are updated nightly. That is, at the end of the working day, credit sales slips are transported to Red River from the various businesses where these source documents are keypunched for further processing. Client managers of Red River each want a printout of the previous day's sales with various sales statistics, credit exceptions, aging of accounts receivable, income statements, and so forth. The management of Red River has been handling their data processing with unit record equipment. You have been commissioned to outline to Red River management a new data processing system for their consideration. In your proposal, be sure to suggest the type of file media and data organization method(s) that should be used.

10.2 Pitts Foundry, Inc., a new business developed to fabricate sheet piling and concrete forms, has hired you as one of their systems analysts. Your job is to set up a filing system for storing over 800 programs for a variety of programming procedures. Nearly all of the data will be processed online, regardless of the type of record accessed or updated. For example, when a job order is released, several programs are retrieved to process various cost and inventory calculations, billing procedures access other routines, bills of material interrogations trigger still other routines, and so forth. A tape program library has been considered to maintain these various programs. Do you agree that a tape library should be used? Why? Why not? Outline your proposal and state its advantages.

10.3 MoParts, an automotive parts dealer, maintains six warehouses scattered throughout the southwest. MoParts carries an inventory of 30,000 different items, each of these items identified by a twelve-digit part number. MoParts management wants to record each transaction affecting each item, as it occurs, so that if any one item in inventory reached or exceeded the reorder point, the buyer(s) would receive an out-of-stock notification. In broad terms, provide a sketch of the computer configuration and description of the system you could suggest to the management of MoParts for implememtation. Specify type of file media and data organization to be implemented in addition to the possible application of management science techniques, such as those described in Appendix A.

10.4 Consider a basic data processing system which performs order processing, invoicing, inventory, and accounts receivable applications. Sales orders are received and a combined invoice and shipping-order form is prepared on the printer. Inventory and accounts receivable master records, on magnetic tape, are updated. The first step is keypunching and key verifying; there are at least five more steps in the computer processing run to maintain this system. Flowchart these six steps and list the requisite hardware. Assume the same system, except, instead of using tapes, the files have been converted to magnetic disk. Flowchart this system. How many steps are required?

10.5 A large manufacturer of children's toys is considering the implementation of a marketing information system to assist its sales force. Approximately 300 salespeople work out of 15 branch offices throughout the continental U.S. and Canada. The goal of the system is to have customer sales history files online at central headquarters, in St. Louis, which can be accessed by remote terminals at each branch office during normal business hours. New customer orders and shipments received from each branch office nightly, will update the sales history file that same night.

Approximately 30,000 customers records are on file at any one time. Fifty customers are added, and twenty customers deleted, daily. History data are maintained for thirteen months by product for each customer. Each customer's master record has 100 characters of descriptive data. The average number of product records per customer is expected to be 20, each having 70 characters of information. Finally, projections indicate that the volume of order and shipment records updating the history file will be 3000 nightly.

Prepare a brief report describing the structure of the required data base you would propose.

10.6 A car manufacturer has implemented a system whereby its customers can call a district representative toll-free to lodge any complaints about dealers. The district representative then attempts to aid the customer by coordination with the dealer, the manufacturer, or both. Phase I of this program was launched by a national advertising campaign. Major objectives of Phase I were to fortify the company's image, in the area of customer service, and to increase customer confidence in the reliability of their product.

The objective of Phase II has been formulated, but the detailed modifications to the original system have not been firmed up. The basic goal of Phase II is to create a feedback from customers to manufacturer. Data flowing through the feedback loop are stored in a data base, where it would be available to various functional areas within the corporation. Two obvious users are the design engineers and quality control people. Apparently information from the field is valuable in quickly replacing defective parts and improving the design of parts and components. The corporation executives see the network of district representatives as a skeletal framework which could be expanded to handle the demands of Phase II.

Bearing in mind the extensive resources available to a major automobile producer, present your ideas about the following aspects of the proposed Phase II system:

1. Specific description of the data which should be collected.
2. How it is should be collected, and by whom.
3. How it should be transmitted to the manufacturer.
4. How it should be stored at the corporations's main office to facilitate retrieval by numerous users.

Additional Background Information

In addition to handling customer complaints, district representatives also serves as watchdogs on the dealers. In this role they must ascertain that the individual dealers, franchised by the company, are complying with the service standards imposed by the corporation. The office staff and facilities of the representatives are presently limited to those needed in the performance of Phase I duties.

Two coding structures utilized by the corporation may be useful in this problem. The first is the serial number affixed to each auto. A sample serial number and its interpretation is given below.

2 G 2 9 R 4 G 1 0 6 1 1 3

2 G	Brand name (major manufacturers produce several brands)
2 9	Body style (station wagon, convertible)
R	Engine (code representing engine model)
4	Year (last digit of year)
G	Factory (factory where produced)
1 0 6 1 1 3	Car's serial number (discrete code depicting one particular car)

A second code structure is used for identifying parts. Each individual part of an automobile is coded with a nonintelligent, seven-digit number. The problems associated with locating a particular part number from the thousands incorporated in one car are obvious. To facilitate the retrieval of part numbers, all the part numbers are structured within a directory code. The directory code is composed of five digits. The first two run from 00 to 15 and identify the major subsystems (i.e., 01 represents Engine Cooling, Oiling, and Ventilating systems). The last three digits are a serial code representing the individual parts incorporated in the major subsystem. An example may provide clarity. Let us assume that we're trying to locate the part number for the oil pump cover gasket for a 1983 six-cylinder Bassethound. The Bassethound is one of the brands produced by the major manufacturer, Dogs, Inc. Searching the directory we find that 01.724 is the directory number for oil pump cover gaskets. This number is the general part number for all oil pump cover gaskets produced by Dogs, Inc. Looking in the parts manual under 01.724 we find the specific part numbers for this particular gasket for the individual years and models. Searching this list we find that the gasket for a 1983 six-cylinder Bassethound has a part number of 3789970. This number identifies the exact part.

In concluding the background information, one point should be emphasized. Under the present system, the district representative only receives information concerned with customer complaints. The details and financial arrangements of warranty service, performed by the dealer in a satisfactory manner, are communicated directly between manufacturer and dealer, by-passing the district representative. You may desire to alter this information flow in your solution.

10.7 A systems analysis study has been completed in a large company which manufactures and markets various types of paper for the printing industry. This study initially was intended to identify the information requirements related to the purchasing function, but was subsequently expanded to include the accounts payable function as well. The justification for expanding the study was based on the similarity of the data required in the data base to support each function.

The study identified the need for purchasing to maintain three files: (1) a vendor master file containing name, address, purchasing terms, and miscellaneous descriptive data; (2) an open purchase order file containing all of the data related to purchase orders placed but not yet completed; and (3) a history file of purchases made in a two-year period, by product, by vendor. At the time of the study, these files were maintained in a manual system.

The accounts payable department on the other hand required the following files: (1) a vendor master file containing the descriptive data necessary to produce and mail a check for purchases received, (2) a file of invoices from vendors received but not yet paid, and (3) a one-year history file of paid vendor invoices. Currently, accounts payable maintains a manual vendor master and open invoice file. A punched card system was used to create checks to vendors and to maintain paid invoice history.

The company leases a medium-sized computer with both magnetic tape and disk storage available in a batch processing mode. Approximately 20 percent of all purchases are considered re-buys from an existing vendor. At any point in time there are 3,000 active vendors; 5,000 open purchase orders; 1,500 open invoices; and annually, the company places 40,000 purchase orders.

From the above facts, your assignment is to determine the following:

1. How many data files are necessary in the required data base?

2. What data fields will be required in each data file? (Prepare a table or matrix which illustrates the relationship of data fields among files.)
3. What storage media should be used for each data file?
4. How should each file be updated, and which department is responsible for keeping the file current?

BIBLIOGRAPHY

Atre, *Data Base: Structured Techniques for Design, Performance, and Management,* New York: John Wiley and Sons, 1980.

Cardenas, *Data Base Management Systems,* Boston: Allyn and Bacon, Inc., 1979.

Hussain and Hussain, *Information Processing Systems for Management,* Homewood, IL.: Richard D. Irwin, Inc., 1981.

Inmon, *Effective Data Base Design,* Englewood Cliffs, NJ.: Prentice-Hall, Inc., 1981.

Kroenke, *Business Computer Systems,* Santa Cruz, CA.: Mitchell Publishing, Inc., 1981.

PART III

Information Systems Development Methodology

CHAPTER 11

Systems Analysis

11.1 ▪ INTRODUCTION

The development of an information system, no matter what its size and complexity, requires many coordinated activities. The systems development methodology is a standard way to organize and coordinate these activities. The analyst who uses this methodology can apply it in any kind of organization regardless of his or her expertise relative to the organization's operations. Obviously, the more one knows about a particular organization, the better one can perform systems work. On the other hand, a systems analyst can enter a totally unfamiliar organization and perform systems work, and develop a viable information system if the methodology is followed.

In Chapter 1 we presented an overview of the systems development methodology. Using a different schematic, we present it here, in Figure 11.1, as it relates to the information system building blocks. You will note that it contains five phases. Each of these phases will be discussed in this part of the text. As supplements to the chapters listed below, an example of the output of each phase has been included to provide structure for the analyst who is doing systems work for the first time. These outputs and their corresponding chapters are:

1. Proposal to Conduct Systems Analysis Report (Chapter 11).
2. Systems Analysis Completion Report (Chapter 11).
3. General Systems Design Proposal Report (Chapter 12).
4. Final General Systems Design Report (Chapter 13).
5. Final Detail Systems Design Report (Chapter 15).
6. Final Implementation Report (Chapter 16).

11.2 ▪ PREPARING TO CONDUCT SYSTEMS ANALYSIS

In this section some of the reasons why systems analysis is initiated are discussed, as well as some of the difficulties of defining the scope of the analysis. Guidelines for preparing a Proposal to Conduct Systems Analysis Report are also given.

298   Systems Analysis

Reasons for Initiating Systems Analysis

Certainly, the first step in any systems analysis is for the analyst to acquire an understanding of why the analysis is being undertaken. A basic understanding can be attained usually through preliminary interviews with the persons requesting or authorizing the systems analysis. The basic reasons for initiating systems analysis are:

1. *Problem solving.* It might be that the present system is not functioning as required and the analyst is called upon to correct this malfunction. Or, it might be that some department in the organiza-

```
                    Demand
                    Blocks
         • Information    • Data Processing
           Attributes       Requirements
         • Systems        • Organizational
           Requirements     Factors
         • Cost/Effectiveness • Feasibility
           Requirements     Requirements
```

Phase	Systems Analysis	General Systems Design	Systems Evaluation and Justification	Detail Systems Design	Systems Implementation	Phase
Activities	• Definition of users problems/ needs • Systems scope • Gathering of study facts • Analyzing study facts	• Broad design of design blocks • Presentation of design alternatives	• Employee impact • Cost/effectiveness analysis	• Detail specification of design blocks	• Training and educating users • Systems testing • Systems conversion • Systems follow-up	Activities
Report	• Proposal to conduct systems analysis report • Systems analysis completion report	• General systems design proposal report	• Final general systems design report	• Final detail systems design report	• Final implementation report	Report

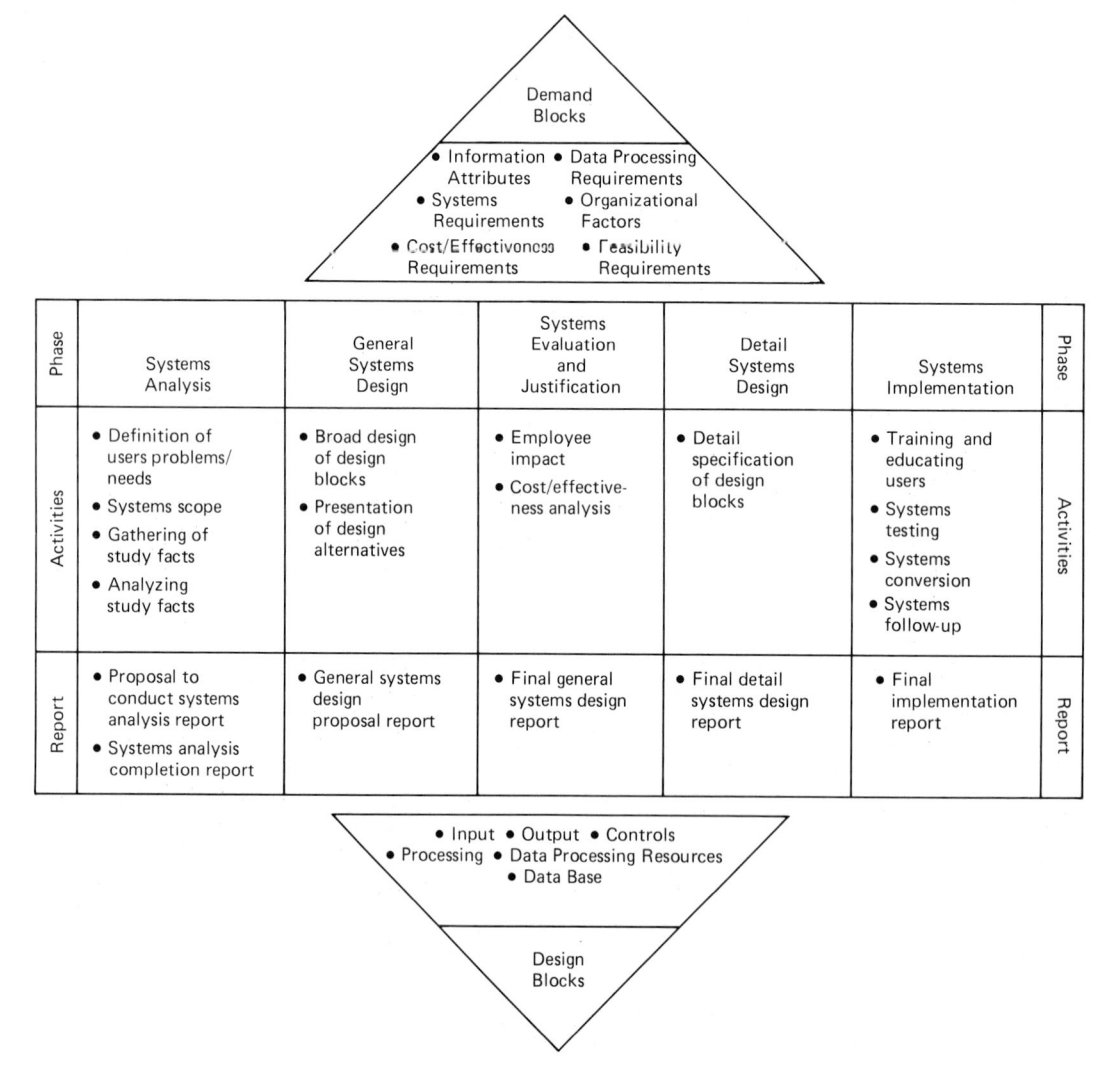

```
         • Input  • Output  • Controls
         • Processing  • Data Processing Resources
                   • Data Base

                    Design
                    Blocks
```

FIG. 11.1 The systems development methodology and its relationship to the information systems building blocks.

tion has a scheduling, forecasting, or inventory control problem which must be corrected or improved upon.

2. *New requirement.* A second reason for conducting systems analysis might be that a new requirement or regulation has been imposed upon the organization. This requirement might be a new law, accounting practice, organizational service, or product, or a new management practice. Regardless of what generates the new requirement, systems analysis will identify the necessary modifications or additions to the information system that are necessary to support the organization in satisfying this requirement.

3. *Implement new idea/technology.* A third reason for conducting systems analysis might arise from a desire to implement a new idea, piece of technology, or technique. For example, starting to use OCR equipment for entering customers' orders will likely result in a new subsystem being designed.

4. *Broad systems improvement.* Finally, systems analysis might be initiated simply because of a desire to find a better way to do what is currently being done. Many of the data processing and information systems now operating in organizations were designed and implemented many years ago. In many instances the reasons for designing these systems in a particular way are no longer valid. General objectives of a broad systems improvement might be cost reduction, increased customer service, and faster reporting.

In many instances the reasons for initiating systems analysis are vague and poorly defined by the initiators. The analyst must be careful, however, to identify any specific objectives stated. Frequently, specific objectives are given to the analyst concerning elements of cost, quality, and timing related to conducting the systems analysis, which will affect any recommendations that result. These stated objectives are a major factor in determining the scope of the investigation.

Defining the Scope of Systems Analysis

The activities and events comprising systems analysis are for the most part directed toward answering the question: What is the new system to include? In many cases this question can be more accurately phrased as: What more is the existing system to include? In answering these general questions the analyst must address many specific questions. What information is needed? by whom? when? where? in what form? how? where does it originate? when? how can it be collected? and so forth.

An overriding criterion, which to a great extent dictates the scope of systems analysis, is the systems structure adopted by the organization. In Chapter 4 three broad alternative approaches were outlined for developing information systems. These are (1) the centralized structure, (2) the distributed structure, and (3) a combination of the two. Any attempt to exceed the scope dictated by the systems philosophy of a particular organization will probably meet with resistance from management. Such a situation does not prevent the systems analyst from making suggestions as to how the total system might be improved, but the analyst still must work within the context dictated by management. Moreover, the scope of systems analysis can vary widely in terms of duration, complexity, and expense. Consequently, the scope must be defined somewhat arbitrarily at times to meet constraints such as time and cost. The primary problem for both the novice analyst and the skilled professional is converting unconsciously an instruction such as "I want to know what yesterday's sales were by 8:00 AM today," into "Develop a new sales reporting system."

Often, in practice, an analyst who fails to define the scope of systems analysis properly, either fails to achieve objectives, or achieves them at a great loss of both time and money. It must be understood, however, that the presence of limiting objectives (or constraints) on the scope of the analysis, limits the potential solutions and/or the recommendations that result from the analysis. As a rule, the initial definition of purpose and scope, as well as any given objectives and constraints, are subject to redefinition at a later date, based on findings in the analysis.

Preparation of a Proposal to Conduct Systems Analysis Report

Once the systems analyst completes the initial interviews and determines that systems analysis should be conducted, an understanding of what must be accomplished and the general approach toward this goal must be communicated formally to both the requestor and the systems analyst's own management. This communication is termed the **Proposal to Conduct Systems Analysis Report.** It provides a checkpoint at which the requestor can evaluate whether or not the analyst clearly understands what is desired, and it gives the analyst's management an opportunity to evaluate the approach and amount of resources to be used during the analysis.

The report should facilitate an initial in-depth understanding, as well as provide reference points that can be accessed when actual performance of the analysis can be periodically reported. It should include the following:

1. A clear, concise definition of the reasons for conducting the analysis.
2. A specific statement concerning the performance requirements of the proposed system.
3. A definition of the scope of the analysis.
4. An identification of the facts that will likely need to be collected during the analysis.
5. An identification of the potential sources where the facts can be obtained.
6. A schedule which lists the major events or milestones of the analysis.

While the analyst should exercise a great deal of care in preparing this report, it should be remembered that the report itself is intended to be only a guideline. As the investigation progresses, the analyst might modify, add to, or delete from the original report. Thus, the resources spent preparing the report must be balanced against the expediency in providing it. An example of how the report can change is illustrated below.

Michael Jay, a systems analyst for a large west coast electronics manufacturer, was given the responsibility of developing a corporate payroll system. Although Michael had been receiving paychecks from companies for many years, he had not before been involved with the payroll function in any assignments. In his Proposal to Conduct Systems Analysis Report he listed the following sources of facts:

1. Manager, Corporate Payroll Department.
2. Supervisor, Salary Payroll.
3. Supervisor, Union Payroll.
4. The payroll check and other documents maintained in the Payroll Department.

5. Ann Brown, the analyst who developed and installed the present payroll system.

After discussing the proposed payroll system with the Manager, Corporate Payroll Department, Michael added the following items to his list of sources to be investigated.

6. The new union contract.
7. Manager, Corporate Benefits.
8. Manager, Corporate Work Scheduling.
9. State Law # 107352.
10. Director, Corporate Planning.
11. Corporate file of requests for information from the National Labor Relations Board.

Next, Michael interviewed the Supervisor, Salary Payroll, and, again, added additional sources of facts to his list. And so it went. After each interview or document review, Michael added and deleted potential sources of facts from his checklist.

11.3 ▪ SOURCES OF STUDY FACTS FOR SYSTEMS ANALYSIS

In this section we discuss the various sources of study facts in and around the organization that are available to the analyst during systems analysis. Three categories of study facts are: (1) the existing system, (2) other internal sources, and (3) external sources.

Studying the Existing System

It is rare indeed when an analyst is provided with an opportunity to develop an information system where one did not exist before. In most cases a system or subsystem exists which serves the organization. As a result, the analyst is confronted with decisions such as: What role does the old system have with respect to the new system? Should I analyze the old system? If so, what subsystems in the old system should I analyze?

Often a great deal of time and money is spent investigating, analyzing, and documenting the old system, with the results seeming to have little benefit in the design of the new system. It is not uncommon to have experienced managers comment, "We spent $20,000 studying the old system only to have them tell us that we were correct in asking for a new system." At the other end of the spectrum, some state emphatically that the first step in all systems studies is to analyze the old system. Again, many managers who have experienced new systems conversions comment, "I will never consent to implementing another new system before I have analyzed thoroughly my present system."

While it may be impossible to reconcile fully these two extreme positions, an examination of the advantages and disadvantages will shed some light on when the old system should be studied and to what extent it should be studied.

The primary advantages of analyzing the old system are:

1. *Effectiveness of present system.* Studying the old system provides an opportunity to determine whether that system is satisfactory, is in need of minor repair, requires a major overhaul, or should be replaced. To design a new system without this consideration might be comparable to purchasing a new car without knowing whether your present car may only be out of gas.
2. *Design ideas.* Analyzing the old system can provide the analyst with an immediate source of design ideas. These ideas include what is presently being done and how, as well as what additional needs or capabilities have been requested over the years. The analyst is able to gain an in-

sight into how the present information system serves the decision-making function as well as to ascertain key relationships.

3. *Resource recognition.* Examining the present system allows the analyst to identify the resources available for the new system or subsystem. These resources might include the management talent, the clerical talent, and the equipment currently owned and operational.

4. *Conversion knowledge.* When the new system is implemented, the analyst is responsible for having previously identified what tasks and activities will be necessary to phase out the old system and begin operating the new system. To identify these conversion requirements, the analyst must know not only what activities will be performed, but also what activities were performed. Studying the present system gives the analyst the "what was" answer.

5. *Common starting point.* When communicating with management, the systems analyst is an agent of change. As such, often the analyst will be confronted with resistance to new techniques, ideas, and methods, lack of understanding of new concepts, procrastination in obtaining decisions, lack of commitment to making the new system work, and other similar manifestations of people being asked to change familiar activities. To minimize these reactions, the analyst can compare and contrast the new system to the old system and demonstrate that it is not entirely new.

The primary disadvantages of analyzing the old system are:

1. *Expensive.* Studying the old system requires time, and in all organizations time can be converted to money.
2. *Unnecessary barriers.* An extensive analysis of an existing system can result in unnecessary barriers or artificial constraints being included in the design of the new system. For example, in the existing system, in a given department, there may be a document flow and a series of actions taken with that document. The analyst can become so involved with improving those actions that the involvement of the department in the first place is left unquestioned. The more familiar an analyst becomes with a given system, the more likely it is that some perspective or objectivity concerning it will be lost. One may argue logically that an *ideal systems concept* should be used in performing systems work. That is, the analyst formulates an ideal system, and then proceeds with his or her systems work using this ideal systems framework.

Internal Sources

The single most important source of study facts available to the analyst is *people*. This includes not only the formal management, but the clerical and production workers as well. Information requirements can best be stated by the users of the information. The analyst, however, can help the users define their requirements by explaining to them what can be provided. It is important to note that most individuals are guided in formulating their needs by arbitrary and often antiquated notions of what they "think" can be provided. The analyst's function, then, is to remove or expand these attitudes so that the real information requirements can be obtained.

A secondary source of study facts for the analyst comes from the existing *paperwork* within the organization. The paperwork in most organizations can be classified as that which describes how the organization is structured, what the organization is or has been doing, and what the organization plans to do. In Figure 11.2 a partial list, by types, has been provided of some of the documents found in organizations.

A word of caution is in order when organizational documents are used as sources of study facts in systems analysis. The documents identified as describing how an organization is structured, and what it plans to do, *do not* necessarily reflect reality. At best, these documents serve to give the analyst an understanding of what management considered its structure and direction to be at one point. It is not uncommon for organizations and plans to change while their documentation remains unchanged.

A third source of study facts important to the analyst can be termed *relationships*. Defining the relationships between people, departments, or functions can provide the analyst with information and insights not formerly known or documented anywhere within the organization.

Throughout the analysis the analyst must guard against overlooking the obvious. Frequently, an analyst may be questioning an individual and uncover some excellent ideas that management has been unwilling to act upon. Similarly, a brief analysis of something as simple as counting the number of occurrences of some event, can result in a finding about that activity not realized or understood by management. In essence, the analyst provides an opportunity to present to management, at a time when their attention is strongly focused on a subject, not only

Documents describing how the organization is organized	Documents describing what the organization plans to do	Documents describing what the organization does
Policy statements Methods and procedure manuals Organization charts Job descriptions Performance standards Delegations of authority Chart of accounts (All other coding structure references)	Statement of goals and objectives Budgets Schedules Forecasts Plans (long- and short-range) Corporate minutes	Financial statements Performance reports Staff studies Historical reports Transaction files (including: purchase orders, customer orders, invoices, time sheets, expense records, customer correspondence, etc.) Legal papers (including: copyrights, patents, franchises, trademarks, judgments, etc.) Master reference files (including: customers, employees, products, vendors, etc.)

FIG. 11.2 Illustration of the various types of documents available to the analyst in an organization from which information may be obtained pertaining to systems analysis.

the analyst's discoveries, but ideas, suggestions, and recommendations from various levels of operating personnel.

External Sources

The systems analyst's work can take him or her outside the boundaries of the segment of the organization for which the analysis is being conducted. Exploring other information subsystems within the organization can be a useful source of data collection, data processing, or information reporting ideas and techniques. Moreover, reviewing other systems provides an opportunity to identify potential interface points when the analyst is involved in a limited or subsystem analysis.

Just as meaningful, though often overlooked, is a review of similar information systems in other organizations. Not only can this be a source of new ideas but it can provide the analyst with an opportunity to actually see systems, subsystems, concepts, techniques, and mechanisms in operation. Many organizations zealously guard manufacturing and marketing techniques, but information processing exchanges are common. In fact many societies and organizations exist whose sole purpose is the exchange of information and data processing experiences, both good and bad.

Textbooks and professional journals provide still another source of study facts for the analyst. Studying this material may entail reviewing known theory and practice, or searching for new ideas, theories, and proposals. Similarly, the analyst can profit from attendance at professional seminars, workshops, and conferences held throughout the country.

Sales brochures from equipment and computer software vendors are an excellent source of concepts and ideas. When we consider that products and services are developed and marketed to satisfy needs, it follows that the brochures and proposals of the vendors offering the products define the needs they propose to satisfy.

The sources of study facts available to an analyst during systems analysis are varied and plentiful. What sources are exploited will differ from analysis to analysis as time and cost constraints are considered. The size and complexity of the system or subsystem under study will also help to determine which sources are utilized. Common sense is often the most compelling factor as to what sources of study facts the analyst actually selects. It is important to recognize, however, what the overall choice of sources can be.

11.4 ▪ FRAMEWORKS FOR FACT GATHERING

Many of the frameworks are dictated by the reason and scope of the study. Others are personal preferences of each analyst. A discussion of the more widely used frameworks for study fact gathering will demonstrate their usefulness and will also provide a basis for other techniques to be conceived by the reader.

Decision Level Analysis

With this approach, the analyst interviews the key managers to categorize the major resources of the organization. Resources include both tangible and intangible assets, such as inventories, plant and equipment, employee skills, and so forth. The major argument for this approach is that managers at all levels need an information system that provides information about resource use.[1]

---

[1] Dr. Germain Boer, "A Decision Oriented Information System," *Journal of Systems Management,* October 1972, pp 36–39. With permission.

Frameworks for Fact Gathering

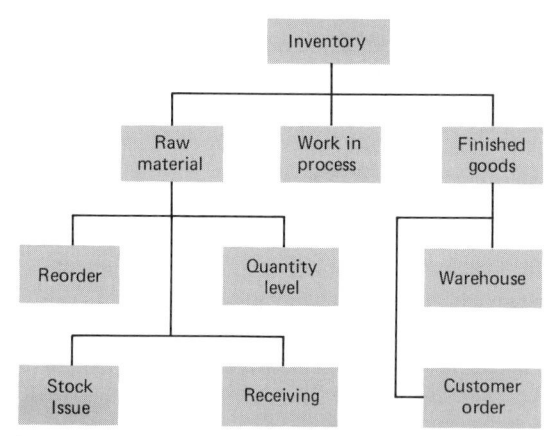

FIG. 11.3 Decision points based on a resource break down.

requirements are fully described, the analyst ascertains the sources of data (e.g., customer order) which generate this information, as shown in Figure 11.4

Identifying the sources of data is useful for illustrating to managers the kinds of decisions that must be made before given subsystems can be developed. For example, before rules for inventory reorder decisions can be incorporated into an inventory control system, a decision rule must first be formulated.[2]

Moreover, this form of analysis graphically illustrates the many interrelationships among the decisions made in separate segments of the organization. For example, production scheduling decisions affect stock issue and stock level decisions, and stock level decisions in turn affect reorder decisions. These decision interfaces must be properly designed into the information system so that data can flow smoothly from one decision point to the other.[3]

For example, one resource area is inventory. As shown in Figure 11.3, this resource (raw material and finished goods only) is broken down into major types of decisions concerned with it.

Once the organization's resources are defined and categorized, the systems analyst breaks each one down into its decision levels so as to identify the information required for each decision level. After the information

[2] Ibid.
[3] Ibid., p. 39.

Customer Order

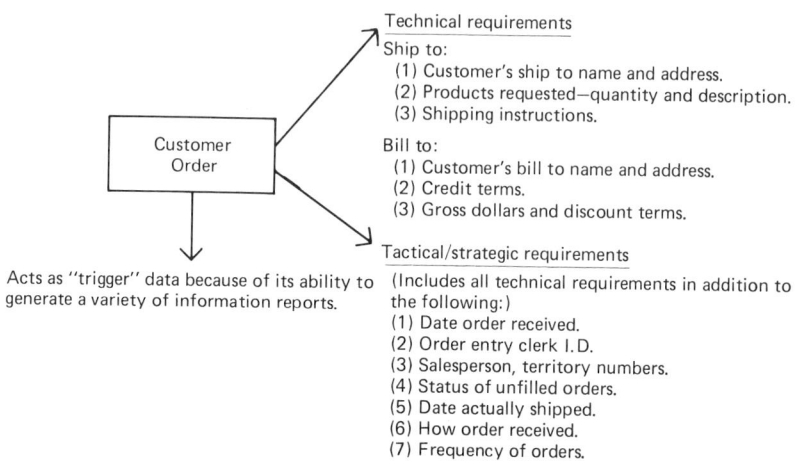

Acts as "trigger" data because of its ability to generate a variety of information reports.

Technical requirements
Ship to:
(1) Customer's ship to name and address.
(2) Products requested—quantity and description.
(3) Shipping instructions.
Bill to:
(1) Customer's bill to name and address.
(2) Credit terms.
(3) Gross dollars and discount terms.

Tactical/strategic requirements
(Includes all technical requirements in addition to the following:)
(1) Date order received.
(2) Order entry clerk I.D.
(3) Salesperson, territory numbers.
(4) Status of unfilled orders.
(5) Date actually shipped.
(6) How order received.
(7) Frequency of orders.

FIG. 11.4 Illustration of the information requirements from a customer's order, as required to fill the order and as a potential source of management information to be used later in planning, controlling, and decision-making activities.

Information Flow Analysis

Information flow analysis is a popular method used by systems analysts when attempting to identify what information is required, by whom, and from where it is obtained. Figure 11.5 illustrates the flow analysis approach as a framework for gathering study facts. As can be seen, the analyst is concerned with what information the individual needs from others (supervisors, peers, and subordinates), and what information is required from him or her by others.

Input/Output Analysis

When the analyst is investigating the old system to gain an understanding of what is presently being done, particularly the mechanized or computerized portions of the system, facts can be collected in terms of inputs and outputs. Figure 11.6 illustrates this approach as a framework for gathering study facts. It should be noted that each input and each output is described. Nothing is said, however, about how the input is converted to output, or about decision making, information requirements, or information flow.

Structured Analysis

In recent years, structured analysis has been available as a tool for analysis and design. The key assumption in this approach is that all organizations are made up of a number of well-defined functions (e.g., marketing, inventory control, production scheduling), and that these functions are, in turn, made up of a group of activities. These activities are performed by people, procedures, and machines. By studying these functions and their supporting activities, the analyst is given a logical way of developing design blocks, especially input, process, data base, and output blocks. In the next chapter a popular technique of structured analysis, called HIPO, is presented.

A rule of thumb in performing structured analysis is to start with the top function and work down to the lowest activity. Big functions are broken down into small activities to allow the analyst to see how functions fit together. As an added comment, some systems experts state that all systems work should be done by following a structured top-down approach to analyzing function, and a bottom-up approach to the study of the political situation.

Application of a structured, top-down approach results in a tree like function diagram. For example, assume that you are an analyst involved in analysis of an inventory control function. Part of this function is shown in Figure 11.7. The top level of the tree states that it represents the function of inventory control. The tree is built by defining all of the activities (or subfunctions) that

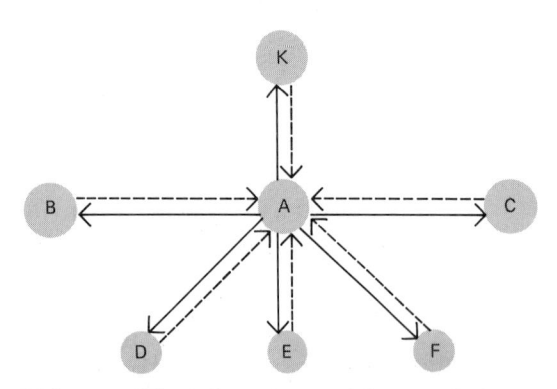

FIG. 11.5 The information need framework for collecting study facts. The solid lines represent what is given to others. The broken lines represent what is required from others. A represents the individual being queried. B and C represent peers (from other departments). D, E, and F are subordinates. K represents superiors or upper level management.

Input/Output Analysis: Plant A, Inventory System

INPUTS:
(1) Production. (Quality, product code, product number, batch numbers, operator numbers.)
  Machine X
  Machine Y (Production ticket prepared by machine operator for each batch of completed goods.)
  Machine Z
(2) Scrap. A scrap ticket is prepared as necessary—same information as production ticket but coded scrap.
(3) Receiving. All receipts are noted with: Product number
  Receipt codes
  Receiver's number
  Product quantity
  Date received
  Purchase order
  Authorization number
(4) Shipments. Finished Goods. Received from billing computer system by product number, including date shipped, quantity shipped, customer order number.
(5) Transfers. Transfers within company recorded with transfer code.
(6) Inventory Adjustments. Inventory adjustments entered by auditors. The correct amount of product is entered with date of physical count.

OUTPUTS:
(1) Input Listing. A listing of all inputs is prepared daily with errors in coding. This report is received by the supervisors of manufacturing, shipping, receiving, and accounting.
(2) Daily Inventory Status. A daily report is prepared indicating the status of all products. Report includes opening inventory, production, shipments, transfers, adjustments, and closing inventory. Report is distributed to production scheduler, shipping foreman, auditor, and inventory analyst.
(3) Monthly Inventory Status. A monthly report is prepared with the same format as daily report, only reflecting that month's activity. This report is issued to plant manager and plant accountant, in addition to daily distribution.
(4) Monthly Scrap Report. A monthly scrap report is issued showing all scrap reported lost by product, by machine operation. This report is issued to plant manager, plant accountant, supervisor of quality control, supervisor of operations.

FIG. 11.6 An example of the input/output framework for gathering.

support the top function. Some of these activities are shown. As you construct the tree in a top-down fashion, the input, processing, data base, and output design blocks required become clear. For example, you will see that an inventory master file is needed to interface with the activity UPDATE INVENTORY MASTER FILE. You will be able to define each of the data elements and state the way they are combined in data structures.

The structure should have a complete definition from a logical viewpoint. In the diagram no reference should be made to technicalities. At this stage no distinction is made to the method of processing or file media.

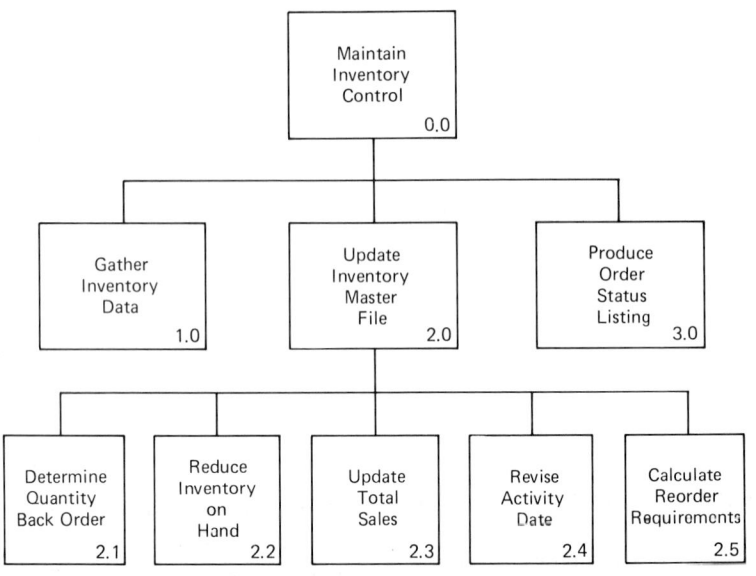

```
                    ┌─────────────┐
                    │  Maintain   │
                    │  Inventory  │
                    │   Control   │
                    │         0.0 │
                    └──────┬──────┘
         ┌─────────────────┼─────────────────┐
  ┌──────┴──────┐   ┌──────┴──────┐   ┌──────┴──────┐
  │   Gather    │   │   Update    │   │   Produce   │
  │  Inventory  │   │  Inventory  │   │    Order    │
  │    Data     │   │   Master    │   │   Status    │
  │             │   │    File     │   │   Listing   │
  │         1.0 │   │         2.0 │   │         3.0 │
  └─────────────┘   └──────┬──────┘   └─────────────┘
                           │
       ┌────────┬──────────┼──────────┬────────┐
   ┌───┴───┐┌───┴───┐  ┌───┴───┐  ┌───┴───┐┌───┴───┐
   │Determ.││Reduce │  │Update │  │Revise ││Calc.  │
   │Quant. ││Invent.│  │ Total │  │Activ. ││Reorder│
   │Back   ││ on    │  │ Sales │  │ Date  ││Requir.│
   │Order  ││ Hand  │  │       │  │       ││       │
   │   2.1 ││   2.2 │  │   2.3 │  │   2.4 ││   2.5 │
   └───────┘└───────┘  └───────┘  └───────┘└───────┘
```

FIG. 11.7 Activities of a portion of an inventory control function.

Less-Structured Analysis

Some systems experts say that since systems work is heuristic in nature, following a set procedure similar to those above, especially during analysis, stifles creativity. They also state that organizations do not have a top or bottom, per se. They contend that organizations are complex entities with complex networks of people and activities. They believe that systems work should take advantage of the combined wisdom of many managers. There is little disagreement between systems people on this last point. Several approaches are used to help extract and analyze this wisdom. One approach is called the Delphi method; the other is known as brainstorming.

1. *Delphi method.* The Delphi method receives its name from the priestess of Delphi, who sent runners into the countryside to get opinions about a particular problem. A concensus of opinions led to her decision. A number of organizations and "think tanks" (e.g., the Rand Corporation) use a similar method to get a "handle on" projects or future trends. A panel of experts answers a series of questionnaires. As results of these questionnaires go back and forth, experts change and adjust their opinion toward a concensus. A similar method could be used to extract ideas and study facts from management and operating personnel. It could be used by the systems analyst at the start of the systems analysis phase, and at the end of each phase through systems implementation. It could even be used again after implementation for review and feedback. Certainly the Delphi method ensures full participation and concensus, an imperative of successful systems development.

2. *Brainstorming.* Since time began, people have worked on the analysis and design of a number of projects by engaging in a free flow of ideas. The purpose of this activity is to stimulate creative thinking,

which in turn is intended to lead to an action solution. Traditionally, this activity was referred to as brainstorming. To make brainstorming sessions productive, an atmosphere conducive to a free flow of ideas must be created. Also, a group leader must be selected. The group leader informs the members of the session of the stated problem and objectives, and emphasizes that all ideas will be considered without criticism. As ideas are consolidated, reviewed, and reconsolidated, a few begin to rise to the top. After several brainstorming sessions, precise alternatives emerge and are discussed. Eventually, one alternative is chosen. Again, this method gives the systems analyst another way to get people involved in systems work, especially during the analysis phase.

A degree of similarity exists between all of the above frameworks for fact gathering and analysis. We do not recommend one method over another. Each has its own strengths. The bottom line to systems work, and in particular the gathering of study facts and their analysis, is to extract from a group of people their knowledge, ideas, and needs. To accomplish this task calls for the use of a combination of methods. A suggested approach is to use the brainstorming method to get things started, and from there, apply more structured methods.

In the next section, we present some specific fact-gathering techniques that are applied once the framework for fact gathering is established.

11.5 ▪ TECHNIQUES FOR GATHERING AND ANALYZING STUDY FACTS

In the analysis phase of the information system's development process the systems analyst relies on specific techniques for gathering study facts. Like any good craftsperson, some analysts rely more heavily on one technique to serve them. In most systems endeavors, however, the systems analyst requires many forms of assistance.

The techniques presented in this section do not represent an exhaustive list of what is available or what is used. It does, however, identify the major techniques used by systems analysts.

The Interview

In many instances, the best way to obtain critical study facts is to conduct a series of interviews. In general, questions such as "Does this report give you what you need?" and "How could this be done better?" allow respondents to contribute to the analysis. (Other questions that elicit the basis for further systems work are "What is your job?" or "What is the objective of your job?" or "What information are you getting now to help you meet these objectives?" or "What additional information do you need?")

It is important that the systems analyst makes sure that each respondent understands that the ultimate objective of systems work is to make the new system more useful. Eliciting meaningful and helpful facts from respondents is a function of a positive attitude by all participants. It is also important that systems analysts actively *listen* to respondents. Subtle overtones and nuances by respondents can be as significant as their direct responses to questions. Ultimately, since the final system developed will, to a great extent, rest upon facts supplied by people, it will be no better than the facts upon which it was based.

Within an organization, interviewing is the most significant and productive fact-finding technique available to the analyst.

Simply stated, the interview is a face-to-face exchange of information. It is a communication channel between the analyst and the organization. Interviewing is used to gain information concerning what is required and how these requirements can be met. The interview can be used to gain support or understanding from the user for a new idea or method. Moreover, the interview provides an excellent opportunity for the analyst to establish rapport with user personnel.

Interviewing is conducted at all levels within the organization, from the president or chief operating officer to the mail clerk or the maintenance engineer. Consequently, the interview proceedings can vary from highly formal to somewhat casual. Even the location where interviewing is conducted is subject to wide variation (e.g., the plant operating floor or an executive suite). Interviewing success is dependent on how well the analyst is able to adjust to these environmental variables. This adjustment is complicated further by the qualities possessed or deficient in the analyst.

Preparing to Interview. Before beginning the interview, the systems analyst should confer with and obtain cooperation from all department managers to be included in the systems project. The analyst should fully explain to the department managers the scope and nature of the analysis and stress that its scope may be subject to change upon further investigation.

We believe that several of the following points would be helpful in preparing an interview and obtaining the necessary cooperation and support:

1. Arrange for an appointment ahead of time. Don't just "drop in."
2. Identify the interviewee's position within the organization and job responsibilities and activities.
3. Prearrange the time and place for the interview. Set up the interview at a time that is convenient to the interviewee and when he or she will not be distracted by interruptions.
4. The primary aim of the interview is to gather study facts. Therefore, prepare an outline of the forthcoming interview, along with pertinent questions. If appropriate, forward a copy of the questions to the interviewee. Do not go into an interview and try to "play it by ear."

Conducting the Interview. In conducting the interview the systems analyst should behave in a manner, and ask questions, that will get the required study facts in as little time as possible. The analyst should not take the position of a "know-it-all" or an interrogator. Before going into the interview, the analyst should have a fair understanding of the duties and responsibilities of the interviewee, along with the individual's working and personal relationships with others in the organization. Additionally, the analyst should have some awareness of the kinds of answers the analyst is looking for and will probably receive. Much of this information comes from other interviews with higher-level management, which assumes a "top-down" approach.

Some points that will be helpful in conducting an interview are as follows:

1. Explain who you are, what the purpose of the interview is, what the systems project is about, and what contribution the interviewee will make in the development of a new system. A typical ques-

[4]John G. Burch, Jr. and Nathan Hod, *Information Systems: A Case-Workbook* Santa Barbara, CA.: John Wiley & Sons, Inc., 1975, pp. 13–15.

tion for clarification subsequent to this introduction is, "At this point, is there anything more you would like to know concerning the systems project?"

2. Make sure that you have a correct understanding of the interviewee's job responsibilities and duties. A typical question is, "It is my understanding that your job is . . . (a brief job description). Is this correct?"

3. It is important to attempt to ascertain the interviewee's decision-making model (i.e., what decisions are made and how the interviewee makes them). Typical questions are, "As a cost accountant, it is my understanding that to prepare a monthly cost-analysis summary, you need to decide how telephone costs are allocated between departments. Can you now decide how this is to be done with the information you are now receiving? If not, what precisely is the information you need and how many days before closing do you need it?"

4. As much as possible, try to ask specific questions that allow for quantitative responses. A typical question: "How many telephones do you now have in this department?"

5. Avoid buzz words, meaningless jargon, and broad generalizations. Typical statements to avoid are, "We will probably interface a CRT with an XYZ front-end, multiplexed in a conversational mode online to a DASD using synchronous broadband channels connected to our 369 Mod 1000 Number Cruncher, which has one megabyte of virtual storage."

6. Develop an awareness of the feelings of the person being interviewed. Learn to listen well. Guard against anticipating answers before the interviewee has had sufficient time to respond.

7. Maintain control of the interview by using tact and discrimination to end ramblings and extraneous comments. A typical response: "Now back to that problem of cost allocation we were talking about earlier: do you propose that we use toll-call usage as an allocation base?"

8. Vague answers to questions should be pursued for full clarification. A typical statement is, "Please bear with me, but I do not quite understand how you propose to handle this."

9. Determine if the interviewee has any additional ideas or suggestions that have possibly been missed. A typical question is, "Do you have any additional suggestions or recommendations concerning the method used to calculate budget variances?" Also, find out if the interviewee wants credit for any suggestions or recommendations. It is very important for the systems analyst to give credit where credit is due. A typical question is, "Do you want your supervisor or others to know of your suggestion?"

10. At the end of the interview, summarize the main points of the session, thank the interviewee, and indicate you will return if you have any further questions.

Taking notes is a traditional and sometimes accepted method for the analyst to use during the interview to record various points, observations, and answers to questions. Similar to taking notes during a lecture in school, the analyst must guard against excessive note taking, thus losing the ideas and responses being presented. The use of voice recorders in place of taking notes is becoming a common practice. While voice recorders eliminate the problems associated with taking notes, the presence of a voice recorder may make the interviewee nervous and overcautious in answering questions. Common sense is usually the best guide to the systems analyst when choosing among fact-recording techniques.

Pitfalls of the Interview. Interviewing is an art, and accordingly, does not always proceed as planned. Normally, people react to an interview in different ways, some favorable and some unfavorable. The following material includes a spectrum of reactions the systems analyst is likely to encounter, along with some suggested stop-gap activities to offset them.[5]

[5]Material adapted from Ronald J. DeMasi, *An Introduction to Business Systems Analysis* (Reading, MA: Addison-Wesley Publishing Company, 1969), pp. 38–39.

Behavior of interviewee	Stop-gap activity
Appears to guess at answers rather than admit ignorance.	After the interview, validate answers that are suspect.
Attempts to tell the analyst what the analyst presumably wants to hear instead of the correct facts.	Avoid putting questions in a form that implies the answer. Validate answers that are suspect.
Gives the analyst a great deal of irrelevant information or tells stories.	In a friendly but persistent fashion, bring the discussion back into the desired focus.
Stops talking if the analyst begins to take notes.	Put the notebook away and confine questions to those that are most important. If necessary, come back later for details.
Attempts to rush through the interview.	Suggest coming back later.
Expresses satisfaction with the way things are done now and wants no change.	Encourage the interviewee to elaborate on the present situation and its virtues. Take careful notes and ask questions about details.
Shows obvious resentment towards the analyst, answers questions guardedly, or appears to be withholding data.	Try to get the interviewee talking about some self-interest, or his or her previous experience with analysts.
Sabotages the interview with noncooperation. In effect, refuses to give information.	Ask the interviewee, "If I get this information from someone else, would you mind checking it for me?" Then proceed on that plan.
Gripes about his or her job, associates, supervisors, and unfair treatment.	Listen sympathetically and note anything that might be a real clue. Do not interrupt until the list of gripes is complete. Then, make friendly but noncommittal statements, such as "You sure have plenty of troubles. Perhaps the study can help with some of them." This approach should bridge the gap to asking about the desired facts. Later, make enough of a check on the gripes to determine whether or not there is any foundation for them. In this way you neither pass over a good lead nor leave yourself open to being unduly influenced by groundless talk or personal prejudice.
Acts as eager beaver, is enthusiastic about new ideas, gadgets, techniques.	Listen for desired facts and valuable leads. Do not become involved emotionally or enlist in the interviewee's campaign.

The Questionnaire

A questionnaire can be used at various times by the systems analyst in the systems development process. It can be used in systems work to obtain a consensus, to identify a direction or area for indepth study, to do a post implementation audit, and to identify specific but varying requirements.

Use of the Questionnaire.

For fact-finding, the questionnaire is a somewhat restricted channel of communication and should be employed with great care. Analysts must identify what it is that they desire to know, structure the questions that will result in the answers to these needs, and prepare and submit the questionnaire to the individual who is to complete it. Unlike the interview, the analyst has no immediate opportunity to readdress comments that are vague or unclear. Moreover, the analyst cannot follow up tangent comments that might well lead to additional facts or ideas.

The questionnaire can be used best as a fact-finding tool when the recipient is physically removed from the analyst and travel is prohibited for either person, where there are many potential recipients (e.g., a sales force), and when the information is intended to verify similar information gathered from other sources.

Limitation of the Questionnaire.

The reasons for recommending a limited use of the questionnaire in systems analysis are numerous. First, it is extremely difficult to structure meaningful questions without anticipating a certain response. Second, the inability for immediate follow-up and redirect tends to limit the real value of this type of communication. Finally, it appears that "blanket" style documents, especially questionnaires, are assigned low priority and importance by most people.

Guidelines for Constructing a Questionnaire.

When the analyst decides to use a questionnaire a few, but important, guidelines should be followed.

1. Explain the purpose, use, security, and disposition of the responses.
2. Provide detailed instructions on how you want the questions completed.
3. Give a time limit or deadline for return of the questionnaire.
4. Ask pointed and concise questions.
5. Format questions so that responses can be tabulated mechanically or manually.
6. Provide sufficient space for a complete response.
7. Phrase questions clearly. For example, the question, "Has your processor stopped malfunctioning?" can be frustrating to answer for the respondent whose processor has never malfunctioned.
8. If a question cannot be responded to objectively, provide an opportunity for the respondent to add a clarifying comment.
9. Identify each questionnaire by respondent's name, job title, department, etc.
10. Include a section where respondents can state their opinions and criticisms.

Question Formats. The following are several formats that can be used to prepare questions for a questionnaire. Note that the content of the sample questions is only illustrative.[6]

1. *Check-off Questions.* These kinds of questions are structured to enable the respondent merely to check an appropriate response(s). Examples are as follows:

   a. Which vendor is the supplier of your CPU?

   _____ Burroughs   _____ DEC   _____ IBM

   _____ CDC   _____ Honeywell   _____ UNIVAC

   Other _____

   b. What access do the application programmers have to the computer center? (check one)

   _____ Unrestricted access

   _____ Restricted acess (e.g, by password, magnetic card)

   _____ Controlled access by permission of data processing manager

   _____ Other

   c. The data base system can be best described as: (check one)*

   _____ A relational structure

   _____ A tree structure

   _____ A network structure

   *You may phrase a similar question and specify in parenthesis, "check all that apply."

In addition to the above formats, a simple checklist can also be used as follows:

Fire Protection Checklist
(Partial)

☐ 1. Smoke and heat detectors are placed at strategic locations.

☐ 2. Excess combustible materials are removed on a regular basis from the data processing center.

☐ 3. Portable fire extinguishers are placed at points for ready access.

☐ 4. All emergency telephone numbers are posted for ready access.

☐ 5. Emergency exit doors are checked daily for obstructions.

☐ 6. Fire drills are conducted monthly.

---

[6]Taken from: Burch and Hod, *op. cit.*, pp. 18–22.

2. *Yes/No Questions.* This kind of question format is quite popular and is used extensively not only by systems analysts but by auditors as well. Examples are as follows:

	Answer		Answer based on		
	Yes	No	Inquiry	Observation	Test
a. Are all out-of-balance or error conditions brought to the attention of the accountant?	___	___	___	___	___
b. Is the EDP department independent of all departments for which it processes data?	___	___	___	___	___

A simple yes/no question, with an explanation, is illustrated as follows:

	Yes	No	Not applicable
c. We use 24-hour service on our communications equipment.	___	___	___

If not applicable, please explain: _____

_____

All yes/no questions should be phrased in such a way that responses run is a predetermined direction. For example:

	Yes	No
d. Do you prepare telephone budgets?	x	___
e. Do you pay toll bills without verification?	x	___

There are two "yes" responses. If the preparer of these questions wanted a preponderance of "yes" answers to indicate good accounting controls, then he or she has failed because the answer to the second question is also "yes." The second question should be rephrased:

	Yes	No
f. Do you verify bills before payment?	___	x

In this case, a "no" answer flags inadequate accounting controls.

3. *Opinion or Choice Questions.* These questions are phrased to allow the respondent to give an opinion or make a choice, but in a very specific area. Examples are as follows:

a. If your operating system is modified, note the relative importance of each of the following goals in your design process (scale them from 1 through 10, where 1 is least important and 10 is most important).

_____ Improve throughput or service level
_____ Maximize number of concurrent processes
_____ Interface to special equipment
_____ Protect operating system from user processes
_____ Increase reliability
_____ Provide special accounting or billing
_____ Protect system files

316 Systems Analysis

    ____ Protect user files
    ____ Simplify command language
    ____ Simplify file access or sharing

b. You are presently receiving enough information to help control the toll calls made from your department. (circle one)

    Strongly   Strongly
    disagree   1 2 3 4 5 6 7 8 9 10   agree

c. Rate on a scale of 1 to 10 the awareness of those who control the cost of telephone usage. (circle one)

    Not   Very
    concerned   1 2 3 4 5 6 7 8 9 10   concerned

d. Circle one of the five numbers to indicate your disagreement or agreement with the following statement.

    1 = strongly disagree
    2 = disagree
    3 = neither agree nor disagree
    4 = agree
    5 = strongly agree

Departments, for which records are maintained on the tabulation of toll calls, maintenance, expense allocation, and equipment costs, should have the following rights:

    1 2 3 4 5   To be informed of the existence of such records
    1 2 3 4 5   The right to review, on demand by department managers, the records' contents
    1 2 3 4 5   To be furnished monthly reports of budgeted toll calls and expenses, as compared to actual expenses incurred for that month

How would you rate your switchboard workload?

- [ ] Too heavy for adequate service
- [ ] Heavy, but not impossible
- [ ] Heavy to average
- [ ] Average workload
- [ ] Light

4. *Fill-in-the-Blank Questions.* This type of question is structured to provide the respondent with the ability to give an unconstrained response or a short, qualitative answer. Examples are as follows:

    a. In what states does your organization operate?
       _____

    b. What percent of the operating budget is allocated to production? ____%

5. *Combination Questions.* The following is an example of how two formats, check-off and fill-in-the-blank, can be combined into one format:

a. Please check the tasks for which you are responsible, and insert in the blank spaces to the right of each checked task, the percent of time in your workday you devote to each task.

    Preparing flowcharts   ____%

    Coding   ____%

    Testing   ____%

    Implementing   ____%

6. *Short Questionnaire.* The following is an example of a short questionnaire:

    TITLE   Report Analysis—Batch EVR   PAGE NUMBER _____

    CODE NUMBER   1274-Batch-Per

    PURPOSE   To determine the usefulness of the Expense Variance Report

1. Do you wish to receive the Expense Variance Report?
   - ☐ Yes   If yes, answer all remaining questions.
   - ☐ No   If no, do not answer the remaining questions, and skip to the bottom.

2. How often would you like to receive the Expense Variance Report?
   - ☐ Daily   ☐ Monthly   ☐ Semiannually
   - ☐ Weekly   ☐ Quarterly   ☐ Yearly

3. What do you do with this report after you receive it?
   - ☐ Use if for budget planning   ☐ Read it only for general information
   - ☐ Use it to control expenses   ☐ Other _____

4. How do you rank this report relative to other reports you receive?
   - ☐ Superior   ☐ Equal   ☐ Inferior

5. Is this report suitable in its present form?
   - ☐ Yes   ☐ No

   or should additional information be provided, such as:
   - ☐ Ratios   ☐ Prior-period figures
   - ☐ Other _____

6. Please list any other comments or suggestions as to form, content, or method of preparation.

   _____

   _____

   Thank you for your participation.

Signed _____Title _____

Department _____Date _____

Observation

Another technique available to the analyst during fact-finding is to observe people in the act of executing their job. Observation as a fact-finding technique has widespread acceptance by scientists. Sociologists, psychologists, and industrial engineers use this technique extensively for studying people in groups and organizational activities. Auditors observe a number of things such as inventory. Items covered in dust or rust, or prior-year inventory tags may indicate excess, slow-moving, or unsalable inventory. The purpose of observation is multifold. It allows the analyst to determine what is being done, how it is being done, who does it, when it is done, how long it takes, where it is done, and why it is done.

The systems analyst can observe in the following manner. First, the analyst may make a walkthrough and take note of people, things, and activities at random. Second, the analyst may observe a person or activity without awareness by the observee and without any interaction by the analyst. Unobtrusive observation is probably of little importance in systems analysis as it is nearly impossible to achieve the necessary conditions. Third, the analyst can observe an operation without any interactions but with the person being observed fully aware of the analyst's observation. Lastly, the analyst can observe and interact with the persons being observed. This interaction can be simply questioning a specific task, asking for an explanation, and so forth.

Observation can be used to verify what was revealed in an interview or as a preliminary to the interview. Observation is also a valuable technique for gathering facts representing relationships. Observation tends to be more meaningful at the technical level of data processing where tasks can be more easily quantified. Technical activities include tasks related to data collection, accumulation, and transformation. Decision-making activities do not lend themselves to observation as easily. Decision-making activities can best be understood through the process of interviewing and use of decision level analysis discussed earlier in this chapter.

To maximize the results obtainable from observation, a number of guidelines should be followed by the analyst.

Preparing for Observation. Before observation begins, the analyst should (1) identify and define what it is that is going to be observed, (2) estimate the length of time this observation will require, (3) secure proper management approval to conduct the observation, and (4) explain to the parties being observed what will be done and why.

Conducting the Observation. Observation can be conducted most effectively by the analyst following a few simple rules. First, the analyst should become familiar with the physical surroundings and components in the immediate area of the observation. Second, while observing, the analyst should periodically note the time. Third, the analyst should note what is observed as specifically as possible. Generalities and vague descriptions should be avoided. Fourth, if the analyst is interacting with the persons being observed, then he or she should refrain from making qualitative or value judgment comments. A final rule that should be followed when conducting the observation is to show proper courtesy and heed safety regulations.

Following Up the Observation. Following the period of observation, the analyst's notes and impressions should be formally documented and organized. The analyst's findings and conclusions should be reviewed with the person observed, his or her immediate supervisor, and, perhaps, another systems analyst.

The benefits to be derived from skillful observation are many. As analysts gain experience, however, they become more selective as to what and when they observe. Observation is often quite time-consuming and thus expensive. Moreover, people in general do not like to be observed. We strongly recommend that when observation is used, it should be used in conjunction with other fact-finding techniques to maximize its effectiveness, particularly with less experienced analysts.

Sampling and Document Gathering

Two additional techniques available to the analyst, particularly during fact-finding endeavors, are sampling and document gathering. Both of these techniques are oriented to paperwork stored throughout the organization. Both techniques provide a source of information unavailable via any other fact-finding approach.

Sampling. Sampling is directed to collecting and accumulating data on problems that are either unmeasurable, or entail a tremendous amount of detail work to obtain a given piece of data. For example, if an analyst wants to find out how long it takes to process 10,000 customer orders in the shipping room, the analyst might measure the time required to process a sample of 40 customer orders, and based on this sample, extrapolate the expected time to process 10,000 orders.

40 orders require T time
$T/40$ = time per order
$10,000 \times T/40$ = time for 10,000 orders

Another practical instance of sampling is illustrated in the following example.

"How many purchase orders required a Vice-President's signature of approval last year?" asked the Manager of Purchasing to Grace Dee, Systems Analyst. "Well," replied Grace, "the policy states that any P.O. greater than $10,000 requires V.P. approval. I checked the P.O. 'dead' file for last year, and found that we have thirteen drawers filled with P.O.'s. I asked Bob, the file clerk, if he kept any records concerning approvals or dollar amounts on P.O.'s and he said he did not. He said there was no particular organization to the 'dead' file. I knew you needed some idea of how many V.P. approvals there were, so I took a sample.

I measured the drawers and found that the file space was about two feet in length. That told me I had twenty-seven feet of P.O.'s and thirty minutes to figure out how many had V.P. stamps. I took about four inches of paper out of one of the drawers and fingered through the documents. I noted seven 'big' ones. I figured that if there was no special handling involved with V.P. P.O.'s, that would be about twenty-one to a foot; twenty-one times twenty-seven feet is about 560–570 purchase orders with Vice-Presidential signatures."

The Purchasing Manager thanked Grace for her help and proceeded to call the President. "Jim, we don't keep records concerning executive signatures required on P.O.'s. A sampling the systems people made on the closed file indicates about 600 a year are required."

The above example is of course hypothetical and may raise a number of questions concerning its mathematical validity. Large transactional files, however, do exist in most organizations. And, surprisingly, in this day and age, statistics similar to that requested by the Purchasing Manager are not available. While Grace might have used more scientific methods to attain her number (certainly we can question the size and representation of the sample), systems analysts often use rules of thumb to arrive at this type of information.

But whether you use rules of thumb or classical algorithms, the technique of sampling can provide valuable facts and insights during the systems analysis phase.

Sampling is also an effective technique for projecting resource requirements. It is again not unusual for an analyst to measure a certain activity on a limited basis, and then project the resources required to perform this function for a complete system.

Document Gathering. Collecting exhibits of source documents, worksheets, reports, etc., (many of these were presented earlier in this chapter) is another way for the analyst to gather facts during systems analysis. From these exhibits or sample documents, the analyst can gain an understanding of what is presently done, how it is structured, what is not available, and, perhaps, get a "feel" for what is considered important. When an analyst is conducting an interview or an observation, if the analyst has a copy of the documents involved, efforts in gathering facts will be enhanced. Moreover, a working knowledge of user documents on the part of the analyst increases the likelihood of smoother communications between the analyst and the user personnel.

Charting

Charting is the technique that pictorially represents some dimension of an organization or an organizational activity. Of all the techniques used by systems personnel, charting is the one technique most closely identified with systems efforts. Indeed, charting is not only an important fact-finding technique but it is also a valuable technique for performing analysis, synthesis, communication, and documentation. Charts are also used extensively as design techniques. Obviously, a technique with many uses is favored over single-purpose techniques.

Organization Charts. Figure 11.8 represents an organizational chart of the management of a medium-sized company.

In most large organizations the analyst can usually secure a copy of the official organization chart. Many times, however, the organization chart is nonexistent or outdated. In the latter cases, the analyst must construct the organization chart.

The **organization chart** provides information concerning reporting relationships, quantities of resources, interrelationships, and levels of authority and responsibility.

Often during fact-finding, the analyst will prepare a brief narrative which is coded to accompany the organization charts. Figure 11.9 provides an example of this combined usage of narrative and organization charts.

The brief annotation relative to each decision-making level provides not only the function of each manager but also an overall insight into the roles that they play in the organization. For instance, the function and responsibility of the sales manager is to hire, fire, and establish training programs for salespeople; set specific quotas for each salesperson; and prepare a breakdown of the sales force and resources by territory, by customer, and by product line. It should be noted, however, that Mr. Andrews devotes half of his time to the selection and training

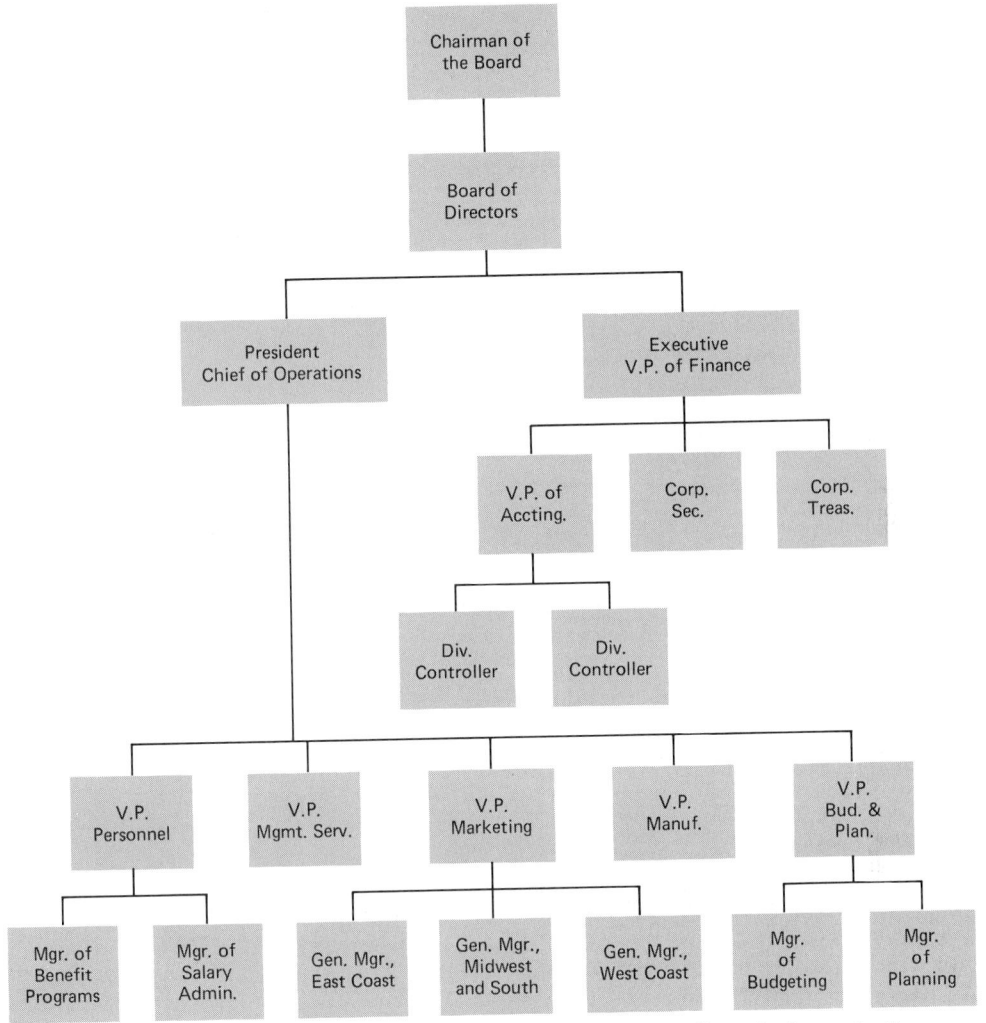

FIG. 11.8 A typical organization chart of upper management of a medium-sized organization.

of salespeople, and nearly all of the remaining time to analyzing salespeople's performance. This additional insight into each decision maker's function and responsibility will be of great value to the analyst later when user requirements are determined, and still later, when the analyst is designing the data base.

The traditional organization charts we have been discussing are often ineffective for portraying the complex structures of modern organizations. This is true even when a narrative is attached to the organization chart. Traditional box charts depict the organization from the point of view of formal reporting relationships. At best this

322 Systems Analysis

A — B. Powell—Office 110—Ext. 205—Establishment of plans and policies—is in charge of the organization, but is sales oriented—is on the road 50 percent of the time helping to open up new markets—makes most decisions in committee meetings.

B — H. Cranford—Office 212—Ext. 207—Establishing of quotas, setting of priorities, and allocation of resources—works closely with advertising, and devotes a great deal of time on development of large government purchases—holds a meeting of all staff the first Monday of each month.

C — E. Andrews—Office 135—Ext. 211—Hires, fires, and establishes training programs for salespeople. Sets quotas among salespeople—breakdown of sales force and resources by customers, and by product line. Devotes about 50 percent of time to selecting and training new salespeople—most of the remainder of the time devoted to salespeople performance—has indicated dire need for "good, up to date" performance information.

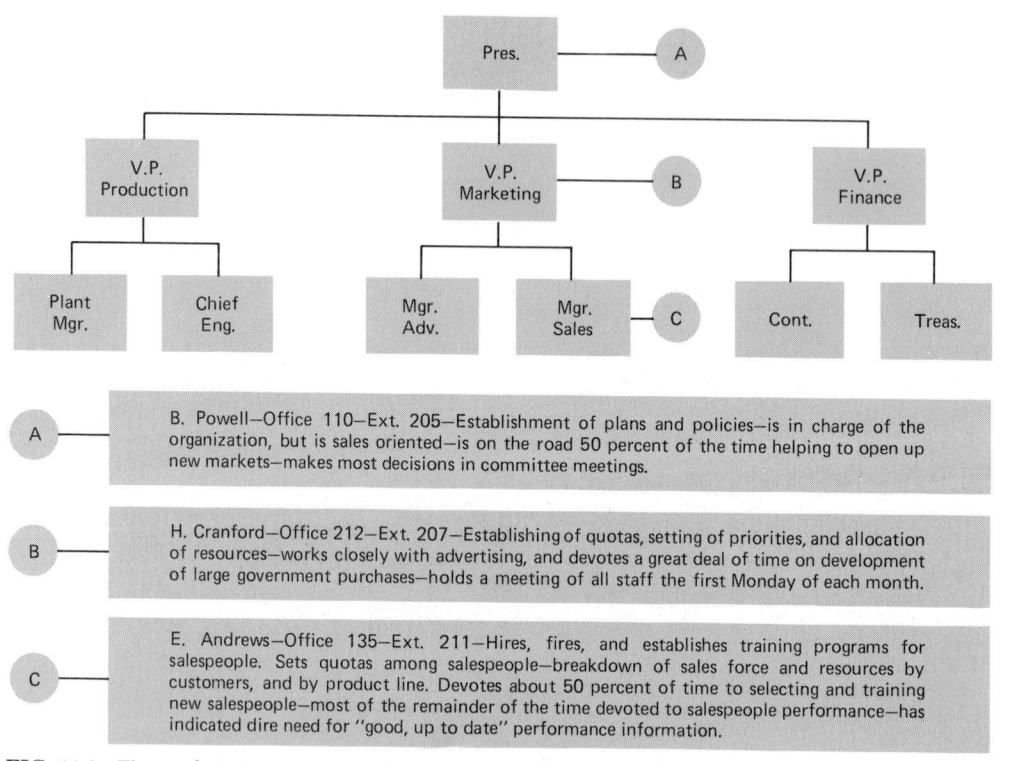

FIG. 11.9 The analyst can combine the narrative with the organization chart to achieve greater understanding and clarity.

portrayal reflects the organization at one point in time, treating the organization structure as though it were static. In reality, however, the organization is a dynamic entity. Additionally, the modern trend to minimize the rigid boundaries of hierarchical structures encourages a great deal of responsibility sharing. To better depict this aspect of shared responsibility or interfunctional relationships, the analyst can develop what is termed a *linear* organization chart (LOC). Figure 11.10 illustrates a linear organization chart reflecting various marketing functions in a medium-sized corporation.

In our example, the activity pertaining to the development and usage of a new product line is a multi-function responsibility. The President, the Vice-President of Marketing, and the Manager of Production Engineering all share in the approval process. Planning is the responsibility of the Manager of Research and Development, the Manager of Product Planning, and the Manager of Product Engineering. Control is exercised by the General Manager of Sales, the Manager of Product Planning, and the various Regional Sales Managers. Operations responsibility is shared by various levels of marketing personnel in addition to supply and transportation, manufacturing, etc.

	New Products	New Markets	Training	Salary and Commission
President	A			A
Vice-President Marketing	A	A		A
General Manager Sales	C	A	A	AP
Regional Manager Sales	C	P	AP	C
Manager Product Planning	PC	P		
Vice-President Personnel				A
Manager Supply and Transportation	O	O		
Manager Product Engineering	APC			
Manager Manufacturing	O			
Salespeople	O	O	PO	
Manager Research and Development	P			
Controller				PC
Manager Information Systems	O	O	O	PO

FIG. 11.10 An illustration of a linear organization chart of some of the marketing functions. Legend: A: approval; C: control; P: planning; O: operation.

To construct a LOC the analyst must delineate the decision makers, the business activities, and the degree of responsibility each decision maker has for each business activity.

The advantages to constructing a LOC include (1) graphically representing the organization, (2) the necessity to develop an indepth understanding by the analyst before charting, (3) displaying redundancies, and (4) reflecting lack of responsibility or potential bottlenecks.

The organization chart is of immense value to the analyst in understanding the makeup of the levels of management, and ascertaining the span of control and chain of command. In short, the organization chart depicts the role of each manager in the decision-making hierarchy.

Physical Layout Charts. A second classification of charting reflects the physical environment which concerns the analyst. Figure 11.11 represents a typical office layout. Figure 11.12 shows the layout of computer components in a data processing installation. Understanding the physical environment in which an activity is executed provides information concerning space and resources available. Additionally, the

324 Systems Analysis

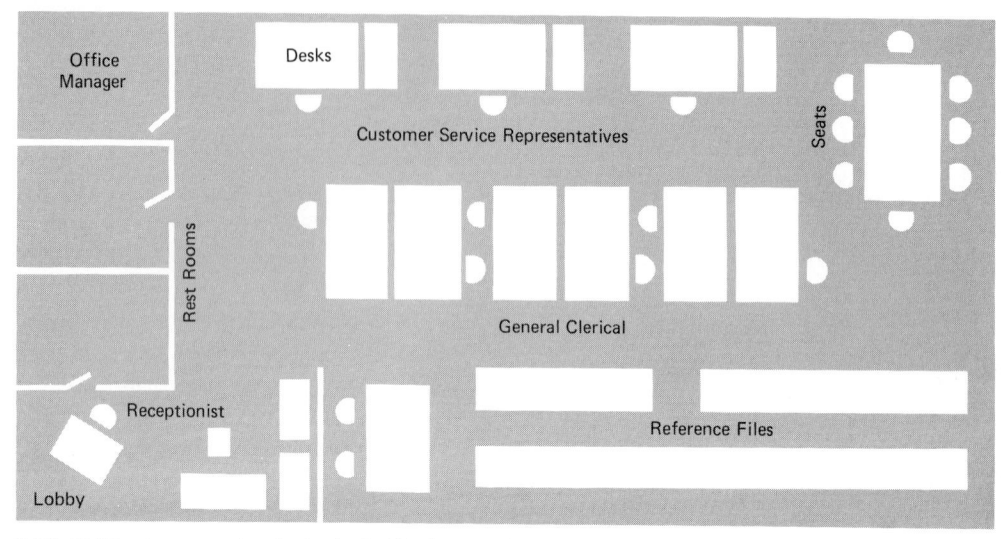

FIG. 11.11 An example of a typical office layout chart.

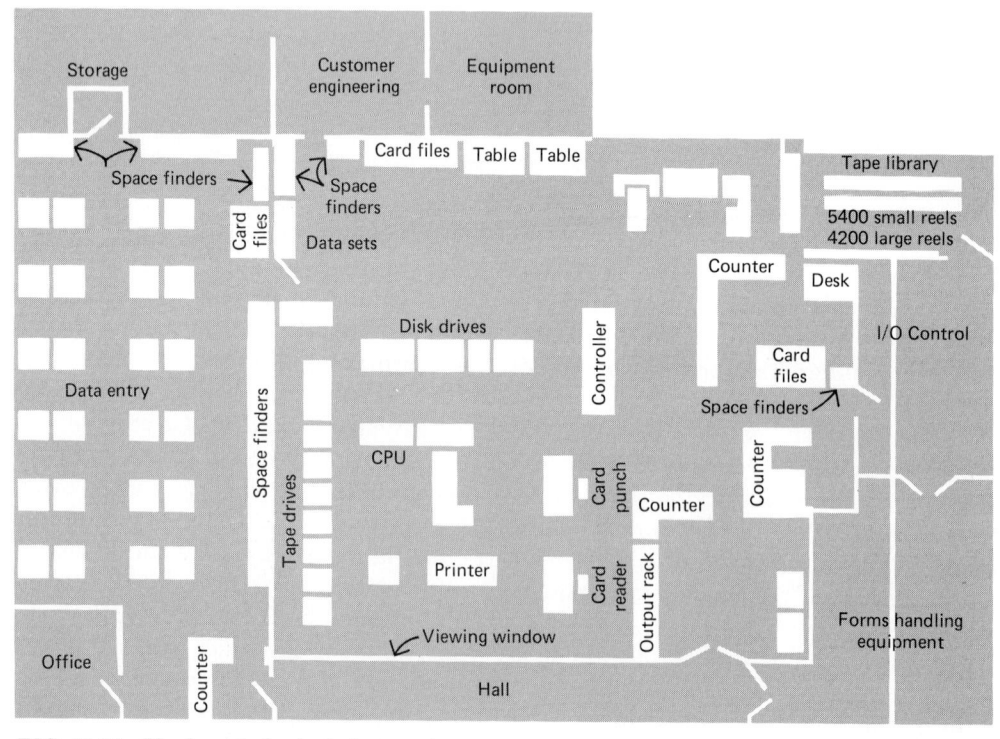

FIG. 11.12 The layout of a typical computer room.

analyst can gain insights into why specific tasks are performed the way they are, as well as possible physical changes that might have an impact on the organization's information requirements.

Traditional Flowcharts. Perhaps the most important of all charting techniques to the analyst is the flowchart. A flowchart is a set of symbols representing an activity. Flowcharts are widely used in systems work because they can represent graphically the interrelationships among elements in a system to varying degrees of detail. Four broad classifications of flowcharts can be distinguished.[7] Please bear in mind that you do not have to understand the details of these specific charts to see how they are used as fact-gathering techniques.

1. *The Systems Flowchart,* as its name implies, is a chart which depicts the system as a whole with only subsystems or major elements shown. Figure 11.13 is a systems flowchart of a payroll processing process.
2. *The Program Macro Flowchart* is a broad graphic representation of a program. An example of a program macro flowchart is illustrated in Figure 11.14.
3. *The Program Micro Flowchart* is a graphic representation of the logic (processing steps) of a program or a part of a program. The micro flowchart illustrated in Figure 11.15 shows the processing steps of a subroutine in which standard earning's deductions are calculated.
4. *The Document Flowchart* is used by the systems analyst to trace the flow of documents and reports through an organization. Figure 11.16 is an illustration of a document flowchart of ordering, shipping, and billing.

The Template. Within the flowcharting examples presented in this section, a variety of symbols have been used to represent certain logical or processing operations. These symbols are used by many systems personnel for a number of reasons: (1) the symbols have specific connotations attached to them, (2) these connotations are standard among computer and technical persons, and (3) these symbols can be drawn quickly through the use of a template. Figure 11.17 illustrates an extensive list of special symbols used in flowcharting.

A template is usually constructed from tinted plastic; however, it may be constructed from any hard-surface material. The special symbols noted in Figure 11.17 are precut into the template. Thus, these symbols may be drawn on paper by simply tracing with a pencil or pen around the edges of the symbol cutout. Templates exist for office and computer layout charting as well.

While it is not necessary to use special symbols when flowcharting, the use of symbols can enhance the viewer's understanding. This is particularly true when the viewer is a computer or technically oriented individual. When the chart is intended for use in communicating with general management or nontechnical personnel, the analyst is advised to use few special purpose symbols. The use of technical symbols can serve as a psychological barrier to effective communications with nontechnical persons.

Data Flow Diagram. A **data flow diagram** is a way of depicting the flow of data through a system. Data flow diagrams are

---
[7]*Ibid.*

326 Systems Analysis

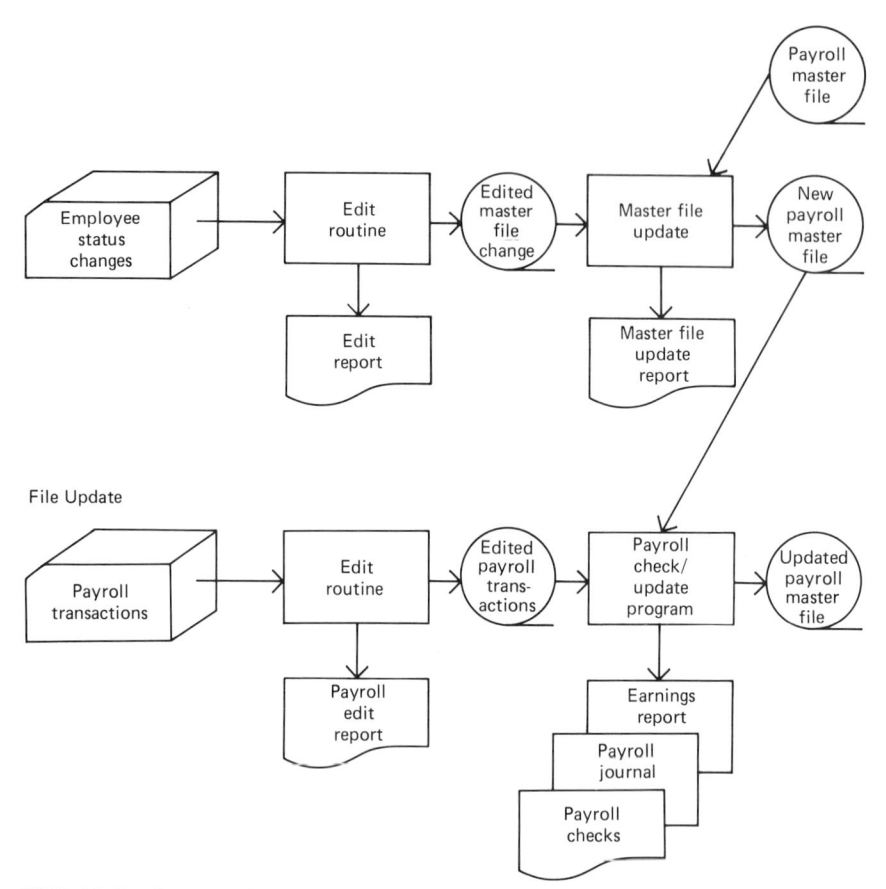

FIG. 11.13 An example of a systems flowchart for a payroll processing process.

intended to help the analyst understand how complex systems work. Figure 11.18 illustrates four commonly used data flow diagram symbols.

1. *External Entities.* Things, systems, or people representing a source or destination of transactions are called external entities. For example, a customer, who is a source of sales orders for our company, is an external entity. Likewise, a supplier, who is a receiver of our company's payment, is an external entity.

By categorizing a thing, person, or system as an external entity, it is being placed *outside* the boundary of the system under consideration. As our understanding of the system under consideration increases, external entities may be brought into our system, or, alternatively, parts within the boundary may be designated as external entities.

The symbol for an external entity is a square. It is identified by labeling it with the thing or person it represents. For example, external entities for customers,

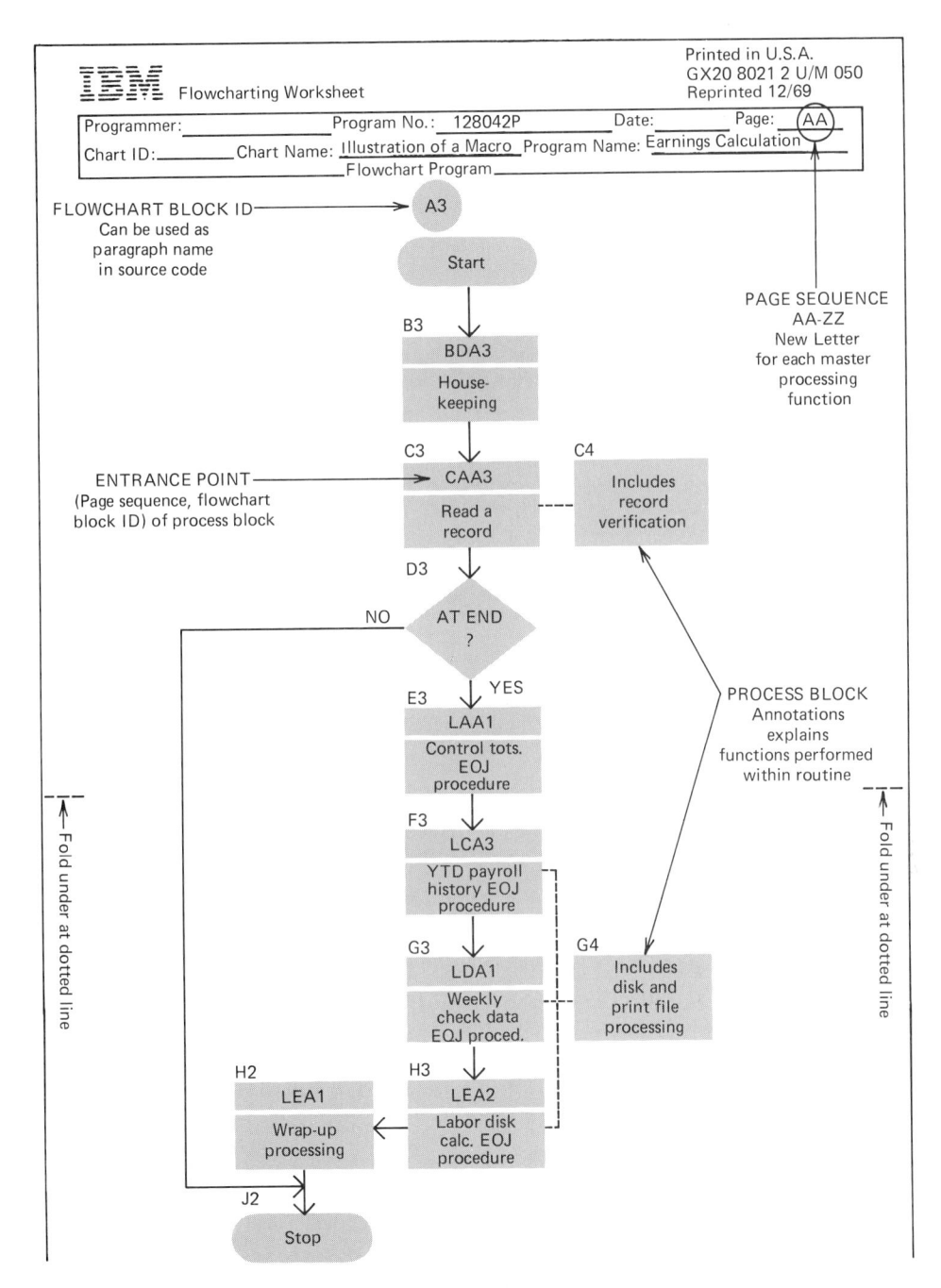

Techniques for Gathering and Analyzing Study Facts 327

FIG. 11.14 An example of a program macro flowchart.

Systems Analysis

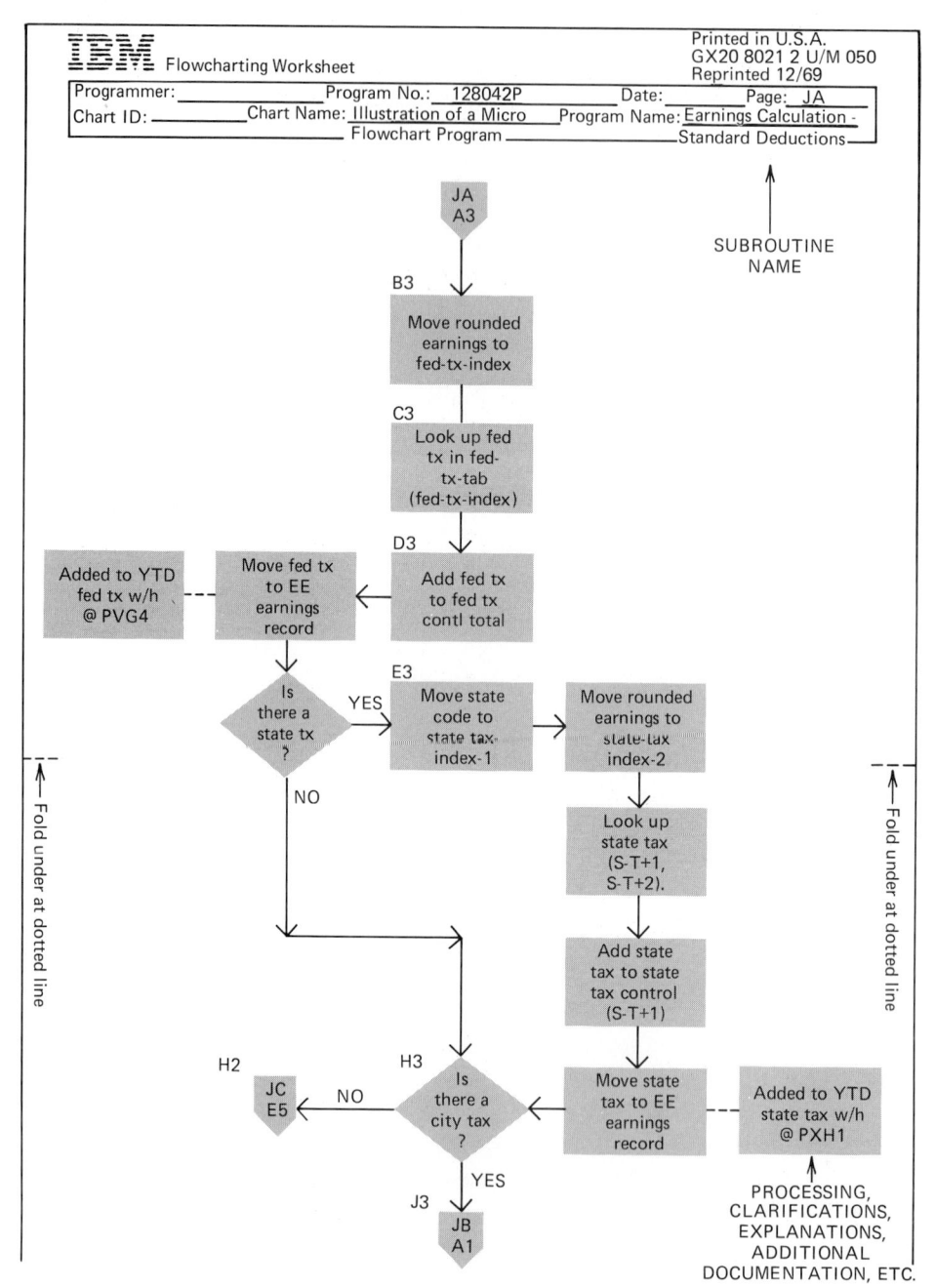

IBM	Flowcharting Worksheet	Printed in U.S.A. GX20 8021 2 U/M 050 Reprinted 12/69
Programmer:	Program No.: 128042P	Date: Page: JA
Chart ID:	Chart Name: Illustration of a Micro Flowchart Program	Program Name: Earnings Calculation - Standard Deductions

```
                        JA
                        A3
                         │
                         ▼
                        B3
                    ┌─────────┐
                    │ Move rounded│
                    │ earnings to │
                    │ fed-tx-index│
                    └─────────┘
                         │
                        C3
                    ┌─────────┐
                    │ Look up fed │
                    │ tx in fed-  │
                    │ tx-tab      │
                    │(fed-tx-index)│
                    └─────────┘
                         │
                        D3
   ┌──────────┐   ┌──────────┐   ┌──────────┐
   │Added to YTD│   │Move fed tx│   │ Add fed tx│
   │fed tx w/h  │---│ to EE     │◄──│ to fed tx │
   │@ PVG4      │   │ earnings  │   │ contl total│
   └──────────┘   │ record    │   └──────────┘
                    └──────────┘
                         │
                        E3
                      ◇ Is ◇         ┌──────────┐   ┌──────────┐
                      there a  YES   │Move state │   │Move rounded│
                      state tx ────►│ code to   │──►│ earnings to│
                      ?              │ state tax-│   │ state-tax  │
                        │            │ index-1   │   │ index-2    │
                        │NO          └──────────┘   └──────────┘
                        │                                 │
                        │                            ┌──────────┐
                        │                            │ Look up    │
                        │                            │ state tax  │
                        │                            │ (S-T+1,    │
                        │                            │ S-T+2).    │
                        │                            └──────────┘
                        │                                 │
                        │                            ┌──────────┐
                        │                            │ Add state  │
                        │                            │ tax to state│
                        │                            │ tax control│
                        │                            │ (S-T+1)    │
                        │                            └──────────┘
                        ▼                                 │
       H2          H3                               
    ┌────┐      ◇ Is ◇        ┌──────────┐   ┌──────────┐
    │ JC │◄NO── there a  ◄────│Move state │   │Added to YTD│
    │ E5 │      city tax      │ tax to EE │---│ state tax w/h│
    └────┘      ?              │ earnings  │   │ @ PXH1     │
                 │             │ record    │   └──────────┘
                 │YES          └──────────┘
                J3
                 ▼
                JB
                A1
```

SUBROUTINE NAME

PROCESSING, CLARIFICATIONS, EXPLANATIONS, ADDITIONAL DOCUMENTATION, ETC.

← Fold under at dotted line

FIG. 11.15 An example of a program micro flowchart.

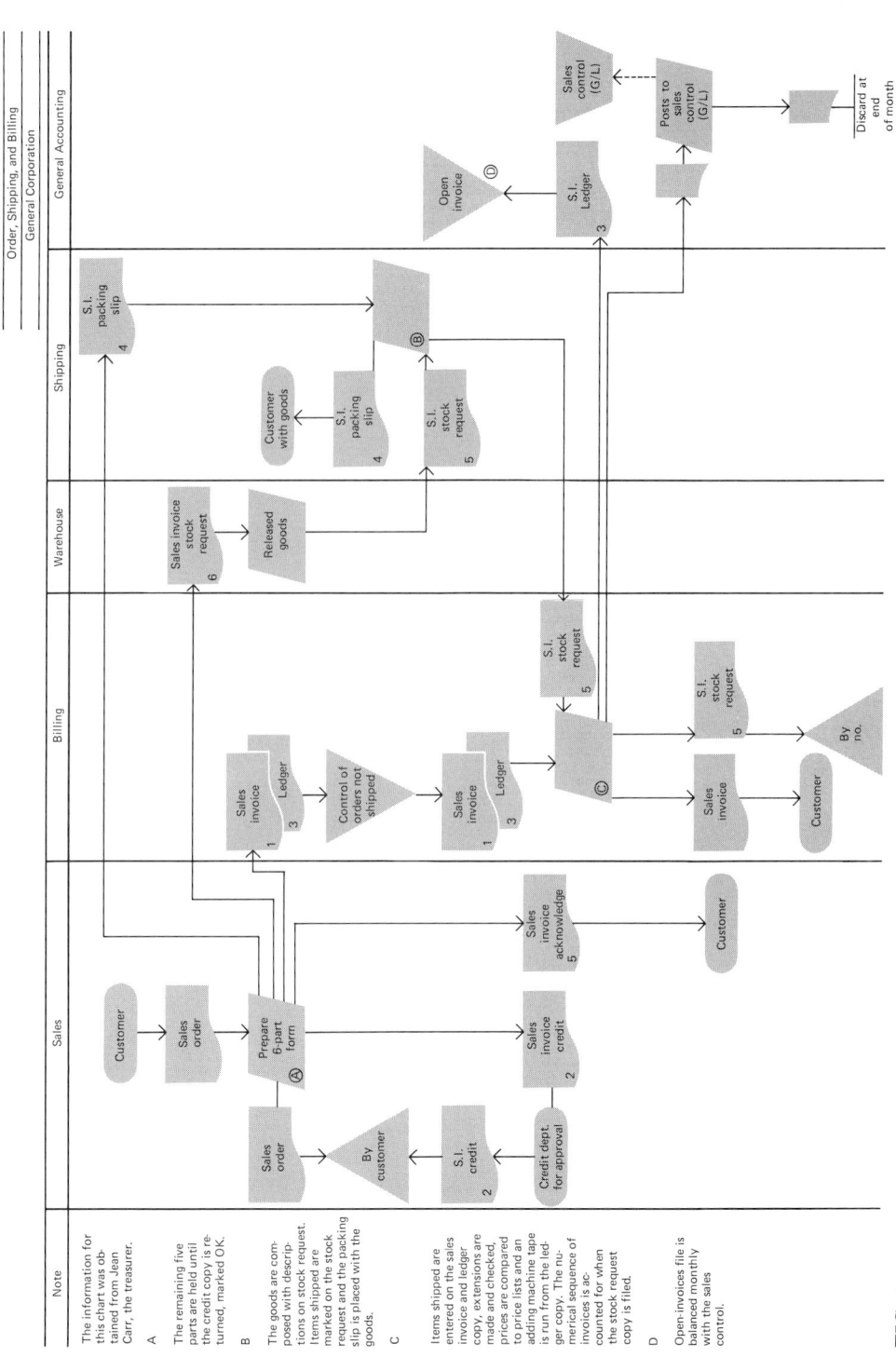

Techniques for Gathering and Analyzing Study Facts   **329**

FIG. 11.16 An example of a document flowchart.

330 Systems Analysis

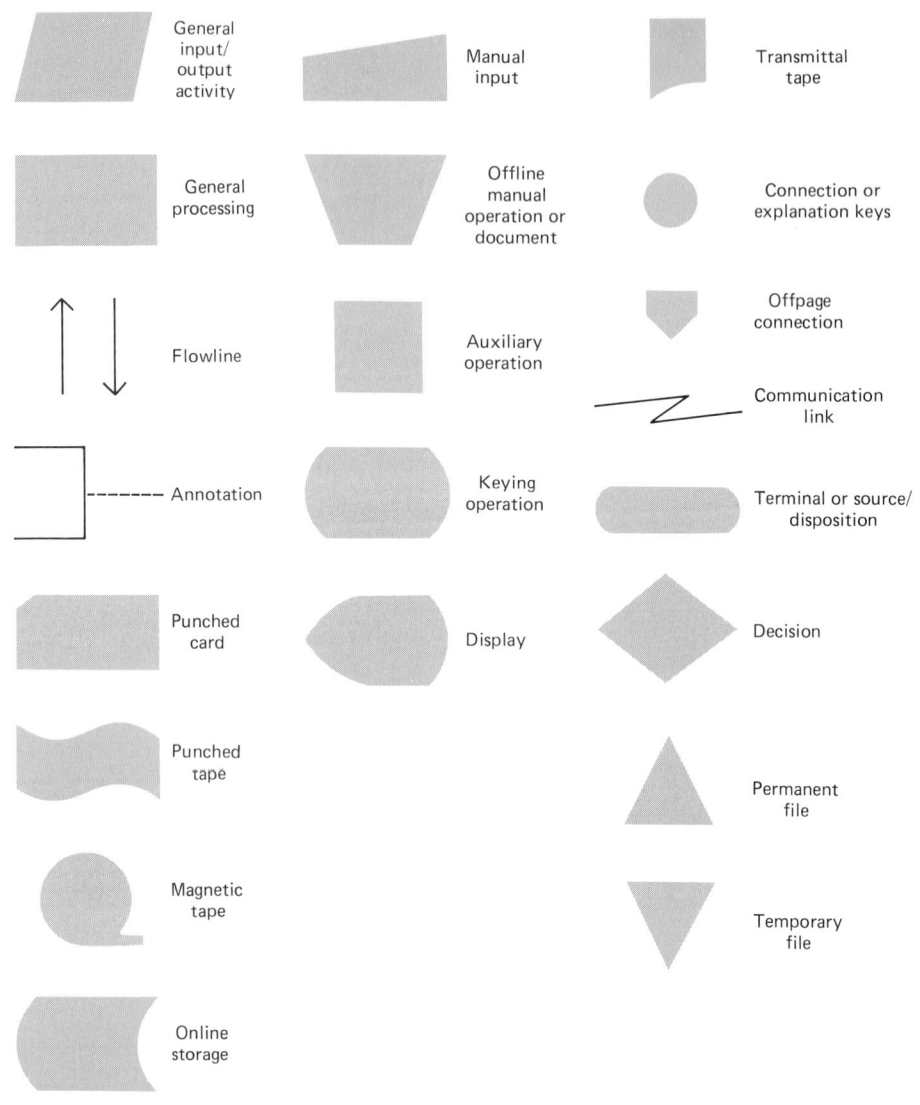

FIG. 11.17 Each of these flowcharting symbols has a special meaning to help the viewer understand the logical process represented by the flowchart.

shareholders, and suppliers are illustrated in Figure 11.18.

2. *Data Flows.* The symbol for a data flow is an arrow, with the arrowhead indicating the direction of the data flow. Each data flow arrow should have a meaningful description written alongside of it.

3. *Processes.* The symbol for a process, activity, or task is a tall rectangle. Depending upon the standards adopted, the rec-

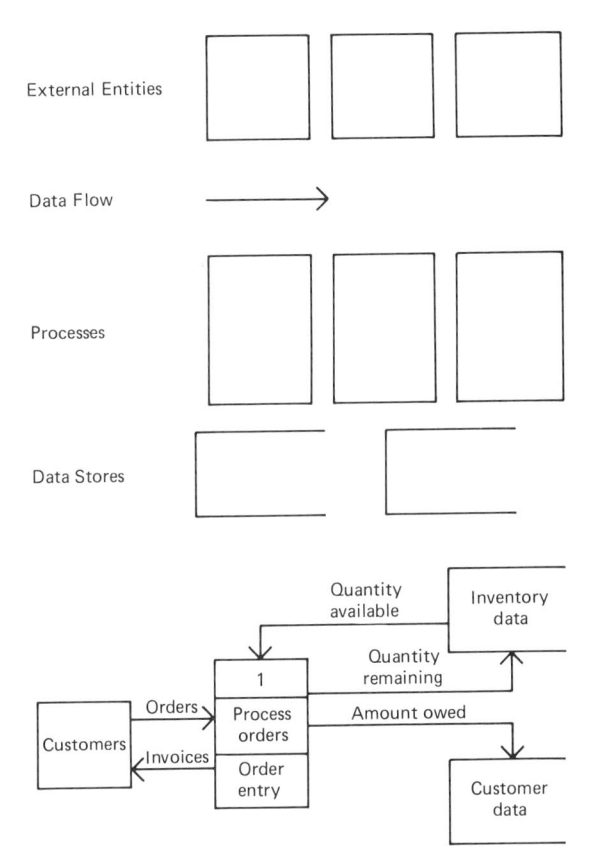

FIG. 11.18 Data flow diagram symbols.

will be performed. For example, the program "Compute GPA," could be used to perform the process of calculating a student's grade point average.

4. *Data Stores.* A pair of horizontal lines, which are closed at one end, is the symbol used to represent data being stored between processes. A descriptive title (e.g., employee master file, cancelled checks, purchase orders pending) should be chosen for each data store.

Other Charting Techniques. There are other charting techniques with which many of us are familiar but which are not necessarily associated with systems work per se. This general familiarity with these charts results in their usage being helpful particularly in communicating with management and nontechnical personnel. Moreover, these charting techniques can be used in problem definition, analysis, and control endeavors. One classification of these charts includes (1) line charts, (2) bar charts, (3) pie charts, and (4) pictorial charts. Figure 11.19 illustrates each of these four types of charts. Figure 11.20 lists the advantages and disadvantages of each charting technique. A second classification of charts generally familiar to management and other business professionals is associated with scheduling and control activities. These include Program Evaluation and Review Technique (PERT), Critical Path Method (CPM), and Gantt Charts. These are presented in Appendix A.

Guidelines for Charting. While it may appear that charting is a relatively simple task, the novice analyst will find that early attempts at charting, particularly flowcharting, can be frustrating, time-consuming, and complicated. Even with experienced analysts, first attempts to chart an organi-

tangle may be split into three areas. The top of the rectangle may contain an identification number. Identification numbers, which are allocated from left to right across a data flow diagram, have the sole purpose of identifying the process. The middle of the rectangle may describe the function performed. An imperative sentence containing an active verb (e.g., compute, store, create) and an object clause (e.g., sales tax, unused credit, payment and record), is a preferred function description. The purpose of the lower part of the process rectangle is to indicate how or by whom the process

332 Systems Analysis

Line Chart

Bar Chart

Pie Chart

Pictorial Chart

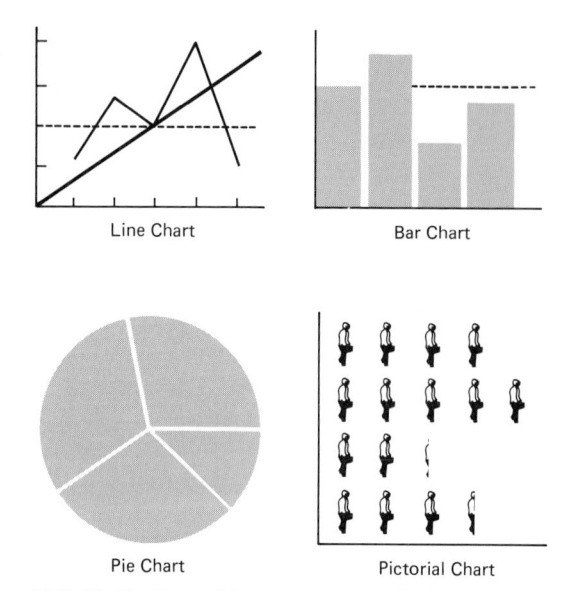

FIG. 11.19 Four of the more universally known charting techniques. The analyst can use these for improving communications with nontechnical personnel.

zation or activity are considered drafts and are quickly redrawn. The usefulness that charts can provide, however, makes them a necessary tool in the analyst's repertoire.

The following set of guidelines are provided to assist the analyst in gaining maximum usefulness from charting attempts:

1. The first attempt at constructing a chart should be freehand.
2. If the chart is for the analyst's use only, then a formal chart need not be drawn.
3. If a chart is not readily understandable to the viewer, then the chart should be either simplified or redrawn as two or more charts.
4. The symbols used in a chart should aid the viewer and not hamper his or her understanding.
5. Charts which are to be used as permanent documentation should be keyed to

	Line Charts	Bar Charts	Pie Charts	Pictorial Charts
Advantages	1. Shows time and magnitude of relationships well. 2. Can show many points. 3. Degree of accuracy adjustable. 4. Easily read.	1. Good for comparisons. 2. Emphasizes one point. 3. Accurate. 4. Easily read.	1. Good for monetary comparisons. 2. Good for part versus whole comparison. 3. Very easily understood.	1. Very easily understood. 2. Easily constructed.
Disadvantages	1. Limited to less than four lines without adding complexity. 2. Limited to two dimensions. 3. Spacing can mislead.	1. Limited to one point. 2. Spacing can mislead.	1. Limited usage. 2. Limited precision. 3 Tends to oversimplify.	1. Limited usage. 2. Limited precision. 3. Tends to oversimplify.

brief narratives or computer programs as appropriate.

6. Charts used in management presentations should minimize symbolism.
7. Charts should be large enough so that all members of the audience can read them.

Decision Tables and Matrices

Very early in our formal education we are introduced to tables and their usage as a technique for representing varied and complex subjects. These same techniques can be valuable to systems analysts for problem definition, analysis, synthesis, procedure and program development, communication, and documentation. A relatively recent development in this area is called **decision tables.**

Decision Tables. A decision table is a tabular representation of the decision-making process. Unlike a matrix, a decision table does not portray static answers or solutions. Instead, the decision table standardizes the logical process and allows the user to insert the values in both the conditions and actions related to the decision. The underlying premise for using a decision table can be structured as an—*if* this occurs, *then* do this—proposition. Figure 11.21 illustrates a decision table which represents the decision logic applied to a paycheck to post its amount to the proper payroll register correctly.

The decision table is read as follows:

Rule 1. If the check code is equal to L, K, F, G, I, R, E, P, or D, post that check amount to Register X.
Rule 2. If the check code is equal to B and the division code is equal to 24, post that check amount to Register Y.
Rule 3. If the check code equals B and the division code does not equal 24, post that check amount to Register X.
Rule 4. If check code is not equal to L, K, F, G, I, R, E, P, D, or B, go to the routine that handles bad check codes.

Register Posting Logic				
IF:	1	2	3	4
Check code = L, K, F, G, I, R, E, P, or D	Y	N	N	N
Check code = B	N	Y	Y	N
Division code = 24		Y	N	
THEN:				
Post register X	1		1	
Post register Y		1		
Go to bad check code				1

FIG. 11.21 Decision tables are techniques that assist the analyst in understanding and communicating complex logic. This decision table represents the logical process applied to posting paychecks to registers.

Each rule is applied to a situation that table users are confronted with until they have made a match of conditions and can take one of the specified actions.

Structure of a Decision Table. Figure 11.22 is a conceptual model of a decision table. The upper half of the table contains the decision conditions, which are expressed in areas called *stubs* and *entries*. Condition stubs are those criteria the decision maker wishes to apply to his or her decision. To incorporate these criteria into a decision table, they must be phrased to follow the word *IF*.

The lower half of the table contains the actions which are to be taken when the specified conditions are satisfied. Actions are also indicated as stubs and entries. To incorporate actions into the table, they must be structured to follow the term *THEN*.

	Decision Table Title	Rules						
		1	2	3	4	5	...	N
A								
B	Condition stub			Condition entry				
C								
D								
E								
F								
G								
I								
J								
K	Action stub			Action entry				
L								
M								
N								
O								

FIG. 11.22 Generalized decision table format.

Combining the conditions with the actions results in: *IF* (these conditions exist), *THEN* (perform these actions).

Single condition decisions do not require decision tables for communication or understanding. Thus, the table allows for multiple conditions. Conditions are listed vertically along the upper left side of the table which is called the stub and are read as—*IF* (condition 1) *AND* (condition 2) *AND* (condition N) *THEN* action 1, action 2, action N.

Again, one alternative in a decision process may not require all conditions nor demand all actions to be taken. Selectivity is accomplished by choosing the correct rule to meet the decision requirements. Rules are numbered horizontally across the top of the decision table and are applied as *OR*. For example, "My situation can match Rule 1 *OR* Rule 2 *OR* Rule N." Any given decision which is appropriate to the decision table can apply to one rule only.

The proper rule is determined by examining the condition entries for each rule one at a time until a rule is identified which matches the conditions in the decision being applied to the table. Condition entries may contain one of three symbols; Y, N or –. If Y is present in the condition entry then that condition must exist in the situation facing the decision maker. If N is present in that condition entry then that condition must not exist in the situation confronting the decision maker. If neither Y nor N is present, the entry should have a –; often the entry is left empty. A – or empty condition entry indicates that the condition does not apply to the situation the decision maker is concerned about.

When all of the condition entries included in the table are evaluated and the proper rule is identified, the table user then performs all of the actions in the order indicated, in the action entry portion of the table.

Decision Table Vocabulary. A set of standard linkage terms has been developed for use with decision tables since complex decision processes cannot always be reflected in one decision table. The four most common terms are:

GO TO	This is an action stub term that tells the table user where to go for further processing.
GO AGAIN	This is an action stub term that directs the table user to return to the first condition entry of the table.
PERFORM	This term links the table users to another table, and when that table has been executed, the users must return to the table where they were instructed to PERFORM.
EXIT	This action entry term is always used with the PERFORM term and is the signal to return to the table where they were instructed to PERFORM.

Figure 11.23 is an example of decision tables where special linkage terms are used.

Types of Decision Tables. Up to this point we have been discussing one type of decision table known as a *limited entry table.* A limited entry table is so called because the conditions or actions required are contained within the appropriate stubs; symbols are used in the entry sections (e.g., Conditions = Y, N or –; Actions = numbers or blanks) to relate to specific rules. This type of table is the most widely used in practice.

A second type of decision table is known as an *extended entry table.* Both the stub and the entry sections of any specific condition must be considered together to decide if a condition is applicable to a given rule. This type of table is applicable in describing problems with few variables which may have many different values. In addition, it may save space. Figure 11.24 is an example of a decision table in the limited entry format and in the extended entry format.

Constructing Decision Tables. When an analyst identifies an opportunity for constructing a decision table, the following guidelines should be followed:

1. Limit the decision process or objective of the decision table with firm boundaries.
2. List all the conditions which must be addressed before a decision can be executed.
3. List all the activities which must be accomplished based on the exact nature of the decision.
4. Identify and define the values of all conditions and actions.
5. Classify and consolidate like conditions and actions.
6. A decision table can have only one entry point into the table.
7. A decision table may have many exits from the table.
8. Only one rule in a table may be satisfied by a situation.

Check Code Table

	1	2	3	4	5
Check code = L,K,F,G,I,R,E,P, or D	Y	N	N	N	N
Check code = B, M, or Y	-	Y	N	N	N
Check code = C	-	-	Y	N	N
Check code = A	-	-	-	Y	N
Post register X	1				
Post register Y		1			
Go to company code table			1		
Go to division code table				1	
Perform error routine					1
Exit	2	2			
Go again					2

Division Code Table

	1	2
Division code = 01	Y	N
Post register X	1	
Post register Y		1
Exit	2	2

Company Code Table

	1	2	3	4	5	6	7
Check code = B	Y	Y	N	N	N	N	
Check code = M	N	N	Y	Y	N	N	
Check code = Y	N	N	N	N	Y	Y	
Company code = A	N	N	Y	N	Y	N	
Company code = B or C	Y	N	N	-	N	N	
Post register X	1			1			
Post register Y			1		1		
Go to pay class table				1			
Perform error routine		1				1	
Exit	2		2		2	2	

Pay Class Table

	1	2
Pay class = hourly	Y	N
Post register X	1	
Post register Y		1
Exit	2	2

FIG. 11.23 An example of linking decision tables together.

9. Rules may be considered in any order. (It is often helpful in reading the decision table if conditions are grouped or sequenced.)
10. Actions must be executed in the order written.
11. If two conditions exist, one of which is the negative of the other, eliminate one of the conditions.
12. If with the exception of one condition, two rules have the same condition entries, and if for that one condition one rule has a Y entry and the other an N entry, the rules may be combined with that one condition becoming indifferent.
13. Each rule in the final table must have at least one condition entry different than any other rule.
14. In a limited entry table, before rule consolidation, the maximum number of rules should equal 2^N, where N is equal to the number of conditions.
15. Test each rule in the table as well as the table as a whole for completeness, accuracy, and proper format.

The construction of meaningful decision tables is an iterative process. Few other analytical tools or techniques result in as complete an understanding as do decision tables. Moreover, as a communication and docu-

Techniques for Gathering and Analyzing Study Facts **337**

Limited Entry

	1	2	3	4
Approved credit	N	Y	Y	Y
Order qty. 0–25 gallons		Y	N	N
Order qty. 26–55 gallons			Y	N
Reject order	1			
Release order		1	1	1
5% discount			2	
10% discount				2

Extended Entry

	1	2	3	4
Approved credit	N	Y	Y	Y
Quantity ordered		0–25	26–55	≥ 56
% discount		0	5	10
Release order		X	X	X
Reject order	X			

FIG. 11.24 Example of an extended entry table compared to a limited entry table.

mentative aid, decision tables not only help understanding but they often eliminate the possibility of misunderstanding. Figures 11.25 to 11.28 provide a detailed explanation of how a decision table is developed from a narrative.

Matrices, Arrays, and Value Tables. Matrices, arrays, and value tables are all terms that refer to similar techniques whose prime purpose is to order or arrange facts. The earliest such technique most of us remember is our addition and multiplication tables. Later, we were introduced to still more uses of this technique in mathematics, science, history, geography, and so forth. In each case a matrix was used to provide easy reference to a value related to certain conditions, or to help foster understanding of a complex subject by reflecting one or more important relationships contained therein.

Unfilled Order File Reporting

    Each record on the unfilled order file must be examined and classified as either a Closed order, Backorder, In-process order, Current order, or a Future order. Any record which has the order quantity equal to the shipped quantity is considered closed. Any record having a to-be-shipped date earlier than the report date is a backorder. A record with the to-be-shipped date equal to the report date is treated as in-process. Any record with a to-be-shipped date more than seven days later than the report date is a future order. All other records are considered current, except any record with net dollars less than zero which are called closed.

FIG. 11.25 An example of a complex procedure in narrative form.

338 Systems Analysis

Unfilled Order File Reporting
 Each record on the unfilled order file must be examined and classified as either a Closed order, Backorder, In-process order, Current order, or a Future order. Any record which has <u>the order quantity equal to the shipped quantity</u> is considered <u>closed</u>. Any record having <u>a to-be-shipped date earlier than the report date</u> is a <u>backorder</u>. A record with <u>the to-be-shipped date equal to the report date</u> is treated as <u>in-process</u>. Any record with <u>a to-be-shipped date more than seven days later than the report date</u> is a <u>future order</u>. All <u>other records</u> are considered <u>current</u>, except <u>any record with net dollars less than zero</u> which are called <u>closed</u>.

FIG. 11.26 An illustration of the analyst identifying *IF-THEN* relationships by underlining conditions once and actions twice.

Conditions	Actions
The order quantity equal to the shipped quantity	closed
A to-be-shipped date earlier than the report date	backorder
The to-be-shipped date equal to the report date	in-process
A to-be-shipped date more than seven days later than the report date	future
Any record with net dollars less than zero	closed
All other records	current

FIG. 11.27 Example where all conditions and actions are listed. Redundancies and ambiguities are eliminated.

IF	1	2	3	4	5	6
Net $ < 0	Y	N	N	N	N	N
Order qty = shipped qty		Y	N	N	N	N
TBS date = rep date			Y	N	N	N
TBS < rep date				Y	N	N
TBS > rep date + 7					Y	N
THEN						
Closed order	1	1				
Backorder				1		
In-process			1			
Current						1
Future					1	

FIG. 11.28 Example of a decision table prepared from a narrative.

This same technique is valuable in systems efforts for analysis, communication, and documentation. Figure 11.29 illustrates the various data elements which might be contained in a data base from which a number of accounts receivable/credit reports are extracted.

Hazards During Fact Gathering

The analyst must be constantly on guard against three hazards while gathering study facts:

1. *Using incorrect or misdirected facts.* Often the analyst will be given misleading facts concerning potential systems requirements. This problem can result from the comments of a well meaning but uninformed manager or supervisor. Or it could result from an erroneous chart, casual observation, or poor sample. The analyst can guard against this hazard by using many sources, or a number of techniques, to cross-validate the study facts.

2. *Making conscious or unconscious assumptions.* Usually the analyst possesses some degree of knowledge concerning the organization function being investigated. With experienced analysts in particular, the notion that the analyst already knows what is needed, or is being

	Customer Statements	Aged Trial Balance	Open Item Ledger	Dunning Letters	Account Analysis
Trigger					
Code in customer master record	X			X	
Transactions	X			X	X
Request		X	X		X
Content					
Customer name	X	X	X	X	X
Customer address	X	X	X	X	X
Account number	X	X	X	X	X
Document number	X		X	X	X
Document date	X		X	X	X
Customer document number	X		X	X	X
Customer document date	X		X	X	X
Customer document amount	X		X	X	X
Account total dollars	X	X	X	X	X
Date due	X	X		X	X
Special message				X	
Sequence					
By customer	X	X	X	X	X
document	X		X	X	X

FIG. 11.29 Illustration of the use of a matrix for an analyzing, documenting, or communicating related logical structures.

done, in that function sometimes replaces fact-finding and results in erroneous facts being analyzed. This hazard can usually be minimized by the analyst identifying his or her study assumptions in writing and having various users or other analysts review them.

3. *Checking and verifying every potential source.* Just the opposite problem from that of using unverified assumptions results from the analyst's checking and verifying every study fact that the analyst feels might have some importance. Obviously, this can result in an excessively expensive and time-consuming analysis. This hazard can be minimized by establishing time objectives for each fact-finding task.

11.6 ▪ COMMUNICATING THE FINDINGS

Throughout the systems analysis phase, the analyst should maintain extensive communications with the requestor, users, management, and other project personnel. This communication begins with the Proposal to Conduct Systems Analysis Report described previously. On a continuing basis this communication effort includes feedback to persons interviewed, or observed, as to what the analyst understands; verification with user personnel as to the findings in other, but related, functions or activities that the analyst identifies; and periodic status meetings to inform management and other project personnel about progress, status, and adherence to schedule.

Preparing the Systems Analysis Completion Report

Perhaps the most important communication of all, however, is the **Systems Analysis Completion Report,** which describes findings of the systems analysis. The format and content of this report include the following:

1. A restatement of the reason for and scope of the analysis.
2. A list of the major problems identified.
3. A restatement of all systems performance requirements.
4. A statement of any critical assumptions made by the analyst during the analysis.
5. Any recommendations concerning the proposed system or its requirements. This step actually is a preliminary general design.
6. A projection of the resources required and the expected costs involved in designing any new system or modification to the present system. This projection includes the feasibility of continuing further systems work.

In general, the Systems Analysis Completion Report is directed to two different recipients. First, the analyst's management uses the report to determine if the analyst has done a competent job in identifying systems requirements and ascertaining how these requirements fit into any overall or master plan for systems development in the organization. Second, the report provides general and user managements with an opportunity to determine whether the analyst has considered all of the organization's requirements.

To provide a meaningful report to both of these interested parties, the analyst should strive to be concise but thorough in preparing the report. Requirements should be quantified and explained specifically. The analyst should avoid technical jargon and acronyms in the report. Exhibits and supporting working papers used in the systems analysis should be attached or an indication given as to their location.

Good communication between the analyst and the user is a key ingredient in successful information systems development. Achieving and maintaining good communications throughout the systems analysis goes far to eliminate two real problems that have plagued practitioners in the development of systems to date. The first problem is the failure to obtain user approval to proceed with development of an improved information system because the proposed system is not clearly understood. The second problem is a need to "sell" the analyst's proposed system to the users.

If effective communications have been established, there should not be any difficulty in obtaining approval resulting from the users' lack of understanding of the proposed system. And there will be no need to "sell" anything, since the proposed system was accepted each time the analyst obtained an agreement pertaining to a user's requirement.

The Feasibility Requirements

Systems work is a continuous cycle, but within this cycle it is also iterative. For example, the systems analyst's steps have to be retraced repeatedly and several Proposal to Conduct Systems Analysis Reports may have to be prepared before total agreement between users and analyst is reached. This situation should be understood when one refers to the feasibility requirements of systems work (introduced in Chapter 1). The systems analyst must continually ask whether something is feasible or not. For example, at the very outset a requestor might indicate that some problem situation should be investigated by the analyst. Evaluating the situation quickly, the analyst might decide that it is infeasible to pursue the matter further at that particular time. Or it may be that the analyst begins the analysis in earnest, but later it becomes infeasible to continue. Moreover, an entire systems analysis can be conducted for the sole purpose of proving or disproving the feasibility of something. For convenience, feasibility analysis is discussed here, and in a different context, in the next chapter. As noted in Chapter 1, *feasibility requirements* are one of the demand blocks that dictate the overall design and development of the information system.

Feasibility analysis helps determine the likelihood that the recommendations proposed in the completion report can be carried out. In other words, that these recommendations, although still at a general or conceptual level, are capable of (1) being specifically designed in terms of input, output, data base, processing, controls, etc.; (2) attaining desired goals, user requirements, and system requirements; and (3) being successfully implemented at a later date.

The feasibility aspect has five primary areas, which are characterized by the acronym *TELOS*.

1. *Technical feasibility.* The technical area can be divided into two sections: hardware and software. To decide technical feasibility, the analyst simply determines if the preliminary design can be developed and implemented using existing technology. Usually this determination includes the technological expertise that exists presently within the organization, but it may include an assessment of the technological state of the art from outside the organization.

2. *Economic feasibility.* In this area, the analyst determines if the benefits to be derived from the systems recommendation are worth the time, money, and other resources required to achieve the recommendation. This aspect of feasibility is often referred to as cost/effectiveness analysis and includes the weighing of costs against the effectiveness of the recommendation. Cost/effectiveness is illustrated in the accompanying table. In Chapter 15 we will present a detailed cost/effectiveness analysis of a computer configuration.

Estimating costs	Assessing effectiveness
Equipment costs	*Direct benefits.* These are a direct result of the recommended system.
Personnel costs	They include reduction in errors, reduction of personnel, etc.
Development costs Operating costs, etc.	*Indirect benefits.* These do not necessarily arise automatically from the system and they are difficult to quantify. Examples of these benefits include increased efficiency, better decision making, more profit, increased customer service, etc.

3. *Legal feasibility.* This factor mandates that no conflicts exist between the system under consideration and the organization's ability to discharge its legal obligations. In this regard the analyst must consider the legal implications arising from applicable federal and state statutes, rules of common law, federal and state administrative agencies (e.g., Internal Revenue Service, Securities and Exchange Commission), and contractual provisions. For example, in considering requirements for records retention, the analyst should know what records must be retained, who must keep them, and how long they must be kept.

4. *Operational feasibility.* This is the determination that the system will be able to perform the designated functions within the existing organizational environment with its current personnel and existing procedures. If not, and changes are required, the analyst must point these out and indicate the level of probability of such changes being achieved successfully. The operational aspect is really a human relations problem. In this regard, Ross and Schuster have identified some Do's of the systems analyst[8]:

Do in the initial stages to gather information on the workings of the emergent social system and the constraints it imposes. Pay particular attention to work group norms (i.e., expected standard of behavior) and emergent status relationships, both of which will be key factors in the acceptance or rejection of the system. *Do* design the information system within the emergent social system constraints,

[8]Dr. Joel Ross and Dr. Fred Shuster, "Selling the System," *Journal of Systems Management,* October 1972, p. 10. With permission.

just as you design it within technical or physical constraints. *Do* consider the social and behavioral aspects of systems design to be as equally important as the technical or physical aspects. In addition to these Do's the analyst must also: (1) develop a tentative work force plan that indicates the probable need for orienting and training employees who will be performing the functions of the new system or subsystem; (2) develop a list of required new skills which will be needed; and (3) develop a tentative plan for relocation of displaced employees; possible changes in overall organization structure; and changes in levels of responsibility, authority, and accountability.

5. *Schedule feasibility.* This means that the analyst must estimate when the proposed recommendation will be operative, assuming that it is eventually accepted. The use of PERT and Gantt charts are helpful to the analyst in this area.

All of these categories must be feasible before systems work can continue. For example, a preliminary design proposal may be feasible based on technical, legal, operational, and schedule analysis, but not be feasible based on economic analysis. Such a design proposal would not be *totally* feasible.

Final Results of Systems Analysis

Five alternative outcomes for any particular systems analysis are:

1. *Stop work.* This outcome means that no further work is to be performed and that systems work and resources should be directed toward other projects. This outcome might result because a proposal(s) does not meet TELOS feasibility considerations, because of a change in manage-

ment's or the requestor's decisions, or through a reshuffling of systems priorities which results in the present project being scrapped.

2. *Wait state.* This outcome is quite common and usually results from a lack of funds or a conservative attitude of management.

3. *Modify.* This outcome means that management decides some aspects of the proposal must either be changed or combined with another subsystem.

4. *Conditional proceed.* This outcome means that systems work will proceed as proposed, but that the final design proposal prior to implementation will have to be justified on a TELOS feasibility basis.

5. *Unconditional proceed.* Many system or subsystem proposals are authorized by management with full knowledge that costs will exceed measurable benefits. For example, severe constraints imposed upon the organization by legislative and judicial action might require the development of a system regardless of cost. Or it may be that broader organizational objectives dictate the development of a system that is not cost/effective. For example, management may be planning to expand in a market area which will not be profitable for a number of years. A subsystem to support this venture would not be cost/effective for some time.

SUMMARY

Four possible reasons for the initiation of systems analysis are: (1) to solve a problem; (2) to take care of a new requirement imposed upon the organization; (3) to implement a new method, technique, or idea; and (4) to make a general system improvement or overhaul. In performing systems analysis the analyst must first define the scope or boundaries within which the analyst will be working. A Proposal to Conduct Systems Analysis Report is then prepared. This report is a communication device that allows both the requestor or future user of the system and the analyst's manager to know what will be entailed during the systems analysis phase.

The study facts come from three major sources: (1) the existing system; (2) internal sources, which include people, documents, and relationships; and (3) external sources, which include other interface points outside the present system, user groups, or societies to which the organization belongs, textbooks and periodicals, seminars, and vendors.

Five major frameworks for fact-gathering are: (1) Decision level analysis breaks a system down based on resources. Decision points which control these resources are defined and appropriate decision rules are formulated by management. (2) Information flow analysis shows what information is required, by whom, and from where it is obtained. (3) Input/output analysis simply shows the data inputs and information outputs of a system without concern for resulting decisions made from the outputs. (4) With structured analysis facts are gathered by starting with the top function and working down to the lowest activity. (5) Less-structured analysis uses Delphi and brainstorming techniques to gather facts. Potential hazards during fact gathering are using incorrect facts, making incorrect conscious or unconscious assumptions, and checking needlessly and slavishly verifying every potential source.

Techniques for gathering and analyzing study facts include organization charts, flowcharts, decision tables, grid charts, etc. These techniques may be used to communicate the findings to various persons and also to prepare the Systems Analysis Completion Report. The two major areas of the completion report are (1) preliminary design recommendations and (2) the feasibility of continuing further systems work. Feasibility concerns five areas (TELOS): (1) technical feasibility, (2) economic feasibility, (3) legal feasibility, (4) operational feasibility, and (5) schedule feasibility.

The final outcome of systems analysis will result in one of the following decisions: (1) stop any further systems work on present project, (2) wait for a period of time until other events occur, (3) modify present systems work and/or combine it into another systems project, (4) proceed with systems work based on further considerations, and (5) proceed with systems work without further restriction.

REVIEW QUESTIONS

11.1 What are the basic reasons for initiating systems analysis?

11.2 Distinguish between the objective and the scope of systems analysis.

11.3 What are the purposes for preparing a Proposal to Conduct Systems Analysis Report? List and explain the major items included in this report.

11.4 Compare and contrast the sources of study facts available during a systems analysis, related to information systems development.

11.5 Distinguish between developing a framework for fact gathering and actually performing analysis. Give an example of each.

11.6 Compare and contrast the use of the various types of study fact-gathering frameworks discussed in this chapter.

11.7 Compare and contrast the advantages/disadvantages of using interviewing, questionnaire, and observation as a technique for fact-gathering.

11.8 What is the purpose of document gathering? What are the basic types of documents available within most organizations?

11.9 What is the basic reason for developing a chart? What are the basic types of charts prepared by systems analysts?

11.10 Describe the Systems Analysis Completion Report. How does this report relate to the Proposal to Conduct Systems Analysis Report?

11.11 What does the term "feasible" mean? What feasibility requirements concern the systems analyst? Explain.

11.12 What are the five possible outcomes of any systems analysis?

QUESTIONS FOR DISCUSSION

11.1 "The systems investigation is a feasibility study." Evaluate this comment.

11.2 "All systems studies are directed to cutting costs." Evaluate this statement.

11.3 "The only thing wrong with the study Jill conducted was that it wasn't what management requested." Comment.

11.4 "The reason we cannot manage inventories any better today than we could five years ago, is that we have the same inventory recording system now as we had then. The only difference is that a computer prepares the reports rather than some inventory clerk." Discuss.

11.5 "Don't ask clerks whether something is necessary or not. They only do what they are told. Management decides what is needed." Evaluate this statement.

11.6 "I never thought to define what would be needed if the system utilized online terminals. I guess I assumed we were not going to have that kind of capability." Discuss.

11.7 "I have found that systems investigations are performed much faster when you fit the pieces together as you receive them." Comment.

11.8 "Just analyzing the entries in a pay stub indicates there is much more to a payroll system than calculating the correct pay." Evaluate.

11.9 "We just couldn't sell management that our study findings reflected the actual situation." Evaluate.

11.10 "The demands for systems analysts' efforts in this company are unending. It seems that no sooner do we have a project completed than somebody wants us to take a look at the activity from a different perspective. It appears that each new manager is looking for a better way to do things." Comment on this statement.

11.11 "Although we only budgeted three months to analyze the requirements on the new Personnel System, we worked the equivalent of fourteen months before Personnel cancelled the project." How could this situation be avoided in future systems efforts in the organization?

11.12 "As a result of considering only the activities in the previous manual order entry system, we missed an opportunity to provide many new benefits to the organization when we designed the new system." Discuss how this situation could arise in any organization.

11.13 "The failure of the systems analyst to challenge outdated corporate policies results in many new systems being designed to satisfy nonsensical requirements." Fully discuss.

11.14 "As we progress from designing data processing systems to designing information systems, the emphasis in the analysis must be changed from what must be produced, to what should be produced as information outputs." Evaluate this comment.

11.15 "To a great extent, systems analysis results in defining the ingredients of the demand blocks." Discuss this statement.

EXERCISES

11.1 The Tricor Manufacturing Company produces and sells several lines of bicycles, tricycles, scooters, and so forth, worldwide. Recently the company president, Anne Williams, announced a major reorganization that will affect all facets of Tricor's operations. Anne has decided to implement the relatively new concept of materials management at Tricor.

The materials management concept places under one person the responsibility for the movement of all products in the company. This involves combining the traditional functions of purchasing, production scheduling, inventory control, traffic, and product estimating.

Ed Bishop has been appointed vice-president of materials management for Tricor. Presently, Tricor's headquarters are in Cincinnati, Ohio. All orders are entered in a centralized order entry system at Cincinnati. Four manufacturing plants are located in Rhode Island, Virginia, Colorado, and Oregon.

Ed has decided to maintain a centralized purchasing staff consisting of six purchasing agents, and a clerical staff of ten persons including the supervisor at Cincinnati. J. Brown has been named manager of central purchasing and will report to Bishop.

Virginia and Colorado contain relatively large plants, whereas Rhode Island and Oregon house smaller operations. Although Bishop is unsettled on the actual persons to appoint, he has decided on the following organization structure. Each plant will be headed by a manager of materials management who will report directly to the vice-president. The larger plants will have supervisors for each of the functional areas being consolidated. These supervisors will report directly to the manager at that location, although the supervisor of purchasing will have an indirect responsibility to the manager of central purchasing.

The smaller plants will consolidate the functions of purchasing and traffic under one supervisor, and the functions of production scheduling and inventory control under one supervisor. Supervising product estimating will be the direct responsibility of the manager at these smaller locations.

Each manager of materials management at Tricor will be assigned a secretary, as will the vice-president. A field coordinator for materials management will report directly to Bishop. Before Bishop assigns specific persons to these positions and designates the size of each staff involved, he would like to review his preliminary thoughts with Anne Williams.

Ed has asked you to draw up an organization chart according to the above facts.

11.2 The order entry system in most commercial organizations provides for shipping products on a delayed payment basis, assuming that the customer has a proven credit record. However, a new customer, in many instances, is subject to credit approval. Consequently, most order entry systems are designed to contain a credit checking operation as a standard procedure. The Tricor Company is no exception.

The centralized order entry system is computerized. A customer master file is used to process all orders. This file contains a record for each approved Tricor customer. Among the many fields of data in each customer record is a customer code, a trade class, a credit limit field, a current accounts receivable dollar field, a past due accounts receivable dollar field, and a credit referral field. Currently, all orders must pass through the credit manager before they can be processed by the computer. A sampling has shown that less than 5 percent of all orders are held by the credit manager. You have suggested that the credit check might be performed by the computer and only problem orders forwarded to the credit manager before shipment. This would eliminate the credit manager having to handle all the orders, as well as decreasing the overall order processing time. The credit manager has agreed to try this approach.

The following narrative represents the credit manager's thoughts on how the credit checking procedure should operate in Tricor.

All orders received at Tricor will have a credit check performed. All orders received from new customers must be forwarded to the credit manager. All orders exceeding $1000 must be forwarded to the credit manager. If the dollar amount of an order plus the present accounts receivable balance for that customer exceeds the credit limit assigned to the customer, then the order must be sent to the credit manager. All orders from customers with past due accounts receivable balances must be forwarded to the credit manager. All orders from customers on "credit referral" are forwarded to the credit manager. Orders from customers coded to class of trade 100 are not rejected unless the account is on "credit referral" or the order exceeds $10,000, or the present accounts receivable balance is greater than $50,000. Orders that pass the credit check are sent directly to the shipping department.

As the systems analyst you have three concerns with the above narrative:

1. You must understand fully what is required.
2. You want to ensure that the credit manager has not forgotten or misrepresented any concern.
3. You want to communicate this credit checking logic to the programmer as clearly as possible.

Develop a decision table to satisfy these requirements.

11.3 The processing of sales adjustments is an essential aspect in the system of The Magic Gadget Company. Potentially, sales adjustments can affect five different data files.

Goods returned to Magic Gadget require an adjustment to be processed to the sales statistics file, the accounts receivable file, the salesperson's commission file, the inventory file, and the financial file.

Invoice pricing errors result in an adjustment to the sales statistics file, the accounts receivable file, the commission file, and the financial file.

Invoice quantity errors result in adjustments similar to pricing errors in addition to an adjustment of the inventory file.

Transfers of goods between customers result in sales adjustments being processed to the sales statistics file and the accounts receivable file only.

Errors in recording the freight charges for shipments result in adjustments to the accounts receivable file and the financial file.

As the systems analyst responsible for this area, you are requested to make a presentation to the Sales Department explaining the processing of sales adjustments.

1. Prepare a decision table representing this procedure.
2. Prepare a flowchart(s) representing this procedure.
3. Prepare a matrix (or array) representing this procedure.

Which method would you recommend for presentation to the Sales Department? Why?

11.4 For each of the following activities, rank the fact-gathering techniques of decision level analysis, information flow analysis, input/output analysis, structured analysis, and less-structured analysis on a most probable-least probable scale:

1. Customer order processing.
2. Expense account reporting.
3. The sales manager's budget.
4. Inventory scrap reporting.
5. Developing market strategy.

11.5 List at least five different sources of facts for each assignment described below.

1. Payroll system.
2. Accounts receivable.
3. Inventory management.

4. Sales forecasting.
5. Employee skill bank.

11.6 Rank the techniques for gathering and analyzing study facts insofar as their usefulness in gaining an understanding of each of the activities listed below:

1. Preparation of the sales budget.
2. Classroom assignments.
3. Recording absences from work/class.
4. Preparing a customer order.
5. Recording inventory movements.
6. Ordering raw materials.
7. Recruiting new employees.
8. Recording birth certificates.
9. Planning for new facilities.
10. Calculating net pay.

11.7 Choose an individual, responsible for a large number of decision-making activities in an organization, and conduct an interview for the purpose of identifying the types of information presently received by this person as well as any additional information this person might require to better perform his or her duties. In preparation for your interview, sketch a rough outline of the questions you will ask. When you complete the interview prepare a completion report that summarizes the proceedings. Lastly, write a brief summary comparing and contrasting what you anticipated in the interview versus what actually was said and done.

Note: The subject that you interview may be part of the administration of your school (e.g., registrar, a dean or department head, student housing director, etc.). Additional ideas for interviewing include a management person in the organization where you are employed, or someone in a local business establishment or government agency. Employed friends and associates provide a third choice for interviewing, although this alternative should be used only as a last resort.

11.8 Select an individual in an organization whose prime responsibility is to process data, and observe his or her activities. Briefly outline what you plan to observe. Take notes as you observe, and prepare a report summarizing what you have observed. Lastly, prepare a brief recommendation for any improvements or alternatives concerning the activity you observed.

11.9 Outline in broad terms the approach you would take to conduct a systems analysis in the following situations:

1. Customer complaints concerning poor quality merchandise.
2. Inability of the shipping department to meet shipping schedules.
3. Inaccurate invoices being sent to customers.
4. High level of obsolescence in raw materials.
5. Excessive amount of returned goods from customers.

PROBLEMS

11.1 Based on facts in the following letter, prepare a Proposal to Conduct Systems Analysis Report.

Barbara D. Student
Systems Analyst
Southwest Oil Co.

Dear Barbara,

    I enjoyed talking with you yesterday and am looking forward to seeing you again next week. I cannot tell you how pleased I am to hear that you are the analyst who will conduct the investigation for developing a forecasting system to assist in operating our lines. I thought I might take this time to provide you with some background on our needs.

    As you are aware, we operate 3600 miles of pipeline throughout the South. We are a contract carrier for petroleum products for ten major oil companies in addition to Southwest, our parent firm.

    Petroleum products enter our lines from five different refineries, from forty different storage tanks, and from four pipeline interface points in batches (we call them tenders). We deliver these products to 174 different bulk stations in addition to the above mentioned storage tanks and interface points.

    Currently we employ over a thousand delivery people whose sole responsibility is to open a valve to withdraw or input a product and close it when the proper amount of a product has been transferred. In a significant number of instances a delivery person will not have any activity during a shift.

    It is our opinion that if we could better forecast when products will be available at a given value, we could reduce the number of delivery people required through consolidation of assignments.

    A few years ago we installed about three hundred meters in strategic locations throughout the lines which measure the product flow and report this information back to our central dispatching station via teletypewriter on demand. Perhaps we could feed this information into one of those computers you have and predict arrivals of our tenders at selected valves.

I know you will need more facts than this before you decide what we need, but I do hope I have given you some insight into what we want.

If I can be of any further help, please call on me.

Until next week,

R. G. Sherman

R. G. Sherman
Director,
Southwest Pipeline Co.

11.2 The selling and exchanging of mailing lists has become a profitable undertaking for many firms, particularly those firms having lists that are computer accessible. The data processing service bureau that you work for has decided to construct a generalized mailing list for the metropolitan areas of Pittsburgh, Pennsylvania; Akron, Ohio; and Cleveland, Ohio.

The potential customers for this list will be small- to medium-sized retail establishments as well as local direct mail companies. Your president feels there will be an improved opportunity to market this mailing list if potential customers can select the type of individual they wish to reach on criteria other than solely geographical.

Your assignment is to conduct an investigation to determine what data will be included in this generalized mailing list, and submit your findings and recommendations to the president. Based on the above facts and any assumptions you deem necessary, prepare a Systems Analysis Completion Report.

11.3 Scheduling the work for professional, semiprofessional, and clerical workers is a modern management practice gaining wide acceptance in government and industry. This technique is usually called work measurement or work scheduling. The basic idea behind this mechanism is the establishment of standard times for performing specific tasks and measuring actual performance against these standards.

One approach to using this technique is to assign persons some measurable quantity of work and periodically check (e.g., every two hours) their progress. Another approach is simply to assign daily or routine tasks on a longer time period basis (such as weekly or monthly), and check progress at some interval.

The key factor that makes this technique attractive to many managements is that a task can be estimated and, depending on the expected volume and time constraints, an approximate staffing level can be projected. Whether or not a person progresses on schedule, the supervisor can evaluate the impact of their progress according to the plan. Where work standards are proven to be loose, they can be tightened, and vice versa. Additional advantages, such as following individual performance trends, evaluating fluctuating volumes, and costing specific activities regardless of who performs them, increase the attractiveness of this technique.

A significant disadvantage is that a seemingly high degree of clerical support is required to calculate performance ratios for each time period, to perform maintenance to schedules of work standards, and to provide periodic summary reporting for middle and upper management.

You are a systems consultant who has been requested to install a work scheduling system in a mail order firm which employs 270 persons to merely open correspondence and forward it to the shipping or production departments. This firm has access to a computer which supports online terminals. Based on the above facts, prepare a Proposal to Conduct Systems Analysis Report.

11.4 A systems analyst for a west coast cosmetic manufacturer called a meeting of the various functional managers to solicit their ideas, experiences, and information requirements, as she was about to initiate a systems investigation project related to sales statistics. The participants of the meeting included the following: Manager, Accounting; Manager, Credit; Manager, Customer Service; Vice-President, Sales; Manager, Market Research; Manager, Budgets; Manager, Manufacturing; and Manager, New Product Development.

The following notes were recorded by the analyst:

Manager, Accounting—Sales statistics provide the financial entry each month—(dollar figure for all sales); basis for paying monthly commissions; basis for paying quarterly bonuses; input to selected analysis and profitability studies; basis for paying state sales taxes.

Manager, Customer Service—Sales statistics used to resolve disputed shipping problems and/or invoicing problems; to assist customer in understanding what was purchased and when; to provide special analyses for salespeople, customers, and sales management.

Manager, Credit—Sales statistics are not directly essential; however, accounts receivable and current and past due balances are important; customer payment history provides analytical insight.

Vice-President, Sales—Historical record of customer purchases for each product; basis for developing future quotas; routine summary reports of different dimensions of performance (i.e., product by customer, total product class, product within territory, actual versus budget, this year versus last year, etc.).

Manager, New Product Development—Provides favorable/unfavorable trends; orders placed for new products; test market results of specific products, advertisements, promotions, etc.

Manager, Budgets—Historical sales provide part of input for preparing new budget, as well as measuring old budget, both at the salesperson level and product level.

Manager, Manufacturing—A history of orders and shipments provides a comparison of supply and demand; potential inventory problems; provides an input to production forecast; reflects prior periods' performance.

Manager, Market Research—Provides a measurement to evaluate competitor sales as reported in journals, studies, etc.

Analyze the above facts and prepare a Systems Analysis Completion Report.

11.5 Charting, Inc., your new client, processes its sales and cash receipts in the following manner:

(a) *Payment on account:* The mail is opened each morning by a mail clerk in the sales department. The mail clerk prepares remittance advices (showing customer and amount paid) for customers who fail to include a remittance with their payment. The checks and remittance advices are then forwarded to the sales department supervisor, who reviews each check and forwards the checks and remittance advices to the accounting department supervisor.

The accounting department supervisor, who also functions as a credit manager in approving new credit and all credit limits, reviews all checks for payments on past due accounts, and then forwards the checks and remittance advices to the accounts receivable clerk, who arranges the advices in alphabetical order. The remittance advices are posted directly to the accounts receivable ledger cards. The checks are endorsed by stamp and totaled, and the total is posted in the cash receipts journal. The remittance advices are filed chronologically.

After receiving the cash from the previous day's cash sales, the accounts receivable clerk prepares the daily deposit slip in triplicate. The original and second copy accompany the bank deposit; the third copy of the deposit slip is filed by date.

(b) *Sales:* Sales clerks prepare sales invoices in triplicate. The original and second copy are presented to the cashier; the third copy is retained by the sales clerk in the sales book. When the sale is for cash, the customer pays the sales clerk, who presents the money to the cashier with the invoice copies.

A credit sale is approved by the cashier from an approved credit list after the sales clerk prepares the three-part invoice. After receiving the cash or approving the invoice, the cashier validates the original copy of the sales invoice and gives it to the customer. At the end of each day the cashier recaps the sales and cash received and forwards the cash and the second copy of all sales invoices to the accounts receivable clerk.

The accounts receivable clerk balances the cash received with cash sales invoices and prepares a daily sales summary. The credit sales invoices are posted to the accounts receivable ledger, and all the invoices are sent to the inventory control clerk in the sales department for posting on the inventory control cards. After posting, the inventory control clerk files all invoices numerically. The accounts receivable clerk posts the daily sales summary in the cash receipts and sales journals and files the sales summaries by date. The cash from cash sales is combined with the cash received on account to comprise the daily bank deposit.

(c) *Bank deposits:* The bank validates the deposit slip and returns the second copy to the accounting department where it is filed by date by the accounts receivable clerk. Monthly bank statements are reconciled promptly by the accounting department supervisor and filed by date.

Required: You recognize that there are weaknesses in the existing system and believe a data flow diagram would be of assistance in evaluating your client's needs. Accordingly, prepare a data flow diagram for sales and cash receipts within the accounting and sales departments of Charting, Inc.

BIBLIOGRAPHY

Boer, "A Decision Oriented Information System," *Journal of Systems Management,* October 1972.

Burch and Hod, *Information Systems: A Case-Workbook,* Santa Barbara, CA.: John Wiley & Sons, Inc., 1975.

Canning, "New Training in System Analysis Design," *EDP Analyzer,* August 1972.

Chapin, *Flowcharts,* Philadelphia: Auerbach Publishers, 1971.

Cleland and King, *Systems Analysis and Project Management,* New York: McGraw-Hill Book Co., 1968.

DeMasi, *An Introduction to Business Systems Analysis,* Reading, MA.: Addison-Wesley Publishing Co., 1969.

Gane and Sanson, *Structured Systems Analysis: Tools and Techniques,* Englewood Cliffs, NJ.: Prentice-Hall, Inc., 1979.

Glans, Grad, Holstein, Meyers, and Schmidt, *Management Systems,* New York: Holt, Rinehart, and Winston, 1968.

McDaniel, *Applications of Decision Tables—A Reader,* Princeton, NJ.: Brandon/Systems Press, 1970.

Murdick and Ross, *Introduction to Management Information Systems,* Englewood Cliffs, NJ.: Prentice-Hall, Inc., 1977.

Optner, *Systems Analysis for Business Management,* Englewood Cliffs, NJ.: Prentice-Hall, Inc., 1968.

Ross and Shuster, "Selling the System," *Journal of Systems Management,* October 1972.

Semprevivo, *Systems Analysis: Definition, Process, and Design,* Chicago: Science Research Associates, Inc., 1976.

Pelican Case

Phase 1 · Systems Analysis

- Proposal to Conduct Systems Analysis Report
- Systems Analysis Completion Report

Phases of Systems Development Methodology

Completed ▨

To be completed ☐

Phase 1	Phase 2	Phase 3	Phase 4	Phase 5
Systems analysis	General systems design	Systems evaluation and justification	Detail systems design	Systems implementation
Proposal to conduct systems analysis report / Systems analysis completion report	General systems design proposal report	Final general systems design report	Final detail systems design report	Final implementation report
Presented and completed in this chapter	Presented at the end of Chapter 12	Presented at the end of Chapter 13	Presented at the end of Chapter 15	Presented at the end of Chapter 16

THE SETTING

Patti Blake, Controller of Pelican Supply Company, dreaded attending today's meeting of top managers. For months she and Danny Loman, Marketing Manager, had been at each other's throats over the use and control of telephone resources. Patti believed that all telephone costs should be accounted for. She wanted to know where the dollars were being spent and who was responsible for spending them. Danny, on the other hand, had taken a rather dim view of controls of any kind, let alone for the telephone network. Other managers conveyed a similar stance.

At several earlier meetings, and also on informal occasions, Patti had mentioned to Danny and other managers that telephone costs ran 30 to 40 thousand dollars per month. Her staff paid telephone costs without verification because she could not get

357

any documentation from user departments. Adding to this accounting pettifog, telephone costs are charged to a general overhead account, instead of being allocated to user departments as they should be.

So far, all Patti's urgings had fallen on deaf and unsympathetic ears. She had even heard through the grapevine that Danny Loman had said, "No one is going to prevent me or my people from using the telephone whenever we please." True or not, this rumor incensed Patti. To keep her professional sanity, she would, in today's meeting, resolve this control weakness, one way or the other. Her diplomatic pleadings had been in vain. Today, she was going to throw down the gauntlet.

The meeting room buzzed with small talk and harmless insults. Patti did not take part. She looked like a thundercloud.

Soon, the meeting coughed to order. The routine agenda was dutifully followed and dragged on until all were glassy-eyed with boredom. Patti sensed that adjournment was imminent.

Patti spoke in a clear and assertive voice. "I know that what I'm about to say isn't on our agenda for today's meeting. But the control weakness in the use of our telephone network must be resolved now."

A chorus of groans cascaded through the room.

The groans told Patti that she should have spoken up earlier. "What lousy timing," she muttered.

Patti continued in a shaky yet strangely forceful voice, "I was hired as the Controller of Pelican, and part of my responsibility is, obviously controlling costs. All costs! I have no way of knowing if the telephone bills are correct. I don't know who is responsible for these costs. I can't, therefore, perform proper cost accounting. If I'm to be effective in my work, I must have support from all of you to correct this apparent control weakness."

Danny sat at the far end of the conference table from Patti. As Patti spoke, a cloud of disgust began to shadow the craggy landscape of his face.

No doubt, Danny Loman had paid his dues. He began as a youngster selling magazine subscriptions door to door to help support his widowed mother and two younger brothers. Later, he sold insurance for several years. Much of his life had been spent outside some prospect's office. He had had his share of insults and rejections.

Danny's few detractors thought he had a Madison Avenue mentality. All conceded, however, that he epitomized the true, natural-born salesman.

Twenty years ago, Danny started at Pelican as a sales trainee. He had worked long and hard hours to become Pelican's top salesman. Five years ago, he was promoted to Marketing Manager. He had done a good job and was well liked by other department managers.

These managers, along with Danny, listened to Patti in controlled disgust. Danny, usually the calmest of men, could contain himself no longer.

Sarcastically, Danny interrupted Patti, "Why do we need to control telephone costs, anyway? I'm making dollars for this company while you're counting pennies. And I use the telephone to do it!" He continued, "You remind me of a bureaucrat who can give you ten ways why something can't be done rather than one way it can be done."

Patti responded, irritably, "If I didn't control the pennies, as you say, this company wouldn't have any dollars left. We have to get a handle on these telephone costs, the same as other costs. Also, I suspect that the telephone is not being used for business purposes."

"You mean you're going to be the one to judge whether or not I use the telephone for business reasons? Ridiculous!" Danny shouted.

Patti glared, eyeball to eyeball with Danny. Neither blinked.

Danny continued, "I called Joe Luciano in New Jersey last month to wish him a happy birthday. We talked for over thirty minutes about everything but business. Yesterday, he ordered one of our TX-1 compressors. Last week, I called Tim Larsen to simply see how he was getting along. Some of you know Tim. He was in a car wreck several weeks ago. He's also one of our best customers. I also . . ."

Patti interrupted, but seemed flustered. "Danny, please pardon me," she said, "but I don't care who you call just so long as it's for business reasons and I can verify the bills and make charges to the right user departments."

Danny fumed, "Yes, but I'm trying to tell you that . . ."

At this point, Martha Pringle, Chief Executive Officer, broke in and said that both Danny and Patti had made their points clear and that she would appoint Ben Snow, Systems Analyst, to look into the matter to see what could be done to solve the problem. She, then, adjourned the meeting. With a rustling of papers, snapping of briefcases, and clanking of chairs, all attendees scurried to their offices.

PRELIMINARY ANALYSIS

First, Ben set up an interview with Patti. Patti did not have to be prodded. She had thought about the problem for a long time and she knew exactly what she wanted. A summary of her requests are listed below.

1. *Reconcile Telephone Bill.* Account for incoming and outgoing calls. Reconcile the logged calls with the telephone bill.
2. *Department Manager Control.* Department managers need to know how calls are distributed and why and when usage of extension phones in their departments occurs.
3. *Cost Allocation.* For accepted cost accounting procedures, the telephone bill should be shared by departments in proportion to their telephone network usage. This allocation becomes an overhead cost to the department and ensures managerial attention to costs above standard.

Before leaving, Ben got from Patti an abridged organization chart of her area of responsibility. This chart is depicted in Figure C.1.

After Ben finished his interview with Patti, he went to see Danny. As soon as he

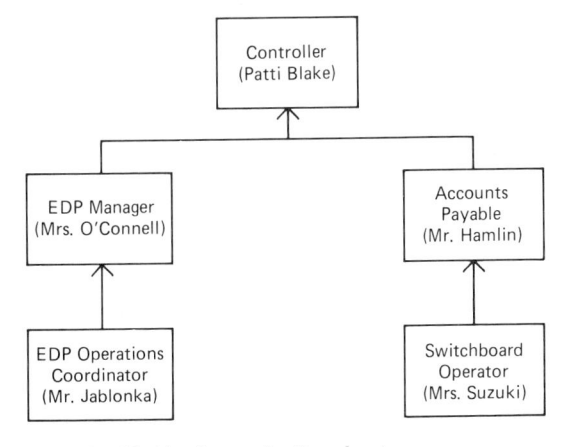

FIG. C1 Abridged organization chart.

entered Danny's office, he sensed a hostile situation. Danny rose to his feet and limply shook Ben's hand. He gave Ben an alert, suspicious glance and then sat down.

"Sit down," Danny said.

"Thanks," Ben said.

"Well, what can I do for you, Jim?" Danny asked.

"The name is Ben," retorted Ben. "I'm here to see what can be done about this telephone control problem," Ben explained.

"I don't care what those bean counters in accounting want, my job is to sell," Danny said. "To do this, me and my people have to use the telephone to call anybody, anytime, and anywhere. Sales pay the bills, and they also pay accountants' salaries," Danny explained.

Ben, after trying unsuccessfully to divert Danny into a discussion about telephone costs and how to control them, let Danny ramble on. During a lull, Ben asked Danny if he would use the telephone network differently if accounting controls were implemented. Danny said that he would not because all he cared about was contacting customers to make sales.

Ben assured Danny that accounting controls were for reconciling telephone bills, allocating costs to user departments, and preventing unauthorized use of telephones. He emphasized to Danny that he was not interested in restricting anyone's authorized use of the telephone.

Danny reiterated that his responsibility was selling but he wished that routine calls to customers could be handled by another method. "Me and my staff handle customer complaints from time to time via the telephone, but most of the time, we're on the road, beating the bushes, trying to drum up business."

Ben took note of this and asked, "How are the complaints handled when you and your staff are on the road?"

Danny replied, "I don't know. Probably, the switchboard operator tells the customer that no one is available. Sometime we get messages from our secretaries."

Danny continued, "At times, we use the telephone to collect names and addresses of prospective customers, to notify customers of new product lines, and to acknowledge customer orders. But all of this is done in a haphazard manner."

Ben noted to himself that not only was it haphazard, but it probably was an expensive way to perform these tasks.

With the above preliminary analysis behind him, Ben prepared the Proposal to Conduct Systems Analysis Report, which follows.

PROPOSAL TO CONDUCT SYSTEMS ANALYSIS REPORT

To: Martha Pringle, Patti Blake, and Danny Loman
From: Ben Snow, Systems Analyst

Definition and Reason for Conducting Analysis

Analysis will be performed to determine if it is feasible to design a system to provide financial controls for the telephone network and at the same time not restrict its use for business.

Requirements for the System

Based on initial interviews with Patti Blake and Danny Loman, the system should provide the following:

1. Improve financial controls.
2. Verify telephone bills.
3. Provide a way to allocate telephone expenses to departments based on their use.
4. Control equipment and service charges.

System Scope

The system should include every aspect that relates to the control and operation of the telephone network for the entire company. Information is needed for two reasons: (1) financial control and (2) effective operations.

Users of this information are the Controller, Accounts Payable personnel, switchboard operator, and various department heads. Some of the information will be available by paper reports on a periodic basis. Other information can be obtained via online interrogation.

Also, I believe that the scope is too restrictive and must extend beyond control of the telephone network. I believe we can design a system that not only provides certain financial control data, but also aids the marketing area. Therefore, the scope may expand as study facts become available.

Study Facts to Be Collected

1. Organizational chart and job description to:
   a. Determine decision points.
   b. Present information flow.
   c. Describe inputs/outputs.
2. Computer configuration and other data processing methods available.
3. Volume of incoming and outgoing telephone calls.
4. Distribution of telephone calls.
   a. Long distance.
   b. Collect.
   c. Credit cards.
   d. WATS.
5. Identification of departments and all extensions.
6. Identification of all telephone equipment including public phones (e.g., lobby phones).
7. Name and duty of all major telephone users.
8. Determination of number and type of customer complaints and how they are routinely handled.

Sources of Study Facts

1. Martha Pringle, CEO.
2. Danny Loman, Marketing Manager.
3. Sales staff.
4. Patti Blake, Controller.
5. Mrs. O'Connell, EDP Manager.
6. Mr. Jablonka, EDP Operations Coordinator.
7. Mr. Hamlin, Accounts Payable.
8. Mrs. Suzuki, Switchboard Operator.
9. All of the major telephone users (department managers).
10. Billing procedures of the telephone company.
11. A sampling of customers.
12. Certain documents, such as correspondence to customers and invoices.
13. Systems literature.

Schedule of Major Events in the Preparation of the
Systems Analysis Completion Report

1.	Interviewing managers and other users	60 hours
2.	Gathering study facts	20 hours
3.	Analyzing study facts	80 hours
4.	Synthesizing study facts	40 hours
5.	Communicating findings	20 hours
		220 hours

The above schedule gives absolute hours, but to give these hours meaning, they have been put into the following Gantt chart. Notice that the number of each event is used rather than duplicating each event description.

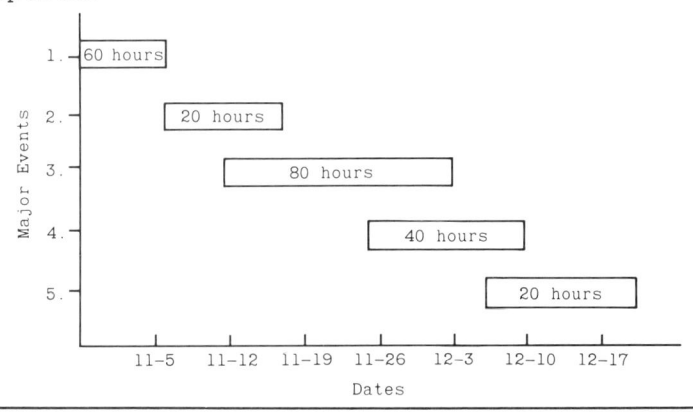

```
                1. ─┤60 hours│
Major Events    2. ─      ┤20 hours│
                3. ─           ┤  80 hours  │
                4. ─                    ┤40 hours│
                5. ─                         ┤20 hours│
                     11-5  11-12 11-19 11-26 12-3  12-10 12-17
                                     Dates
```

GATHERING AND ANALYZING STUDY FACTS

At Pelican, all incoming and outgoing calls must go through a central switchboard. Ben asked Mrs. Suzuki, the switchboard manager, and her assistants to log all calls for a period of one typical week of operation for the following categories: (1) long-distance outgoing calls not using WATS lines, (2) incoming collect calls, (3) outgoing nontoll calls, and (4) WATS calls. Here are the results of the study:

The study was done the first part of November, which represents an average time period in terms of business volume at Pelican. However, the volume of calls will increase by 25 percent during December and January, the months of heavy promotion.

This study indicates some underutilization of the WATS line. It appears that many callers do not use the WATS line, but instead dial directly. Ben started to investigate this by interviewing randomly selected telephone users. His findings are listed below:

1. WATS lines cover only ten states (a need for additional coverage may exist).

2. After requesting a WATS line from a switchboard operator, users wait five or more minutes for a free WATS line. Impatience or urgency cause users to dial directly rather than wait for WATS availability.
3. Some callers are unaware of the existence of the WATS lines.

Ben analyzed telephone traffic at Pelican in many different ways. He examined the destination of long distance calls to determine if additional lease-line coverage was necessary. A representative of the telephone company had told Ben that the WATS network could be expanded either to include more states or to provide more lines within the existing geographical area covered. Also, Ben analyzed incoming collect calls and credit card charges in an attempt to determine if incoming WATS line coverage was appropriate.

From Ben's perspective, he was interested in the part of the analysis which specified telephone activity by department. This part of the analysis showed Ben that while Marketing had less than 10 percent of the installed telephones, they were the originator or destination of more than 80 percent of telephone activity. Manufacturing, purchasing, and accounting had more equipment but used it for mostly internal or local calls.

As Ben reflected on these relationships, a smile crossed his face. He thought to himself, "I'll just bet both Patti and Danny suspected this all along. Danny knows that a proper cost allocation procedure means that his department will pay a lion's share of the telephone bill. It makes sense why these two are the most vocal and emotional concerning telephone costs." He wondered if Danny would try to throw a monkey wrench into the development of a new system.

The identification of departments, extensions, and equipment turned out to be a simple matter. When interviewing Mr. Hamlin from Accounts Payable, Ben asked what was done with the equipment installation bills. As it turned out, it was a critical question, since Mr. Hamlin was new in the department and did not know of the equipment information available. He found out that one of his bookkeepers logs all this information, so it was available to Ben in an organized manner within two hours. Of course, that discovery saved Ben a great deal of time.

In addition to internal people who must be interviewed by the systems analyst to

Category	Number of Calls	Total Time	Average Time
Long distance calls	6,520	34,200 min.	5.245 min.
Collect calls	3,800	25,020 min.	6.548 min.
Nontoll calls	12,040	124,580 min.	10.347 min.
WATS calls	400	2,080 min.	5.200 min.

gather study facts, external organizations and individuals also represent an important source of study facts. For example, while Ben was interviewing the telephone business office communications consultant about some routine matters, he was told that the telephone company will furnish to an organization, for a fee, a regenerated bill of all toll calls made, what number made them, to what number they were made, the time duration (in minutes) of the call, the date, and so forth. All the data on these calls could be on a punched card or a magnetic tape. The initial charge for this service was $60.00 (setup cost), plus a one cent charge for each record (variable cost).

Ben was elated over this discovery because he considered that these computer-prepared records might serve as valuable input for some of the control reports that he had in mind to develop. He would need to perform further investigation to determine if the regenerated data would be cost/effective; but at this point, Ben felt he had discovered a procedure that could be quite beneficial to the development of the new system. He incorporated this alternative into his general systems design proposal so that management could ultimately decide on the best alternative.

Ben also visited personnel in the computer center several times to become better acquainted with equipment and the programming skills available. The computer configuration at Pelican is shown in Figure C.2.

After the above fact gathering had been done including additional interviews, Ben still felt that a big piece of the puzzle was missing. He felt depressed. He wasn't really doing anything creative. He knew he could build a good system to provide control information about the telephone network.

But, so what? Ben felt that he needed to give something to Danny, the main user of the telephone network, to take the sting out of the cost allocation proposal.

Ben wondered how he could design a system to help the company as a whole, including Danny's area. To this end, Ben requested that he get together with Danny and his salespeople next Monday to see what the new system should do for them. Ben thought this appropriate since the missing part of the puzzle seemed to revolve around the Marketing area. Danny said that he and his "bunch" would be on the road Monday, but that many of them usually got together on the first Saturday morning of each month, and that next Saturday they would be meeting. Danny told Ben that he was welcome to come by.

In the meantime, Ben gave a great deal of thought to the system and what shape it would eventually take. He began to peruse the systems literature. He was looking forward to meeting with Danny and his people. Maybe after this meeting he would have some better ideas and a sense of direction. Presently, he felt like he was treading water.

Ben arrived at the meeting a little early. He did not know most of the salespeople. Danny introduced him to them and proceeded to tell them that Ben wanted to develop a computer system to control the use of the telephone.

Ben laughed and said, "That's not quite right. I'm here to get some fresh ideas from you on how we can make the system serve Marketing better. I thought that if everyone is agreeable, we could have a brainstorming session to ferret out some of those ideas."

"During my analysis, I've called thirty or so customers to get their reaction on how well 'things' are handled at Pelican," Ben

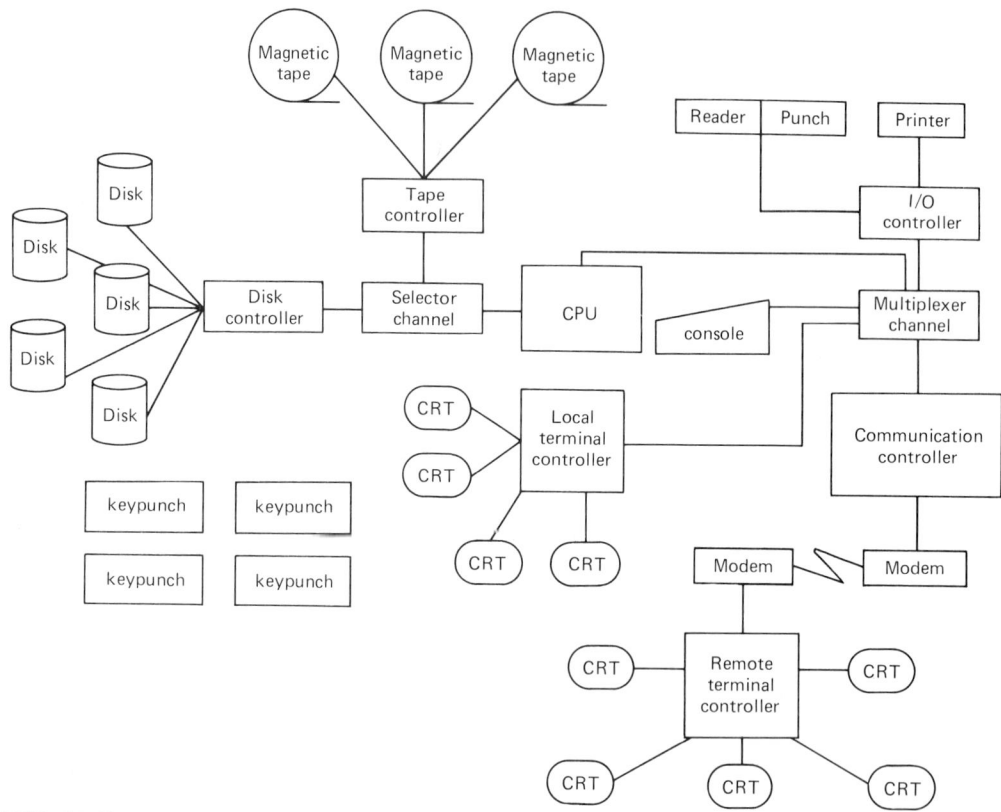

FIG. C2 Computer configuration at Pelican.

continued. "Most of these customers like the way delivery of product and other services are handled. They have few complaints about accounting. It's the 'little' things that bother them."

"For example," Ben stressed, "they say that they seldom receive acknowledgment of their orders. Also, they want early notification of new products and services. Some of them don't see their salesperson but every sixty to ninety days. Often, when they do see their salesperson, he or she doesn't have enough time to go over everything with them."

With the above as background, Ben stated that he wanted to get ideas from the group as to how they think the system could respond to these criticisms. He impressed on them that if the system could take care of routine chores, they would have more time for direct customer contact. Ben said he wanted their ideas to flow freely and they should not feel constrained by any preconceived notions.

Herman Dingle, one of the salespersons, said, "Most people think that salespeople have good memories. I don't. I have a lousy memory. I wonder if you could design a system to keep up with my appointments and remind me of such things as my customers' birthdays. I like to give them a call on their birthdays. It's good business."

Beverly Misty, another salesperson, said, "I would like to be able to call in 'notes' that I make about prospective customers I meet on the road. Maybe, the system could help qualify them as suspects or true prospects. If they turn out to be bona fide prospects, then someone in the system could write them a letter informing them about Pelican's products and services. I do some of this, but I don't have time to cover everything. Also, a follow-up call could be made as a courtesy and to get additional information about a product. This information could be kept in a file and a copy given to me. The more information I have about a prospect, the better."

"I hate to write all those routine letters to my customers every week," Melvin Comatose, another salesperson, interjected. "All of them say the same thing."

"How much time do you spend getting these letters out?" Ben asked.

"Ben, at least thirty or forty percent of my time is spent in nonsales work such as letter writing," Melvin responded. "Even worse, sometimes I forget to write a letter, or write the same letter to a customer more than once. All this routine work is the worst part of my job. I want to be out selling, not writing letters and maintaining filing cabinets."

Others echoed their agreement.

Tyrone Reynolds, considered to be Romeo of the sales staff, said, "I need a system to help keep up with the names and addresses of my girlfriends. I would like the system to schedule me at these addresses for the weekends. I'm tired of spending most of my weekends in places like Hondo, Texas."

Thomas Knapp, was was sitting in the back of the room, said, "This is the kind of bull you get during brainstorming sessions."

Ben countered, "Tyrone's remarks may have some relevance. Certainly, I will look into scheduling problems. Anyway, the whole reason for brainstorming is to generate ideas and note them no matter how ridiculous they seem."

Tyrone countered, "I don't think my ideas are so ridiculous."

A few more ideas were expressed and then the brainstorming session began to drift into another kind of Saturday morning sales meeting. Above the din, Ben tried to thank everyone for their participation, closed his briefcase, and left the room. As he was walking down the hall, he heard hurried footsteps approaching from the rear. He turned and saw that it was likeable, old Bud Wiser, the elder statesman of Pelican's sales force. Through hard breathing, Bud asked if he could take a few minutes of Ben's time. Ben said, "You bet."

Bud explained that he was getting tired of the road and had been planning for sometime to change jobs and get something closer to home. He suggested that he would be more than willing to consider any opening that might result from development of the new system. Bud said that he was especially interested in learning more about computers and still dealing with customers. Ben said that at this point, things were not clear in his mind how the system would turn out, but he would keep Bud in mind.

PREPARATION OF THE SYSTEMS ANALYSIS COMPLETION REPORT

After the brainstorming session was over and Ben had gotten back to his office, his head was literally buzzing with facts and ideas. For the first time since he began this systems project, he began to zero in on what kind of system might be workable and do something more than merely control telephone expenses. He knew that much work lay ahead to define the design blocks, but at least they were taking shape. Ben was ready to prepare the Systems Analysis Completion Report. He felt that he had done enough analysis and if everyone agreed with his report, he would, after additional research of the systems literature and consultation with vendors, proceed to general systems design. He felt pleased with himself because he had already conceptualized some alternative designs, although they were still hazy. What follows is the Systems Analysis Completion Report prepared by Ben.

SYSTEMS ANALYSIS COMPLETION REPORT

To: Martha Pringle, Patti Blake, Danny Loman

From: Ben Snow, Systems Analyst

Reason and Scope for Conducting the Analysis

Concern has been expressed about loose controls over telephone usage, payment of telephone bills, and allocation of telephone expenses to appropriate departments. An improved reporting system can be developed to alleviate this concern. Marketing has presented reasons for expanding the scope of this system to incorporate routine marketing chores. An attempt will be made to combine telephone and computer technology to handle most, if not all, of these chores. A general examination was made in other areas of the information system such as accounting and inventory control. It appears that these areas are working well, and no change to them is planned at this time.

Major Problems Identified

1. Insufficient allocation of expenses to appropriate departments.

2. Poor discipline in the use of the telephone system.
   a. Employees use the telephone to make personal long distance calls.
   b. Equipment installation and relocation are not controlled.
   c. Managers do not know their telephone expenses.
3. A large number of users are not aware of the availability of the WATS line.
4. Telephone bills are paid without verification.
5. Customer complaints and call-ins are handled improperly. Often, the switchboard operator has no one to transfer the calls to.
6. Routine communications with customers are treated in a haphazard way.
7. Background customer information is not systematically given to salespeople on the road.

Requirements of the System

Based on complete analysis, the new system should provide the same requirements as originally listed in the first report. Additional requirements have also been defined, based on what was learned in meetings with the staff. Following is a list of all requirements defined to date:

1. Improve financial controls.
2. Verify telephone bills.
3. Provide a way to allocate telephone expenses to departments based on their use.
4. Control equipment and service charges.
5. Handle all customer complaints.
6. Correspond and by other methods notify customers of new products, product changes, price changes, availability of new services, and so on. Routinely, acknowledge customers orders.
7. Collect data about old customers and prospective customers and provide information about them to appropriate salespeople.

Critical Assumptions

A number of things must be present to make the system viable. Since I have no control over some of these, to proceed further on this project, I must assume that the following will be in place and will be done.

1. Sufficient funds will be available to develop and support the system if it proves to be cost/effective.
2. Managers will support the systems development with time and personnel.
3. Personnel from the computer center will be made available for programming, equipment evaluation, and other tasks for systems development.
4. Personnel will be provided to operate and manage the new system.
5. All personnel who provide input to the system will do so when required. For example, sales personnel will provide data from the field and the switchboard operator will log and time all long distance and collect calls.
6. Department managers will be motivated to control telephone usage in their departments if provided with timely and accurate information.

General Recommendation

At this point, I recommend that we proceed further. I believe that a system can be developed that will meet the requirements outlined in this report. The system will integrate data processing with word processing. A coordinator of the system is needed to answer customer complaints and, in general, manage the system. I recommend Bud Wiser for this position.

Several leading vendors of word processing equipment, desktop computers, and software packages should be asked to demonstrate and explain their products. These systems' compatibility with the present computer configuration will be evaluated. Such attributes as growth potential, cost/effectiveness, and maintainability of these systems will also be checked. At this time, it is not known whether or not a standalone system is appropriate. It may be more feasible from a technical and operational viewpoint to interface the new system with the computer center to gain additional storage space. General design alternatives will be presented in my next report.

CHAPTER

12

General Systems Design

12.1 ▪ INTRODUCTION

Systems design is concerned with the development of specifications for the proposed new system or subsystem which satisfy the demands identified during the systems analysis phase. Eventually, therefore, the systems design becomes a detailed elaboration of the Systems Analysis Completion Report. In this chapter broad principles of systems design are presented, and in Chapter 14 detailed design considerations are discussed. The flowchart of steps applicable to general systems design are shown in Figure 12.1.

12.2 ▪ THE DESIGN PROCESS

In analyzing the design process we will define what it means to design, summarize the elements of knowledge the systems analyst requires for designing a system, describe the basic steps in the design process, and present an approach to systems design.

Definition of Design

Systems design can be defined as the drawing, planning, sketching, or arranging of many separate elements into a viable, unified whole. Whereas the systems analysis phase answers the questions of what the system is doing and what it should be doing to meet user requirements, the systems design phase is concerned with how the system is developed to meet these requirements. In the design process, the analyst develops alternative solutions and eventually ascertains the best design solution. The design phase is technically oriented to the extent that the analyst must answer the question: "How do we do it?" On the other hand, design is an art, and creatively oriented, to the extent that the analyst continually asks: "What if?" and "Why not?" questions.

At a broad systems design level, conceptual specifications are prepared which outline a complete systems design proposal. At this point, the design proposal is reviewed against the detailed values of the demand blocks as determined during the systems analysis phase. It can be cancelled, modified, or continued. If the systems work continues, then the next level of design is concerned with detailed technical design specifications such as, selection of I/O media, file size, controls, programs, and so forth. Once again, based on further systems work and additional information, a decision is made by management to cancel, modify, or continue the project. If the project is continued or modified, then the next step in systems work is implementation, a subject discussed in Chapter 16.

The Elements of Knowledge Related to the Design Process

To participate in the design of an information system, an analyst must be knowledgable about a variety of elements as illustrated in Figure 12.2. The bulk of this knowledge is acquired during the systems analysis phase and should be readily recognized as the detailed values for the demand blocks discussed throughout this text. To satisfy these demands, it is necessary to organize or arrange a variety of data processing resources. Thus, knowledge of the capabilities of data processing resources is an essential prerequisite to beginning the design process. An understanding and an adeptness in using various design tools such as charting, decision tables, and modeling facilitate transforming concepts and ideas into physical activities. Finally, an individual's powers of reason and creativity applied to these elements of knowledge produce the system's design.

The Basic Steps in the Design Process

In practice the application of the design process is an iterative endeavor. As each of the design process elements is addressed by the analyst, he or she is usually forced to reexamine whatever structure or relationship had been developed to date, and to modify it to satisfy the new requirement. This repetitive activity continues until each dimension of the proposed system has been considered and a final design proposal is formulated. The basic steps in the design process can be

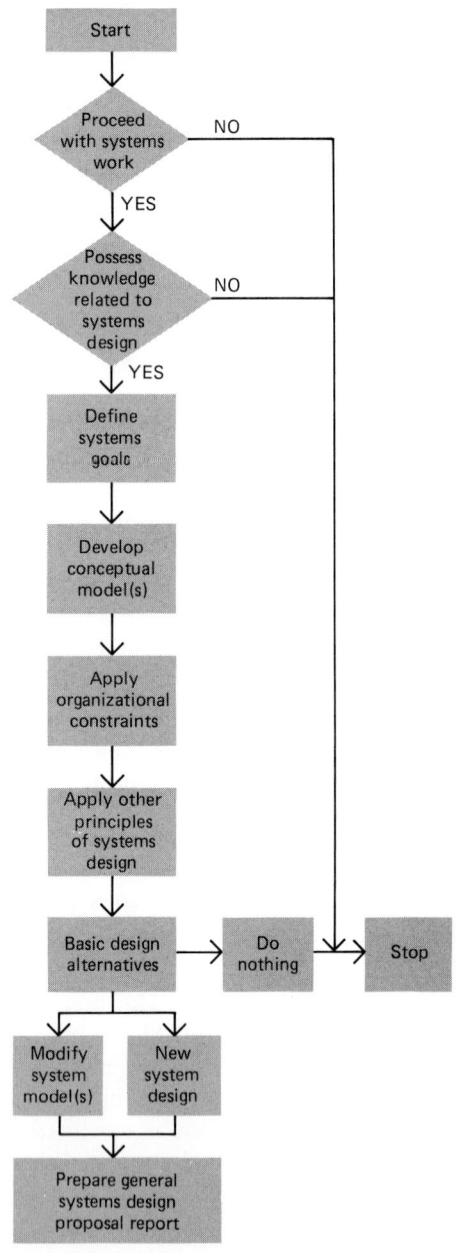

FIG. 12.1 A flowchart of steps applicable to general systems design.

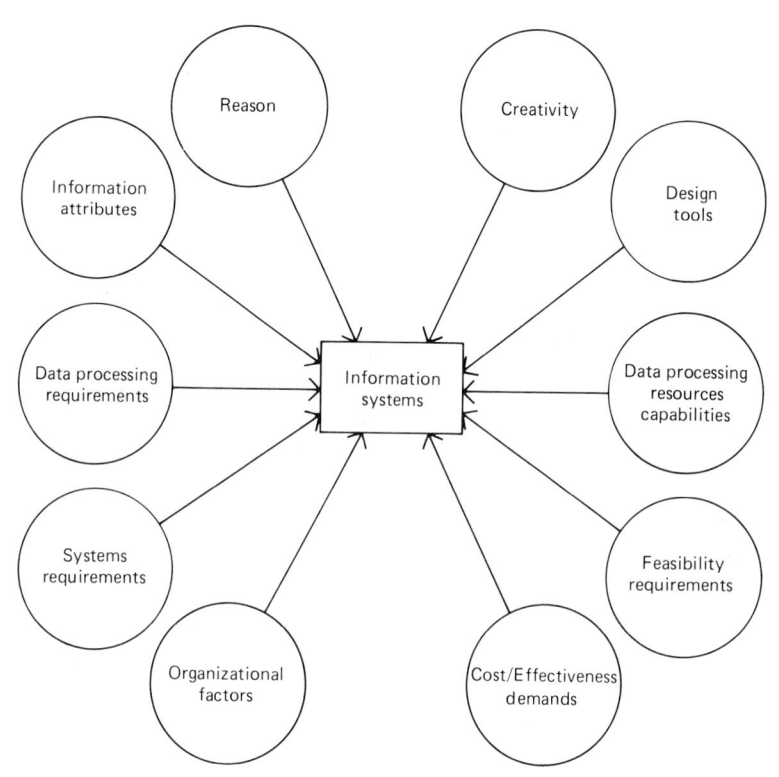

FIG. 12.2 The elements comprising the design process for an information system.

termed: (1) defining the systems goal, (2) developing a conceptual model, (3) applying organizational constraints, (4) defining data processing activities, and (5) preparing the Systems Design Proposal Report, which contains a broad definition of the design blocks presented earlier. The first three steps noted will be discussed next. The remaining steps will be discussed in the following sections.

1. *Defining the systems goal.* Defining the systems goal results from reviewing and evaluating the requirements described in the Systems Analysis Completion Report. It is important to note that the systems goal is not always equated with a specific user information requirement. The goal of a system can usually be defined by abstracting certain common characteristics from all of the information requirements. The difference between the systems goal and specific user or systems requirements can be illustrated using an accounts payable system. The goals of an accounts payable system can be stated as: (1) to maintain efficiently an accurate and timely account of monies owed by the organization to its vendors; (2) to provide internal control mechanisms that will ensure the reliability of the system performance; and (3) to produce a variety of technical, tactical and strategic information to support the organization's overall objectives and operations.

By definition, the goal of the accounts payable system is not subject to change. The content and format of each specific input, output, and processing requirement, however, is subject to change as organizational needs change. Let us examine briefly the various alternatives the analyst might consider when designing the specific design blocks required to support the systems goals.

The basic inputs to the accounts payable system are identified in Figure 12.3 as the purchase order, the receiving report, and the vendor's invoice. Purchase order data can be input to the system directly from a computer-based purchase order system, or it can be input via a hardcopy of the purchase order. The receiving report can be input via a hardcopy document or from an online terminal at the receiving depot. Finally, the vendor's invoice can also be input either online or offline. The specific data content can also vary in two different ways. First, the purchase order can contain all descriptive input data, while the receiving report and invoice could contain only variable data, such as actual quantity received and dollars owed. Second, the quantity of descriptive data associated with the payables function can vary from that required to satisfy basic technical requirements to that used to produce related tactical and strategic information.

The basic technical information produced by the system includes the check to vendor and the accounts payable financial entry for the balance sheet. The number and composition of control reports (e.g., input registers, error reports) is dependent on both the stated needs of the users as well as the type of data processing logic included in the system. Finally, tactical and strategic information outputs (e.g., vendor performance, departmental usage) will vary continuously with the operating environment and demands of the organization as a whole.

When a system is designed to attain a goal, it generally provides some flexibility as to how this goal can be reached. This built-in flexibility results in the system being able to absorb continous modifications

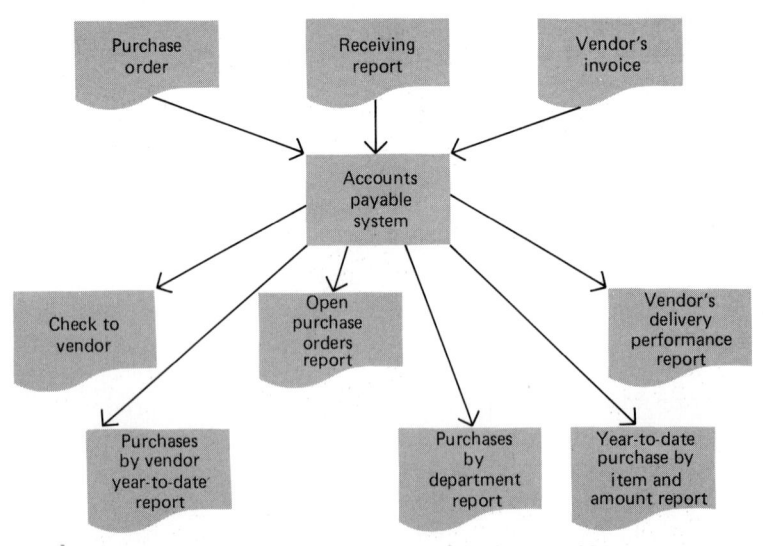

FIG. 12.3 A conceptual design model of an accounts payable system.

from changing user requirements. On the other hand, when a system is designed to produce specific output(s), it is likely that it will have to be redesigned each time there is a significant change in the format, or the content, of that output.

2. *Develop a Conceptual Model.* Developing a conceptual design model of a system is the second step in the design process. Often, if the analyst is experiencing difficulty in identifying a system's goal, then an attempt to develop a conceptual design model will aid in defining the goal. Figure 12.3 represents a conceptual model of an accounts payable system. To constuct this conceptual model of the payables function does not necessarily require the analyst to review any specific organizational requirements, unless the classical accounts payable function is not understood. When the analyst considers the specific values of the demand blocks as identified in the systems analysis phase, the model can be quite detailed, as illustrated in Figure 12.4.

3. *Applying Organizational Constraints.* Developing and operating information systems requires the extensive use of organizational resources. Many activities are pursued within the organization which also require use of organizational resources. Thus, the information system must compete with these other activities to obtain necessary resources. Organizational resources are usually allocated to those activities which will provide the greatest cost/effectiveness to the organization.

Applying systems requirements to the development, performance, or operation of the information system is management's technique for attempting to obtain the maximum cost/effectiveness from the information system. This is also applicable when the analyst must use data processing resources that are less than what available technology allows.

The task of obtaining a good or optimum mix of resources and requirements is an extremely significant problem confronting the analyst in the systems design phase. The overall objectives of a particular systems design are usually quite complex, vary widely, and depend on specific requirements.

The short-term view normally considers cost, performance, and reliability. The long-term view, on the other hand, considers the installation schedule, the developmental and operational resources, the flexibility of the system to accommodate changing user demands, the growth rate of the organization, and the life expectancy of the system.

All of the above-mentioned systems requirements are interrelated. For example, it may be that more flexibility and higher reliability can be achieved if the cost factors are increased. Conversely, the cost of the system can be decreased at the expense of flexibility and reliability. Depending upon the application and management needs, some systems stress reliability, others flexibility, and so on. Because of these different emphases, it is necessary to consider each system separately and to evaluate the relative importance of the various requirements in their proper perspective. Models from other organizations, manuals, and texts can serve as guides, but the major part of every system has to be designed to meet the particular requirements of each individual organization and its managers. An illustration of how the different requirements are related to provide optimization of a system is shown in Figure 12.5.

The inputs to the information system model illustrated are: the system's requirements; and data processing resources in the form of people, machines, money, material,

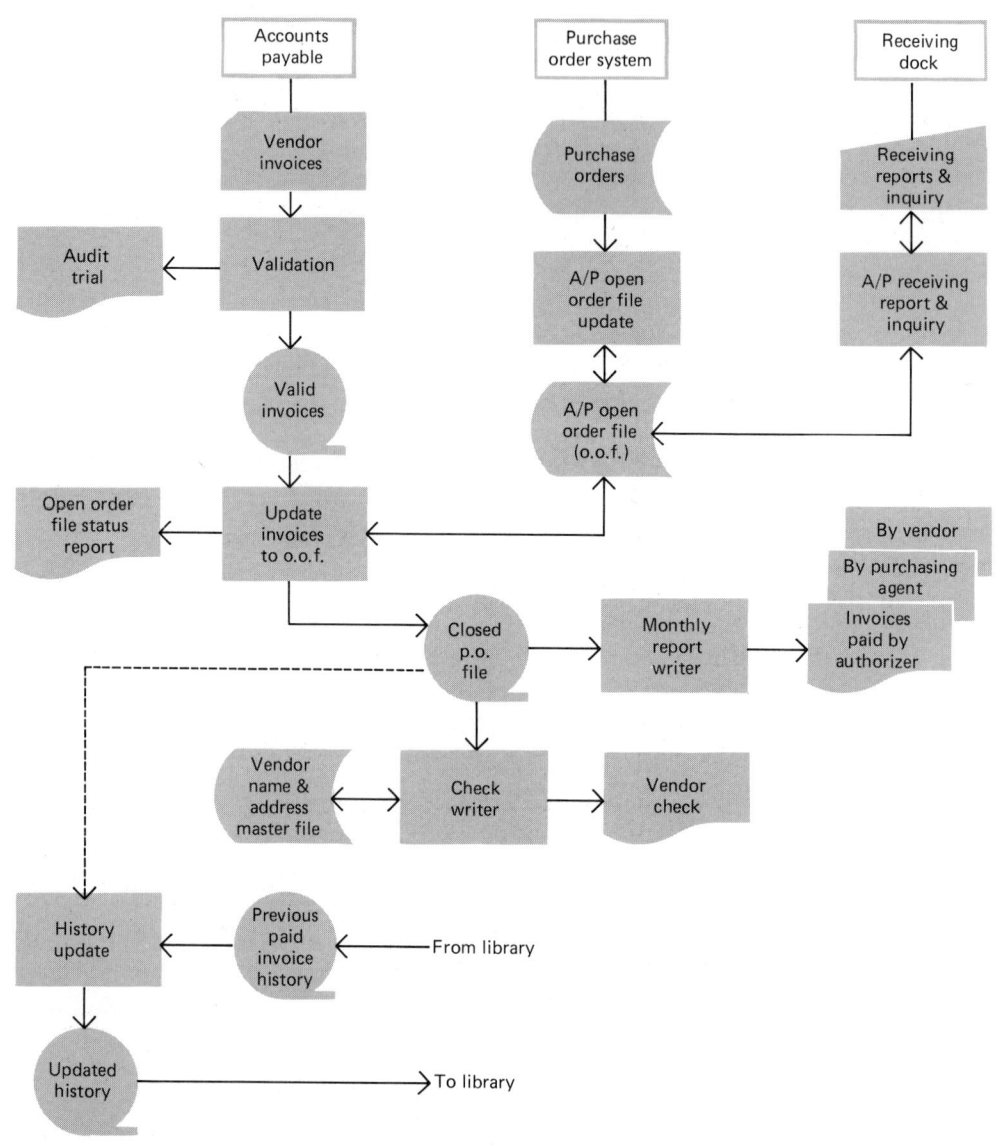

FIG. 12.4 A detailed design of an accounts payable system.

and methods. A weighting factor is applied to each requirement, giving a set of weighted system requirements. This results in the criteria for an optimum system for the particular organization. The derived weighting factors for performance, reliability, cost, installation schedules, maintainability, flexibility, growth potential, and life expectancy, are denoted W_R, W_C, W_I, W_M, W_F, W_G, and W_L, respectively. It is from the

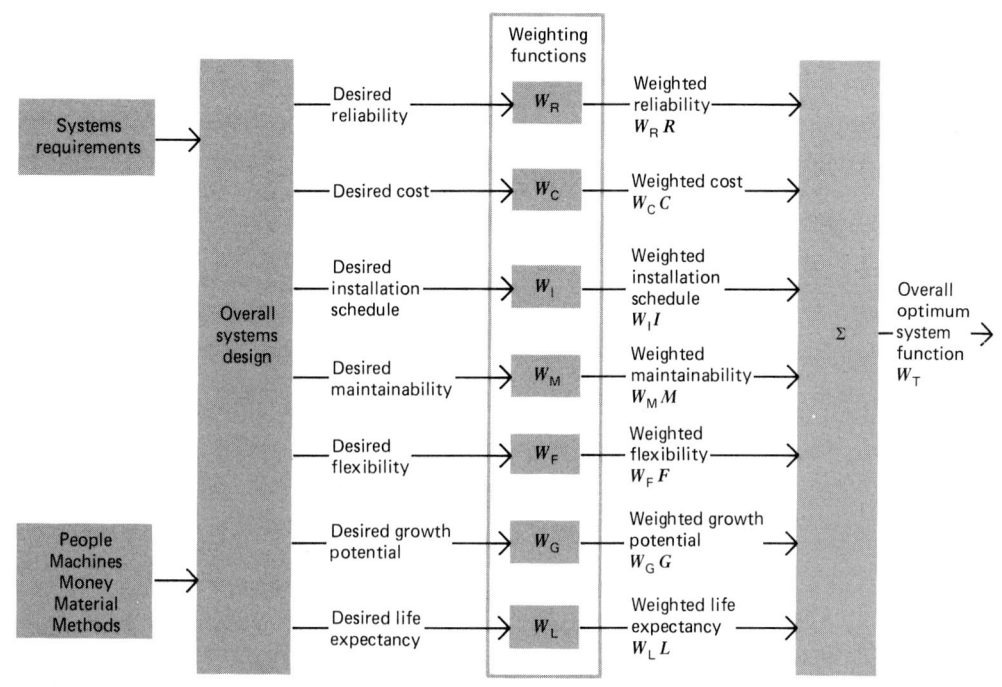

FIG. 12.5 Model for optimum systems design.

output of these weighted objectives that W_T, the total optimum system function is derived.[1]

For example, in a dynamic, growing organization, an optimum match of a proposed computer configuration to information systems requirements means that the power and capabilities of the computer configuration should exceed by some margin the present information system requirements. This margin allows the growing information systems requirements to be met adequately during the useful life of the computer configuration. Otherwise, growing system requirements will soon produce processing demands that cannot be met by a computer configuration precisely matched to today's requirements.

Predicting the useful life of the computer configuration is a critical factor in optimum matching and must be coupled with a clear understanding of the systems requirements. Otherwise, one of two conditions will exist: (1) overmatching, where the organization is paying excessively for capabilities not needed; or (2) undermatching, where the organization is paying for inadequate capabilities, and the system is growth-restricted.

An Approach to Systems Design

Many experienced analysts believe that obtaining an adequate definition of user requirements is the key activity in preparing

---

[1]Adapted from Stanley M. Shinners, *Techniques of System Engineering*, New York: McGraw-Hill Book Co., 1967, Ch. 1. Used with permission of McGraw-Hill Book Company.

General Systems Design

design alternatives. They argue that if user requirements, in the form of detail specifications, are miscommunicated or omitted from the proposed system, costly modifications and corrections will be required later, and users will fail to gain many of the possible benefits of the proposed system.

One approach that is directed toward defining users' needs is HIPO.[2] HIPO, an acronym for **hierarchy plus input, processing, and output,** is a graphical method of describing a system, program, or procedure in terms of functions to be performed.

The hierarchy portion of HIPO involves a tree structure of functions or actions. Top-level functions contain the control logic.

Lower-level functions, which are subsets of higher-level functions, contain increasing degrees of detail.

Each function in the structure is named by an objective or by the data affected (e.g., payroll master, year-to-date gross pay, overtime rate, etc.), and described by a verb or an action (e.g., update, compute, revise, etc.). To complete the visual description, every function has a corresponding input, process, and output.

For example, consider the HIPO of an inventory control application as illustrated in Figure 12.6. At the top of the hierarchy, the name and the purpose of the task are identified. The function, "Maintain Inventory Control," is then divided into subfunctions devoted to obtaining the input ("Gather Inventory Data"), processing it ("Update Inventory Master"), and generating output ("Procedure Order Status Listing"). Then these subfunctions are subdivided further.

[2]Summarized from Martha Nyvall Jones, "HIPO for Developing Specifications," *Datamation,* March 1976, pp. 112–114 and 121, 125. Reprinted with permission of *Datamation®,* copyright © 1976 by Technical Publishing Company, Greenwich, Connecticut 06830.

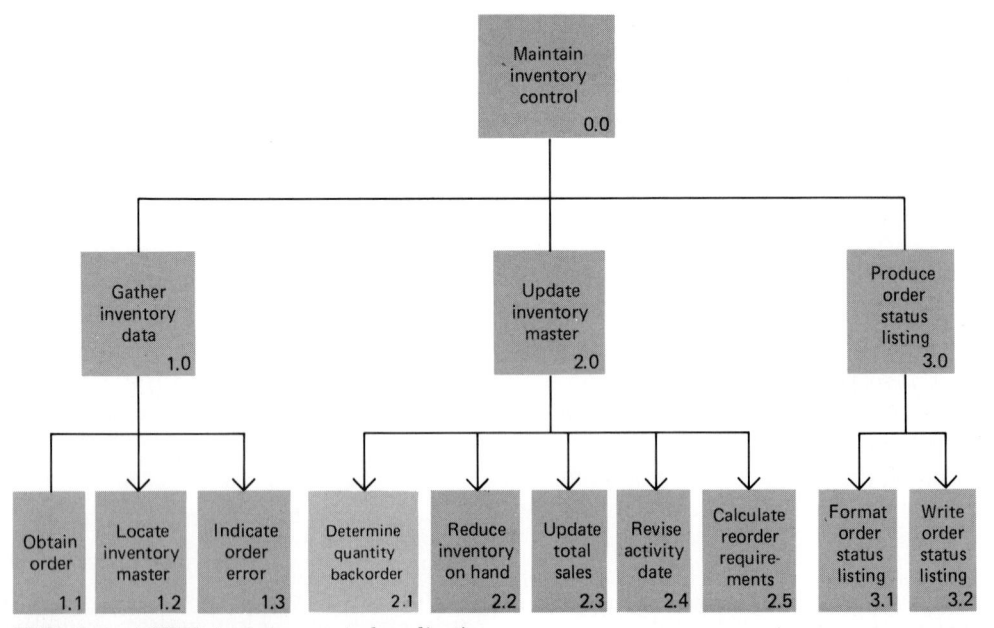

FIG. 12.6 A HIPO inventory control application.

Exploring the function "Update Inventory Master" (as illustrated in Figure 12.7) reveals the following details:

1. The master field of ON-HAND and output field of QNTY-REQD are used in the first process to produce the output field of QNTY-AVAIL.
2. The subfunctions "Reduce inventory on hand," "Update total sales," and "Revise activity data" are performed sequentially.
3. The subfunction "Calculate reorder requirements" is performed conditionally (notice the arrow to it in Figure 12.6), depending on the master fields of ON-HAND, ON-ORD, and REORD-LVL.

To begin defining the functions required, the analyst should discuss with users the generalities and desired outputs of the proposed system. By clarifying vague areas, a preliminary list of probable functions can be established. Working from this tentative hierarchy of functions the analyst should next determine what circumstances will trigger the performance of each function, what data will be acted on, and what output will be produced from the processing that will occur. At this point the analyst should be alert to the appearance of new functions and the need for alteration of relationships among functions. Control functions should be established at upper levels; function names should reflect the actions taking place and the objects being acted upon; and the hierarchy should have the correct number of levels and subfunctions. Once the analyst is satisfied that little more can be revised, a walkthrough meeting should be scheduled with the user. At this time, HIPO is evaluated critically, from top to bottom, for errors and omissions.

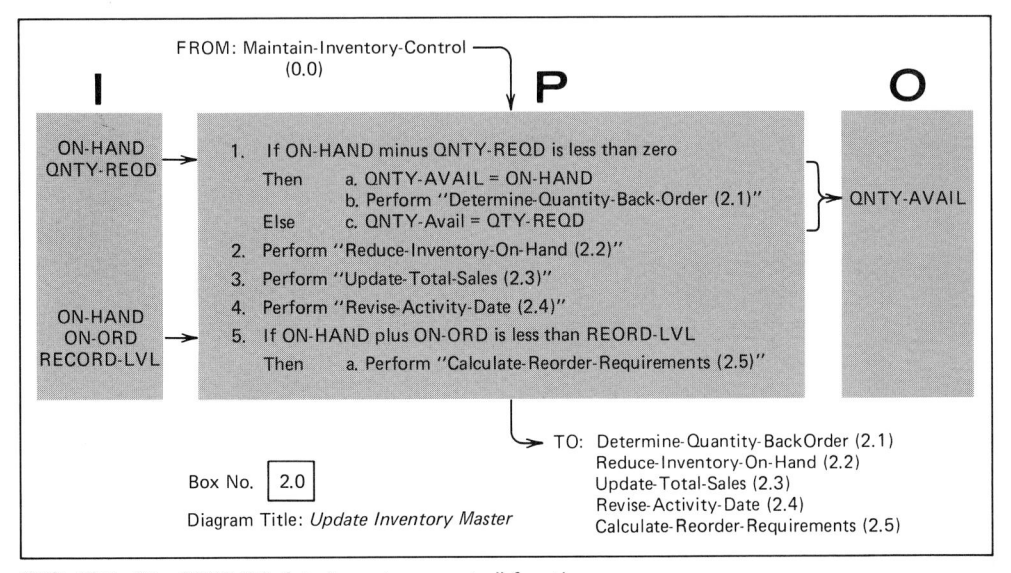

FIG. 12.7 The HIPO "Update inventory master" function.

12.3 ▪ BASIC DESIGN ALTERNATIVES AND THE GENERAL SYSTEMS DESIGN PROPOSAL REPORT

Thus far it has been assumed that the identified systems requirements, and users' information needs, must be met by the design of a new system. However, this is not always true. The analyst should be aware of other available alternatives. Moreover, when a new systems design is required, additional decisions are made concerning the manner in which the new system is to be developed and operated. In this section we will examine the basic design alternatives available to the analyst as well as some major guidelines for preparing the General Systems Design Proposal Report.

Basic Design Alternatives

The analyst has at least three basic design alternatives each time a set of systems and user requirements are evaluated: (1) to recommend doing nothing, (2) to modify an existing system, and (3) to design a new system.

1. *The do nothing alternative.* In every systems decision as to how to satisfy users' information requirements or requests for systems improvements, the analyst has an opportunity to recommend that no action be taken at this time. The reasons for choosing this alternative include: (1) poor identification and definition of requirements or needs; (2) a determination that it is infeasible to develop a meaningful system or solution to the user's needs; (3) other systems requests have higher priorities and developmental resources are fully allocated; or (4) the user's needs as stated are not real needs.
2. *Modify an existing system alternative.* The majority of all systems investigations conducted in organizations include some consideration of existing systems and subsystems. To effectively satisfy new or revised user requirements, the analyst often recommends modifying existing systems rather that designing new systems. Depending on the size of the organization and the particular subsystem being evaluated, systems modifications can have a larger impact on an organization than the development of an entirely new subsystem. This impact can result from either the size of the systems effort expended or from the change resulting in the organization.

   When systems support is applied to solving an organizational problem, the emphasis is on immediate results. Thus changes are often implemented to existing systems until a new system can be defined and developed. In addition, the level of information systems development that exists today in many medium-to-large organizations has reached a point where new user demands often require relatively small changes to data collection and storage elements, and the emphasis is placed on accessing available data in a new format or on a more timely basis.
3. *Design a new system alternative.* The final alternative available to the analyst for recommendation is to design a new system to satisfy users' requirements. This alternative is obviously the most complex and difficult solution to implement. This alternative can be viewed as a combination of two further choices of action. When an analyst recommends that a new system be implemented, a decision must be made whether this system is to be developed from the very beginning, or whether an acceptable system can be purchased from other sources. Traditionally, this is termed the "make or buy" decision.

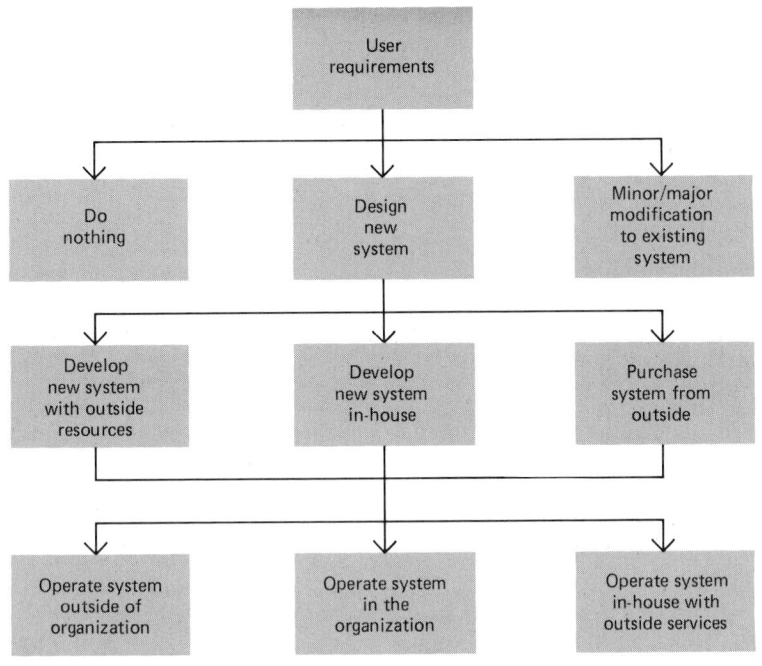

FIG. 12.8 A chart showing the major design alternatives available to the analyst.

Summary Points of Basic Design Alternatives

Figure 12.8 is a chart which demonstrates the various decision points that analysts must address themselves to when recommending the best use of organization resources to satisfy user information requirements.

Analysis of Make or Buy Decision

Make or buy decisions are not new to the management process. Manufacturing management continually review their operations to determine if a certain product or assembly can be manufactured as efficiently as it can be purchased. In the area of information systems, however, the make or buy decision is becoming increasingly important. The development of computer-based information systems is an expensive proposition in any organization when weighed against the resources available to that organization. Until recently, only very large organizations could afford extensive computer-based systems development. As a result, many consulting firms and service bureaus have been established to provide data processing systems for implementation in an organization. In many cases these firms actually assume responsibility for operating a selected portion of an organization's data processing requirements.

But over time, as the manufacturers of data processing equipment, particularly computers, were able to greatly reduce the initial cost of equipment, many smaller organizations acquired the equipment necessary to process their own data. The cost of redoing the payroll or accounts payable applications in every organization (i.e., "reinventing the wheel"), however, became even more expensive. Consequently, organizations began to purchase their basic data processing systems from consultants, computer manufacturers, and software houses, whose primary function is to design, develop, and/or operate data processing systems for universal application.

The make or buy decision is less important in large organizations or where an information requirement is somewhat unique or unusual. In most medium-to-small-sized organizations, however, the choice between making or buying, for at least the basic data processing system, represents a very important decision.

The advantages and disadvantages of purchasing or building a specific data processing system or subsystem are illustrated in Figure 12.9.

Preparing the General Systems Design Proposal Report

The **General Systems Design Proposal Report** is prepared to communicate to management and users in the organization how, at a broad level, the designed system will satisfy their information, systems, and data processing requirements. Assuming, at this point, that management authorizes continuation of the project, it is the forerunner of the Final Systems Design Report. Otherwise, the project is modified to the extent that the analyst must retrace some steps, or it is abandoned. The following guidelines are offered for assistance to the analyst in preparing the General Systems Design Proposal Report:

1. Restate the reason(s) for initiating systems work, including specific objectives. Relate all original user requirements and objectives to the present systems design proposal.

2. Prepare a concise but thorough model of the proposed systems design. Always try to include design alternatives from which management can make choices, rather than presenting only one approach. Not only does the presentation of alternatives allow management to choose, but often it

In-House Development	Purchase System
Advantages	
1. System tailored to requirements.	1. System tested and proven.
2. High degree of design integration possible.	2. Implementation time reduced.
3. Optimum use of organizational resources possible.	3. Advantages/disadvantages known.
4. Advanced state of the art techniques utilized.	4. Developmental resources freed for other efforts.
	5. Usually less cost.
Disadvantages	
1. Lengthy developmental time.	1. Does not meet all requirements.
2. Costs and benefits uncertain.	2. Inefficient use of resources.
3. Developmental talents are scarce and not always available.	3. Maintenance and modification are a greater problem.
4. Debugging and other problems occur long after implementation.	4. Less integration with other systems.
5. Usually more expensive.	5. Demoralizing to developmental staff.
	6. Generally, not latest state of the art.

FIG. 12.9 Advantages and disadvantages related to the systems make or buy decision.

can be shown that a different alternative will make a significantly different impact on the organization. For example, design proposal B may meet 90 percent of the requirements of design proposal A, but B may cost only 40 percent of A. The analyst should never get into a situation where the only choice is one particular design or nothing.

3. Show all of the resources required to implement and maintain each alternative.
4. Identify any critical assumptions or unresolved problems that may affect the final systems design.

Certainly, the format of the General Systems Design Proposal Report is subject to wide variation from organization to organization. The main thing to keep in mind when preparing a design proposal, however, is that the person(s) who must authorize the development of one of the alternatives must have sufficient facts on which to base a decision.

12.4 ▪ SYSTEMS DESIGN— AN EXAMPLE

Throughout this chapter the general guidelines and method to be used in designing systems have been discussed. In this section the design of a system that is required in almost all organizations, the Accounts Receivable/Credit System, is examined.

Accounts Receivable/Credit System— An Overview

From a financial viewpoint, the accounts receivable system is designed to maintain a permanent record of monies owed the organization by its customers. The credit function may or may not be performed in conjunction with the accounts receivable operation. The purpose of the credit function is to control the issuance of credit to customers as well as to follow up the collection of monies owed. As a rule, the credit function is the primary user of technical and tactical information produced from the data accumulated by accounts receivable.

Many organizations use the cash flow analysis concept for the development of both short- and long-range planning. This strategic information can, at least in part, be obtained from an Accounts Receivable/Credit system.

Accounts Receivable/Credit— Data Collection

The two primary inputs to the Accounts Receivable/Credit System are the customer payments for goods and the organization's invoices to its customers. Figure 12.10 illustrates how these data are collected and input to the system.

Customer payments are entered to the accounts receivable Open Item File via online keyboard devices. At this time the operator enters the account number, payment amount, and the document number of the item being paid. If a problem occurs, such as input with an invalid account number, then an error message is produced and the transaction is voided. The operator can verify the account number or place the payment document in a manually maintained file of problem payments. A second level of reconciliation would have to occur before that payment could be entered into the system.

At the completion of inputting specified payment batches, the operator requests a control total from the system and to this total adds any error documents. This com-

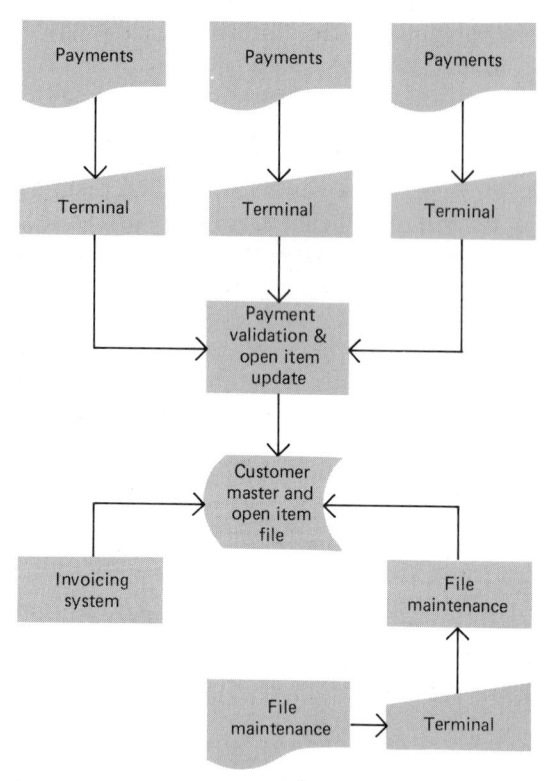

FIG. 12.10 Illustration of the accounts receivable data collection operation.

bined total must equal the batch control total given to the operator by another function (e.g., accounting).

The second primary input to the system is the organization's invoice. In our systems design note that this input is a direct update to the accounts receivable Open Item File from the billing system. In other words, as an invoice is produced for the customer the invoice data required for accounts receivable processing is produced and updated simultaneously. This integration of data flow eliminates the need to produce an additional copy of the invoice for internal use and a subsequent reentering of this data into the computer portion of the accounts receivable system. Absolute financial control is maintained by a daily comparison of the total (dollar and quantity amounts) of invoices produced in the billing system to the total (dollar and quantity amounts) of invoices updating the accounts receivable system.

A secondary input to the system is file maintenance. In our design this is shown as being an online operation; however, it could as easily be performed in an offline batch mode. This input allows any file descrepancies caused by erroneous input to be corrected.

Accounts Receivable/Credit—Data Base

As Figures 12.10 through 12.12 illustrate, the data base contains a (1) Open Item File, (2) Closed Item File, and (3) Customer Master File.

The Open Item File is designed for direct updating and access. All three figures show this file as being resident on a DASD. The

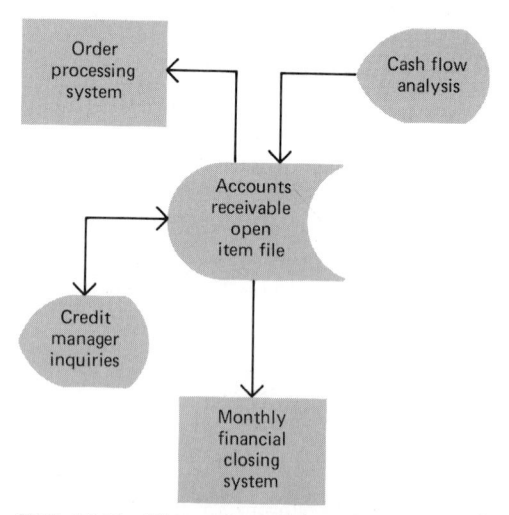

FIG. 12.11 Illustration of the online status of the accounts receivable open item file. This file provides management with significant tactical information for short-term planning and control.

Closed Item File, however, is shown as being a tape file, which is primarily oriented to sequential or offline batch processing. Figure 12.12 shows the ability to interrogate the Closed Item File from a remote terminal. The difference is reflected in the fact that the Open Item File is used for technical requirements, whereas the Closed Item File is used to produce tactical and/or strategic information requirements as needed.

The Customer Master File is a source of reference data for our system. Thus, it is shown here only as a source of information with no updating or maintenance requirements. Again, this systems design demonstrates an integration of systems as being desirable, since duplicate data processing operations pertaining to customer data have been eliminated.

Accounts Receivable/Credit—Output

In our systems design, examples of the various types of information that can be produced, as well as the different ways in which it can be represented, have been provided.

Technical information is provided to the order processing system (Figure 12.11) in various ways. When a customer order is entered, the order processing system uses the Customer Master File to determine the customer's account balance. The account balance, in conjunction with a preestablished credit limit field on the customer master file,

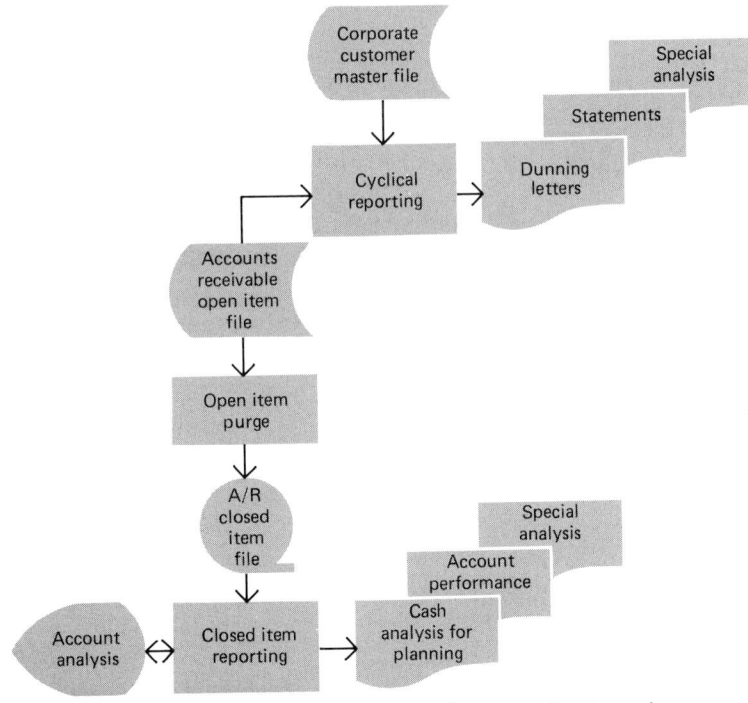

FIG. 12.12 An accounts receivable system which provides strategic information as well as meets technical requirements.

for example, permits automatic credit checking on every order processed. Additionally, the credit manager has the capability of interrogating open items for an indepth analysis of one or more customer accounts. Routine technical requirements such as dunning letters and customer statements are also produced by the system. In these latter cases, however, the processing is accomplished offline.

Tactical and strategic information, representing cash flow and payment performance, is also produced both offline and online for management's use. For example, sales management can see what effect the establishment of a service charge would have on cash flow. Another example might be to assess the effect of a special marketing promotion for smaller accounts. The payment performance of small accounts might affect adversely the short-term cash flow, in which case management might have to look to another source of short-term financing.

Accounts Receivable/Credit—Summary

The accounts receivable system, traditionally viewed by management as a necessary bookkeeping evil, can become the key element supporting technical, tactical, and strategic information requirements. Unless the systems analyst is able to show management how the use of new technology can be profitable, not only from the standpoint of reducing operating cost, but also in providing an opportunity to produce needed tactical and strategic information systems, many organizations will continue to operate without this valuable resource.

Another Example

A local business has installed a large time-sharing computer facility available for use by families. Figure 12.13 illustrates the proposed general systems design. Each family leases a small CRT terminal and keyboard connected to this facility. Lease payments by a family are based on the terminal, CPU time, storage costs, and consultation services. The system provides various analyses of expenses versus budget, a worksheet for income tax preparation, other operating information, and a complete library of video games. A systems analyst is hired to prepare a General Systems Design Proposal Report to be used in presentation to prospective users. What follows is an example of this report. In actual practice, several alternative designs would be prepared.

GENERAL DESIGN

① INPUT

    A. Each family enters their budget forecasts by account numbers at least monthly. Data entries required include:
- account number
- account name
- dollars per month (maximum 12 months)

The system automatically updates forecasted expenses each month as they are entered, and tracks year-to-date expenses.

    B. Actual expenses are entered as incurred. Update may occur immediately, daily, weekly, or monthly. In some instances, these expenses may be recorded by the system automatically (see other output).

② PROCESSING
   A. Each user is trained to use the system. Thirty minutes of training is sufficient.
   B. A background form appears on the terminal. All a user has to do is "fill in the blanks."
   C. Budget models and programming are handled by the staff of the computer service company.

③ DATE BASE
   A. Physical files are stored on a DASD.
   B. Each family is furnished the following three logical files:
      1. The Budget Master File contains the annual budget data as well as the actual expenses (summarized) incurred by account. This file is organized indexed sequentially to support both sequential and direct access. The records in this file are owners of the records in the Expense Detail File.
      2. The Expense Detail File contains all individual expense records either input to the system or generated by the system. This file is organized randomly.
      3. The Address File is accessed by the Budget Master File and contains the address for all the expense detail records that support a given budget master record.

④ CONTROL
   A. System controls include the following:
      1. A highly trained, professional staff.
      2. A set of contingency plans in case of system failure.
      3. Various input controls.
      4. Programming controls, such as limit checks and arithmetic proof.
      5. Data base controls, which include copies of all files stored in an underground storage facility. Moreover, all logical files have a lockout system to prevent unauthorized access.
      6. The central computer facility is housed in an environmentally secure location.
   B. Terminal control is achieved by issuing all users personal identification numbers and passwords.

⑤ OUTPUT
   A. A variance report is produced by comparing budgeted with actual expenses. Output is produced either by direct inquiry from the family terminal, or as the result of the system monitoring expenses related to budget and automatically notifying the user of significant variances.
   B. In the event a user wants to see a projection of expenses to budget estimates for the remaining part of the year, a request is made of various simulated expense projections. The system can also be queried to provide a detailed account of transactions affecting a given account.
   C. The accumulation of expenses reported in a calendar year permits the system to produce a simulated detail income tax return. Output is achieved by relating the expense account codes in the Budget Master File to an Income Tax Schedule Coding System, updated and maintained by the service company management.
   D. Other optional features include such things as automatic check writing. Certain family obligations that are constant from month to month (e.g., utilities, insurance payments,

loan obligations, rent or mortgage payments) are paid automatically by the system. The family is billed by the system for the total value of checks it issued, plus a service charge. Expenses are updated to each account as they occur, thus eliminating the need for reentry of each expense item by the family.

⑥ DATA PROCESSING RESOURCES

Each family is required to lease a CRT and keyboard for input/output purposes. A computer with telecommunication capabilities is furnished by the service company. A multiplexer or front-end processor handles communication and switching requirements.

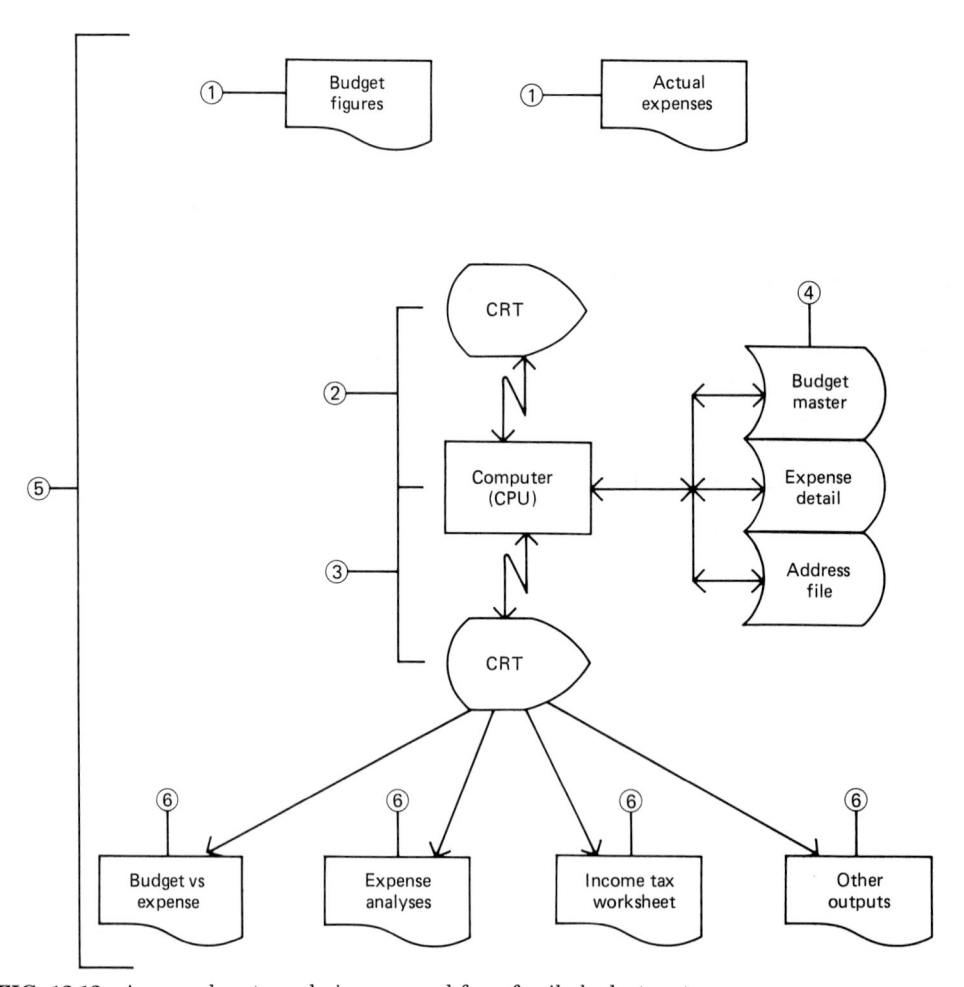

FIG. 12.13 A general systems design proposal for a family budget system.

SUMMARY

General systems design entails the bringing together of separate elements into a viable whole and illustrating how something purposeful can be accomplished. Basic steps in the design process include: (1) definition of systems objectives, (2) development of conceptual design models, and (3) application of organizational constraints.

Design alternatives include: (1) do nothing (no change), (2) systems modification, and (3) new systems design. The final step in general systems design is the preparation of the General Systems Design Proposal Report.

REVIEW QUESTIONS

12.1 Explain what is meant by the term "design."

12.2 What types of knowledge must a systems analyst possess to successfully design an information system?

12.3 Distinguish between user requirements and systems requirements.

12.4 List and explain the basic steps in the design process.

12.5 Compare and contrast systems requirements with organizational constraints.

12.6 List the steps an analyst should follow when defining a system using the HIPO approach.

12.7 List and explain the basic design alternatives.

12.8 Describe the logic behind the "make or buy" decision, as it pertains to the development of information systems.

12.9 What is the primary purpose of the General Systems Design Proposal Report? In your own words, what should this report include?

QUESTIONS FOR DISCUSSION

12.1 Compare and contrast the design of an information system with the design of an automobile. With a political system.

12.2 "There is only one real resource, and that is money." Discuss this comment.

12.3 Identify at least one major difficulty an analyst might experience in using conceptual design models.

12.4 The following is a comment made by a middle manager: "I just attended a presentation by systems regarding our new sales reporting system. They are 'blue skying' again." Discuss fully.

12.5 "We will have a new system within five months of starting work and the president will be pleased and satisfied; that is, until she understands what it costs to operate the system." Based on this comment, what criteria were given priority in selecting the final design?

12.6 After having viewed a series of flowcharts reflecting segments of a new system proposal report, the following remark was made: "The design of the system is basically the same as the existing system but with up-to-date technology." Comment on this remark.

12.7 "We have had computers for over twenty years. We have only begun designing systems in the last two or three years." Explain this statement. Do you agree or disagree? Why?

12.8 "We no longer design any new systems in our shop. We have found that we can buy a completely developed system for a much lower cost than if we designed it ourselves." Discuss fully.

12.9 "Information systems should be designed by management, not by technicians." What, most likely, prompted this comment?

12.10 "You can't teach someone how to design a system. Design is a creative act. You can't teach creativity." Discuss.

12.11 "The costs of operating the payroll system are somewhat deceiving. Each small change in either the law or management's information needs requires extensive programming modifications." Discuss.

12.12 "Before you begin programming a new system, it is important to 'lock' the users in on what format the output reports will take." Do you agree or disagree with this statement?

12.13 "Implementation schedules do not directly affect systems design." Discuss.

12.14 "Eighty percent of the effort to implement the new system resulted from the requirements of less than 10 percent of the information outputs." Evaluate this comment.

12.15 Define the terms "turnkey operation," "facilities management," and "proprietary systems."

EXERCISES

12.1 Define the HIPO function to determine the gross earnings of an employee. Assume that regular and overtime pay rates are available from a master employee record and that regular and overtime hours are available from an employee time card record.

12.2 Prepare a conceptual design model showing the relationships between an inventory control system, a purchasing system, and an accounts payable system in a manufacturing organization.

12.3 From the library, research information systems literature which describes at least two data base management systems. Based on your readings, prepare a report describing how these systems will affect the design of a system such as payroll or sales reporting.

12.4 Many software packages are available for the purpose of providing documentation for computer programs. Routinely, many of the data and information processing magazines publish articles which evaluate these packages. Select one such article and prepare a report describing how the analysis was performed.

12.5 Design a data record(s) that could be used in a data base to record the activities performed by the following types of persons:

1. An automobile mechanic in a large garage,
2. An intern or resident in a large hospital,
3. A specialist who prepares individual income tax returns,
4. A typewriter salesperson,
5. A trainer of dogs to assist the blind.

PROBLEMS

12.1 You have been hired by a large country club to design an information system for its golfing activities. This system is to accept golf scores from members and their guests and automatically update the members' handicaps. In addition, the system is to have the capability of providing members with a complete analysis of all matches they participated in for a given year showing their strokes per hole. Finally, the club's management would like to have the ability to analyze activity on the course by day.

You are given the following information: The course has a teletype tied into a large timesharing computer system. The teletype is operable from 6 AM to 10 PM. The course uses a handicap system which assigns a golfer a handicap equal to 80 percent of the difference between actual scores and par based on the last ten rounds played. Prepare a General Systems Design Proposal Report for your proposed system.

12.2 In many small-and medium-sized organizations, telephone expenses are a significant part of the total business expense. Although the telephone company provides a detailed list of charges each month, this data, as presented on the bill, are not readily adaptable for controlling individual telephone users. In many organizations a company telephone operator places all long distance calls and accepts all incoming collect calls. In each case the operator is able to log which extension user in the company placed or received the call.

The telephone bill each month shows the total cost of all installed equipment (e.g., extension phones, switchboard, multiple lines on phones, etc.). A separate inventory list is provided monthly which details equipment costs. Long distance, collect, third party calls, and credit card charges are shown in detail on the monthly bill. Often these charges, however, are a month or two late in being billed. Credit card numbers are issued by the telephone company and are usually logged by a clerk in the accounting department. The monthly telephone bill shows detail fields for each line item as follows: (1) date call placed or received, (2) number called or number called from, (3) code for type of call, (4) city called or called from, (5) credit card number if applicable, (6) length of call, and (7) charge for call. Analyze the above facts and provide the following:

1. A detailed design of an information system which collects, processes, and reports telephone expenses. Assume the organization has a computer which operates in batch processing mode utilizing punched cards, magnetic tape, and magnetic disk.
2. The forms and procedures required to collect input data.
3. The records and files to be contained in the data base.
4. Your recommendations for the information outputs to be received by each department manager and the company controller.

12.3 A small midwestern state plans to experiment with a new way of dispensing drugs required by doctors' prescriptions. In general, each hospital, doctor's office, and pharmacy will be required to purchase or lease a small terminal which is capable of accessing a large, centralized computer. Rather than write prescriptions in the traditional sense, the doctor will enter the prescription into the terminal and forward the data to the computer. A data base maintained at the central computer will contain inventory records for each pharmacy in the state. Patients can request that the prescription be filled at a pharmacy of their choice, or at one of the several pharmacies in a specified geographical area based on some criteria such as price, availability, etc.

The goals of this system are to reduce the mishandling and misinterpretation of patients' prescriptions, reduce the costs related to obtaining prescriptions, and provide a method for exercising control over illegal drug dispensing.

Prepare a General Systems Design Proposal Report for this system as you visualize it operating. Prepare a two- or three-page report discussing the advantages and disadvantages of this type of information system.

12.4 A food manufacturer has traditionally relied on "money back coupons" for promoting its products. This means that when consumers purchase a manufacturer's product, they simply return the label from the product with their name and address to the manufacturer who, in turn, refunds part (25 to 50 cents) of the purchase price to the consumer. As business has grown, however, the vice-president of marketing has had two concerns: (1) this type of promotion is not very successful in many parts of the country, and (2) the cost of operating the promotion is nearing $1,000,000 annually.

The cost includes approximately $150,000 for manually processing refunds and $850,000 in payments. The firm has a large computer with online processing capabilities via teletypes or CRTs. The vice-president believes processing costs can be reduced by 50 percent if the computer were used to replace the manual processing.

Analyze the above facts and make any assumptions you deem necessary; then prepare a General Systems Design Proposal Report. Your design should include not only the processing of consumer claims but considerations for informing management as to the success/failure of the promotion through specific analytical reports.

BIBLIOGRAPHY

Gane and Sarson, "Data Flow Diagrams Ease Planning of Any Systems," *Computerworld*, October 3, 1977.

Jones, "HIPO for Developing Specifications," *Datamation,* March 1976.

Laden and Gildersleeve, *System Design for Computer Applications,* New York: John Wiley & Sons, Inc., 1967.

Matthews, *The Design of the Management Information System,* Philadelphia: Auerbach Publishers, 1971.

Ross and Brackett, "An Approach to Structured Analysis," *Computer Decisions,* September 1976.

Sarson, "Structured Systems Development," *Computer Decisions,* August 1977.

Shinners, *Techniques of System Engineering,* New York: McGraw-Hill Book Co., 1967.

Teichroew and Gackowski, "Structured Systems Design," *Ideas for Management,* Cleveland, Ohio: Association for Systems Management, 1977.

Pelican Case

Phase 2 · General Systems Design
· General Systems Design Proposal Report

Phases of Systems Development Methodology:

Completed ▨▨▨
To be completed ☐

Phase 1	Phase 2	Phase 3	Phase 4	Phase 5
Systems analysis	General systems design	Systems evaluation and justification	Detail systems design	Systems implementation
Proposal to conduct systems analysis report Systems analysis completion report	General systems design proposal report	Final general systems design report	Final detail systems design report	Final implementation report
Completed in Chapter 11	Presented and completed in this chapter	Presented at the end of Chapter 13	Presented at the end of Chapter 15	Presented at the end of Chapter 16

PHASE 2

INTRODUCTION

For the first time since the project began, Ben believed he had a sense of direction. All of the respondents he interviewed agreed that he was on the right track. Those who had read his reports, agreed with them totally. Martha and Danny were enthusiastic about a system being designed to help with customer communications. Even Patti considered the recommendations to be feasible and a vast improvement over what they had now. Both Patti and Danny seemed to have more respect for each other and a better sense for the other person's job demands. All parties wanted to see something on paper that would give them a better definition of what Ben had in mind. What follows is the General Systems Design Proposal Report prepared by Ben.

397

GENERAL SYSTEMS DESIGN PROPOSAL REPORT

To: Martha Pringle, Patti Blake, Danny Loman, and Bud Wiser

From: Ben Snow, Systems Analyst

Restatement of Reasons for Initiating Systems Project

In the beginning, this project was started because a system of internal control was needed to prevent the misuse of telephone network resources. The system's main output was to be expense information, so that Accounting and the managers throughout Pelican could control the telephone resource.

Current Reasons for Performing Systems Project

The need for a system to provide unbiased and accurate information about telephone usage still exists. The scope of the system, however, has expanded to meet additional needs of management. Several managers have indicated a need to use the system not only to control the telephone network, but to exploit it to the company's advantage.

Introduction to General Systems Design

The underlying objective of the new system is to combine digital, word, voice, and image processing to meet all demands previously ascertained. The new system integrates the telephone network with computer technology to control expenses, to improve sales effectiveness and efficiency, and to handle routine customer service and communication activities.

Demands on this system are for more timely, accurate, and unbiased information for accounting control and to aid Marketing. The volume of transactions and messages are sufficient to dictate the need for a computer-based system to provide this information. Published research about the technology of the new systems indicates a high level of reliability. To increase noncomputer reliability, a training program will be started to train users and operators. Before implementation, all the design blocks will be tested separately and then together before the system is put "on the air." The projected cost of the system appears at this time to be well within budget.

Assuming approval is given by the first of next month, the system can be operational within two to three months. The system is flexible because it serves to control the telephone network, performs routine tasks for Marketing, and provides communications between customers and Pelican. By performing similar tasks for other departments, the system can be expanded in the future. Life expectancy of the system appears to be about four years. The potential to handle greater volumes is considerable because of modularity. For example, more terminals or storage can be easily added. Implementing standards for documentation, programming, and procedures will help to ensure maintainability. Moreover, all prospective vendors have local offices and provide overnight maintenance service.

All managers have expressed support for this project. No organizational factors appear to restrict its final implementation. It is technically, economically, legally, operationally, and schedule feasible. Our Legal Department indicates, however, that we could have a legal problem if we sell our customer mailing list. Top management have said that they will issue a policy statement on the confidentiality of the data base.

Another strong demand on the new system is its cost/effectiveness. Management's guidelines state that effectiveness must be at least 1.5 times cost for a project to be approved. Once it becomes approved, sufficient funds will be made available for detail design and implementation. If the system passes all tests and satisfies all users, then a budget for its operation will be approved.

General Systems Design

The following is a general design of the new system for your consideration. Bear in mind that a number of variations could be made on this design. In this report, two alternatives are considered. Alternative I is based on a standalone, highly distributed structure. The standalone processor does not share any logic with the mainframe host computer. Once each month, summary data are transmitted to the mainframe computer for archival storage.

Alternative II is a hybrid structure. A remote processor is connected to the central host computer for online processing. It shares the logic and storage of the host processor.

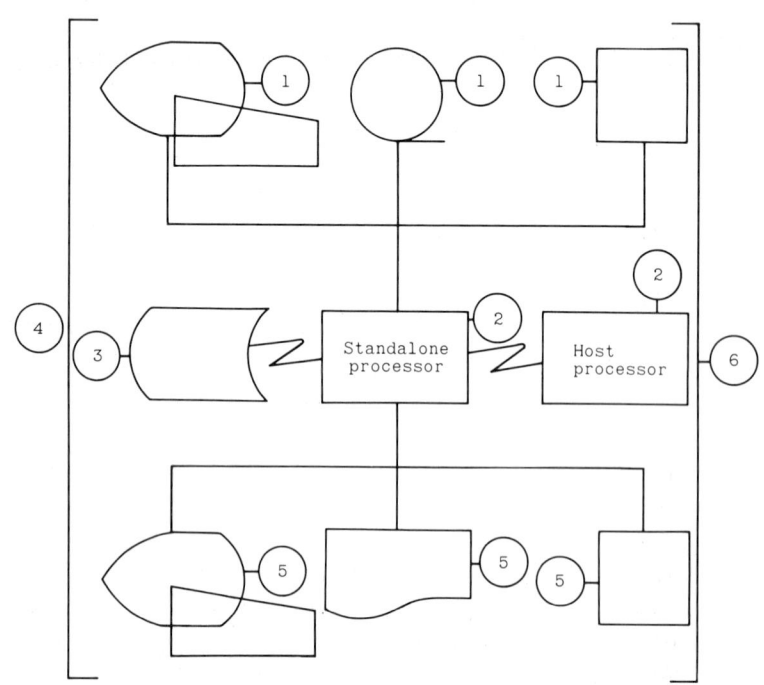

① <u>Input</u>. Input includes a variety of business transactions, captured by a number of data collection devices and techniques. For example, a switchboard operator uses OCR devices to input toll calls. A regenerated bill is supplied by the telephone company on magnetic tape. Voice messages are transmitted by telephone lines from remote locations and recorded automatically on cassettes. CRTs are available for operators to transcribe and input a variety of budget, customer, and sales data.

② <u>Processing</u>. Data, word, voice, and images are processed by this system to provide output. For example, budgeting procedures provide telephone usage and cost information. Also, text material is sorted and merged by menu-driven programs.

③ <u>Data base</u>. Cassettes, minicassettes, floppy disks, and hard disks comprise the physical files. Logical data association is handled by pointers and chains. Data reflecting telephone resources and usage, and customer activity, are structured in tree form, wherein descriptive data comprises the parent record and variable data comprises the child records. Also, the system has the capability of storing variable data for a two-year period, thereby permitting comparison reporting of this year to last year.

④ <u>Controls</u>. Appropriate administrative, operations, documentation, and security controls are used. Moreover, preformatted inputs help the terminal operators enter correct data. Also, if an error is detected during data entry, the transaction is flagged and placed in an error file where it is retained until it is corrected.

⑤ <u>Output</u>. A variety of output will be provided by the system. This output consists of telephone cost and usage reports, customer profiles, sales performance reports, and letters and other material for mailing to customers. Besides periodic accounting reports, several methods are used to tailor information outputs. For example, comparison of actual to budgeted amounts, provides an opportunity for variance or exception reports as desired. Also, users may interrogate the system for an assortment of status information.

⑥ <u>Data processing resources</u>. Hardware components are made up of telephones, telecommunication channels, CRTs, processors, magnetic storage media, and printers. Most software packages are vendor supplied. Programs developed internally will be written in a standard, universal language such as COBOL. The system can be operated by terminal operators and managed by Bud Wiser. Mrs. Suzuki and her assistants will be under Bud Wiser's direction. In addition to supervision and coordination of the new system, Bud Wiser's other major responsibility will be to handle customer complaints.

Special Features of the General Systems Design

The common elements of both designs are CRTs, storage, and printers. The remote processor can be a small standalone minicomputer, which does its own processing. Or, the minicomputer with its peripherals can be connected to a larger host, which satisfies heavy processing and storage demands.

All terminals have a regular keyboard, with function keys that allow operators to make special selections from a menu-driven program. Also, the function keys permit users to create, revise, print, and store documents automatically.

Printers for word processing jobs vary from vendor to vendor. Two broad categories of printers are: impact, those that actually strike the page; and nonimpact, those that do not put pressure on the page. The two types of impact printers considered are element and print wheel (also called a daisy wheel) printers. Both give letter-quality output. The daisy wheel printer is recommended because it prints at higher speeds than the element printer. Although nonimpact printers can print at high speeds, at this time, their adoption is not recommended. Their application for printing Pelican's catalogs and price lists in the future, however, should be studied further.

Listed below are some special features available in either system alternative:

1. _Automatic text wraparound_. This feature eliminates the need to keystroke carrier returns. Words that do not fit on one line are moved to the next line automatically.

2. _Text modification_. Portions of text can be taken out, moved, or changed without having to rekey the entire document. This is known as electronic "cutting and pasting." For example, when the sales staff sends out mailings, they simply call up appropriate letters and have the operators insert, delete, and change the text as necessary. Or, often, a new letter can be constructed by just combining paragraphs from letters already in storage. To overcome the appearance of a form letter, personalized paragraphs or sentences can be added easily. Also, Bud Wiser can follow up mailings with telephone calls through the use of an automatic notification feature.

3. _Aligned margins_. The printer can make the right-hand margin even by minutely adjusting spacing between words or characters.

4. _Indexing_. Data can be indexed and retrieved based on a number, title, originator, or department. Also, by sorting the file, data can be retrieved by customer name, customer address, Zip Code, or salesperson.

5. _Pagination_. Pages are numbered automatically. If new material is inserted or eliminated, pagination is redone automatically.

6. _Global searches_. The system searches a set of data for a specific term such as UT and replaces it with the University of Texas everywhere it occurs. Also, files can be interrogated for a specific person, company, product, service, and address. This feature will be

especially helpful in handling "bingo cards." These cards allow magazine readers to request information on a variety of products and services Pelican offers. Now, these leads can be stored in our mailing list and the system can search for product/service information requested on the bingo card. Bud Wiser can also make follow-up calls to qualify these leads.

7. <u>Merging</u>. This feature permits one or more sets of data to be created from separate, previously recorded data. For example, a paragraph from one letter can be combined with a paragraph of another letter to form a new letter. The operator keys in a list of names and addresses, and the system merges all the data to print any number of the same letter, each with a separate name and address.

8. <u>Dictionary lookup</u>. A dictionary is online to verify spelling and automatically change misspelled words. This feature eliminates the loathsome chore of proofreading for typos. Also, an operator can store in the dictionary special words. For example, Andersen Supply is spelled with a "sen" not a "son."

Both system alternatives will have dictation units available for sales personnel. These units can be used by salespersons to take "notes" while on the road and calling on customers. These units are pocket size with minicassette storage. These minicassettes will be mailed to Bud Wiser's office for transcription and storage in the data base under a name or number supplied by the originator.

Other remote dictation will be handled by telephone, which in turn, feeds into a central recorder. As we see it now, portable dictation units will handle quick notes made in the field. Telephone dictation will then be used for transmission of more detailed and lengthy notes, (e.g., at night from a motel room). Also, the system includes a voice message capability. The sender keys in a special code number on a telephone, then dials the receiver's phone. When he or she presses the listen key, the message is played back. These phones will be installed in Bud Wiser's, Danny Loman's, and the Ordering and Shipping Department offices. Also, we strongly recommend the use of teleconferencing. When the need arises for several people to meet but they are in different locations, this technique will allow them to communicate immediately, rather than waiting to meet at the monthly sales meeting.

Videodisk, facsimile, electronic mail, computer graphics, and micrographics are being investigated to determine if they can be added after the system is implemented.

CHAPTER 13

Systems Evaluation and Justification

13.1 ▪ INTRODUCTION

In this chapter the process the analyst must go through to prepare a Final General Systems Design Report is discussed. This report is the basic document that management uses to make a decision as to what proposed general systems design should be implemented. A computer configuration serves as a vehicle for our discussion in this chapter, but the same kind of process could be followed for any type of system evaluation and justification. The flowchart for the steps in this process is outlined in Figure 13.1.

13.2 ▪ GENERAL SYSTEMS DESIGN REQUIREMENTS

Not all systems designs call for computer equipment selection and acquisition. Assume, however, that it has been concluded at this point that some kind of a computer configuration is necessary to meet the user, data processing, and systems requirements identified in the systems analysis phase.

Within these categories, certain requirements are either *imperative* or *desirable*. The imperatives are essential to the implementation and operation of the new system and, no matter how one changes the overall systems design, are always present and must be adhered to. For example, an imperative might be that the system must process X number of payroll checks, produce a payroll register, and update all employee files, by noon each Friday. Desirables, on the other hand, aid and enhance the system but are not absolutely necessary for the system to become operative. For example, while it might be desirable to enter data via keyboard-to-storage devices, it may be determined that, because of a variety of circumstances, data must be prepared by keypunches, and entered via a card reader.

It is the job of the analyst to select from a wide range and class of equipment a specific computer configuration which will meet all of the imperatives and as many of the desirables as possible, at the lowest possible cost.

13.3 ▪ APPROACHES TO OBTAINING EQUIPMENT PROPOSALS

The various requirements of the systems design help to determine the computer config-

408 Systems Evaluation and Justification

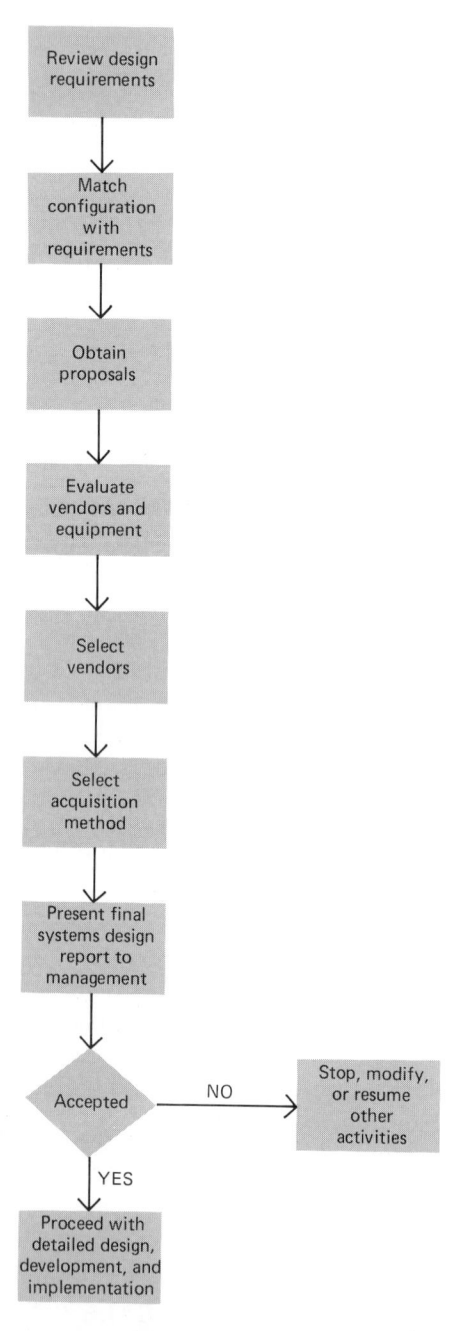

FIG. 13.1 A flowchart of the systems evaluation and justification process.

uration needed (e.g., processor, peripherals, and data communication devices). Although other ways are available to obtain computer processing, such as service bureaus and remote computing networks, it is assumed here that the final computer configuration will be acquired (rented, leased, or purchased) from one of the computer vendors. The selection methods outlined in this chapter have universal application.

The analyst may choose from the following three basic approaches when obtaining equipment proposals:

1. *Proposal for a specific configuration.* With this method, the analyst specifies a particular computer configuration and requests that vendors submit proposals based on these particular specifications. One advantage of this approach is that it tends to reduce the complexity of evaluating different vendors' proposals. Secondly, it reduces the time period required by the vendor to prepare a proposal. The primary disadvantage is that this approach generally rules out a vendor offering a new or different equipment configuration not known to the analyst.

2. *Proposal for performance objectives.* With this approach the analyst translates the systems requirements into performance objectives and submits them to several vendors, requesting proposals for the type of equipment that they feel can best satisfy these objectives. For example, instead of stipulating that a computer must be able to support 12 online terminals, the analyst indicates that online information will be required by 12 different physical departments, and lists the types of information required, expected frequency, volume of inquiries, etc. The advantages of this approach are

that it minimizes the effect of the analyst's lack of equipment knowledge, permits the most knowledgeable persons (i.e., the vendor personnel) to configure the equipment, and provides further alternatives for performing an activity or satisfying an objective. The disadvantages of this approach are that the vendor usually requires a long period of time to prepare a proposal, the evaluation process is complicated, and the analyst's organization might not possess the expertise to implement a given vendor proposal.

3. *Proposal from one vendor.* A third approach which has widespread popularity, especially in smaller organizations, is to pick one vendor and allow this vendor to propose one or two alternatives for meeting the systems requirements, based on the vendor's available technology. The advantage to this approach is that an organization spends very little time and money choosing and evaluating equipment, and thus is able to concentrate its resources on other developmental activities. The obvious disadvantage is that a particular equipment manufacturer will seldom (never?) recommend adopting another vendor's equipment, in whole or in part.

13.4 ▪ THE EVALUATION PROCESS

For our evaluation analysis, it is assumed that bids, based on a specific configuration, have been submitted to several vendors. The general process one goes through to evaluate these proposals follows.

First Level Evaluation

At this level, the analyst simply determines which vendors have met the mandatory requirements. Figure 13.2 is an example, in the form of a decision table, of how this evaluation is made. In our example, vendors A, B, and C meet the imperatives and are, consequently, included for further evaluation. Vendor D fails to meet at least one of the imperatives and is rejected from further consideration. Bear in mind that the list in Figure 13.2 is not inclusive, but is intended simply for illustrative purposes.

Criteria Comparisons

The easiest way to make a broad comparison of selected vendors is to place basic criteria

	Vendor A	Vendor B	Vendor C	Vendor D
Imperative Conditions:				
1. Costs less than X dollars per month	Y	Y	Y	Y
2. Offers family series of computers	Y	Y	Y	N
3. Offers COBOL compiler	Y	Y	Y	N
4. Printer speed equal to or greater than 1200 LPM	Y	Y	Y	N
5. Handle direct access storage of X characters	Y	Y	Y	Y
Actions:				
1. Accept for further analysis	1	1	1	
2. Reject				1

FIG. 13.2 A first level evaluation of vendors.

side by side in a matrix, as shown in Figure 13.3. Not all possible criteria are listed, but enough are listed to indicate how such a comparison is made.

Methods for Testing Equipment

Besides reading literature published by vendors and independent services, and querying users about vendors' equipment, two primary methods of testing equipment performance are benchmarking and simulation.

1. *Benchmark method.* Test problems are prepared and run on the equipment configuration proposed by the vendor. Overall, the benchmark programs test: (1) anticipated workload, (2) compilers, (3) operating system, and (4) application and utility packages. To apply benchmark programs, the systems analyst can obtain an agreement with the vendor to run the programs at the vendor's location, run the programs on some other user's computer system (assuming it is the same as the one proposed), or hire a consulting firm to perform the benchmark testing. The elapsed operating time required to run the test problems is the main determinant. If the test problems are representative of the future processing workload, then required times for future operations can be extrapolated. The method is usually effective for evaluating operating time requirements for typical batch processing configurations but is not particularly applicable to analyzing large total systems in an online environment. Figure 13.4 is an example of the results of benchmark tests for an accounts receivable application. It must be emphasized that these results are strictly a function of the mix of programs chosen

Vendors Criteria	Vendor A	Vendor B	Vendor C
Processor monthly rental	$52,000 (1536K bytes memory)	$86,000 (1310K bytes memory)	$85,000 (1573K bytes memory)
Processor purchase price	$2,500,000	$3,900,000	$3,600,000
Processor monthly maintenance	$5,600	$7,800	$2,500
Cycle time (μsec.)	0.080	0.100	0.600
Characters per access cycle	2	4	6
Max. memory capacity (K bytes)	3,072	1,310	3,145
Extended core storage	No	Yes	Yes
Max. I/O channels	12	36	18
Disk capacity (Megabytes)	800	838	2,000
Transfer rate (K bytes/sec.)	806	418	248
Average access time (msec.)	30	60	60
Max. magnetic tape transfer rate (K bytes/sec.)	320	240	240
Max. printer speed (lines/min.)	2,000	1,500	1,200
Max. card reader speed (cards/min.)	1,000	1,200	1,400

FIG. 13.3 Criteria comparison of vendors.

Vendors Program	Vendor A	Vendor B	Vendor C
AR card to tape edit	63 sec.	60 sec.	78 sec.
AR sort	93	106	70
AR master file update	306	652	491
AR file purge	175	94	96
AR aging report	453	400	417
Total	1090 sec.	1312 sec.	1152 sec.

FIG. 13.4 Results of accounts receivable benchmark tests.

to represent the application. For example, had a sample of processor-constrained programs been chosen for benchmarking, then Figure 13.4 results would not apply, since the major constraint on the given accounts receivable application is input/output.

2. *Simulation method.* This method incorporates mathematical models which accept a number of measurements such as sizes and structures of files, frequency of access to files, transaction volume, etc. These models are then run on computers to predict time considerations such as turnaround time, clock time, response time, and so forth. In addition, simulation models help to predict systems capacity (used and unused), and to define optimal equipment configurations. Simulation packages can be purchased or leased from various suppliers of software.

Other Criteria for Hardware/Software Evaluation

In Chapter 4, we discussed systems requirements and how they can be transformed into desired performance capabilities for data processing resources. These performance capabilities are then used as criteria for evaluating various vendor proposals. Some criteria that might be developed, for example, include: (1) modularity, (2) compatibility, (3) reliability, (4) maintainability, and (5) general vendor support.

1. Modularity. The concept of modularity allows the addition of components to the configuration, thereby allowing it to change and grow to meet changing systems needs. This concept permits the organization to start with an initial installation of a less expensive, slower system and then increase the size of the mainframe, and to add peripherals as the need arises.

2. Compatibility. In some instances the installation of one computer system to replace an old system means major program rewrites (i.e., two different computers are incompatible if they cannot operate together or handle the same input data and programs). The term "compatibility" has three facets: (1) *flexibility;* computers are designed for a variety of purposes, allowing them to be used for business data processing applications, communications, and timesharing; and for scientific applications; sometimes all with equal facility; (2) the design concept of a *family* of computers that allows a small "child" (e.g., IBM 3031) to grow into an "adult" (e.g., IBM series H) without necessitating major software changes; and (3) the concept of machine-independent languages, such as COBOL, that permit programs written in this language to be run on a variety of computers with minimal changes.

In selecting a computer configuration, the concepts of modularity and compatibility play important roles. Some models on the market are considered to be "dead end" machines. That is, they are not part of a standard product series. In a standard product line computers are compatible all the way up the line, peripherals are interchangeable throughout the line, and primary storage is expandable. Because of these features, upward transition from a small computer to a larger computer is rather simple and straightforward. Selection of a dead end computer can, on the other hand, significantly increase conversion costs and transition time, once it becomes inadequate to meet systems requirements.

3. Reliability. All computer configurations must be reliable, especially integrated configurations. If the configuration breaks down ("crashes"), not only do all processing operations come to a halt, but restarting an integrated configuration is an involved, complicated process. High reliability is based on the type of production control and testing methods used by the vendor. This area is difficult to measure, but any change in production methods, production facilities, and new technologies should be closely observed by the prospective computer user. The measure of reliability used by engineers is MTBF (Mean Time Between Failure). To minimize the probability of failure, the concept of redundancy is used. Redundancy uses two parallel components to decrease the probability of failure. For example, if the probability of failure of one component over a given period of time is .04, then the probability of failure of two parallel components, given that they are independent, is $.04^2$, or .0016.

4. Maintainability. MTTR (Mean Time To Repair) is the basic measure of maintainability. The MTTR consists of the time required to accomplish the following: detect the nature of the failure; isolate the malfunctioning element; remove the malfunctioning element; obtain a replacement for it; replace it; verify its operability; initialize the replacement; proceed to an operable state. The accomplishment of these actions is influenced by the physical construction, the level at which replacements can be made, the training of the maintenance technicians, the ability to detect and isolate malfunctions, the extent and quality of diagnostic tools, the built-in test and diagnostic facilities of the system, and the repair facilities of the complex.

5. General Vendor Support. The support of the vendor is of primary importance when making an equipment selection decision. In the long run the equipment is no better than the general support from the vendor. This support includes such things as: (1) availability of training facilities; (2) installation support; (3) system development, conversion, and testing assistance; (4) experience level and competency of vendor's personnel; (5) duration of time any support is available after installation of equipment; (6) availability of a user group; and (7) availability of specialized software systems, such as data base management systems.

The concept of **bundling** has come to the fore in the past several years. This term means the degree to which vendors offer educational programs, compilers, application programs, and system engineers to the user free of charge. Some manufacturers are "semibundled," which means that certain services are provided without charge relative to the amount of rental payments (i.e., the greater the amount of payments, the more services the organization receives). Other companies are totally "unbundled," which means that they charge for education, application programs, compilers, and system engineers as required.

It may be that the resulting quantitative measurements derived from criteria comparisons, benchmarks, and simulations are, within a prescribed cost range, quite similar. In such situations qualitative criteria of modularity, compatibility, reliability, maintainability, general vendor support and others, may, in the final analysis, dictate the selection of a particular vendor. To make a proper selection, the analyst uses a rating matrix as shown in Figure 13.5.

To prepare the rating matrix, the analyst first determines the relative weight of each criterion using a base of 100. Next, based on the best information about the criteria applicable to each vendor, the analyst assigns a value to each criterion. The weights are then multiplied by the criteria values. Each resulting score is finally summed to give a total score for each vendor. In our example it appears that Vendor C has the highest score.

Professional service companies[1] are in business to gather a wealth of information about all of the computer manufacturers and their equipment. They, in turn, sell this information to subscribers. The history and a management summary of each manufacturer is provided. Other information consists of main storage capacity and cycle time, control storage, registers, instruction repertoire, instruction timing, and input/output control. Also, peripheral devices are described and their speed is given. The operating system software is described, along with available utilities and application program languages. Support provided by the manufacturer, such as training, installation, and maintenance, is covered together with items that are bundled/unbundled. A complete price list of all equipment is supplied. Responses are compiled from surveys of customers who use the equipment (i.e., "ask the person who owns one"). An example of results from these surveys is shown in Figure 13.6. In some surveys, technical support, responses to trouble-shooting, education, and documentation are included. This informa-

[1]Datapro Research Corporation, Delran, N. J.

Criteria	Weight	Vendor A Value	Vendor A Score	Vendor B Value	Vendor B Score	Vendor C Value	Vendor C Score
Modularity	10	6	60	7	70	5	50
Compatability	10	7	70	7	70	5	50
Reliability	30	8	240	6	180	7	210
Maintainability	30	5	150	4	120	5	150
Vendor Support	20	2	40	5	100	7	140
Total	100		560		540		600

FIG. 13.5 A rating matrix.

Performance Criteria	Ratings of Users				
	Excellent	Good	Fair	Poor	WA
Ease of operation	7	5	2	0	3.4
Reliability of mainframe	7	5	2	0	3.4
Reliability of peripherals	4	8	1	1	3.1
Maintenance service:					
Responsiveness	4	7	1	2	2.9
Effectiveness	2	7	5	0	2.8
Technical support	4	5	4	0	3.0
Manufacturer's software:					
Operating system	3	6	4	1	2.8
Compilers and assemblers	3	6	5	0	2.9
Applications programs	2	5	4	1	2.7
Ease of programming	4	6	3	0	3.1
Ease of conversion	4	3	5	0	2.9
Overall satisfaction	4	6	4	0	3.0

FIG. 13.6 Example of 14 user responses to a survey about a particular computer manufacturer (conducted by Datapro Research Corporation). (Weighted average on a scale of 4.0 for excellent.)

tion, plus the information presented above, assists the prospective computer user in making an informed decision.

13.5 ▪ ACQUISITION CONSIDERATIONS

The analyst must be aware of financial and legal considerations involved in acquiring computer equipment.[2] The four alternative financial means of acquiring computer equipment are: (1) rent from vendor, (2) purchase from vendor, (3) lease from third party, or (4) a combination. Legal considerations involve the negotiation of a strong, enforceable, low-risk contract.

Methods of Acquiring Computer Equipment

The method of acquisition is considered an economic question related to the cost of money to a particular organization and the useful life of the acquired equipment. The method of acquisition should be determined independent of the selection of the equipment itself. The four methods are defined as follows:

1. Rent from Vendor. Usually, rental is on a month-to-month basis sometimes with a minimum of a one-year contract. The rental rates are such that the basic purchase cost of the computer is recovered by the vendor within 45 to 60 months. The user can also receive purchase credits which range from 10 percent to as much as 50 percent of rental payments, depending on the vendor.

Vendors typically offer either an unlimited use rental contract, or a prime shift rental contract. The first type provides for a fixed monthly price regardless of the number of computer hours used. The prime shift rental contract establishes a fixed monthly rental for one predetermined eight-hour period each day. The rental is proportionately

[2] See, for example, *Computer Decisions,* March 1974.

increased by the number of additional eight-hour shifts used during the month. For example, the prime shift (first eight-hour shift) may be charged at $100 per hour; additional hours of usage beyond the prime shift may be charged at $10 per hour.

2. Purchase from Vendor. With this method the computer equipment becomes the property of the user. This method is usually the most popular where the equipment is to be kept over five years. Over half of federal government equipment is purchased, and this percentage is expected to increase substantially in the future.

3. Leasing from Third Party. Third party leases can be either operating or financial. The operating lease is usually of relatively short-term duration (two to five years) and is cancellable, or terminable, before the lease payments have equaled or exceeded the equivalent purchase price. The principle underlying the operating lease is that third party companies assume a longer leasable life for the equipment than does the vendor. Consequently, third parties can offer lower rates than vendors and still realize a profit.

The financial lease (analyzed later) is of longer duration, is noncancellable, and obligates the lessee to lease payments which in total may equal or exceed the purchase price of the equipment leased. This method guarantees the leasing company a full return on its equipment. Obviously, many leasing companies prefer this method over the operating lease.

4. Combination. This method allows the user additional flexibility. A user may purchase those components of the computer configuration that have the longest useful life (over five years) and may rent or lease the remainder. For example, an organization might purchase its central processor and rent or lease the peripheral devices. Or if cash flow is a problem, the organization might lease a central processor and rent peripherals.

Analysis of the Financial Lease

The financial lease decision is complicated because each rental payment is comprised of the implicit interest charged by the lessor and the amortization of the principal sum. In effect the lessor is a seller of an asset and a lender of money. The rental payment, therefore, provides the vendor with a recovery of the selling price of the equipment plus interest on the money advanced.

In actuality, the decision is not whether to "lease or purchase," despite the fact that most of the literature states it this way. But rather, the basic decision pivots on the point of whether to acquire the equipment or not to acquire the equipment (at this point the decision is to acquire), and whether to actually lease or borrow.[3]

> Since the lease is presumed to require a contractually predetermined set of payments, it is reasonable to compare the lease with an alternative type of financing available... that also requires a contractually predetermined set of payments (i.e., a loan). It follows that the interest rate at which the firm would actually borrow, if it chose to acquire the asset by buying and borrowing, is an appropriate discount rate to use in this analysis. The recommendation holds even if the firm chooses to use some other discount rate for ordinary capital budgeting decisions.[4]

---

[3]Charles T. Horngren, *Cost Accounting: A Managerial Emphasis,* Fourth Edition, Englewood Cliffs, N.J.: Prentice-Hall, Inc., 1977, pp. 446–448.

[4]Harold Bierman, Jr. and Seymour Smidt, *The Capital Budgeting Decision,* Fourth Edition, New York: The Macmillan Company, 1975, p. 216. Used with permission from the Macmillan Company.

An Illustration: The ABC Company has chosen a computer configuration which will provide benefits in its information system operations measured at $980,000 per year over the equipment's useful life of five years. The equipment has zero resale value. The purchase price of the equipment is $2,500,000; it is also available on a five-year, noncancellable lease at $720,000.00 annually. ABC's cost of capital is 25 percent. Should ABC lease or purchase? Disregard taxes.

1. Investment decision:

    (a) Discount future cash flow:
    $980,000 at 25 percent for five years,
    $980,000 × 2.690 = $2,636,200
    (b) Net present value of system:
    $2,636,200 − $2,500,000 = $136,200
    Therefore, continue analysis.

2. Financing decision:
    Equivalent purchase price is $720,000 at cost of borrowing money (assume 18 percent) for five years: $720,000 × 3.127 = $2,251,440, which is less than the purchase price by $248,560. Therefore, it seems that the decision would be to lease. Additional considerations, however, are discussed in the next section.

Advantages/Disadvantages of Acquisition Methods

The advantages and disadvantages of the four acquisition methods are summarized in Figure 13.7.

Legal Considerations

Managements of organizations must establish more effective policies than those used in the past for negotiating contracts pertaining to the acquisition of computer equipment. Many organizations cannot afford the potential losses resulting from poor contract compliance, delays in delivery dates, component failures, and so forth. To guard against such losses, management must establish basic principles of contract procurement. The establishment of such principles may or may not be met by the vendor's "standard" contract. Normally, these standard contracts are drawn more in favor of the vendor than in the interest of the user.

Most organizations sign standard contracts provided by the vendors when acquiring computer equipment. If delivery schedules are missed, and promised performance never materializes, historically very little has been done by either party except to trade accusations and develop bitter feelings. Today, those acquiring equipment are urged to employ the services of professional purchasing agents and attorneys when negotiating the final contract. The contract should spell out clearly the duties, rights, and responsibilities of each party as well as any appropriate penalty clauses to be assessed.[5]

Two important points to include in every contract are an acceptance test and a delivery date. Some 60–90 days prior to the delivery date, the analyst should furnish the vendor with the acceptance test required by the contract. It is in the vendor's interest to see that the computer configuration passes the test before it is shipped.

The focal point in the contract is the scheduled delivery date. Usually the vendor will offer a choice of two or more dates for delivery. Before choosing a date, however, the analyst must consider what his or her organization has to do to accept delivery in a meaningful and systematic fashion. While

---

[5] For the details that should be contained in a contract, see Dick Brandon, "Does Your Contract Really Protect You?", *Computer Decisions*, December 1971, pp. 21–25.

Methods	Advantages	Disadvantages
Rent	1. Helpful to user who is uncertain as to proper equipment application. 2. Normally psychologically more acceptable to management. 3. High flexibility. 4. If an organization does not have past experience with computers, this may be the safest method. 5. Maintenance charges included in rental payments. 6. Allows a favorable working relationship with the vendor. 7. No long-term commitment. 8. Avoids technological obsolescence.	1. Over approximately five years, this is the most expensive method. 2. Rental payments increase by some factor less than one if usage exceeds a specified number of hours per month, assuming prime shift contract.
Purchase	1. The more mature users no longer need to depend on the security of renting. 2. Stabilization of computer industry means that changes in technology are not as disruptive as they once were. 3. Lower costs for an organization with a fairly stable growth pattern that will keep the equipment relatively longer than a growth company (i.e., not subject to operational obsolescence). 4. Investment credit offers certain tax advantages. 5. All other advantages accruing to ownership.	1. Organization has all the responsibilities and risk of ownership. 2. Usually if equipment is purchased, separate arrangements must be made for maintenance. 3. In a growth company there is a high probability of being locked into a computer configuration that fails to meet the changing requirements of the system. 4. Must pay taxes and insurance on equipment. 5. If the organization has better alternative investment opportunities, it would be more profitable for it to use the funds for these alternatives. 6. Ties up capital, thereby impinging upon cash flow. 7. Increased risk of technological obsolescence. 8. Low resale value.
Lease	1. In long run, can save 10–20 percent over the rental method. 2. Tax benefits. 3. Conservation of working capital because of low monthly payments. 4. Allows users to select their equipment, have it purchased, and then have it leased to them.	1. Lessee is obligated to pay a contracted charge if lease is terminated before end of lease period. 2. Little support and consulting service. 3. Lessee loses a great deal of negotiating leverage. 4. For maintenance, the lessee must depend upon a service contract from the vendor, not from the leasing company.
Combination	1. Optimizes the best of other methods. 2. Flexible.	1. More recordkeeping. 2. Might have to deal with several vendors in case of breakdown.

FIG 13.7 A list of the advantages and disadvantages of the four methods of equipment acquisition.

Three-Tier Acquisition System

awaiting delivery, the analyst must make sure that all interface equipment is ready for connection. Test programs and data must also be prepared for use when the configuration is delivered.

Three-Tier Acquisition System

Many information system managers use a three-tier acquisition system, as shown in Figure 13.8. At the base of the pyramid is equipment purchased and owned outright by the organization. This level represents the basic equipment required to operate the information system (e.g., the CPU, line printers).

The second level of the pyramid is for systems growth potential, both in terms of capacity and capability. The planning horizon is from five to ten years. Once the basic system is established, this level allows the addition of more or a different mix of equipment as the long-term need arises.

The third level of the pyramid is for a crisis situation, in which the level of operations of a particular area or function has been grossly underestimated. This level of acquisition allows the short-term rental of additional equipment. It lasts from 6 to 12 months, and gives management room to maneuver and time to reassess their total acquisition pyramid and system needs.

13.6 ▪ COST/EFFECTIVENESS ANALYSIS

Justification of a proposed computer configuration, or anything else requiring a capital investment, should always be stated in terms of **cost/effectiveness**. This analysis weighs the effectiveness derived from the direct and indirect benefits of a proposed sys-

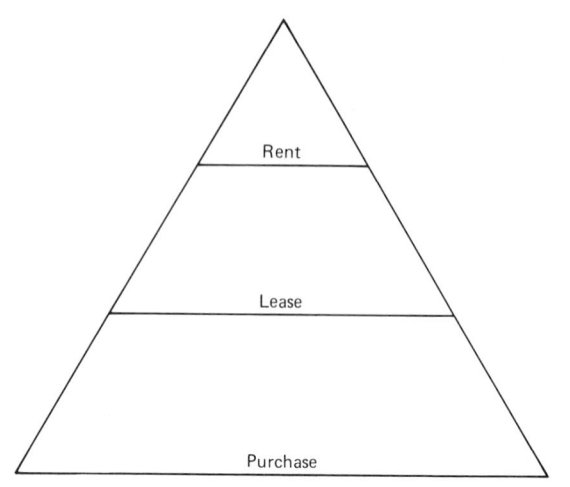

FIG. 13.8 Three-level system of acquisition of computer equipment.

tem against resource constraints which, in this analysis, equate to costs. This analysis determines if the proposed system produces benefits which outweigh costs. Normally, this analysis is performed on a number of desirable alternative systems and by comparison indicates which one is the best. The aim in this section, however, is to show generally how to conduct a cost/effectiveness analysis. Again, remember that one of the keys to successful decision making is for management to be able to select from a number of alternatives.

Consideration of Cost and Effectiveness

Earlier, when the feasibility analysis based on TELOS considerations was performed, preliminary cost figures were estimated. After the analyst has proceeded further with the systems work and made equipment evaluations, however, these cost figures are much more precise. The next task is to identify all costs, classify them, and estimate effectiveness over the useful life of the proposed system. In Figure 13.9 we illustrate a variety of ways to categorize costs.

Measurement of Effectiveness

The effectiveness of any proposed system is measured in terms of two kinds of benefits: (1) direct benefits, sometimes called *tangible* benefits; and (2) indirect benefits, sometimes called *intangible* benefits. These benefits occur over the useful life of the system, which runs from the point of start-up to the point of operational obsolescence (the time at which the system is due for an overhaul).

1. Direct Benefits. These benefits are cost savings resulting from the elimination of an operation, or from the increased efficiency of some process. For example, in the present system it may cost $2.00 to process each transaction whereas the proposed system will process the same transaction for $1.50. Since direct benefits are traceable to, and are a direct result of the proposed system, they are relatively easy to measure.

2. Indirect Benefits. Many benefits are intangible and cannot be easily traced to the system. An attempt should be made to express, however, in quantitative terms, those which can be identified. For example, an analysis of customer sales might show that the organization is losing 5 percent of its gross sales annually due to stockouts. The present system has an 85 percent customer service level whereas the new system, because of the implementation of better inventory control methods, will achieve a 95 per-

Costs by Behavior	Costs by Function
1. *Variable Costs.* These costs fluctuate with volume changes in a direct manner. Examples are electrical power and supplies (i.e., if the volume of work increases, the use of electrical power and supplies will also increase). 2. *Fixed Costs.* These costs might vary from period to period, but this fluctuation is not in response to volume changes in a particular period. Examples are depreciation, rent, taxes, and management salaries.	1. *Development Costs.* These are costs incurred to bring something into being or to make something better, more useful, etc. 2. *Operational Costs.* These are costs that must be expended to make something work or perform. The employment of a computer operator involves operational costs.
Costs by Time	**Costs by Type**
1. *Recurring Costs.* These costs are repeated at regular intervals. Examples of these costs are payroll and computer rental payments. 2. *Nonrecurring Costs.* These are one-time costs or costs that will end at some specific point in time. The cost of computer program development is a nonrecurring cost. (The cost of maintaining computer programs is recurring.)	1. *Direct Costs.* These costs represent expenditures that result directly from the proposed system. 2. *Indirect Costs.* These are overhead costs which cannot be directly identified with the elements of the proposed system and are apportioned among various areas in the organization. Examples are rent, insurance, taxes, management salaries, and employee benefits.

FIG. 13.9 A variety of categories for costs.

cent customer service level. It is estimated that this expected increase in customer service will increase annual sales by 3 percent due to fewer stockouts.

Examples of benefits that increase the effectiveness of a system are: (1) increased labor productivity; (2) better work scheduling; (3) better quality control; (4) better accounts receivable control, reduction in bad debts, and increased cash flow; (5) better inventory control and fewer stockouts; (6) quicker response to customer inquiries; (7) reduced clerical costs; and (8) reduced data processing costs. All these benefits, direct or indirect, can be reduced to quantitative measurements, though some of these measurements may be estimates. In all cases, benefits eventually increase profits or decrease costs. The analyst can always relate benefits to one or the other of these parameters showing, in quantifiable terms, how a particular benefit either increases profit or decreases costs.

Two basic methods used in estimating costs and effectiveness are:

1. *Objective Calculations.* These calculations result from a compilation of those costs, in bids and price lists, submitted by vendors. Such costs or benefits are simply compiled and easily verified.

2. *Estimations.*[6] Any alternative proposal under consideration is by its very nature future oriented. Costs and benefits will occur that are to some degree uncertain, because future events can seldom, if ever, be predicted with certainty. Usually costs are easier to predict than benefits, especially indirect benefits, but to derive a cost/effectiveness analysis, both sides of the equation must be estimated.

---

[6]Adapted from Burch and Hod, *op. cit.*, pp. 130–132.

Two problem areas are relative to estimation: (1) the reluctance of some systems analysts to attempt to measure or quantify the "unmeasurable," and (2) for those who do attempt to measure, a tendency to underestimate costs and overestimate benefits.

The second aspect we recognize as a psychological tendency, beyond complete treatment in this text. The techniques of estimating which we present later, however, will help to lessen the impact of this tendency to some degree. At this point, we suggest that you be on guard and try to avoid this pitfall. As for the first aspect, the conscientious systems analyst must set up an approach that will formalize the estimated measurement of both the cost side and the effectiveness side.

How does one go about measuring the unmeasurable? Many people will say it should not be done or it is a waste of time. But the point is that without some formalized approach to determine the cost/effectiveness of proposed systems projects, management will be making decisions based strictly on guess and intuition.

One approach to measurement is by the use of *probabilities* and *expected value*. The use of probabilities formalizes and quantifies the hunches and intuitive judgments of management that would have been used in any event. By formalizing the measurement process, the combined wisdom of all decision makers can come into play.

Even though we believe that some approximation is better than no approximation, a full disclosure of how measurements were derived should be given to management, with a warning that they should accept the figures cautiously. If the cost/effectiveness analysis were a precise process, then there would be no need for the management function. Consequently, management's responsibility is to obtain the best information available. Then, using their ability as decision makers, they must select the "best" alternative. In our opinion, this best information for management is provided when the systems analyst attempts to measure and quantify all recognized costs and benefits, no matter how intangible.

One technique used to formalize estimation is shown in Figure 13.10. Values are estimated by participants based on optimistic, pessimistic, and most likely categories.

To effect the estimation process, the following steps should be taken:

1. Employ a participative approach. In addition to advantages already alluded to, the diversity of participants will help to even out the underestimation/overestimation problem.
2. Once the participants have been selected, they must address themselves to the recognition and definition of both costs and benefits. An open discussion should be held during this step, so that each member of the group gains understanding of what the process is about and can interact and debate with others about all the ramifications of the proposed systems alternatives. The main purpose of this step is to recognize and define all costs and benefits pertinent to each alternative.
3. Each participant gives his or her own estimate. These estimates can be gathered and calculated by a designated person. During the estimation process, participants should not be allowed to review others' estimations. Such a constraint guards against any individual exerting undue influence on the other members of the group. You might liken this step to part of the Delphi procedure mentioned in a previous chapter.
4. Steps 2 or 3 are repeated until all participants are satisfied with the result.
5. Presentation of final estimations are made, including a full disclosure of estimation methods and each participant's input into the estimation process.

Preparation of Cost and Effectiveness Summaries

Management is most interested normally in direct costs (i.e., those add-on costs that relate directly to the proposal). For example, housing of the computer configuration in the home office building, on which the amount of rental will not change as a result, is an indirect cost, and might not be considered. The rental charges of the computer configuration itself, however, are a direct cost

Direct Benefit Estimates	Strength of Subjective Categories	Odds for Occurring	Amount
$10,000	Optimistic	3/10	$3,000
4,000	Pessimistic	1/10	400
6,000	Most likely	6/10	3,600
		Expected Value:	$7,000

FIG. 13.10 General example of calculating an expected value using optimistic, pessimistic, and most likely categories.

which is obviously relevant to the cost/effectiveness analysis. If, however, the installation of the computer in the office building caused another group to move to other quarters, then such relocation costs would be considered. Also, the opportunity cost for using the part of the building that the computer configuration requires might also be considered; but opportunity cost considerations are beyond the scope of our analysis and, thus, are excluded. Also, organizations are concerned with discounting factors and the net present value of proposed investments. In most instances, if a systems analyst does not have the financial background, we recommend that the cost/benefit analysis be reviewed by a financial analyst prior to presentation to management.

Our major aim here is to define those costs that will be *different* because of the implementation of the proposal. We are answering the question: "What difference will the development, implementation, and operation of the proposed system make?" Many people mistakenly think that the cost of the computer configuration itself is the major cost of the information system. Many other costs are incurred to support the computer configuration which, in total, amount to much more than the equipment. Computer configuration costs, and then all these additional costs, are discussed next.

Computer Configuration Costs. First, for an overview of possible computer configurations, we suggest that the reader review Appendix B. As discussed earlier, a computer configuration can be acquired by one or a combination of financial methods. We will assume for illustrative purposes that the configuration is rented, and that we have negotiated an unlimited use rental contract rather than a prime shift rental contract. Also, we include an "other equipment" category for miscellaneous equipment which does not fall into the computer category.

Environment Costs. These costs include all aspects involved in preparing the site not only for the equipment, but for offices, storage space, and conference rooms. The efforts in preparing this site can range anywhere from the minor renovation of an existing site to the construction of a new building. In addition to the site itself, other features are needed such as:

1. *Power requirements*. Different system configurations require different power requirements. The power parameters for any system, however, are measured in KVAs, volts, and kilowatts. For an approximate cost for power the total average KVA per month would be computed, based on the number of hours of use per day.

2. *Air conditioning*. Newer computer systems have reduced to some extent the total need for air conditioning, but even with the newer generation of equipment, the need for air conditioning is still a major consideration. Not only does air conditioning ensure proper functioning of equipment, but it provides comfortable working conditions for operating personnel.

3. *Furniture and fixtures*. Proper equipment must be provided for personnel operating the system.

4. *Miscellaneous features*. Other features that may be included in the environment costs are false flooring, special lighting, fire prevention equipment, lead-lined walls, and off-premises storage.

Physical Installation. In some cases the physical installation may present problems that require the use of special equipment such as cranes. Installing a system on the tenth floor of a building is not an easy task, but the cost is often overlooked until actual installation. Also, another charge not considered in some cost estimates is freight. It should be determined whether the vendor prepays freight. The freight charges for even a very small system, frequently sent by air freight, can run as high as $1500.

Training Costs. The training costs are normally high at the beginning and level off to a fairly constant rate. Training costs, if not provided "free" by the vendor, can range from $500 for a five-day introduction to programming, to over $2000 for a ten-day seminar course. This cost includes payment for the course only, which means that a company might spend $1200, or more, to send one employee out of town to a five-day introductory course.

Program and Program Testing Costs. As different systems design applications are developed, programming is initiated. The implementation of a new system will require a great deal of programming, but the need for programming does not stop after implementation. Changes are being made constantly to old programs, and new design applications are being developed. Total programming time can be reduced sometimes by the use of application and utility programs, but these packages cost money and, in many instances, require major modification before they can be applied to a specific system.

Cost of Conversion. The cost of conversion depends upon the degree of conversion. The degree of conversion depends on how many applications included in the first system are to be changed, and how much is to be handled as in the past. Several aspects need to be included in the estimate of cost of conversion:

1. Preparing and editing records for completeness and accuracy as, for example, when they are converted from manual media to magnetic disk.
2. Setting up file library procedures.
3. Preparing and running parallel operations.

Cost of Operation. The cost factors discussed above are basically setup costs. Most of the costs do not recur until another major systems conversion is made, except for the recurring rental charge of the computer equipment. Cost of operation, however, includes all factors necessary to keep the system working. These factors are listed below:

1. *Staff costs.* These costs include the payroll for all employees in the information system and for occasional consulting fees. This staff consists of the information systems manager, systems analysts, accountants, programmers, systems engineers, computer operators, data preparers, the data base administrator, the security officer, and general clerks.
2. *Cost of supplies.* As the system operates, it consumes supplies. These supplies are in the form of punched cards, printer paper, ribbons, paper tape, magnetic tape, and so forth. These items are drawn from inventory and as such, should be subject to management control procedures. Often control on these supplies is inadequate, causing waste and unnecessary costs.
3. *Equipment maintenance.* Maintenance of a system may be performed by the organization's own engineers and technicians, by the manufacturer's personnel, or by a combination of the two. In any

event, maintenance is a recurring expense.

4. *Systems maintenance.* These costs are incurred in debugging the system, adapting the system to meet new requirements, improving the system on the behalf of users, and enhancing the system for operations.

5. *Power and light.* After the initial electrical equipment for servicing the system is installed, there is a recurring charge, based on amount of use, for power and light.

6. *Insurance.* For purchased equipment, it is sound policy to obtain insurance for fire, extended coverage, and vandalism. For equipment rented, determine whether to obtain similar insurance while the equipment is in your possession. To safeguard against disgruntled employees who might be inclined to do injury to the system, it is advisable to obtain a DDD (disappearance, dishonesty, destruction) bond.

Further Systems Work. If it is decided, after the cost/effectiveness analysis has been performed, that the proposed system will be implemented, then additional systems work will be required. This work includes detailed systems design, control specifications, procedure writing, and so forth.

Preparation of Final General Systems Design Report

Prior to considering further detailed systems work and implementation work, management must make a final decision concerning implementing the proposed system. The document upon which management relies is the **Final General Systems Design Report,** which includes, among other things, the cost/effectiveness analysis. The supplement at the end of this chapter provides an example of this report.

SUMMARY

The general systems design requirements will dictate what kind of system is finally implemented. In this chapter we have assumed a computer configuration as a vehicle for discussion.

After proposals have been received from vendors, each vendor is evaluated on the basis of imperatives. Any vendors not meeting all imperatives are automatically eliminated from further evaluation. Next, to gain further insight into what the remaining vendors have to offer, criteria comparisons are made. Performance of equipment can be determined by benchmarks and by simulation. Having evaluated the vendors, the analyst grades each vendor using selected criteria.

Four methods of acquiring a computer configuration are rent, purchase, lease, and a combination of the preceding. Management selects a particular method based on advantages applicable to the organization. If a computer configuration is acquired, then management should strive to sign a "risk-free" contract.

The major consideration as to whether or not an organization acquires a computer configuration, or undertakes any project, should be stated in cost/effectiveness terms. If the effectiveness of a proposed system sufficiently outweighs costs of that system, then it is likely that the proposed system will be implemented. To receive a go/no-go decision from management, the analyst should prepare a Final General Systems Design Report containing, among other things, the results of the cost/effectiveness analysis.

REVIEW QUESTIONS

13.1 Draw a flowchart of the steps one must take to evaluate and justify any general systems design proposal.

13.2 List and explain general systems design requirements.

13.3 Explain the meaning of "imperatives" and "desirables."

13.4 List and briefly discuss the methods used to obtain computer equipment proposals.

13.5 What are the methods used to evaluate computer equipment? What are the advantages/disadvantages of these methods?

13.6 Select eight criteria of computer selection and rank them, in order of priority, from one to eight (one being the most important). You are not restricted only to those mentioned in the text.

13.7 Give a brief definition of: (1) modularity, (2) compatibility, (3) reliability, (4) maintainability, and (5) general vendor support.

13.8 List and explain the four methods of acquiring computer equipment.

13.9 Define costs by type, behavior, function, and time. Give an example of each.

13.10 Effectiveness can be equated to two types of benefits. Discuss and give an example of each.

13.11 Discuss the basic methods of estimating costs and effectiveness.

QUESTIONS FOR DISCUSSION

13.1 "The problem of quantifying benefits, especially indirect benefits, normally is quite difficult. Nevertheless, to perform meaningful cost/effectiveness analysis, all aspects should be quantified." Discuss.

13.2 The Department of Transportation evaluates alternative highway safety measures by "cost per reduced fatality." How would you quantify the benefits?

13.3 If the amount of research funds to be allocated to various diseases could be analyzed in terms of costs related to reductions in mortality, how, then, would you compare these costs to benefits?

13.4 Discuss the comment, "A reasonable, educated approximation is better than nothing at all."

13.5 "There is a propensity, by even the most competent people, to underestimate the cost of doing something new and to overestimate the benefits to be derived." Do you agree? Disagree? Why?

13.6 "There is a tendency to place a great deal of confidence in anything that is quantified and printed on paper. So we constantly remind our managers to be skeptical about any quantifications concerning the future and to assume a large margin of error." Discuss.

13.7 "Regardless of uncertainties, decisions must be made. If we have done a conscientious job in our cost/effectiveness analysis, then we do not hesitate to make a decision. We feel that postponing action is, in reality, a decision to continue business as usual, which in many instances may be the worst decision of all." Discuss.

13.8 The relevant costs in any decision are those costs that would be incurred if a system were implemented, but that would not be incurred if it were not implemented. Elaborate on this statement and give several examples for illustrative purposes.

13.9 Discuss the statement, "Cost calculations are only half the picture in a cost/effectiveness analysis."

13.10 A basic principle in preparing a cost/effectiveness analysis for management is to provide alternatives. Explain.

13.11 We may look at costs as being disadvantages and benefits as being advantages. Therefore, for proper decision making, there must be a systematic attempt to determine, quantify, and weigh the advantages and disadvantages of each proposal alternative. Discuss.

13.12 Some authorities believe that not all factors involved in a cost/effectiveness analysis can be measured and quantified. Do you agree? Why? Why not? If a factor is material, then the analyst either quantifies it or leaves it unquantified. If the analyst chooses not to quantify it, then how is it incorporated into the decision-making process?

13.13 "Measurement of the system is far more significant and meaningful in the long term than measurement of the CPU." Comment on this statement.

13.14 "You can't design a system until you know what kind of computer you are going to have." Discuss the merits of this statement.

13.15 "The most important consideration in choosing a vendor is the level of support provided after you install the machine." Evaluate.

13.16 "The manufacturer apologized for failing to install the new machine on time. But, in the meantime, it was necessary to rent an outside computer for six weeks." Discuss the implications of this comment.

EXERCISES

13.1 Classify each of the following cost items by behavior (variable or fixed), by function (development, operational, or maintenance), and by time (recurring or nonrecurring):

1. Rental charges for the computer mainframe based on $150/CPU hour.
2. Rental charges of $1000/month for a line printer.
3. Cost of installation of one-way emergency doors.
4. Delivery charges on the computer mainframe.
5. Wages of a special instructor to train a class of programmers in the new virtual storage operating system.
6. Programming charges of $36,000 for conversion of accounts receivable application package from an IBM 1401 to an IBM 3032.
7. Analyst costs of $3500 for preparing a Proposal to Conduct Systems Analysis Report on a sales analysis package.
8. Operator payroll fringe benefit charges of $1900.
9. Charges for repairing three broken keypunch machines this month.

13.2 Barry Bright, systems analyst for Graphics, Inc., has just completed his systems design proposal report. Included in this report is some information concerning the acquisition of a computer configuration. This information is listed as follows:

1. The purchase price of the computer is $1,200,000. Maintenance expenses are expected to run $60,000 per year. If the computer is rented, the yearly rental price will be $370,000, based on an unlimited use rental contract with free maintenance.

2. Mr. Bright believes it will be necessary to replace the configuration at the end of five years. It is estimated that the computer will have a resale value of $120,000 at the end of the five years.
3. The estimated gross annual savings derived from this particular alternative computer configuration are $450,000 the first year, $500,000 the second, and $550,000 each of the third, fourth, and fifth years. The estimated annual expense of operation is $190,000, in addition to the expenses mentioned above. Additional nonrecurring costs are $70,000.
4. If Graphics decides to rent the computer instead of buying, the $1,200,000 could be invested at a 25 percent rate of return. The present value of $1.00 at the end of each of five years, discounted at 18 percent is:

End of Year	Present Value
1	$0.800
2	0.640
3	0.512
4	0.410
5	0.328

Based on the above financial considerations alone, ignoring tax impact, which method of acquisition do you recommend?

13.3 The following are results of benchmark problems run on configurations A, B, and C. The benchmark problems run on each configuration are representative sample workloads, which test for both I/O and internal processing capabilities of each configuration. The monthly rental, based on projected usage of at least 176 hours per month, is $30,000 for configuration A, $34,000 for configuration B, and $32,000 for configuration C.

Benchmark Results: CPU Times (in Seconds) for Compilation and Execution of Different Programs

Vendor	Process-Bound Problem	Input/Output-Bound Problem	Hybrid Problem
A	400.5	640	247.5
B	104.9	320	260.3
C	175.4	325	296.8

Required: Which configuration should be selected? Why?

PROBLEMS

13.1 Clayborn Mines is contemplating installing a computer system that will save them an estimated $96,000 per year in operating costs. Clayborn estimates that the useful life of the system will be four years and that it will have no residual value. The computer system may be purchased from Honeywell for $260,000, or it may be leased from a third party for $80,000 payable at the end of each year. The noncancellable lease would run for four years.

Clayborn Mines is a fast-growing corporation and requires that all capital investments earn a rate of return of at least 26 percent. Through a favorable agreement with a large Chicago bank they are able to borrow funds for capital investment projects at 20 percent.

Required: Ignoring tax effects, what should Clayborn do? (*Note:* the present value of a $1.00 annuity for four years is $2.588 and $2.300 at rates of 20 and 26 percent, respectively).

13.2 A computer center has four jobs whose processing times are directly related to the speed of the input/output components and the volume of data being processed. The input medium is cards and the card reader has a rated speed of 1000 cards per minute. On the output side, the printer is rated at 1100 lines per minute, and the card punch has a rated speed of 600 cards per minute.

Since these devices share a single multiplexer channel, simultaneous operation of the components results in interference, and consequently, degrades each component's level of efficiency (rated speed).

	Level of Efficiency (in Percent) of Components with			
Components	Card Reader	Card Punch	Printer	Both Other Components
Card reader	100	90	85	70
Card punch	90	100	87	70
Printer	85	87	100	70

The volumes of the four jobs are as follows:

JOB	INPUT CARDS	OUTPUT CARDS	LINES
(1)	3,000	400	4,000
(2)	50,000	1,000	1,000
(3)	5,000	300	10,000
(4)	50	800	800

Required: Assuming that output is not dependent on input, determine the shortest processing time for each of the four jobs.

13.3 Tidex Manufacturing is planning to acquire a computer system. The costs for the undertaking have been projected over a five-year period. Year 0, the first year, is prior to the computer installation, while the remaining four years represent the life of the system. The costs and savings have been estimated as follows:

	0	1	2	3	4
1. Initial systems and programming	74,000				
2. Environment preparation	7,000				
3. Conversion	15,000	14,000	3,000		
4. Parallel operations		9,000	6,000	1,000	
5. Equipment rental		75,000	81,000	85,000	115,000
6. Systems and programming		70,000	70,000	70,000	70,000
7. Operations		60,000	64,000	70,000	72,000
8. Reduction in service bureau costs		65,000	95,000	125,000	130,000
9. Reduction in clerical costs		12,000	18,000	24,000	55,000
10. Reduction in inventory costs		35,000	150,000	160,000	160,000
11. Reduction in rental of old equipment		10,000	15,000	20,000	25,000
12. Reduction in overtime			6,000	30,000	40,000
13. Increased customer service level		6,000	58,000	95,000	100,000
14. Improved management planning		8,000	45,000	50,000	50,000
15. Improved management control		9,000	50,000	50,000	50,000

Required: Analyze these costs and benefits and indicate when total benefits exceed total costs, and where total direct benefits exceed total costs.

13.4 A large fabricator and marketer of customized aluminum products has a sales force of 400 people throughout the continental United States and Canada. A traditional problem in the company has been the delay of entering orders (via mail) from each of these salespeople to a centralized data processing center in St. Louis, Missouri. In addition the salespeople are unable to respond to a customer's inquiry concerning the status of an in-process order in less than two days. A marketing study has estimated that delays in order entry cost the company $200,000 in lost sales annually. Moreover, customer frustration with late shipments resulted in a loss of $300,000 from cancelled orders in each of the last two years. The average profit margin for the company is 30 percent.

A recently completed systems analysis has revealed the following facts:

1. Each salesperson can be assigned a small portable terminal to access the corporate computers directly at an initial cost of $500 per terminal.
2. Special communication networks to permit toll free calls can be installed at a cost of $20,000 initially and $3500 per month.
3. Maintenance for all the terminals is estimated at $10,000 annually.
4. System development and implementation costs are estimated at $250,000.
5. To operate the system with the centralized computer is estimated at $20,000 annually.
6. Corporate guidelines require new projects to pay back within five years or less.

Analyze the above facts and prepare a report describing the economic feasibility of implementing the new system.

13.5 The Wing Commander of a tactical fighter wing has requested the implementation of a formal information system to assist him in evaluating the quality of aircrew members. Although many factors are related to determining an individual's quality level, it has been recommended that one source of objective data is from the testing process administered by the Standardization/Evaluation Section in the fighter wing. Each flight crew member is tested periodically either by an instrument check or by a tactical/proficiency check to detect violations of standardized operating procedures or errors in judgment. The result of a test is either pass or fail and discrepancies such as single-engine landing, dangerous pass, incorrect holding pattern, and so forth are noted where applicable. A general feeling exists in the Standardization/Evaluation Section that if these reports were prepared and disseminated in a timely fashion, the Wing Commander could take swift corrective action to prevent a hazardous practice or critical weakness from causing a decline in mission performance or even an accident from occurring. Further analysis indicates that such a report can be prepared daily, five days a week throughout the year, at a cost of $14.10 per day per report. This time period for reporting is judged acceptable by the Standardization/Evaluation Section.

While many benefits are anticipated from implementing such a system, the Wing Commander has requested that all new information systems be justified initially on economic grounds alone. As the systems analyst assigned to this project, you have decided to take the approach that the proposed system will help change the probability of a major accident per flight from .00002 (without the report) to .000015 (with the report). From your investigation you have gathered the following statistics concerning major accidents:

Costs of a Major Accident

Certain costs:	
Aircraft	$1,600,000
Accident investigation	6,000
Property damage (impact point)	2,000
Total	$1,608,000
Possible costs (both crew members are lost):	
Invested training in crew members	
2 @ $25,000	$ 50,000
Survivors benefits and mortuary costs	
2 @ $50,000	100,000
Total	$150,000
Probability of crew loss .25	

Required: Can the proposed system be economically justified using this approach? (*Hint:* it may be helpful to calculate the number of flights that would have to be made each year by the wing to cover the cost of generating the report.) Identify other economic factors not considered in this problem.

BIBLIOGRAPHY

Beizer, "The Viability of Computer Complexes-Reliability and Maintainability," *Modern Data,* December 1969.

Bierman and Smidt, *The Capital Budgeting Decision,* Fourth Edition, New York: The Macmillan Company, 1975.

Bibliography

Brandon, "Does Your Contract Really Protect You?" *Computer Decisions,* December 1971.

Burch and Hod, *Information Systems: A Case-Workbook,* Santa Barbara, CA.: John Wiley & Sons, Inc., 1975.

Cantania, "Computer System Models," *Computers and Automation,* March 1972.

Horngren, *Cost Accounting: A Managerial Emphasis,* Fourth Edition, Englewood Cliffs, NJ.: Prentice-Hall, Inc., 1977.

Joslin, *Analysis, Design and Selection of Computer Systems,* Arlington, VA.: College Readings, 1971.

Kanter, *Management Guide to Computer Systems Selection,* Englewood Cliffs, NJ.: Prentice-Hall, Inc., 1970.

"Operating Leases Seen Leading to 'Financial Suicide'," *Computerworld,* June 13, 1977.

Pelican Case

Phase 3 · Systems Evaluation and Justification
· Final General Systems Design Report

Phases of Systems Development Methodology:

Completed ▨
To be completed ☐

Phase 1	Phase 2	Phase 3	Phase 4	Phase 5
Systems analysis	General systems design	Systems evaluation and justification	Detail systems design	Systems implementation
Proposal to conduct systems analysis report / Systems analysis completion report	General systems design proposal report	Final general systems design report	Final detail systems design report	Final implementation report
Completed in Chapter 11	Completed in Chapter 12	Presented and completed in this chapter	Presented at the end of Chapter 15	Presented at the end of Chapter 16

FINAL GENERAL SYSTEMS DESIGN REPORT

To: All Managers

From: Ben Snow, Systems Analyst

Purpose and Scope of Report

The purpose of this report is to compare the cost/effectiveness of Alternatives I and II. With the exception of a few minor differences, both systems alternatives require the same computer configuration. Based on a specific hardware configuration with appropriate software packages, a thorough evaluation was made of six candidate vendors. This report also contains an analysis of employee impact and an implementation plan and schedule.

Summarized Request for Proposal

Analysis and design efforts determined the general nature of a system that would meet a variety of demands. Based on these efforts, a Request for Proposal (RFP) was mailed to six Original Equipment Manufacturers (OEMs) who appeared able to meet the specifications summarized below. (Note that for simplicity purposes, several technical details are left out.)

1. The hardware configuration should include four CRTs, a desktop processor, two printers, 100 portable dictation units, one OCR reader, one hard disk unit, four floppy disk drives, 100 double density floppy disks, four magnetic tapes and one magnetic tape unit, 200 minicassettes, and a central recording system for remote dictation via telephone.

2. The processor must be compatible with Pelican's present host computer configuration. Connection to the host must be made by a direct-connect modem. Because of noise and other disturbances, an acoustic coupler connection is unacceptable. The communication interface must have an industry-accepted standard protocol; handshaking capabilities; and be able to transmit digital, voice, word, and image data.

3. Transmission mode must be full duplex.

4. A 16-bit processor will be considered, but a 32-bit processor is preferred. The processor must retain data in the event of a power failure or power loss. Random access memory (RAM) must be a minimum of 192K; RAM must be expandable to at least 384K.

5. The system must be able to handle more than one user/job at a time and perform simultaneous input/output.

6. The hard disk must be able to store a minimum of 10 megabytes. The system must have the expansion capability to add three more hard disk units.
7. The system must be able to print at least 10,000 one-page letters per month plus other reports of approximately equal volume. Printers should be able to print at least 400 words per minute.
8. Letter-quality output is required. A daisy wheel printer is preferred over conversion kits for dot matrix printers.
9. Although no immediate application is planned, the system must be able to produce graphic output with a minimum of six colors.
10. CRTs must be high-resolution, 12-inch monitors. They must have an automatic scrolling feature and the ability to display upper and lower case characters and output graphics. The keyboard must be detachable from the monitor and must contain special keys for delete, insert, repeat, and like functions.
11. The system must have four floppy disk drives online. Their total capacity must be at least 2 megabyes.
12. Two utility programs or library commands are imperative. The first is a program to copy data from disk onto magnetic tape for backup. The second necessary utility program is spooling. Spooling saves printer output in a disk file for later printing and also allows printing while other operations are being performed. The system's operating system should also have password or lockout features to control access.
13. The data base management system must allow direct, indexed sequential, and sequential access to the data in disk files. Also, access by attribute value is a desirable feature.
14. The OCR reader must be capable of reading hand-printed data.
15. Cost of the hardware and appropriate software packages must be less than $60,000 per year if not purchased; $200,000 if purchased.
16. The system must have a COBOL compiler.
17. A central storage system for remote dictation must

be available online 24 hours per day with continuous loop recording media.

18. All conventional word processing features must be available, such as: automatic text wraparound; text modification, sorting and merging; automatic margin alignment; indexing; pagination; global searching; automatic hyphen; automatic carriage return; automatic decimal alignment; and dictionary lookup.

19. Backup of 10 megabytes of data from hard disk to magnetic tape should not exceed 20 minutes

All vendors responded to the proposal. One vendor presented a configuration that did not have a COBOL compiler or the ability to add memory. This vendor was eliminated from further consideration.

Questionnaire

The next step in selecting a specific configuration involved preparation and mailing of questionnaires. Following is a sample of the questionnaire sent to the remaining five vendors. Note that some comments have been added at the end of each question. These comments are for internal use and were not included in the original questionnaire.

<u>Vendor Questionnaire</u>

1. How long have you been in the computer business? ____

   If a vendor was in the business less than three years, they were eliminated from further consideration. For the purpose of assurance that a vendor will be able to service our system over the next four to five years, a three-year existence is minimal.

2. Is the computer business your only business? ____Yes ____No
   We do not want our vendor to be a subsidiary of a larger corporation or be involved in other business

activities. We want a total commitment to computers and research and development in this area.

3. Over the past two years, how much have your sales increased in percentage and absolute dollars? _____%
_____$

We are seeking vendors who have a healthy growth pattern.

4. How many similar configurations have you installed? _____

Anything less than 20 indicates a lack of experience. The more experienced a vendor is, the better able the vendor is to serve us.

5. Will you furnish us with names and addresses of users who are located within 200 miles of our home office and whom we may contact? ____Yes ____No
A negative answer is sufficient to eliminate a vendor from further consideration. The purpose of this question is twofold. One, we can ask these users what they think about the system. Two, we may be able to form or become a member of a user's group to exchange ideas, problems, and solutions.

6. Will you run benchmarks which simulate our processing requirements using our data? ____Yes ____No
A negative answer eliminates the vendor from further consideration. We do not want prepared "samples" and "dog and pony" shows. We want to benchmark our programs.

7. Will you commit to a training and implementation schedule? ____Yes ____No

8. Will your staff maintain the system? ____Yes ____No
A negative answer eliminates the vendor from further consideration. Vendors can be manufacturers, distributors, or third parties. We are dealing directly with manufacturer representatives because we want direct support by people who work for the manufacturer.

9. Are complete service and maintenance facilities and personnel available locally? ____Yes ____No
An affirmative answer is required.

10. Are hardware and software warranted? ____Yes ____No For how long? _____

The answer must be yes and for over 60 days after implementation.

11. Are your manuals fully documented and understandable to the average reader? ____Yes ____No
    We expect a positive answer. These manuals will be examined and inquiries will be made of other users.

12. Do you provide experienced implementation personnel? ____Yes ____No
    An affirmative answer is required.

13. Do you provide training for all users from operators to managers? ____Yes ____No
    A positive answer is required.

14. Will you provide a copy of the service and maintenance contract before we acquire the system? ____Yes ____No
    A positive answer is required.

15. What is your projected Mean Time Between Failure (MTBF) of your weakest component? _____

16. What is your projected Mean Time To Repair (MTTR)? _____

17. How often is preventive maintenance performed? _____
    We strongly believe in preventive maintenance. Twice a year is acceptable. Monthly would be desirable. Over a year or never is enough to eliminate a vendor from further consideration.

18. Will you perform major repairs "on-site" or "in-shop?" _____
    We prefer on-site repairs if possible.

19. Do you offer a toll-free hotline? ____Yes ____No
    A positive answer is obviously preferable. Our experience indicates that many calls about minor "bugs" occur for several months after implementation. A toll-free hotline provided by the vendor can save a substantial amount of money.

One vendor did not respond to the questionnaire. Another's response was unfavorable. The three remaining vendors were evaluated further on the basis of performance material furnished by a computer research

440 Pelican Case—Phase 3

company.[1] An example of the results of this evaluation on one of the vendors is shown in the following chart. This chart is based on 14 user responses.

Performance Criteria	Ratings of Users				WA*
	Excellent	Good	Fair	Poor	
Ease of operation	7	5	2	0	3.4
Reliability of mainframe	7	5	2	0	3.4
Reliability of peripherals	4	8	1	1	3.1
Maintenance service:					
Responsiveness	4	7	1	2	2.9
Effectiveness	2	7	5	0	2.8
Technical support	4	5	4	0	3.0
Training availability	7	5	2	0	3.4
Training manuals	7	7	0	0	3.5
Software upgrades	7	7	0	0	3.5
Availability of equipment	7	5	2	0	3.4
Manufacturer's software:					
Operating system	3	6	4	1	2.8
Compilers and assemblers	3	6	5	0	2.9
Applications programs	2	5	4	1	2.7
Ease of programming	4	6	3	0	3.1
Overall satisfaction	4	6	4	0	3.0

*Weighted average on a scale of 4.0 for excellent.

In addition, a number of companies using the vendor's hardware and software were called. Their evaluation responses were consistent with the above material.

[1] For example, see Datapro Research Corporation, Delran, New Jersey.

Benchmarks

Two of the vendor's weighted average scores were remarkably close. The third vendor's score was so low that it was eliminated at this point. For the two remaining vendors benchmarks were prepared and run on configurations similar to those specified in their proposals. Results of these benchmarks are shown below:

Vendors / Program	Vendor A	Vendor B
Paragraph merging	15 sec.	22 sec.
Addressing and printing	106	138
Backup from disk to tape	412	470
Sales report	417	498
Expense report	392	427
OCR reading of handwritten documents	60 (with no rejects)	74 (with one reject)

Some of the peripheral devices, such as dictation units, were simply demonstrated and not benchmarked as such.

To this point, both vendors were relatively equal. The results of the above benchmark helped to decide in vendor A's favor. After checking with accounting, it was concluded that Pelican should lease vendor A's configuration. Leasing gives Pelican certain tax benefits and prevents a cash flow problem from occurring. Also, it appears that Pelican will be in a better position for equipment and software upgrades with a leasing arrangement than if equipment and software were purchased. If need be, one or two CRTs can be rented during peak promotion months.

Employee Impact

Bud Wiser has been designated as manager in charge of the new system. With Alternative I, he would have to hire his own programmer; with Alternative II, a programmer from central processing will work part time for Bud on a loan-out basis.

Additional training is required of all operators and users. Mrs. Suzuki and her assistants will be trained to complete special OCR forms. All salespeople will have to be trained to use dictation facilities and to interact with the system. Training sessions will be conducted by vendor A. All of the users of CRT equipment must spend one-half day learning how to use this equipment. Because of scheduling problems, it is projected that this training session will have to be conducted over a three-week period.

It is recommended that Sally Worth and an assistant be transferred from the secretarial pool to handle transcription of dictation minicassettes.

Bud Wiser will have general management responsibility of the telephone network. For internal control purposes, Bud Wiser is not authorized to pay any telephone bills. Accounting will do this. Allocation of telephone equipment and resources among and between departments will be under Bud Wiser's authority. Any major conflicts will be arbitrated by Martha Pringle.

Implementation Plan and Schedule

The following PERT-type chart shows the projected schedule for detail design and implementation. If Alternative II is chosen, the schedule may have to be increased by one or two weeks because of potential interface problems with the host computer. The probability of this occurring is low.

Cost/Effectiveness Analysis

It is estimated that no major modifications will have to be made to either alternative for a period of four years. Consequently, the analysis is based on a four-year period.

Pelican Case—Phase 3

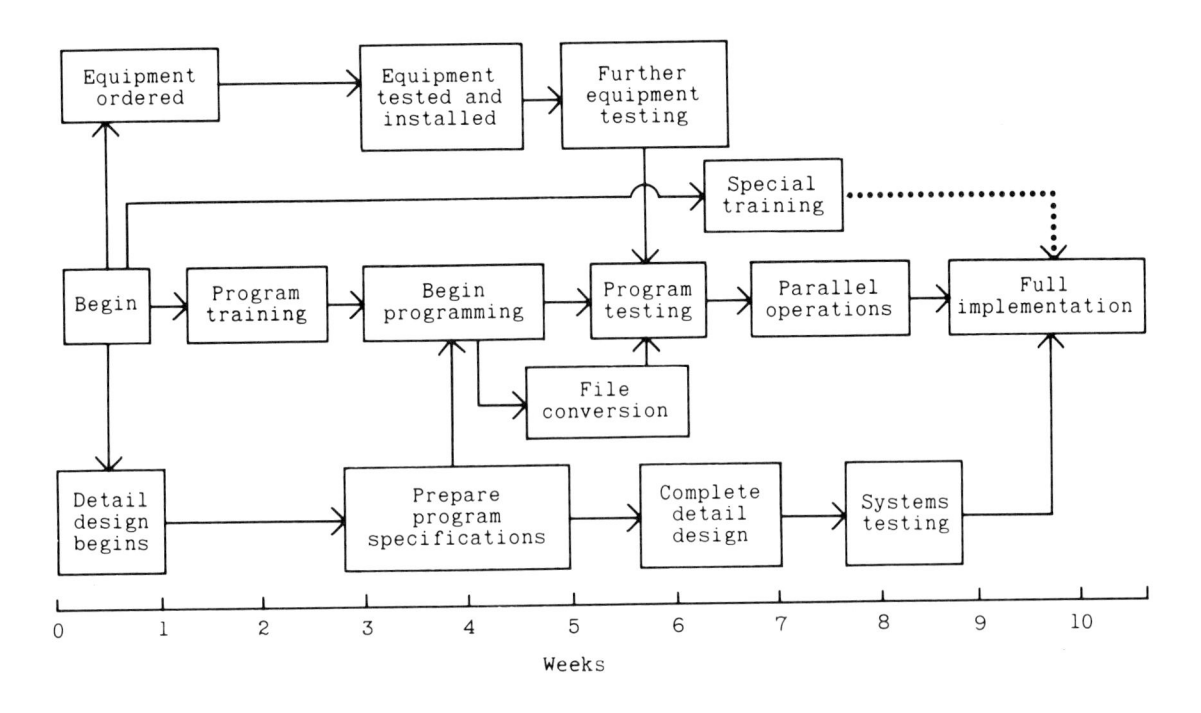

```
Equipment  →  Equipment     →  Further
ordered       tested and       equipment
              installed        testing
                                  ↓
                               Special
                               training ·········┐
                                  ↓               ⋮
Begin → Program  → Begin       → Program → Parallel   → Full
        training   programming    testing   operations   implementation
                      ↑            ↑
                      │         File
                      │         conversion
                      │
Detail       →  Prepare       →  Complete  →  Systems
design          program           detail       testing
begins          specifications    design
```

Weeks: 0 – 10

Costs for Alternative I

Cost Items	Year 1	Year 2	Year 3	Year 4
Computer system	$60,000	$60,000	$60,000	$60,000
Systems work	20,000			
Programming	25,000	27,000	30,000	32,000
Training	10,000			
Testing	5,000			
Conversion	10,000			
Operation	250,000	300,000	320,000	350,000
Total	$380,000	$387,000	$410,000	$442,000

Notice that the lease, programming, and operating costs of the computer system are recurring, while all others are one-time, setup costs. Computer system costs are certain by lease agreement. Other costs are estimated with a built-in inflation factor.

Pelican Case—Phase 3

Costs for Alternative II

Cost Items	Year 1	Year 2	Year 3	Year 4
Computer system	$6,500	$6,500	$6,500	$6,500
Systems work	20,000			
Programming	5,000	6,000	7,000	8,000
Training	10,000			
Testing	5,000			
Conversion	10,000			
Operation	200,000	240,000	250,000	280,000
Total	$315,000	$311,000	$322,000	$353,000

The reduction in programming and operation costs as compared to Alternative I stems from the fact that a programmer from the central system can be used on a part-time basis. Also, other skills such as computer operations, librarians, data clerks, and so forth, can be used in the same way.

Benefits are listed below. They are the same for both alternatives. All the figures were derived using statistical methods applied to management's best guesses. For example, a profit figure was derived by getting a number of estimates from different managers, and from these estimates computing an expected value.

Direct Benefits	Year 1	Year 2	Year 3	Year 4
1. Reduction in telephone costs because of correction of billing discrepancies.	$ 4,000	$ 4,000	$ 4,000	$ 4,000
2. Reduction in unauthorized long distance calls.	10,000	10,000	10,000	10,000
3. Reduction in long distance charges by increased use of WATS.	10,000	12,000	14,000	18,000

4. Increased profit through more effective sales promotion.	100,000	110,000	130,000	150,000
5. Increased profit through sales efficiency.	186,000	206,000	226,000	266,000
Total Direct Benefits	$310,000	$342,000	$384,000	$448,000

Indirect Benefits	Year 1	Year 2	Year 3	Year 4
1. Better allocation of telephone calls.	$10,000	$15,000	$10,000	$25,000
2. Increased profit through improved customer service.	100,000	150,000	200,000	250,000
Total Indirect Benefits	110,000	165,000	220,000	295,000
Total Benefits	$420,000	$507,000	$604,000	$723,000

Given the estimated system's costs and benefits, a comparison of alternatives is performed below. These figures can be analyzed using a number of accounting and financial models, such as present value analysis. Also, tax benefits, which would include tax credits and depreciation expense, are not included. The several methods presented below, however, should be sufficient to highlight major points and draw a cost/effectiveness comparison between the two alternatives.

Pelican Case—Phase 3

Analysis for Both Alternatives

	Year 1	Year 2	Year 3	Year 4
Total Benefits	$420,000	$507,000	$604,000	$723,000
Less Cost I	380,000	387,000	410,000	442,000
Effectiveness (+, −) I	+$40,000	+$120,000	+$194,000	+$281,000
Less Costs II	315,000	311,000	322,000	353,000
Effectiveness (+, −) II	+$105,000	+$196,000	+$282,000	+$370,000
	1	2	3	4
Accumulated Direct Benefits	$310,000	$652,000	$1,036,000	$1,484,000
Accumulated Costs I	380,000	767,000	1,177,000	1,619,000
Direct Benefits (+, −) I	−$70,000	−$115,000	−$141,000	−$135,000
Accumulated Costs II	315,000	626,000	948,000	1,301,000
Direct Benefits (+, −) II	−$5,000	+$26,000	+$88,000	+$183,000
Accumulated Indirect Benefits	$110,000	$275,000	$495,000	$770,000
Accumulated Costs I	380,000	767,000	1,177,000	1,619,000
Indirect Benefits (+, −) I	−$270,000	−$492,000	−$453,000	−$531,000

Accumulated Costs II	$315,000	$626,000	$948,000	$1,301,000
Indirect Benefits (+, −) II	−$205,000	−$351,000	−$453,000	−$531,000
Total Accumulated Benefits	$420,000	$929,000	$1,531,000	$2,254,000
Accumulated Costs I	380,000	767,000	1,177,000	1,619,000
Effectiveness (+, −) I	+$40,000	+$160,000	+$354,000	+$635,000
Accumulated Costs II	$315,000	$626,000	$948,000	$1,301,000
Effectiveness (+, −) II	+$105,000	+$301,000	+$583,000	+$953,000

Notice that neither alternative has high indirect benefits. Also, Alternative I must combine both direct and indirect benefits before effectiveness exceeds cost. And, then, it is only 1.40 times greater than total costs. On the other hand, direct benefits alone for Alternative II are 1.14 times greater than total costs. Total benefits are 1.73 times total costs, a fairly good ratio. This means that risk of meeting economic demands is reduced, if not eliminated. Certainly, with an excess of direct benefits, Pelican has a substantial cushion to absorb fairly large estimation errors. Also, an item that is not factored into the analysis is the additional operating capacity the host provides. That is, Pelican has the potential to grow without incurring significant variable costs because of the more effective use of a fixed-cost resource. Alternative II, therefore, is recommended for detail design and implementation.

CHAPTER 14

Detail Systems Design—Controls

14.1 ■ INTRODUCTION

Earlier in Part III, the design of an information system was discussed at a conceptual level. To transform a general or conceptual design into a unified system of people and machines that collects and processes data and produces information, the systems analyst must perform some additional activities. Many of these activities were discussed in Part II as they were related to the development of a data base. In this chapter the control points necessary to ensure reliable processing of data are identified and explained, and the important aspects of security, which must be considered during detailed systems design, are discussed.

14.2 ■ CONTROL POINTS

The information system is a large and valuable resource to the organization. Ensuring that this resource is performing as required, and protecting its operation from both internal and external misuse, is essential. For effective administration and control of an information system, an overall framework of organizational and procedural controls must be designed and implemented. Such a framework helps to ensure the stewardship of assets, reliability of operations, and general integrity of the system. The importance of controls was not always recognized in the early days of computerization. This failure to recognize the importance of controls led to many of the early computer systems' failures and resulted in the "anticomputer mentality" of many organization users.

In Chapter 1, controls were introduced as a design block component of the information system. Throughout the text, we have alluded to the use of and need for controls. Figure 14.1 is a schematic of the information system showing its major control points. All of these major control points are grouped into nine general categories, discussed below. Security controls are discussed in a separate section.

External Controls

These control functions emanate from, and are performed by, such groups as indepen-

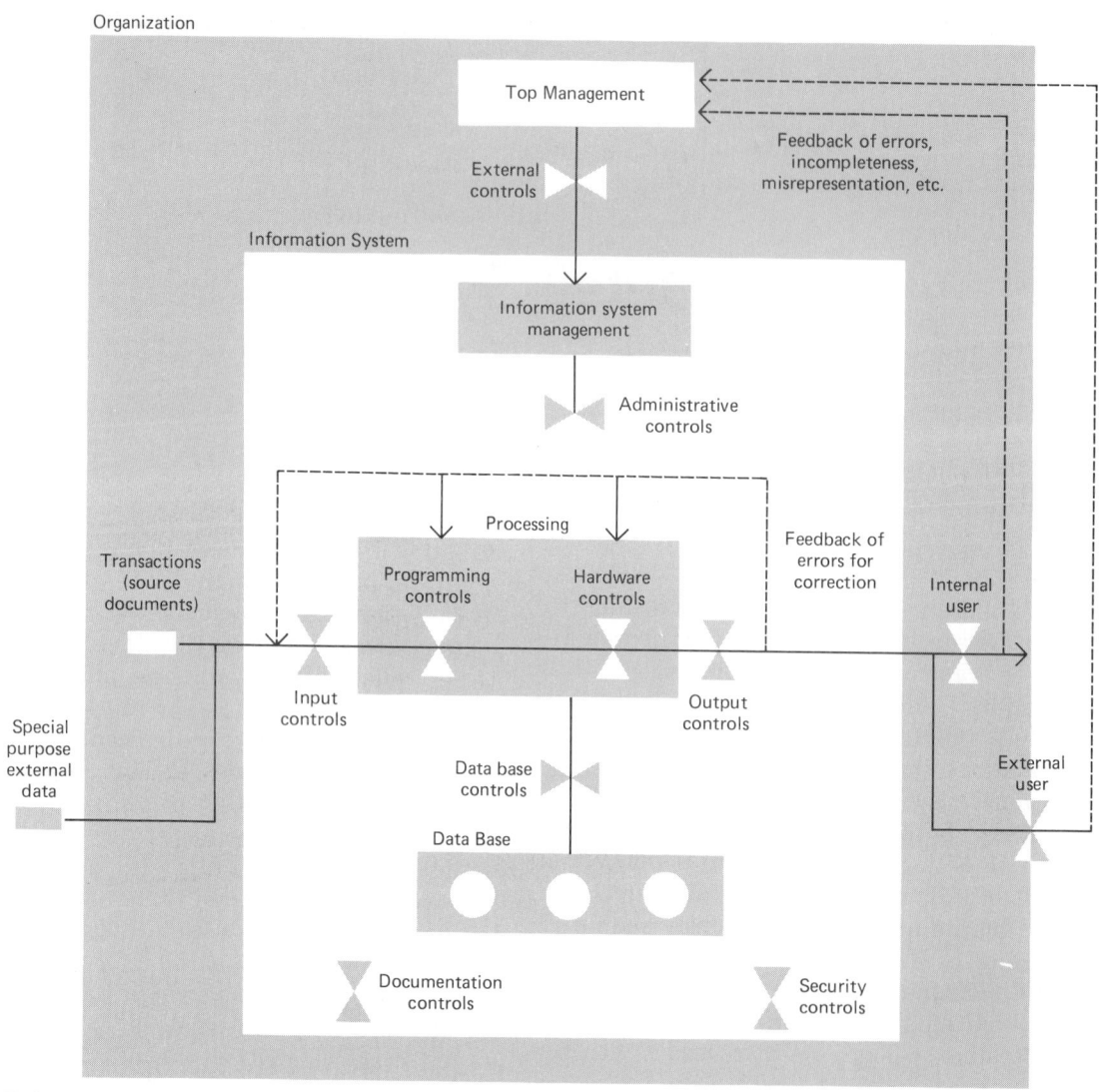

FIG. 14.1 Control points relative to the information system.

dent auditors and consultants, user departments, top management, special staff control groups, and various other constituents of the organization. They establish an independent check on the overall activities of the system through observation and feedback. This control point is discussed further in the last chapter of this part.

Administrative Controls

These controls emanate directly from the management of the information system and are traditional management functions, such as setting of plans, selection and assignment of personnel, delineation of responsibilities, preparation of job descriptions, establishment of performance standards, and so forth. Management should establish both *master* and *contingency plans*. The overall benefit of a master plan is organizational goal congruence. The master plan provides a sense of direction. It unifies and coordinates personnel and other resources. It also reduces the number of isolated, noncompatible subsystems which might otherwise be developed. It establishes benchmarks and gives a means of controlling activities and projects.

A contingency plan is a set of procedures that instructs personnel what to do in the event of abnormal circumstances. For example, in a computer-based information system, what does management do if the computer stops working? If no backup system exists, or if management has not signed a contingency contract with another organization to use their computer as backup, then a serious situation can develop if the computer is down for an extended period.

Good personnel control includes hiring the right people initially. These employees should have the technical ability, character, and past performance records necessary to contribute to the organization. A new employee should never be thrust into an organization without some form of orientation and training. Management should establish a program not only to train new employees, but also to update the expertise of all employees.

Once personnel are hired and trained, they must be managed properly. Controlling a computer system is basically a matter of controlling computer personnel. Not only should standards be established, but a system should be in place to report to management any significant deviation from standards. Measurement bases for standards are comprised of procedures, quality, quantity, time, and money. These standard measurements relate to personnel, hardware, software, and the data base. More about management of the system will be discussed in the last chapter.

Input Controls

Input controls are comprised of the following items:

1. *Transaction codes.* In any organization, data (transaction documents, fields, records, files, etc.) represent people, events, assets, objects, and so forth. Codes provide an abbreviated structure for uniquely classifying and identifying data. The assignment of unique and specific codes to transactions will aid in the control of input.

2. *Forms design.* When a source document is required for the collection of data, this form can be designed to force more legible entries by the use of individual blocks for each character to be recorded. Figure 14.2 is an example of a source document which shows explicitly where each data item is to be entered. Care should be taken, however, to avoid creating a form that is so difficult for the user to complete that it becomes a new source of error.

3. *Verification.* Source documents prepared by one clerk can be verified or proofread by another clerk to improve accuracy. In a data conversion operation such as keypunching or keyboard-to-storage, each document can be verified by a second operator. The verifying operator goes through the same keying operation as the original operator; his or her keying efforts are compared logically by the machine to the previous entries. A discrepancy in the data entered by the first and second operators is indicated by lights on the machine. Verification is a duplication operation and, therefore, doubles the cost

452 Detail Systems Design—Control

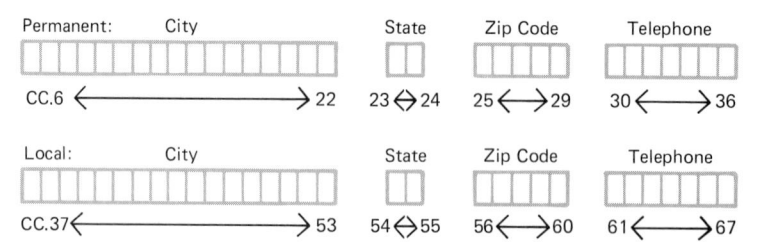

FIG. 14.2 An example of a source document layout for a keypunch operator.

of data conversion. To reduce this cost, it may be possible to (1) verify only critical data fields, such as dollar amounts and account numbers, while ignoring such fields as addresses, names, etc.; (2) prepunch or machine duplicate constant data fields while keying only variable fields; and (3) use programming logic to provide verification.

4. *Control Totals.* To minimize the loss of data when they are transported from one location to another and to check on the results of different processes, control totals are prepared for specific batches of data. For example, a batch of source documents, such as time cards from a division of a plant, are sent to a control clerk in the information system. The control clerk produces an adding machine tape containing a total of employee numbers (a *hash total*) and hours worked. These totals are recorded on a control sheet. The source documents are then transferred to the keypunching unit for conversion to cards. These cards, along with other batches, are converted to magnetic tape as payroll transactions. After each step is completed, the control totals generated in that step are compared. This ensures that all data can be accounted for through to the completion of processing and the issuing of outputs. By establishing control totals at input time, the remaining processing controls, either manual or programmed, can be implemented on the same basis.

5. *Other Controls.* During the design of input collection, the systems analyst also should evaluate the use of check digits for important codes such as customer account number. The use of *check digits* was discussed in Chapter 7. The labeling of data files is another important control point. *Labels* contain information such as file name, date created, date updated, retention period, etc.

Programming Controls

Input controls are established primarily to prevent errors from entering into subsequent processing activities. Using programming controls the computer can also help detect input errors, as well as to detect error conditions that occur as a result of processing the input. Entries are not posted to the files until all controls are passed. The ability to edit and validate the accuracy of entries directly affects the integrity and reliability of the systems data base and outputs. Various ways that the computer can be programmed to provide control are:

1. *Limit or reasonableness check.* This control is used to identify data having a value higher or lower than a predeter-

mined amount. These standard high/low limits are ascertained and established from research performed by the systems analyst. This control technique detects only those data elements that fall outside the limits. Examples of how this technique can be used are:

a. If the higher account number in a customer file is 6000, but CUSTOMER-NUMBER 7018 is read, then CUSTOMER-NUMBER of this particular record is in error.
b. If the minimum/maximum hourly rate for employees is $3.50/$10.50, any rate which falls outside this range is in error.
c. All authorized B coded purchase orders cannot exceed $100.
d. An exception notice is printed or displayed if a customer order exceeds twice the customer's average order.

2. *Arithmetic proof.* Various computation routines can be designed to validate the result of other computations, or the value of selected data fields. One method of arithmetic proof is *cross-footing*, which entails adding or subtracting two or more fields and zero balancing the result against the original result. This control method is applicable where total debits, total credits, and a balance forward amount are maintained for each account. For example, in the cash account, if the debits equal $5000 and the total credits equal $4000, then the balance of cash should equal $1000.

Another example uses approximation techniques. If fairly homogeneous items such as steel or grain are shipped to a customer, the billable amount can be checked for approximate accuracy. The average price for all steel stock may be $0.08 per pound. This rate is multiplied by the total weight of the shipment to derive an approximated billable amount. If this amount is not within 4 percent of the billed amount, then a message is displayed for subsequent investigation to determine if the billed amount is actually in error. As a final example, net pay for employees is determined by subtracting certain deductions from gross pay. In a separate routine the deductions could be added back to the derived net pay. Then the resulting gross pay could be checked against the original gross pay to see if it matches.

3. *Identification.* Various identification techniques can be designed to determine if the data being processed are valid. This can be done by comparing data fields from transaction files to master files, or to constant tables, stored either internally to the program or on a peripheral device. Some examples of this technique are:

a. A chart of accounts may designate current assets with a number range of 100–199, where Cash is 100. If the cash register is being processed, then all cash credits or debits must contain the identifier 100.
b. The warehouse that handles steel stock and pipe is coded with a 1. If issue and receipt transactions of steel and pipe inventory do not have the warehouse code of 1, then the transaction has either been entered in the wrong location or a keying error has been made.
c. Each customer number entered in the order transaction file is compared to the customer master file. If a customer

master record is not found, then the order transaction record is rejected.

4. *Sequence check.* Files are often arranged in ascending or descending sequence by employee number, account number, part number, etc. Instructions written in the processing program compare the sequenced field of the preceding record or transaction. With this technique, any *out-of-sequence error* can be detected and the file can be prevented from being processed incorrectly. Typical reasons for an occurrence of an out-of-sequence error are use of an incorrect file, failure to perform (correctly) a required sorting operation, hardware malfunctions, and incorrect merge operation.

5. *Error log.* A vital control technique used during processing is the maintenance of an error log. This log contains a record of all identified errors and exceptions noted during processing. As the errors are identified, they are written onto a special file, thus enabling the processing of that particular step to continue uninterrupted. At the completion of that processing step the error log can be checked, either by the computer or by the operator, and a decision made whether or not to continue processing.

   The error log is then forwarded to either the department or group who prepared the original input, or to a specially designated control group within the information system where the entries are corrected, reconciled, and resubmitted for processing.

6. *Transaction log.* A transaction log provides the basic *audit trail.* For audit and control purposes, the transaction log should indicate where the transaction originated, at what terminal, when, and the user number. For example, in an insurance company the transaction log supports all entries to the general ledger accounts. An entry into the general ledger that debits accounts receivable and credits written premiums, is simultaneously recorded in the transaction log and contains the following detail support: user, terminal, and user identification numbers; time of day; day of week; policy number; premium; and other identifying data. At any time the auditor can have the system produce a hardcopy listing of the transaction log for manual review, or have the software print specific audit information.

Data Base Controls

Great care should be exercised with the data base. To guard against complete loss or destruction of the data base, preplanned procedures should be in place to recreate lost data or other vital documents. We divide data base controls into physical controls and procedural controls.

1. *Physical controls.* To withstand stress and disasters (e.g., fire), a strongly constructed storage vault should be available to store files and documents that are not in use. In addition, all backup files, programs, and other important documents should be stored in secure off-site facilities. Fire, flood, theft, disgruntled employees, riot, vermin, or even nuclear attack represent hazards to an organization's vital records. Their secure storage is of utmost importance for the continued operation of any business. Several sites are available to management that guarantee safekeeping of records. Some of these storage centers are in mountains. One is in a 500-acre limestone cave that

is 175 feet underground.[1] This installation provides a dirt-free environment with a year-round temperature of 70°F and relative humidity of 35 percent. In addition to secure storage, many off-site installations provide services such as microfilming, telecopier long-line transmission of stored paper documents, copying and shipment of stored paper records, and 24-hour emergency shipment of stored documents. Records may be sent to an installation by truck, express, courier service, or United States Postal Service.

File protection devices (e.g., *file protect rings* for magnetic tape) should be used to prevent accidental erasure. All storage devices, especially magnetic tape and disk, should be kept free of air pollutants. Temperature and humidity conditions should be strictly controlled.

2. *Procedural controls.* Again, all files should be stored in the library (sensitive files in a vault) when not in use. The *librarian's* function should be independent and segregated from other functions (e.g., programmers and computer operators). The librarian should inventory all files and documents, listing the person to whom they are assigned, their status, and when they are due back. All files should contain external labels for identification. These labels, however, should be coded and understandable only by authorized personnel. For example, it would be unwise to label a file as CUSTOMER-ACCOUNTS-RECEIVABLE; preferable is some code like 14927.

The librarian should ensure that all backup copies are properly maintained off premises. Unusable magnetic tapes and disks should be segregated from those that are usable until they can be cleaned, repaired, or replaced. This maintenance procedure, done on a regular basis, minimizes read/write errors, and ensures an adequate supply of usable storage media. It should be noted that in many computer installations procedural controls that are adequate for the first shift are reduced for the second shift, and quite often, cease to exist during the third shift.

A simple, yet important file reconstruction procedure that is recommended for important sequential files contained on magnetic tape is illustrated in Figure 14.3. This backup system is usually referred to as the *grandfather-father-son* file reconstruction procedure. With this procedure, three versions of a file are available at any time. File A (father) in Update Cycle I produces File B (son). Update Cycle II, File B (now a father) produces File C (son of B). During this cycle, File A becomes the grandfather.

The advantage of this control procedure is that recovery is always possible. For example, if File C contained errors or was damaged during processing, then the job could be repeated using File B with transaction data from transaction File 2. If both File B and File C are damaged or destroyed, File A (stored off premises) is still available along with transaction File 1 to create File B, which in turn can be used to create File C.

In our discussion of DBMSs in Part II, we mentioned that the contents of a DASD file be written periodically (dumped or copied) on a backup file (e.g., magnetic tape), and stored at another location. In addition, a before and after image log should be maintained for any DASD whose update occurs by overlay (i.e., a write command erases the previous value and puts the new value in its

---

[1] For example, Inland Vital Records Center, 6500 Inland Drive, P.O. Box 2249, Kansas City, Kansas 66110.

456 Detail Systems Design—Control

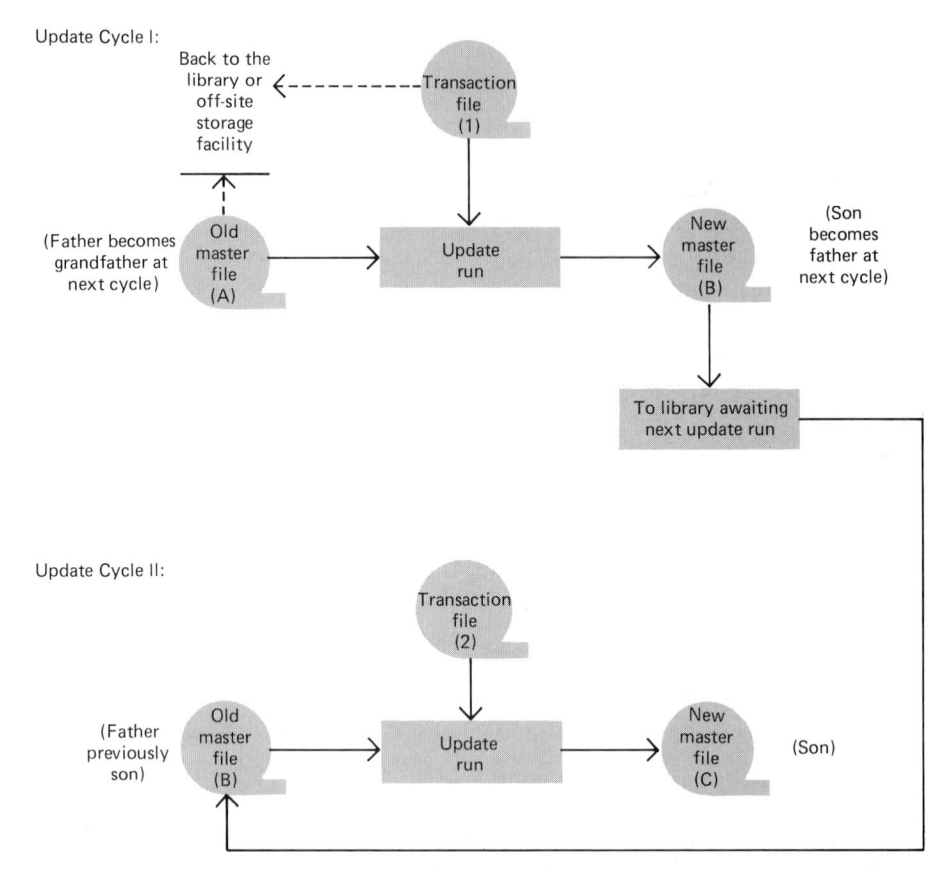

FIG. 14.3 An example of grandfather–father–son file reconstruction for sequential files. If one file is lost or destroyed, enough data are available to reconstruct it.

place). The log in essence provides a link from the backup file to the current file.

If the system goes down or a file(s) in the data base is destroyed or incorrectly modified, the DBMS may automatically reconstruct the file. In Figure 14.4, an example is illustrated of a file reconstruction plan for overlay files. In this example, assume that the online direct access file (master file) is destroyed sometime during Period II. With Backup File A, which is a copy of the online master file as of the end of Period I, and Log 2, which recorded all before and after images of master file records changed by transactions, a new online master disk file can be rolled forward or reconstructed. First, all master file data from Backup File A is written on the new master disk file. Then, all after images from Log 2 are recorded, thus bringing the master file to a correct present state.

As mentioned previously in Part II, in an online data base environment, controls should be written in the DBMS to protect against two programs concurrently updating the same record. This consideration is significant in a multiprogramming mode where many users are simultaneously pro-

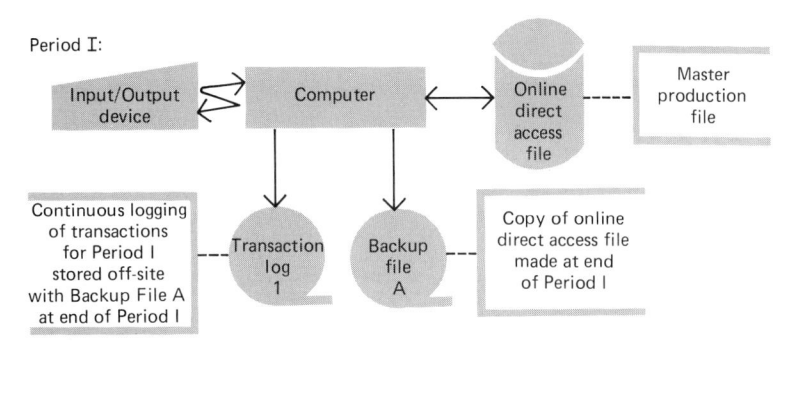

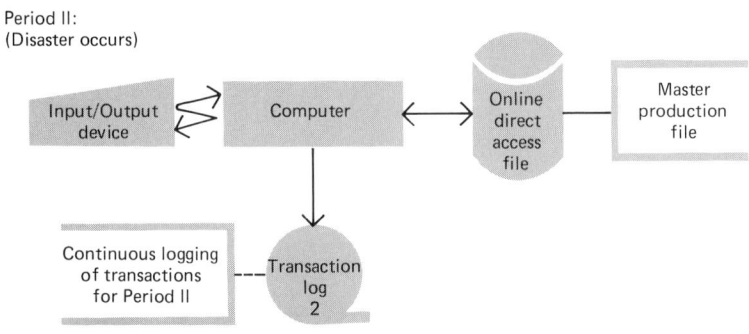

FIG. 14.4 An example of a file reconstruction plan for an overlay file.

cessing against the data base. The procedure should allow all active users to gain access to the data base through one active copy of the data base software. Data held for update by one user, however, cannot be accessed by another user until the other user releases the data.

Output Controls

Output controls are established as final checks on the accuracy and completeness of the processed information. The following control procedures are related to output:

1. An initial screening should be conducted to detect obvious errors.

2. Output should be immediately routed to a controlled area and distributed only by authorized persons to authorized persons.

3. Output control totals should be reconciled to input control totals to ensure that no data have been changed, lost, or added during processing or transmission. For example, the number of input records delivered for processing should equal the number of records processed.

4. All vital forms (e.g., paychecks, stockholder registry forms, passbooks, etc.) should be prenumbered and accounted for.

5. Any highly sensitive output that should not be accessible by computer center per-

sonnel should be generated via an output device (e.g., a printer) in a secure location away from the computer room.

6. Despite all the precautions taken, some errors will slip through. The major detection control point for detecting such errors is, of course, the user. Therefore, procedures should be established by the auditor to set up a channel between the user and the control group for the systematic reporting of occurrences of errors or improprieties. Such a systems design would employ a feedback loop where users would report all errors to the control group, and the control group, in turn, would take action to correct any inaccuracies or inconsistencies that might be revealed.

Documentation Controls

The overall control feature of documentation is that it shows the manager, auditor, users, etc., what the system is supposed to be and how it should perform. Besides improving overall operating, management, and auditing controls, documentation also serves the following purposes: (1) it improves communication; (2) it provides reference material for what has happened in the past; (3) it provides a guide for systems maintenance, modification, and recovery; (4) it serves as a valuable tool for training and educating personnel; and (5) it reduces the impact of key personnel turnover.

As many systems authorities have said, the documentation area is really the "Achilles' heel" of information systems. Some of the consequences of not having appropriate documentation are: (1) an increase in the "fog index," (2) creation of inefficient and uncoordinated operations, (3) an increase in redundant efforts, and (4) disillusioned systems personnel and users.

The documentation that directly relates to the computer-based information system and its operation is made up of three types: general systems, procedural, and program. **General systems documentation** provides guidance and operating rules for users when interfacing with the system. This part of documentation includes a *users' manual* that describes what the system is and how to receive services from it. It provides names and addresses of key personnel to contact, prices, and overall objectives. It also states the systems development method that was used and both the systems analyst's and users' responsibilities relating to it. The reports (e.g., General Systems Design Report) prepared during the development of the system provide for the overall documentation of the system itself.

The **procedures manual** introduces all operating, programming, and systems staff to the master plan of the system; computer operating standards, controls, and procedures; and programming standards and procedures. It is updated by the use of periodic guidelines.

Program documentation consists of all documents, diagrams, and layouts that explain aspects of the program supporting a particular systems design. The following comprises a typical program documentation manual:

1. The program manual should start with a general narrative describing the system. Also, a general systems flowchart should be included. This material links the program manual to the systems manual.

2. Program flowcharts, showing the input/output areas, source and main flow of data, entrance and exit of subroutines and program modules, and sequence of program operations, should be clearly

illustrated. Also, supporting notes, narratives, and decisions tables should be understandable and properly organized.

3. The *job control language* (JCL) used to interface the program with the computer operating system should be included, together with a complete explanation of the purpose of each job control statement. Without this explanation, many JCL statements are difficult to understand.

4. All programming aids used should be described (e.g., librarians).

5. Program listings of both the source program and the object program should be included.

6. Program testing procedures should be described.

7. Sample printouts of all reports generated by the program should be included.

8. All controls (explained in programming controls) written into the program should be clearly noted.

9. All operating instructions, operator console commands, and execution time parameter values should be defined. Computer operator instructions are contained in what is called a **console run book** (also called operators' manual, etc.). This book should contain (1) flowcharts and decision tables relative to that part of the system to which the program applies, (2) identification of file media required for input/output, (3) all console switch settings, (4) list of program halts and required action, (5) description of any exceptions to standard routines and input of parameter values (e.g., current date, titles, constants), and (6) authorized disposition of output.

10. An approval and change sheet should be included and kept current. In addition, the names of persons who wrote, tested, and approved the program should be listed.

Hardware Controls

Most computers have a variety of automatic control features to ensure proper operation. These controls come in the form of built-in hardware controls or vendor software controls. They are standard in most computers; where they are not, management should require that these control features be incorporated in the computer system by the vendor before installation.

1. *Built-in hardware controls.* These controls are built into the circuitry for detection of errors that result from manipulation, calculation, or transmission of data by various components of the computer system. These equipment controls are required to ensure that only one electronic pulse is transmitted through a channel during any single phase, that data are encoded and decoded accurately, that specific devices are activated, and that data received in one location are the same as were transmitted from the sending location. Examples of some of these internal equipment control features follow.

   a. *Parity checks.* To ensure that the data initially read into the system have been transmitted correctly, an internal self-checking feature is incorporated in most computer systems. In addition to the set of bits (e.g., a byte) used to represent data, the computer uses one additional bit for each storage position. These bits are called parity bits, or check bits, and are used to detect errors in the circuitry when a bit is lost, added, or destroyed due to an equipment malfunction. The parity bit makes the number of bits in the set either even or odd, depending on the parity used by the computer.

b. *Validity check.* Numbers and characters are represented by specified combinations of binary digits. Representation of these data symbols is accomplished by various coding schemes handled by the circuitry of the computer system. In a single computer system several different coding schemes can be used to represent data at various stages of processing. For example, the Hollerith characters of an input card are converted to Binary Coded Decimal (BCD), or Extended Binary Coded Decimal Interchange Code (EBCDIC), or to U.S.A. Standard Code for Information Interchange (USASCII). If output is written on a printer, for example, then the data will have to be converted to yet another code. Therefore, a message being either transmitted or received goes through an automatic encoding and decoding operation that is acceptable to the sending or receiving device in question.

c. *Duplication check.* This control check requires that two independent components perform the same operation and compare results. If any difference between the two operations is detected, an error condition is indicated. For example, punch cards being read by a card reader pass two read stations. If the two readings are unequal, an error is indicated. The same principle of duplication is used in nearly all computer system components. For example, much of the circuitry of the arithmetic-logical unit of the CPU is duplicated. This requires calculations to be performed twice, thereby increasing the probability of accurate results.

d. *Echo check.* This control feature authenticates the transmission of data to and from components of the computer system. The data transmission is verified by echoing back the signal received by the component and comparing it with source data for agreement. For example, the CPU transmits a message to a card punch to perform an operation. The card punch returns a message to the CPU that is automatically checked to see if the correct device has been activated.

e. *Miscellaneous error checks.* In addition to the control checks discussed above, the computer system should also contain controls to detect various invalid computer instructions, data overflows, lost signs, zero division, and defective components.

f. *Firmware controls.* Firmware or hardwiring implies the use of solid state techniques to represent instructions. Unlike programing instructions, a hardwired instruction cannot be modified. In the early years, boards were hardwired. An individual would plug various wires into different holes in the board permitting different operations to be performed. New technology, however, permits many hardwired instructions to be placed on a single chip, called **read only memory** (ROM). For example, the logic that performs functions like square root in a calculator is permanently contained on a chip. The logic cannot be modified with conventional software techniques. The chip itself, however, may be physically altered or replaced.

The concept of firmware is extremely important because it removes from the programmer the ability to alter programs, which includes the highly vulnerable operating system. Furthermore, due to the increased complexity and sophistication of computer systems, there is a requirement to place a greater reliance for internal control upon the computer itself.

Unfortunately, not all computer equipment installed today has a total complement of built-in hardware controls. In making equipment selection, the individual charged with this responsibility must evaluate the completeness of the control features incorporated in a particular component. If equipment is selected with a limited number of these controls, then the probability of errors occurring due to equipment malfunction is increased.

2. Vendor Software Controls. These controls are designed into the operating system and, to a great extent, deal with the routine input/output operations of the system. These controls are as follows:

a. *Read or write error.* In the event of a read/write error, the machine will halt the program and allow the operator to investigate the error. For example, the system will stop if a writing operation is attempted to defective tape or if the printer runs out of paper.

b. *Record length checks.* In some instances, blocks of records are defined that are too long for the input buffer area of the computer. This control feature, therefore, ensures that data records read into the computer from tape or disk are the correct length (no longer than permissible).

c. *Label checking routines.* Header and trailer are two kinds of labels. At a minimum, the *header* label should contain: file serial number, reel serial number, file name, creation date, and retention date. The *trailer* label should contain the block count, record count, control totals, and end-of-reel or end-of-file condition. For input files the header label is used to check that the file is the one specified by the program. The trailer label is used to determine if all data on the file were processed and whether physical or logical file is at end. For output files, the header label is used to check whether the file may be written on or destroyed (e.g., today's date is after the file retention date).

d. *Access control.* An error condition occurs when reference is made to a storage device that is not in a "ready" status.

e. *Address compare control.* An error condition occurs when a storage address referenced by one component does not compare properly with the component's address that is referenced. For example, the core storage address does not agree with the address referenced by a disk drive.

Computer Operations Controls

The computer is one of the key components in the information system. It is essential that it be properly maintained and controlled. Moreover, it is imperative that the personnel who operate computer equipment be subject to the same stringent controls. This area of controls is divided into physical and procedural controls.

1. Physical Controls. These controls pertain to the environment in which the computer system is housed. Common sense and the establishment of simple physical controls can guard against the occurrence of many errors and mishaps.

a. *Computer site.* The location of the computer system and site construction are fundamental. Cases have been documented where computer systems have been housed next to steam boilers, radio stations, carpentry shops, radar towers, on the first floor of a building on a busy street in view of all passersby, and so forth. The construction of the site should be of high quality, fireproof material.

b. *Environmental control.* Adequate and separate air conditioner, dehumidification, and humidification systems should be installed. Regardless of what vendors say, computer systems still need a great deal of air conditioning to operate properly. For example, although equipment manufacturers often suggest that their equipment will operate in a temperature range of 50° to 95°F, a stricter guideline of 72°F ± 2° is advised to avoid malfunctions due to temperature. Similarly, with respect to relative humidity (RH), the manufacturers cite the range of 20 percent to 90 percent RH. A much safer guide is 50 percent RH ± 5 percent. Semiconductor life in a computer's logic and memory unit is very sensitive to temperature fluctuations. High RH levels (e.g., 80 percent and above) can cause problems in computer systems in various ways, including the corrosion of electrical contacts or the expansion of paper. The latter effect can cause printers and card readers (or any equipment that uses paper) to malfunction. Low RH, on the other hand, can result in a buildup of static electricity causing paper to stick and jam. With technology becoming more and more sensitive, an almost surgically clean environment is necessary.

c. *Uninterruptible power systems.* In many areas, power supply is erratic during extreme weather conditions. It may be cost/effective to acquire and install an emergency power source. Also installed should be an emergency power shutoff in the event of fire or other disaster. Computers, like most highly sophisticated systems, demand the continued operation of their functionally contributive subsystems. One obviously important subsystem is electric power.

It is generally considered that the quality and quantity of utility power are diminishing daily. In some geographical areas, brownouts (a sustained reduction of electrical power) have become the norm during peak demands, and total power loss may occur. But the increased sophistication of computer systems requires the utilization of "clean" electric power. "Dirty" electric power implies short-term transients and line instability (i.e., fluctuations in voltage and/or frequency of electricity).

To ensure the continuous availability of "clean" electric power, **uninterruptible power systems** (UPS) have been developed. A UPS generally consists of rectifier/charger, a battery, and an inverter. The rectifier/charger normally converts AC utility power to DC, and maintains a full charge on the battery. Should utility power fail, the battery provides DC to the inverter which converts the DC power into clean and continuous AC power. Transfer of the critical load from the utility power source to the battery and back is generally accomplished by a static bypass switch. A static switch is electronic (unlike a mechanical switch) and therefore permits critical load transfer within the acceptable tolerances required by most mainframes and peripherals (4 msec.).

The power support time available from batteries is a function of the number and size of batteries available. The recommended maximum support time, however, is 5 min. This figure may be increased, of course, but calculations should be performed to determine if it is cost/effective to do so. If continuous computer processing is critical, such as in hospitals or for air traffic control, it might be appropriate for the installation to consider the addition of emergency motor generators to supplement utility power for extended power outages.

2. Procedural Controls. Procedural controls relate to the performance of tasks in the system. Management must establish how the tasks are to be performed and close supervision must be effected to see that the tasks are being performed accordingly.

All computer center staff, especially operators, should be under direct supervision. Supervisors should establish job priorities and run schedules for every working day, and all computer operators should be required to sign the computer operating log at the beginning and end of their shifts.

Supervisors should require equipment utilization reports and maintain accurate job cost records of all computer time, including production, program listing, rerun, idle, and downtime. On a periodic basis, the auditor should review these reports.

No business transactions should be initiated by any computer center staff. Only computer operators should operate the computer, but operator intervention to processing should be limited. Access of computer operators to sensitive tapes, disks, programs, and documentation should be tightly controlled.

Access to computer room facilities should be restricted to authorized personnel only. For example, many programmers request "hands-on" testing. Any hands-on use of the computer by programmers should be limited and closely supervised.

Good housekeeping procedures are fundamental to any system, especially a computer system. Along with good housekeeping, preventive maintenance procedures should be established. These procedures help to forestall a deterioration in performance or a failure of the various computer components by an ongoing system of detection, adjustment, and repairs. Basic to preventive maintenance is an inventory of spare parts. (It would be foolish to halt operations of a million-dollar system for want of a one-dollar part.) All service of equipment should be performed by qualified and authorized service engineers.

The console terminal, either typewriter or CRT, and the switches and buttons on the console control panel, enable the computer operator to enter messages or commands into and receive information directly from the storage unit of the CPU. Using keys, switches, audible tone signals, and display lights on the console unit, the computer operator can: (1) start, stop, or change the operation of all or part of the computer system; (2) manually enter and display data from internal storage; (3) determine the status of internal electronic switches; (4) determine the contents of certain internal registers; (5) alter the mode of operation so that when an unusual condition or malfunction occurs the computer will either stop or indicate the condition (e.g., a jam in the card reader or the wrong tape file mounted) and proceed after the condition or malfunction has been corrected; (6) change the selection of input/output devices; (7) load programs and various routines; and (8) alter the data content of specific storage locations.

The operating log (also called the *console log*) can be in the form of a continuous paper printout from the console typewriter, or in some large installations, from a printer dedicated to printing the operating log. This latter alternative is preferable when the console typewriter is not fast enough to handle high volume output. In some installations the operating log may be written out on magnetic tape, especially if a CRT is used instead of a console typewriter. In any case, the operating log is a valuable control document because it gives a running account of all the messages generated by the computer and of all the instructions and entries made by the computer operator. In addition, it can indicate the beginning or end of various stages of processing and intermediate or final results of processing.

14.3 ▪ SECURITY CONTROLS

Ordinarily, security controls do not affect the proper and accurate processing of transactions as much as the controls discussed earlier. Conceptually, a secure system is one that is penetration-proof from potential hazards. Security controls help to assure high systems standards and performance by protecting against hardware, software, and people failure. Absence of security controls can increase the probability of such things happening as (1) degraded operations, (2) compromised system, (3) loss of services, (4) loss of assets, and (5) unauthorized disclosure of sensitive information.

Security controls, as well as all of the controls discussed so far, apply to both small and large computer centers and to in-house and outside computer services. Security controls are a key ingredient in the system of controls and are an area that cannot be neglected.

In this chapter our discussion of security controls is divided into three categories: hazards, physical security techniques, and procedural security techniques.

Hazards

What follows are the classic hazards of a computer-based information system, arranged by their probability of occurrence and their impact on the system. The rationale for this hierarchy is, in part, based on research, intuition, and generalizations. It cannot be proved or disproved. Therefore, not only is it a subject for debate, but in any particular system, the arrangement of these hazards may be quite different.

1. Malfunctions. People, software, and hardware error or malfunction cause the biggest problems. In this area humans are frequently the culprits by acts of omission, neglect, and incompetency. Some authorities have said that simple human error causes more damage than all other areas combined. We read of one incident where a disk pack was warped from being dropped; the warped pack was mounted on a disk drive and damaged the access mechanism. The same pack was then moved to another drive, and a different pack was mounted on the first drive, and so on, resulting in several damaged drives and unusable disk packs.

2. Fraud and Unauthorized Access. This hazard or threat is the attainment of something through dishonesty, cheating, or deceit. This hazard can occur through (1) infiltration and industrial espionage, (2) tapping data communication lines, (3) emanation pickup from parabolic receivers (the computer and its peripherals are transmitters), (4) unauthorized browsing through files via online terminals, (5) masquerading as an authorized user, (6) physical confiscation of files and other sensitive documents, and (7) installation of Trojan horses (those things that are not what they appear to be).

3. Power and Communication Failures. In some locations this hazard may occur with greater frequency than other hazards. To a great extent, the availability and reliability of power and communication facilities is a function of location, as mentioned earlier in this chapter under the heading of "Uninterruptible power systems." In heavily populated areas brownouts occur frequently, especially during the summer. Conversely, there have been instances where power surges have occurred, burning out sensitive components of a computer. This particular hazard can be easily controlled with a power regulator. Also, during each working day, communication channels are sometimes busy or noisy.

4. Fires. Fires occur with greater frequency than many people realize, and they are one of the worst disasters.

5. Sabotage and Riot. Components of computer centers have been destroyed by disgruntled employees and damage has occurred to computer centers installed in or near decaying urban areas that later become scenes of riots.

6. Natural Disasters. Relatively speaking, natural disasters (so-called Acts of God) do not occur often, but when they do the results can be devastating. These disasters include earthquakes, tornadoes, floods, and lightning. Preplanning can help to reduce their impact. For example, one organization installed its computer complex in a quiet suburban center only to find later that the center was constructed on a lot beneath the flood plain—something that should have been ascertained prior to installation.

7. General Hazards. This category covers a number of random hazards that are difficult to define and anticipate. Normally, general safeguards will lessen the probability of their occurrence. For example, one Sunday morning, a vice-president arrived at his office to find a fully loaded gasoline truck, with its brakes on fire, parked next to the computer center. Better isolation of the computer site from this type of traffic could have prevented this incident from occurring.

Goals of Security Controls Against Hazards

Goals of security controls against hazards can be viewed as a level of controls. That is, if one level fails, then another control level takes over, and so forth.

1. *Deter.* At this level, the goal is to prevent any loss or disaster from occurring.
2. *Detect.* Complete deterrent often cannot be achieved. Therefore, the goal at this level is to establish methods to monitor hazard potential and to report this to people and equipment for corrective action.
3. *Minimize impact of disaster and loss.* If an accident or mishap occurs, then there should be procedures established and facilities that help reduce the loss. For example, a backup master file would help mitigate the destruction of a master file.
4. *Investigate.* If a loss does occur, an investigation should be started immediately to determine what happened. This investigation will provide study facts that can be used for future security planning.
5. *Recovery.* A plan of action to recover from the loss and return operations to normal as soon as possible should exist. For example, if the data processing operation for a bank could not operate for a week or two, financial failure would likely result. Recovery procedures can

range from backup facilities to insurance coverage.

Physical Security Techniques

Physical security techniques include devices and physical placement of computer facilities that help guard against hazards. Some of these techniques are (1) physical controlled access, (2) physical location, and (3) physical protection devices.

1. Physical Controlled Access. Access control protection is basic to a security system. If a potential penetrator cannot gain entry to the computer facilities, then the chance for harm is reduced considerably. The following items help to control access.

a. *Guards and special escorts.* Guards should be placed at strategic entry points of the computer facility. All visitors who are given permission to tour the computer center should be accompanied by a designated escort.

b. *Sign-in/sign-out registers.* All persons should be required to sign a register indicating time of sign-in, purpose, and time of departure. An improvement upon the standard signature register incorporates devices that analyze signatures as a function of time and pressure. Thus a counterfeiter may be able to duplicate the outward appearances of a signature, but take more time and apply less pressure during the signing.

c. *Badges.* Color-coded (e.g., red for programmers, blue for systems analysts) badges, with the badgeholder's picture when possible, can be used to readily identify authorized personnel and visitors.

d. *Cards.* Card control entry equipment, used alone or in conjunction with other measures, is probably the most popular access control device. Doors can be opened by either optical or magnetic coded cards. Authorization for entry can be dynamically controlled by individual doors, time of day, day of week, and security classification of individuals to whom the card is issued. Authorizations can be added or deleted easily, and entry activity logs and reports can be prepared and displayed to a control officer. Open or closed status of all doors can be monitored and attempts at unauthorized entry can be detected immediately and an alarm sounded.

e. *Closed-circuit monitors.* Devices such as closed-circuit television monitors, cameras, and intercom systems, connected to a control panel manned by security guards, are becoming increasingly popular. These devices are very effective in controlling a large area, rather than concentrating only on entry and exit points.

f. *Paper shredders.* Sensitive reports should never be disposed of by simply being thrown in waste containers. Numerous cases have been reported where penetrators were able to steal confidential information by gaining access to waste disposal facilities. Any sensitive reports should be shredded before being thrown away. A disintegration system that converts an end product into unclassified waste or microconfetti that cannot be reconstructed, works even better than a shredder. These machines will disintegrate bound manuals, computer printouts, carbons, microfilms, and microfiches, EDP cards, plastic binders, printer circuits, and mylar computer tape.

g. *One-way emergency doors.* These doors are for exit only and are to be used in case of emergency situations such as a fire.

h. *Combination of control devices.* The above devices can be combined with other safeguards that we will be discussing in following sections to increase security even further. Card systems can be combined with a hand geometry identifier. In another example, entry through one door, equipped with a card reader, leads to a man-trap area that is sealed from the computer system by bulletproof glass. To get through the second door leading to the computer room, a valid card has to be used, plus identification over a combination intercom and television monitoring system.

2. Physical Location. Location of the computer system is an important consideration in security planning. Note the following guidelines:

a. *Remote location.* The computer site should be away from airports, electrical equipment (e.g., radar and microwave), decaying urban areas, heavy traffic, steam boilers, and so forth. The more removed the computer system is from these kinds of hazards, the better. If the site cannot be as distant as desirable, then some remoteness can be achieved by clearing a 200- to 300-foot radius around the site, and installing floodlights and a perimeter fence.

b. *Separate building.* Many security specialists recommend that the computer system be housed in a separate building. The advantage of doing this is that access control is easier and there is less risk from general hazards. For example, there would be less risk from fire caused by flammable products used by other building occupants. A disadvantage is that deliberate attack on the power source, the communication lines, and the air intake, could be made easier because of specific identification. If the computer system is not housed in a separate building, then it should be centered in the building, away from the outside walls, and not located on the top floor, on the street floor in view of passersby, or in the basement. It should not be displayed as a showcase.

c. *Identification.* The computer site should not contain any signs that identify it to outsiders.

d. *Carrier control.* Power and communication lines should be underground. Air intake devices, compressors, and cooling towers should be protected by fences and placed at heights that cannot be reached easily. Manhole covers should be locked.

e. *Backup facilities location.* Backup plays a major role in many areas of a total system of control. Backup is the key element to recovery. As far as location is concerned, a backup facility should be far enough away from the main facility so that it is not subject to the same hazards, but close enough to provide quick recovery. When possible, the backup facility should be located in a place that uses a different power source. The location of the backup facility should be kept confidential.

3. Physical Protection. Additional protective devices should be considered in an overall protection plan. These items are:

a. *Drains and pumps.* Sometimes water pipes burst or water enters the site from a fire or flood. To help reduce these mishaps, drains and pumps should be installed.

b. *Emergency power.* Again, backup plays an important part in control. Uninterruptible power systems (UPSs) should be installed for power backup to provide continuous processing. The decision to install a UPS depends upon the frequency and nature of the power disturbances and the effect they have on the computer system. Power failure or disturbance can range anywhere from transients of a few milliseconds' duration to long-term power outages. These power fluctuations can result in loss of data, processing errors, downtime, equipment malfunction and damage, and so forth. A complete study of any power failures should be made to determine the causes of the disturbances. For example, a study may reveal a number of short-term transients and line instability, rather than real power outage. Power fluctuations may be caused by extreme load changes (e.g., air conditioning, elevators) within the building and consequently are beyond the control of the utility. In such cases an approach less expensive than a UPS, such as a *motor generator set* (also referred to as a M-G set), or a voltage regulator, may be more applicable. The primary objective of the UPS and other power control devices is to supply precise, smooth, steady, and clean power to the computer system at all times.

c. *Coverings.* All equipment should be covered with plastic covers when not in use. In several cases water damage to computer equipment was reduced during a fire because some alert individual covered the equipment.

d. *Fire control.* Basically, there are three kinds of fire: Class A—cellulosis, Class B—flammable liquid, and Class C—electrical. Consultation with fire department personnel and fire control equipment vendors should be made to determine the appropriate fire and smoke detectors and extinguishing methods. Normally, methods recommended will be a combination of (1) portable fire extinguishers, (2) fluoride gas, (3) Halon (causes no permanent damage to office material and equipment), (4) CO_2 (carbon dioxide, good for extinguishing electrical fires but dangerous in that it can suffocate personnel), (5) water sprinklers, and (6) smoke exhaust systems. Smoke exhaust systems are a necessary element of fire control methods because smoke, in many instances, is the biggest problem, especially where there is a preponderance of vinyl and other plastic material.

Insurance companies report that more insurance claims for water and flooding damage are from putting out fires, than from damage caused by the fires themselves. This situation reinforces the need for drains, pumps, and coverings.

When various detection and extinguishing systems are used, it is important that the detectors not release a fire extinguishing agent immediately. To do so is wasteful, and in the case of CO_2, it can be hazardous to personnel in the area. The detectors should trigger audible and visible alarms locally and at appropriate fire or guard stations. A control panel should be available to indicate which detector(s) triggered the alarm. By zeroing in on the fire, some designated individuals (no one should be sent alone) can go directly to the source of trouble, determine the extent of the fire, and put it out with a portable fire extinguisher if it is small and localized.

e. *General building safeguards.* Walls of the building should be constructed from slab. Walls and ceilings should have at least a one-hour fire rating. The number of doors should be limited and there should be no windows. All ducts should be filtered and contain fire dampers.

Procedural Security Techniques

It is difficult to draw a precise line between physical and procedural security techniques because a great deal of overlap exists between the two. Both, for example, limit access of unauthorized penetrators. One technique can work in conjunction with and enhance the effectiveness of the other. One is more device oriented while the other is more logic oriented. In many instances a procedural security techniques is the use of a physical one. To think in terms of one instead of the other will not lead to a good security control system. For example, as the following indicates, a bank can be secure against physical access to its information system but still be vulnerable to unauthorized access.

> Recently, many banks have opened the floodgates to theft of confidential financial information through the information systems designed to give bank tellers real-time access to customer accounts. In many cases, virtually no safeguards have been erected to prevent unauthorized access to these files. Many of these systems are ordinary touch-tone telephones and automatic-dial cards provided by the telephone company to gain access to the central files of all depositor accounts. It is not even necessary for the information thief to acquire one of these automatic-dialing devices. All he needs is an ordinary touch-tone telephone. The dial codes employed are generally the most obvious and straightforward; anyone watching a bank teller's operation for about ten minutes can learn them. Once they are learned a simple telephone tap anywhere within the bank's telephone system is all that is needed to read (and in a limited way, modify) any account in the bank, to ascertain whether an account is being used or not (for purposes of forgery or kiting), and to gain detailed information as to deposits and withdrawals in that account. All this can be done without ever setting foot in the bank.[2]

Whereas physical security techniques deal with a number of hazards, including fire, natural disaster, and so forth, procedural security techniques deal almost exclusively with access control. In some cases, a procedural technique will require the application of a physical technique.

Our discussion on procedural security techniques will cover the six concepts of integrity, isolation, identification, authorization, authentication, and monitoring.

1. Integrity. As a concept within the context of security controls, integrity is basically the assurance that the system is functionally correct and complete. Otherwise, the absence of integrity will cause implementation of all the other concepts to be ineffective.

If a user is authorized to retrieve item A from a file, then the system must be depended upon to provide item A, and only item A, to the user. Analogous to this idea of integrity is where an authorized user is given a key intended to unlock door A, but not doors B, C, and D. Therefore, the locking mechanism system should guarantee that the key does in fact unlock only door A. As another example, if a user is supposed to be in *read only* mode, then the system should guarantee that the user cannot do something else (e.g., write).

Another aspect of where integrity procedures apply is during simultaneous job processing. The system should function in such a way that after one authorized job is com-

---

[2]Stephen W. Leibholz and Louis D. Wilson, *User's Guide to Computer Crime*, Radnor, Pa.: Chilton Book Company, 1974, p. 27.

pleted, information from that job is sanitized (e.g., erased, scrubbed), so unauthorized penetrators cannot read it via browsing. Without sanitizing procedures, confidential information would be exposed to unauthorized access at various points during processing.

2. Isolation. In any system where a high level of security is to be maintained, no individual or part of the organization should be in a position to have available all the components or subsystems that can be put together to make a whole. This isolation is sometimes referred to as **interface isolation** or **compartmentalization,** and is a concept used in the design and construction of secret weapons. In computer-based information systems, this isolation should be maintained between users and information, as well as between hardware and software resources and processes. Several procedures that effect isolation are listed below.

a. *Disconnection and separation.* One form of isolation is achieved by geographical or logical distribution, where certain elements of the system are unconnected. For example, terminal 1 is not connected to computer A. This procedure employs total isolation where two or more elements are disconnected.

In most situations some connection or interfacing among elements has to exist to make the total system operative. Several examples of key interface points that require logical separation procedures and tight control are (1) computer operator/console, (2) computer operator/programs, (3) computer operator/data base library, (4) programmer/computer, (5) systems analyst/programs, and (6) user/terminal.

Similar to traditional accounting internal control, separation procedures, for example, mean that no single individual should have access to computer programs and operation of the computer, and to the design of the system. Also, this means that those individuals who input transactions into the system should not also be those who have access to programs.

b. *Least privilege access.* To make a system operative, certain privileged states and instruction sets must be assigned to appropriate users. This assigned privilege should be the minimum access authority necessary to perform the required process. For example, an order clerk may be given the privilege to access only quantity on hand and price of items in an inventory file. The clerk would not be able to access cost, vendor, vendor performance, and so forth. Another example of least privilege access is where programmers are required to use compiler languages such as COBOL, which automatically isolates them from the computer equipment and operating system.

c. *Obfuscation.* This procedure means to isolate by confusing, bewildering, obscuring, or hiding something from, a potential penetrator. For example, a simple method of hiding the computer system from would-be penetrators is to not list the access telephone number of the computer system in the building directory. Scrambling devices are also used.

d. *Location of terminal.* Based on location, terminals are given different classifications and levels of security. For example, a terminal located in a warehouse, easily accessible by a variety of personnel, may be given few access privileges and permitted to perform only low-level tasks. A major problem with this kind of identification is that if terminals later need to be switched, authorization changes must be made. Consequently, it may be better to rely primarily on one or a combination of the other identification methods discussed.

3. Identification. If a system incorporates isolation procedures, then the system must also have the ability to identify authorized and proper interfaces. The system must have the ability to distinguish between those users to whom access is permissible and those to whom it is not. Based on the level of security required, either the person, the terminal, the file, or the program must be identified so that the right to use the system can be verified and the user can be held accountable. Methods to effect identification are listed below:

a. *Something the user has.* A user is identified by something in his or her possession. Identification items can consist of (1) codes (also called passwords, keywords, or lockwords), (2) keys to locks, (3) badges, (4) magnetic striped or optical cards, (5) phone numbers, (6) terminal ID number, and/or (7) encryption key. The main disadvantage of these items is that the probability is relatively high that they could be obtained and used by others.

b. *Something the user knows.* Here, a user is identified on the basis of something the user knows (the identification item is not physical). Examples of these items are personalized codes that are changed regularly, and sequences where the user answers a prearranged set of questions (e.g., previous address, birthplace, family member birthday, color of spouse's eyes). Effectiveness of this identification item is related directly to its rate of change; the more often an item is changed (e.g., password, prearranged question), the less likely it will be appropriated by others.

c. *The user's characteristics.* The user is identified on the basis of some physical characteristic uniquely his or her own. These characteristics can be divided into two categories, neuromuscular, such as dynamic signatures and handwriting, and genetic. The genetic category covers (1) body geometry (e.g., hand shape identification is being used to a limited extent), (2) fingerprints, (3) voice response patterns, (4) facial appearance (primary use is on badges), (5) eye iris and retina, (6) lip prints, and (7) brain wave patterns.

Human behavior may be more significant in slowing down or preventing the commercial application of this kind of identification than the advance of technology. People normally resist an invasion of privacy and personal self. If this kind of identification technology is viewed as a personal invasion, then people will resist. Stories are told about an unauthorized user "kissing" a computer terminal and a clamp attaching his lips to the terminal until a security officer arrives. Or, about users having to stick their finger through a tiny guillotine for fingerprint identification. Unauthorized user? Goodbye finger!

4. Authorization. Once a person has been identified as a valid user, the question becomes, what authority does this person have? That is, what does he or she have the right to do? For instance, in the security of a data base, procedures must be set up to determine who has access to what files, who has the right to make additions and deletions, and who is responsible for administration of the data base. The following items help to deal with the concept of authorization.

a. *Categorize authorization.* This step determines the specific authority of users, programs, and hardware. That is, each category is limited in what it can and cannot do. Classes of authority can include user to documentation, user to equipment, user to program, user to file, terminal to program, program to file, program to program, and so forth. Those activities that must be designated in conjunction with classes of authority are read, write, add, change, delete, copy, create, append, display, and so forth. For example, Joe Clerk may be given the right to use program 1 to read (entirely or a specific part of) file A. An example of how the categorization step can be performed is illustrated in Figure 14.5.

b. *Use of codes.* Codes are linked to the authority table and the authority table is, in turn, linked to an identification table. That is, the validity of the user (or terminal, etc.) is first identified, then it is determined what the valid user can do. For example, Joe Clerk may be permitted to read only parts of file A. Therefore, codes may have to be assigned not only to files, but to a category of records within files, or even to individual fields within records.

c. *Security program.* The computer system itself must be programmed to identify not only valid users but to ensure that proper authority is granted. To do so requires installation of a security program. What follows is a general, hypothetical example of the type of instructions contained in a security program.

User/Relation
DEFINE RELATION (INVENTORY)
AUTHORIZE USER (JONES) RELATION (INVENTORY)
FOR (READ, CHANGE)

User/Program:
AUTHORIZE USER (JONES) PROGRAM (UPDATE)
FOR (READ, CHANGE = QUANTITY-ON-HAND DOMAIN)

In addition, the security program should have the ability to change readily the identifications and authorizations, as well as to change security requirements based on time of day, day of week, weekends, holidays, and so forth. For example, certain users would lose their authority over weekends, vacations, or holidays. Included in the program should also be a routine to report immediately the source of any attempted violations.

User \ Authorized to	Authorization Access for File A				
	Read Only	Write Only	Read Write	Delete	Add
1	X				
2		X		X	
3		X			X
.					
.					
.					
N			X		

FIG. 14.5 An example of designating authority.

5. Authentication. Authentication is an action intended to determine whether something is valid or genuine. Someone or some facility may be identified appropriately and be given authority to access information or perform some activity. The system cannot be assured that the user is valid, however, especially if the user is identified on the basis of "what he has" (e.g., magnetic card) or "what he knows" (e.g., code or password). Periodically, especially for usage of sensitive files (as well as other resources), the user should be confirmed. This confirmation may include some or all of the following authentication procedures: (1) physical observation (e.g., sending someone to confirm the identity of the user), (2) periodic disconnects and call back procedures (e.g., a terminal is disconnected and called back to see if the appropriate terminal responds), and (3) periodic requests for further information or reverification from the user.

6. Monitoring. Monitoring is the act of watching over, checking, or guarding something. This activity recognizes that eventually, either accidentally or intentionally, controls will be neutralized or broken. Some specific systems capabilities to support the monitoring concept procedure include the following:

a. *Detection of security violations.* A security system should be installed to detect any security violation as soon as it occurs. Examples of violations are mismatch of user or terminal identification code and unauthorized request for a file.

b. *Locking of system.* If certain security violations are serious, then the system should be set up to lock the system automatically from further use. For example, a terminal would be locked automatically after N unauthorized attempts.

c. *Exception reporting.* All exceptional conditions should be reported to the internal auditor for review. Auditors should be skeptical if they receive no reports. The absence of any attempted violations may indicate that users are subverting controls.

d. *Trend reporting.* The system should collect data concerning all user access. Typical data in this report would indicate (1) user, terminal, etc.; (2) type of processing (demonstration, training, testing, normal operations); (3) date; (4) time of day; and (5) items accessed (e.g., name of file). These reports should be reviewed systematically by auditors and security officers.

SUMMARY

An important part of the overall design of an information system is the establishment of effective controls. During the specific design phase, the systems analyst must identify and implement a series of processing controls to ensure the integrity and reliability of the information system. These processing controls can be categorized as follows: (1) input controls, (2) programming controls, (3) data base controls, (4) output controls, and (5) hardware controls.

Security, another form of control, must also be considered during the design of an information system. In large information systems a separate group responsible might be for establishing security. More often, the systems analyst must implement many security controls into the system. Some security considerations include (1) access to data files, (2) access to physical components, (3) transmission intervention, and (4) software disruption. Procedures for recovery after intentional or unintentional disasters must be designed and implemented.

REVIEW QUESTIONS

14.1 List and describe the major control points of an information system.

14.2 What techniques can be applied to control input? Give an example of each input control technique.

14.3 Give an example of at least five different programming controls.

14.4 List several control techniques related to the data base and describe how they operate.

14.5 What is the final control point in the information system? Explain.

14.6 Why is documentation control important?

14.7 What are hardware controls? What is their purpose? List and explain three different types of hardware controls used in computers. Can you identify at least one type of hardware control not discussed in this chapter?

14.8 What factors are pertinent to the environment in which the computer system is housed?

14.9 What is the purpose of an operating log?

14.10 Give an example of each of the various types of hazards. What physical security techniques can be used to help guard against hazards? What procedural security techniques can be used to deal with access control?

QUESTIONS FOR DISCUSSION

14.1 Give examples of control totals that can be used in the preparation of a payroll.

14.2 A master inventory file was destroyed by inadvertently writing over it in another processing run. What elementary control procedure was not used to prevent incorrect mounting of the file? What elementary item was not used to prevent the computer from writing on the wrong file? What method can the system use to recreate the file?

14.3 As long as the operator can mount the correct tape reel or disk pack by referring to its external label, why should it be necessary to also have internal header and trailer labels written on the files?

14.4 List at least ten different types of processing controls which might be included in an inventory control system.

14.5 List several advantages of Keyboard-to-tape and keyboard-to-disk devices as compared to a keypunch (refer to any journal related to data processing, programming, or systems in the library) from the aspect of improved control.

14.6 Describe how a master file of customer information can be used to provide control when processing orders.

14.7 "Equipment checks are more effective in ensuring the accuracy of processing than programmed control checks." Discuss the merits of this statement.

14.8 "Many control procedures in the information system are based on the principle of duplication." Discuss this comment.

14.9 "The extent and cost of implementing control procedures should be proportional to the vulnerability and risk of loss in the absence of such control procedures." Discuss the merits of this statement.

14.10 "Improved data entry devices must be evaluated not only according to what they do, but also according to how much less the computer will have to do to ensure accurate data." Evaluate this comment.

14.11 Discuss how most operating systems include various types of file protection controls.

14.12 "We verify everything that is input to our computer. Keypunching is inexpensive compared to rerunning jobs because of bad input." Evaluate this comment.

14.13 "Many users have become disenchanted with the computer because systems designers often fail to ensure the reliability of the systems performance with adequate control procedures." Discuss fully.

14.14 "Today, it is infrequent that we hear a programmer blame a systems problem on the hardware failing, and not detecting this failure. While this situation reflects a tremendous improvement in hardware today, it also indicates that most systems failures can be prevented during systems design." Explain.

14.15 "One sign that the computer has become an important resource in many organizations is the absence of viewing windows." Discuss.

EXERCISES

14.1 For account number 67001, prepare a check digit(s) using the following approaches and moduli:

1. Arithmetic progression—Modulus 11.
2. Geometric progression—Modulus 13.
3. Prime number weighting—Modulus 15.

14.2 The following are questions designed to determine if adequate controls exist for the organization's data processing operations. Indicate the most appropriate categorization of control (input, programming, data base, output, and hardware) for each question.

1. Are all control totals produced by the computer reconciled with control totals on input plus control totals on files to be updated?
2. If one processing program requires more than 20 minutes of continuous computer time, are provisions adequate for restarting the program if interrupted?
3. Is sequence checking employed to verify that the master files are in the correct order?
4. Is adequate use being made of the computer's ability to test for alphabetics or blanks in a numeric field?
5. Are all program files stored in temperature and humidity controlled fireproof storage areas?
6. Does dividing by zero cause an interrupt?
7. If data are being transmitted between locations, are message and character counts adequate to determine correctness and completeness of transmissions?
8. Are data that have been corrected and reentered into the system subject to the same control as applied to original data?
9. Are comparison checks being made of different fields within a record to see if they represent a valid combination of data?

14.3 What physical and procedural security techniques would be effective in preventing instances of the following type:

1. A teenager in Atlanta used a long distance telephone call to tap the lines of a time-sharing firm in Macon,

Georgia, extracting data from its ledgers as well as records of its customers.
2. An employee of a popular weekly magazine was able to walk off with a tape containing a subscriber list. Subsequently, he used a service bureau to duplicate the list for sale.
3. The data processing manager was able to steal $81,000 from a brokerage house by making program changes that caused fraudulent payments to be made to her account.
4. A 300-watt bulb overheated a fire resistant ceiling and touched off a blaze that engulfed both the tape library and the adjacent computer room.
5. It was reported that several reels of magnetic tape were erased by energy emitted from the radar equipment of a nearby Air Force base.
6. War protesters invaded Dow Chemical's unmanned computer center in Michigan. A thousand tapes were damaged and cards and manuals were ransacked. Damage was estimated at $100,000.

PROBLEMS

14.1 A bank in Pittsburgh must relocate its data processing facilities, within the next two years, due to anticipated growth and the concomitant need for more physical space. Four possible sites for the new computer center are being evaluated: (1) the ground floor of the main office in the center of town which recently has been renovated with exterior walls of plate glass; (2) the basement of the same building cited in alternative (1) above; (3) the twelfth floor of the same building described in alternative (1); and (4) an old, converted warehouse about two miles from the main office at the edge of the business district.

Considering the criteria of (1) sabotage—internal, (2) sabotage—external, (3) fire—explosion, (4) flood—water, (5) transmission, and (6) electrical interference, evaluate each alternative described and rank them in order of most to least desirable. If a criterion applies equally over all alternatives, it may be omitted. Support your conclusions.

14.2 A steel products fabricator in the Midwest is in the process of installing a computer-based order entry system. Upon receipt, customers' orders will be coded and batched for processing on an hourly basis. The order information will be maintained on a magnetic tape, where it will provide the means for producing shipping papers, invoices, and, later, sales statistics. Because of this significant impact on all stages of the company's operations, the analyst has designed an extensive validation process early in the processing of customer orders. A customer master file exists on magnetic tape which contains a customer code, name and address, salesperson identification, credit limit, and special shipping instructions for all approved customers. Similarly, a product master file exists on magnetic disk which contains the product number, market price, cost, unit of measure, current inventory amount, and miscellaneous information concerning weight, size, volume, etc., for all approved products.

Required:

1. With a customer master file and a product master file online, identify the minimum data that would comprise a customer order.
2. In conjunction with manual control procedures, what program control procedures should be implemented?

14.3 An inventory control system servicing ten auto parts stores is operated in an online mode. As supplies are received the status of the inventory is updated. In addition, as various stores request the withdrawal of items their quantity on hand is reduced. The inventory status is maintained on a magnetic disk. The file is accessible from 6 A.M. to midnight seven days a week. Define a file backup procedure as part of the overall security program for this system.

14.4 The marketing department is planning a special sales promotion for the fall. This program involves a certain trade class of customers who will be given a special 1 percent discount on all products they purchase, if they purchase a certain group of products and promote them with advertisements in newspapers or magazines. The promotion will last one year. The special discount, however, will be paid each quarter on sales that qualify in that quarter. Each customer in the designated trade class will be given an opportunity to participate in the promotion. The company, through its salespeople, must verify that the customer advertised the required products each quarter before the special discount will be paid.

The information system maintains sales history by product for each customer in time increments of a month for a total of two years. In addition, this file contains customer account number, trade class, name, and address. A check writing system is also available to prepare checks from data stored in the data base.

The sales manager has expressed a desire to have a complete control reporting package for this promotion. Your assignment is to analyze the above notes and prepare a proposal for a series of control reports to present to the sales manager. (*Hint:* The earliest control report could show all the customers who are eligible for the promotion. Another control report might show the customers who have received their special discount as evidenced by a cancelled check being returned.)

BIBLIOGRAPHY

Alexander, "Waiting for the Great Computer Rip-off," *Fortune,* July 1974.

Allen, "Danger Ahead! Safeguard Your Computer," *Harvard Business Review,* November–December 1968.

Allen, "Computer Fraud," *Financial Executive,* May 1973.

Bates, "Security of Computer-based Information Systems," *Datamation,* May 1970.

Becker, "Network Security in Distributed Data Processing," *Data Communications,* August 1977.

Canning, "Security of the Computer Center," *EDP Analyzer,* December 1971.

Canning, "Computer Security: Backup and Recovery Methods," *EDP Analyzer,* January 1972.

Canning, "Recovery in Data Base Systems," *EDP Analyzer,* November 1976.

Computer Services Executive Committee, *The Auditor's Study and Evaluation of Internal Control in EDP Systems,* New York: American Institute of Certified Public Accountants, 1977.

"DP Bureau Establishes 'Secure' Facility," *Computerworld,* September 12, 1977.

"Electronic Detectors Guard Operations," *Computerworld,* June 27, 1977.

Exton, "Clerical Errors: Their Cost and Cure," *The Office,* December 1970.

Fitzgerald, Eason, and Russell, *Systems Auditability & Control Report: Data Processing Control Practices Report,* Altamonte Springs, FL.: The Institute of Internal Auditors, Inc., 1977.

Gentile and Grimes, "Maintaining Internal Integrity of On-Line Data Bases," *EDPACS,* February 1977.

Hoffman, *Modern Methods for Computer Security and Privacy,* Englewood Cliffs, NJ.: Prentice-Hall, Inc., 1977.

Leibholz and Wilson, *User's Guide to Computer Crime,* Radnor, PA.: Chilton Book Company, 1974.

Mair, Wood, and Davis, *Computer Control & Audit,* Third Edition, Altamonte Springs, FL.: The Institute of Internal Auditors, Inc., 1978.

Shankar, "The Total Computer Security Problem: An Overview," *Computer,* June 1977.

"$3 Million in CPUs Damaged as Fire Rages Installation," *Computerworld,* April 19, 1976.

Weber, *EDP Auditing: Conceptual Foundations and Practice,* New York: McGraw-Hill Book Co., 1982.

CHAPTER

15

Detail Systems Design—Forms, Programs, and Procedures

15.1 ▪ INTRODUCTION

In Part I, our analysis of data provided some insights into the alternatives for recording and collecting data for processing in the information systems. Also, we described a variety of ways information outputs are tailored to satisfy user needs. In this chapter we discuss many additional considerations that enter into the detailed design of forms. A description is provided of the activities involved in preparation of formal, written documentation that serves to communicate the ideas of the systems analysts to the personnel operating and programming the system.

15.2 ▪ FORMS/REPORTS DESIGN

Forms and reports (i.e., paperwork) provide the primary interface between users and the information system. Forms for collecting data are the physical manifestations of the input design block; reports that provide information are the physical representations of the output design block. Interactive dialogue via a terminal such as a CRT, also follows a forms/reports concept. The importance of good forms design cannot be overemphasized. This is true whether we are referencing a paper form or a menu displayed on a CRT. The true cost of a form is difficult to determine, but some experts indicate that, in addition to any EDP processing cost related to the form, $20 worth of clerical expense is incurred gathering, entering, and reviewing data for each dollar actually spent on the form. In this section, we discuss various types of forms and provide some basic guidelines in providing a forms analysis.

Types of Forms

Many types of forms exist in a large information system. For example, an organization may have a form for paychecks, invoices, shipping papers, work assignments, budget worksheets, checks to vendors, purchase orders, sales reports, customer lists, routing files, and so forth. To deal with this multiplicity of forms and reports it is common to categorize each form as it relates to the information system. Inputs are generally termed **forms,** while outputs are called **reports.** A special type of form that is used both as input and output to the system is termed **turnaround form.**

Input Forms. The primary purpose of this classification of forms is to record data for subsequent processing. The first determination the analyst must make is what data are to be recorded. It is suggested that the analyst compose a list which includes the purpose for collecting data related to this activity, the specific data fields required, and the anticipated length of each field.

Secondly, the analyst must consider whether the data will be recorded by an employee of the organization, by one person or by many different people, written or typed, inside or outside of a building. Once these questions are answered, the analyst is in a position to design a form which will aid the recording process.

Since this type of form will require subsequent processing, the analyst must consider next the method that will be used to process the data. If the analyst designs a form that captures all of the necessary data efficiently, and can be processed subsequently with a minimum of reformatting or reproducing into another media, most likely the ideal form has been designed.

In most cases the analyst chooses a final forms design after going through a series of tradeoffs between the ease of recording the data and the efficiency of processing it. Most of the forms used to record data are designed first to aid the recorder, and second to facilitate processing. Moreover, the majority of forms designed today require further reformatting or reproduction into another media before the data are processed as discussed in Chapter 4. The analyst should always be mindful of newer and more efficient ways of capturing and recording input data due to advances in technology. **Source Data Automation** (SDA), for example, allows data to be recorded on two different media simultaneously. One medium is clearly understood by a human recorder and the second medium is available for processing on a computer.

A good example of SDA is the electronic scratch pad.[1] It works in the following way. A (multipart) form is placed on a pressure sensitive pad which is able to interpret a pen's movement. As the form (e.g.; sales order, employment application, search request, etc.) is completed, the data are fed back to the operator for visual inspection. Errors can be corrected by overwriting, adding, or deleting characters as necessary. After the validation process is complete, not only is a hardcopy record generated but also the data are in an acceptable form for further processing by a computer.

Source data entered on paper forms can also be processed readily when optical scanning equipment is employed. Optical scanning is often termed **OCR** (Optical Character Recognition). The use of special inks and character construction, as in **MICR** (Magnetic Ink Character Recognition), provides still another alternative for designing better forms.

Additional design considerations which affect the final form of an input document might be (1) number of copies required, (2) loose or padded forms, (3) multicolored, (4) type of carbons desirable, and (5) number of

---

[1]Quest Automation Limited Brochure, *Datapad*™ *Puts Your Pen On-Line to a Computer.*

forms required. We will consider these ideas and many others in the Guidelines for Forms Analysis section.

Output Forms. The design of output documents can be subdivided further into designing operational or legal documents, or designing information outputs. The design of legal or operational documents such as paychecks, invoices, shipping documents, etc., involves a reasoning process similar to that applied in the design of input documents. The design of information outputs such as budgets, performance summaries, trends, and the like, however, is not as concerned with the quality of paper and type of print font. Information outputs must have meaningful content, and be in a format that assists the reader in understanding what is contained therein.

When designing information outputs, the analyst must choose between using preprinted forms or using stock paper. The current trend is to use preprinted forms only when a document is prepared for use by persons outside of the organization. The performance capabilities of modern printing devices allow columnar headings of every description to be produced on stock paper. Preprinted forms, however, do permit more characters to be printed per line than does stock paper. This occurs because a preprinted form can use vertical lines to separate the information, but spaces must be used to separate information on stock paper.

Some additional guidelines for designing information outputs are:

1. Each page should have a brief, descriptive title.
2. Report pages should be numbered. A report that is prepared for functional use should begin each function's section with page 1.
3. Reports should contain a report identification. Many different identification schemes can be used that represent a specific organizational function (e.g., ACC, MFG, SAL, etc.), or a specific production cycle (e.g., day, week, month, etc.), or the computer program number that generated the report. Although the first two identification schemes cited may seem most relevant, in a large organization the last scheme is more practical.
4. Reports should contain two dates in the heading. The first date shows the time period covered by the report and the second is the date the report was produced.
5. Columnar headings should be brief but descriptive. Usually they appear at the top of each page in the report. The exception to this is when a report is extremely voluminous, produced often, and used by the same individuals.
6. Reports to upper management should always include very descriptive headings.
7. Multiple formatted lines can be used in a report. Columnar headings can be included once at the top of each page in a group, or printed each time the line format changes. Readability of the former approach can be enhanced by carefully using report spacing techniques.
8. Forms that will contain similar output should be placed side by side, to the limit of printer capacity, to increase printing efficiency. For example, if a printer can accommodate three payroll checks abreast, then printing time is decreased by two-thirds.

Turnaround Forms. The third classification of forms, turnaround forms, contains both input and output aspects. The enclosures we receive with our utility bills or charge accounts are examples of turnaround forms. Turnaround forms are produced as output from the processing of one system, and when returned to the organization that created them, are used as input to another system.

The turnaround form can be used in various ways. For example, many organizations produce these documents when a product is received and recorded in an inventory system. As the product is removed from inventory, the forms are input to record the depletion transaction. Other organizations produce checks to employees and vendors that are in reality punched cards, that are used later as input for cash reconciliation purposes.

Guidelines for Forms Analysis and Design

In our discussion of types of forms, we indicated some of the considerations the analyst must include when designing a form or report. In this section, some additional guidelines for analyzing and designing forms are provided.

1. Forms Functions. Perhaps the first step in analyzing a form is to determine its function. The eighteen basic forms functions are[2]:

to acknowledge	to identify
to agree	to instruct
to apply	to notify
to authorize	to order
to cancel	to record
to certify	to report
to claim	to request
to estimate	to route
to follow up	to schedule

2. Forms Distribution. The distribution of a form can be either a sequential or a parallel flow. These distributions are illustrated in Figure 15.1. The approach used to distribute a form is important since it determines (1) the number of forms required, (2) the total throughput time, (3) preparation time and costs, and (4) filing and retention procedures.

3. Physical Considerations. A complete discussion of the physical aspects of forms design is beyond the scope of this text. We provide, however, the following list of elements to be considered:

form width	form length
horizontal spacing	vertical spacing
field size	marginal perforations
bindings	carbons
colors	font type
paper weight	special features

To summarize our presentation of forms analysis we present a number of suggestions for analyzing, designing, and implementing efficient forms.[3]

First, in the design of the component parts of the form:

1. Determine the proper size that is consistent with printing production standards, and be certain that the form is reduced to the minimum practical size.
2. Determine the necessary number of copies to be included in the form, since unneeded copies represent extra cost.
3. Reduce or eliminate costly part-to-part composition changes within the form.
4. Guarantee that spacing on the form will be adequate for handwriting and prop-

---

[2]Beiden Menkus, "Designing a Useful Form," *Business Graphics*, September 1972, p. 32. Used with permission.

[3]Albert F. Tiede, "2 Ways to Save Money on Forms," *Information and Records Management*, June/July 1968, pp. 24–26. Used with permission.

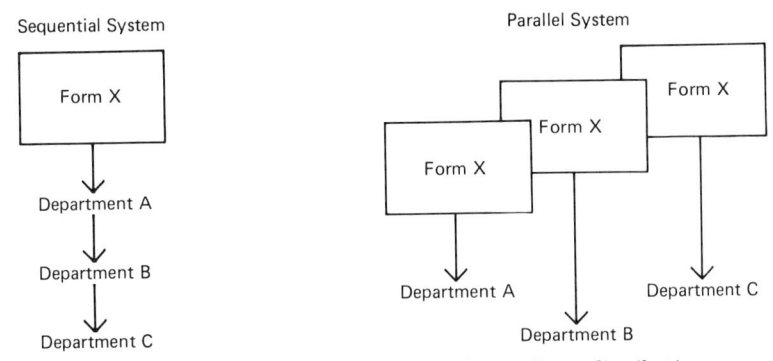

FIG. 15.1 An illustration of the two approaches to forms distribution.

erly arranged for the machines on which the form will be processed.

5. Assure an arrangement of items in the same sequence as the source or the subsequent form arrangement.
6. Preprint repetitive items to eliminate typing operations.
7. Design for use in window envelopes whenever applicable.
8. Streamline the copy for use of tab stops.
9. Give consideration as to how the form will be filed, for how long, and what information on it will act as reference for retrieval.
10. Determine the need for a new form. Examine the possibility of using a substitute form before designing or approving any new form.

Second, in the materials specifications and construction of the form:

11. Specify the correct grade, weight, and color of papers to be used. All of these factors affect the ultimate cost.
12. Determine the carbon specifications necessary to supply the needed number of legible copies. Weight, color, grade, size, striped, pattern, finish, all can affect the cost of the form.
13. Keep to a minimum, or eliminate completely, colored inks, matching colors, or special nonstandard colors.
14. Select the best type of binding to hold the form together, for processing through various machine operations, and for the ultimate separation of parts and removal of carbons. This requires careful consideration of types of gluing, stapling, crimping, perforations, and sizes both of margins and stubs.

Third, in the cost of the forms:

15. Set up the proper reordering points and quantities to assure a continual stream of supplies, requisitioned in quantities that should result in the lowest price of each item.
16. Combine requisitions for forms of like size and construction for group purchasing to secure maximum savings.
17. Furnish "guideline prices" to the purchasing department, on new forms, as a reference against bids submitted.
18. Determine whether a form can best be produced by an outside vendor or an in-house printer. This will assure the proper type of orders flowing to the internal print shops and eliminate so-called "bootleg" forms.

Finally,

19. Ensure that normal quantities of existing forms will be reordered only when no changes are contemplated in the system that may result in making one or more forms obsolete.
20. Be aware of new developments in the business forms and business machines industries.

15.3 ▪ HUMAN PROCEDURES

In Chapter 14, documentation was classified as a form of control. Documentation was also classified previously as (1) the communication prepared by the systems analyst throughout the developmental cycle of the information system (e.g., Proposal to Conduct Systems Analysis Report, Systems Analysis Completion Report, various project status reports, and so forth); (2) the formal description of the many human activities required in the information system; and (3) the formal description of the logical processing required in each computer program of the information system.

In this section we will discuss category (2) above, the writing of human procedures. This documentation formally describes what each person who is part of the information systems operations is to perform. In the next section we will discuss the design of program specifications (i.e., the documentation that formally describes the logic performed by a computer program).

As previously stated, design implies planning or arranging. The activities performed by persons operating the information system must be identified by the systems analyst. No better way exists to ensure that these activities are clearly understood by the analyst, and by the individuals assigned to perform them, than to describe the activities formally. In this section we will (1) analyze the purpose and use of human procedures, (2) describe guidelines related to the format and content of procedures, and (3) discuss general considerations for compiling a procedures manual.

The Purpose and Use of Written Procedures

The purpose of written procedures is to communicate uniformly management's desires—what activities are to be performed, when, how, and by whom. In short, written procedures are one way for management to exercise control over the activities of the organization.

It is also important to understand the various ways in which written procedures are used. First, written procedures are used to achieve standardization. Second, written procedures are used to assist in the training of new persons. When used for these purposes, written procedures should be supplemented by other methods, such as observing the activities being performed by another person, special training manuals and films, and so forth. Some additional approaches to personnel training are discussed in the next chapter.

A third use for written procedures is as a guideline and reference for auditors and analysts.

Guidelines for the Format and Content of Written Procedures

Ideally, a written procedure should be provided for each distinct activity which must be performed in the operation of the information system. Some examples of the many activities that should be described in a written procedure included (1) adding a new customer to a customer master file, (2) entering a customer remittance for accounts receivable, (3) modifying a product sales record, (4) balancing the daily labor distribution report, (5) issuing a credit memo for defective merchandise, (6) setting up the computer to process payroll, (7) distributing commission checks, (8) preparing a request for processing a special profit analysis, (9) recording the interplant transfer of raw material, and (10) entering annual departmental budgets.

Written procedures are used for reference material and for a communication link between personnel. While the specific content of each procedure depends on the activity it describes, in general the procedure should supply the answers to the following questions:

1. *What* activity is being described?
2. *Who* must perform the activity?
3. *Where* is the activity performed?
4. *When* is the activity performed?
5. *Why* is the activity performed?
6. *How* is the activity performed?

Figure 15.2 illustrates one approach to preparing written procedures. As can be seen, the format is directed to answering an individual's specific question or problem, rather than for reading as a novel at one sitting. Each section of the procedures answers one or more of the above questions clearly but concisely. The terminology used is somewhat arbitrary. For example, the section labeled "Title" might also be labeled "Subject," or "Purpose."

Title	Procedure Number	175
Cash Discounts	Effective Date	MM-DD-YY

Policy Statement: All customers are entitled to a cash discount of 2 percent on purchases as follows:
  a. The order exceeds $1000, or
  b. The order is paid in full within 10 days of shipment, or
  c. The order is received as part of a special promotion which grants the cash discount as part of the promotion.

Locations Affected: All sales divisions.

Authorization: Vice-President, Marketing.

Specific Instructions:

  Salesperson
  1. Enter the words "Cash Discount Due" on all orders eligible for cash discount.
  2. If only selected items are eligible for cash discount on an order, circle the line item number and place the letters "C.D.D." next to that line item.

  Order Entry Clerk
  1. If an order contains the words "Cash Discount Due," enter an "X" in column 7 of the order total line.
  2. If an order contains the letters "C.D.D." and the appropriate line item number is circled, enter an "X" in column 17 of the line item line.
  3. All other orders are to be left blank in these columns.

FIG. 15.2 An illustration of a cash discounts procedure.

Considerations in Compiling a Procedures Manual

A system may include hundreds of individual procedures. It is not necessary, nor even desirable, to give each person involved with the system a complete set of procedures. As a rule, procedures are combined into manuals representing specific jobs, activities, or department responsibilities. A master procedures manual for the system is usually maintained in a special library within the information system, and is readily accessible to both the systems analyst and other authorized users. Each departmental level procedures manual should contain an index, however, which identifies all procedures included within the system.

When procedures are written, compiled into manuals, and implemented in the organization, they will be discarded quickly or rendered obsolete if the analyst has not identified a simple method for modifying the contents of the manual. Although the written procedure represents management's desires, and therefore requires some level of management approval to become official, many changes normally will be identified at the user's level. Consequently, each manual should have a self-contained, simple maintenance procedure for updating the system's procedures.

Assigning identification codes to procedures is a common practice in many organizations. This identification code not only helps to minimize ambiguity among similar or related procedures, but it also helps to expedite modifications to the manual.

15.4 ▪ PROGRAM SPECIFICATIONS

Describing the activities to be performed manually in a system was treated in the last section on writing procedures. Describing the activities to be performed on a computer in a system is referred to as preparing program specifications, and is discussed in this section. The formal preparation of program specifications by the analyst provides three distinct benefits: (1) an opportunity for the analyst to rethink the systems design logic at a low level of detail; (2) a vehicle for communicating, to one or more programmers, that which is required of the programmer; and (3) a permanent record which describes or documents the activities performed by each program in the system. The importance of having complete and accurate program specifications increases as systems become large, complex, and integrated.

Programming—A Definition

The writing of computer programs is usually the largest single activity in the development phase of a system. **Programming** can be defined as the preparation of procedures to be executed on the computer. The actual tasks performed by a programmer differ little today from what they were when computers were first introduced. What has changed is the relative emphasis that a programmer gives each task as a program is developed. We can define the tasks that constitute writing a program as follows:

1. The first task in writing a program is to identify the purpose and scope of the logic to be executed by the computer. This step can be accomplished by reviewing the program specifications.

2. Defining the sequence in which the logic is to be executed is the second task in writing a program. Various techniques such as flowcharts, data flow diagrams, and decision tables can be of immense value to the programmer at this time.

3. Task three involves the translation of the identified logic into a coding structure which can be executed by the computer.

To perform this task a programmer must possess a working knowledge of one of the many programming languages (or coding structures) available for execution by the computer.

4. The fourth task is related to checking out the written program to determine if all the rules of the programming language were adhered to. This task is normally termed **compiling** or **assembling** the program. That is, the computer translates the source program written by the programmer to an object program of machine language instructions which guide the computer's processing. As a rule, a programmer will require two or three attempts to compile before a "clean" (no detectable syntax errors) status is achieved for processing.

5. Testing is the task where the programmer attempts to validate that the program logic equates to the program specifications. The programmer submits simulated input and attempts to perform all of the related processing steps to produce the required output. The number of test attempts required is a function of both the programmer's ability and the specific complexity of the program. The process of resolving and reconciling errors detected during testing is called **debugging**.

6. The sixth task performed by the programmer is the preparation of JCL instructions that will link this one program to the other software (i.e., operating system, master program, monitor, etc.). A debugging process is also required to achieve the proper JCL instructions for processing.

7. The final task performed by the programmer before the program is installed is to prepare the written procedures describing the activities to be performed by data center personnel (e.g., computer operators) to execute the program.

With this basic understanding of the programming function, we will now discuss the major form of communication between the systems analyst and the programmer; that is, the program specifications. Figure 15.3 is an illustration of a table of contents for a program specification that will serve as a guide to our presentation.

Program Control Sheet

Figure 15.4 is an illustration of what we will call the Program Control Sheet. This part of the specifications package presents the programmer with all administrative information related to the program.

1. A program name and program identification number are provided. This might be completed as:

   "Daily Update"   SA 1234
   "Monthly Master File Purge"   093-B
   "Check Printer"   Pay 110

2. In large organizations the system is given an identification number in addition to a name. The number would then be used to allocate costs to proper user departments.

3. The testing authorization number also might be used to assess charges or as a security measure.

4. "Completion Date Scheduled" and "Personnel Hours Scheduled" defines the timing of the schedule within which the programmer is expected to complete the assignment.

5. "Assigned to" and "Approval" signatures are both control and security measures.

6. The remaining entries on the form are self-explanatory and are required for general administrative and security purposes.

490   Detail Systems Design-Forms, Programs and Procedures

Table of Contents
Specifications for Program _____
Prepared by _____ Date _____
_____ Program Control Sheet
_____ Procedural Overview
_____ Systems Flowchart
_____ File Descriptions
_____ Record Formats
_____ Report Formats
_____ Specific Record Logic
_____ General Logic
_____ Reference Tables
_____ Users Variables
_____ Processing Controls
_____ Test Data
_____ _____
_____ _____

FIG. 15.3 Table of contents for a program specification package.

Program Control Sheet
Program Name _____ I.D. _____
Systems Name _____ I.D. _____
Testing Authorization Number _____
Completion Date Scheduled _____ Actual _____
Personnel Hours Scheduled _____ Actual _____
Assigned to _____ Date _____
Approval _____ Date _____
Analyst Acceptance _____ Date _____
Operations Acceptance _____ Date _____

Modifications/Revisions

Date	Programmer Initials	Approval Initials	Revision Code
_____	_____	_____	_____
_____	_____	_____	_____
_____	_____	_____	_____
_____	_____	_____	_____
_____	_____	_____	_____

FIG. 15.4 An illustration of a program control sheet.

Procedural Overview/Systems Flowchart

Figure 15.5 is an illustration of a form which gives the programmer an overview and quick understanding of a specific program's purpose and scope. Logical "File Assignments" information is required as part of the program.

A systems flowchart, illustrated in Chapter 11, may or may not be included in every package of specifications given to a programmer. It is desirable that this flowchart be available in at least one specification package for each system with which the programmer is involved.

Procedural Overview

Systems
Identification

Program
Identification

Procedural Flowchart

The Purpose of This Program

File Assignments

File I.D.	Status	Log Assg.	Phy Assg.	File I.D.	Status	Log Assg.	Phy Assg.

FIG. 15.5 An illustration of a program considered as a procedure.

Record Formats/Report Formats

Figure 15.6 illustrates one approach to formatting record layouts. Traditionally, record layouts have been provided in a horizontal format resembling the media that is being used (e.g., 80 column cards, magnetic disks, and tapes). The vertical format illustrated here is more desirable for many reasons. First, this layout does not require a special form. Second, this layout lends itself to being typed, which is desirable from a documentation viewpoint. Finally, a change in field sizes or positions can be penciled in and given to a typist for correction, thus eliminating programmers spending exorbitant amounts of time redoing outdated documentation.

Record Format

Record	Record I.D.		Record Length
File Name	File I.D.	Organization	Blocking Factor

Record Created in Program _____
Record Used in Programs _____

Field Description	Field Mnemonic	Field Position	Value/Comments

Latest Revision Date ___/___/___

FIG. 15.6 An illustration of a vertical record layout.

Logic, Tables, and User Variables

Up to this point we have been able to make use of special forms to describe the type of information that must be contained in program specifications. The narrative, however, is probably the most universal method of describing the processing logic to be performed in a program, although many analysts have described complex logic using techniques such as software-generated flowcharts of program statements ("automatic" flowcharts) and decision tables.

Reference tables refer to highly variable information that must be used at program execution time. Consequently, it is desirable that the table entries not be included within the program structure itself. Reference tables may or may not be loaded into primary storage at execution time. Where constant data are required in many different programs, this data can also be accessed from reference tables rather than coded into each program.

User variables are similar to reference tables, in that it is desirable to exclude them from the program logic. Examples of user variables might be instructions as to what reports to prepare, what fields are to be used, and in what sequence reports are to be printed. This type of entry is important where programs have "what if" or multiple reporting capabilities.

Processing Controls

The analyst should always provide the programmer with a list of the controls that are to be implemented within the program. Many of the different controls that can be implemented into each program were discussed in the previous chapter.

Test Data

Many analysts find it highly effective to provide a programmer with prepared test data. **Test data** are a series of system inputs which are used to ascertain whether or not the program is performing as planned. Using test data prepared by the analyst, or under the analyst's guidance, reduces the time a programmer must spend in achieving an error free program and minimizes the total time taken to review test results in preparation for accepting a completed program. Testing of program procedures is expanded on in the next chapter.

15.5 ▪ PROGRAMMING TECHNIQUES

Over the last 35 years we have learned that the application of certain programming techniques increases programmers' efficiency and makes their code more maintainable. Moreover, programmers' productivity can be improved if management creates an atmosphere wherein programming errors are not taken personally and programmers are not defensive about their programs (i.e., "egoless" programming).

Structured Programming

Structured programming is an approach to writing code that gets along without the use of unconditional (i.e., GO TO) program statements. Since the flow of logic through a program is more linear, without detours, productivity of both development and maintenance programmers increases.

Structured programming is comprised of three types of instructions: sequential, decision, and repetition. The logic flow of each structured programming instruction is illustrated in Figure 15.7.

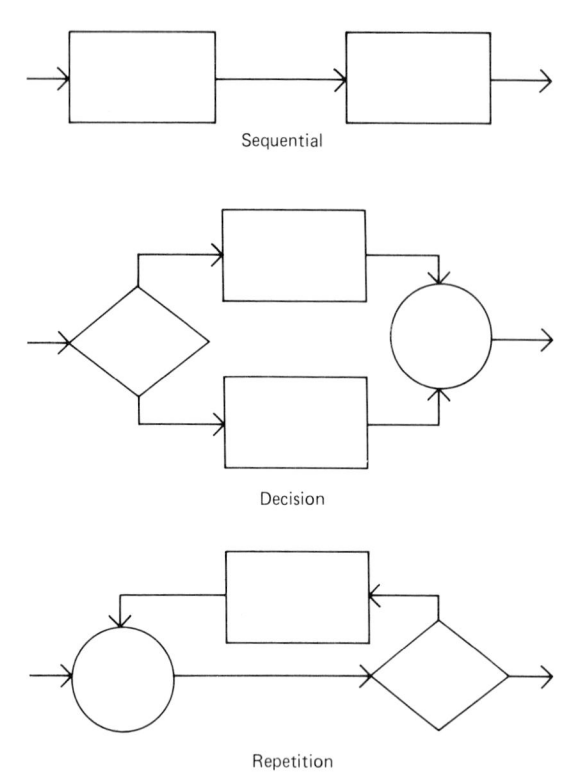

494 Detail Systems Design-Forms, Programs and Procedures

FIG. 15.7 Logic flow of structured programming instructions

1. Sequential Instructions. Sequential instructions are instructions that have no repetition or branching built into them. Examples of sequential instruction include: "MULTIPLY regular-hours-worked by regular-hourly-rate to get regular-pay," "READ XYZ-5555 record from the motor-vehicle file," or "STOP program."

2. Decision Instructions. The standard format for a decision instruction is as follows:

    IF condition
    THEN action A
    ELSE (not condition) action B

To illustrate decision instructions consider the following example:

    IF Accounting 311 is passed
    THEN register for Accounting 312
    ELSE (Accounting 311 is not passed) register for Accounting 311 again.

Each action in the decision instruction can be a group or *block* of sequential instructions, a repetition instruction (to be discussed next), or another decision instruction. An example of a decision instruction nested within the above decision instruction would be

    IF Accounting 311 is passed
    THEN IF grade in Accounting 311 is B or better
        THEN register for Accounting 329
    ELSE (grade in Accounting 311 is not B or better) register for Accounting 312
    ELSE (Accounting 311 is not passed) register for Accounting 311 again.

3. Repetition Instructions. Repetition instructions apply to the situation in which an instruction or group of instructions is repeated until a specific condition is satisfied. For example, suppose that we want to code a program that calculates a student's grade point average. The sequential set of instructions, called "Grade-Point," might be coded as follows:

Grade-Point.
    MULTIPLY hours-taken by grade-obtained to get grade-hours
    ADD hours-taken to total-hours-taken
    ADD grade-hours to total-grade-hours

To obtain a student's overall GPA, we would then specify

    REPEAT Grade-Point UNTIL all classes extended
    DIVIDE total-hours-taken into total-grade-hours giving overall-gpa.

By structuring our code in the above way we have specified exactly what is to be repeated (the set of sequential instruction entitled "Grade Point") and when to stop (when all hours taken by a student are extended).

Modular Programming

When structured programming is used, an assumption is made that the total program will be made up of a number of program modules. These modules should be relatively easy to write, debug, change, and maintain without having to know anything about other modules, and certainly without having to modify the code in other modules. Using a conventional approach to programming results in Jell-O programs that "shake all over" when one part has to be changed. Modular construction permits a programmer to unplug a module of a previously written program and plug in a new module without causing other parts of the program to be affected. Anyone who has had his or her TV or stereo repaired will appreciate the modular approach.

Probably, humans deal with, and comprehend better, things that are hierarchical and modular rather than those things that are unorganized and cluttered. For example, look at Figures 15.8 and 15.9. The first figure represents an unorganized design. The second figure illustrates a hierarchical, modular design.

Now imagine anything you wish to relate to these figures (e.g., an organization chart of a company, a procedure on diesel engine maintenance, or the design of a computer program). Then, decide which one is easier to work with and understand.

It is not necessary to have perfect symmetry in a structure, as indicated in Figure 15.9. The span of control from one level to the next, however, must be reasonable.

Moreover, the modules must have a logical connection and cohesion.

For a 200-line, one-programmer program, it is not imperative to follow the modular approach exactly. For large programs that

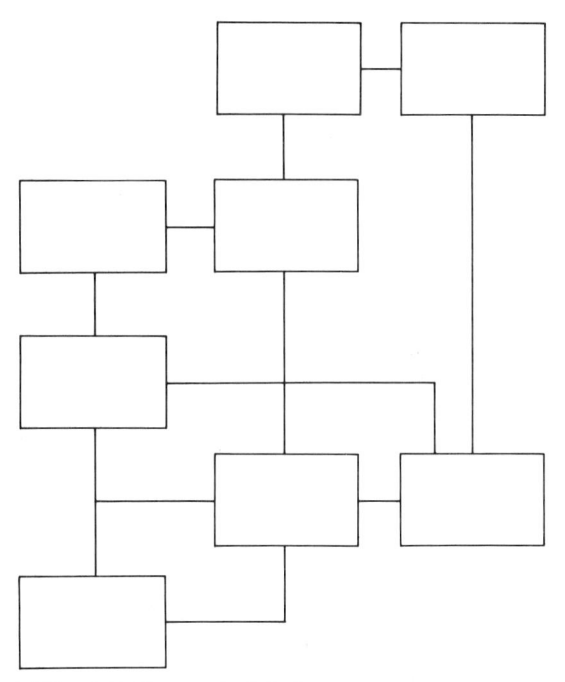

FIG. 15.8 Unorganized design.

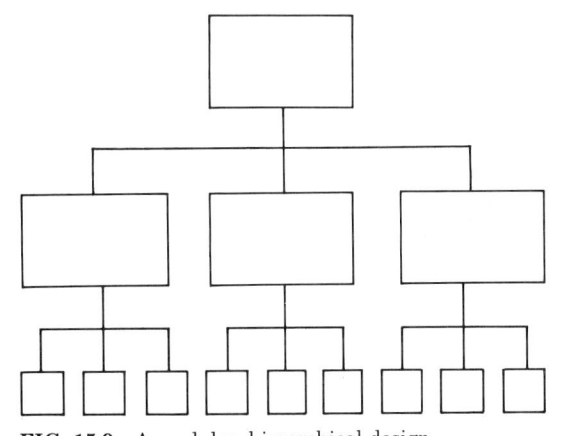

FIG. 15.9 A modular, hierarchical design.

entail thousands of hours of programmer effort, however, this approach is highly desirable. It breaks the big, complex program into small, independent, viable pieces, that when "divided," can be "conquered."

Three tests must be met to divide the program into modules. First, each module should solve one clearly defined part of the program such as input, input edit, process, or output. For example, one module of a payroll program may compute FICA. Second, each module should be manageable and easy to understand. Many programmers feel that a module should be no more than 50 lines of instruction code, which means that a listing of its source code can be contained on one page of printer output. Third, the modules should be connected logically. For example, the results of modules for FICA calculation, along with other payroll deductions, should connect to the GROSS-PAY module. The results of the GROSS-PAY module should be passed, in turn, to another module where computations are made to produce NET-PAY.

An Example

A simple example of how a total program is put together is illustrated in Figure 15.10. The accounts receivable and sales program is broken down into various modules, such as invoice preparation, connected to each other via CALL statements. The invoice preparation module is further divided into input, process, and output modules. Each programmer is assigned a module with minimum complexity so that it can be coded in a reasonable time. For example, one programmer could be assigned the invoice prep-

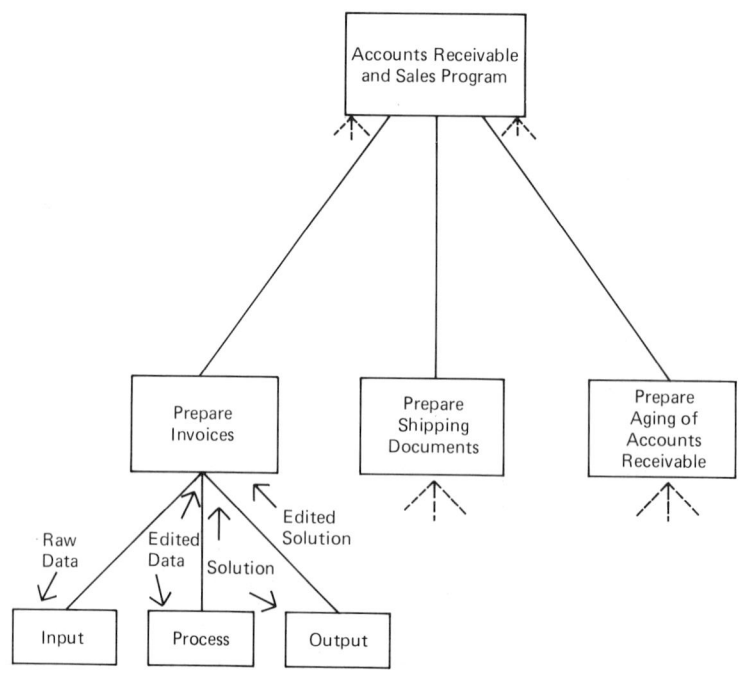

FIG. 15.10 Example of a modular program.

aration module, another the shipping documents module, and yet another the accounts receivable aging program. When a programmer completes a module, it is tested and debugged. After all modules are completed, they are connected together to form the total program, which, in turn, is tested.

Programming Standards

Programming calls for stringent standards. *Data dictionaries* with data names and data references, complete documentation, standard conventions for program comments, standards for flowchart and decision table preparation, rules for forming characters (e.g., letter versus number 0), rules for pagination and indentation (e.g., all PICTURE clauses must begin in column 40), rules for line numbering, and standards for programming techniques (e.g., use numeric fields in packed format, subscript with literals), are standards that facilitate program development and maintenance.

The Programming Team

A large program is developed by a programming team consisting of: (1) a chief or lead programmer who manages all tasks required to develop the program; (2) a documentation specialist who develops program documentation including flowcharts, decision tables, file layouts, table of contents, program control sheets, etc.; (3) a program librarian who performs functions that interface the program with the total system and place it in program library residence; and (4) a number of application programming specialists who work independently on program modules. Assistants to any of the above are added if span of control warrants it.

SUMMARY

An important activity during detail design is the design of all the forms and reports required in the information system. Forms can be categorized as input, output (reports), or turnaround documents. To design effective and economical forms, the analyst must perform an analysis of the form, identifying its purpose, distribution, and physical attributes.

Human procedures are formal descriptions of the activities to be performed by the people component of the system. Program specifications are formal descriptions of the activities to be performed by the computer.

Pelican Case

Phase 4 · Detail Systems Design
· Final Detail Systems Design Report

Phases of Systems Development Methodology:

Completed [////]
To be completed [ ]

Phase 1	Phase 2	Phase 3	Phase 4	Phase 5
Systems analysis	General systems design	Systems evaluation and justification	Detail systems design	Systems implementation
Proposal to conduct systems analysis report / Systems analysis completion report	General systems design proposal report	Final general systems design report	Final detail systems design report	Final implementation report
Completed in Chapter 11	Completed in Chapter 12	Completed in Chapter 13	Presented and completed in this chapter	Presented at the end of Chapter 16

PHASE 4

OVERVIEW

Like the architect who converts blueprints to brick and mortar, the systems analyst transforms general design to detail design. Like the architect who relies on builders to perform the construction, Ben Snow relies on others to give specific shape to every design block. He must, for example, depend on programmers to write and test the actual program code.

The detail of the final system is presented in the Final Detail Systems Design Report. In the example that follows, not every item of the system is given. We believe that you can gain an appreciation of how and why this report is prepared without having to wade through volumes of detail. We stress, however, that in a real world situation every aspect of the final system must be described in detail for complete systems documentation.

FINAL DETAIL SYSTEMS DESIGN REPORT

To: All managers and various systems personnel

From: Ben Snow, Systems Analyst

Input

Dictation communication is handled by telephoning and speaking into the dictation recording unit. Dictation can also be done in the field by using portable recorders and then mailing the recorder cassettes to the office for transcription.

Transcribers receive and playback dictation of sales personnel. Transcribing equipment consists of the recording/transcribing unit, headset and separate speaker, and foot control. The transcriber operator can scan the cassette for special instructions, plus control speed, backspacing, degaussing, and tone/volume.

To input long distance and collect calls, a log form which is completed by hand, is read by optical character recognition (OCR) units.

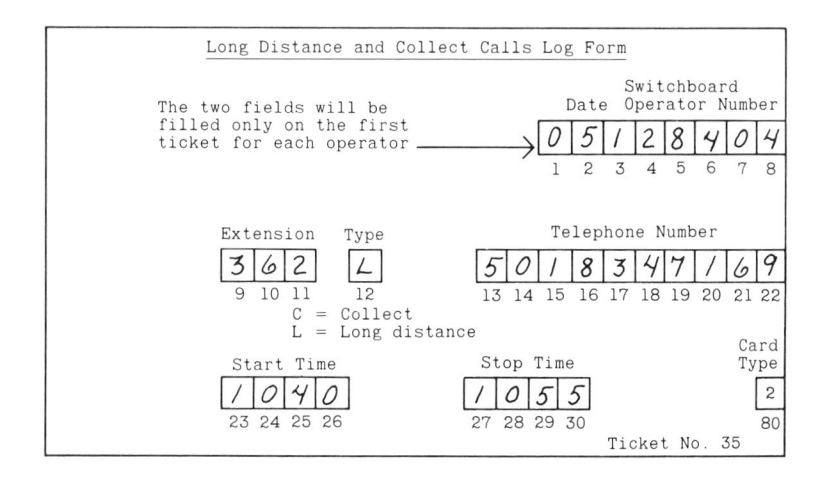

```
        Long Distance and Collect Calls Log Form

                                          Switchboard
   The two fields will be        Date   Operator Number
   filled only on the first    ┌─┬─┬─┬─┬─┬─┬─┬─┐
   ticket for each operator ──→│0│5│1│2│8│4│0│4│
                                └─┴─┴─┴─┴─┴─┴─┴─┘
                                 1 2 3 4 5 6 7 8

          Extension  Type              Telephone Number
          ┌─┬─┬─┐   ┌─┐          ┌─┬─┬─┬─┬─┬─┬─┬─┬─┬─┐
          │3│6│2│   │L│          │5│0│1│8│3│4│7│1│6│9│
          └─┴─┴─┘   └─┘          └─┴─┴─┴─┴─┴─┴─┴─┴─┴─┘
          9 10 11   12           13 14 15 16 17 18 19 20 21 22
                 C = Collect
                 L = Long distance
                                                       Card
          Start Time              Stop Time            Type
          ┌─┬─┬─┬─┐              ┌─┬─┬─┬─┐             ┌─┐
          │1│0│4│0│              │1│0│5│5│             │2│
          └─┴─┴─┴─┘              └─┴─┴─┴─┘             └─┘
          23 24 25 26            27 28 29 30                80
                                            Ticket No. 35
```

To log toll calls, an employee asks the switchboard operator to dial a long distance call. The operator then fills in the following fields: "extension requesting the call; "type" which contains the letter "L" for long distance, or "C" for collect; "telephone number" requested; "start time" of the conversation; and "stop time" when it ends. (Note that seconds are not accounted for and a 24-hour clock is used.) When the conversation begins, the form is attached with a spring clip to a connecting plug; when the conversation is over, the plug is unplugged and "stop time" is added. "Card type" for this form is always "2."

Another input of the system is the telephone bill. Telephone equipment and service charges are provided by the telephone company on magnetic tape ready to be input in the system. These charges are matched against a charge file prepared by Pelican. Differences are investigated and reconciled. Then, actual charges are allocated to user departments.

A customer profile form is used as input to the customer mailing and promotion file. A copy of this form is illustrated below. These forms are partially filled in by field sales personnel or from bingo cards mailed in by customers. A credit rating, is generated by Credit Department clerks. Once the form is complete, data from it are input via a CRT.

Processing

The procedures here involve preparation of form letters and documentation of a report generator program.

The form-letter procedure produces documents which are made up of constant data and variable data stored on a disk file. In form or acknowledgment letters, the variable data are names and addresses of customers or prospective customers. The main content of the letter consists of constant data or boiler plate, (i.e., standard paragraphs or sentences that do not vary from one letter to the next). Variable data, such as names

```
                        CUSTOMER PROFILE FORM

NAME OF RESPONDENT:                    POSITION:
COMPANY:                               TELEPHONE:
ADDRESS:
CITY:                    STATE:                    ZIP:
CREDIT RATING:  ____EXCELLENT  ____GOOD  ____FAIR  ____POOR

TYPE OF BUSINESS (CHECK ALL THAT APPLY):
☐ Drilling Contractor
☐ Independent Oil Producer
☐ Refinery
☐ Industrial
☐ Building Contractor
☐ Common Carrier
☐ Other _____

RESPONSE REQUESTED (CHECK ALL THAT APPLY):
☐ Send Sales Literature and Prices
☐ Have Salesperson Call on Us Regularly
☐ Have a Production Engineer Call Us Right Away

INTERESTED IN (CHECK ALL THAT APPLY):
☐ Drilling Equipment
☐ Oilfield Supplies
☐ Foundry and Fabrication Work
☐ Compressors
☐ Industrial Equipment and Supplies
☐ Earthmoving Equipment
☐ Large Equipment Repair, Parts, and Maintenance
☐ Pipe and Fittings
☐ Storage Tanks
☐ Heaters/Treaters
```

and addresses, are inserted or merged where appropriate to print a new letter.

An example of a letter sent to a customer is shown below. Other customers will get the same letter, but with appropriate company name, address, and salutation.

> BARNHILL DRILLING COMPANY
> ONE OILFIELD PLAZA
> SHREVEPORT, LOUISIANA 71161
>
>
> DEAR MR. BARNHILL:
>
>
> We would like to announce that we offer sales and service on a complete line of Decat Diesel Engines.
>
> This line of engines offers no-adjustment fuel system, low maintenance, and top fuel efficiency. Also, power can be easily upgraded. Engines can be reset for 1800, 1900, or 2100 RPM operation at any time without major rework or overhaul. Ask one of our sales persons about these engines or call Bud Wiser direct, 800-839-7100.
>
> Sincerely,
>
>
> Danny Loman
> Director of Marketing

To prepare the above letter, the boiler plate part of the letter, is keyed in and becomes a temporary working file. A data file called CUSTOMER MAILING AND PROMOTION FILE is stored on diskette. This file contains the variable data necessary to provide variables for each letter printed.

The next procedure detailed is a report generator program. A systems flowchart and narrative follows.

The major logic of this procedure is a proper match of the telephone bill to the switchboard log record. The telephone bill contains LD—long distance call, CO—collect incoming call, CR—credit card call, SC—service charge, and EQ—equipment charge codes.

If a CR code is read from the telephone bill, there will be no matching entry on the switchboard log since the

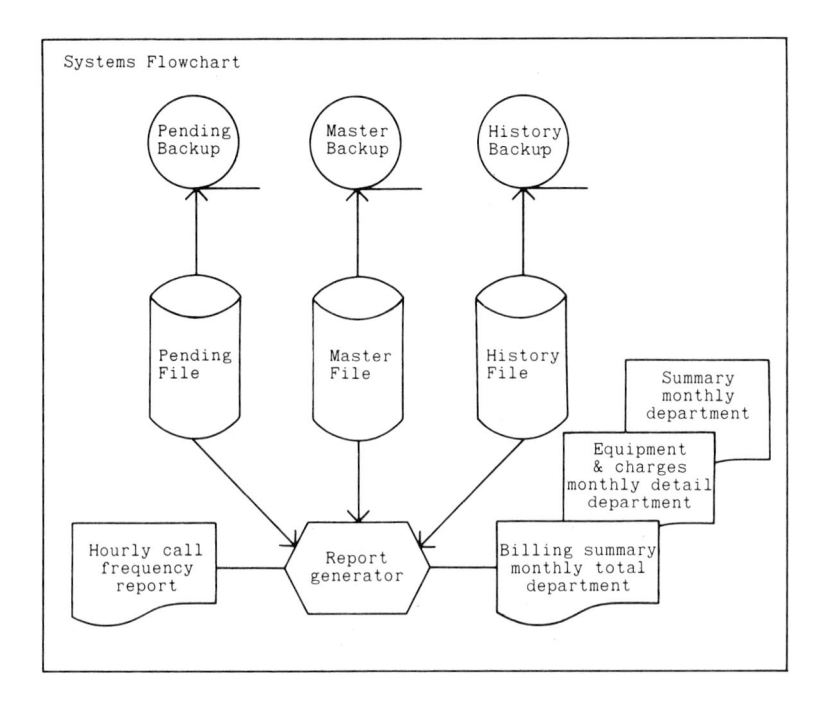

```
              Systems Flowchart

                Pending    Master    History
                Backup     Backup    Backup
                   ▲         ▲         ▲
                   │         │         │
                   │         │         │
                Pending    Master    History
                 File       File      File                Summary
                                                          monthly
                                                         department

                                                     Equipment
                                                     & charges
                                                    monthly detail
                                                     department

                Hourly call      Report          Billing summary
                frequency       generator        monthly total
                  report                           department
```

call originates outside of the organization. For a
record of this type, the credit card holder's name and
department are extracted from the appropriate master
file record, and the information is written directly on
the report. EQ and SC types also have no matching entry,
but are assigned to a department and are written
directly on the report. LD and CO codes must have a
corresponding entry in the switchboard log. If
unmatched, the record is written to the error list. A
matching entry causes the caller's name and department
to be extracted from the appropriate pending file
records and the information is written on the report.
The validation procedure is described in the following
decision table.

Data Base

In addition to the many dictation minicassettes and
various working files, four major physical files make up

Pelican Case—Phase 4

		1	2	3	4	5	6	7	8	9	10	11	12	13	14	15
If:	Long distance?	Y	Y	Y	Y	N										
	Switchboard pickup?	Y	Y	Y	N	Y	Y	Y	N							
	Collect?	–	–	–	–	N	Y	Y	Y	Y						
	Credit card?	–	–	–	–	–	–	–	–	Y	Y	Y				
	Service charge?	–	–	–	–	–	–	–	–	–	–	–	Y	Y	N	
	Name on file?	Y	Y	N	–	–	Y	N	Y	–	Y	N	Y	–	–	–
	Department valid?	Y	N	Y	–	–	Y	Y	N	–	Y	Y	N	Y	N	–
Then:	Write report	1				1				1			1			1
	Write pending file		1	1	1	1		1	1	1		1	1		1	2
	Write error list		2	2	2	2		2	2	2		2	2		2	

the data base. These are: (1) customer mailing and promotion file, (2) pending file, (3) history file, and (4) master file. The master file is described below.

This file contains every extension and credit card number in the company. All telephone charges entering the system are validated against this file. Also, year-to-date (YTD) charges are accumulated in specific fields called "YTD total charges," "YTD credit charges" (see record layout below). These fields are used for generating information on various reports.

Department, extension number, and credit card number are concatenated to form the primary key. If an employee does not have an extension but has a credit card, the extension field will be zero filled. If an employee has an extension but not a credit card, the credit card field will be zero filled. Each department will have a header record with zero extension, zero credit card, and blank employee name. This header record contains department equipment charges and is used to discriminate between department equipment charges and extension equipment charges.

If an extension is not in use, then the field "date closed" will contain an expiration date in it and no charges can be allocated to that extension.

Controls

Department and extensions are verified by matching to records on the master file. Date is checked for reasonableness (i.e., day is greater than zero and less than 32 and month is greater than zero and less than 13). Name is not verified. Equipment and service charge field is checked for a numeric value. Credit card number is verified by reading the master file and searching for a matching credit card number. All files contain header and trailer labels as an added control.

The switchboard log is verified as indicated above. Also, the switchboard operator can be any number between zero and ten. Telephone number, start time, and stop time are checked for numeric values. The ticket number is checked manually to determine if it is one greater than the previous record. This check detects missing tickets.

Preplanned backup procedures are established for the four major files to safeguard them from loss or destruction. Copies of these files are made on magnetic tape, which are, in turn, stored in an offsite vault.

The switchboard operator is controlled by the fact that an operator number is part of the input. This way, all logs deviating from the telephone bill will be challenged by Bud Wiser. Also, the billed calls not logged can be traced to the operator, since time of the call is part of the input.

Computer operation is controlled by messages displayed on the console. Instructions relate to the appropriate disk drive to mount, how many parts of printer paper to use, and other control checkpoints requiring operator response.

Control clerks are provided with a list of report recipients and must account for every report distributed. Once the list is completely checked off, it is handed to the operations manager for filing.

Output controls are established as a final check on the accuracy and completeness of the processed information. The control clerk scans the reports to detect obvious errors. Communication channels between users and control clerks are established so that user satisfaction or dissatisfaction with reports is acknowledged. The control clerk is also responsible for report distribution to users on time.

Output

An example of a management report produced by the system is shown on the last page of this report.

Data Processing Resources

Data, as previously mentioned, come from a variety of sources. Specifics that relate to these data are described in the INPUT and DATA BASE sections of this report.

Hardware that supports the system includes a processor, four CRTs, two printers, one hard disk, four floppy disk drives, 100 floppy disks, one magnetic tape drive, four magnetic tapes, 200 minicassettes, one dictation and transcription unit, one central system for remote dictation, and one OCR unit. Specifications of some of the components are detailed below.

1. <u>Processor</u>. A 16-bit system with clock speed of 2 MHz with interrupt capabilities; 192K RAM expandable to 384K; connection to host mainframe computer is via telephone line using standard binary synchronous communication protocol; full duplex at data rates of up to 19,200 baud; performs EBCDIC/ASCII conversion; power: 120 VAC, 60 Hz, 140 W.

2. <u>CRTs</u>. A high-resolution 12-inch display; 24 lines of 80 upper and lower case characters (i.e., 1920 character screen); direct-connect modems; 53 keys including up, down, right, left arrows, and BREAK and CLEAR commands; 6K RAM; power: 120 VAC, 60 Hz, 50 W.

3. <u>Printers</u>. "Letter perfect" copies are printed at over 500 words per minute; interchangeable daisy wheels of 124 characters (96 ASCII plus international); Courier 10 pitch; forward and reverse paper feed and selectable print densities; up to 16-inch paper with original plus five carbons; friction feed; acoustic cover for quiet printing; power: 120 VAC, 60 Hz, 140 W. W.

4. <u>Hard disk</u>. Fast access to over 10 megabytes of data; easily add three units for combined total of over 40 megabytes of data; one Winchester unit provides two, 10-inch platters permanently sealed in a dust-free environment; both surfaces of each platter are accessed by their own read/write head, forming a cylinder of four tracks under the head at any one time; SAVE command automatically copies data from disk onto a tape and writes it back with the RESTORE command; data transfer rate is 4.5 megabytes per second; disk rotation speed is 3200 RPM; latency is 9.3 msec., average; track-to-track access time is 18 msec.; power: 120 VAC, 60 Hz, 140 W.

Some of the salient features of software include a DBMS, which uses trees to associate data. The operating system offers many features such as CREATE to allocate a working file, or SPOOL to save printer output in a disk file for later printing and also to allow printing while other operations are being performed.

Standard COBOL is available with an interactive DEBUG feature for program development and testing. CRT control with extended ACCEPT/DISPLAY commands provide screen formatting. Other features include advanced string handling; multidimensional arrays; full editing; and program line renumbering.

Application of software is described in the PROCESSING section. Documentation of these programs are in program manuals provided by the vendor or by the internal programmer.

The people who work directly on this system are as follows: Bud Wiser, Manager; Mrs. Suzuki and her assistants; Sally Worth, and her assistants who perform transcription work and operate the CRTs; Travis Cook, part-time programmer; and John Tinker, computer operator. Other tasks such as librarian work is handled by personnel from the central system.

```
RUN DATE MM/DD/YY                                                                                    PAGE NO XX OF XX
AS OF DATE MM/DD/YY               COMMUNICATIONS BILLING SUMMARY
                                     MONTHLY DEPARTMENT XXXXXXXX

                    SERVICE DESCRIPTION  NUMBER OF CALLS  COST OF CALLS  TOTAL FOR GROUP
                    LONG DISTANCE        XXXXX            $ZZZZZ.00
                    COLLECT              XXXXX            $ZZZZZ.00
                    CREDIT CARD          XXXXX            $ZZZZZ.00
                                                                         $ZZZZZZ.00
                    WATS                 XXXXX            $ZZZZZ.00
                    TELEGRAPH COLLECT    XXXXX            $ZZZZZ.00
                    TELEGRAPH STANDARD   XXXXX            $ZZZZZ.00
                                                                         $ZZZZZZ.00

                    EQUIPMENT CHARGES    XXXXX            $ZZZZZ.00
                    MONTHLY RENTAL       XXXXX            $ZZZZZ.00
                                                                         $ZZZZZZ.00
                                            DEPARTMENT TOTAL  $ZZZZZZ.00
```

	YEAR XX	JANUARY	FEBRUARY	MARCH	APRIL	MAY	JUNE	JULY	AUGUST	SEPTEMBER	OCTOBER	NOVEMBER	DECEMBER	YTD SUMMARY
TOLL WATS TWIXS EQUIP		$ZZZZ.00	$ZZZZ.00	$ZZZZ.00	$ZZZZ.00	$ZZZZ.00	$ZZZZ.00	$ZZZZ.00	$ZZZZ.00	$ZZZZ.00	$ZZZZ.00	$ZZZZ.00	$ZZZZ.00	$ZZZZ.00
TOTALS		-	-	-	-	-	-	-	-	-	-	-	-	
BUDGET		-	-	-	-	-	-	-	-	-	-	-	-	
BUDGET VARIANCE		-	-	-	-	-	-	-	-	-	-	-	-	

CHAPTER 16

Systems Implementation

16.1 ▪ INTRODUCTION

In the previous two chapters many of the specific design activities necessary for the development of an information system were discussed. To implement the new system successfully, a few activities must be performed by the systems analyst and others that are not generally classified as design work, per se. These activities involve the training and educating of personnel, and testing of the system. Moreover, because of the dynamic environment of an organization, a special consideration, termed **systems conversion,** is required to achieve implementation of the new system. Finally, efforts of the systems analyst do not end with the implementation of the system. An implementation follow-up is often vital to eventual acceptance of the system. Each of these subjects is discussed in this chapter.

Final activities required to implement a new system are illustrated in Figure 16.1.

16.2 ▪ TRAINING AND EDUCATING PERSONNEL

It has been emphasized throughout this text that the key ingredient in every system is

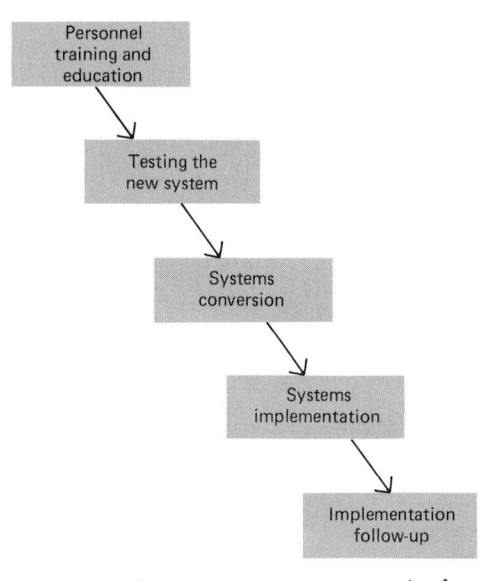

FIG. 16.1 Final activities necessary to implement a new system.

people. People design, develop, operate, and maintain the system, and they use the output generated by the system. If a new information system is to be implemented successfully, then everyone who is affected by the system must be made aware, first, of their individual responsibilities to the system, and second, what the system provides to them. The prime responsibility for effecting this educational process rests with the systems analyst.

In our analysis of training and educating personnel, we discuss types of personnel requiring training or educating, various approaches to educating and training, and some general considerations in choosing approachs.

Training and Educating Categories

Users of information and operating personnel represent two broad categories of people who must receive education and training.

Users of Information. This category of personnel includes general management, staff specialists, and personnel in various functional areas, including salespeople, accountants, production schedulers, and so forth. Also, this category might include customers, vendors, government officials, and other constituents of the organization. It is generally termed "education" when the users of the information are informed of what the system requires and provides. The educational process for many members of this group actually begins in the analysis phase when they identify their information requirements. The emphasis at this later point in development is directed toward explaining how these requirements are met by the system.

Providing this kind of education is often overlooked or its value underestimated during the implementation of a system. The systems analyst, who has spent nearly every day for several months thinking about and working with the new system, fails to realize that most of the potential users of the system have spent relatively little time thinking about the new system. Furthermore, when plans are presented to management by systems personnel for what appears to be massive educational efforts, they are often reduced or eliminated on the grounds of being too expensive. Although it is fairly easy to calculate the costs of providing education, it is often quite difficult to identify the benefits of such education; or, the costs incurred when resources, such as information, are not used due to lack of understanding. The first problem can be corrected by systems analysts who recognize the need, and who plan for, user education as part of the system's implementation process. The systems analyst can overcome the second problem by the preparation of well-thought-out educational plans presented to management as integral to the systems implementation process.

Operating Personnel. This category of personnel includes all individuals involved in preparing input, processing data, and in operating and maintaining both the logical and physical components of the system. It also includes those persons responsible for direct control over the system. Generally, we call their educational process "training." Training operating personnel has two dimensions that must be considered by the analyst. First, operating personnel must be trained initially to run the new system. Second, training must be provided to this general category of personnel on a continuing basis as the system is modified, or as new personnel are required. The importance of recognizing this second aspect of training will become clear as we discuss the various methods that might be used to provide acceptable training when the system is implemented initially.

Approaches to Educating and Training Personnel

Psychologists and educators have demonstrated that different educating and training objectives call for a variety of educating and training approaches. A lecture is appropriate to explain to a group of users generally how the new system operates, whereas a "learn-by-doing approach" might be used to train new operations personnel. Likewise, many people can perform any given job satisfactorily after they have performed that job once or a relatively few number of times. Some approaches used by the systems analyst include:

1. *Seminars and group instruction.* This approach allows the analyst to reach many people at one time. It is particularly useful when the analyst is presenting an overview of the system. Additionally, this approach is worthwhile in large organizations where many people perform the same tasks.

2. *Procedural training.* This approach provides an individual with the written procedures describing his or her activities, as the primary method of learning. Usually the individual has an opportunity to ask questions and pose problems concerning the procedure, either in a group session or individually. An extension of this technique is to provide a formal writeup of the system, particularly of the outputs, to each affected user.

3. *Tutorial training.* As the term implies, this approach to training is of a more personal nature and, consequently, is fairly expensive. In conjunction with other training approaches, however, this technique can eliminate any remaining void which prevents a satisfactory understanding of the system. In systems where certain tasks are highly complex or particularly vital to successful operations, tutorial training may be necessary to achieve the desired results. In practice, the analyst provides personal training or education not only to operating personnel, but also to users of the system's outputs.

4. *Simulation.* An important training technique for operating personnel is the simulated work environment. This environment can be created relatively easily by reproducing data, procedures, and any required equipment, and allowing the individual to perform the proposed activities until an acceptable level of performance is attained. Although simulation seems to be an expensive training method, fewer errors and less rework usually result when the individual is later placed in an operating environment.

5. *On the job training.* Perhaps the most widely used approach to training operating personnel is to simply put them to work. Usually the individual is assigned simple tasks and given specific instructions on what is to be done and how it is to be done. As these initial tasks are mastered, additional tasks are assigned. The learning curve in this approach can be quite lengthy and, in many cases, what appears to be immediate results or production can be very deceptive. Moreover, if a particular operation is highly complex and difficult to master, the individual designated to carry it out may become frustrated and request a transfer.

The first step in determining training requirements and training approaches is to compile a list of all the tasks required by the new system and the skills needed to perform them. The next step is to prepare an inventory of skills already available. The difference between these lists indicates the number of skilled personnel to be trained (some may also be hired who are already trained). The amount of time spent in train-

Systems Implementation

ing relates to levels of difficulty and complexity of each task.

Much of the training effort is directed toward human/machine dialogues.[1] These dialogues are categorized in terms of how easy they are to use and, thus, the time necessary for training. Figure 16.2 shows a spectrum of examples ranging from dialogues that are difficult to understand and use on the right side of the scale, to dialogues that are child's play to learn on the left. For example, simple dialogues can be learned in 5 minutes, while dialogues for airline reservation systems may require three weeks of training. To become skilled at using the full facilities of some interactive programming languages takes several months, although a basic subset of most of these languages can be learned quickly!

General Considerations When Choosing Training Approaches

The analyst's primary objective during the systems development is to provide training for existing personnel so that the new sys-

[1]This material plus Figure 16.2 is adapted from James Martin, *Design of Man-Computer Dialogues*, Englewood Cliffs, N.J.: Prentice-Hall, Inc., 1973.

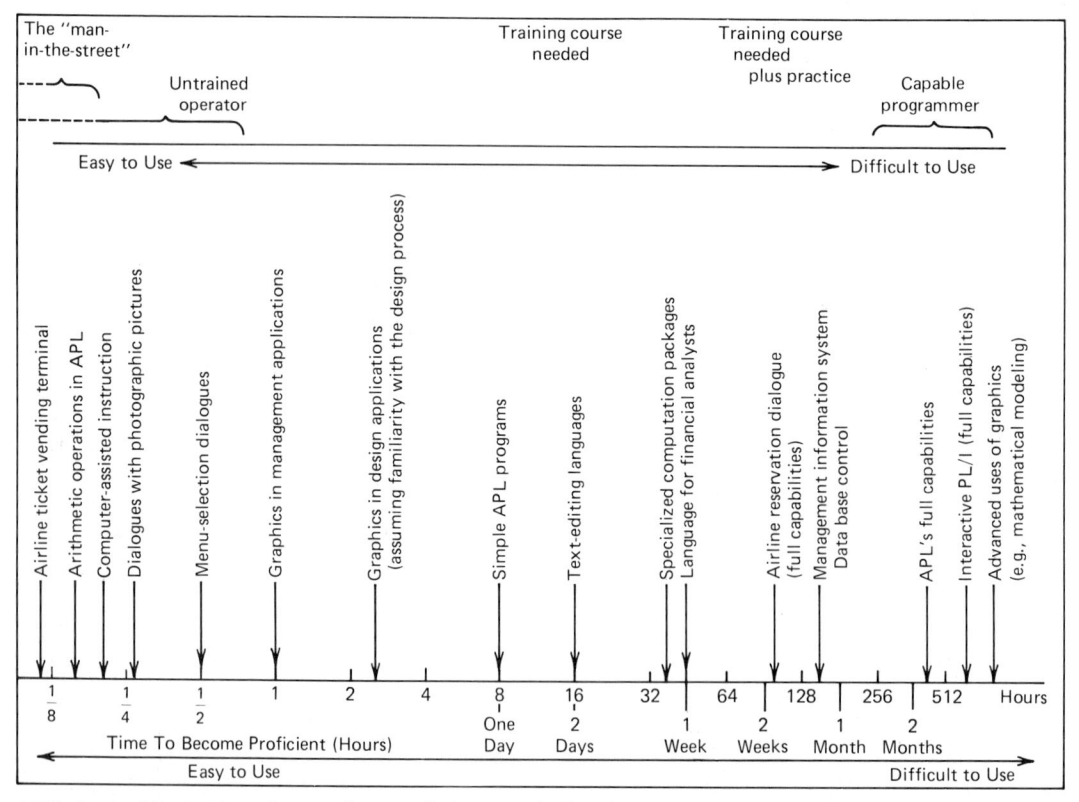

FIG. 16.2 Illustration of ease of use and time required to learn a variety of human/machine dialogues.

tem can be implemented. Careful planning at this time, however, can result in a meaningful training mechanism that should reduce employee turnover and that can be used by the organization on a continuing basis. This consideration is important since employee turnover is expensive and affects all levels in the organization. When a training approach is developed that meets both objectives, the analyst should not hesitate to construct more expensive aids and programs for this initial requirement. For example, full scale training sessions, simulated facilities, and learning manuals such as programmed instruction courses, rarely can be justified for a one-time effort. The real benefit to constructing these mechanisms lies in their reuse on a continuing basis.

A second, corresponding consideration might be termed *direct* versus *indirect* training. Once a system is implemented, the systems analyst often is reassigned to an entirely new area of the organization. Consequently, the analyst is not available to assist with the day-to-day systems problems with either operating personnel or users. To ensure that these problems can be addressed satisfactorily and resolved, the analyst can take a more indirect role during initial training. In other words, a select group of supervisors might be trained in the areas of data preparation and operations, and allowed to conduct individual training for both clerical workers and user personnel. With this approach the analyst is rapidly removed from all but the exceptional problems related to the system. In most organizations this approach is highly desirable. The failure of many analysts in using this technique seems to be related to what we might call "pride of ownership." Having spent many long hours during the developmental phases, the analyst is quite often reluctant to give away this last-minute control over the new system.

One final note is in order concerning the training activity. It is generally recognized that if individuals are provided with an initial overview, they can better relate to the significance of each task and activity required of them. Often, without thinking, an analyst will begin to provide training, starting with a single task and moving from task to task until the whole job has been presented. Regardless of which approach is finally selected to accomplish the educating and training of personnel, the effort should begin with the preparation of an overview.

16.3 ▪ TESTING THE SYSTEM

Testing the newly developed or modified system is one of the most important activities in the systems development methodology. It is an implementation activity that, similar to training personnel, requires careful planning and application. The goal of testing is to verify the logical and physical operation of all design blocks to determine that they operate as intended. Often, testing is given lip service, or is abridged as cost overruns occur or schedules slip. Inevitably, failure to test adequately leads to problems with the systems operation. In our analysis of testing, we discuss specific techniques that can be used to test each of the individual design blocks. An overview of the testing activity is portrayed in Figure 16.3. Prior to conversion, the test plans, data, and procedures, along with the test results, are filed with systems documentation.

Test of Input

The major tests of input are to determine if the various forms meet design rules and are

514 Systems Implementation

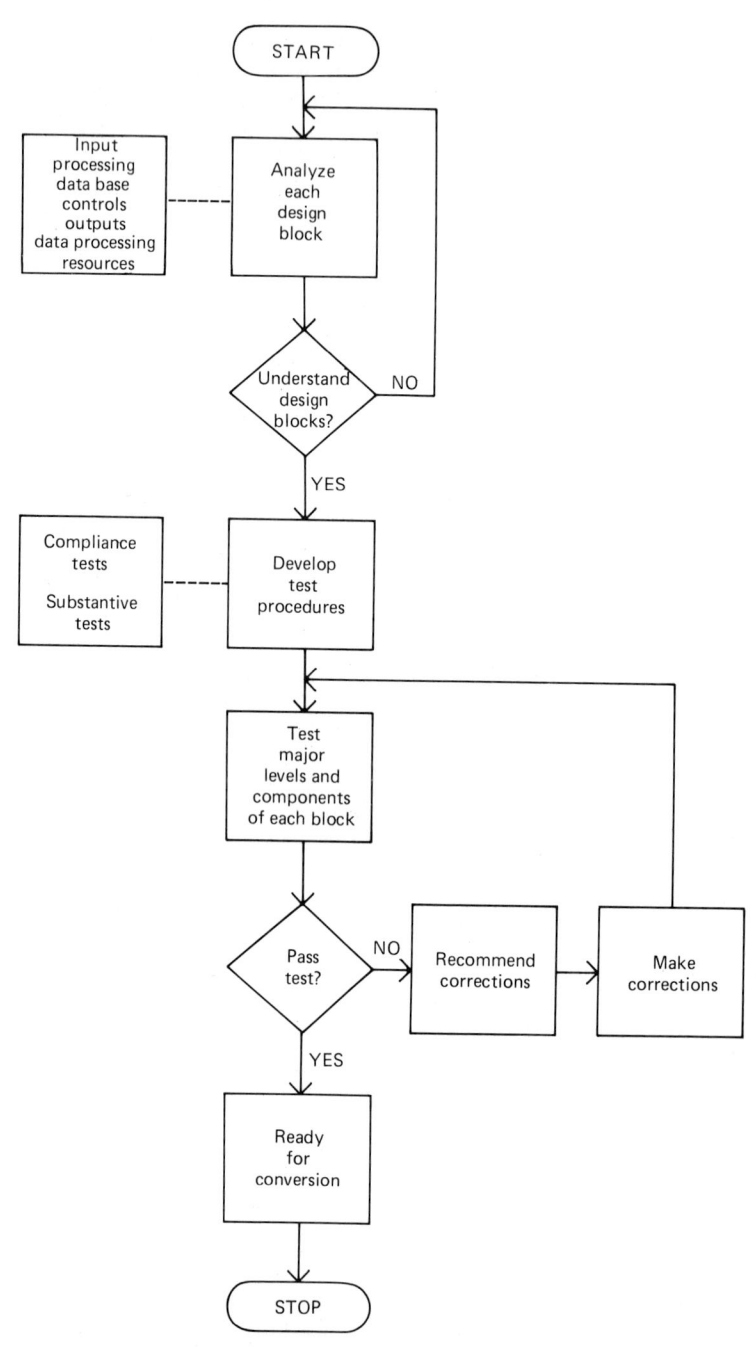

FIG. 16.3 Overview of testing the system.

completed correctly by users of the system. Much of this testing can take place during training. Also, additional testing is performed while procedures are being tested.

If input is handled by a POS device, for example, a simple random sample of products is selected and passed by the reader to determine correctness of price and description. If certain products do not contain a bar code, then a keyboard must be available to enter the data manually. If input entered via keyboard is displayed on a CRT, proper layout on the screen is important. Any screens that are cluttered and contain unnecessary data should be identified and corrected.

Many organizations hire people whose only function is to enter data. It is important that these people receive adequate training in data entry. For example, by testing the performance of order entry personnel, additional on the job training can be given to correct inadequacies.

Test of Processing

Testing the processing design block involves both computer programs and human procedures. The objective of testing computer programs is to ensure that they perform intended functions and only those. A program may appear to be operating properly because it is processing input and producing what appears to be valid output. Or, it may be producing valid output but performing additional unauthorized tasks. For example, a utility company used a formula for computing electric bills that appeared to be correct. Several months later it was discovered that the formula had undercharged the company's customers. To their dismay, the customers had to make up the difference between the correct and erroneous charges in one lump sum. In another company, a programmer wrote a program that correctly performed all the functions specified in the design. She also, however, inserted unauthorized routines that accessed sensitive data for her personal gain.

A program can be tested in two ways. One way is a walkthrough of the program where the tester plays the role of the computer. The other way is to install the program on the computer and test it against a combination of test transactions.

1. Walkthrough. To perform a complete walkthrough, three sequential phases are covered. First, the tester obtains a listing of the program and compares it to a checklist of potential errors. Some of the errors that may exist are: improper use of subscripts to reference arrays, improper initialization and declaration of variables, a variety of computational errors, mixing modes, endless loops, improper initialization or termination of loops, disagreement between files that are described in the documentation and those that are designed in the program, and improper labels and end-of-file indicators.

Second, the tester develops several transactions and "walks" these through the program as if he or she were the computer. The number of test transactions the tester can handle is limited; at a minimum, both proper and improper transactions should be tested. This phase bears directly upon testing the program logic and ensures the correct use of formulas and accurate computations.

In the third phase of the walkthrough, the tester reviews key program statements. If the program is written in COBOL, for example, the tester makes notes of OPEN and CLOSE commands. The tester should be aware of all the files that are OPENed and CLOSEd. In most programs decisions are made by IF instructions. The tester needs to ask for an explanation of all IFs that appear to be illogical or confusing. No IF statements are unimportant. If something is amiss, it will normally involve an IF statement. Next in importance are the PERFORM statements. The IFs control logic and the PERFORMs direct the processing flow. The tester should scan the program, make a list of all PERFORM statements, and then determine what they do to the transfer of control and why.

2. Computer execution. A number of errors and unintended functions uncovered by walkthroughs cannot be found by running the program on the computer, and vice versa. Testing the program on the computer is appropriate when the number and variety of transactions are large. To aid the tester in producing a variety of test transactions, a **test data generator** is useful to create permutations and combinations of test transactions.

After walkthroughs and computer testing are done, the program should be subjected to tests of various functions (e.g., accounting or marketing). For example, Figure 16.4 illustrates an overview of a sales, accounts receivable, and cash receipts test. Also, much of the data base and output blocks are tested at this time. Note that if this is a totally new system, all of the data will have to be simulated.

Human procedures include all the things users do to interact with the system. Users range from order entry clerks to the chief executive officer. The purpose of training is to set up a viable interface between all the users of the system and the system itself. The reason for testing is to see if this objective has been achieved and, if not, to see what has to be done. The tester should heed two areas.

(a) *Human/Machine dialogue.* In batch processing systems, the user does not interact with the system directly. A number of intermediaries (i.e., programmers) aid the user in obtaining information from the system. In online information systems, most users engage in a fairly direct dialogue with the computer. As discussed previously, dialogues range from those where the system guides the user, to those where users tell the system what they want. Both users must understand how to operate the system. The tester simply wants to make sure that they do so by asking questions and observing how they interact with the system.

(b) *Written procedures.* Procedures that guide users in their workings with the system are written and compiled in what is normally called a procedures or users manual. This manual is also used as a key training aid. It is tested by reviewing and editing as is any other written material. Its contents should be checked for correctness by all concerned personnel.

Test of the Data Base

An organization's data base is one of its most vital resources. If the data base is inoperative, business may come to a standstill. The data in the data base must be secure, accurate, and in many instances, private. **Substantive tests** to determine if the contents of the data base meet users' conditions are, to a large extent, performed when the output block is tested.

Compliance tests to ensure a secure data base are performed in the control block. Ad-

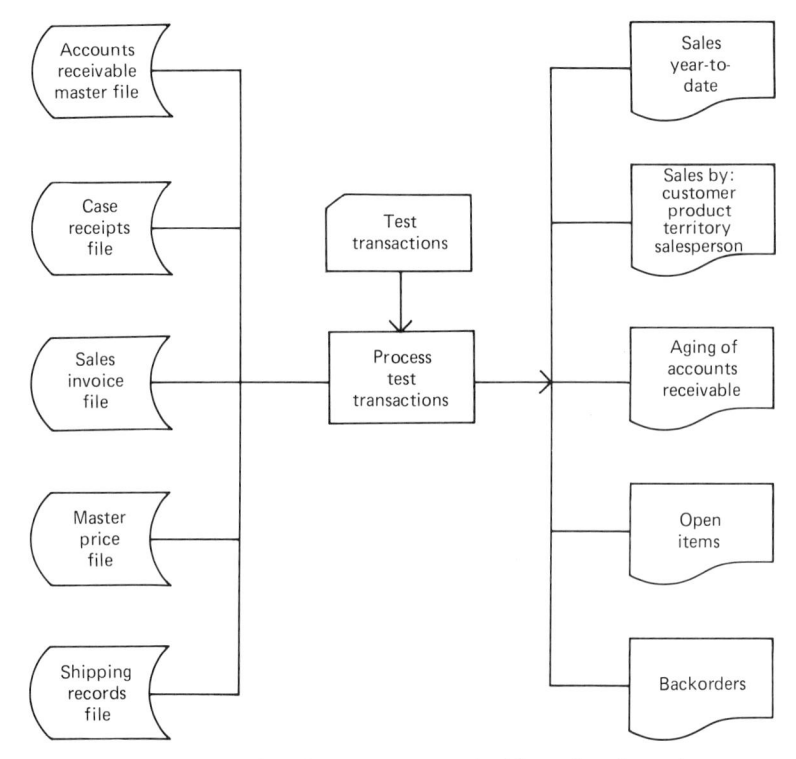

FIG. 16.4 Overview of a sales, accounts receivable, and cash receipts test.

ditional tests, however, can be done to make sure that the data base meets all demands placed upon it. The tests might include creating a new record before the first record on a master file, creating a new record after the last record, creating a record for a nonexistent division or department, trying to read from or write to a file with the wrong header label, attempting to process past an end-of-file indicator, and trying to create a record that is incomplete.

Files should be checked for completeness. Predetermined control totals should be compared with totals produced from the new files. For instance, predetermined totals might be checked against the number or records in a file or the total amount of a specific amount field, such as AMOUNT-OWED in an accounts receivable master file. File description and layouts should be compared to the ENVIRONMENT and DATA divisions in COBOL programs for agreement.

Test of Controls

The purpose of testing controls is to ensure that they are in place and are working as intended. This is called **compliance testing.** Three phases involved in compliance testing are: (1) study and observe controls, (2) conduct the actual tests of compliance, and (3) evaluate how effectively the controls meet these compliance tests. As always, by testing other design blocks, some tests of controls will be already done. For example, when testing program procedures, programming controls are also tested.

Test transactions help ensure programmed controls, such as limit and reasonableness checks, arithmetic proof, identification, and so forth, are in place and working correctly. These tests also help to cross-test other design blocks. For example, some of the test transactions prepared by clerks and terminal operators for special processing not only test the program and its ability to detect errors, but also check the way the transactions are prepared and entered.

Some of the controls that would normally be tested by a series of test transactions are as follows:

1. Check to see if control totals are prepared and reported back to the control group. For example, if 100 test records are processed, the number of transactions processed should read 100.
2. Try to process a sensitive transaction without proper authorization (e.g., change of customer's credit limit) and see if the system rejects it.
3. Make numeric, alphabetic, and special character checks. For example, if all characters in a customer number are supposed to be numeric, input an alphabetic character in this field. A properly working check will detect this mistake before processing is performed.
4. Input a field with a negative sign and see if it is handled as a negative value. In some systems, without proper control, the negative sign is converted to a positive sign. Divide an amount by zero.
5. Perform validity checks on key data fields. For example, input an invalid code or try to process one department number as another department number.
6. Make limit and reasonableness checks. If no employee can work more than 60 hours per week, process a time card with more than 60 hours worked.
7. Check for proper transaction sequence. Where transactions are supposed to be in sequence, shuffle the order of several test transactions so they are out of sequence.
8. Include an account number with a predetermined self-checking digit and see if it is processed by the computer system properly.
9. Use units of measure (e.g., feet for pounds) different from those allowed.
10. Input several fields with incomplete or missing data.
11. Insert characters in fields that cause an overflow condition.
12. Try to read from or write to a wrong file.

The study of controls includes a review of documentation found in the systems development reports. Observation and walk-throughs are required for an on-site study of controls. Always a key tool used to study controls is the questionnaire. An excerpt from a *general control questionnaire* is shown in Figure 16.5.

Although questionnaires provide effective means of gathering evidence on controls, more must be done. Often, respondents give automatic answers that will put them in a good light. For this reason, the tester must conduct compliance tests to determine whether or not answers to the questionnaires are true.

Testers may be able to satisfy themselves that a number of controls are working

Security Control Questionnaire
(Partial)

	Answer	
	Yes	No
1. Are sign-in/sign-out registers maintained for visitors?	_____	_____
2. Are controls adequate over the removal of materials from the data processing area? Are sensitive reports shredded?	_____	_____
3. Does the system make use of:		
(a) guards?	_____	_____
(b) cards?	_____	_____
(c) badges?	_____	_____
(d) closed-circuit television?	_____	_____
(e) limited entry points?	_____	_____
(f) central monitoring?	_____	_____
(g) detection devices?	_____	_____
(h) alarms?	_____	_____
(i) intercoms?	_____	_____
(j) man-trap doors?	_____	_____
(k) fire emergency exit-only doors?	_____	_____
4. Is the system backed up with power, air conditioning, and redundant equipment?	_____	_____
5. Are air conditioners adequate for peak thermal loads?	_____	_____
6. Are terminals located in secure areas to prevent access to the terminals by unauthorized users?	_____	_____
7. Do terminals include locking devices to prevent unauthorized use?	_____	_____
8. Are there hardware erase or sanitizing features? That is, are memory and peripherals cleared of residue between jobs?	_____	_____
9. Is the computer area housed in a fire-resistant, noncombustible structure?	_____	_____
10. Do all the materials used in construction of the computer area (e.g., walls, doors, ceilings) have at least one-hour fire rating?	_____	_____

FIG. 16.5 Excerpt from a security control questionnaire.

merely by *observation*. For example, they can observe a fire suppression system and inspection tags. Testers may even "try out" particular control techniques to see if they work (e.g., various access controls). In other cases, the only way to tell that particular controls work is to set up a test situation and see what happens. For example, a "disaster simulation" may be run on a surprise basis. To run disaster simulations, the tester seals certain master files and tells the computer center manager the system is "down." This simulated situation requires data processing personnel to bring the system to a current status by using cycled and backup files, other backup facilities, and contingency procedures. If they fail, reasons for failure are ascertained and swift corrective action is taken. Also, with executive approval, the tester "pulls the power switch" to the computer center to test recovery procedures. Sometimes, professional penetrators are hired to attempt to obtain access to the computer center and data base. Unexpected fire drills are performed to see if standard operating procedures are followed.

Test of Output

The output design block, to a great extent, dictates how the other design blocks are developed. Some tests of output are a by-product of testing other design blocks. For example, while testing input, procedures, and data base, the resulting output is reviewed for accuracy and appropriateness.

A substantive test of output involves nothing more than generating a report, giving it to the user, and seeing if it meets his or her information needs. In general, a good test to determine if the output format is understandable is to show the output to a person who is not involved in the system. If the person can "explain" the report, then the format is likely to be understandable by appropriate users.

Technical tests include checking for proper headings, edited amounts (e.g., leading zero suppression, debit/credit notation, dollar signs), correct page number sequence, clear end-of-report indicators, and correct dates (e.g., date the report was prepared and the current date).

Test of Data Processing Resources

Here we assume that the major processing is performed by a computer. In Chapter 13, we presented a section on testing computer hardware and software. Also, because the design blocks are highly interrelated, the computer system is tested to a degree during the testing of other blocks (e.g., program procedures). A few additional remarks, however, are warranted here.

A computer must be able to process the variety of jobs that make up the total system. Benchmark tests should also be conducted to see how efficiently these jobs run. Many times, minor adjustments in the configuration, software, or scheduling can correct any known problems before the system is implemented. Some of the tools available to do these tests are: job accounting systems, hardware and software monitors, and various performance utilities. These tools should also be used on an ongoing basis by management after the system is implemented.

1. Job Accounting System. This system can be used to test design efficiency, help in capacity planning, and project growth patterns. IBM's System Management Facilities (SMF) is an example. Among many things, it can be used to obtain large amounts of useful test information about a computer system's operating environment. It shows who used the system and how long they used it, along with the data files then accessed. SMF indicates the amount of available space on direct access storage devices and gives basic error statistics for magnetic tape files. This information helps to utilize file space better.

2. Hardware Monitor. A hardware monitor consists of a number of sensors connected to the innards of the computer. They measure CPU active, CPU wait, disk seek, disk data transfer, disk mount, tape active, tape rewind, and core storage timings and utilization. The sensors are, in turn, connected to a small computer which records various signals. With sufficient utilization statistics, properly evaluated, the total computer equipment budget may be reduced by improving overall efficiency through changing the CPU, dropping channels, or reconfiguring tapes and disks. The broad purpose of using a hardware monitor is to match the "horsepower" of the computer to the demands of the information system.

3. Software Monitor. To evaluate overall system performance, a software monitor can be used in conjunction with a hardware monitor and a job accounting system. A software monitor is a program that resides in the computer system to be tested. Software components commonly measured are operating systems, support software, and application programs. Measurement of the operating system identifies inefficient sections of code. The existence of such sections could compel management to ask the vendor for improvement, or if this is not possible, other commercially available software might be considered as a replacement.

Support software falls in the gray area between user programs and the operating system. Although handled in the system much like user programs, support software is written by the vendor and appears to the ordinary user as part of the operating system. Compilers, communication programs, and utilities are examples of support systems. With compilers and communication programs, the user is not seeking to modify the code of such complex programs, but rather to know what they cost in terms of resources. The aim is to ask the vendor to improve the program or to investigate the feasibility of using alternative software.

Application or user programs are measured to determine resource utilization and code efficiency. These measurements record and report the amount of time a program used each resource, such as core, disk,' and tapes. For example, a program may request eight tape drives, even though it would normally need only four. If the installation rations tape drives, the tester should ask the programmer to change the program.

Another important aspect of resource analysis is the determination of input/output (I/O) activity and block sizes. Sometimes, for example, a program might require ten more physical I/Os than necessary because records are improperly blocked.

A software monitor can isolate heavy **paging** areas in virtual storage systems. Heavy paging occurs when application programs use a number of IF statements incorrectly, causing a "thrashing" condition of pages to occur. The CPU is forced to spend a disproportionate time accessing pages from and storing pages on disk. With some analysis and program rewrites, this program inefficiency can be reduced.

4. Performance Utilities. Data set reorganizers reduce wasted file storage on disk and improve throughput by reducing access time. *Virtual storage code reorganizers* reduce resources used in paging. *Code optimizers* reduce consumption of resources by eliminating unnecessary program statements. *Schedulers* help meet timing demands and balance job mix.

The Growing Importance of Testing

Testing, as a major development activity, is increasing in importance for a number of reasons.

1. The trend toward a higher degree of integration of systems within an organization requires each new system implemented to perform successfully initially, not only for its own purposes, but so as not to degrade other existing systems.

2. The increased dependency upon computer-generated information, by all lev-

els of users within the organization in their decision-making and problem solving activities, relates the organization's performance directly to the systems performance.
3. Increased usage and familiarity with computer-based systems has resulted in higher expectations by users of the system.
4. The inflationary trend in the cost of other development activities can be halted with improved testing procedures.
5. The investment in systems maintenance resources can be reduced with improved testing procedures before the system is installed.

In an attempt to improve the testing procedure for a system, the analyst must exercise a great deal of creativity. The involvement of user personnel during testing is one method being used in many organizations. Other organizations have developed, or have purchased, testing aids that during systems testing, use the computer itself to detect potential shortcomings (or flaws) in the system.

The use of a *test team,* comprised of user department managers, internal auditors, and various systems personnel, should be independent from the designers and programmers who developed the system. While this may not always be practical or operationally feasible, it should be recognized that individuals are less than completely effective when they test their own work. For instance, often a programmer will debug a program enough to get it to run (i.e., function). A program that runs, however, is not necessarily a program that runs the way it should. If individuals have programmed routines that allow them to commit fraud, designed illogical or incorrect procedures, or have not installed required controls, then their involvement in testing gives them the opportunity to ensure that test procedures do not uncover these abuses and weaknesses.

16.4 ▪ SYSTEMS CONVERSION

The conversion process puts the system "on the air." As we analyze this systems conversion process, we can identify different approaches to accomplishing the conversion, the special considerations for the data base, and the importance of planning the conversion.

Approaches to Systems Conversions

Four basic approaches toward accomplishing the conversion of a new system are: (1) direct, (2) parallel, (3) modular, and (4) phase-in. Figure 16.6 is a graphic representation of the four approaches to conversion.

1. Direct Conversion. A direct conversion is the implementation of the new system and the immediate discontinuance of the old system, sometimes called the "cold turkey" approach. This conversion approach is meaningful when: (1) the system is not replacing any other system, (2) the old system is judged absolutely without value, (3) the new system is either very small or simple, and (4) the design of the new system is drastically different from the old system and comparisons between systems would be meaningless. The primary advantage to this approach is that it is relatively inexpensive. The primary disadvantage to this approach is that it involves a high risk of failure. When direct conversion is to be used, the systems testing activity discussed in the previous section takes on even greater importance.

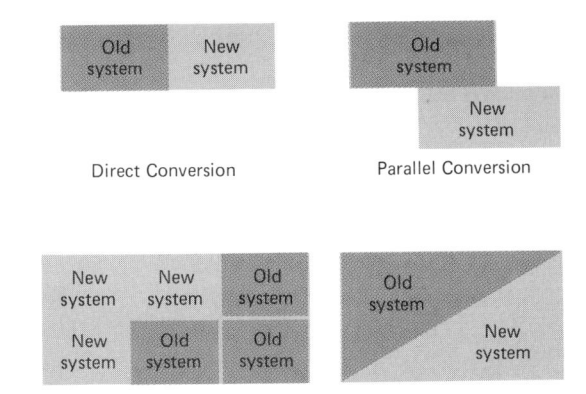

FIG. 16.6 A graphic representation of the basic approaches to systems conversion.

If the design blocks have been thoroughly tested with simulated test data and cases, and they have passed all tests, the risk of direct conversion is low. The system has already updated files, written payroll checks and vouchers, checked procedures, investigated the completeness and accuracy of the data base, checked the viability of controls, and determined the appropriateness of the output.

2. Parallel Conversion. Parallel conversion is an approach wherein both the old and the new system operate simultaneously for some period of time. It is the opposite of direct conversion. In a parallel conversion mode the outputs from each system are compared and differences reconciled. The advantage to this approach is that it provides a high degree of protection to the organization from a failure in the new system. The obvious disadvantages to this approach are the costs associated with duplicating facilities and personnel to maintain the dual systems. But because of the many difficulties experienced by organizations in the past when a new system was implemented, this approach to conversion has gained widespread popularity. When the conversion process of a system includes parallel operations, the analyst should plan for periodic reviews with operating personnel and users concerning the performance of the new system and designate a reasonable date for acceptance of the new system and discontinuance of the old system.

Because of faulty training and testing activities, conversion projects are often burdened with additional tasks of training, testing, procedure and documentation rewrites, file changes, attempts at retrofitting controls, and major computer configuration adjustments. If this is the case, then parallel conversion is really the only sensible approach to use. Some would contend that parallel conversion is a form of testing. We do not argue with this contention. Other situations may exist, however, where this approach is not feasible. Where different production methods, decision rules, accounting procedures, and inventory control models are to be used in the new system, parallel conversion makes little sense and, obviously, will not work. In this case, and in all cases, we recommend stringent training and testing procedures before the conversion process begins.

3. Modular Conversion. Modular conversion, sometimes termed the "pilot approach," refers to the implementation of a system into the organization on a piecemeal basis. For example, an order entry system could be installed in one sales region and, if proved successful, installed in a second sales region, etc. An inventory system might be another example. The inventory system might be converted with only a selected product grouping or with all products in one location of a multiple-location organization.

The advantages to this approach are (1) the risk of a system's failure is localized, (2) the problems identified in the system can be corrected before further implementation is attempted, and (3) other operating personnel can be trained in a "live" environment before the system is implemented at their location. One disadvantage to this approach is that the conversion period for the organization can be extremely lengthy. More importantly, this approach is not always feasible for a particular system or organization.

4. Phase-in Conversion. The phase-in approach is similar to the modular approach. This approach differs, however, in that the system itself is segmented, and not the organization. For example, the new data collection activities are implemented and an interface mechanism with the old system is developed. This interface allows the old system to operate with the new input data. Later, the new data base access, storage, and retrieval activities are implemented. Once again, an interface mechanism with the old system is developed. Another segment of the new system is installed until the entire system is implemented. Each time a new segment is added, an interface with the old system must be developed. The advantages to this approach are that the rate of change in a given organization can be minimized, and data processing resources can be acquired gradually over an extended period of time. The disadvantages to this approach include the costs incurred to develop temporary interfaces with old systems, limited applicability, and a demoralizing atmosphere in the organization of "never completing a system."

Data Base Considerations During Systems Conversion

The success of a systems conversion depends to a great degree upon how well the systems analyst prepares for the creation and conversion of the data files required for the new system. This preparation is of particular importance in an organization where the information system has a high degree of integration through its data base. In some large organizations where an integrated information system exists, the analyst may work closely with the data base administrator to prepare for data base creation and conversion. For our purposes, however, we will assume that the systems analyst must make all the preparations for the systems conversion. Additionally, to simplify the explanation of the many complexities of data base conversion, we will cast the data base in terms of file units.

By creating a file, we mean that data are collected and organized in some recognizable format on a given storage medium. By converting a file, we mean that an existing file must be modified in at least one of three ways: (1) in the format of the file, (2) in the content of the file, and (3) in the storage medium where the file is located. It is quite likely in a systems conversion that some files can experience all three aspects of conversion simultaneously.

When creating a file which is to be processed on the computer, it is sometimes necessary to provide special start-up software that defines and labels a specific physical or logical storage location for the file. This process is referred to as creating a "dummy" file. Once the "dummy" file is created, the new system will process and store the designated data in this file.

When converting a file which must be processed on the computer, the special start-up software, which may be part of a DBMS, contains logic that permits existing data to be input in the old format, or on the old medium; and output in the new format, or on the new medium. With regard to the aspect of converting the contents of a file, the special start-up software may simply initialize (e.g., set to zero) the new fields in the file so that these fields can be updated correctly when the system begins processing transactions.

Often, during the conversion of files, it is necessary to construct elaborate control procedures to ensure the integrity of the data available for use after the conversion. Using the classification of files introduced in Chapter 10, several general observations pertinent to each type of file during a conversion can be noted:

1. *Master files.* Master files are the key files in the data base and usually at least one master file is to be created or converted in every system conversion. When an existing master file must be converted, the analyst should arrange for a series of hash and control totals to be matched between all the fields in the old file and all the same fields in the converted file. Special file backup procedures should be implemented for each separate processing step. This precaution is to prevent having to unnecessarily restart the conversion, from the beginning, in the event an error is discovered in the conversion logic at a later date. Timing considerations, particularly in online systems, are extremely important. If the converted file is not to be implemented immediately after conversion, special provisions must be made to track any update activity occurring between the time of conversion and the time of implementation.

2. *Transaction files.* Transaction files are usually created by the processing of an individual subsystem within the information system, and can, consequently, be checked thoroughly during systems testing. The transaction files that are generated in areas of the information system other than the new subsystem, however, may have to be converted if the master files they update change in format or media.

3. *Index files.* Index files contain the keys or addresses that link various master files. Therefore, new index files must be created whenever their related master files have undergone a conversion.

4. *Table files.* Table files can also be created and converted during the systems conversion. The same considerations required of master files are applicable here.

5. *Summary files.* Summary files are created during the processing of the new system in a manner similar to transaction files. Summary files created in other areas of the information system, however, do not usually have to be converted when a new subsystem is implemented.

6. *Archival files.* Archival files are another category of files similar to master files. The considerations which apply to master files during the system conversion are applicable to archival files with two exceptions: the timing considerations are not as severe with archival files as they are with master files, even in an online processing mode; and the volume of data records in archival files is usually far greater than that contained in master files.

7. *Backup files.* The purpose of backup files is to provide security for the information system in the event of a processing error or a disaster in the data center. Therefore, when a file is converted or created, it is necessary to create a backup file. The backup procedures for the converted file more than likely will be the same as the procedures which existed for the original

file. The one exception to this might be where a change in file media took place. For example, a card file which was previously backed up by another card file, when converted to magnetic disk or tape would probably be backed up on disk or tape also.

Determining which files are to be created or converted when a new system is implemented, and how these files will be created and converted, is part of the thinking process required to prepare a conversion plan.

Planning the Conversion

Although a system may be well designed and properly developed, a major part of its success is contingent on how well the conversion is executed. When a new system produces information that is inaccurate or untimely due to certain activities within the system not being performed as designed, it can create a stigma which remains long after the problems have been resolved. To avoid the creation of a "credibility gap" between a new system and the users of the system's outputs, the systems analyst must plan the systems conversion carefully.

In practice, the conversion plan is usually developed in two stages. The broad conversion plan dictates the scheduling of the systems work performed during the systems development phase. The specific conversion plan, prepared during the last stages of testing, identifies any special start-up procedures for personnel, the plan and schedule for file creation and conversion, establishment of acceptance criteria, and any special start-up control procedures. Figure 16.7 illustrates the relationship of the conversion plans to the developmental and implementation activities.

Preparing formal plans for executing the systems conversion is another vital communication task for the systems analyst. It is important that the management of the organization understand fully the approach that is to be taken for systems conversion. As a rule, the analyst's recommendations will be carefully weighed with other organizational commitments and activities that are also due or planned during the same time period. The preparation of carefully thought-out conversion plans that are communicated to and understood by all affected personnel in the organization, will help to ensure a successful systems implementation.

16.5 ▪ FOLLOW-UP TO IMPLEMENTATION

Once the new system has been implemented, the systems analyst's participation does not necessarily end. In Chapter 17, many of the continuing activities performed by systems analysts during the life of a system are discussed. At this time, we will simply highlight the many different tasks the systems analyst must perform in the time period immediately following the implementation.

At first, the analyst should check regularly that input, processing, and output schedules are being met. After it appears that a routine has been established, these checks can become less regular and can be directed only toward any trouble spots identified.

The activities of input preparation personnel (e.g., key punchers, order entry clerks) should be reviewed periodically. A high probability exists that some manual procedures will need additional clarification. A programming bug might be identified which requires immediate resolution. On occasion, certain procedures, manual or computer, might be identified as being some-

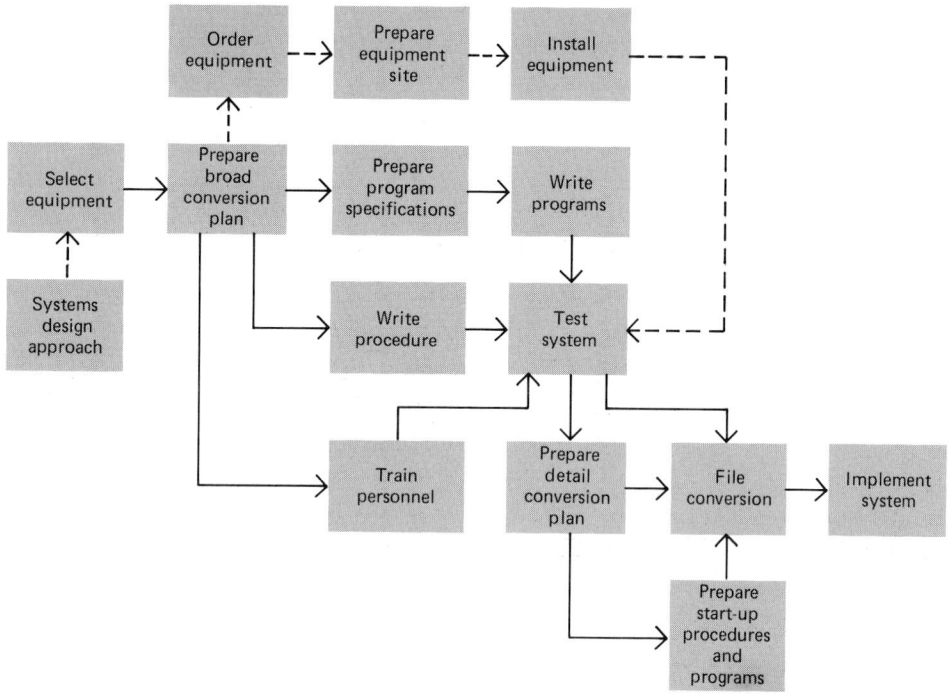

FIG. 16.7 A scheduling chart illustrating the relative position of the conversion planning activities as they relate to the systems development and implementation activities.

what inefficient, and a minor change will eliminate a bottleneck situation in the systems operations.

Perhaps the most important follow-up activity the analyst performs is to verify that the systems controls are functioning properly. In some instances where a large system is implemented many input errors are initially processed into the system without detection. Usually, an efficient file maintenance mechanism for large quantities of errors does not exist. During the learning period, the analyst can assist the operations of the system either by providing a quick method for the reconciliation of errors, or by recommending to the appropriate supervisors where additional clerical support is required.

One problem the analyst will have during the follow-up period is distinguishing between suggestions for improvements and additional "niceties" in the system, and the identification of actual systems problems. During the education of systems users, the analyst should explain that when the information outputs are reviewed initially, the primary emphasis at that time will be placed on correcting errors. Other suggestions for improvements to the system are welcomed and encouraged; however, these suggestions will be compiled and evaluated after implementation is complete. In this way all output users will be given an opportunity to be heard and further improvements to the system can be effectively implemented in total, as they relate to specific subsystems (or modules) of the new system. Without this distinction, the implementation activity of the system will continue indefinitely.

A final activity that the analyst might perform during the follow-up period is to remove all outdated and start-up procedures, programs, forms, etc., that were part of the old system or conversion effort. This action will eliminate the possibility of someone inadvertently referring to (or using) the wrong procedure or program.

An **acceptance meeting** should be held, attended by the systems analyst, systems operating management, and user personnel. At this time an official termination of the developmental project is given and a final systems "sign-off" is obtained. The systems analyst then becomes available for a new assignment.

SUMMARY

People are the key ingredient in any system. Providing adequate educating and training, both initially and on a continuing basis, is absolutely essential if a system is to achieve its objective.

Testing the system is the final activity before implementation. The goal of testing is to determine whether all design blocks are operating as intended. Testing is becoming a more and more important activity in the implementation of a new system.

The implementation of many new systems involves a conversion process from an existing system. Four basic approaches to conversion are: (1) direct, (2) parallel, (3) modular, and (4) phase-in. The data base requires special considerations during the conversion process. Planning is an important aspect of conversion. Generally, a broad conversion plan is prepared before specific design and developmental activities begin. A specific conversion plan is prepared shortly before the actual implementation of the new system.

Once the system has been implemented, the systems analyst serves as a consultant. The analyst is available to assist operations and user personnel in understanding the new system, and in solving any problems.

REVIEW QUESTIONS

16.1 For whom must the systems analyst provide training and educating before implementing a new or modified system? Give at least two practical examples of each personnel category as related to: (a) an inventory control system, (b) a manufacturing budget system, (c) a payroll system, and (d) an order entry/billing system.

16.2 List and explain the major considerations when choosing a training approach.

16.3 Compare and contrast the major approaches to the educating and training of systems users and operations personnel.

16.4 What is the purpose of testing in the development of a system?

16.5 Compare and contrast the various procedures used by the analyst to test the design blocks.

16.6 Why does the testing of newly developed information systems promise to be even more important in the future?

16.7 What is the systems conversion?

16.8 Compare and contrast the four approaches to systems conversion.

16.9 How is the data base affected during systems conversion? Be specific.

16.10 What is the primary importance of preparing a broad systems conversion plan? A specific plan? In which plan is the conversion approach selected?

16.11 Describe the major activities performed by the systems analyst as a follow-up to the implementation of a new system.

16.12 What is the importance of an acceptance meeting?

QUESTIONS FOR DISCUSSION

16.1 Discuss the merit of using operating procedures as training manuals.

16.2 Explain how you would prepare for training personnel in a department which annually experiences a turnover rate of over 10 percent; 40 percent; 80 percent.

16.3 "We spend about $20,000 annually preparing formal presentations for management to explain new or modified systems. This investment is returned many times over by the enthusiastic support most of our new systems receive from management." Discuss.

16.4 Excerpt from a programmer's standards manual: "Programmers are responsible for testing each of the programs they have written. The project leader is responsible for testing the system in its entirety." Evaluate this statement.

16.5 "Desk checking is a waste of my time. I would rather let the computer test my programs." Discuss the pro's and con's of this statement.

16.6 "I don't care how much testing a programmer performs on a program, the first time they try real data, they receive a surprise." Comment.

16.7 "The cost associated with performing corrective maintenance on an operating system correlates with whether or not the system was tested using controlled data." Discuss the implications of this statement.

16.8 "The file conversion was going along smoothly until we discovered that one of the special programs we wrote for the conversion was putting garbage into part of the record. We had to rerun the entire eighteen hours of processing, although the error occurred in the last two hours or so." Discuss.

16.9 "We never completely finish installing a system." Evaluate.

16.10 "One really important advantage to this new computer is that it requires no reprogramming to process your existing program." Comment.

16.11 "Never implement a new system without a period of parallel operations with the old system." Discuss the rationale behind this statement.

16.12 "They have been implementing the new sales reporting system for three years now." What situation might have prompted this statement?

16.13 "We will not be able to implement the new payroll system for three more months. Although all the reporting programs have been tested, we still have to write the data collection programs." How might this situation have been avoided, at least in part?

EXERCISES

16.1 Analyze the following situations. Which approach to systems conversion would you recommend for each? Note that you may elect to use more than a single conversion approach to each situation. Explain fully your recommendations.

1. Implementing a check deposit system utilizing OLRT (online real time) devices into a bank with 40 area branches.
2. Implementing an inventory control system for 50,000 items at three warehouses.
3. Implementing a centralized order entry system servicing 40 sales offices.
4. Implementing a sales statistics system to be accessed by CRT devices.
5. Implementing a lottery system (where one had not ex-

isted before), with 250 ticket offices and remote batch entry.
6. Implementing a computer-based accounts receivable systems, where a manual system existed previously.
7. Implementing an integrated system that includes order entry, inventory control, accounts receivable, sales statistics, and product forecasting, into a multiple-plant organization with sales of more than $100,000,000.

PROBLEMS

16.1 The manual accounts receivable system of Calico Pet Supply is being converted to a computer-based system. The present, manual accounts receivable system has the following characteristics: (1) each customer with a nonzero accounts receivable balance has a folder containing a copy of all unpaid invoices and credit notes issued; (2) when a payment and accompanying remittance is received from a customer, the remittance is matched to an unpaid invoice and both documents are placed in a "current closed" file, which, in turn, is purged every six months; (3) a "permanent closed" file, comprised of purged "current closed" file documents, is maintained for a period of seven years, and (4) at month's end, the balance of each customer's account is classified according to the age of the balance outstanding. This is done by a clerk tallying and dating folder amounts.

The frequency of access to the three files varies considerably. The "folder" file is accessed frequently. The "current closed" file is accessed periodically, normally at the request of the credit manager or a customer. The "permanent closed" file is accessed very infrequently.

The new system to be implemented will contain three files: (1) a customer master file, containing information pertinent to each customer; (2) an open item file, corresponding to the "folder" file of the manual system; and (3) a closed item file, assembling a combined "current closed" and "permanent closed" file.

Assume you were given the responsibility of converting the old system to the new system. Please answer the following questions:

1. Would you suggest a direct or a parallel conversion approach? Why?
2. Is a phase-in conversion approach appropriate? Why?
3. What special clerical procedures would need to be established to validate the correctness of the new system's operation against the old system?

4. What special initialization and validation programming is required for the data base conversion?

16.2 An employee time card contains the following data:

FIELD	LENGTH	COMMENT
Employee number	10	(1) First character must be alphabetic. (2) Next nine digits are his or her social security number.
Department	2	(1) Must be numeric. (2) Must match valid department table.
Shift	1	(1) Must be numeric. (2) Day = 0; Afternoon = 1; Midnight = 2.
Start time	4	(1) Must be numeric. (2) First two digits must be between 00–23. (3) Last two digits must be between 00–59.
Stop time	4	(1) Must be numeric. (2) First two digits must be between 00–23. (3) Last two digits must be between 00–59.

This card is punched daily and submitted for computer processing. Only time cards with valid data, based on an edit subroutine, are accepted for further processing.

Required: Prepare a set of decision tables that describes the subroutine for editing the time cards. Also, format the time card error report and provide examples of several types of errors.

BIBLIOGRAPHY

Couger and McFadden, *Introduction to Computer Based Information Systems,* New York: John Wiley & Sons, Inc., 1975.

Lucas, *The Analysis, Design, and Implementation of Information Systems,* New York: McGraw-Hill Book Co., 1976.

Scharer, "Improving System Testing Techniques," *Datamation,* September 1977.

Taylor, "AICPA Testing Guidelines Seen in Need of Clarification," *Computerworld,* April 25, 1977.

Pelican Case

Phase 5 · Systems Implementation
· Final Implementation Report

Phases of Systems Development Methodology:

Phase 1	Phase 2	Phase 3	Phase 4	Phase 5
Systems analysis	General systems design	Systems evaluation and justification	Detail systems design	Systems implementation
Proposal to conduct systems analysis report / Systems analysis completion report	General systems design proposal report	Final general systems design report	Final detail systems design report	Final implementation report
Completed in Chapter 11	Completed in Chapter 12	Completed in Chapter 13	Completed in Chapter 15	Presented and completed in this chapter

INTRODUCTION

Ben sat back in his chair and fingered through the draft of his implementation report. It had been several months since Martha had asked him to study the telephone cost system at Pelican. The final system was considerably different from his first perceptions of the problem and its likely solution.

Patti seemed satisfied with the accounting control features about to be implemented. Danny was excited about some of the options that the new technology offered his department. Danny said jovially, "Hell, since I'm paying for most of the telephone network and everything else, I ought to be getting something good out of it."

Ben could hardly believe that the project was nearly over. After what seemed like a hundred endless meetings, dozens of compromises, and an infinite number of fine tunings, everything was falling slowly into place.

As Ben received the proposal for training, testing, and conversion, his mind began to wander over his next assignment which Martha mentioned only this morning. As far as he knew now, the new project dealt with production scheduling.

The telephone shattered his daydreaming. Bud Wiser's excited voice reminded him that the project was not yet implemented.

What follows is Ben's Final Implementation Report.

FINAL IMPLEMENTATION REPORT

To: All managers, systems, and operating personnel

From: Ben Snow, Systems Analyst

Educating and Training

Primary user education about the new system will follow the schedule below. Other management personnel can attend if they desire. Education will be handled by my staff.

Primary Users	Dates of Sessions	Location
1. Patti Blake and staff	8:00–11:45 AM 1:00–5:00 PM JUNE 1–13	Conference Room 2A
2. Danny Loman and staff	8:00–11:45 AM 1:00–5:00 PM JUNE 18–30	Conference Room 9B

These sessions will be conducted as seminars. Group discussion is encouraged. Also, all sales personnel will receive special tutorials on the use of the dictation system.

A variety of training programs are needed for operating personnel. All personnel will be provided with a copy of the Final Detail Systems Design Report plus manuals furnished by the vendor. Training will be provided by my staff and the vendor. Training objectives are listed below.

Tasks to be Performed	Basic Skills Required to Perform Tasks	Training Approaches
1. CRT operations.	1. Touch knowledge of keyboard. Input of 60 or more words per minute. Use of all function keys. Understanding of all input and transcription procedures.	1. One day procedural and tutorial training session provided by the vendor for all CRT operators. On-the-job training provided by my staff.
2. Preparation of forms.	2. Understanding of all forms and how to fill them out.	2. One-half day tutorial and on-the-job training conducted by my staff for all clerks and CRT operators.
3. Use of special COBOL features.	3. Travis Cook is a skilled COBOL programmer. But he needed training in special features that pertain to the new system.	3. Travis to attend three-day training session to become skilled in the use of these special features.

| 4. Operation and preventive maintenance of all equipment. Does not include repairs. | 4. John Tinker already has skills in equipment operations and maintenance. However, different technology requires some training. | 4. The vendor will provide a systems engineer to work with John several days using procedural manuals and tutorials as training aids. |

Test Group

The test group is comprised of Theresa Lightfoot, Internal Auditor; Jack Daniels, Lead Programmer from the Central System; and Barney Carbuncle, from the Systems Analyst Group. None of these people have worked on, or have in any way been connected with the design and development of the system being tested. Also, Nancy Nuance from Marketing, and Joel Scribe from Accounting were selected to serve as user representatives to advise and consult with the test group.

Test of Input

The following tests of input will be conducted:

1. Several telephone dictation inputs will be made from the field to check the dictation system. Portable units were tested during the training sessions and they worked well.
2. All forms will be checked again to ensure that they include all necessary entries and that they are correct. Also, several OCR forms will be prepared and entered to ensure proper processing.
3. The regenerated telephone bill will be tested for completeness and compatibility with our computer system.

Test of Processing

As a minimum, a promotion letter and an acknowledgment letter will be prepared and scrutinized for accuracy and completeness. Also, all the special word processing features such as automatic text wraparound, text modification, aligned margins, indexing, pagination, global searches, merging, and dictionary lookup, will be tested to be sure that they are working as promised. Vendor-supplied manuals will be tested for precision, accuracy, comprehensiveness, and clarity.

All of the programs will be tested with both valid and invalid transactions. Also, walkthroughs will be made of several application programs which pertain to the generation of telephone usage reports.

Test of Data Base

While input and processing are being tested, the data base will also be tested for correct posting to appropriate files. Records will be printed before and after a transaction updates them. Also, a sampling of files will be printed for verification purposes.

Test of Controls

All of the controls listed in the Final Detail Systems Design Report will be tested for compliance. Especially important is the test of backup procedures for the master file.

Test of Output

While testing the input and processing blocks of this system, a number of valid transactions will be processed to generate reports and other output of this system. This output will be reviewed by users, especially Nancy

Nuance and Joel Scribe for precision, accuracy, verifiability, comprehensiveness, appropriateness, and clarity.

Test of Data Processing Resources

By performing the above tests, most aspects of the data processing resources will be tested. Recommendations for additional tests include transmission between the new system and the host, ability of the printer to produce five carbons, and the spooling function.

Results of Testing

Company policy requires that all tests are documented and prepared as a report. A cover letter signed by all members of the test group must accompany the report. This cover letter contains an opinion as to the fitness of the system. The letter should contain one of the four following opinions.

1. <u>No reservations or qualifications</u>: ''We have tested 'X' system as of 'Date.' Our tests were made in accordance with the recommendation of the Final Implementation Report which included tests of all design blocks and any other tests that we deemed necessary, all of which are documented in the enclosed report.

In our opinion, 'X' system has passed all tests and we hereby recommend that it be made ready for conversion to full operations.''

2. <u>Opinion with minor exception or qualification</u>: ''We have tested 'X' system as of 'Date.' Our tests were made in accordance with the recommendations of the Final Implementation Report which included tests of all design blocks and any other tests that we deemed necessary, all of which are documented in the enclosed report.

In our opinion, except for 'qualification,' the 'X' system has passed all tests and we hereby recommend that it be made ready for conversion to full operations."

3. <u>Opinion that recommends the system be postponed until certain weaknesses have been corrected</u>: ''We have tested 'X' system as of 'Date.' Our tests were made in accordance with the recommendations of the Final Implementation Report which included tests of all design blocks and any other tests that we deemed necessary, all of which are documented in the enclosed report. Also, in this report are a list of all the tests failed, plus recommendations to correct these failures.

In our opinion, 'X' system has failed a large number of tests and we hereby recommend that it's conversion be postponed until all failures have been corrected.''

Company policy dictates that all failures and recommendations to correct failures be prepared based on the following format:

Test Failures	Recommendations to Correct Failures
1.	1.
2.	2.
.	.
.	.
.	.
N.	N.

4. <u>Opinion to scrap system</u>: "We have tested 'X' system as of 'Date.' Our tests were made in accordance with the recommendations of the Final Implementation Report, which included tests of all design blocks and any other tests that we deemed necessary, all of which are documented in the enclosed report. The system failed all significant tests. We found the system to be so lacking in performance and inadequate to make it unreasonable to expect corrections can be made for operations.
  In our opinion, 'X' system has failed so many tests and its design is so deficient, we hereby recommend it to be scrapped and not considered further."

Conversion Recommendations

It is recommended that after the tests have been made and if the system is cleared for operations that we bring the system up the following Sunday afternoon and be ready for full operations the following Monday morning.

Follow-up Recommendations

It is recommended that a senior auditor from internal auditing be assigned the responsibility of performing a post implementation audit 180 days after conversion.

CHAPTER 17

Management Considerations of the Information System

17.1 ▪ INTRODUCTION

The purpose of this text is to analyze and discuss the many aspects of information system design. We have addressed the role of the information system as the primary interface between the management subsystem and the operations subsystem within the organization. However, the information system is itself a large, complex resource that requires managing. We conclude Part III by providing several suggestions concerning management activities related to the effective use of the information system resource. Discussed specifically in this chapter are guidelines for the development of more maintainable systems, methods used to audit systems, types and pitfalls of project management systems, and managing change from a human perspective.

17.2 ▪ MANAGING MAINTENANCE

As discussed in Part I, organizations and their information systems are dynamic resources. All resources are subject to deterioration, malfunction, and the need for periodic upgrading. *Maintainability* is a systems requirement which is receiving more and more attention from both information systems designers and management. More maintainable systems require less attention, fewer modifications and changes, and are easier to change when maintenance is needed. In this section an analysis is provided on the causes of maintenance work, the problems it presents, and some ideas how to deal with maintenance.

Causes of Maintenance Work

What follows are some of the causes why programs, data files, documentation, and general procedures must be changed in existing systems.

Emergency Maintenance. Emergency maintenance is directed toward resolving a malfunction or "bug" in the system. This maintenance is urgent and usually calls for immediate attention. Normally a system malfunctions because it has not been tested

541

completely. In fact, it may be a system that has run perfectly for months or even years. Although this type of activity is associated with programming, frequently the information system user is the one who identifies the malfunction. Then a team of analysts and programmers must determine if the malfunction is in a computer program or caused by a system input. The ability to diagnose rapidly and remedy the malfunction is of considerable value to the organization.

Routine Maintenance. Routine maintenance activities are required to keep systems performance relevant as it reflects the organizational environment. This activity may take the form of rewriting manual procedures, conducting training sessions, altering information report formats and contents, and defining new processing logic for computer programs. For example, a new tax law may require a change in the calculation of net pay, the production of a new report from the system, or the adoption of a new accounting depreciation method.

Special Reporting Requests. Special reporting requests are periodic requests for tactical and strategic management information not scheduled for routine production from a system. The analyst must define what is being requested, what is required to produce the information, and, finally, the most efficient way to produce the information based on available resources. While many of these special requests can be satisfied directly by a user via a data base management system, often the analyst assists in preparing the necessary parameters for the request. Even in an online environment users may be unfamiliar with all aspects of the data base available to them. Examples of special requests might include an analysis of pay rates during labor/management bargaining sessions, a special report on selected products during a sales promotion, or a special analysis of a particular vendor's delivery performance.

Systems Improvements. After a new system is implemented, users may suggest additional improvements to the system. In short, many users' information requirements are subject to a rapid rate of change. To accommodate these changing requirements, an analyst must define what is needed, if it can be met with the existing data base, and develop the necessary manual and computer procedures to satisfy these requirements. The approach used by the analyst in this activity differs only in duration when compared to the development of a system.

Problems of Maintenance

Given the above causes for change, it is little wonder that existing systems are subject to almost continuous modification. Unfortunately, this can result in a number of problems.[1]

Cost. Changing existing application systems can be very expensive, requiring in some instances up to half of an organization's allocated funds for systems. Many organizations have adopted the principle of setting a budget for maintenance and then performing only the highest priority maintenance work.

Personnel Morale. Personnel working in the information system, especially programmers, often object to the amount of maintenance work they are asked to do. They do not want to spend most of their time maintaining or trying to patch up systems designed and implemented years ago. In some organizations, programmers are rotated

---

[1]Summarized from "That Maintenance 'Iceberg'," *EDP Analyzer,* October 1972, pp. 4–8. Used with permission.

from one project group to another on a one- to three-year cycle. This policy of rotation has a number of advantages. First, it means new assignments for the programmer, even if much of the work is maintenance. Second, such a policy provides backup, since the experience base of the personnel is broadened. Third, rotation brings fresh outlooks, increasing the chance of better ideas being proposed. And, fourth, evaluation of personnel becomes more objective because a comparison can be made of the performance of two or more persons on the same job, and the performance of a person under several project leaders.

Failures. Maintenance programming has a history of causing more catastrophic failures than the original development programming. If the maintenance programmer is not familiar with the program or if the documentation is poor, then it is possible that some changes made will result in serious failures. To remedy the first shortcoming, management should assign complex maintenance problems to the most knowledgeable people. For the second, it is the responsibility of management to ensure that all programs are properly documented.

Extra Training Costs. To maintain older applications that use outdated programming languages and run under primitive operating systems, means extra training for persons who will be working on such applications.

Unmanageable Conditions. Management may find itself faced with a complex and unwieldy problem; a problem that was not fully appreciated as it developed. This situation is characterized by inadequate documentation, rambling designs, a variety of incompatible hardware/software configurations, and outdated equipment and procedures. In such a situation information system management can rarely keep user departments satisfied. Few, if any, personnel hours are available. Practically no budget amounts are available for allocation to remedy the situation. In such a case, the severe problems of maintenance (and dissatisfied users) will continue indefinitely.

Procedures to Achieve More Maintainable Systems

The rate of change most organizations and their information systems experience is increasing rather than decreasing. Providing more maintainable systems and more efficient maintenance efforts are also likely to gain more emphasis. To achieve these goals within a dynamic environment requires action from both systems designers and managers.[2]

Designing for Change. This aspect encompasses a variety of procedures, some of which are:

1. *Standard data definitions.* The trend toward data base management systems underpins the push for standard data definitions. Many organizations now have redundant and inconsistent data definitions. These inconsistent data definitions are found in procedure manuals, source program documentation, data files, and so forth, and only add to the problem of maintenance. A glossary or data dictionary of terms for data elements and other items in the system should be provided. For example, all data elements should have a name, description, size, source, location, and maintenance responsibility designation. It is also important to use the name, precisely as stated. ACC-REC-1 is not the same as ACCT-REC-1.

[2]*Ibid.*, pp. 8–14.

2. *Standard program languages.* The use of a standard language, such as COBOL, makes the maintenance task easier.

3. *Standard set of configuration resources.* Standards should be developed, and the use of stipulated resources (such as core memory and peripherals) by a program should be enforced.

4. *Modular design of programs.* As with the maintenance of home appliances, where a repairman can determine which module is causing trouble and quickly replace it, the maintenance programmer can change modules of a program much easier than trying to deal with the total program.

5. *Use of decision tables.* Decision tables support modular program design. They make program logic clear to the maintenance programmer. Also, decision table preprocessors[3] provide a means for automatically converting decision tables into source code, thus reducing the chance for error.

6. *Documentation standards.* System, program, and operation documentation is needed so that all the information required to operate and maintain a particular application is available. Since documentation is so essential, it is imperative that procedures be established and enforced for producing the documentation and keeping it current.

Design Changes. Even when programs are designed to facilitate change, maintenance programmers need other tools to aid them in making and testing the changes. One tool that is needed is cross-reference listings of commonly used subroutines, files, records, and so forth. For example, when a change is to be made to a subroutine, the maintenance programmer wants to know all of the programs that use that subroutine.

Configuration Design. The total configuration of an installation is subject to almost continual change. Maintenance requirements will be eased if the information system adheres to the policy of interchangeability (plug-compatibility), when making these configuration changes. If a noninterchangeable alteration is made in the configuration, then some or all of the programs will not run. A great deal of maintenance work is, therefore, necessary to make these programs run on new, noncompatible equipment.

Organizing for Maintenance. The issue here is whether maintenance should be performed by the development group, or whether it should be performed by a separate maintenance group. Some thoughts on this issue are as follows:

1. *Arguments for combined development and maintenance.* If both development and maintenance are performed in the same group, then the user departments will have one point of contact with the information system personnel who can effect change. User departments often do not know if a request for work will be classified as development or maintenance, since large revisions or system improvements are often treated as development. Furthermore, the analysts and programmers who originally developed the application systems have the best knowledge of those systems, and can best assess the full impact of changes. Some systems are so critical and complex that maintenance must be handled by only the most capable people and, in many

---

[3]See, for example, R.N. Dean, "A Comparison of Decision Tables Against Conventional COBOL as a Programming Tool for Commercial Applications," *Software World,* Spring 1971, pp. 26–30. Also see, "COBOL Aid Packages," *EDP Analyzer,* May 1972.

instances, the most capable people are the ones who developed the system in the first place.
2. *Arguments for separate maintenance.* Separate maintenance tends to force better documentation, formal transfer procedures, and formal change procedures. Senior maintenance programmers may be promoted to development project leaders, since they have a good knowledge of documentation requirements, standards, operations, and so forth. And, for junior programmers, it is a good training ground.

17.3 ▪ AUDITING CONSIDERATIONS

Auditing is not only a legitimate form of systems work, but it affects directly the way systems work is performed. Consequently, the systems analyst should be aware of the different types of audits that the information system is subjected to, and the general approach taken by auditors, particularly when a computer is the heart of the system.

It is, however, the ultimate responsibility of management to see to it that the information system maintains a high degree of integrity. Therefore, all information systems should be audited both periodically and randomly. The general purpose of the audit is to detect inadequacies in the system and pinpoint defective operating procedures.

Types of Audits

A number of types of audits can be performed in the information system, each with its own particular objectives. All, however, are performed to ensure the integrity and operational efficiency of the system.

Post Implementation Audit. The basic purpose of this audit is to identify what actually occurred, versus what was projected during the development phase. In a large information system, a systems analyst may perform the post implementation audit. The audit, however, should not be performed by any analyst who was involved with the analysis, design, development, and implementation of the system. In many organizations a management consulting group is commissioned to perform the post implementation audit to ensure that a high degree of objectivity prevails.

From the perspective of the systems operations, this audit should determine that manual procedures are documented formally, that all computer programs are documented properly, all operating personnel are trained, and that the level of accuracy and reliability of information outputs is acceptable to users. With regard to developmental projections, actual costs of each phase should be compared to projected costs. Likewise, actual developmental schedules should be compared to previously projected schedules.

Depending on the size and magnitude of the system implemented, the post implementation audit should not be conducted until the system has been operating for six months or more. This delay factor is intended to eliminate or minimize any learning curve effects on the system, which might distort unduly the auditor's findings.

Routine Operational Audit. In a large information system the routine operational audit is performed by a specially designated control group within the system itself. In a smaller information system, the routine operational audit may be performed by analysts or maintenance programmers. In either case the primary purpose of this audit is to determine how well operations are adhering to established control procedures (see

Chapter 14) and to provide assurance that the system is operating as designed. This audit involves such tasks as comparing output totals to input totals; reviewing console logs and error registers; verifying that input, processing, and output schedules are being met; and comparing actual procedures against standard procedures.

Financial Audit. The financial audit is a unique function of independent accountants. The primary purpose of this audit is to examine the organization's financial statements and express an opinion as to their fairness, their conformity with generally accepted accounting principles, and the consistency with which the accounting principles have been applied from year to year. Since one of the major outputs of the information system are the financial statements, this type of audit serves as an excellent control over general operations of the system.

> ... If the CPA firm that performs the annual audit does not detect the inadequacies, and if serious losses result, the CPA firm can be sued by stockholders. If the CPA firm does detect the inadequacies, it will probably feel compelled to qualify the company's financial statements by noting such inadequacies in the statements. If such qualifications are made, and if there is not sufficient time to correct the control system and insure the integrity of the records, the company will be faced with the embarrassment of the notes in the annual statement.[4]

Systems Audit. Another service to top management is in the area of the systems audit. A systems audit generally involves review and evaluation of the following: (1) overall systems logic and design; (2) programming logic, operating system, and compilers; (3) computer configuration design and selection methods; (4) computer operation and utilization; (5) systems backup and contingency plans; (6) security and procedure controls; and (7) documentation.

In summary, the post implementation audit simply answers the question posed by management: "Does the system do what the development people said it would do within projected schedule and cost?" The routine operational audit aids supervisors in ensuring that day-to-day operations meet standard operating procedures. Although CPA (certified public accountant) auditors are primarily concerned with satisfying themselves to the extent necessary to express an opinion on the financial statements, they may also be commissioned to perform many functions relative to a systems audit. During the course of the financial audit, the auditor may develop helpful comments and suggestions on improving the effectiveness and the efficiency of policies, procedures, and controls which pertain to the information system. Recently, the most significant advance in the role played by the external auditor is this extension from the traditional financial audit. Often, the auditor is charged with a broader responsibility encompassing many aspects of the systems audit.

Computer Auditing Approaches

In a computer-based information system, the auditor must determine how to validate that the processing done on the computer is correct. Auditing around the computer and auditing through the computer are two approaches to testing the processing logic of the computer.

Auditing Around the Computer. Previously, the typical auditor, being unfamiliar with computer technology, programming,

---

[4]"Computer Security: Backup and Recovery Methods," *EDP Analyzer*, January 1972, p. 11. Used with permission.

and other techniques used in electronic data processing, developed audit procedures to review input documents and output reports only.

For example, the auditor selected source documents to be tested (e.g., employees' time cards), traced them through computer printouts (e.g., payroll accounts), and then reversed the order by tracing from summary accounts through computer printouts to source documents. The rationale behind this approach was that if source documents were properly reflected in the master files, and in turn the master files were properly supported by source documents, then the processing functions of the computer (e.g., the black box) must be performing correctly. Therefore, a review or test computer programs or computer operations was unnecessary. These steps were bypassed completely as if the computer printouts were prepared manually, hence the term auditing around the computer. This approach is illustrated in Figure 17.1.

Auditing Through the Computer. As limitations of the above approach became more significant, as audit trails began to disappear with more sophisticated applications (e.g., the monitoring method), and as auditors became more knowledgeable in computer operations, auditing procedures also changed. Transactions began to be tested through the computer. With this approach, illustrated in Figure 17.2, the auditor verifies the effectiveness of control procedures over computer operations and computer programs, and the correctness of internal processing.

Summary Comparison of Both Computer Auditing Approaches

Figure 17.3 is a matrix which gives the advantages and disadvantages of both approaches. It should be pointed out, however, that many auditors use a combination of both approaches for effective procedures.

Using the Computer as an Audit Tool

To perform meaningful and comprehensive audits, the auditor should use an array of audit techniques rather than one technique alone. Most of these techniques require the computer to support their application. For example, to make compliance tests of pro-

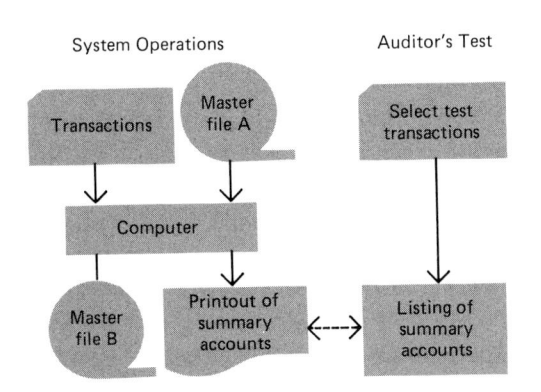

FIG. 17.1 Test of transactions around the computer.

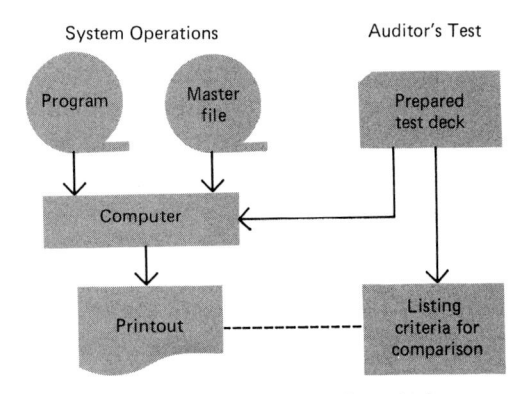

FIG. 17.2 Test of transactions through the computer.

Approaches	Advantages	Disadvantages
Around the computer	1. Logic is plausible. 2. Simple to use and is familiar to auditors. 3. Lessens need for specialized training. 4. Does not interfere with the normal operations of the system. 5. Applicable for audits of fairly small, simplistic systems.	1. Input data goes through many changes, limiting true comparisons. 2. A wide variety of transactions makes this approach tedious and time consuming. 3. Auditors fail to exploit the computer as a tool to help in auditing chores.
Through the computer	1. Applicable for larger, more sophisticated systems. 2. Gives a more detailed review of computer processing programs and procedures. 3. Uses the computer as a tool for performing auditing functions.	1. Requires highly skilled personnel. 2. High cost of processing test transactions. 3. Often interferes with normal operations of the system.

FIG. 17.3 Advantages and disadvantages of auditing approaches.

gram controls, test transactions (traditionally called **test decks**) are prepared and run through the computer. Further tests (e.g., substantive tests), however, must be performed to test the accuracy and existence of records in the data base, and to retrieve from it various audit information. The following is a list of computer-assisted audit techniques.

Test Deck. Real data are simulated by dummy transactions (test data) that ideally include every possible type of condition, including those that the system, because of lack of proper controls, is incapable of handling. That is, the list of simulated transactions should test for both valid and invalid conditions.

Generalized Audit Programs. Nearly all large accounting firms have at least one generalized audit program to help them in their audit work. Normally, these programs are written in a compiler-level language. Functions that audit programs perform, along with practical examples of audit results, are as follows:

1. *Search and retrieve.* The auditor can have the program scan large files and retrieve specified data segments that have audit significance. For example, it can search depositors' accounts for unusual charges, or identify dormant accounts.
2. *Selection of samples.* The program can select a sample of records from a file population. Stratified sampling can be specified based upon upper and/or lower limits. Systematic sampling can be performed in which every nth record is selected for further review or confirmation. Or simple random sampling can be specified for record selection. Some programs select a sample to meet desired statistical confidence levels. Furthermore, programs calculate the arithmetic mean and variance of the population. Inferences can be made from these sample statistics, such as an estimate of the total book value of inventory.
3. *Perform basic calculations.* The audit program performs the arithmetic opera-

tions of addition, subtraction, multiplication, and division. It also performs the logical operations of less than, greater than, or equal to.

4. *Prepare subtotals.* Totaling functions enable the auditor to print subtotals and item counts. For example, in payroll, auditing the program can give levels of subtotals, by department, by plant, by state, by region, and so forth. It can also give end-of-file totals, such as numbers of records in the file and total debits and credits.

5. *Compare, sort, and merge.* Data, either alphabetic or numeric, can be sorted or merged in ascending or descending order. The auditor can match files on a given sequence, and compare the data in one file with that of another file. For example, a confirmation reply file may be compared with the confirmation log file, and a second mailing printed of those accounts not responding. In another instance, the auditor can compare payroll files for different periods to see if there has been any significant change in pay rates, salaries, etc.

6. *Copy data.* This function simply copies records or fields from one file to another. It can produce a tape file of all accounts to receive positive confirmation. The auditor may have the program create a work file of items that are of special interest, such as selling prices, item costs, pay rates, and commission rates.

7. *Summarize.* Large volume computer files can be summarized quickly to lessen the burden of making detailed reviews. This function creates desired totals and subtotals for a group of related records in a file.

8. *Print.* This function allows the auditor to specify the audit results in almost any format desired with descriptive major and minor column headings. Moreover, a great deal of flexibility is provided to the auditor for spacing, paging, and ordering of the output. This function enhances the organization and readability of the audit information.

Tagging and Tracing. With application of tagging and tracing routines in the programming logic, any transactions and related data can be traced through the system. As each processing step is performed, the interaction of the selected transaction with other data and related tests is displayed. Control and selection of tagged transactions can be specified by the auditor through a terminal in his or her office.

The tagging and tracing audit technique flags, by some special notation or code, selected transactions. These transactions are processed as normal transactions by the programming logic. Displays of the status of these transactions are made to the auditor as they flow through the system. This technique, if installed into the programming logic while the programs are being developed, requires relatively little extra time and cost, and provides a powerful technique to obtain a comprehensive transaction trail.

Three aspects to the tagging and tracing technique are: (1) some identifier must be used to tag the selected transactions, (2) program instructions must be embedded in the application programs to recognize the tagged transactions, and (3) routines must be prepared to print the results of the tagged transactions and related data at key points in the system.

General display points are: (1) where the transaction enters the system, (2) where the transaction enters each program module, (3) where the transaction exits each program module, (4) interface points between each transaction and a secondary record in the system, and (5) before and after displays of the master records changed by the transaction.

Integrated Test Facility (ITF). The ITF involves the establishment of a fictitious entity (e.g., customer, department, division, employee) in the data base, against which test transactions, unknown to the systems personnel, can be processed as if they are regular, live transactions. This approach integrates permanent test data into the system and permits the auditor to monitor continuously the performance of the system. The ITF requires the auditor to supply a system for recording and processing the test transactions so that predetermined results can be checked against the actual results produced by the computer system. Furthermore, the ITF gives the auditor a strong computer audit technique for auditing on-line systems, in that it tests the system as it is operating versus after the fact.

Monitors. Software companies and computer vendors (e.g., IBM's System Management Facilities—SMF) provide packages that can be put to good use by auditors to provide computer usage, control, and equipment performance information. This information is collected as a by-product of the normal operations, without requiring extensive programming or special work by the auditor. Six general categories of information furnished by monitors such as IBM's SMF package are as follows:

1. *Accounting records.* This category consists of records that show who used the system and for how long. The information contained in these records includes: (a) identification of job or job step, user, and hardware features; (b) job priority; (c) date and time of job initiation; (d) date and time of job termination; (e) type of job termination (for abnormal terminations, the reason for the ABEND is indicated); and (f) amount of main storage, in bytes, used to execute the job. These records provide an audit trail of the system resources used and the jobs or personnel responsible for the use of these resources. Information contained in these records is used by the accounting department as the basis for developing EDP cost allocation and charging users accordingly.

2. *Data set activity records.* These records provide information about which portions of the data base were used to perform a computer job or job step, and who requested the use of the data sets. The records furnish an audit trail of data usage. This trail is one of the principal benefits the auditor will derive if SMF is used. These records also supply considerable information about the characteristics of the data base.

3. *Volume utilization records.* These records indicate the amount of available space on direct access storage devices and give basic error statistics for tape files. They also record the number of records contained in each file. These records are used by the data processing department in its efforts to obtain better utilization of space within direct access storage devices. In the case of tape files, the error statistics are helpful in assessing the quality of a particular reel of tape. For example, when the number of errors on a tape reaches a certain level, the tape should be either cleaned or discarded. The information in the volume utilization records has little meaning for auditors. They might want to review this data in an attempt to determine whether or

not the data processing department is making effective use of this information. Usually the auditor has no reason to look at these records, unless there are symptoms of a problem at the installation which such a review might clarify.

4. *System usage records.* This category contains records that show the portion of the hardware configuration being used by each job and job step. These records can be used to develop some appreciation of how effectively the resources of the system are being applied. Much of the information is technical in nature; for example, the amount of time the processor is idle. The auditor might want to be certain that this information is being used by the data processing department to achieve maximum system efficiency. Information that would be of particular interest to the auditor includes date and time of all file dumps, terminal initiation times, and times when a system halt command was initialized.

5. *Subsystem records.* Whenever a job requires a subsystem (subroutine, program, or module) for some processing operation, that fact can be recorded by SMF. This information is of value to the auditor for two reasons. First, it provides an audit trail of which subsystems are being utilized by what jobs. Second, it gives the auditor an opportunity to determine what activity is being entered and from where it is being entered.

One particular type of record will be of interest to most auditors. This record is written whenever a sign-on attempt fails because of an invalid password. A limited number of invalid passwords are normally allowed because of keying errors at the terminal. An abnormal number of such errors could indicate that someone is trying to penetrate the system. This error data are a potential signal for audit investigation.

6. *User written records.* When needed information cannot be obtained from one of the categories described above, SMF provides the user with the option of incorporating his or her own analysis routines into the system. The extensive capabilities for performing further analysis should provide the auditor with unlimited possibilities for evaluating data processing. Auditors can build routines to review every transaction for conformity with organization policies and procedures, to detect violations of systems standards, or to perform special analysis in support of audit objectives. In spite of performance degradation of the system, the use of analysis routines is an important technique because it potentially allows the auditor to analyze the operation of a system during execution time, without the specific knowledge of any other person or group. This could improve audit integrity, security, and independence in a computer environment.[5]

17.4 ▪ PROJECT MANAGEMENT SYSTEMS

The activities required to analyze, design, and develop an information system or subsystem are generally termed a project. As discussed in Chapter 1, the project concept is an effective technique for managing change. A project management system

---

[5]This presentation on SMF summarized from William E. Perry and Donald L. Adams, "SMF—An Untapped Audit Resource," *EDPACS*, September 1974, pp. 1–8, and William E. Perry, "Using SMF as an Audit Tool-Accounting Information," *EDPACS*, February 1975, pp. 1–17.

(PMS) is a system that supports the tasks of planning, scheduling, controlling, and accounting for projects. The essential feature of a PMS is a mechanism for delineating a project into measurable work units. What follows is a discussion of the types of PMS and an analysis of the problems they can create.[6]

Types of Project Management Systems

Project management systems can be classified into four general categories: (1) manual structured systems, (2) project tracking systems, (3) project networking systems, and (4) full project management systems. Many commercial packages are available for organizations to use.

Manual Structured Systems. These systems normally impose a standard structure of eight to twelve phases on all projects. Each phase is identified with work products and documentation. Project progress is reviewed at specific checkpoints where, relying on revised estimates of remaining costs and estimated benefits, management must make the decision on whether to proceed.

Project Tracking Systems. Project tracking systems produce reports showing actual schedule realization and cost accumulation, based on a list of project activities and their corresponding time estimates and budgeted expenditures. Project tracking systems do not include a facility for project planning.

Project Networking Systems. Project networking systems use the well-known techniques of PERT and CPM (see Appendix A). Since time is the focus of these techniques, project networking systems are best suited for planning and controlling schedules; they are not particularly suited to controlling costs.

Full Project Management Systems. Full PMSs perform (or have the potential to perform) most of the functions (e.g., planning, work definition, tracking, and reporting) that were listed for the other categories of PMSs. Aspects of the planning function include (1) a work breakdown structure; (2) network capability, considering all projects; (3) resource scheduling; and (4) "What if?" analysis capability. This last aspect of the planning function is especially intriguing. When a project gets in trouble or a management redirection alters a plan, the "What if?" capability should help management analyze alternative courses of action and the concomitant impacts on the project.

A second feature of a full PMS is its work definition function. This includes aspects of (1) structuring projects based on phases, activities, and checkpoints; (2) preparing a precedence relationship among the activities (i.e., a network); (3) setting performance time standards for activities; (4) creating procedures describing how to perform the activities; and (5) defining documentation standards for the activities.

The tracking function of a full PMS entails collecting and validating data concerning work progress, schedule revisions, and resource allocation changes. Finally, the reporting function encompasses preparation of project reports to management, project leaders, project employees, and accounting. These reports detail actual versus plan for the last period, as well as planned activities for the next period. Furthermore, reports may be prepared on a departmental basis, showing the time distribution for all staff members over all activities.

[6]Adapted from "Project Management Systems," *EDP Analyzer,* September 1976.

Pitfalls in Implementing PMS

If suppliers of full PMSs were polled and they were candid in their comments, it is likely that they would report that over half of their full PMS installations have been failures. Moreover, an additional number of installations are making only limited use of a full PMS. This underscores that a full PMS is no panacea. It is not a solution to inadequate systems design procedures or poor programming practices. A full PMS is only of value in helping a smooth-running operation run even more smoothly.

Installing a project management system is like installing any other management procedure. If an organization does not have any sort of PMS at present, then it would be unwise to install a full PMS at the outset. Regardless of the type of PMS implemented, it needs to be accompanied by large doses of management commitment, encouragement, and endorsement. Management sets the tone by either using, or not using, the reports that the system generates.

Impediments to Installing a Successful Full PMS

When installing a full PMS, three major problem areas to avoid are:

1. *Insufficient support.* Who will benefit from the successful installation of a full PMS? Not the analysts and programmers; while the chance of their being overloaded is reduced, the system can be a source of embarrassment, since their deficiencies will be highlighted. Not the project leaders; while the impact of schedule slippages will be pointed up, the mechanics of supporting the system can easily take up to 10 percent of their time. So the only people in the organization with a real incentive to make the system work is management. With an investment of little personal effort, the system can provide them with who is doing what and where each project stands.

2. *Costs out of proportion.* As a rule of thumb, no more than 5 percent of the annual salaries of analysts and programmers should be spent on the purchase of a full PMS package. The purchase price of a full PMS system, however, is only the tip of the iceberg. Attention must be given to installation costs, and then to the annual costs of operating the system. For example, in a unit of 25 programmers and analysts, installation costs may be twice the purchase cost; operating costs may be four times the purchase cost.

3. *Lack of a realistic understanding.* The most common misunderstanding seems to be that the full PMS reports will provide a complete picture of the status of a project. This is clearly just not the case. Two important types of information missing from PMS reports are *quality of work completed* and *expected problems*. Quality of work done can only be assessed by conducting technical reviews. For example, at a checkpoint the programs that have been completed might be reviewed from the standpoint of ease of conversion, ease of maintenance, effective utilization of computer resources, and so forth. Information on expected problems might be obtained by instituting a hierarchy of periodic, manual reports. These reports could indicate the activities worked on during this period, what is planned to be worked on next period, and what are some of the anticipated problems where assistance may be needed.

17.5 ▪ MANAGING CHANGE

Many systems analysts, as well as managements, make the mistake of assuming that information systems development is controlled only by technical, economic, legal, and schedule constraints. A fifth constraint, *operation,* deals mainly with the people element in the organization. In the long run operational feasibility often has a greater impact on systems development than the other four constraints combined. Much of the current literature related to the field of information systems reflects a concern that a preoccupation with technology and techniques has replaced the systems analyst's ability to deal effectively with people. While the dramatic and rapid developments in technology require an inordinate amount of attention from the analyst, these developments have also resulted in a greater need to pay attention to the human element of systems work.

All too often technical specialists have blind spots in dealing with people. Much of their work requires changes in the work of other persons, but they often do not recognize the social problems they cause. They are convinced that the technical part of their change is correct, and therefore any opposition to it must come from bullheaded or ignorant people. When they talk to workers, they sometimes use jargon and theories that do not "make sense" to the practical people of the shop. Further, they do not discuss; they tell—convinced that change is logical, they ignore the psychological![7]

The major result of the systems analyst's work is change, and many of the users or personnel in an organization cannot deal effectively with the changes which they are being asked to accept. This problem is more acute in the areas of the organization that traditionally performed many of the operations now done automatically by the information system. Moreover, these problems are found at each level of the organization.

People and their social systems often resist change in organizations. In fact, the fear of change can be as disrupting to the organization as the change itself. The reasons for this latter type of resistance are summarized as follows.

1. *Economic.* An individual fears becoming technically unemployed, demoted, or asked to work fewer hours at a reduced wage rate.
2. *Personal.* Change, by definition, imputes criticism that the present system is inadequate. The individual fears that, because of greater systematization, his or her skill will be diminished or lost, and the personal pride derived from it will be lost or reduced. Moreover, most people dislike being required to relearn.
3. *Social.* Change frequently affects human relations and brings about new social situations. Old social ties must be severed and new ones must be made. The employee feels that the change, while perhaps benefiting the organization, does little to benefit the individual or fellow employees.[8]

Participative Versus Coercive Change Strategy

Hersey and Blanchard[9] outline a four-tiered diagram of change: (1) knowledge changes,

---

[7]Keith Davis, *Human Behavior at Work,* New York: McGraw-Hill Book Co., 1972, p. 517.

[8]*Ibid.* For a more detailed list of human factors that contribute to resistance to change, see Ephraim R. McLean. "The Human Side of Systems: The User's Perspective," paper presented to the 1976 Western Systems Conference, Los Angeles.

[9]P. Hersey and K.H. Blanchard, *Management of Organization Behavior,* Englewood Cliffs, N.J.: Prentice-Hall, Inc., 1972, p. 160.

(2) attitudinal changes, (3) individual behavior changes, and (4) group or organizational performance changes. The time duration and the degree of difficulty in effecting change at each tier is illustrated in Figure 17.4.

The systems analyst, when acting as a change agent, may attempt to move individuals from one tier to the next by employing a participative change strategy, a coercive change strategy, or a combination of both. If a participative change strategy is to be successful, then the analyst must possess a certain amount of influence over the individuals who will experience the impact of the change. Additionally, the group targeted for the change must be self-motivated and relatively independent.

Participative change begins when the systems analyst educates the individuals affected by the new system. It is hoped that this introduction of new knowledge (tier 1) will cultivate the development of the appropriate attitude toward the new system (tier 2). This attitude will, in turn, shape individual behavior via participation in such activities as goal-setting exercises (tier 3). Finally, individual behavior patterns will lead to formalized group participation (tier 4). While participative change may be slow and evolutionary, if effective, it is enduring.

Coercive change, on the other hand, is initiated from a position of power; its permanency is a function of the strength of the rewards, punishments, and sanctions it is able to impose. As one would expect, coercive change is most effective when the target group is composed of dependent people.

Coercive change begins with a direct order being issued by an authoritative figure. This brings pressure to bear on the group to alter its behavior (tier 4). Consequently, the individual's behavior can be expected to change (tier 3), which in turn, can influence

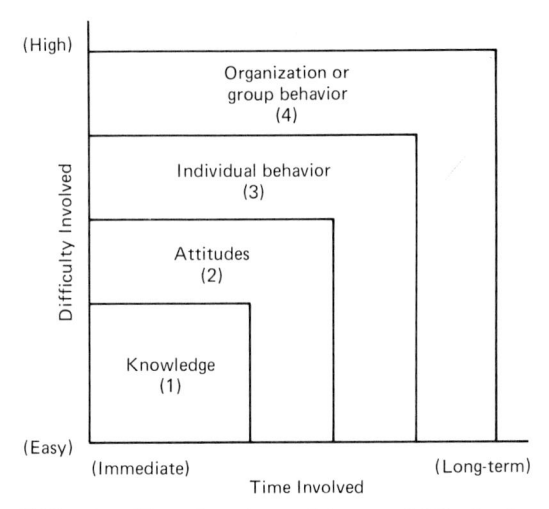

FIG. 17.4 Time duration and degree of difficulty in effecting change at each tier.

that individual's attitude (tier 2) and what he or she believes (tier 1). As beliefs are reinforced attitudes are confirmed, and individual and group behavior patterns are verified through experience.

Tactical Guides for Implementing Change

The systems analyst should be aware that a number of simple tactics can be applied profitably when change is desired.[10]

1. *Spaced practice.* Improvement in performance of a new task occurs more quickly, is mastered in greater depth, and is more permanent, if learning is introduced in relatively short periods with ample provision for rest. This can be contrasted to situations in which continuous or massed practice learning sessions are employed.

2. *Rehearsal.* Performance improves constantly with continued practice, until a

[10]Condensed from M. Kubr (ed.). *Management Consulting,* Geneva, Switzerland: International Labour Office, 1976, pp. 36–41.

plateau is reached. Practice beyond this point can lead eventually to overlearning, a condition in which the change routine or procedure becomes virtually automatic.

3. *Knowledge.* Considerable evidence indicates learning of a prior skill can have a negative transfer effect on the acquisition of a new skill. If the analyst moves directly to the new approach without first addressing established practices, negative transfer is likely to take place. In short, when introducing change, move from the known to the unknown.

4. *Goal setting.* Targets should be realistic, neither too easy nor impossible, but such that when attained they provide a feeling of achievement.[11] Moreover, they should be expressed, if possible, in numerical terms, described specifically, and be time-phased. "Net retail sales of Product X are expected to increase in the next calendar year by one million dollars," is one example of such an expression.

5. *Feedback.* Successful introduction of change requires that appropriate feedback information be presented to permit necessary adjustments to be made by those undertaking the change process. The systems analyst must provide for review and reporting sessions, not merely to boost morale, but as a control and correction requisite.

[11] D.C. McClelland and D.G. Winter, *Motivating Economic Achievement*, New York: The Free Press, 1969.

SUMMARY

To achieve effective information systems, management must be concerned with the activities of maintenance, auditing, project control, and introducing change.

It is inevitable that in working to get the information system developed, certain errors will be made and a variety of expedients employed. Moreover, users of the information system may suggest certain improvements. What is needed then is a plan of action that increases the maintainability of the information system.

Auditing activities are performed to ensure that management objectives are being met and that the integrity of the system is maximized. Many auditors, especially the independent certified public accountant (CPA), are extending the bounds of their traditional financial audit to include additional operational aspects of the system.

Project management systems are integral to the tasks of planning, scheduling, and controlling projects. Although project management systems may vary in their degree of sophistication, their successful introduction into an organization will be a function of the commitment, encouragement, and endorsement given them by management.

In performing effective systems work and ensuring that changes in the system are accepted by the personnel in the organization, both the systems analyst and the management of the information system must be acutely aware of human needs. If the technical potential of the information system is to be realized, then the various factors that relate to people and their social systems must be satisfied first.

REVIEW QUESTIONS

17.1 Why are more maintainable systems a major objective of management? Discuss fully.

17.2 List and discuss the four main causes of program, data files, documentation, and procedure changes. Prepare your own example for each of these causes.

17.3 Why do you think most people dislike maintenance work?

17.4 List and fully discuss the procedures for achieving more maintainable systems.

17.5 Define modular design of programs.

17.6 Should maintenance be performed in the development groups, or in separate maintenance groups?

17.7 List and discuss the types of audits.

17.8 Why should the post implementation audit be delayed until several months after implementation of a system?

17.9 List and discuss computer auditing approaches. Give advantages and disadvantages of each approach.

17.10 Prepare a list of computer-assisted audit techniques.

17.11 List and give examples of the functions that comprise a generalized audit program.

17.12 In what way does the integrated test facility differ from the test deck and tagging and tracing audit techniques?

17.13 Describe how auditors can use different types of records produced by system monitors.

17.14 Describe four general classifications of project management systems.

17.15 Who will benefit most from a successful PMS, and why?

17.16 List the reasons individuals resist change.

17.17 Discuss some tactics that systems analysts might find useful when change is desired.

QUESTIONS FOR DISCUSSION

17.1 How can one differentiate between maintenance work, such as systems improvements, and new development work?

17.2 "We wrote all our programs in LOGELNUM, the language promoted by the vendor we acquired our computer from. Now, we are planning on changing to another vendor but we are in a real bind because LOGELNUM is not compatible with the proposed new equipment." Comment on several ramifications applicable to this statement.

17.3 Compare and contrast systems work performed by a systems analyst, and the auditing function performed by an auditor. Discuss fully.

17.4 "During the course of the financial audit, the auditor may develop helpful comments and suggestions on improving effectiveness and efficiency of policies, procedures, and controls which pertain to information systems. In recent times, the most significant advance in the role played by the auditor is in this extension from the traditional financial audit." Discuss.

17.5 "Many systems analysts, as well as managements, make the mistake of assuming that information systems development is controlled by technical, economic, legal, and schedule constraints. There is a fifth constraint which might be more severe." What is this fifth constraint? Discuss fully.

17.6 Is technological development a boon or a curse to mankind?

17.7 "Our programmers operate the computer themselves during testing periods." Discuss.

17.8 "The manager of systems development is a tough negotiator. When he disagrees with the users, he does it his way or not at all." Discuss fully.

17.9 "All your planning and control problems would be solved if only you were to install a full project management system." Comment on this generalization.

17.10 "The marketing system I have implemented is the most sophisticated one of its kind. Now if only the sales force were bright enough to recognize this fact. . . ." Comment on this approach to introducing change into the organization.

17.11 "Because of its many advantages, we rely solely on the ITF auditing technique." Indicate the conditions under which this might be an unwise course of action.

17.12 Comment on the statement, "When introducing change use the carrot first, and if that fails, use the stick!"

17.13 "Our goal is to increase the size of our membership by 5 percent." How could this target statement be improved?

EXERCISES

17.1 What follows is a network with corresponding activity times estimated:

Activity	Optimistic	Most Likely	Pessimistic
A	5	8	16
B	3	4	9
C	2	5	7
D	6	8	10

Required:
1. Calculate expected times for each activity.
2. Determine the critical path.
3. Calculate the cumulative variance along the critical path.
4. For each event, indicate the earliest, latest, and slack time.

17.2 Classify the following maintenance situations as emergency, routine, special reporting requests, or system improvements. You may feel that some of the situations cannot be appropriately classified under a single category; in this case use as many classification categories as necessary.

1. An order entry system has been operational for 18 months. During this period, the company's product line has been expanded, two new warehouses have been added, and three sales offices have been opened in Canada. Additionally, users have indicated that the report showing backorders would be of greater value if it were to reach their desk before noon, rather than by 4:00 PM.
2. You, as the maintenance analyst for the payroll system, have just received a memorandum from the Vice-President of Public Affairs. She has requested information on the year-to-date number of minority hires. It is indicated further in the memorandum that henceforth this information will be required on a quarterly basis.
3. As you leave the tennis courts, there is an urgent message requesting you to call operations immediately. It

seems the sales analysis program, which had been running smoothly for the last six months, has just abnormally terminated.

4. Due to the sharp decline in the cost of color CRTs, you are requested to modify the traffic control system, presently using black and white CRTs, to accommodate color.

17.3 Past experience has shown that a particular type of program has an expected time of completion equal to 200 hours. David Wilson is assigned to prepare this program. The plan provides the following tasks and related times for each task:

Design program logic	50 hours
Code program	40 hours
Test program	70 hours
Document program	40 hours

After reviewing the program and developing a program macro flowchart, Wilson begins to code. At the end of several days, Wilson reports the following:

	Planned	Actual	Remaining
Design program logic	50	20	0
Code program	40	4	27
Test program	70	0	15
Document program	40	0	12

You are the chief programmer. What is your reaction to Wilson's revised plan?

17.4 Conduct a post implementation audit of some system in your school or a local business. Prepare a report of your findings, highlighting the discrepancies between any projections and actual results.

PROBLEMS

17.1 Donna Henry, a systems analyst, in developing a production control system for Apex Products, needed to conduct some routine studies of machine utilization and downtime in the manufacturing plant. Without explaining her purpose she set up records to be kept by each operator of a lubricant capper machine. These operators were paid on a piece-rate basis. The machine operators were told to report the length, time of day, and cause of all capper machine downtime. The supervisor was directed to require the operators to maintain these records for 30 days.

Both the supervisor and the operators stalled and complained, and finally, kept such inadequate records that they turned out to be unusable. Donna Henry concluded that the department was full of obstructionists who did not have the best interests of the organization at heart.

Required: Identify the human aspects that Donna Henry has failed to recognize in dealing with the supervisor and the operators.

17.2 Heath Corporation is a manufacturer of quality sound components. It has a number of plants located in California and Oregon. Recently, a new labor recording system was installed in three plants in Oregon. A brief description of the labor recording system follows.

Automatic time recording devices are located throughout the shop areas. For 2000 employees covered by this system, these devices completely replace human timekeepers and manually prepared time cards. Data from the system flows through to the company's payroll and job-order cost accounting and control records. Basic timekeeping tools are plastic employee badges, prepunched with charge number and other information about a particular job.

The badge is assigned permanently to each employee. The job cards follow the parts or assemblies to be worked on. Exceptions are indirect labor and other special cards, which are located in racks adjacent to the input devices. Clock-in on reporting for work requires only insertion of the badge and one or more job cards, and depression of other keys.

All input devices are linked electrically to a central control box, a master clock, and an online keypunch that creates a punched card for each entry. The cards are converted to magnetic tape for passing through computer processes. The first of these, a match against an employee identification master tape, begins after the beginning of each shift.

Within an hour after shift start, an exception report has been prepared for distribution to shop foremen. This report indicates absences, tardy clock-in, preshift overtime, and failure to check in on a job. Each exception must be approved by the shop foreman. Transactions accepted in this first processing routine plus transactions accepted for the remainder of the shift are "posted" to a direct access file arranged by employee.

Transactions rejected must be analyzed and corrected for reentry into the processing cycle.

To evaluate the labor recording system, the internal auditors decided to use simulated transactions designed to test not only routine processing, but also various exception conditions. Since the auditors wanted to perform the tests under normal operating conditions, using actual shop locations and job cards, a special set of employee badges and corresponding master records were created.

Required: For the labor recording system, prepare a set of transactions to test routine processing and exception conditions.

17.3 Listed below are the activities necessary to complete a project. For each activity lettered A through M, an optimistic, most likely, and pessimistic time estimate is included (O, M, and P, respectively). Additionally, predecessor and successor activities are indicated.

				Activities	
Activity	O	M	P	Predecessor	Successor
A	5	8	19	—	B, C, E
B	5	8	10	A	F, D
C	3	5	7	A	G
D	0	0	0	B	G
E	6	9	12	A	M
F	4	8	18	B	H, K
G	5	7	12	D, C	I, J
H	0	0	0	F	L
I	0	0	0	G	L
J	0	0	0	G	M
K	4	7	10	F	—
L	7	10	25	H, I	—
M	4	6	8	E, J	—

Required:

1. Construct a network for the project.
2. Compute the expected completion time for each activity.
3. Determine the critical path and the slack present in the network.
4. What is the probability of completing the project within 40 days from the day it started?

5. A $1000 late penalty fee is assessed if the project is completed after day 42. Is it cost/effective to purchase a new tool for $275 that will change the optimistic, most likely, and pessimistic time estimates of activity L to 6, 9, and 15, respectively? Assume that the tool, after being used in activity L, can be sold for $175.

17.4 Patty Randall, one of your more experienced and better maintenance programmers, has requested a meeting with you (her supervisor) to discuss the possibility of transferring to the systems development area.

"I'd like to move to the development area because I'm tired of cleaning up someone else's mess. And I would like to get over to development because there is a greater chance for exposure to top management and, consequently, I might be able to progress a bit faster," she began.

"My progress here has been quite good and I have nothing against you or the people in this area. It just seems that I might be able to do something more important—something I could call my own—over in development. I mean, that's where the action is and that's where they're creating all the new systems that are really going to contribute to the company," Patty continued. "Besides, development works with new equipment and new languages. It is not very exciting to be stuck here in maintenance and have to work with second generation languages and outmoded equipment."

Required: How would you respond to Patty to convince her of the value of the maintenance function to the company, and the important role she can play within that function?

17.5 In establishing performance requirements for a proposed magnetic ink character recognition (MICR) demand deposit system, management indicated that the following qualitative factors were important:

1. "The system should result in the most economical operation possible."
2. "Items should not be posted to the wrong account."
3. "The system must be able to handle unexpected future changes with minor difficulty."
4. "System downtime should be infrequent and cause as little disruption as possible."
5. "Customers should feel comfortable with the new system."

6. "The system should operate in a timely fashion."

Required: For each of the qualitative factors listed above, provide a corresponding quantitative measure that might be used to evaluate the new system when implemented.

BIBLIOGRAPHY

"Approach Trains User to Read 'Alien' Code," *Computerworld,* September 12, 1977.

Auditing Standards and Procedures, Committee on Auditing Procedure Statement No. 33, New York: American Institute of Certified Public Accountants, 1963.

Canning, "COBOL Aid Packages," *EDP Analyzer,* January 1972.

Canning, "Computer Security: Backup and Recovery Methods," *EDP Analyzer,* January 1972.

Canning, "Project Management Systems," *EDP Analyzer,* September 1976.

Canning, "That Maintenance 'Iceberg'," *EDP Analyzer,* October 1972.

Davis, *Human Behavior at Work,* New York: McGraw-Hill Book Co., 1972.

Dean, "A Comparison of Decision Tables Against Conventional COBOL as a Programming Tool for Commercial Applications," *Software World,* Spring 1971.

"DP Auditing Viewed as Art Form Instead of Science," *Computerworld,* July 11, 1977.

Hersey and Blanchard, *Management of Organization Behavior,* Englewood Cliffs, NJ.: Prentice-Hall, Inc., 1972.

Kubr (ed.), *Management Consulting,* Geneva, Switzerland: International Labour Office, 1976.

"'Ideal' DP Auditor Needs Range of Experience," *Computerworld,* September 5, 1977.

McClelland and Winter, *Motivating Economic Achievement,* New York: The Free Press, 1969.

McLean, "The Human Side of Systems: The User's Perspective," paper presented to the *1976 Western Systems Conference,* Los Angeles.

Perry, "Using SMF as an Audit Tool-Accounting Information," *EDPACS,* February 1975.

Perry and Adams, "SMF—An Untapped Audit Resource," *EDPACS,* September 1974.

Perry and Fitzgerald, "Designing for Auditability," *Datamation,* August 1977.

Porter and Perry, *EDP Controls and Auditing,* Third Edition, Belmont, Calif.: Wadsworth Publishing Company, Inc., 1980.

Study Group on Computer Control and Audit Guidelines, Toronto, Canada: The Canadian Institute of Chartered Accountants, 1971.

Thierauf, *Data Processing for Business and Management,* New York: John Wiley & Sons, Inc., 1973.

Toffler, *Future Shock,* New York: Random House, Inc., 1970.

Wadsworth, *The Human Side of Data Processing Management,* Englewood Cliffs, NJ.: Prentice-Hall, Inc., 1973.

Wilkinson, "An Application Audit," *Datamation,* August 1977.

PART IV

Appendixes

Introduction to Appendixes

In the beginning of this text it was stated that two basic components are required in modern information systems. These components are logico-mathematical models and data processing methods, especially the computer and its related technology.

The text part of this book has dealt with information system concepts and practice. These two appendixes provide the underlying techniques which give efficacy to this theory and practice.

APPENDIX A

Logico-Mathematical Models

INTRODUCTION

Many information needs of an organization can be met by establishing a common data base and from it, providing timely reports or online responses to the users, via remote terminals such as CRTs. An information system is also comprised of a number of information subsystems such as traditional accounting, inventory control, process control and production scheduling, shipping and transportation, sales analysis, and so on. The total information system is management oriented; thus, in addition to being a data processing center, it also uses logico-mathematical models to aid management in its planning, controlling, and decision-making functions. In addition to developing reports and systems for historical record-keeping and to satisfy business and governmental requirements, it is also the responsibility of the information systems analyst to select, test, and implement these models to provide alternative, predictive, optimizing, and performance information. A systems analyst, therefore, needs a working knowledge of the various logico-mathematical models. In this appendix several models that over the years have proven to be valuable in converting raw data elements into meaningful information are presented.

TRADITIONAL ACCOUNTING MODELS

The traditional accounting function, in addition to handling routine data processing activities, also provides a great deal of information to both internal and external constituents. Much of the information provided by this function is historical, and is stated in terms of money. Traditional accounting, however, also provides information that is performance oriented. In the following subsections most of the traditional accounting models are presented.[1]

Accounting reports derived from models aid management (as well as others) in:

1. Planning, because reporting information on past periods helps the user to make predictions about future events.
2. Controlling, because budgets and standards are set, and performances are mea-

[1]For a tutorial treatment of these methods, we refer you to Robert N. Anthony and James S. Reece, *Management Accounting*, Fifth Edition, Homewood, Ill.: Richard D. Irwin, Inc., 1975, and Charles T. Horngren, *Cost Accounting: A Managerial Emphasis*, Fifth Edition, Englewood Cliffs, N.J.: Prentice-Hall, Inc., 1982.

sured against these budgets and standards.
3. Decision making, because the reporting of possible outcomes based on alternative inputs allows the decision maker to select the best alternatives.

The accounting function also acts as an overall control device for external constituents such as stockholders. It provides performance measurement via position statements, earnings statements, and funds statements, which together help to indicate how management is doing. It also helps asset control (e.g., cash, securities, receivables, and so on) by promoting efficiency and internal control, which reduces loss through error or fraud. Moreover, it limits needless expenditures by establishing a decentralized system of budgets.

Bookkeeping Model

The bookkeeping model is an equation which sets up a procedure for classifying, recording, and reporting financial transactions of an organization. It can be stated as follows:

Assets (A_t) = Liabilities (L_t)
   + Contributed Capital (CC_t)
   + Retained Earnings (RE_t)

Each category represents some financial amount at some point in time. All transactions are classified and recorded in such a way that the total assets equal the sum of the liabilities, contributed capital, and retained earnings.

Retained earnings, at some point in time (usually stated at the end of an accounting period), is the algebraic sum of the retained earnings of the previous period, RE_{t-1}, the earnings for the period, E_t and the dividends declared during the period, D_t. This equation is stated as:

$$RE_t = RE_{t-1} + E_t - D_t$$

Earnings are determined by matching the inputs for the period with the outputs for the period. In business organizations the inputs are measured in terms of revenue, (R), and the outputs are measured in terms of expenses (EXP) required to generate this revenue. Income tax (TAX), is not recognized as an expense, per se, but as a social cost of doing business. The equation for earnings is stated as:

$$E_t = R_t - EXP_t - TAX_t$$

Accounts

Accounts are set up which represent each category in the above equations. These accounts are merely a place to receive transactional data, and to show increases or decreases where, at certain periods, the current amount balance of an item is available. All accounts can be algebraically summed, in accordance with the procedures dictated by the equations, to provide financial statements whenever needed.

These accounts take a variety of forms, depending on whether they are recorded on paper for manual data processing methods, or recorded on punched cards, magnetic tape, magnetic disk, etc., for computer processing. The basic procedures in classifying, recording, and reporting are the same whatever data processing method is used.

The essential features of an account can be shown in the form of a classical T-account, as follows:

Debit	Credit

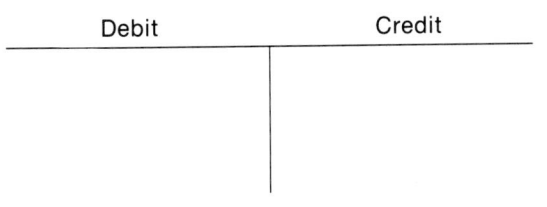

The rules of recording are as follows:

1. *Debits* increase assets, and decrease liabilities, contributed capital, and retained earnings.
2. *Credits* decrease assets, and increase liabilities, contributed capital, and retained earnings.

Retained earnings represent the "meter" for earnings (i.e., revenue increases retained earnings, therefore a credit increases a revenue account). Conversely, an expense decreases retained earnings, so a debit increases an expense account.

Accounting data can also be structured in the form of an m by n matrix with the following general notation:

$$A = \begin{vmatrix} a_{11} & a_{12} & \cdots & a_{1n} \\ a_{21} & a_{22} & \cdots & a_{2n} \\ \vdots & \vdots & & \vdots \\ a_{m1} & a_{m2} & \cdots & a_{mn} \end{vmatrix}$$

Such a matrix is usually represented by the following abbreviation

$$A = (a_{ij}) \quad \begin{matrix} i = 1, 2, \ldots, m \\ j = 1, 2, \ldots, n \end{matrix}$$

where i = rows and j = columns.

An accounting matrix, using 16 common accounts, is shown in Figure A.1. Notice that the increases and decreases in the accounts work the same as previously explained and that a current balance can be determined at any time. For example, look at Sales (column 10), a revenue account. It obviously has a credit balance (unless there were sales returns, which would be another account) and that balance is $90,000 (row 19). But how were the sales made, cash or credit? Looking at the Cash and Accounts Receivable accounts (rows 1 and 2) under the Sales account, one can readily determine that $30,000 of the sales were for cash and $60,000 were for credit.

Cost-Volume-Profit Model

Costs react on the basis of activity. We can categorize costs into three basic behavior patterns, which are:

1. *Variable cost behavior.* These costs react in direct proportion to changes in activity.
2. *Fixed cost behavior.* These costs remain the same within a specified range of activity.
3. *Semivariable cost behavior.* These costs vary with the level of activity, but not in a strict proportional way. For example, two shifts might be required to produce X units. However, to produce $X + 1$ units would require another entire shift.

In knowing cost behavior, we can simulate those profits which might be obtained with changes in volume (activity). This simulated activity can be illustrated in a cost-volume-profit (CVP) graph, as shown in Figure A.2. In this graph, for simplicity, we delineate only two categories of cost—variable and fixed.

Debits \ Credits	01 CASH	02 AR	03 INV	04 PR	05 PE	06 AD	07 AP	08 CS	09 RE	10 S	11 COGS	12 WAGE	13 DEP	14 RENT	15 OTH	16 DIV	17 BEG DR	18 Σ DR	19 END DR
01 Cash		10000						400000									440000		266000
02 Accounts receivable																	60000		50000
03 Inventory							150000										60000		150000
04 Prepaid rent	12000																12000		12000
05 Plant and equipment																	150000		150000
06 Accumulated depreciation							25000										100000		100000
07 Accounts payable	65000																65000		0
08 Capital stock																			
09 Retained earnings									60000										
10 Sales									30000										
11 Cost of goods sold																			
12 Wages expense	22000																22000		22000
13 Depreciation expense																			
14 Rent expense																			
15 Other expense							8000										8000		8000
16 Dividends																			
17 Beginning credit balance																			
18 Σ Credit totals this period	174000	10000					183000	400000		90000									
19 Ending credit balances	0	0					118000	400000		90000									

FIG. A.1 An accounting matrix.

572

Figure A.2 shows the relationship between cost and profit at various volume levels. The measure of volume is the number of units produced and sold. At lower volumes, a loss is expected; at higher volumes, a profit is expected; somewhere in between a breakeven point exists where total cost equals revenue.

The cost-volume-profit relationship provides a useful way for simulating the profit factors of any organization. The factors which increase profit are:

1. Increased selling price per unit.
2. Decreased variable cost per unit.
3. Increased volume.
4. For a multiproduct company, a change in its product mix.

A typical question from management may be: What would the profit picture look like if we decreased selling price by 5 percent, variable cost remained constant, decreased nonvariable cost by 8 percent, and increased volume of sales by 20 percent? A variety of questions such as this, proposed by management, could generate information which could effectively enhance planning and decision making.

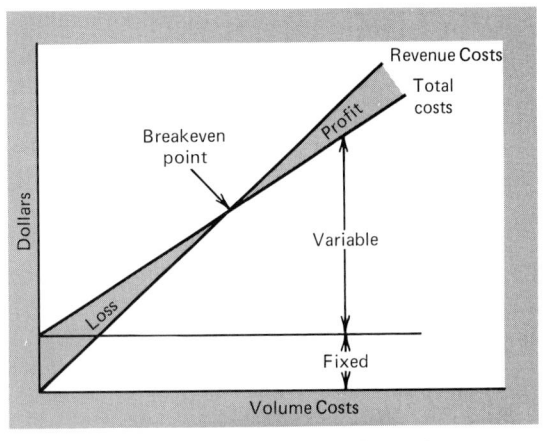

FIG. A.2 The cost-volume-profit relationship.

Budget and Performance Analysis Models

A budget is a plan of action, expressed in quantitative terms, which covers some specific time period. The key concept of a budget is to structure it in terms that equate to the responsibility of those who are charged with its execution. In this way the budget is used not only as a planning device but also as a control device. Budgets are of three types[2]:

[2]Anthony and Reece, *op. cit.*, p. 721.

1. An operating budget showing planned operations for the forthcoming period.
2. A cash budget showing the anticipated sources and uses of cash.
3. A capital budget showing planned changes in a variety of fixed assets.

The budgeting process involves a planning-control-planning life cycle, which is described as follows:

1. Planning which entails selecting objectives and means for their obtainment.
2. Controlling encompasses two activities:
    (a) Translate objectives into units of output and determine specific inputs to
    (b) Comparison of actual operations with budgeted operations.
3. Planning at this stage uses performance reports for evaluating past operations for planning future operations.

Budgets can also be viewed as being prepared for different levels in an organization.

Typically, budgets may relate to four levels: (1) entire organization (master budget), (2) division, (3) department, and (4) subunit. For example, a typical performance report at one level is structured as follows:

	Budgeted	Actual	Variance[a]
Material	XX	XX	XU
Labor	XX	XX	XF
Other	XX	XX	XU

[a] U: Unfavorable; F: Favorable.

Budget is a macro concept whereas standards are a micro concept. For example, the standard cost per labor hour may be $5. The budget for 20,000 hours would show a total labor cost of $100,000. The standard itself is a predetermined estimate of what performance should be under stated conditions. In preparing performance information based on standards, we can use three models:

Quantity Variance = (Actual Quantity
        − Standard Quantity)
        × Standard Cost Per Unit
Cost Variance = (Actual Cost − Standard
       Cost) × Actual Quantity
Total Variance = Quantity Variance + Cost
       Variance

Payoff Graph Analysis Model

The payoff graph is another tool that can be used effectively by the analyst to enhance the information received by management. Payoff analysis is a simple, straightforward technique which can be used by analysts to compare costs and savings of alternative systems. For example, examine the set of figures given in the table below.

These figures represent the costs of both systems and the resulting savings (or dissavings) when compared to each other. Figure A.3 depicts a payoff analysis graph that, in a meaningful manner, makes this comparison.

The present system's costs are represented by the cross-hatched areas. Savings are calculated by subtracting the proposed system's costs from the present system's costs. The savings are:

YEAR 1: 450,000 − 700,000 = −250,000
YEAR 2: 500,000 − 510,000 = −10,000
YEAR 3: 570,000 − 480,000 = 90,000
YEAR 4: 720,000 − 410,000 = 310,000
YEAR 5: 810,000 − 410,000 = 400,000

The plotted points in the graph indicate the accumulated net annual savings. These points are calculated as follows:

Point 1:   0 + (−250,000) = −250,000
Point 2: (−250,000) + (−10,000) = −260,000
Point 3: (−260,000) + 90,000 = −170,000
Point 4: (−170,000) + 310,000 = 140,000
Point 5: 140,000 + 400,000 = 540,000

Although this is a useful model in making gross estimates, it ignores the time value of money and a desired rate of return on investments. For these considerations we now

	Year 1	Year 2	Year 3	Year 4	Year 5
Costs: Semi-automatic (present system)	$450,000	$500,000	$570,000	$720,000	$810,000
Automatic (proposed system)	$700,000	$510,000	$480,000	$410,000	$410,000
Savings:	($250,000)	($ 10,000)	$ 90,000	$310,000	$400,000

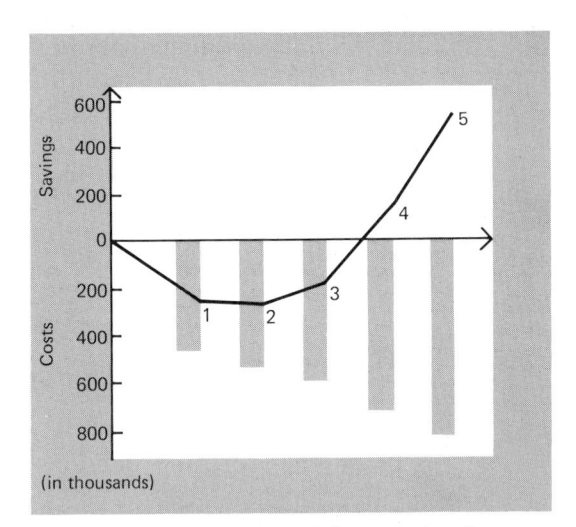

FIG. A.3 Payoff analysis graph comparing the proposed system to the present system.

turn to the model presented in the next section.

Net Present Value Model

The net present value model can be used to help management make decisions about investment proposals if such a proposal can be reduced to monetary amounts. Stated simply, neglecting nonmonetary considerations, an investment proposal is accepted if the present value of its earnings or cost savings equals or exceeds the amount of the investment required at some desired rate of return.

For example, suppose that management is thinking of purchasing a computer system for $200,000. The useful life of the computer is five years. The cost savings for the first year is $30,000, for the next three years $100,000, and for the last year $80,000. The minimum desired rate of return is 30%. Neglecting other quantitative or qualitative considerations, should management purchase the computer?

In the example below, the net present value of $-5716 means the investment has not earned what it should at a minimum desired rate of return of 30%. Therefore, the investment is undesirable. If the present value were positive or zero, the investment would be desirable because its return either exceeds or meets the desired minimum.

	Present Value of $1 Discounted at 30%	Present Value
Annual Cost Savings:		
$36,000 ×	.769	$ 27,684
100,000 ×	.592	59,200
100,000 ×	.455	45,500
100,000 ×	.350	35,000
80,000 ×	.269	26,900
Present Value of Future Cost Savings		$ 194,284
Initial Investment	1.000	− 200,000
Net Present Value		$− 5,716

Cost Savings Streams

0	1	2	3	4	5
$200,000	$30,000	$100,000	$100,000	$100,000	$80,000

ADDITIONAL MODELS

In addition to some of the basic, traditional accounting models presented above other models also help management in planning, controlling, and decision making. In many organizations, these functions are performed on an intuitive basis. That is, minimal effort is made to define and measure variables affecting the organization. Logico-mathematical models help to systematize and quantify certain variables in a manner where management can make more knowledgeable decisions. In this section, we discuss some of these models.[3]

Probability Concepts

The following concepts of probability and random variables represent the basic knowledge that a systems analyst must have in formulating successful models.

Probability of an Event. The probability that an event E will occur is the ratio between the number, n, of cases in which E occurs and the total number, N, of the elementary cases, all equally likely,

$$P(E) = \frac{n}{N}$$

where the assumption of equally likely outcomes describes such processes as tossing coins, rolling a die, and so on.

Random Variable. A random variable, X, assumes the values

$$X_1, X_2, \ldots, X_n$$

---

[3]For an in-depth treatment of a variety of models, refer to H. Bierman, C.P. Bonini, and W.H. Hausman, *Quantitative Analysis for Business Decisions*, Fourth Edition, Homewood, Ill.: Richard D. Irwin, Inc., 1973, and Howard Raiffa, *Decision Analysis*, Reading, Ma.: Addison-Wesley, 1968.

with each of these values having a probability of

$$P(X_1), P(X_2), \ldots, P(X_n)$$

where

$$\sum_{i=1}^{n} P(X_i) = 1$$

and the expected value of X is

$$E(X) = X_1 P(X_1) + X_2 P(X_2) + \ldots + X_n P(X_n)$$

For example, "what will sales revenue be for the next quarter?" is a typical question an analyst might ask. The estimator states a range of possibilities together with an estimate of the probability each will occur. The sum of the possibilities $(X_1, X_2, \ldots, X_n)$ multiplied by the applicable probability $(P(X_1), P(X_2), \ldots, P(X_n))$ equals the expected value $(E(X))$. The expected value of sales for the next quarter is computed as follows:

Sales (X_i)	Probability $P(X_i)$	Amount $X_i P(X_i)$
$100,000	.1	$ 10,000
120,000	.4	48,000
160,000	.3	48,000
200,000	.2	40,000
	Expected value	$146,000

Compound Probability. This is the probability that both A and B will occur and is written: $P(A, B)$. Compound events are shown in a tree diagram model below.

The probability of a compound event is determined by multiplying branch probabilities. The probability of compound event $A_1 C_2$ is:

$$P(A_1 C_2) = P(A_1) \times P(C_2) = (.3) \times (.2) = .06$$

Tree Diagram

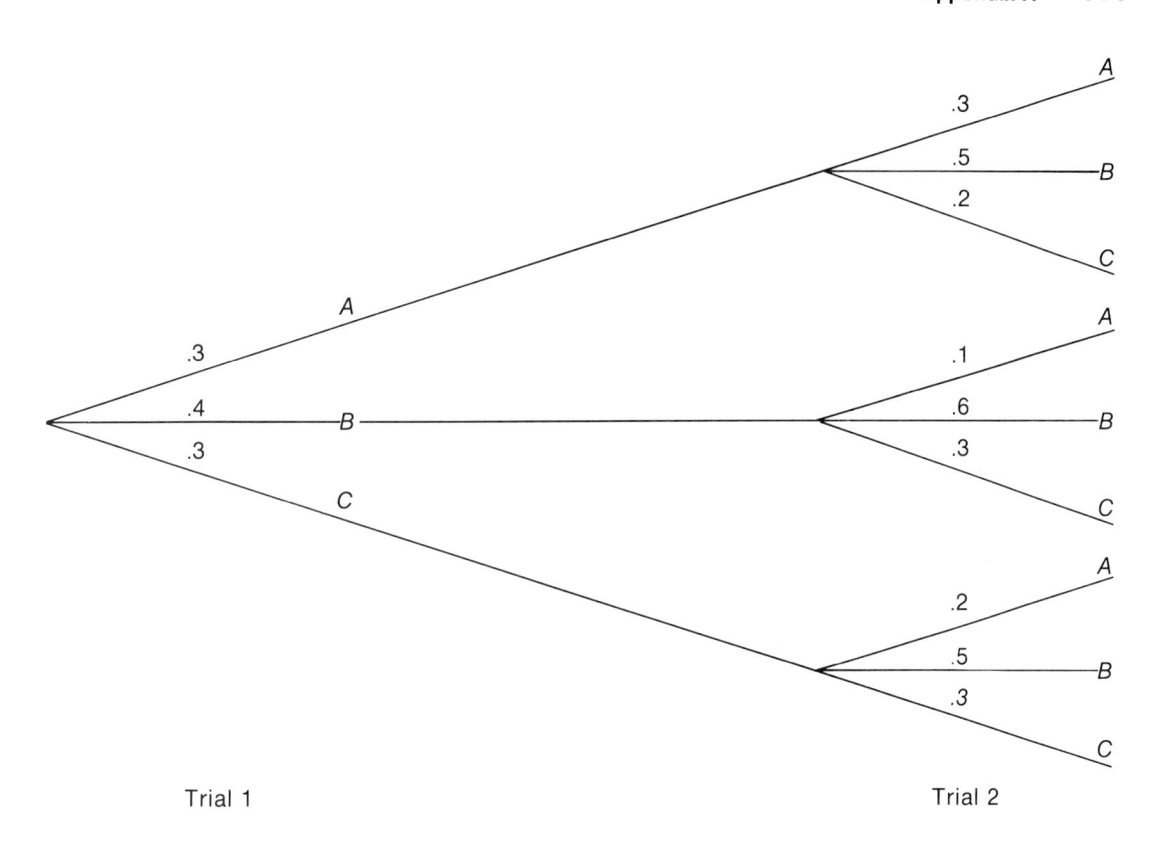

```
                    Trial 1                                Trial 2

                                                              .3      A
                                                         ────────────
                              A                          .5
                    .3    ────────                      ────────────  B
                         /                               .2
                    .4  /                               ────────────  C
              ─────────── B ──────────────────
                    .3  \                                .1      A
                         \                              ────────────
                          C                              .6
                                                        ────────────  B
                                                         .3
                                                        ────────────  C

                                                         .2      A
                                                        ────────────
                                                         .5
                                                        ────────────  B
                                                         .3
                                                        ────────────  C
```

Conditional Probability. The probability that an event A will occur, if it is known that event B has occurred is written $P(A/B)$. For our tree diagram, $P(A_2/B_1) = .1$.

Total Probability. This is the probability of mutually exclusive (nonoverlapping) events occurring. In our example the probability of A_1 or C_1 occurring, written as $P(A_1 + C_1)$ is .6.

Cumulative Probability. This is the process of accumulating the values of $P(X)$ which results in the cumulative probability function,

$$P(\chi) = P(X \leq \chi) = \sum_{\chi_1 \leq \chi} P(\chi_1)$$

Customer Demand χ	Probability of χ
3	.1
4	.2
5	.3
6	.2
7	.2
	1.0

P (number of units sold ≤ 5) = P (number of units sold = 5) + P (number of units sold = 4) + P (number of units sold = 3) = .3 + .2 + .1 = .6

Statistical Concepts

Statistical concepts represent additional methods of manipulating data to provide information. Some of these basic concepts are indicated here.

Histogram. This is a table showing the number of individual observations falling within each interval or class; this number is called the frequency. Before constructing a histogram, the following must be defined:

1. The limits of the group studied.
2. The data or characteristics measured for each individual.
3. The conditions under which the measurements were made.

Mean. Given a population consisting of N individuals, if f_1 is the frequency of the variate χ_1, then the mean, $\bar{\chi}$, is given by the formula:

$$\bar{\chi} = \frac{1}{N} \sum_{i=1}^{k} f_1 \chi_1$$

where k is the number of classes and

$$N = \sum_{i=1}^{k} f_1$$

Mean of the Means. If m measurements are taken in populations of the same nature:

$$\bar{\bar{\chi}} = \frac{n_1 \bar{\chi}_1 + n_2 \bar{\chi}_2 + \ldots + n_m \bar{\chi}_m}{N}$$

Mode. The mode is the value of χi for which fi is greatest (i.e., the most frequently occurring value).

Median. The median is the value of χi (or lying between two consecutive χi) for which

$$\text{cum } f = \frac{1}{2} N$$

Two Measures of Dispersion. The standard deviation, or mean square deviation:

$$\sigma \chi = \sqrt{\frac{1}{N} \sum_{i=1}^{k} f_1 (\chi_1 - \bar{\chi})^2} \quad \begin{array}{l} \sigma = \text{standard deviation} \\ \chi = \text{observations} \\ \bar{\chi} = \text{mean} \end{array}$$

and the variance is $(\sigma \chi)^2$.

Random Sample. A sample is considered to be random if it consists of observations that are independently drawn from an identically distributed population.

Network Model

PERT[4] (Program Evaluation and Review Technique) is an example of a network model used for planning and controlling projects with well-defined activities and events. PERT is based on a network composed of activities that take time to accomplish. Between the activities are instantaneous events, which designate the completion of each activity. Probably a better interpretation indicates that events represent a start or finish of the activities.

The activities are placed on a network and are represented by arrows. Generally, the arrows or activities flow from left to right. Four rules to follow when placing an activity on the network are:

1. A determination must be made to see if any activities logically precede the activity that is under consideration.

---

[4]For full treatment of PERT, refer to Russell D. Archibald and Richard L. Villoria, *Network-Based Management Systems (PERT/CPM)*, New York: John Wiley and Sons, Inc., 1967. Harry F. Evarts, *Introduction to PERT*, Boston: Allyn and Bacon, Inc., 1964.

2. A determination must be made to see if any activities are logically concurrent with the activity under consideration.
3. A determination must be made to spot activities which are logically subsequent to the activity under consideration.
4. Events must be clearly defined relative to their beginning and end.

Expected Time

The activity time should be estimated by someone knowledgeable about particular processes. The three time estimates furnished are:

1. *Most likely time.* How long do you expect it would take to complete this particular activity?
2. *Optimistic time.* What is the minimum possible time in which this particular task or activity can be completed?
3. *Pessimistic time.* What is the longest time this particular activity or task has ever taken?

The goal in getting three subjective estimates is to use them to calculate a single weighted average or mean time and variance. This average or mean time is called the expected time of the activity. Briefly, the three time estimates are related to the expected time and standard deviation by the following formulas:

$$t_e = \frac{O + 4M + P}{6}$$

$$\sigma_{t_e} = (P - O)/6$$

where O = optimistic time estimate
M = most likely time estimate
P = pessimistic time estimate
t_e = expected time (weighted average)
σ_{te} = standard deviation of t_e

The above formulas are based on the assumption that the time estimates approximate a beta distribution.

Critical events on the network are those which have zero slack time. Slack time equals the latest event time (T_L) less the earliest event time (T_E). The latest event time is the latest time that an event can occur without disrupting the project. Earliest event time is the earliest time that an event can occur. A heavy line connecting the critical events represents the critical path for a network. An increase in time along this path will extend the completion date by the same amount. A decrease in time along this path will shorten the time to completion by the same amount or change the critical path.

The network for a batch-project of okra/tomatoes/corn is shown in Figure A.4. The activities and time estimates are listed in Table A.1.

Frequently, estimates are required concerning the probability of completing an activity on the critical path by a certain date. Based on the assumption that possible completion times for an activity are approximately normally distributed, PERT has the capability to provide such estimates. The probability of completing an activity is determined by the number of standard normal units between the completion deadline and the earliest time the activity can be completed. The formula is as follows:

$$Z = \frac{T_D - T_E}{\sqrt{\Sigma \sigma_{t_e}^2}}$$

where Z = number of standard normal units between T_D and T_E
T_D = completion deadline
T_E = earliest completion time
$\sqrt{\Sigma \sigma_{t_e}^2}$ = the square root of the sum of the variances of the pertinent activities on the critical path.

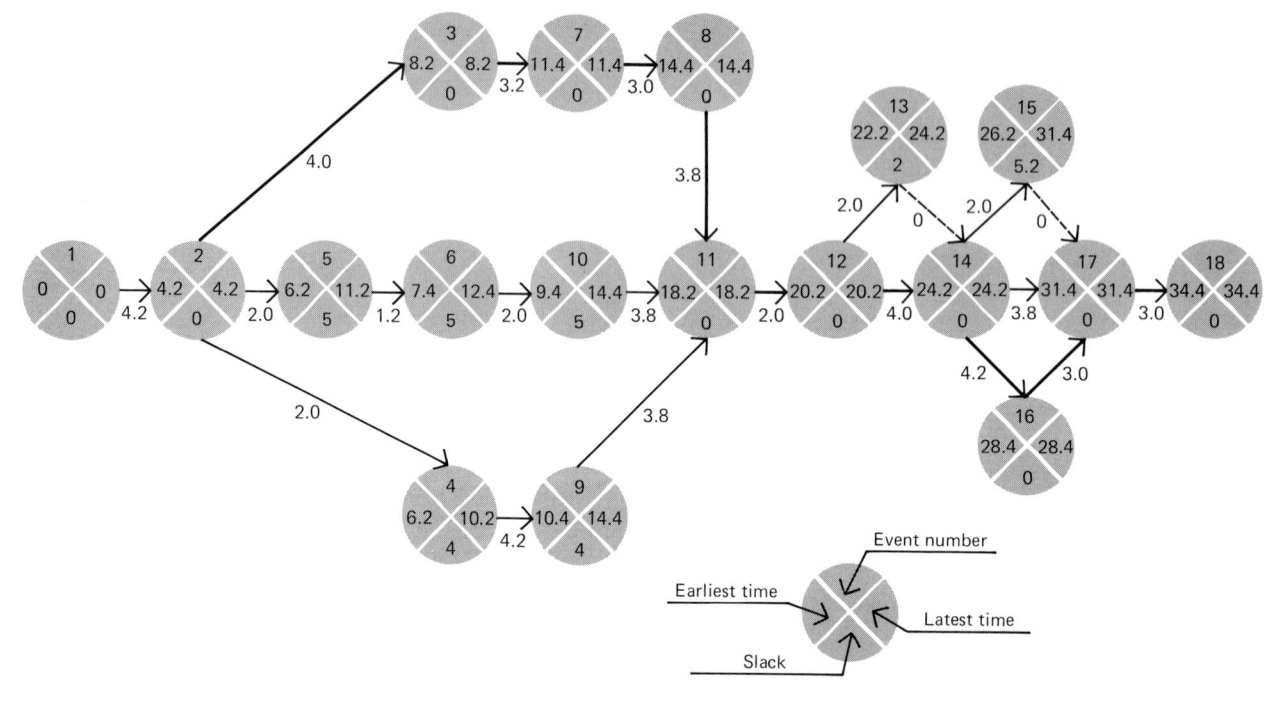

FIG. A.4 Network showing earliest and latest time and slack. The heavy line represents the critical path.

Once Z has been calculated, reference is then made to a standard normal table. The probability that time to completion will exceed the deadline date is equal to the area under the normal curve to the right of the Z value.

For example, we may ask the question, "Can activity 3,7 (cutting okra) be completed by day 13?" The variances associated with the pertinent critical path activities are as follows:

Activity	σ_{t_e}	$\sigma^2_{t_e}$
1,2	.83	.69
2,3	.67	.44
3,7	.50	.25
	Total	1.38

Substituting into our formula for Z,

$$Z = \frac{13 - 11.4}{\sqrt{1.38}}$$

$$= 1.36$$

The area under the normal curve to the right of 1.36 is .0869. Therefore, we can say that the probability of completing activity 3,7 later than day 13 is less than 8.69 percent. Stated another way, the probability that activity 3,7 will be finished by day 13 is 91.31 percent.

Decision Model

The elements of a simple decision model consist of actions, outcomes, probabilities of out-

Activity	Description	Optimistic	Most Likely	Pessimistic	t_e
1,2	Unloading/testing raw produce	2	4	7	4.2
2,3	Washing okra	2	4	6	4.0
2,4	Washing/stemming tomatoes	1	2	3	2.0
2,5	Loading can racks	1	2	3	2.0
3,7	Cutting okra	2	3	5	3.2
4,9	Blanching tomatoes	3	4	6	4.2
5,6	Mixing device changeover	1	1	2	1.2
6,10	Preparation of corn for mixing	1	2	3	2.0
7,8	Preparation of okra for mixing	2	3	4	3.0
8,11	Loading of okra	2	4	5	3.8
9,11	Loading of tomatoes	2	4	5	3.8
10,11	Loading of corn	2	4	5	3.8
11,12	Canning process	1	2	3	2.0
12,13	Quality control-testing	1	2	3	2.0
12,14	Pressure cooker process	2	4	6	4.0
13,14	Dummy	0	0	0	0
14,15	Quality control-testing	1	2	3	2.0
14,16	Cool bath process	3	4	6	4.2
14,17	Warehouse preparation	2	4	5	3.8
15,17	Dummy	0	0	0	0
16,17	Stacking in warehouse	2	3	4	3.0
17,18	Cleanup and retooling	2	3	4	3.0

TABLE A.1 Activities and time estimates for the okra/tomatoes/corn project.

comes, and utilities. Let us define the following:

A = set of alternative resource commitments, or actions ($a \in A$),

O = set of future states or outcomes ($o \in O$),

$p(o)$ = set of probabilities that describe the outcome occurrence,

$U(o, a)$ = utility of an outcome occurring given the selection of an action. If an expected utility approach is taken, then the alternative with the highest expected utility would be selected.

$E(U/a^*)$ = MAX Σ ($U(o, a) \cdot p(o)$)
$\qquad\qquad a \in A\ o \in O$

An example may make this clearer. Suppose you are a raw material inspector for the Swill Wine Co. Your job is to either accept (a_1) or reject (a_2) incoming shipments of grapes. The shipments can either meet standards (o_1) or be substandard (o_2). From past experience you know that the probability of a substandard shipment is .2. Conversely, you know that the probability a shipment will meet standards is .8. Now suppose further that the following utility matrix, in terms of dollars, is applicable:

	Outcomes	
Actions	o_1	o_2
a_1	2	−4
a_2	0	1

Then the expected dollar utility for the alternative resource commitments is as follows:

$E(U/a_1) = U(o_1,a_1) \cdot p(o_1) + U(o_2,a_1) \cdot p(o_2)$
$= \$2 \cdot .8 + (\$-4) \cdot .2$
$= \$1.60 - .80$
$= \$.80$
$E(U/a_2) = U(o_1,a_2) \cdot p(o_1) + U(o_2,a_2) \cdot p(o_2)$
$= \$0 \cdot .8 + \$1 \cdot .2$
$= \$.20$

Maximizing over alternatives leads us to choose action a_1, accept the shipment.

Many different types of questions can be answered within this decision framework. One of the most interesting is, "What would be the most you would pay for correct information about the contents of a shipment?" Let us answer this question by again referring to our example.

Suppose your "perfect" information source was a trained German Shepherd dog, who by sniffing the crate could tell with certainty whether or not the grapes were substandard. Your expected utility function would now be,

$E(U) = U(o_1,a_1) \cdot p(o_1) + U(o_2,a_2) \cdot p(o_2)$
$= \$2 \cdot .8 + \$1 \cdot .2$
$= \$1.60 + .20$
$= \$1.80$

Notice that the probabilities of the outcomes have not changed. What has changed is that you are no longer making incorrect decisions. You should be willing to pay up to $1.00 ($1.80 − .80) per crate sniffed for this canine's services.

Contribution-by-Value Analysis Model

A very simple, but quite effective, logical model that can be used in almost any kind of performance analysis is termed contribution-by-value analysis (also called ABC analysis). This analysis is based on Pareto's Law, which states that in most situations a relatively small percentage of certain objects contributes a relatively high percentage of output.[5] For instance, it can be shown that in most areas approximately 15–30 percent of the population contributes 70–90 percent of the tax revenue. Or, for example, that 20 percent of the employees in an office do 80 percent of the work. Many systems analysts find that when inventory items are plotted on a cumulative percentage graph, in order of descending value, Pareto's relationship usually exists. Relative to such a phenomenon, one frequently hears a rule of thumb quoted as: 20 percent of the items in inventory account for 80 percent of the sales. Such an analysis is quite effective in that it reveals very clearly the performance of any situation analyzed. For inventory analysis, the contribution-by-value analysis can be applied to sales by customer, by salesperson, by product item, by territory, by warehouse, and so on.

An example of contribution-by-value analysis relative to sales by warehouses is discussed and illustrated in Figure A.5.

To prepare the analysis, the following steps are taken.

1. Dollar annual sales are calculated for each warehouse by multiplying sales price times quantity sold for each product and computing a grand total for all products in each warehouse.

2. All warehouses are arranged by dollar annual sales in descending sequence.

3. A list is printed from these ranked warehouses. Included in this report is such information as warehouse number, warehouse count, percentage of total, annual

---

[5]C. Jay Slaybaugh, "Pareto's Law and Modern Management," *Management Services*, March–April, 1967.

Warehouse Number	Warehouse Count	Number of Warehouses Percentage of Total	Annual Sales	Cumulative Sales	Cumulative Percentage of Total Contribution
1	1	2.00	4,331,927.34	4,331,927.34	56.00
2	2	4.00	1,331,521.32	5,663,448.66	73.20
41	3	6.00	271,765.00	5,935,213.66	76.70
3	4	8.00	189,880.05	6,125,093.71	79.10
50	5	10.00	157,450.05	6,282,543.76	81.20
94	6	12.00	145,175.00	6,427,718.76	83.10
45	7	14.00	123,044.65	6,550,762.41	84.60
14	8	16.00	98,355.30	6,649,117.71	85.90
48	9	18.00	94,579.75	6,743,697.46	87.10
43	10	20.00	86,769.56	6,830,467.02	88.30
42	11	22.00	75,180.12	6,905,647.14	89.20
25	12	24.00	68,287.65	6,973,934.79	90.10
67	13	26.00	66,245.20	7,040,179.99	91.00
26	14	28.00	60,040.40	7,100,220.39	91.80
64	15	30.00	58,352.45	7,158,572.84	92.50
38	16	32.00	42,587.50	7,201,160.34	93.10
39	17	34.00	36,915.80	7,238,076.14	93.50
15	18	36.00	35,601.80	7,273,677.94	94.00
29	19	38.00	32,322.60	7,306,000.54	94.40
36	20	40.00	29,919.65	7,335,920.19	94.80
4	21	42.00	29,322.25	7,365,242.44	95.20
24	22	44.00	29,184.10	7,394,426.54	95.60
19	23	46.00	28,548.05	7,422,974.59	95.90
57	24	48.00	27,129.90	7,450,104.49	96.30
95	25	50.00	24,260.13	7,474,364.62	96.60
62	26	52.00	23,379.75	7,497,744.37	96.90
47	27	54.00	23,088.10	7,520,832.47	97.20
16	28	56.00	22,110.39	7,542,942.86	97.50
17	29	58.00	19,293.90	7,562,236.76	97.70
66	30	60.00	18,705.50	7,580,942.26	98.00
71	31	62.00	17,925.20	7,598,867.46	98.20
46	32	64.00	15,764.25	7,614,631.71	98.40
58	33	66.00	14,306.00	7,628,937.71	98.60
18	34	68.00	13,304.20	7,642,241.91	98.80
35	35	70.00	12,741.70	7,654,983.61	98.90
28	36	72.00	11,347.80	7,666,331.41	99.10
65	37	74.00	10,164.25	7,676,495.66	99.20
34	38	76.00	10,087.15	7,686,582.81	99.30
61	39	78.00	9,422.20	7,696,005.01	99.50
27	40	80.00	6,463.10	7,702,468.11	99.50
91	41	82.00	6,196.60	7,708,664.61	99.60
54	42	84.00	5,592.55	7,714,257.16	99.70
55	43	86.00	4,507.80	7,718,764.96	99.70
5	44	88.00	4,049.70	7,722,814.66	99.80
70	45	90.00	3,356.00	7,726,170.96	99.80
37	46	92.00	3,262.10	7,729,433.06	99.90
60	47	94.00	2,402.35	7,731,835.41	99.90
49	48	96.00	1,694.50	7,733,529.91	99.90
23	49	98.00	558.35	7,734,088.26	99.90
68	50	100.00	252.50	7,734,340.76	100.00

FIG. A.5 Contribution-by-warehouse sales report.

sales of each warehouse, cumulative sales, and percentage of total contribution. The relevant points of this report are:
a. The top 10 percent of the warehouses account for 81.20 percent of the dollar sales. In other words, a mere 5 out of 50 warehouses account for over four-fifths of the sales of the entire business or close to $6.28 million annually.
b. The upper 20 percent of the warehouses account for 88.30 percent of the sales. An additional 10 percent increase in the number of warehouses increased sales by 5.20 percent.
c. The upper 50 percent of the warehouses account for 96.60 percent of the sales.
d. The upper 74 percent of the warehouses account for 99.20 percent of the sales. Conversely, the lower 26 percent of the warehouses account for only .80 percent of the sales.

The information from the report is plotted to assist management in visualizing the relationships between number of warehouses and their relative contribution to sales volume. A plot of the results of this analysis, with the percentage of cumulative annual sales on the vertical axis, and the percentage of warehouses on the horizontal axis, appears in Figure A.6.

The contribution-by-value analysis shows that the company is operating several warehouses which are probably not necessary for efficient and streamlined operations. As surprising as the above relationships are on first exposure, however, they will probably be found in many organizations. It should also be noted that the discernment of such relationships provides management with valuable information even though the contribution-by-value analysis model is, itself, simplistic.

Forecast Models

Good forecasts are vital to the success of every organization. The sales forecast, for example, is a basic source of information for production, inventory, procurement, and employment plans. Even though inherent errors exist in any forecasting model, an organization that bases its operations on intuitive decision making is ignoring the possibilities for a more efficient operation.

The Least-Squares Model

As an extrapolative forecast model, the least-squares technique uses historical data exclusively. When a model of this type is used, two basic assumptions must be made: that the recent level of activity will continue and that the recent rate of change will remain about the same. The least-squares line approximating the set of points $(X_1, Y_1), (X_2, Y_2), \ldots, (X_n, Y_n)$ has the equation

$$Y = a_0 + a_1 X$$

where the constants a_0 and a_1 can be found from the formulas

$$a_0 = \frac{(\Sigma X^2)(\Sigma Y) - (\Sigma XY)(\Sigma X)}{N \Sigma X^2 - (\Sigma X)^2}$$

$$a_1 = \frac{N \Sigma XY - (\Sigma Y)(\Sigma X)}{N \Sigma X^2 - (\Sigma X)^2}$$

Here, X is the independent variable and Y is the dependent variable. The least-squares line passes through the point $(\overline{X}, \overline{Y})$, called the centroid or center of gravity of the data.

Suppose the value of X represents time, such as months, and the value of Y represents quantities of products sold each

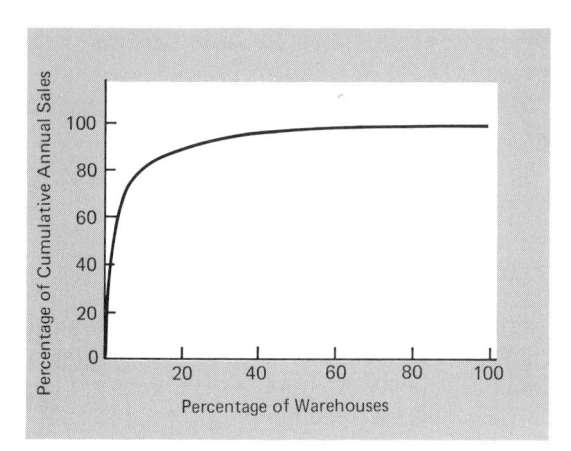

FIG. A.6 Graphic representation of the contribution-by-warehouse sales report.

month. The value of Y can be extrapolated according to some value of X. In other words, if the independent variable X is time, then the data show the values of Y at various times in the future.

Since Y is estimated from X, $\hat{Y}$ represents the value of Y for given values of X as estimated from the least-squares regression line of

$$\hat{Y} = a_0 + a_1 X$$

From this, a measure of the scatter about the regression line of X on Y is supplied by the quantity

$$S_{Y,X} = \sqrt{\frac{(Y - \hat{Y})^2}{N}}$$

which is called the standard error of the estimate of Y on X.[6]

---

[6]The above discussion of the least-squares method represents a summarization of several comprehensive textbooks. For example, see Samuel B. Richmond, *Statistical Analysis*, New York: The Ronald Press Company, 1964, Chapters 2, 7, 18, and 19.

The Exponential Smoothing Model

Exponential smoothing is similar to a moving average; however, where applicable, exponential smoothing is normally chosen as a forecasting method for the following two reasons:

1. With the moving average all data in the series are weighted equally. In other words, recent data are given the same weight as older data.
2. Forecasting by the moving average method requires that a great deal of data be maintained.

Exponential smoothing is a form of weighted moving average. All that is needed to use the exponential smoothing model is a smoothing constant, the current forecast, and a new observation.

The computational procedure of exponential smoothing is shown by the following formula:

New Average = Old Average
        + α (New Demand − Old Average)

where α designates a smoothing constant between 0 and 1.

The new average represents the forecast of demand for the subsequent forecast interval. The old average is the new average of the preceding forecast interval, and the new demand is the actual demand for the present period. Said another way, the forecast is part old forecast and part forecast error. If the forecast had been completely accurate, then the new average would equal the old average.

By controlling the weight of the most recent data, α simultaneously determines the average age of the data included in the estimate of the average. The value chosen for the smoothing constant can be such that the estimate is very stable, or reacts very quickly. For example, α = 0.5 would give a greater weight to the new data than α = 0.1. Regardless of the value of α, the weighting of data follows what is called an exponential curve; therefore, the name exponential smoothing.

One of the crucial questions that arise when one uses exponential smoothing is the size of the smoothing constant that should be used. Conceptually, the answer is simple. Enough weight should be given to provide system stability, but it should be small enough so that real (not random) changes in the level of demand will be recognized.

Inventory Control Model

The problem of planning, scheduling, and controlling production in the face of uncertain market conditions, and of maintaining reasonable levels of inventories, is almost universal. In many organizations with a wide product line, the inventory clerks as well as management may not know with reasonable accuracy what the levels are, and an investigation into the inventory will often indicate a wide variation between the actual conditions, and what is thought to be the inventory. When an inventory item is overstocked, the error may not become evident for a long time, if at all. When an item is understocked and a stockout occurs, customer goodwill is reduced. Any organization with inventory problems, therefore, needs an inventory management system that accomplishes two things: (1) it makes certain that items are available when they are needed, and (2) it prevents an increase of inventory beyond proper limits. Inventory management assures that an adequate supply of inventory is maintained and requires an optimum balance between shortage and overstock. Too many shortages decrease the customer service level. Conversely, an overstock of items ties up working capital that can be used more profitably elsewhere.

Replenishment, Lead Time, and Safety Stock

The first of two approaches to replenishing inventory is shown in Figure A.7 and is termed a periodic system wherein an order is placed on a specific date. The disadvantage of this method is that stockouts are risked. The second approach, illustrated in Figure A.8, is termed reorder point system in that an order is placed when the inventory level of an item reaches a predetermined level L_{RE}.

The time T in the periodic method is always the same, whereas T in the reorder point method is unequal. Of the two methods, the second one is used more often. It consists of placing a constant order quantity when the inventory level reaches the reorder level. The reorder level is computed as follows:

Reorder Level =
  Lead Time × Forecast of Demand
          − Safety Stock

The lead time t_1 to t_2 is that time interval between placement of an order and receipt of that order. In Figure A.8, it was assumed that lead time was zero. Such an assumption is normally not realistic. Lead time would probably be similar to that shown in Figure A.9. The safety stock allows for a margin of error in estimating lead time or demand.

The Problem of How Much to Order

The best known model of how much to order is the classic EOQ (economic order quantity)

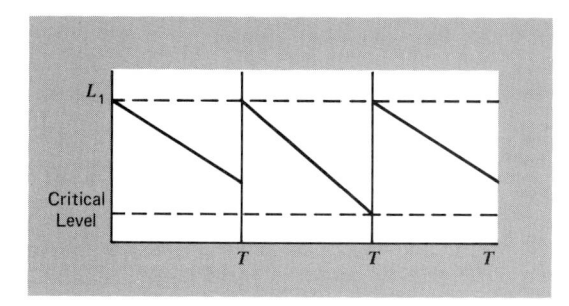

FIG. A.7 Periodic replenishment system.

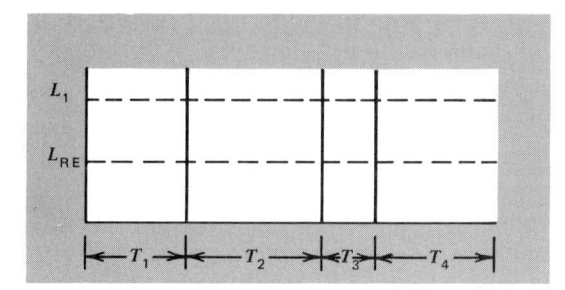

FIG. A.8 Reorder point replenishment system.

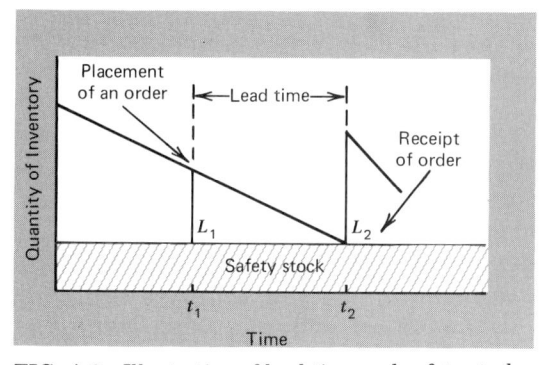

FIG. A.9 Illustration of lead time and safety stock.

model. This model reveals to the inventory clerk how much to buy (or order) when a reorder point is reached.

The order quantity chosen will incur certain costs. Two different sets of cost factors are considered. If a greater or lesser quantity is ordered, then some costs will increase, while others decrease. Among those costs that increase are interest, obsolescence, risk, and storage, while the set of decreasing costs includes such items as freight and procurement costs. These costs can be lumped into the categories of cost to carry and cost to purchase inventory. The goal is to balance the opposing costs, and thus, obtain a minimum total cost. For an illustration of annual costs versus number of orders, see Figure A.10. Two facts are illustrated:

1. As orders are placed more frequently, carrying costs decrease because the cycle stock (cycle stock is one-half the order quantity) is less.
2. As orders are placed more frequently, purchasing costs increase.

The total operating cost is the sum of purchasing and carrying costs, and Figure A.10 shows that it is lowest when these two are equal. Notice a relevant range of choices between A and B where the resultant total cost is not greatly affected by slight deviations from the best ordering frequency.

The literature normally handles the cost of purchasing as a constant amount for each order placed, and the cost of carrying is lumped into one percentage figure represented by P. Let Y designate the expected yearly demand in physical units (determined from the forecast model), let Q be the economic lot size in physical units, C be the unit cost, and S be the cost of making one purchase order. Then total annual variable costs (TVC) are expressed as follows[7]:

$$TVC = \frac{QC}{2}P + \frac{Y}{Q}S$$

---

[7]For example, see Thomson M. Whitin, *The Theory of Inventory Management*, Princeton, N.J.: Princeton University Press, 1957, pp. 32–34. Martin K. Starr and David W. Miller, *Inventory Control: Theory and Practice*, Englewood Cliffs, N.J.: Prentice-Hall, Inc., 1962.

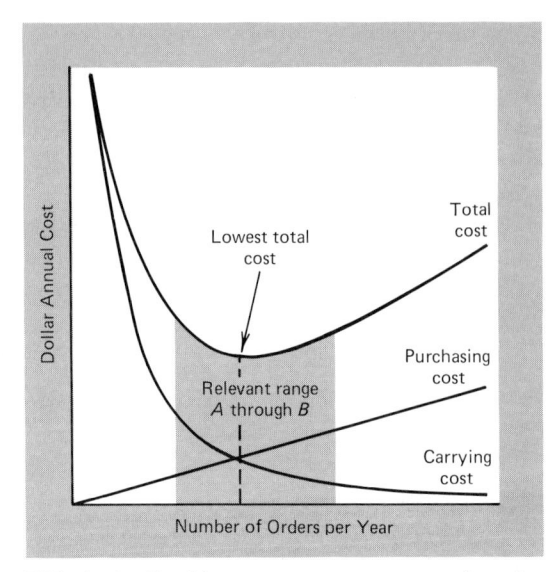

FIG. A.10 Total inventory costs versus number of orders.

In the absence of safety allowances, inventories vary from Q to zero. The average value of inventory is therefore $QC/2$ if the new order quantity replenishes stock at the time the inventory is depleted. The quantity $QC/2$ times P represents the annual carrying cost. Y/Q represents the number of times a year that orders are placed. Therefore, $(Y/Q)S$ represents the total annual purchasing costs.

To determine the amount of Q which minimizes total cost, the above equation is differentiated with respect to Q and set equal to zero. The following equation is obtained:

$$\frac{PC}{2} - \frac{YS}{Q^2} = 0$$

which, when solved for Q, equals:

$$Q = \sqrt{\frac{2YS}{PC}}$$

This formula states that Q, the economic order quantity, varies directly with the square root of the forecasted demand and the square root of the purchasing costs and varies inversely with the square root of the cost of carrying.

Material Yield Analysis Model

In a number of industries, particularly of the process type, material yield plays a significant role in effecting cost reduction and production improvement. Material yield standards are generally set for various types of raw material. In most cases the yield standards are based on laboratory tests or company records. A substantial cost reduction is achieved through the improvement of the yield of good products based on proper procurement and production efforts. A variance analysis program pointing out and evaluating causes of low yield aids management in minimizing shrinkage and waste in purchasing and production. If, for example, the procurement personnel purchase defective raw material, then an excess of shrinkage will occur during preparation of this material for processing. Consequently, a yield analysis and reporting system should be installed to determine the degree of shrinkage or waste.

Standards for material usage during the production phase are of paramount importance to top management. The plant manager and top management personnel need to have feedback which will enable them to detect and measure losses of raw produce during the production process. Not only do the reports of material yield disseminate information to responsible persons, but they ensure a significant degree of control of the processing function.

The basic question is whether the standard amount of raw material is used to obtain a given output of the finished product. The difficulty here is that computation of variances is delayed until the production process is completed. At the Yummy Company, however, production is set up so that a number of subbatches comprise an overall batch.

An example of yield information reporting is shown in Figure A.11.

The yield analysis report of Figure A.11 does not tell why the yield of this particular batch of pimiento is unfavorable. It does, however, give feedback to the plant manager, the manager of procurement, the president, and other responsible persons that particular phases in the processing function may be faulty. A retracing of the overall process must be set into motion to isolate the cause of the unfavorable variances and take necessary corrective action.

Quality Control Analysis and Reporting

Every organization, large or small, faces the problem of attaining and maintaining satisfactory quality of their output. First, the quality attributes must be identified. Next, accurate standard measurements must be set. Finally, the allowable departures from such standard measurements must be determined. Moreover, satisfactory quality must be obtained at a reasonable and competitive cost level.

Product quality variation arises out of the variables which constitute a given process. The following are basic:

1. The raw materials which enter a process themselves vary in form and composition.
2. The production process itself varies and the resulting output may be below satisfactory quality.

The obvious objectives, therefore, are to reduce the amount of defective raw materials going into production and to eliminate defective finished products. These objectives are never fully possible, but a reduction in the number of defectives in the total operation must be sought.

Statistical sampling and control tables can be used effectively in implementing

---

Material Yield Report—Sliced Pimiento

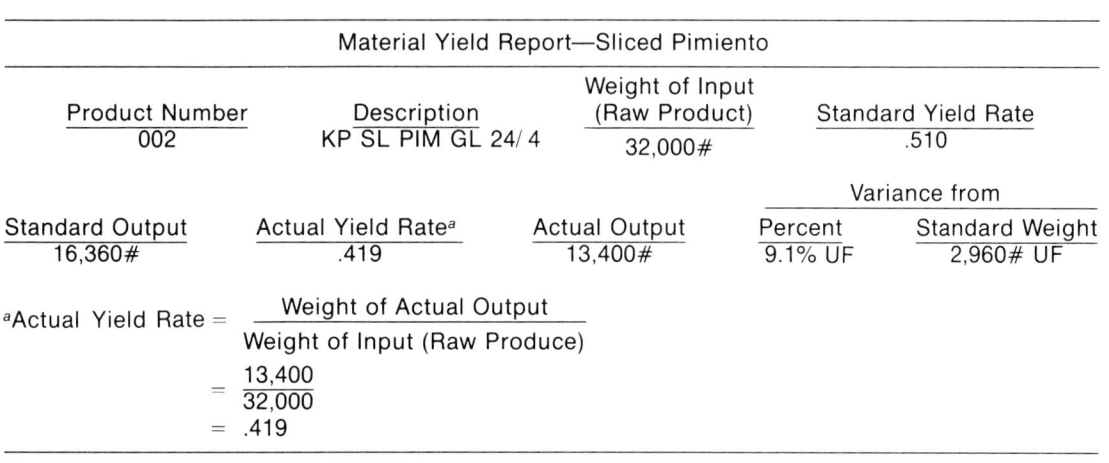

Product Number	Description	Weight of Input (Raw Product)	Standard Yield Rate
002	KP SL PIM GL 24/4	32,000#	.510

Standard Output	Actual Yield Rate[a]	Actual Output	Variance from Percent	Variance from Standard Weight
16,360#	.419	13,400#	9.1% UF	2,960# UF

$$^a\text{Actual Yield Rate} = \frac{\text{Weight of Actual Output}}{\text{Weight of Input (Raw Produce)}}$$
$$= \frac{13,400}{32,000}$$
$$= .419$$

FIG. A.11 Yield analysis report.

quality control in organizations. A simple table for this purpose is shown in Figure A.12.

The table indicates that if 5 or more defectives are in the first sample of 25 from some population (batch or lot), then that population being tested is rejected. If more than 0 and less than 5 defectives are found, then another sample of 25 is taken. If in this next sample the cumulative total of defectives is 3 or less, then the population is accepted. If the number of defectives is greater than 3 but less than 8, then another sample is taken. If the cumulative total of defectives at the second sample is 8 or more, then the population is rejected, and so on.

Basic Queuing Models

Many types of problems are described by the buildup of queues of some input to a service facility. The queues result from stochastic or probabilistic phenomena. In all cases inputs arrive at a facility for processing, and the time of arrival of individual inputs at the service facility is random as is the time of processing. The randomness of one or more parameters in a queue system is responsible for the uncertainties associated with it. In all organizations the queuing phenomena is ever present. In production, machines are idle or overburdened. Patients wait for hours in hospitals. Trucks wait in long lines at loading docks. At times inventories are excessive; at other times, too many stockouts occur. And so it goes. Management must strike a balance between costs of idleness and costs of overburdened service facilities. Consequently, management must know something about the activity and length of a queue, the demand on the service activity, the capacity of the service facility to handle the random demand, and the time spent waiting in the queue plus the time in the service facility.

Four basic structures of queuing situations describe the general conditions of a service facility. The simplest situation is where arriving units from a single queue are to be serviced by a single service facility;

Sequence of Samples Which Show Sample Size and Acceptance and Reject Numbers

Sample	Sample Size	Combined Sample Size	Acceptance Number (Cumulative)	Rejection Number (Cumulative)
First	25	25	0	5
Second	25	50	3	8
Third	25	75	6	11
Fourth	25	100	9	14
Fifth	25	125	12	17
Sixth	25	150	15	20
Seventh	25	175	18	23
Eighth	25	200	21	26
Ninth	25	225	24	29
Tenth	25	250	27	32

FIG. A.12 A table of acceptance and rejection numbers.

for example, a car in a car wash. This structure is called a single-channel, single-phase condition. A simple assembly line has a number of service facilities in series or tandem and represents the single-channel, multiple-phase condition. If the number of service facilities is increased (two or more car washes) but still draws on one queue, then this is represented by a multiple-channel, single-phase condition. Finally, the last structure is a multiple-channel, multiple-phase condition which might be illustrated by two or more parallel production lines.[8] These structures are illustrated in Figure A.13.

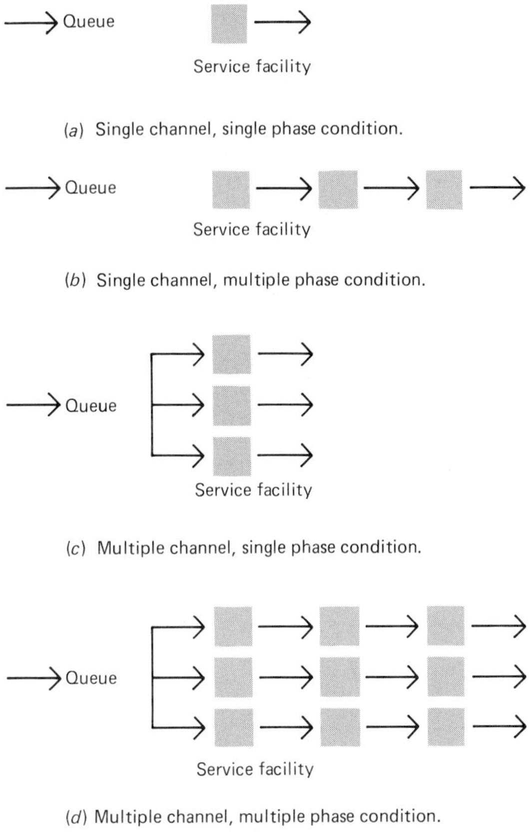

Simulation Models

In a probabilistic model some dimensions are known while the value of others is based on phenomena of a stochastic nature. The randomness of one or more parameters in a system is responsible for the uncertainties that exist. Random machine breakdowns, customer demand, labor strikes, and competitor price changes, all occur.

Simulation models help to organize disjointed data and activities, and to illustrate interrelationships previously unknown. The perception of combinational aspects of a complex problem and their effect on a system can, in many instances, be handled only by a model. For example, the problem of smog control is amenable to simulation techniques. A complete understanding of the problem involves the interrelationship of climate, the molecular behavior of gases, the chemistry of engine exhaust, the number of vehicles, the geographic layout of the city (including the location of the homes, work places, and highway arteries), the availabil-

(a) Single channel, single phase condition.

(b) Single channel, multiple phase condition.

(c) Multiple channel, single phase condition.

(d) Multiple channel, multiple phase condition.

FIG. A.13 Four basic structures of queuing conditions.

ity of alternate means of transportation, the speed of traffic and the timing of traffic lights, the incomes of the population, the chemistry and biology of the lungs and blood stream, and problems of microbes and virus growth under chemical, light, and temperature conditions produced by smog—among other problems.[9]

The above smog control problem can be attacked through the use of simulation. De-

[8]Elwood S. Buffa, *Operations Management,* Third Edition, New York: John Wiley and Sons, Inc., 1972, p. 465.

[9]Alfred Kuhn, *The Study of Society: A Unified Approach,* Homewood, Ill.: Richard D. Irwin, Inc., and The Dorsey Press, 1963, p. 4.

cision makers can see more clearly the aspects of the problem and how they interrelate. By so doing, the information produced by the model can aid the decision maker in choosing among a number of alternative courses of action.

Linear Programming Model

The purpose of linear programming is to provide a method of optimizing the allocation of scarce resources to competing demands.

Following is a list of kinds of problems which have been solved by linear programming methods. These are the kinds of problems that systems analysts encounter in most organizations; however, this list is not exhaustive and indicates only a few examples.

1. Allocation of energy sources in electrical power generation.
2. Determining optimal mix of food products for beef cattle production.
3. Adapting production to variable and seasonal sales.
4. Allocation of limited raw materials and production facilities to the production of a multiple product line.
5. Optimum multiple plant and warehouse location.

The viewpoint that the analyst should take is to concentrate on the definition of the problem and formulation of the model and leave the technical intricacies and solution of the model to the technical staff of the information system. The technical staff would include, among others, mathematicians, operations research specialists, and application programmers.

Two major assumptions are required in using linear programming techniques: linearity and certainty. Linearity means all the relationships involve variables of the first degree and can be illustrated graphically by straight lines. Certainty requires that the value of all variables must be known and that all variables are non-negative.[10]

An example of the general form which a linear programming problem may take on, follows:

maximize $p_1 x_1 + p_2 x_2 + \cdots + p_n x_n$

subject to
$$a_{11} x_1 + a_{12} x_2 + \cdots + a_{1n} x_n \leq b_1$$
$$a_{21} x_1 + a_{22} x_2 + \cdots + a_{2n} x_n \leq b_2$$
$$\vdots$$
$$a_{n1} x_1 + a_{n2} x_2 + \cdots + a_{nn} x_n \leq b_n$$

The p_i's in the objective function may refer to profit contributions of the given products $x_1, x_2, \ldots, x_n$. On the other hand, the a_{ij}'s may refer to the required amounts of manufacturing material for the given products, which are in limited supply according to $b_1, b_2, \ldots, b_n$. The linear programming problem would then be to maximize the profit contribution subject to the given limitations on manufacturing material.

Let us consider a simple graphical example of a linear programming problem, as follows:

maximize $3x_1 + 2x_2$

subject to
$$2x_1 + 3x_2 \leq 10$$
$$3x_1 + x_2 \leq 6$$
$$x_1 \geq 0$$
$$x_2 \geq 0$$

---

[10]For detailed analyses of linear programming models, refer to S.I. Gass, *Linear Programming,* Second Edition, New York: McGraw-Hill Book Company, 1964; G. Hadley, *Linear Algebra,* Reading, Mass.: Addison-Wesley Publishing Company, 1961; F.S. Hillier and G.J. Lieberman, *Introduction to Operations Research,* Second Edition, San Francisco: Holden-Day, 1974; and H.M. Wagner, *Principles of Operations Research,* Second Edition, Englewood Cliffs, NJ: Prentice-Hall, Inc., 1975.

Consider the $x_1 x_2$ coordinate system. Any point (x_1, x_2) can be plotted in this system. For example see Figure A.14. All points lying on or to the right of the x_2 axis satisfy the constraint that $x_1 \geq 0$. Similarly, all points lying on or above the x_1 axis satisfy the constraint $x_2 \geq 0$. Therefore a feasible solution to the problem must be contained in the first section (quadrant) of the coordinate system. Now let us consider the other two constraints. If we allow equality to hold, then we would have equations for straight lines and any point on these lines would satisfy the equations. Refer to Figure A.15. Observe also, that any point (x_1, x_2) in the first quadrant, which lies on or below one of the given lines, satisfies that inequality. For example, the point $(1, 2)$ substituted into the equation $2x_1 + 3x_2 = 10$ yields the value 7, which is less than 10. Therefore, the points satisfying all the constraints lie in the region bounded by $2x_1 + 3x_2 = 10$, $3x_1 + x_2 = 6$, and the x_1 and x_2 axes (the shaded areas).

We must now find the point in the region that maximizes the objective function, $3x_1 + 2x_2$. Allowing this function to take on different values produces straight lines which are parallel. We must then find the

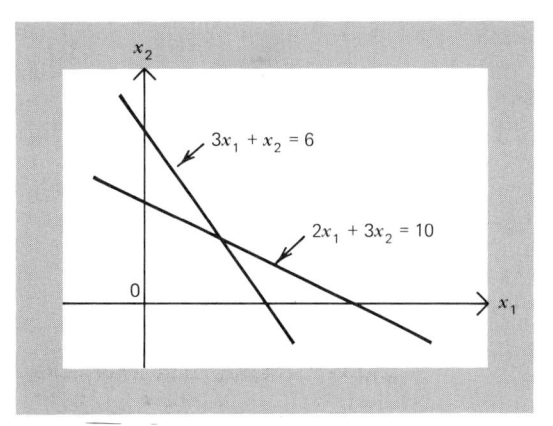

FIG. A.15 Graphical example of constraints in a linear programming problem.

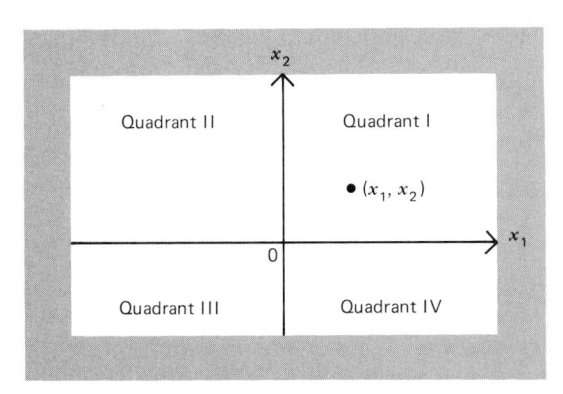

FIG. A.14 The x_1, x_2 coordinate system.

line that gives the objective function its greatest value and at the same time has at least one point in the constrained region. Let us give $3x_1 + 2x_2$ the value 6 and plot this line in the $x_1 x_2$ coordinate system. See Figure A.16. This line has many points within the constrained region, but it should be obvious parallel lines exist above this line that give the objective function a greater value and still have at least one point within the constrained region. In fact, the line that gives the objective function its greatest value and still contains at least one point within the given region, passes through the point of intersection of the two lines $2x_1 + 3x_2 = 10$, and $3x_1 + x_2 = 6$. Solving these two equations simultaneously, we find $x_1 = 8/7$ and $x_2 = 18/7$. It is these two values that, when substituted into the objective function, give it its maximum value of $= 60/7$.

For a "real world" application of the linear programming model, assume a company manufactures two products. P_1 and P_2, which are processed by three departments. The products can be processed in any order. Pertinent data are shown in the table above.

The number of minutes each department

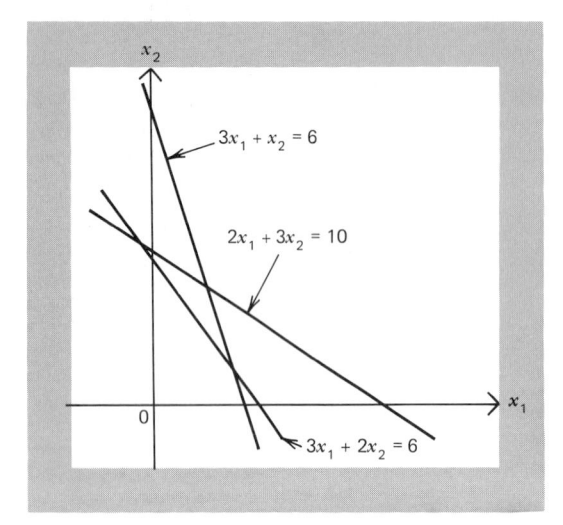

FIG. A.16 Graphical example of the objective function taking on one of many values.

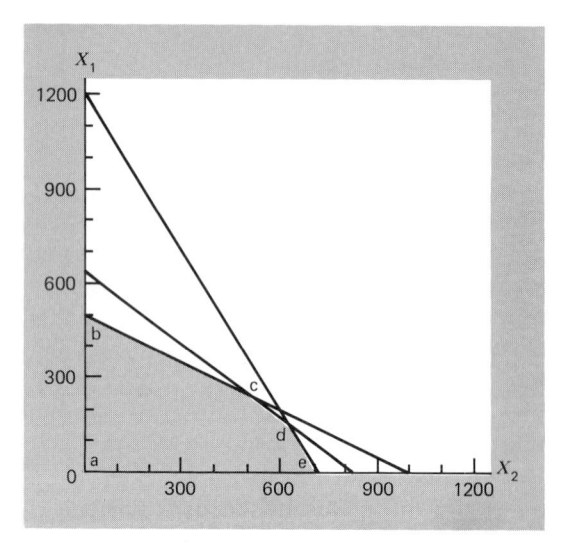

FIG. A.17 Graphical solution.

will be available for operation during the month are as follows:

12,600 minutes for D_1
14,400 minutes for D_2
13,000 minutes for D_3

The questions to answer is, how much of Product P_1 and Product P_2 should be produced to maximize the total contribution margin? The objective function, therefore is $Z = 8X_1 + 10X_2$, where X_1 is the number of units of product P_1, and X_2 is the number of units of P_2. Then: $Z = 8X_1 + 10X_2$ the function to be maximized with the conditions $X_1 \geq 0$, $X_2 \geq 0$.

The constraints are:

$20X_1 + 15X_2 \leq 12{,}600$ for department D_1
$12X_1 + 20X_2 \leq 14{,}400$ for department D_2
$26X_1 + 13X_2 \leq 13{,}000$ for department D_3

An infinite number of feasible solutions exist; among them is one or more for which Z is maximum. The graph in Figure A.17 illustrates a graphical solution of the above problem.

The area enclosed by abcde includes all feasible solutions to the production problem. The maximum solution can be found by computing the values at each corner of the polygon. These computations are made in the table below.

	D_1	D_2	D_3	Contribution Margin[a]
P_1	20 min.	12 min.	26 min.	8.00
P_2	15 min.	20 min.	13 min.	10.00

[a]Contribution Margin = Sales Price − Variable Cost.

The maximum Z is represented by a straight line for a particular value of Z equal to $7600. Since the coefficients $8 and $10 are invariant, this line will remain parallel to itself when the value of Z is changed. The maximum will always correspond to one of the extreme points of the constrained region that is furthest from the point of origin. Therefore, the further this line moves from the origin, the greater the value of Z, and vice versa.

Probably the most important single development in the solution of linear programming problems took place in the late 1940s when George Dantzig devised the Simplex Method. Consider for a moment the graphical example of a linear programming problem treated above. Note that a line drawn between any two points in the constrained area lies entirely within that area. This fact holds for any linear programming problem in which a feasible solution exists and this constrained region is said to be convex (bulges outward from the origin). Also note that an optimal point for the objective function will be at one of the corners of the convex region. The Simplex Method gives us a procedure for moving step by step from a given corner (extreme point) to an optimal corner (extreme point).[11]

[11] G. Hadley, *op. cit.*

	Corner	Product P_1	Product P_2	(Objective Function) Total Contribution Margin
a	0,0	0	0	$Z = \$8.00(0) + \$10.00(0) = \$0.00$
b	500,0	500	0	$Z = \$8.00(120) + \$10.00(0) = \$4000.00$
c	250,510	250	510	$Z = \$8.00(250) + \$10.00(510) = \$7000.00$
d	150,640	150	640	$Z = \$8.00(150) + \$10.00(640) = \$7600.00$[a]
e	0,720	0	720	$Z = \$8.00(0) + \$10.00(720) = \$7200.00$

[a] Optimum solution.

BIBLIOGRAPHY

Anthony and Reece, *Management Accounting,* Fifth Edition, Homewood, IL.: Richard D. Irwin, Inc., 1975.

Archibald and Villria, *Network-Based Management Systems (PERT/CPM),* New York: John Wiley & Sons, Inc., 1967.

Bierman, Bonini, and Hausman, *Quantitative Analysis for Business Decisions,* Fourth Edition, Homewood, IL.: Richard D. Irwin, Inc., 1973.

Brown, *Smoothing, Forecasting, and Production of Discrete Time Series,* Englewood Cliffs, NJ.: Prentice-Hall, Inc., 1963.

Buffa, *Operations Management,* Third Edition, New York: John Wiley & Sons, Inc., 1972.

Burch, "Computer Application of Contribution Analysis," *Journal of Systems Management,* August 1970.

Demski, *Information Analysis,* Reading, MA.: Addison-Wesley Publishing Co., 1972.

Dutton and Starbuck, *Computer Simulation of Human Behavior,* New York: John Wiley & Sons, Inc., 1971.

Evarts, *Introduction to PERT,* Boston: Allyn and Bacon, Inc., 1964.

Gass, *Linear Programming,* Second Edition, New York: McGraw-Hill Book Co., 1964.

Hadley, *Linear Algebra,* Reading, MA.: Addison-Wesley Publishing Co., 1961.

Hillier and Lieberman, *Introduction to Operations Research,* Second Edition, San Francisco: Holden-Day, 1974.

Horngren, *Cost Accounting: A Managerial Emphasis,* Fifth Edition, Englewood Cliffs, NJ.: Prentice-Hall, Inc., 1982.

Kuhn, *The Study of Society: A Unified Approach,* Homewood, IL.: Richard D. Irwin, Inc., and The Dorsey Press, 1963.

Maisel and Gnugnoli, *Simulation of Discrete Stochastic Systems,* Chicago: Science Research Associates, Inc., 1972.

Martin, *Computer Modeling and Simulation,* New York: John Wiley & Sons, Inc., 1968.

Raiffa, *Decision Analysis,* Reading, MA.: Addison-Wesley Publishing Co., 1968.

Richmond, *Statistical Analysis,* New York: The Ronald Press Company, 1964.

Slaybaugh, "Pareto's Law and Modern Management," *Management Services,* March–April 1967.

Starr and Miller, *Inventory Control: Theory and Practice,* Englewood Cliffs, NJ.: Prentice-Hall, Inc., 1962.

Wagner, *Principles of Operations Research,* Second Edition, Englewood Cliffs, NJ.: Prentice-Hall, Inc., 1975.

Whitin, *The Theory of Inventory Management,* Princeton, NJ.: Princeton University Press, 1957.

APPENDIX B

The Computer and Related Technology

INTRODUCTION

The computer and related technology can be divided into three major sections, which are: (1) the central processor, (2) devices peripheral to the central processor, and (3) data communication devices which connect peripheral devices to the central processor.

THE CENTRAL PROCESSOR

The heart of any computer configuration is the central processing unit, or CPU. First, we will analyze the central processor and then present a few techniques which help to increase its processing power.

Overview of the Central Processor

The central processor is really the "computer" in a computer configuration and all computer configurations perform the following five basic functions:

1. *Input.* The data to be operated upon and the instructions are made available to the central processing unit via input media.

2. *Primary storage.* From the input media, data and instructions are transferred to the main storage section of the central processor. Other storage media (e.g., magnetic tape, magnetic disk) are considered auxiliary to primary storage.

3. *Arithmetic-logic.* The processor manipulates the data in accordance with the set of instructions. These manipulations are performed in the arithmetic-logic section, one operation at a time, with intermediate results being placed back into primary storage. The arithmetic-logic section performs addition, subtraction, multiplication, division, and certain logical operations such as comparing the magnitude of two numbers.

4. *Control.* Control is required inside a computer system to: (1) tell the input media what data to enter into primary storage and when to enter the data; (2) tell the primary storage section where to place these data; (3) tell the arithmetic-logic section what operations to perform, where the data are to be found, and where to place the results; (4) tell what file devices to access and what data to

598 The Computer and Related Technology

access; and (5) tell what output media on which to write the final results.

5. *Output.* This function refers to the results of the data processed within the central processor. This final result is written on various output media.

A schematic of a computer system, emphasizing the central processor, is illustrated in Figure B.1. All digital computers, regardless of size, speed, and details of operation, follow this same basic logical structure.

Size of the Central Processor

When manufacturers state the size of their processor, they are referring to the size of the primary storage. Size of a processor's primary storage helps to determine the maximum size of programs and the amount of data available for processing at any one time. Each primary storage location has a unique address, analogous to a mailbox in a post office. The address identifies the location of the data for both storing and accessing operations. Although all data are represented as binary digits or bits, the smallest addressable location in main storage differs from one computer to another. Depending on the design of the computer, each addressable location is a character or the beginning of a computer word. These storage locations may be designated as follows:

1. *Byte-addressable combination.* The basic storage unit of some computers is called a byte. The byte is made up of eight bits and an additional parity bit. Although the byte itself is a fixed binary composition, it can be strung together in different ways to provide structures of varying length. The byte-addressable system is flexible in the sense that each

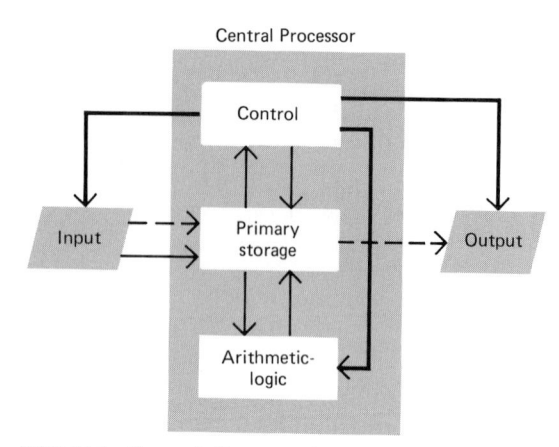

FIG. B.1 General diagram of a central processor. Broken line indicates data flow; solid line indicates instruction flow; and heavy line indicates control flow.

byte is addressable and can represent two numbers or one character. This means that a computer with 64K memory (where K, or kilo, means thousands) has approximately 64,000 bytes of addressable main storage.

2. *Character-addressable.* In a character-addressable system, it may require a six-bit set (not including control bits) to encode a character. If the number 47 is in storage, the 4 will take up one storage location having an address; the 7 is in another contiguous storage location with a separate address. An eight-bit byte would provide greater storage than a six-bit character because two decimal digits may be packed in a byte.

3. *Word-addressable.* A computer word consists of an ordered set of bits, which may be of fixed or variable length, depending on the particular computer. Commonly, computers which are designated as word-addressable, have fixed word sizes of 24, 30, 32, 36, 48, 54, and 64 bits.

Speed of the Processor

Other aspects to consider when evaluating primary storage are: access and cycle time. These aspects are discussed here.[1]

1. *Access time.* Access time refers to the time it takes for the control section to locate instructions and data for processing. It represents the time interval between initiating a transfer of data to or from storage and the instant when this transfer is completed. This time interval varies from one computer to another. In most primary storage devices, access time is measured in microseconds (one-millionth of a second); however, in some large-scale computers access time is measured in nanoseconds (one-billionth of a second).

2. *Cycle time.* A computer performs its operations on a cycle basis. The computer operates on pulses per length of time like a clock. At any one time, the computer is either in the instruction cycle or the execution cycle. An instruction is obtained from a main memory location and transferred to the arithmetic-logic unit. Here it is decoded according to its operation code, specifying what is to be done, and its operand, specifying the address of the data to be operated upon. The computer then moves into the execution cycle. Here the decoded instruction is executed using the data specified by the instruction. When the execution cycle is complete, the computer automatically goes back into the instruction cycle, and the process begins again.

The amount of data accessed in one cycle depends on the computer design, and is expressed in bytes, characters, or words. For example, Model X may have a slower basic access time than Model Y, but Model X may access four bytes at a time whereas Model Y accesses two bytes. Therefore, two factors combine which result in effective access time: the amount of data accessed during each cycle and the time required to perform each cycle.

Size of storage used is normally based on cost, and cost of storage in turn is based on speed (i.e., as access speed increases, the cost per bit stored also increases). This speed mismatch and cost variation between various storage media have caused a number of processor configuration innovations manifested in different storage hierarchy systems. For example, a hierarchy of storage might consist of very high-speed (nanosecond) semiconductor storage; medium-speed (microsecond) core storage; and large, slow-speed (millisecond) magnetic disk or drum. The hierarchy of storage concept can be illustrated by the virtual storage and buffer storage techniques which are discussed in the following sections.

Virtual Storage Technique

The basic idea behind virtual storage is the dynamic linking of primary storage of the processor to auxiliary storage so that each user (several may be using the system concurrently) appears to have very large primary storage, usually measured in megabytes, at his or her disposal. Parts of a program, or data associated with the user's program, may be broken up and scattered both in primary storage and on magnetic disk or drum, thus giving the "virtual" effect of much larger primary storage to the programmer.[2] This technique is illustrated in Figure B.2.

---

[1]Gordon B. Davis, *Computer Data Processing*, New York: McGraw-Hill Book Company, 1969, p. 150. Used with permission of the McGraw-Hill Book Company.

[2]Robert Haavind, "A User's Guide to System Evolution," *Computer Decisions*, June 1971, pp. 26–30. Used with permission.

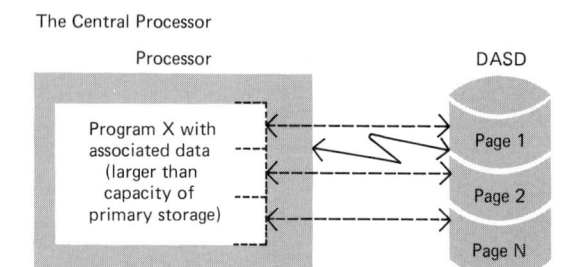

FIG. B.2 Illustration of the virtual storage concept.

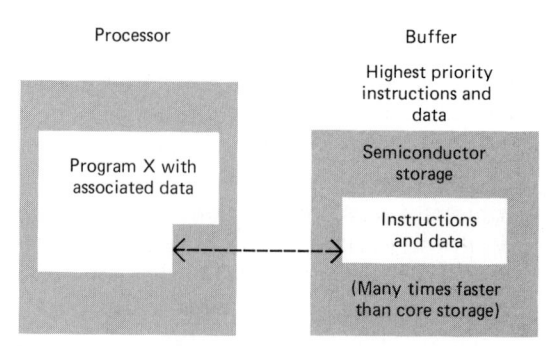

FIG. B.3 Illustration of the buffer storage concept.

Normally only the instructions and data necessary for immediate processing will be located in primary storage, in the form of "pages" which are transferred between primary storage and slower auxiliary (DASD) storage automatically.[3] With this approach, jobs are loaded into partitions or regions of auxiliary storage. During processing, small blocks or pages of instructions and data are transferred between auxiliary storage and processor storage according to the momentary needs of each job.[4]

Buffer Storage Technique

This technique, also called cache memory, uses a limited-capacity but very fast semiconductor storage combined with less expensive, slower, large-capacity core storage to give the overall effect of a faster primary storage. This technique requires careful look-ahead procedures to get the correct data into semiconductor storage when it is required.[5] The buffer storage technique is illustrated in Figure B.3.

It is the function of the buffer to fetch frequently used instructions and data to be used by the arithmetic-logic part of the central processor. In most cases, these instructions and data will be available at the buffer rate, rather than at the slower primary storage rate. This technique is based on the theory that adjacent bytes in primary storage will usually be used at the same time. If the required data are in the buffer, they are transferred to the arithmetic-logic unit at buffer speed. If the required data are not in the buffer then they are obtained from primary storage. On the subject of buffering, studies revealed that the required data are in the buffer 90 percent of the time. As with the virtual storage technique, the buffer storage technique provides increased performance without adding new responsibilities to the programmer (i.e., the operation of buffer storage is "transparent" to the programmer).

Multiprocessors

It should be recognized by the reader that a computer configuration, in many applications, operates with more than one processor unit (multiprocessing). While one can configure a total computer system in endless ways, for one typical illustration of a multiprocessing system, refer to Figure B.4.

[3]*Ibid.*

[4]"Key to Enhanced Application Development," *Data Processor,* September 1972, pp. 2–9. Used with permission.

[5]Haavind, *op. cit.,* p. 26.

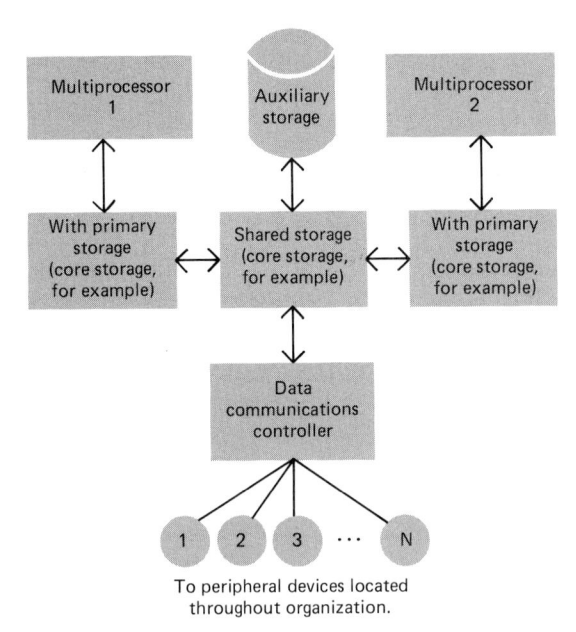

FIG. B.4 Illustration of a multiprocessor configuration.

The system above, for an example, could be used as a fail soft backup system where each processor is equipped with its own dedicated core memory, shares common partitioned storage that is used to access the data base files, and is connected to various peripherals. The partitioned core storage configuration allows either processor to operate the entire system in the event the other processor fails.

Minicomputers

Minicomputers are distinguished from large computers on the basis of cost, processor speed, memory size, and software. Today, a typical minicomputer falls within a $15,000 to $75,000 price range. Over three-quarters of all minis support business applications, while about one-half are designed for use in scientific applications.[6]

Features such as virtual memory and small, high-speed cache memory are becoming increasingly popular in minis. The most common size of main memory is from 128K to 512K bytes. Most minicomputers have 16-bit word sizes. The norm of cycle times for a minicomputer is 700 nanoseconds.

Minicomputers typically support up to four languages, with BASIC being the most popular, followed by FORTRAN, COBOL, and RPG.

Microcomputers

The advances in microelectronics that made possible the minicomputer in the early 1970s, have led to the creation of the microcomputer. A system of large-scale integration (LSI) chips contains the CPU, internal memory, and input/output interfaces of the microcomputer.

While microcomputers were originally designed for hobbyists, they have become a viable alternative to manual systems for small businesses. This trend will accelerate as hardware prices fall and as the amount of business software for micros grows.

Though the line of distinction between minicomputers and microcomputers is blurred on the dimensions of physical appearance and size, we can generally characterize microcomputers as having 4K to 64K bytes of internal memory, data entry via keyboard, and a video screen for output. Beyond a basic configuration, a small business microcomputer system may have additional internal memory, external memory in the form of cassettes or minifloppy disks, and a low-speed printer.

[6]*Minicomputer Review,* Lexington, Mass.: GML Corporation, 1981.

Types of Storage

We will conclude this section by presenting a summary classification of storage media. This classification is presented in Figure B.5.

DEVICES AND APPLICATIONS PERIPHERAL TO THE CPU

In Figure B.6 we present a general schematic of devices peripheral to the computer. In this section we will discuss from a systems application viewpoint five basic areas: (1) aspects of auxiliary storage media, specifically magnetic tape, magnetic disk, mass storage, and microfilm; (2) terminal devices; and (3) data entry techniques.

Name of Storage Media	Primary Storage	Online Auxiliary Storage	Offline Auxiliary Storage
Bubble	X		
LSI	X		
Semiconductor	X		
Magnetic core	X	X	
Thin films	X		
Holographic	X	X	
Plated wire	X		
Magnetic drum	X	X	
Magnetic disks	X	X	X
Mass storage		X	
Magnetic tape			X
Punched paper tape			X
Punched cards			X

FIG. B.5 Types of storage media.

Analysis of Auxiliary Storage Devices

Primary storage is expensive and can only be used economically to hold programs and data that the computer is presently processing. Auxiliary storage devices are used to store other programs and data which are made available to the computer when needed. Popular storage devices which transfer data or instructions rapidly between primary storage and an input/output drive unit are: magnetic tape, magnetic disk, magnetic drum, and mass storage. Computer output microfilm (COM) can also be considered as auxiliary storage. We will treat, in this section, four of these devices, namely: (1) magnetic tape, (2) magnetic disk, (3) mass storage, and (4) COM.

Magnetic Tape

Magnetic tape is a very popular medium for storage of voluminous amounts of data. It is a sequential medium and is used widely in batch processing environments.

Physical Characteristics of Magnetic Tape

Data are recorded on seven-, eight-, nine-, or ten-channel tape in the form of magnetized spots. Tape widths are normally $\frac{1}{2}$ inch, although some tapes are $\frac{3}{4}$, 1, and 3 inches in width. Some new tapes are being marketed which record data in a fashion similar to videotape, (i.e., data are recorded across the tape rather than along it). This technique allows bits to be much smaller and closer together. Some manufacturers claim that packing density is 40 times greater than on regular tape. Usually, reels hold 2400 to 3600 feet of magnetic tape; however, shorter tapes are sometimes used. Further discussion will be based on nine-channel tape.

Coding Scheme

The recording of data on magnetic tape is similar in concept to a tape recorder. Mag-

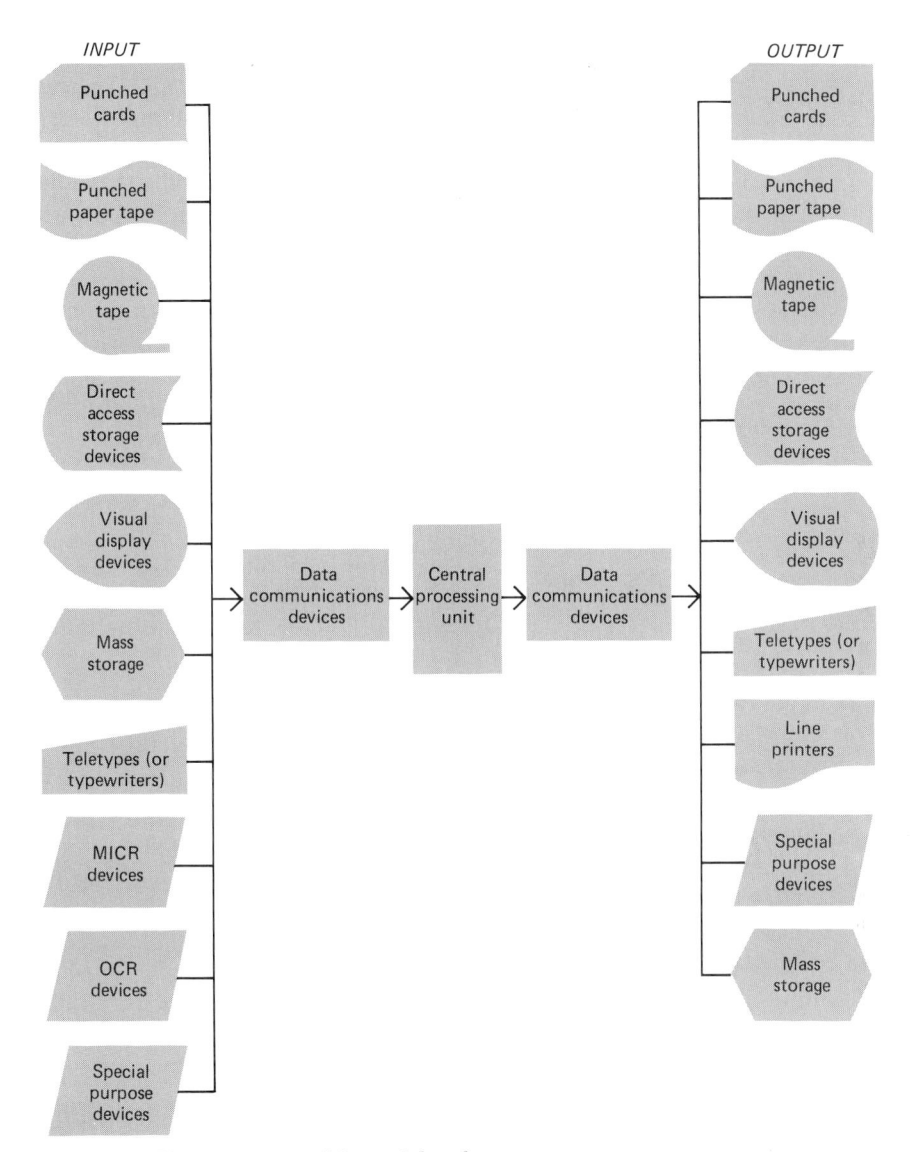

FIG. B.6 The computer and its peripherals.

netic tape for data processing, however, records numbers, and alphabetic and special characters. These data are recorded on tape in channels as shown in Figure B.7.

Density

The density of magnetic tape is represented by the number of characters or bits recorded per inch (CPI or BPI). The most common

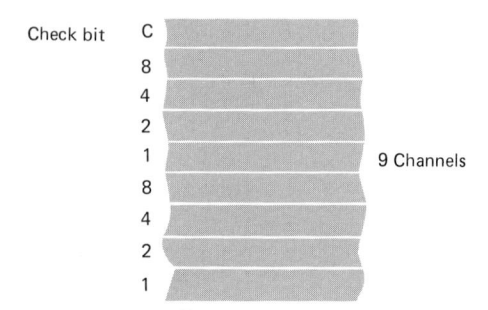

FIG. B.7 Magnetic tape using EBCDIC.

tape density is 1600 BPI. Higher density tapes can record up to 6250 BPI.

Magnetic Tape Transfer Rate

The transfer rate is determined by the speed of a tape drive unit and the density of characters recorded per inch. The tape drive unit functions in much the same way as a home tape recorder (i.e., the tape is wound from one reel to another, passing through a read/write unit where it can be read repeatedly without destroying the data stored). New data can be written over old data, when desired, and the tape can be rewound and backspaced. If the speed of a tape unit is 112.5 inches per second and the characters per inch are 800 then the data transfer rate is 90,000 characters per second (CPS). The common speeds of tape units are: 18.75, 22.5, 36.0, 37.5, 75.0, 112.5, 125.0, and 200.0 inches per second. Some manufacturers use vacuum systems rather than capstan systems. These vacuum systems literally suck the tape from one reel to another at speeds of 1000 inches per second.

Blocking Records

Each physical record that is written on a tape is separated by a blank ($\frac{1}{2}$ inch, $\frac{3}{4}$ inch, etc., according to the particular tape system) referred to as an interblock gap (IBG). The IBG has three purposes, which are: (1) it separates a record or block discussed below, (2) it allows space enough for the tape unit to reach its operating speed (i.e., one-half of the IBG is used for starting speed), and (3) it allows space enough for the tape unit to decelerate after a read or write operation. The tape must be moving at its designated speed before it can be read from or written on. Therefore the IBG gives enough space to get the tape moving at full speed. By the same token, when the end of the record (or block) is reached, in reading or writing, the tape cannot be stopped immediately; therefore, space must also be provided to allow the tape to stop.

The IBG contains no data. For example, if a recording density is 1600 BPI this means that a $\frac{1}{2}$-inch IBG could hold 800 characters of data. Or looking at it another way, approximately the data found in 20 80-column cards could be stored in two $\frac{1}{2}$-inch IBGs. The records in a tape with each record separated by an IBG are shown in Figure B.8. The records contain 800 characters and are unblocked.

Tape economy is realized by combining the records into a block of records by a blocking factor of N, where N equals the number of records within each block. The block itself becomes a physical group of characters separated by IBGs and the data records within the block become a logical record. A block is therefore said to be a tape-recording concept, whereas a record within the block is a logical record, or a data processing concept. Figure B.9 represents records with a blocking factor of 5.

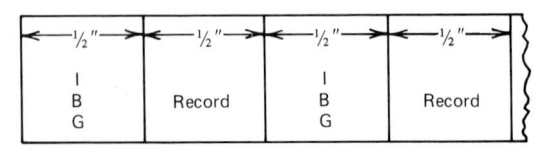

FIG. B.8 Unblocked records.

FIG. B.9 Records with a blocking factor of 5.

The concept of transfer rate is a little misleading because, as a tape unit reads blocks of logical records, it stops each time it comes to an IBG. Consequently, when blocks are being read or written, a certain amount of time is spent at each IBG. The total amount of time required to read or write a given number of blocks is equal to the sum of the time spent reading or writing the data plus the time spent starting and stopping at the IBGs. To realize the effect that start/stop time has on reading and writing speeds, consider the following example:

Tape density = 1600 BPI
Tape unit speed = 75.0 inches per second
Therefore, stated transfer rate = 120,000 CPS
Number of blocks on tape = 8000
Blocking factor = 10 where each record contains 30 characters; therefore, each block contains 300 characters or a total of 2,400,000 characters.
Number of IBGs = 8000
Size of IBG = ¾ inch
Time to pass over IBG = .010 sec.
Therefore,
Total start/stop time = 8000 × .010
    = 80 sec.
Total time for reading data = 2,400,000
    ÷ 120,000
    = 20 sec.
Therefore,
Total time to read all records = 80 + 20
    = 100 sec.
Effective transfer rate = 1,200,000 ÷ 100
    = 12,000 CPS

Consequently, it takes 80 sec. to start and stop the tape, and only 20 sec. to read the data. A waste of tape space and, accordingly, processing time results. To reduce this waste more records should be placed in a block. If the blocking factor is 40, then the number of IBGs would be reduced to 2000 instead of 8000. The total time to read the records is 20 sec. for reading data plus 20 sec. (2000 × .010), or 40 sec. When an installation has thousands of tape reels, reducing wasted space becomes quite significant. The reduction in wasted space results in:

1. *Less cost for tape.* Typical costs for tape reels are between $10 and $100. If a system has 1000 tapes with a cost of $80,000 and the space can be reduced 50 percent then a cost savings of $40,000 can be effected.

2. *Saves time.* Reduction of wait-time of the processing unit resulting either from tapes being moved from the tape units and/or space in the tape itself. Obviously, an increased blocking factor increases I/O speeds.

3. *Saves storage.* In older systems that have not had proper data management, an increasing number of applications, combined with increasingly stringent requirements for data retention, have resulted in a squeeze on available storage space. In some instances this squeeze has caused an expenditure for a new wing of the tape library. The principle of large blocking factors can be applied to many older systems on two levels: (1) The software system should be investigated to ascertain if the largest possible blocking factor is being used by every program. This would be particularly applicable in those installations that have upgraded their central processor storage capacity. (2) The reblocking of archival files should be done to contain the highest blocking factor that the hardware can handle. It

is often found that multiple-reel tape files can be reduced to a single reel. The recompilation of source programs to increase blocking factors, the necessary deblocking and file extraction run, and the reblocking of tapes are methods that use computer time, but the time lost on this fairly infrequent procedure would be more than balanced by the overall cost savings. Incidentally, physical space occupied by tapes can be reduced by writing short files on small reels, which are then stored on special racks to maximize the space savings.

Advantages/Disadvantages of Magnetic Tape

The advantages of magnetic tape are as follows:

1. It has a much faster transfer rate than punched cards.
2. Tapes play an important role and remain unchallenged for backup storage and for low-cost, high-capacity applications requiring only sequential access.
3. It requires less storage space than other media such as cards.
4. It is erasable and can be used over and over again for many different applications.
5. Tape manufacturers offer a wide range of specifications to meet particular applications.
6. Relatively speaking, tapes are inexpensive where one cent can buy enough tape capacity to store tens of thousands of characters.
7. In card systems, one or more records can be lost from a file. A tape file is continuous, which means that no record of the file can be lost.

The disadvantages of magnetic tape are:

1. Since tape is a sequential medium, the access of a particular record is made only after all records preceding it have been read. It is, therefore, not applicable for jobs which require rapid, direct access to specific records.
2. Since the tape is also continuous in design, a clerk cannot physically remove, insert, or change a record without reading from the original and rewriting it with the change to another tape.
3. The magnetized spots are unreadable by humans. A printed listing of the tape is required to read or verify tape data.
4. The temperature, humidity, and dust content of the tape environment must be tightly controlled. Particles of dust on a tape can cause improper processing. Temperature and humidity conditions that fall outside of prescribed ranges can cause peculiar and mysterious results from processing.

Magnetic Disk

Magnetic disks have now become the medium of choice to serve as auxiliary storage. The price per character or byte stored continues to decrease, and the direct access capability of disks gives the systems analyst far more options and flexibility in designing systems (e.g., capability of online inquiry of large files) than does magnetic tape.

Physical Characteristics of Magnetic Disk

A magnetic disk is made up of a stack of rotating metal platters on which records are stored. Direct access to any record can be made without having to read through a sequence of other, irrelevant records. This direct access capability allows random entry of transaction data and random inquiry into the file from a user. The different disk models range from 5 to 100 disks measuring from 1.5 to 3 feet in diameter. The IBM 3330 Disk Storage Facility is used to illustrate the physical characteristics of magnetic disk. A schematic of it is shown in Figure B.10.

The illustration portrays a disk unit in which 10 of the 12 surfaces are used for recording data. Each surface is divided into 404 tracks, which are analogous to flattened, circular sections of magnetic tape. Each track has a capacity of 13,030 bytes. The read/write mechanism positions the read/write heads over a separate track which forms a vertical cylinder. Since each surface consists of 404 tracks, we can see that the disk unit is composed of 404 concentric cylinders. In Figure B.10, the read/write heads are positioned over the tracks which make up cylinder 013.

Addressing

In Figure B.11 we have four 3100-byte records stored on cylinder 013, track 02. These records, although not shown, are coded in EBCDIC. Each record on the track is numbered sequentially. Therefore, each data record is preceded by a small address record.

With these addresses, it is possible to access directly any desired record stored on the disk. Note that records are separated by gaps, similar to an IBG in magnetic tape. Since the addresses and gaps require a portion of the track, it is impossible to store a full 13,030 bytes of data on a track when more than one record per track is stored. As the number of records per track increases, the number of gaps and addresses increases, causing the data per track to decrease. For example, if the record size is 500 bytes, then the track capacity would be 20 records, for a total track capacity of 10,000 bytes of data.

Magnetic Disk Transfer Rate

The disk pack rotates clockwise on a spindle as the access mechanism moves in and out.

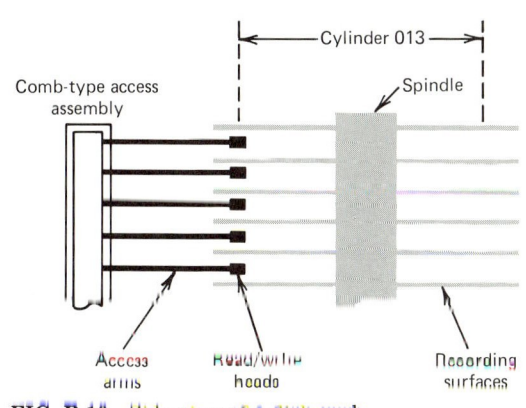

FIG. B.10 Side view of a disk pack.

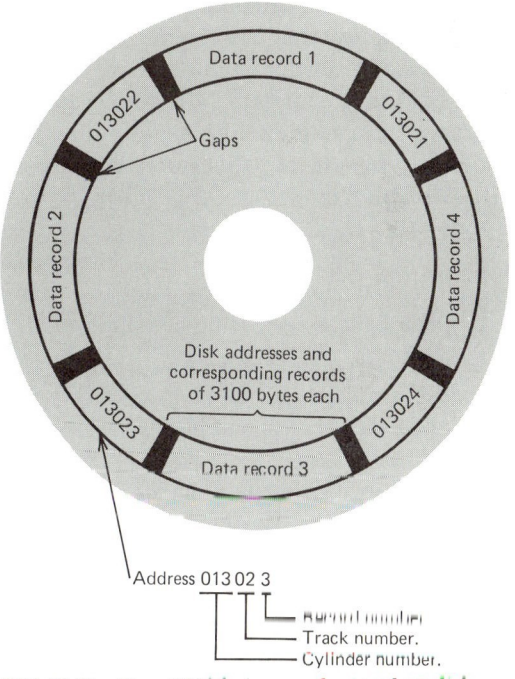

FIG. B.11 Four 3100-byte records stored on disk showing an address for each record.

The speed with which data are read or written is dependent upon these two factors plus read/write head selection and data transfer. These factors are discussed below:

1. *Access mechanism movement time.* This is the time it takes for the access assembly to move the read/write heads to a specified cylinder (called seek time or access time). The access movement time is based on the number of cylinders the read/write heads travel over to reach the one specified, and the speed of the mechanism itself. The movement rate is not uniform because the mechanism is electromechanical and does not move at constant speed (notice the movement of the player arm of a record; the naked eye can detect a somewhat irregular movement). For a movement of one cylinder, minimum time is 10 milliseconds (msec.); across all 404 cylinders, maximum is 55 msec. The average movement speed over the entire pack is 30 msec. If the read/write heads are already at their proper position during access, they do have to be moved, therefore, the access movement time is zero. On some disk systems the read/write heads are fixed in position over each track (e.g., the IBM 2305 Fixed Head Storage Facility). This eliminates the seek time consideration.

2. *Read/Write Head Selection.* After the access mechanism has been properly positioned on the specified cylinder, the head that is to read or write is switched on. This switching is electronic and the amount of time, therefore, is negligible in all cases.

3. *Rotational Delay.* Before data are read or written the proper location on the track must rotate to the read/write heads. The time spent in rotating to a proper alignment of the read/write heads with the specified location is called *rotational delay*. For the IBM 3330 Disk Storage Facility, a full rotation requires 16.7 msec. If, after positioning the access mechanism over the desired track, the desired record has just passed, then the rotational delay is 16.7 msec. If, on the other hand, the desired record has just reached the read/write head, then the rotational delay is zero. For timing calculations, an average rotational delay of 8.4 msec. is used.

4. *Data transfer.* After the disk pack has been rotated to its proper location, the record can be read or written. The time required to transfer the record between the disk pack and the main storage is the transfer rate and is a function of rotation speed, the density at which the data are recorded, and the length of the record transferred. The transfer rate of a 3330 unit is 806K bytes per second.

In timing a read or write operation, the actual direct accessing consists, therefore, of access mechanism movement time, rotational delay (using average time), and data transfer rate. The total time for a complete processing job requires, in addition, the consideration of additional factors such as program processing time, access method processing time, and control program time.

For example, again using the IBM 3330 as the storage medium, Figure B.12 presents

---

Per record:

Average access time	30.0 msec.
Average rotational delay	8.4 msec.
Data transfer time	6.2 msec.
Total	44.6 msec.

1000 records—44.6 sec.

FIG. B.12 A timing summary.

an approximate timing summary to read a thousand 5000-byte records randomly distributed over an entire disk pack.

Floppy Disks

Floppy (flexible) disks were introduced by IBM in 1972 as a low-cost, random access storage medium for minicomputers. Floppy disks are punched out of a polyester film that is coated with an iron oxide compound. The flat, 8-inch circular magnetic diskette rotates freely within a jacket that is intended to prevent both data loss and the diskette from being damaged.

The jacket has access and index holes to accommodate the read/write head (which actually touches the disk) and the data timing transducers of the disk drive. Each diskette contains 77 tracks, and has a storage capacity of 512K bytes (double-sided diskettes or "flippies," single density). Track-to-track access time is 3 msec.; average access time over all tracks is approximately 90 msec.

Advantages/Disadvantages of Magnetic Disk

The advantages are as follows:
1. Besides having a direct access capability, a disk file may be organized sequentially and processed like a magnetic tape.
2. All transactions can be processed as they occur, thereby keeping the system current.
3. Multiple files can be stored on a single disk pack.
4. Multiple and interrelated files may be stored in a way which permits a transaction to be processed against all pertinent files simultaneously.

The disadvantages are as follows:
1. Magnetic disk is still more expensive than magnetic tape. Falling prices and improved recording densities, however, have given real economies to users of magnetic disks (and tapes, too, as far as costs are concerned).
2. For many applications, sequential tape processing is as acceptable and effective as disk.
3. In accounting work, a clearly discernible audit trail is needed. In updating a file on a magnetic disk, the record is read, updated, and written back to the same location, thus destroying the original contents. If no provision for error detection and file reconstruction is made, costly errors may go undetected.

Mass Storage

Although magnetic tape is being replaced by disk units as the medium immediately below processor memory, large data files, backup files, and seldom-used files still need to be stored on a low-cost, medium-to-slow access medium. One such system is Control Data Corporation's 38500 Mass Storage System (another is IBM's 3851).

This system is intended for processing large active files within an environment where performance and equipment costs are the key criteria for evaluation. Storage capacity of the system ranges from 16 billion to over a trillion bytes. A maximum of 5, and an average of 2.5 sec., is required to access data.

The Control Data 38500 system is built around magnetic tape cartridges. Each enclosed cartridge contains a 150-inch-long, 2.7-inch-wide magnetic tape, capable of storing up to 8 million bytes of data. Within a single-file unit, 2052 tape cartridges are clustered in beehive fashion. To retrieve data, an X-Y selector is positioned at the addressable location, the cartridge is picked by the selector, and the cartridge is then moved to a tape transport. At the transport, the cartridge is opened, and the tape is unwound fully and inserted into vacuum columns. It can then be moved past the read/write station at approximately 129 inches per second, effecting a data transfer rate of over 800,000 bytes per second.

Computer Output Microfilm (COM)

COM provides another medium for storing large amounts of data. This approach is shown in Figure B.13. Data output from the central processor is read into a microfilm recorder which is connected to a film developer. The final microfilm output is in two basic forms: (1) microfiche and (2) roll film. Either one can be viewed directly through special readers.

Advantages of COM are:

1. Although CQM is generally considered as a replacement for data on paper, in many situations it can be considered as a replacement for magnetic tape.
2. COM is quite applicable for archival files (five or more years), whereas magnetic tape is not made for long-term storage of data. Tape deteriorates over a long period of nonuse and, in addition, the recorded magnetic signals must be insulated from possible damage caused by environmental conditions such as radiation, heat, humidity, and random signals from electrical fixtures.
3. COM significantly reduces the need for storage space because it reduces the paper explosion.
4. Information is available directly from storage in human readable form with the aid of a microfilm reader.
5. It is relatively inexpensive.

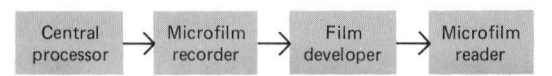

FIG. B.13 An illustration of the processes involved in producing COM.

6. COM, as a replacement for distributed reports, reduces significantly mailing costs.

The major disadvantages of COM are:

1. It is not economical where records within a file require updating continuously.
2. A COM reader is necessary.
3. A COM file cannot be read by a computer.

Summary Characteristics of Auxiliary Storage Devices

We have discussed in detail the four popular auxiliary storage devices—magnetic tape, disk, mass storage, and COM. In seeking the best mix of devices, the high-speed devices such as magnetic drum, magnetic disk, and mass storage are generally the best for quick processing of large quantities of data. In archival files where minimum access speed and high data storage capacity are important, microfilm may be the best choice. Applications that require voluminous amounts of data processed on a periodic basis, requiring little, if any, inquiry capability, are handled best by magnetic tape.

At the slower and lower cost end of the spectrum are punched cards and punched paper tape. It is quite difficult to make a sensible comparison between these two media and other media listed above, because of the great difference in cost, transfer rate, storage capacity, and so on. The decision as to which of the two to select, however, often depends on how the data are to be organized. Paper tape is preferable when files are organized sequentially and there is no need for insertions, modifications, or deletions. On the other hand, punched cards are preferable when the unit-record concept is to be used (i.e., the punched card serves as a record where each card is designed to contain data about a certain transaction).

Terminal Devices

Terminals actually represent devices which are used to get the data into the system and the information from the system. They are fundamental to an online system. Terminal hardware will vary with the needs of the different users throughout the organization. Terminals vary from simple teletypewriters to card readers, high-speed printers, CRTs, magnetic tape units, and so on. The distance of the terminal from the central processor has no effect on its function. Move a magnetic tape unit to a plant 500 miles from the central processor, add a communication data control unit, connect it to a communication channel, and it becomes a remote job entry (RJE) terminal. Hook up a CRT to the data base and one has an interrogative terminal, and so on.

In this section, we will devote our discussion primarily to two types of terminals: (1) telephone terminals and (2) intelligent terminals.

Telephone Terminals

The Touch-Tone® telephone is an example of a low-speed terminal in the sense that it can handle effectively only low volumes of data. It can be used to update files, retrieve response information by voice answerback, printout, or visual display on other devices. For example, it can be used to provide credit status on credit card customers. Clerks type in to the central processor an access code, the customer's account number, and the amount of the purchase. By voice answerback, heard only by the clerk, the transaction is either approved or the clerk is instructed to call the credit department for further instructions. A similar system to this could be used as an order entry system in conjunction with reporting inventory availability to incoming calls from customers and/or salespersons.

Intelligent Terminals

An intelligent terminal incorporates a processing capability usually in the form of a microcomputer. This microcomputer has the capability to perform operations on the data it handles in addition to transmitting it to a central processor.

Applications of Intelligent Terminals

Intelligent terminals are used to (1) extend the power of the central computer and (2) accept data at its origin and perform some level of processing. Many of the intelligent terminals include microcomputers which can be used for different purposes based on how they are configured and programmed. For instance, by using one set of peripherals and programs, a remote job entry (RJE) system is developed, and by using a different set of peripherals and programs a data entry system, such as a remote key-to-disk system, is created.

With the advent of lower costs and greater availability of computers and data communication systems, the use of RJE systems have become cost/effective for small users who cannot economically justify their own data processing systems. Also, this RJE technique is applicable to the distribution information systems structure.

Also, intelligent terminals provide a form of backup for the central computer. With nonintelligent terminals connected to the main processor, if this processor were to fail, the terminals would be disabled, and for all practicable purposes, the entire system would be down. Transactions could not be entered and processed. At most, transactions might be captured on paper tape or magnetic tape for later transmission to the computer. With an intelligent terminal, it is feasible for the terminal to accept transactions and perform some of the processing if the main computer were down or the data communications system were disrupted. This capability is one of the main reasons why banks and retail stores select intelligent terminals. Sales transactions in a store, or savings transactions in a financial institution, can still be recorded at the terminal for processing and later transmission if necessary, even though the central computer is down.

Another reason for using an intelligent terminal is that it can relieve the central processor of some of the processing workload. This situation helps to reduce an overload on the central processor, allowing the system to get along with a smaller central processor than would otherwise be the case.

Data Entry Techniques

More than half the cost of using computers in many organizations is incurred in the capture and conversion of data. Probably no other aspect of computer processing offers more potential for cost savings than does this one area. The preparation of data for computer processing is truly the big bottleneck in the entire system and, as a result, it substantially decreases throughput.

In this section on data entry techniques we will direct our attention to five main areas: (1) keyboard-to-storage, (2) point of sale (POS), (3) optical character recognition (OCR), (4) magnetic ink character recognition (MICR), and (5) voice recognition (VR).

Keyboard-to-Storage

The keyboard-to-storage technique consists of several keystations (CRT) connected to a minicomputer or programmed controller which collects the data input, verifies it, provides various other functions, and writes it on tape or disk for processing. Some of the functions that this kind of data entry system performs are:

1. Keyed-in data are input to an edit program to filter out errors.
2. CRT input terminals provide sight verification for the operator; if an error is made, backspacing and deletion allows the operator to correct the error quickly.
3. Operators can work at higher keying rates than is possible with keypunches.
4. Productivity statistics for monitoring and checking operators' efficiency are supplemented by means of a program in the system.
5. Check digits and batch totals are prepared automatically.
6. Certain reasonableness checks and relevancy checks are made.
7. True modular input of data is allowed because blocks of data are merged together into proper sequence for further processing.

The typical keyboard-to-storage system is referred to as key-to-tape or key-to-disk. It consists of a low-cost minicomputer; direct access intermediate storage; and magnetic disk, tape, floppy disk, or cassette for final output. Most manufacturers of these systems offer 8 to 64 keystations per system. Studies indicate that at the present cost levels, disregarding any other benefits, a system has to replace from 10 to 14 keypunches before a key-to-tape system is cost/effective. With falling prices, in the near future, the same basic system may be cost-effective at a five or six keypunch level. A key-to-tape system is shown in Figure B.14.

An online data entry system works basically the same way except the data flows directly into the central processor. For an example, refer to Figure B.15.

Advantages/Disadvantages of Keyboard-to-Storage Systems

The advantages are as follows:

1. Editing, formatting, combining input data, and dumping data are automatic functions.
2. Supervisors are provided various operational statistics on such things as operators' performance, work in progress, and work completed.
3. Productivity is increased because the operations of card feeding, duplication, skipping, and stacking are eliminated.
5. Operators' acceptance is good because it eliminates menial tasks such as card handling and the creation and use of drum cards, and it furnishes a quieter environment.

The disadvantages of keyboard-to-storage systems are:

1. Buffered keypunch/verifiers perform many of the functions that the key-to-storage systems perform.
2. Practically everyone understands the ubiquitous punched card.

Point of Sale (POS)

Point of sale systems provide a method by which vital data are captured at the point

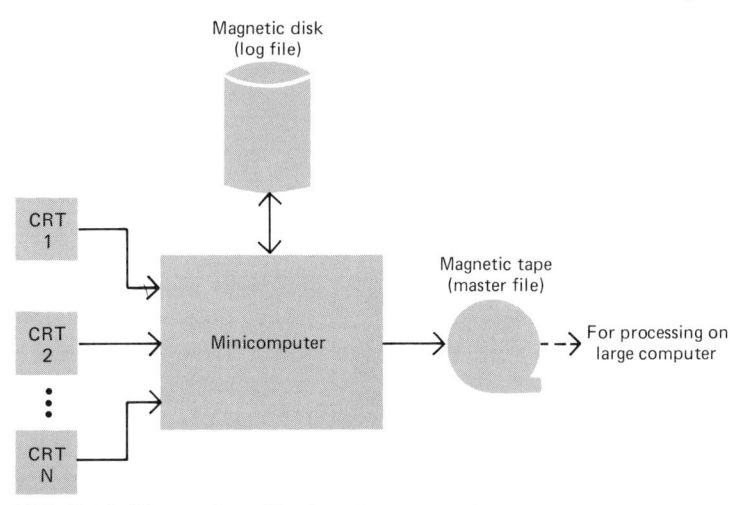

FIG. B.14 Illustration of keyboard-to-tape system.

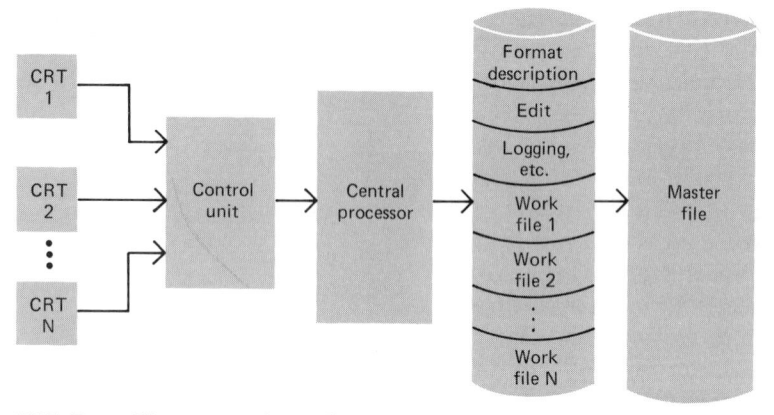

FIG. B.15 Illustration of an online entry system.

of transaction in department stores, supermarkets, and large discount stores. The same technique is applicable to other user categories where it is important to capture data at the time of an event or transaction.

This technique uses either hand-held "wand" readers or stationary sensors, which capture data from merchandise tags or tickets containing optical or magnetic characters. All readers are linked either to a central processor or an intelligent terminal. The main advantages of POS are as follows:

1. Provides large-scale data collection and online capabilities.
2. The method of reading optically or magnetically encoded characters on tickets and product items speeds up the sales transaction to the mutual benefit of the buyer and seller.
3. Input errors are eliminated.

The disadvantages of POS systems are:

1. Currently, many of the systems are too expensive.
2. Requires major revisions to the system in a number of areas (e.g., retagging and recoding).

Optical Character Recognition (OCR)

The purpose of OCR is to decrease the input bottleneck by reducing the number of keying operations and errors in transcription. Ideally, OCR equipment will read any document and transmit the data to a computer, thus eliminating any intermediate data preparation tasks. Most OCR devices being used in organizations are designed to read marks or machine-printed characters. They operate on the basis of sensing a mark in a specific location in the document. Applications for this device are test scoring, surveys, questionnaires, order entry, inventory control, and payroll. Character readers read characters generated by computer printers, accounting machines, cash registers, typewriters, and precisely written handprinted characters. A general flow of data using OCR devices is shown in Figure B.16.

The advantages of OCR are as follows:

1. Since data conversion is handled photographically, data errors are decreased.

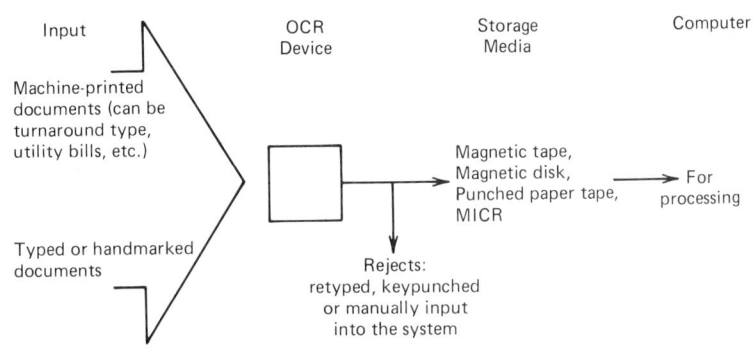

FIG. B.16 Illustration of an OCR application.

2. Increases throughput.

The disadvantages are as follows:

1. Standardization problems in type fonts and document inputs.
2. Reject rate is sensitive to the condition of the document (i.e., smudges, creased documents, dirt, and poor quality paper).
3. Low-cost OCR devices have limited throughput and a single-font reading capability. Devices with the capability to read several fonts are expensive.
4. The installation of OCR equipment usually requires complete forms redesign.

Magnetic Ink Character Recognition (MICR)

Magnetic ink character recognition (MICR) is used primarily by financial institutions for sorting and routing financial documents. The MICR characters are preprinted on documents and are composed of the ten decimal digits and four special characters.

Voice Recognition (VR)

On the floor of a commodities exchange, a transaction is completed between two brokers. The reporter speaks into a wireless microphone, "July silver four-four-four." A visual confirmation is given and he says, "Go." Using voice recognition (VR),[7] the data have been captured for further computer processing.

Where a limited amount of data in the form of words and alphanumeric characters are involved, a number of users are finding voice data entry to be cost/effective. By bypassing the writing or keying operations traditionally used to encode data, time may be saved and the cost associated with error correcting minimized. Moreover, VR can serve an important control function, recognizing only those commands of authorized personnel.

Operationally, VR systems consist of a microphone or telephone receiver to accept voice input, a spectrum analyzer to filter the audio signal, and an analog-to-digital converter to change the signal to digital code. The digital code is then matched using a minicomputer to specific code patterns stored on disk or cassette.

Most VR systems have a number of characteristics in common. Normally, VR sys-

[7]Edward K. Yasaki, "Voice Recognition Comes of Age," *Datamation*, August 1976, pp. 65–68.

tems are discrete or isolated. This means that the speaker must pause for a fraction of a second between each sound. Second, each user of the system must train it through repeated utterances to recognize his or her particular enunciation of sounds. Finally, basic voice recognition systems have a limited memory capacity (vocabulary) of 20 to 40 words.

DATA COMMUNICATIONS

Data communications systems transmit data between peripherals and the central processor and, thus, allow people and equipment to be geographically dispersed rather than being at one central location. In computer-based information systems, nearly all of the information produced must be disseminated to a variety of users, some many miles away. This transmission load is increasing each year, making the interdependency of computers and data communications systems even more apparent. Data communications control systems, equipment, and services have, cumulatively, become possibly the fastest growing area of information systems activity.

Typical applications which require design, selection, and implementation of data communications systems are as follows:

1. *Timesharing.* This application allows a number of remote users to gain access to the computational services of a central computer system. Data flow is in both directions (i.e., the terminal is both sending and receiving).
2. *Computer job load sharing.* This application permits the interconnection of two or more computers.
3. *Remote job entry (RJE).* This application entails the linkage of a central large computer with two or more small computers in separate locations, each of which is equipped with high-speed printers, card read-punches, and magnetic disk and tape. The purpose of RJE is to transmit voluminous amounts of data to a central processor for further processing.
4. *Interrogation.* This application requires the implementation of an online inquiry system using such terminal devices as CRTs and teletypewriters to gain access to the data base. Also, similar to RJE, the user may update records within certain integrated files.

The three major areas of data communications systems are:

1. *Communication channels.* These channels provide a path for electrical transmission between two or more points. These channels are also called circuits, lines, or links.
2. *Modems.* The term modem is a contraction of modulator-demodulator. These devices modulate and demodulate signals transmitted over communication channels.
3. *Line management.* Line management encompasses the procedures and equipment necessary to connect several terminals to the same line. Multiplexers, concentrators, and programmable communications processors are devices that enable many different terminals to share a single communications line.

Communication Channels

Communication channels are comprised of one or more of the following: telegraph lines, telephone lines, radio links, coaxial cable, microwave, satellite, laser beam, and helical waveguides. Depending on the terminal equipment and the application required, the channels can be arranged for operation in one or more of the three basic transmission modes:

1. *Simplex.* Transmission is made in one direction only.
2. *Half duplex.* Transmission can be in both directions, but not at the same time.
3. *Full duplex.* Transmission can be made in both directions at the same time.

Data Transmission

Data are transmitted over a wire line (or microwave system) by an electrical signal. It is comprised of three elements: (1) amplitude-strength of the signal, (2) phase-duration of the signal, and (3) frequency-number of times a wave form is repeated during a specified time interval. These elements are illustrated in Figure B.17.

When the binary numbering system is used to represent characters, a pulse for a defined time interval represents a 1-bit, and no pulse is used to represent a 0-bit. The pulse or no pulse is based on the amplitude, phase, and frequency of the signal, which is termed the "state."

Data transmission is either asynchronous or synchronous. Asynchronous transmission, such as in telegraph communication, is the slower of the two. Signal elements are transmitted to indicate the start and stop of each character. Three common asynchronous codes are:

1. *Baudot.* This is a five-level code with 32 possible combinations. With the use of a shift code (shift from a code for numbers to a code for alphabetics and special characters), it is possible to code 64 combinations. The term, baud, is used for measurement. For example, one baud per second, means one pulse or code element per second. This coding method uses five bits for the character plus a start and stop bit.
2. *Binary Coded Decimal.* The BCD method is similar to the Baudot method. It is, however, a six-level code.
3. *American Standard Code for Information Interchange.* This code, termed ASCII, uses seven- or eight-character bits.

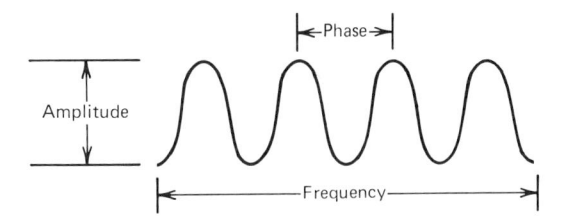

FIG. B.17 Schematic of a wave form.

Synchronous transmission is normally used where the transmission rate exceeds 2000 bits per second. The synchronous data transmission requires the receiving terminal to be synchronized bit-for-bit with the sending terminal. This eliminates the need for start and stop bits, thereby improving the efficiency of data transmission. This system requires, however, a clocking mechanism at both the sending and receiving ends.

Grade of Channels

The above discussion considered the directional flow of data and types of transmission and codes used. Another very important consideration is the grade of the channel. Channels are graded on speed of transmission and this attribute is directly proportional to bandwidth. For example, telegraph lines are narrowband, telephone lines are voiceband, and coaxial cable or microwave are broadband. The bandwidth of a channel is measured by a unit called a Hertz (Hz), which means cycles per second. It has been shown that the bandwidth of a channel should be approximately twice the number of bits to be transmitted per second. For example, if one is to transmit data at 1200 bits per second (bps), then a channel with a bandwidth of 2400 Hz is required. Channels may be classified as low-speed, medium-speed, and high-speed.

Low-Speed Channels

This grade was originally developed for use with teletypewriters (TTYs). It transmits data in the range of 55, 75, 110, 150, and 300 bits per second. Data can be transmitted via the teletypewriter online, or paper tape can be prepared offline and transmitted during slack periods. These systems normally use five-channel (Baudot) code, but, at higher speeds, they also have available the eight-channel ASCII Code.

Medium-Speed Channels

This grade is voiceband and is provided by the Bell System and the independent telephone companies. They are used for voice and data communications, interchangeably. Their typical transmission rate is 300 to 9600 bits per second. There are three types of services available: (1) private line, (2) the dial-up network, and (3) WATS.

1. *Private Lines.* The major difference in this system and a dial-up system is that the channel remains connected for the duration of the lease, the routing can be chosen, and the line can be electrically conditioned so that the transmission rate can be increased up to 9600 bits per second. Private lines are leased on a monthly basis with unlimited usage and the rate is a function of airline miles from point to point.

   Conditioning refers to the process by which the quality of a specific, privately leased line is maintained at a certain standard permissible error rate. Such conditioning adjusts the frequency and phase response characteristics of the channel to meet more exact tolerance specifications.

2. *Dial-up or public switched network.* The dial-up or switched network is currently the most commonly used method of transmitting data. The channel is available as long as the connection is made, and payment varies according to mileage, time of day or night, and duration of connect time. The rate approximates the rate for a normal voice telephone call. The average speed of transmission is generally from 2000 to 2400 bits per second.

   Since each dial-up connection may involve a unique combination of channels, the telephone company does not guarantee the characteristics of dial-up channels. Consequently, to achieve high transmission rates on a dial-up network, the required conditioning must be performed within the modem. Such a modem rapidly determines the channel characteristics and compensates for them at the start of the connection and then continuously adapts to any changes during connect time.

3. *Wide area telephone service (WATS).* WATS is a pricing arrangement for users of large volume data (and voice) transmission over long distances. WATS offers two billing plans: (1) a full period service,

and (2) a measured time service. Under full period service, the subscriber has unlimited use of the channel at a fixed monthly rate in the geographical area for which he or she subscribes. Under measured time service, the basic monthly rate covers the first ten hours of use per month for calls to Data-Phones (or telephones) within the subscribed service area. An additional charge per hour of actual use is levied beyond the first ten hours; however, the tariff which governs this service is extremely complicated and a full explanation is beyond the scope of this text.

High-Speed Channels

Where data are to be transmitted at high speeds and very high volumes, then a broadband service should be used. Both the Bell System and Western Union offer leased broadband services. These broadband lines comprise a group of channels of voice grade. Each channel, when properly arranged, can carry voice, computer data, or facsimile signals. Two classes of services are offered.

1. *Type 5700 line.* Has a base capacity of 60 voice-grade channels and a maximum equivalent bandwidth of 240 kHz (kilohertz).
2. *Type 5800 line.* Has a capacity of 240 voice-grade channels and a maximum equivalent bandwidth of 1000 kHz.

This service is quite flexible because it can be used as a single broadband channel for fast and voluminous data transmission or as several individual lower-speed channels. In certain cases a user group with similar needs may share a line, whereas on an individual basis, they could not afford such a service. A flat monthly rate is charged for this service, regardless of the volume of data transmitted. This rate is based on the number of channels, total capacity, and distance between transmission points.

Some companies have found it more economical and efficient to develop and use their own private-line microwave systems. The First National Bank of Boston, for example, has a microwave link between its head office and its operations center four miles away. The microwave link consists of a 1.544-megabit system that is capable of handling data transmission between the two points at speeds up to 19,200 bits per second.

Massachusetts General Hospital has a microwave link between it and Logan Airport in Boston. Doctors at the hospital, through audiovisual contact with patients at the airport, direct tests performed by technicians at the airport medical facility. This system is being extended to nursing homes throughout the Boston area so that expert medical care can be brought to patients who are unable to come to the hospital for treatment.

Arthur C. Clarke, an author of several books on space, believes that satellites will have at least the same impact on people as have telephones. Most major telecommunications companies (e.g., AT&T, GTE) have launched or will launch their own satellites. Western Bancorp for instance, uses satellite links to connect three remote data centers to its corporate data center in Los Angeles. The system supports a bankwide teller-transaction processing system consisting of 5000 terminals in 700 banking offices covering 11 western states.

Fiber optics are AT&T's terrestrial answer to satellite communications. Optical fibers are embedded in cables and carry communications by bending and bouncing light waves through tiny strands of glass. Fiber optics the size of a human hair offer 1000 times the carrying capacity of today's copper wire pair. The benefits associated with fiber optics as a transmission medium include high bandwidth, little noise interference because they are nonelectrical, high security since they cannot be tapped, and suitability for digital transmission because light pulses lend themselves well to binary coding.

A data transmission medium of the 1980s and 1990s is infrared. Infrared is an optical transmission system that uses the infrared spectrum of light-emitting diodes. Like microwave, it is a "line-of-sight" system that is most useful for building-to-building data communications up to 1 kilometer apart. A system called Lite-Link operates at a speed of 500 kilobits per second.[8]

Modems

Modems, also known as data sets, are used to handle the data stream from a peripheral device to the central processor, or vice versa, through the common carrier network. The modem can operate in simplex, half duplex, or full duplex mode.

Telephone channels were developed for analog voice transmission. In communication applications involving digital data, the modulator portion of a modem converts digital pulses, representing binary 1's and 0's, generated by the computer or peripheral equipment, into an analog, wavelike signal acceptable for transmission over analog channels. The demodulator reverses this process, converting the analog signal back into a pulse train acceptable to the peripheral or computer at the other end. This is illustrated in Figure B.18. If a modem was not used to convert/reconvert data signals, and the computer or peripheral was directly connected to the telephone channel, the signal would be degraded and the data would be made unintelligible by the electrical characteristics of the channel.

Line Management

Often a single terminal connected to a dedicated line is not active enough of the time to keep the line busy. A common solution to this problem is to connect several terminals to the same line. Because the terminals are "dropped off" the communications line, the configuration is called a multidrop. A multidrop configuration, while decreasing line costs, can produce a garbled message if two or more terminals use the line simultaneously. To overcome this potential problem a polling or contention method of line management is used.

With polling, the central computer asks each terminal if it has something to transmit. If it does, then it is directed to send its

---

[8]Summarized from William R. Synnott and William R. Gruber, *Information Resource Management,* New York: John Wiley & Sons, Inc., 1981, pp. 237–240.

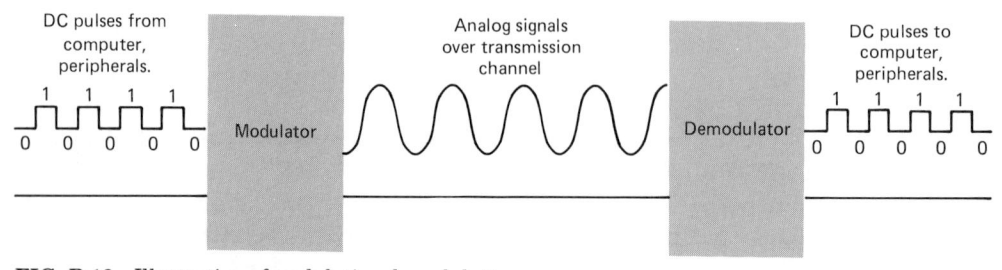

FIG. B.18 Illustration of modulation-demodulation.

message. After transmission of a terminal's message is complete, the computer asks the next terminal if it has something to transmit. This polling continues in turn until all the terminals on the line have the opportunity to transmit. Then, the computer polls the first terminal and the entire polling process is repeated. While polling allows the line to be busier, it can waste processor time if terminals do not have messages to send. An alternative method that overcomes this disadvantage is called contention.

With contention, each terminal listens to the communications line before transmitting its message. If the line is free it sends its message. If the line is busy the terminal wishing to send a message waits awhile before listening again. A serious disadvantage of the contention method of line management is that terminals may experience long delays in sending messages because the communications line is too busy or messages are too long.

Multiplexers, concentrators, and programmable communications processors are devices that permit connection of more peripherals to the central computer using fewer channels.

Multiplexer

Where a number of terminals are in one or more areas outside the toll-free zone of the central processor, the common carrier tariff structure makes it economically attractive to operate a group of such terminals through one voice-grade channel, instead of connecting them separately to the central processor via a number of narrowband channels. In most situations of this type multiplexing will reduce the cost of the communication network by allowing one voiceband grade channel to substitute for many subvoice (slow-speed, telegraph) channels that might otherwise be poorly utilized. Figure B.19 illustrates a communication system before and after multiplexing.

As shown in Figure B.19, the multiplexer accepts input from several terminal sources, combines these inputs, and then transmits the combined input over one channel. At the other end (not shown), a similar unit again

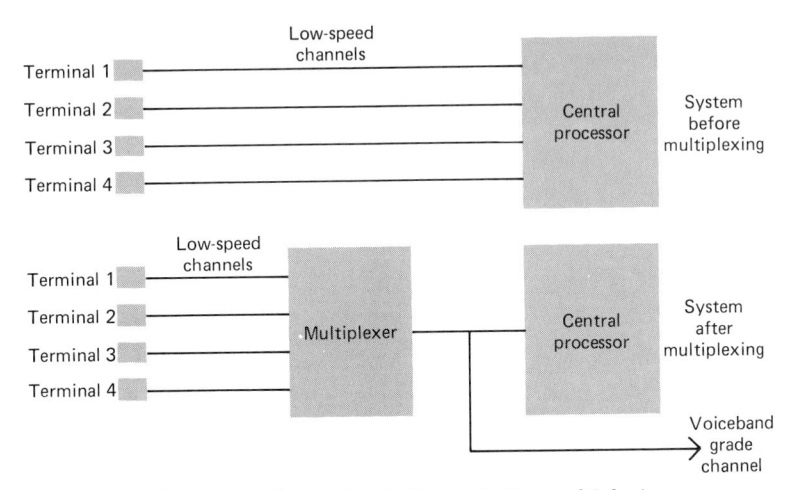

FIG. B.19 Communication system before and after multiplexing.

separates the discrete data inputs for further processing.

Two basic techniques are used to multiplex data: (1) frequency division multiplexing (FDM), and (2) time division multiplexing (TDM). In FDM, the digital pulse signal from each terminal is converted by a modem into an analog signal having a frequency unique to the individual terminal. Each separate signal is allocated its own portion of the frequency of the available band. All the signals are electrically combined and then transmitted over the line. The receiving end of a FDM device demultiplexes the individual signals by using a set of filters, each designed to "hear" a particular tone. The tone is then demodulated by a modem back into a digital pulse signal.

The TDM approach uses transmitting capability according to available time elements. Digital inputs from each terminal are continuously sampled, one by one, for a fixed time period. The sampling time per input corresponds to the time expended to designate a bit (bit-interleaved TDM) or a byte/character (byte-interleaved TDM) by the terminal signal. The bit or byte signal so sampled is time compressed and placed into a time slot in the TDM output signal.

FDM is probably better where the system has a number of low-speed terminals, geographically dispersed with less than 16 channels. If the transmission rate is 2400 bits per second or more, or a great many channels are used, then the system should use TDM.

Concentrator

A concentrator differs from a multiplexer in that a concentrator accommodates X number of terminals but allows only a portion of them to transmit their data over the available lines. That is, 12 terminals may compete for only six channels. All terminals must contend for the channels and those which do not make connection are busied out. With a multiplexer, all terminals can be accommodated because the basic assumption is that all terminals are used all of the time.

The concentrator works as a normal switching device that polls one terminal at a time. Whenever a channel is idle, the first terminal ready to send or receive gets control of one of the channels and retains it for the duration of its transaction. If several transactions occur simultaneously, then each terminal must wait its turn on a first in, first out basis.

The cost savings in using a multiplexer are based on combining the data while the cost savings using a concentrator are based on the amount of data traffic in the system. In effect, the use of a concentrator is based on the assumption that all of the terminals will not contend for the available facilities at the same time.

Programmable Communications Processors

As long as the total number of peripherals, local and remote, and the amount of data transmitted are maintained at a certain level, the computer control program (in residence) can execute the interrupts, move the data into and out of storage, and perform the necessary housekeeping without significant throughput penalty. If the number of terminals and volume of data increase to a point beyond that level, however, then computer throughput is reduced significantly. At this point, it may be more economical to move these functions out of the computer mainframe and into a communications processor.[9] These processors perform some, if not all, of the following functions:

1. Housekeeping—the handling of message queues and priorities, processing of addresses, data requests, message blocks, file management, and updating the executive on peripheral activity.
2. Error checking and retransmission requests to prevent incomplete messages from reaching the host processor.
3. Code translation into the "native" code of the host CPU.
4. Preprocessing and editing.
5. Communications analysis processing—error analysis, the gathering of traffic statistics, and so forth.
6. Establishing and acknowledging the required channel connections including automatic dialing, if this is a feature of the system.
7. Verifying successful completion of the message, or detecting line breaks, and either calling for or executing remedial action.
8. Disconnecting after a completed message, to permit polling to resume.
9. Assembling the serial bit stream into a bit-parallel buffered message.
10. Routing messages to and from required memory locations and notifying the software as required.

The major factor in moving these functions from the central processor (host computer) to a communications processor is economic. With a large number of terminals or communications lines, as much as half the processing time of the host computer (even a large one) can be spent in input/output processing and line control. A separate, specialized computer can perform the same functions with fewer steps and simpler software, reducing direct processor time costs, programming costs, and debugging time. The lease or purchase price of the communications processor is often one or two orders of magnitude lower than that of the main computer; if it can assume work which formerly occupied half the main computer's time, it can obviously be economically justified. In Figure B.20, a typical configuration is illustrated.[10]

The increased use of programmable communications processors can be directly attributed to the current proliferation of low-cost flexible minicomputers and microcomputers, and also to the developments in integrated circuit technology that have enabled digital computers to be manufactured at greatly reduced costs.

[9]"Smart Users 'Deemphasize Host'," *Computerworld*, Supplement, July 27, 1972, p. 10. Used with permission. Copyright by *Computerworld*, Newton, Massachusetts 02160.

[10]R. L. Aronson, "Data Links and Networks Devices and Techniques," *Control Engineering*, February 1970, pp. 105–116. Used with permission.

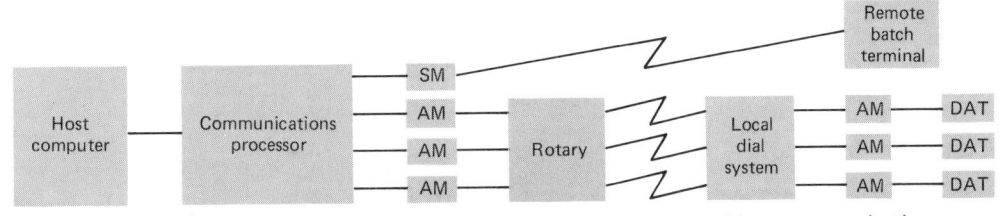

FIG. B.20 Computer system with multiple communication ports served by a communications processor. SM: synchronous modem: AM: asynchronous modem; DAT: dial-up terminal.

BIBLIOGRAPHY

"All About Minicomputers," *Datapro 70,* Delran, NJ.: Datapro Research Corporation, December 1976.

"Control Data 38500 Mass Storage System, *Datapro 70,* Delran, NJ.: Datapro Research Corporation, September 1975.

Davis, *Computer Data Processing,* New York: McGraw-Hill Book Co., 1969.

Haavind, "A User's Guide to System Evolution," *Computer Decisions,* June 1971.

Howard, "Telecommunications: 1970–1990," *Computerworld/Extra,* March 18, 1981.

"Key to Enhanced Application Development," *Data Processor,* September 1972.

Martin, *Telecommunications and the Computer,* Second Edition, Englewood Cliffs, NJ.: Prentice-Hall, Inc., 1976.

Minicomputer Review, Lexington, MA.: GML Corporation, 1981.

Sardinas, *Computing Today,* Englewood Cliffs, NJ.: Prentice-Hall, Inc., 1981.

"Smart Users 'Deemphasize' Host," *Computerworld,* Supplement, July 27, 1972.

Synnott and Gruber, *Information Resource Management,* New York: John Wiley & Sons, Inc., 1981.

Yasaki, "Voice Recognition Comes of Age," *Datamation,* August 1976.

INDEX

ABC analysis, 157, 582-584
Access, 173-174
   control, 155-156, 461
   time, 608
Accounts, 570-571
   payable system, 376, 378
   receivable/credit system, 385-388
Acquisition of computers methods:
   leasing, 415-416
      combination, 415-417
      third-party, 415
   legal considerations, 416-418
   purchasing, 415, 417
   renting, 414-415, 417
Activity ratio, 278, 282-283
Acts of God, 465
ADABAS, 175-176
Addressing methods, 241-245
Administrative controls, 450-451
Air conditioning, 422
Algorithm method of addressing, 243-244
American standard code for information interchange (ASCII), 617
Application approach, 167-172
Application programs, 105
Approximation, 453
Arithmetic proof, 453
Assembling, 489

Asynchronous transmission, 617
Audit:
   financial, 546
   operational, 545-546
   post implementation, 545
   systems, 546
   trails, 155, 454
Auditing, 545-551
   around the computer, 547-548
   through the computer, 547
Authentication, 473
Authorization, 471-472
Automatic notification, 72-73
Backup, 156-175
   facilitity, 467
Badges, 466
Bar charts, 332
Bar codes, 193-195
Batch processing, 38, 273-276
Baudot, 617
Benchmark testing, 410-411
Binary coded decimal (BCD), 617
Binary search, 202
Block code, 191-193
Blocked, 166
Blocking factor, 239, 604-606
Block search, 203-204
Brainstorming, 308-309

Brownouts, 465
Browsing, 464
Bubble sort, 199-200
Budgets, 573-574
Buffer storage, 600
Building, 467
Building blocks, *see* Design blocks,
  Demand blocks
Bundling, 412-413
Byte-addressable, 598

Cache memory, 600
Centralized structures, 110-123
Central Processing Unit (CPU), 102, 597-601
Chains, 245-246
Change, 554-598
Character-addressable, 598
Charting, 320-333
  see also specific types
Check digits, 188-189, 452
Chunking, 188
Closed-circuit monitors, 466
Codes:
  capacity, 189-190
  defined, 185-186
  design, 187-190
  functions, 186
  symbols, 186
  transactions, 451
  types, 190-198
Coercive change strategy, 554-555
Color codes, 197-198
Communication:
  channels, 616-620
  process, 48-49
Compartmentalization, 470
Compatibility, 411-412
Complexity, 125, 146
Compiling, 489
Computational demands, 126, 146
Computer:
  based information, 383
  operations control, 461-464
  operators, 107
  site, 461-462
Computer Output Microfilm (COM), 240, 610
Concentration, 622

Concurrency, 175
Concurrent access, 175
Console, 463
  log, 463-464
  run book, 459
Contention, 620-621
Contingency plan, 451
Contribution-by-value, 582-584
Controlling, 41-42
Controls, 154-156
  check digits, 452
  labels, 452
  programming, 452-454
Control totals, 452
Conversion:
  costs, 423
  planning, 526-527
  systems, 522-526
  see also specific types
Corporate war room, 82-85
Cost, 147
Cost/effectiveness analysis, 147, 418-423
Coverings, 468
Credits, 571
Cross-footing, 453
Cycle time, 599

Data:
  attributes, 164-165
  attribute value, 164-165
  communications, 616-623
  defined, 4, 485
  descriptions, 164, 165
  dictionary, 165
  entry, 612-616
  flow diagrams, 325, 331
  flows, 325-331
  hierarchy, 165
  independence, 172
  input, 98-102
  operations, 7-8
  representation, 164-165
  set, 166
  stores, 331
Data base, 152-154, 163-167
  administrator (DBA), 107
  approach, 167-173

controls, 454-457
conversion, 524-526
management system (DBMS), 173-177
DBMS, 173-177, 456
Debits, 571
Debugging, 489
Decimal codes, 193
Decision level analysis, 304-305
Decision making:
   levels, 44-45
   nonprogrammed, 43
   process, 42
   programmed, 43, 70-72
   requirements, 44-47
   strategic, 44
   tactical, 44
   technical, 44-45
Decision model, 580-582
Decision support center, 82-85
Decision tables, 333-337, 486
   constructing, 335-337
   structure, 333-335
   types, 335
   vocabulary, 335
Delphi method, 308, 421
Demand blocks, 14-15, 143
Design blocks, 13-14, 449
Design process, 373-381
Desktop computers, 103
Detail, levels of, 64
Dial-up lines, 618
Direct access storage device (DASD), 239-240
Direct addressing, 241-243
Direct conversion, 522-523
Directory, 249
Direct processing, 174, 276-278
Disconnection, 470
Disk addressing, 607
Dispersion, 578
Distributed structures, 110-123
Documentation, 103
   controls, 458-459
   general systems, 458
   procedures manual, 458
   program, 458-459
Document gathering, 319-320
Domains, 219-223

Drains, 467
Drucker, *see* Key variable reporting
Duplication check, 460

Echo check, 460
Economic feasibility, 147, 341
Economic order quantity (EOQ), 586-588
Edit checks, 174-175
Educating personnel, 510-513
Emergency doors, 466-467
Encryption, 175
Environmental control, 462
Environment costs, 422
Equipment proposals, 407-409
Error check, 460
Error log, 454
Estimations of costs and benefits, 420
Evaluation process, 409-410
Event processing, 276-278
Expectations, 41
Expected value, 420-421
Expected time, 579
Exponential smoothing, 585-586
Extent, 166
External controls, 449-450
External entities, 326-330
External sorting, 200-202

Faceted code, 192
Fact gathering, 304-309
   hazards, 338-339
Feasibility requirements, 147, 340-341
   economic, 341
   legal, 342
   operational, 342
   schedule, 342
   technical, 341
Feedback, 498
Fiber optics, 619-620
File:
   conversion, 524-526
   design considerations, 284-285
   organization methods, 281-284, 525-526
   protection rings, 455, 456
Filtering, 64-67
Financial lease, 415-416
Final General Systems Design Report, 424
Fire, 465

control, 468
Firmware, 105
  controls, 460-461
Fixed cost, 571
Flat file, 219-223
Flexibility, 127
Floppy disks, 609
Flowcharts:
  symbols, 330
  traditional:
    document, 325, 329
    program macro, 325, 327
    program micro, 325, 328
    systems, 325, 326, 491
Forms:
  design, 451, 481
  distribution, 484
  guidelines for, analysis and design, 484
  input, 482-483
  output, 483
  physical considerations, 484-486
  turnaround, 482, 483-484
  types, 481-482
Frameworks for fact gathering, 304-309
Fraud, 464
Frequency Division Multiplexing (FDM), 622
Full duplex, 617
Furniture and fixtures, 422

Generalized audit programs, 490-491
General Systems Design Proposal Report, 382, 384-385
Goal setting, 498
Grandfather-father-son, 455, 456
Graphs, 84-85, 331-332
Growth, 147
  potential, 127
Guards, 465

Half duplex, 617
Hardware, 102-103
  controls, 459-461
  monitor, 550-551
Hashing, 243-244
Hash total, 452
Hersey and Blanchard, 554-555
Hertz, 618

Hierarchical block codes, 192-193
Hierarchical structures, 216-218
HIPO (hierarchy plus input, processing, and output), 380-381
Histogram, 578
Host language, 174
Hybrid structures, 110-123

Identification, 453-454, 471
IDMS, 175-176
IMS, 176-177
Indexed sequential addressing, 241
Information:
  attributes, 5-7, 145-146
  classification, 35-38
  defined, 4
  flow analysis, 306
  formal, 5
  informal, 5
  requirements, 31-38, 45-47
  status, 52-53
  subsystem, 10
  systems:
    concept, 12
    controls, 449-454
    methodology, 298
Infrared, 620
Input data, 98-102, 148-149
  controls, 451-452
  input/output analysis, 306
Installation schedule, 127
Integrated test facility (ITF), 550-551
Integrity, 469-470
Intelligent terminals, 611-612
Interblock gap, 239
Interface isolation, 470
Interrogation, 282
Interrogative, 79-82
Interview, 309-312
Inventory control, 586-588
  chart, 308
Inverted lists, 257-259
Isolation, 470-471

Job control language (JCL), 459, 489
Join, 225

Keyboard-to-storage, 612-613
Key verification, 451
Key success factors, 67-68
Key variable reporting, 67-68

Labels, 452, 461
Languages programming, 104
Leasing computer equipment, 415-416
Least privilege access, 470
Legal feasibility, 342
Librarian, 455
Life expectancy, 127
Limit check, 452-453
Linear programming, 592-595
Line charts, 332
Line management, 620-623
Load sharing, 616
Location, physical, 467
   of terminal, 470-471
Lockout, 175
Logical data organization, 213-228
Logical files, 166-167
Logico-Mathematical models, 569-595
Logs, 174
Low-speed channels, 618

Magnetic disk, 239-240, 606-609
Magnetic Ink Character Recognition (MICR), 482, 615
Magnetic tape, 238-239, 602-606
Mainframe, 102
Maintainability, 127, 412-413, 541
Maintenance, 541-545
Make or buy decision, 383-384
Malfunctions, 464
Management:
   functions, 38-40
   subsystem, 10
Managing change, 554-556
Mass storage, 609-610
Material yield analysis, 588-589
Matrix 333, 337-338
Mean, 578
Media, input, 99-102
Median, 578
Medium-speed channels, 618-619
Menus, 155

Microcomputers, 103, 601
Microfilm, 100
Microprogramming, 105
Microwave, 619
Minicomputers, 103, 601
Mnemonic codes, 195-196
Mode, 578
Modeling:
   building process, 77-79
   classification, 74
   definition, 74
Models, 569-595
   accounting, 569-575
   bookkeeping, 570
   cost-volume-profit, 571-572
   forecast, 584-588
   least-squares, 584-585
   payoff, 574-575
   queuing, 590-591
Modems, 616, 620
Modular conversion, 522, 523-524
Modular programming, 411, 486, 495
Monitoring, 68-74, 473
Monitors, 550-551
Multiple key retrieval, 251-257
Multidrop, 620
Multiplexer, 621-622
Multiprocessors, 600-601

Net present value, 575
Network:
   model, 578-580
   structures, 218
Noise, 48
Nonprogrammed decision making, 43
Normalization, 219-223
Notification, 175

Obfuscation, 470
Observation:
   conducting, 318
   following up, 319
   preparing for, 318
Online, 38
On the job training (OJT), 511
Operational feasibility, 147, 341
Operating systems, 104-105

Index

costs, 423-424
Operations:
   control, 461-464
   requirements, 47-53
   subsystem, 10
Operators, computer, 107
Optical character recognition (OCR), 482, 614-615
Order processing system: 144-145
Organization charts, 320-323
Organization factors, 144
   management style, 35
   nature, 33
   size, 33-34
   structure, 34-35
Organization methods, 281-284
Organizational constraints, applying, 377-379
Output, 156
   controls, 457-458
Overflow, 243-244

Parallel conversion, 522-523
Pareto's law, 582-584
Parity checks, 459-460
Partially inverted lists, 257
Participative change strategy, 554-555
Passwords, 155-156, 174
Performance analysis models, 573-574
Peripherals, 102
Personal computers, 103
Phase-in conversion, 524
Phonetic code, 196-197
Physical data organization, 237-257
Physical files, 166-167
Physical layout charts, 323-325
Physical record, 165-166
Pictorial charts, 332
Pie charts, 332
Planning, 40-41
Plex structures, 218
Pointers, 245-246
Point of sale (POS), 613-614
Polling, 620-621
Power:
   emergency, 467-468
   requirements, 422
Practice, 497

Price/performance ratio, 103
Primary key, 214
Private lines, 618
Probability concepts, 576-577
Procedural controls, 455
Procedures:
   human, 486-488
   manual, 488
   written, 486-487
Processes, data flow, 325-331
Processing, 149-152
   controls, 493
   test, 515-516
Program Evaluation and Review Technique (PERT), 578-580
Programmable communications processor, 622-623
Programmed decision making, 43, 70-72
Programmers:
   application, 107
   maintenance, 107
   systems, 107
Programming:
   controls, 452-454, 489-490
   definition, 488-489
   languages, 104
   standards, 497
   team, 497
Project management systems (PMS), 551-553
Project networking systems, 552
Projects, 17-18, 224-225
Project tracking systems, 552
Proposal to Conduct Systems Analysis Report, 297
Pumps, 467
Punched cards, 238
Punched paper tape, 238

Quality-control analysis, 589-590
Query-by-Example (QEB), 228
Query language, 173-174
Questionnaire:
   formats, 314-317
   guidelines for constructing, 313
   limitation, 313
   use, 313, 518-519
Queuing, 590-591

Random code, 190-191
Randomizing method of addressing 243-244
Random processing, 38
Read only memory (ROM), 460
Read/write error, 461
Real time, 38
Reasonableness check, 452-453
Record length checks, 461
Recovery, 175
Rehearsal, 497-498
Relational operators, 223-228
Relational structures, 219-223
Reliability, 126, 147
Remote job entry (RJE), 616
Reorder point, 587
Reports, 482
Requirements:
   data processing, 125-126
   systems, 126-128, 146-147
   user, 382
Requirements:
   volume, 125
Resources, data processing, 97-108, 148
Response time, 283-284
Rings, 245-246
Riot, 465
Roll backward, 175
Roll forward, 175

Sabotoge, 465
Safety stock, 586-587
Sample, 578
Sampling, 319-320
Satellites, 619
Schedule feasibility, 342
Schema, 214-216
Searching data, 202-204
Security, 174-175, 466-467, 468-470
   controls, 464-465
   fires, 465
   hazards, 464, 465-466
   malfunctions, 464
   natural disasters, 465
   power failures, 464-465
   sabotage, 465
   unauthorized access and fraud, 464
Seminars, 511

Semivariable cost, 571
Sequence check, 454
Sequential addressing, 241
Sequential code, 190-191
Sequential processing, 174, 273-276
Sequential search, 202
Shredders, paper, 466
Sign-in/sign-out registers, 466
Simplex, 617
Simulation, 411, 511, 591-592
Small computers, 103
Software, 103-105
   monitor, 521
   vendor controls, 461
Sorting:
   internal, 198-200
   purpose, 198
   selection, 199
     with interchange, 199-200
Sorting and merging using auxiliary devices, 200-202
Sort/merge, 200-202
Soundex code, 196-197
Source Data Automation (SDA), 100-102, 482
Source document, 100
Standards, 486
Steering committee, 106-107
Step cost, 571
Strategic decision center, 82-85
Strategic decision making, 44
Status information, 52-53
Storage media, 237-240
Structured analysis, 306-309
Structured programming, 493-495
Study facts, 301-304, 309-339
Subschema, 214-216
Subsystem, 9, 299
Synchronous transmission, 617
Synonyms, 243-244
System management facility (SMF), 550-551
System 2000, 176-177
Systems:
   analysis, 297-355
     input/output, 306
     reasons, 298-299
     scope, 299-301

632 Index

    sources, 301-304
      structured, 306-309
  analyst, 19-21
  concept, 8-10
  design, 373-388
    model, 376-377, 379
  development life cycle, 18-19
  development methodology, 18-19, 298
  flowchart, 491
  goals, 375
Systems Analysis Completion Report, 340

Tables, 219-223
Tactical decision making, 44
Tagging and tracing, 549-550
Technical decision making, 44-45
Technical feasibility, 147, 341
Telephone terminals, 611
Template, 325
Terminals, 611-612
Test:
  of controls, 517-518
  data, 493
    base, 516-617
      generator, 516
      processing resources, 520-521
  deck, 548
  of output, 520
Testing:
  costs, 423
  growing importance, 521-522
  system, 513-515
Three-tier acquisition system, 418
Time constraints, 125-126, 146
Time division multiplexing (TDM), 622

Timesharing, 616
Total, 176-177
Training:
  categories, 510-513
  costs, 423
Transaction:
  log, 454
  process, 49-52
Tranformation method of addressing, 243-244
Tree structures, 216-218
Trojan horses, 464
Turnaround documents, 483-484
Tutorial training, 511

Universal Product Code, 194-195
Uninterruptible power system (UPS), 462
Utilities, performance, 521

Validity check 460
Variable costs, 571
Variance reporting, 69-70, 157-158
Variances, 574
Vaults, 455
Vendor:
  software controls, 461
  support, 412-414
Verification, 451-452
Virtual storage, 599-600
Voice recognition (VR), 615-616
Volatility, 283
Volume, 146

Walkthrough, 515-516
Wide area telephone service (WATS), 618-619
Word-addressable, 598